Byzantium

Pergamum

oles

Athens
Sparta

CRETE

CYPRUS

Jerusalem

Alexandria

A HISTORY OF
WESTERN ART

NEW YORK · HOLT, RINEHART AND WINSTON

A HISTORY OF
WESTERN ART

REVISED

JOHN IVES SEWALL

with a chapter by JOHN CANADAY

The art in the National Gallery, London, reproduced in this book is used
by courtesy of the Trustees of the National Gallery, London. The air view
of Mont St. Michel on the title page is reproduced courtesy of Aéro-Photo.
The rose window of the western façade of the Chartres cathedral at the
beginning of Chapter 11 is reproduced courtesy of Marcel Bovis, Chartres.
The cathedral sculpture from Chartres at the beginning of Chapter 12 is
reproduced courtesy of Archives Photographiques.

CL

Preface

The revision of *A History of Western Art* is an attempt to make the book more practical and more useful. The whole matter of coverage was carefully reconsidered, with the main result that the chapter on the 17th century is much longer and the chapter on the Early Middle Ages shorter. The final chapter is the work of Mr. John Canaday, the Art Critic of *The New York Times;* my own views on modern art remain as stated in 1953.

Otherwise, the text is much as it appeared in the earlier edition, except that the order of presentation has been rearranged and various passages have been rewritten to suit. With cautious regard for maintaining clarity, some passages have been cut and others expanded.

Although most of the original illustrations appear again, there is also a large number of new illustrations, particularly in Chapters 15 and 17. As with the text, the arrangement has been improved, and the plates now appear where first cited. Many new engravings have been made, with consequent improvement in quality, and many of the architectural drawings have been refined and redrawn.

In preparing the revised edition, I have had the benefit of advice from many colleagues. This amounted to several hundred separate and specific suggestions, great and small. Some I was grateful to accept. Others I felt compelled to reject, often with regret. The interval between the two editions has, however, provided time for consideration of every thought that was communicated to me, and I take the greatest pleasure in expressing my appreciation.

I want to renew the statement of appreciation made in 1953 to Dean Julian Park, Miss Louise Lucas, Mrs. Barbara Ives Beyer, Dr. W. D. Richmond, Dr. Patrick J. Kelleher, the late Edgar C. Schenck, and Professors H. W. Janson, Clarence Kennedy, Ulrich Middeldorf, and Clarence Ward. The gracious memory of my former teachers has likewise been with me as I worked.

In preparing the present edition, I have had significant help on theological problems from Dean John C. Bennett. Dr. George Landis put at my disposal his mastery of Hebrew. Dr. Frederic C. Lane answered some difficult questions in the tricky field of economic history. Professor Bernard Heyl and

Professor S. L. Faison, Jr., helped me wrestle with the vexing problem of High Renaissance Mannerism, a subject about which we hear much and about which no one, at this date, may dogmatize.

There are no words adequate to express my gratitude to Professor G. H. Huntley. My friend for more than thirty years, he labored altogether beyond the call of both friendship and scholarship. He read and criticized the entire manuscript, but no suggestion is made that he endorses it in its entirety, and he may be blamed for nothing.

For improvements and additions to the architectural drawings, I am once again indebted to Dr. Richmond. All architectural drawings that appear without credit are his work.

Unless acknowledged to a particular photographer, the copy for the plates was obtained direct from the museum or collection cited in the caption. I share with my publisher a cordial sense of gratitude for this and many another courtesy.

As before, Flaminia Guerrini made herself invaluable.

J. I. S.

South Bristol, Maine
July 8, 1961

Contents

A HISTORY OF
WESTERN ART

Chapter 1

THE SEVERAL DIVISIONS OF THE SUBJECT

Let us begin by defining our field.

The history of art as conceived today in the American university is an all-embracing subject; the name means much more than the words say. In a strict and narrow sense art history is merely a department of all history; and the first duty of the art historian is to explain the monuments of architecture, sculpture, and painting in so far as they stand as records of the past. As such, works of art are often more accurate than any other indication about the state of affairs at some remote but crucial juncture in the progress of humanity. When men speak or write, they are often guarded and devious. But when they build or paint, they are usually perfectly open about what they want. By studying the visual arts from any society, we can often tell what the people lived for and for what they might be willing to die.

As just defined, the history of art is surely a legitimate and rewarding field of knowledge, but no one could possibly accept the limitations implied by what we have so far said. Over and above the attractions of political, military, and social history, art history has the special advantage of dealing with material that tends to expand the personality, refine the emotions, and increase the domain where the sympathies are at home. Art is a product of man's creative impulse. It is as old as the race. A society without artistic taste and standards is a society forever yearning and confused. For reasons like these, art history merges by imperceptible degrees with philosophy, psychology, and religious impulse. We find ourselves constantly involved with ideals and aspirations, and with questions of hope, pride, tragedy, exaltation, and a host of other experiences having to do with the soul's welfare or defeat. Only in part are we concerned with the problem of beauty, although we must labor

THE STUDY OF ART

hard over it. The fundamental concept with which we should begin is this: the visual arts are a means of communication and record; they open straight into the heart and mind of all humanity, both living and dead.

The matters just mentioned are not susceptible of measurement on any numerical scale, but art history, like all other modern studies, nevertheless depends for its validity upon a solid foundation of fact. Except for the research of countless scholars, a book like this one would be an impossibility. It is important for the reader to have some picture of the process by which our knowledge has been built up and of the present state of the subject. In general, it may be said that scholarly activity has tended to divide itself into various specialties, each making an essential contribution to the field as a whole.

Archeology is the field work of art history. Its business is to recover objects preserved from earlier times. *Anthropology* does the same thing; but as ordinarily understood, it implies research into remote and primitive mankind while archeology deals with material from periods of high civilization. Both activities result in the accumulation of *artifacts* (objects worked by the hand of man) and *monuments* (artifacts construable as cultural expression) in our museums.

Archeological scholarship, as distinct from field work, is the further study of the monuments we possess with the purpose of establishing relations of cause and effect between the earlier monuments and the later. Such scholarship deals indiscriminately with objects unearthed yesterday and with monuments that have never been out of sight, but we must not overlook the insight it offers into the creative process. The most original artist is incapable of total creation; all are necessarily creatures of their own past and their own present.

3

We can tell much from the work of art alone, but it is folly to overlook the connotations and overtones opened up for our understanding by apposite if collateral evidence.

Whenever he can locate it, the archeological scholar depends upon evidence external to the work of art itself. The ideal thing to have, of course, is a receipted bill from someone like Titian saying in unmistakable language that he has, on a certain date, received payment for such and such a Madonna. Sadly for the scholar, elaborate bookkeeping is a very recent addition to our civilization, and efficient filing systems are still largely unknown and unpopular except in the United States of America and in Germany. Neat and conclusive proof in documentary form is rare indeed when artistic monuments are being traced to their source. As a general statement, it is probably fair to say that, for any period earlier than the 16th century, such documents exist only by the merest chance. After that, one can usually locate something or other if he hunts long enough.

The *archivist* is the man who makes a specialty of finding such papers. With respect to getting covered with dirt, his daily task is not unlike that of the archeologist in the field; and his patience must be even greater because there is less drama in his life. Devoted men and women are nevertheless at work every day in the libraries of Europe and in the repositories where public and private records are stored, usually in indescribable lack of order. The archivist must not only be an expert linguist in the ordinary sense; he also has to know tricks of script and abbreviation with which most of us are never concerned. Once in a while, he finds himself reading words that settle a question long vigorously debated.

An immense amount of work remains to be done in the archives, but conceivably at some future time we shall have assembled all the apposite documents on earth. In the meanwhile, life goes on and decisions must be made about works of art about which we know nothing except what we may properly infer by inspecting the object itself; or, to put it in technical language, we have to base our judgment upon *internal* or *stylistic evidence*.

The situation will be clear if we attempt to visualize the problem of a museum director who is considering the purchase of a painting for the collection under his care. Works of art are unique; the opportunity to purchase may never come again. The art market is also unique; and the price of a painting depends upon a number of things extraneous to its absolute value as a picture, but most of all upon its authenticity as the work of a great master. If public funds in a large amount are to be disbursed, a heavy responsibility rests upon the man who must decide whether to purchase or whether to let the offer go.

Because there are all kinds of pictures, no individual can possibly be intimately familiar with every class and variety. It is customary, therefore, to seek the advice of some scholar known to be an expert, or *connoisseur,* of the particular category in which the contemplated purchase falls.

Connoisseurship is that branch of archeological study which deals entirely with the single work of art and depends altogether upon stylistic evidence. As before, the purpose is to establish the *provenance* (place of origin), the date, and the authorship of a given picture or statue. After thorough study, the professional connoisseur signs an affirmation of authenticity or the opposite. This amounts to an assertion that he risks his reputation upon his belief that the work of art is truly what he says it is.

Every once in a while, the public prints burst forth with an announce-that the connoisseurs have been fooled. A great museum pays $100,000 for a marble tomb; it turns out to have been made, not in the 15th century and at Florence as confidently supposed, but a year or two ago by a forger in Milan. Paintings celebrated as newly discovered works by a great Dutch master are presently found to be nothing but a psychopath's pitiful attempt to gain recognition.

Such news makes exciting headlines, and at times even good reading. As ordinarily presented in the papers, however, it is all too commonly false in emphasis and interpretation, if not in fact.

It is conceivable that a forger might so perfectly imitate the work of an earlier great master as to fool everyone forever. If so, his work would be as "good" as that of the great master even if discovery of the fraud destroyed its value on the market. In effect, the forger would actually have brought about a resurrection of the dead master's personality; we would be dealing with the work of the same mind once again set into motion. Such a thing is certainly difficult to credit; but no one can prove it has never happened. Most indications suggest that genius sufficient for success in so devious and unrewarding an enterprise ordinarily finds a more direct and legitimate outlet.

It should be noted, moreover, that in the several instances where important forgeries have recently been detected, the fraud has come to light within a year or two—certainly no very great interval of time. If we look behind the scenes, we can appreciate that even the curator of a public collection may at times feel compelled to take a chance: to buy something, that is, without waiting for the report of a connoisseur who might need several months to arrive at his opinion. It takes great courage to announce that one has been fooled, but such announcements are the rule rather than the exception.

The reader must realize that any attribution based only upon internal evidence is necessarily a statement of probability. General confidence in the authenticity of an undocumented work of art is established only over a substantial period of time. Things that stand up for years to the repeated inspection of experts are either genuine or miraculous in their power to deceive.

Connoisseurship, it must also be understood, cannot be undertaken effectively except by direct contact with the originals. Photographic reproductions are among the tools of the trade, of course, but they merely aid the memory in matters of comparative study. A sound attribution on stylistic evidence demands that the eye be close to the surface of the picture. Chemical tests, X-ray, and other laboratory techniques extend one's power to observe, but to date nothing has the scope and reliability of the trained eye aided, perhaps, by a simple magnifier.

There is nothing occult about the method. Everyone who recognizes a signature on a check is to that extent a connoisseur. In general it is believed that authenticity is best indicated by the minute physical characteristics of the picture. The master under review might, for instance, have had a favorite sort of brush with hairs that left a special kind of mark. Small details of every kind tend to be handled in the same way by the same man, like, for example, a routine trick for drawing the corner of the eye or a favorite contour for the fingernails.

Obviously such indications of manual usage are often so insignificant that the painter himself might not recognize them as his own. All indications point to the likelihood that such data are all the more reliable for the very reason of their being the product of unconscious habit.

By its nature, connoisseurship is intensively specialized. The professional is ordinarily compelled to limit himself to the work of a single school, or even to the work of one or two masters within a school. And because he must deal with the minutiae of so narrow a field, the connoisseur is hardly ever a reliable guide on the broader and more philosophical aspects of art history and criticism.

Connoisseurship is obviously most reliable when applied to works of art in perfect condition; but such condition is rare. Art objects wear out. Statues erode in the weather. Wooden panels get infested with worms. Canvas rots. Paints fade. Hence it is likely that any monument of considerable age has been subjected to restoration; and the more famous or important the monument, the more certain we must be that it has been tampered with from time to time. How else are we to account for the remarkable condition of certain well-known statues on the medieval cathedrals, statues which stand in immediate juxtaposition to others which have all but weathered away? And why are some celebrated frescoes fresh and clean when others are nearly illegible?

The reader must understand that restoration, as such, imputes no intention to deceive. The procedure often goes on quite openly in public places; and the motives are of the best. But no matter how well disciplined the workmen may be, the effect of their operation is to make the original surface obscure, and to substitute something modern for something old. Thus, the more important we think a work of art, the more scrupulous we must be to assure ourselves that we see it in something like its original condition. That good intention, as every scholar will testify, is nearly impossible to carry out in every case; and the best we can do is to warn the reader.

Once the work of art is installed in a museum—by purchase, by gift, by bequest, or however else it got there—its worth to the community may or may not be instantly self-evident. Before accepting anything as an important cultural monument, people require to know something about it. What does the picture represent? Is it beautiful, or is it important and moving in some other way? Such questions bring us to still other departments of our general field.

Iconography (from *icon* or *ikon,* an image or representation) is the study of the subject matter of the visual arts. Except for modern art of the so-called nonobjective sort, almost every picture and statue has content. It was produced, that is to say, for the purpose of expressing something or communicating something. Narrative subject matter is only the most obvious type of content. Pictures that tell no story may possess great devotional significance. Upon occasion, abstract design carries a symbolic meaning for those who know the key. Inasmuch as many things that once were common knowledge are now obscure, an immense effort of research has been required and still goes on with the simple purpose of enabling us to make sense of what we see.

It has been fashionable for the past thirty years or so to declare that an interest in iconography is beneath the dignity of the true art critic. He should, we are told, confine his attention to the problem of beauty which, according to this school of thought, is to be sought solely in the abstract organization of mass, line, light and dark, and color. Such study is of course both legitimate and necessary, to say nothing of its fascination. The error in the view just summarized is in what it denies, not in what it asserts.

Under the name *esthetics,* philosophers have long recognized that art criticism formed part of their responsibility. By analogy to such absolutes as good and evil, it has been presumed that beauty might be isolated from other and extraneous elements, and contemplated, defined, and understood by and for itself. This study deals primarily with the professional competence of the artist; not with what he does, but with how well he does it. Its ultimate achievement would be to explain why some artists are great, some merely good, and some not worthwhile.

As generally understood, esthetics aims to solve the problem of beauty on a universal basis. If successful, it would presently furnish us with an explanation of the quality common to Greek temples, Gothic cathedrals, Renaissance paintings, and all good art from whatever place or time. As distinct from this grand approach, we shall find it convenient to limit our objectives now and again, and think in terms of *historical criticism*. Making no attempt to find the common denominator between Greek and Gothic beauty, the historical critic undertakes to explain both styles by reference to their own internal logic. He takes either as a law unto itself, and tries to show how things must work so long as we accept the Greek or Gothic premises and follow them out to the end.

The *theory of art,* sometimes called the *theory of design,* is another important department of esthetics which attempts to make tangible progress by similar limitation of its field of inquiry. The facts of the visual universe are the beginning of all artistic theory. The second level of its foundation rests in the physiology and psychology of sight. Beyond that, theory studies the tools and materials of the artist, their special powers and limitations, and the consequences of such. By studying what the great artists have done with their materials, one builds up an idea of what is artistically appropriate, what can be done, and what had best be avoided.

Linear perspective, worked out at Florence during the early part of the 15th century, is the most familiar part of artistic theory. Without some fairly clear notion of its laws, one cannot draw anything. Another branch of theory studies the properties of color, and of light and dark, both as they act in nature and as they may legitimately be applied in painting. From such fundamental beginnings, the further study of theory involves the arrangement of pictorial materials into *compositions,* an investigation involving the interrelation of masses, lines, colors, statics and dynamics, and all the harmonies, rhythms, balances, tensions, and compensations that may enter into the exhaustive effort of a great artist as he struggles to produce a perfect thing. It is important to understand that theory proceeds inductively; it deals not with artistic law, but with the actual practice of artists and with the phenomena of nature.

Art criticism is the process of arriving at a just estimate of the cultural value of artistic monuments. If he is to command respect, the critic must be vigilantly alert to the implications of anything and everything that may shed light upon the work of art under review; he cannot afford to neglect any department of art study as we have described it above. Walter Pater's estimate of Leonardo is considerably weakened today, for example, because we know that Pater accepted, as genuine, paintings which have not stood the test of connoisseurship. Romanesque sculpture was once considered barbarous, and the very name Gothic originated as a term of contempt; today, on the basis of comparative study and historical criticism, both are recognized at what is probably their true and permanent worth. During the early centuries of Christendom when the Roman polity was crumbling, there was no place for artistic theory and little for technical skill. We nevertheless can make out a very strong case for Early Christian sculpture as a human and historical document of priceless value. And in the same voice, we may admire the dazzling accomplishment of many a baroque artist while deploring the essential vulgarity of the display. In short, it is not the business of the critic to further the popularity of any particular style or kind of art at the expense of any other kind. His obligation lies, rather, in the direction of exhausting all resources in an effort to be fair.

THE STATE OF THE SUBJECT

Modern art history is almost exactly two centuries old. It began with the work of the German scholar J. J. Winckelmann, who published his *Geschichte der Kunst des Altertums* (*History of the Art of Ancient Times*) in 1764. At that time, factual knowledge was in an appalling state. Winckelmann's statements about date and authorship are often wrong almost beyond belief. His critical estimates, however, have become part of our folklore; the man in the street who has never heard of Winckelmann will nevertheless quote him if asked to express an opinion about art. No other art historian has had a comparable influence upon European taste.

Since Winckelmann, our factual knowledge has steadily increased. Under his inspiration, classical art was the first field to be systematically worked. The Italian Renaissance next claimed attention; and during the second half of the 19th century, the art of the Middle Ages, until then the province of a few independent thinkers who refused to accept the notion that an era of darkness separated the enlightenment of Rome from the felicity of modern times, came strongly into its own.

As things stand today, the narrative chronicle of European art history will probably remain forever much as we find it set forth. The important buildings are known. Most of the great pictures and statues have gravitated into the public domain and are generally accessible in museums or elsewhere. Debate still takes place about matters of historical probability; but the contention has to do with particulars and details rather than with fundamentals: the major historical forces have been identified, and the main trend of their operation is clear.

Two things combined to forward the grand program of research. Both were impossible until the Industrial Revolution had done its work. Western Europe became crisscrossed with a network of railways. Photography was invented. Travel for the first time became safe, fast, and inexpensive. Photography made it possible to make trustworthy records and gradually to accumulate a reference file of reproductions. The net result was to open art history to any one who might be interested.

The efficiency of the study has also been tremendously improved. It is still necessary for the specialist to inspect the originals no matter how far he must travel to see them, but he can prepare himself for the experience by the study of photographs and thus make his firsthand investigation more intelligently. Even more important, comparisons are now conveniently made which, for Winckelmann, would have required the expenditure of tremendous energy. At Harvard, at Princeton, in the Frick Library in New York, in Sir Robert Witt's library in London, or in the files of Marburg University one can have a look at almost anything merely by consulting the card catalogue. The required photograph awaits him in its proper place in a drawer that runs on wheels. Valid conclusions on many matters are as easily made in Chicago as in Vienna or Rome.

What remains to be done?

There is probably more classical art underground than we have yet dug up. One of the great outstanding issues in medieval archeology, to name another possibility, is the likelihood that the Near East in some way furnished the inspiration for the architectural styles common in Western Europe during the later Middle Ages; but only a few competent persons have toured the back country of Syria where Christian cities existed until the Arab conquest of the 7th century. Almost nobody has seen the lands between the Black and Caspian seas, to say nothing of the Oxus River valley further east and the Altai region still further on to the north and east. And yet important secrets are to be solved by anyone who can look at visible monuments with a trained eye. Where travel is difficult and dangerous, art history hangs fire.

But that does not mean that new information can be acquired only by heroic methods. Spain and Portugal still offer the chance for significant achievement, as distinct from refining what has already been done. Latin America contains much important art of which we are all but ignorant. The papers of more than one major artist of the 19th century merely await the arrival of the student who has the skill, the time, and the patience to explore them.

Even so, it would seem that the opportunity to make a further contribution to factual knowledge is small in comparison with the vistas that beckon in esthetics, theory, and criticism. These matters have occasionally received the attention of some of the greatest men in our intellectual history, but none of them possessed anything like our facilities for arriving at sound judgments. It seems hard on Plato, for instance, to search his words for statements that might be definitive with regard to the Gothic cathedral at Amiens—Plato died in 347 B.C., or about sixteen hundred years before the church was built, and never saw anything remotely like it. On the other hand, both Plato and Aristotle have left us remarks that stand as capital instances of historical criticism: about the Greek style with which both were familiar, they speak with clarity and authority. What would such men have been able to say if, like ourselves, they had had the whole history of European art spread out before them?

In the field of theory, progress of the most obvious and practical kind may be expected within the next generation, for it is here that scholar, scientist, and artist meet on common ground. Painters no longer need to learn their art in the narrow channel of the local school to which they happen to belong; the museums, of which there were none before the 19th century and few good ones until the last part of that period, offer all the wisdom of the past to the young artist trying to work out his own mode of expression. The ultimate historical position of Paul Cézanne (died 1906), the founder of modern art, will probably rest upon the intelligent use he made of such sources. Had Cézanne chosen to write down his ideas, we might have been closer to a theory of art which would compare in utility and profundity to the theoretical understanding of music that is now accepted as essential for all well-educated musicians.

In the publications of D. W. Ross and Arthur Pope, we already have a color theory which has now stood the test of about fifty years of practical application to the problems of painting. The same theory, because of its simplicity and substantial accuracy, is gaining increasing popularity among scientists.

The theory of architecture is being pursued even more enthusiastically. Eminent practitioners of the art, like Le Corbusier and the late Frank Lloyd Wright, feel obliged to explain their buildings; each new project is accompanied by a statement of the philosophy behind it—one need not agree with what is said in order to appreciate the profound sense of responsibility felt by the architect. In this general effort, the writings of social thinkers, like Lewis Mumford and Sigfried Giedion, supplement the utterances of the active designers.

The end result of artistic theory should be twofold. All those who look to art for wisdom and for esthetic nourishment need a more reliable method of procedure. The artist—and all 19th-century Romanticism to the contrary, the creative process is as much rational as intuitive—should find a mature artistic theory extremely useful; it would set forth the possibilities and the limitations, and save much trial and error.

Chapter 2

THE PALEOLITHIC CAVE PAINTINGS

THE EXTREME ANTIQUITY of the visual arts was dramatically demonstrated in 1880 by the announcement that paintings of Paleolithic date had been discovered on the roof of the cave of Altamira near Santander on the Biscay coast of Spain. In 1879, a gentleman named Sautuola had explored the cave in company with his small daughter. The child was the first to discern the pictures on the ceiling above her, and delightedly shouted out to her father, "Toros! Toros!"—having mistaken some ancient bisons for modern bulls.

Sautuola's discovery naturally stimulated interest in the exploration of other caves. In all, about fifty are now known which contain important paintings. They lie mostly in the general region of southwest France and the northeasterly section of Spain. A great many bits of bone and ivory, some of them carved or incised with drawings, have been unearthed from strata of Paleolithic date. We thus possess a considerable body of material from that remote era.

The assertion that any artistic material whatever falls between 40,000 B.C. and 20,000 B.C. is not one to be accepted lightly; but as a matter of fact, it rests upon data considerably more sound than the evidence we often depend upon to set the period of objects only a few centuries old. Some of the animals represented are extinct, but are known to have been native to the region before the last glacier. Many of the caves, moreover, were closed by gravel deposits laid down as the glacier retreated, thus furnishing proof that the cavern behind had not been entered since.

Because we know nothing of the people who painted the pictures and because the pictures themselves came to light so recently, Paleolithic art hardly forms part of the European tradition. Certain general conclusions may

FORERUNNERS OF THE
WESTERN TRADITION

be drawn from the paintings, however; and these are perhaps more cogent for the very reason that historical continuity is not involved.

In the first place, it is interesting to see that the Paleolithic artists knew all the fundamental techniques of drawing and painting. In one place or another, we may find instances of pure *delineation,* of *form drawing* (line plus modeling in monotone), of *line and local tone* (line plus flat washes of color), and of complete painting (Figs. 2.1–3).

In the manipulation of all techniques, moreover, these early and forgotten artists reached a level of skill which must be described as superb. They understood how to vary the character of their line to express the sleek grace of the antelope and the bumpy stance of the buffalo; for a similar demonstration we must look to the great painters of China and Japan. Their modeling was equally subtle. They graded their tones from light to dark in a way that defined contour in no uncertain fashion. More than that, they managed to work the brush so as to suggest textures without actually describing them.

Splendid as they were in the rendering of single animals, these remote artists appear to have had no notion of the artistic possibilities inherent in the arrangement of several figures in relation to each other and in relation also to a setting. The art of *composition,* that is to say, seems not to have been conceived. Many of the best animal figures overlap others, and a general view of any large number together furnishes us with a definition for *helter-skelter* (Fig. 2.4). Composition aside, however, Paleolithic painting stands as irrefutable proof that the history of art is by no means equivalent to an upward evolution of technique. As more than one competent critic has felt

13

Fig. 2.1 Dordogne. Bison on roof of cave.   Fig. 2.2 Altamira. Deer's head.

Fig. 2.3 Altamira. Wild boar.

Fig. 2.4 Altamira. Drawing to show the arrangment of animal paintings on the ceiling of the cave. (Fig. 2.1 is from Capitan, Peyrony, & Breuil, *Font de Gaume*, Monaco, 1910. Figs. 2.2–4 are from Carthaillac & Breuil, *La Caverne d'Altamira à Saintillane près Santander*, Monaco, 1906.)

impelled to declare, these artists were as skillful as anybody since. One cannot paint better; he can only paint differently.

EGYPTIAN ART

The Pyramids are the most conspicuous and famous of all Egyptian monuments. The three biggest stand at Giza on the western bank of the Nile a short distance upstream from modern Cairo. In the old days, a prodigious and romantic antiquity was assigned to these imposing piles, but more modern research has sobered our estimate. Reasoning largely from astronomical events recorded in the written history of Egypt, scholars have found it possible to fix the chronology within broad but sure limits. It is now generally believed that King Khufu, or Cheops, who dedicated the biggest pyramid, reigned about 3000 B.C.

The monument he left us remains to this day the largest of man-made structures. It is the largest, that is, ever raised from a level footing, as distinct from the application of masonry to a hill or mound. Originally it measured approximately 755 feet square on the base, rose to an apex 481 feet above the ground, and defined a volume of about 85,000,000 cubic feet. It has been estimated that 2,300,000 blocks of cut stone went into its construction, each weighing two and a half tons or thereabouts.

The mere act of raising such a structure bespeaks a prosperous and highly organized society, but the expenditure of so much labor upon a single monument also declares the existence of a compelling motive in any society whatever, no matter how rich. The accurate orientation of the pyramids, each with its sides facing the cardinal points of the compass, has suggested to some that astronomical observations might have been part of the intention. But accurate surveying was commonplace in Egypt, having developed early because landmarks were so often washed away by the inundations of the Nile. Casting aside this and other suggestions of an equally ingenious kind, we come back in the end to the traditional explanation; namely, that the pyramids were no more and no less than royal tombs.

As such, they reflect several aspects of the Egyptian character. More than power and social leadership was centered in the person of the pharaoh. He was believed to be something very close to a deity on earth; and yet, by a paradox, he was mortal enough to make it of supreme importance that his immortality be guaranteed by a tremendous effort devoted to the permanent preservation of his body. The body itself was elaborately embalmed, and the great mass of the pyramid did no more than secrete and shelter it.

The student of social history might well pause at this point to consider the implications of so immense an investment for such a purpose, but it is our present business to learn artistic lessons from the pyramids. In some ways they are peculiarly useful simply because they are extreme. They illustrate better than any other monuments, in fact, the three-part nature of architecture. Because we must look at it, architecture is an art of form, like sculpture. Because we must build it, architecture is a department of mechanics and may be assessed as good or bad by reference to the efficiency with which physical problems are solved. And because we must use it, any building is a device devoted to the functions of human life. Every structure on earth represents a balance of some kind among these three elements.

The designers of the pyramids chose to emphasize form at the expense of engineering and utility. The construction they used, while simple in principle, was wasteful of material to an almost unbelievable degree. There are no buildings that contain a smaller volume of useful space in proportion to their bulk; and for the special function of safeguarding the royal mummy, the pyramids proved a complete failure—every tomb chamber was rifled at an early date. But over against these faults, we must list the tremendous effect of a simple, lucid shape rendered on the colossal scale. Geometric beauty has never been made more impressive.

In addition to that virtue, we must mention still another that might at first escape attention: the virtue of permanence. In some form and to some degree, every great artist has always intended that his work should last forever. Indeed, it may be questioned whether greatness is a psychological possibility without the sobering discipline of a beckoning eternity. In any case, it is an obvious probability that the pyramids will remain in plain sight long after every other work of our race has passed into nothingness, for in durability those great landmarks surpass anything and everything else in the history of art.

Even so, the pyramids remain a historical curiosity. As an architectural type, they did not survive the so-called Old Kingdom (about 2980-2475 B.C.), and except for the three big ones at Giza, there are no others of general interest or importance. Thus even in Egypt, these celebrated buildings must be thought of as a passing episode in art history.

The Egyptians built houses, palaces, and public buildings, but their temples were the only type of building besides the pyramids where the urge for permanence governed design and construction. The elements of the standard Egyptian temple are illustrated by Figure 2.5. The important divisions are four. One enters by way of an immense gate, or *pylon;* ordinarily this consists of two masses of masonry to either side of the opening, and of a peculiar shape: broader at the bottom than at the top, and capped by an overhanging *cornice* usually in the form seen here, and called the *Egyptian gorge* or *cavetto cornice.* (Fig. 2.6). Having passed through the pylon, one then finds

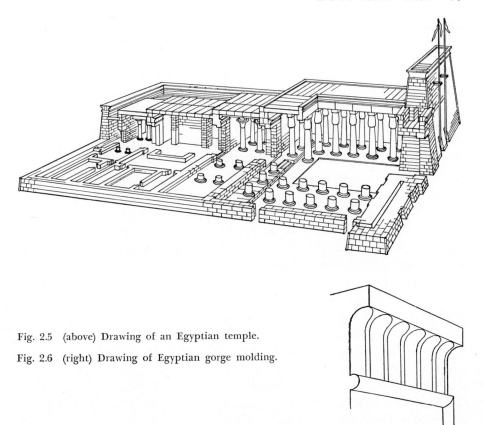

Fig. 2.5 (above) Drawing of an Egyptian temple.

Fig. 2.6 (right) Drawing of Egyptian gorge molding.

himself in the second section, an open courtyard surrounded by a double row of columns which carry a flat roof. Beyond the courtyard, we find the *hypostyle hall,* so-called, which is very nearly filled with columns and entirely roofed over. And beyond that is the sanctuary, a small chamber probably quite without natural lighting where the sacred image or sacred object was installed.

The reader will understand that individual temples may vary from the norm. One or more of the elements cited may be omitted or repeated, the latter being illustrated by the complexity of the two great temples to Amon, at Karnak and at Luxor, both of which reflect the building enterprise of numerous pharaohs.

As an architectural type, the Egyptian temple is of local interest only; but certain of its characteristics were destined to have an important history.

At some early date, the Egyptians decided to engineer their temples on the post-and-lintel system (see Appendix I, *Structural Principles*). They were familiar with the arch, which in many ways is a better method for spanning an opening between vertical supports; but with characteristic fixity of mind, they made a convention of the lintel and used nothing else for nearly four thousand years.

The peculiar form given the post and lintel by the Egyptians probably served as an example to the Greeks. The typical Egyptian post was a column, which is to say, a vertical support with a circular or nearly circular cross-section; and the typical Egyptian lintel was finished off at the top with an overhanging cornice. Columns were destined to be standard in Greek work, although direct adaptations of the several Egyptian types are almost unknown. All Greek architecture used the cornice; and during its later, or Hellenistic period, there occur occasional adaptations of the Egyptian gorge.

But more interesting than these physical details is the religious concept reflected in the plan of the temple. The pylon may be said to shut the court-yard away from the world, and the hypostyle forms a transition between the semiprivacy of the courtyard and the complete privacy of the sanctuary. While a direct historical connection may or may not exist, it is a fact that the plan for the standard Christian church follows a similar theory of pro-gression: from the less toward the more sacred. The earliest churches, indeed, usually had an *atrium,* or open court, which related to the position of the altar (page 235) very much as the Egyptian courtyard related to the Egyptian sanctuary.

Egypt produced an immense amount of sculpture. Usually the motive was religious. It had to do with the belief that survival of the soul depended upon preservation of the body, and statuary furnished a method of providing the soul with extra bodies in the shape of portrait figures. Sometimes these were duplicated and reduplicated in job lots in the apparent hope that at least one might survive.

Accurate portraiture was the prime desideratum for such a purpose, and it developed early and remained a distinctive feature of Egyptian art through-out its long history. It is notable that the bodies and legs of Egyptian statues are often rendered in perfunctory fashion, and that attached to these rather nondescript torsos we find heads modeled with such subtlety that they seem to be literally alive. The Egyptian sculptors thus furnish us with the first demonstration of the artistic philosophy we may recognize as *objective realism*.

The objective realist starts out by subjecting some living model to minute scrutiny. He then attempts to describe that human being in straightforward fashion, without permitting either prejudice or preference to guide his hand. Because neither sculpture nor painting can reproduce the conditions of nature, a strict copy of the model may not be attempted and never results in any normal studio. But within the simple limitations of his medium, the artist sticks to the facts as best he can.

The strength of objective realism is the same as the strength of science. In those few periods where it has flourished, the greater artists were in fact scientists engaged in the investigation of optical phenomena. The weakness of objective realism is made all too apparent, however, by the general run of Egyptian portraiture. As a philosophy, it tends to chain the artist to the particular person or object he is attempting to describe and record. He is unlikely to permit the intrusion of ideas, much less to make positive suggestions of an idealistic sort. The net result is all too likely to be no more than a mere statement of fact, without discrimination between the importance of facts.

For our better understanding of objective realism, it is necessary to remark that the word *realism* (without the adjective) has attained a special meaning through its frequent application to the work of artists and authors who deliberately select unlovely and even sordid subject matter. Without suggesting that their philosophy lacks a legitimate place in art, we must recognize that they employ the hideous or the morbid for reasons of their own which have to do with the expression of particular ideas—not with the reality of the visual world. Nature, so far as we can tell, is impartial. The rain falls on the just and the unjust alike, and both beauty and the opposite are brought into being in equal measure.

As objective realists, the Egyptian portrait sculptors showed as little bias as nature herself. Given an elderly sitter (Fig. 2.7), they described him as he was, disdaining to omit the physical deterioration of the body. Such work may be unlovely; but it has a certain integrity nevertheless, a point illustrated in more subtle fashion by the well-known bust of *Queen Nefertiti* (Figs. 2.8–9). Too often photographed in what the lady herself might have called a favorable light, the piece is generally thought to be an example of idealism. A closer examination of the surface tells us of a woman no longer young. Her beauty remains, but it depends upon the structure of the skull. It would have been easy for the sculptor to smooth over the nascent wrinkles, and to alter the angle and proportion of the oddly elongated neck; but obviously, his philosophy forbade such tampering with fact.

In all departments of life, it was the Egyptian habit to work out a solution to some problem and thereafter to solve the same problem always in the same way. It is not surprising, therefore, to find that Egyptian sculptors settled very early upon certain artistic conventions which they maintained almost without change for some forty centuries. By their very nature, those conventions were restrictive with respect to freedom and originality of expression. At the same time, one must concede that their adoption in the first place was reasonable, and resulted in an uncommon measure of clarity.

Desiring permanence in their sculpture as in everything else, the Egyp-

Fig. 2.7 (left) Boston, Museum of Fine Arts. Head of a priest. Ptolemaic. Basalt.

Fig. 2.8–9 (opposite) Berlin, Staatliche Museum. *Queen Nefertiti.* Painted limestone, rock crystal eyes. 14th century B.C. (Photographs taken for the U.S. Military Government)

tians favored the harder and stronger stones like basalt or diorite, although metal, wood, pottery, and other materials were used for less important examples.

When statues were carved in the round, certain other measures were taken to insure their durability. It was customary, for example, to leave part of the original block attached to the back of the figure in the shape of a slab (Fig. 2.10). The familiar way of dressing the hair in the form of a long, wide bob is not reflective of contemporary fashion, but signifies the artist's desire to brace the head against being broken off at the neck. The wisdom of these arrangements is attested by the fact that most Egyptian figures have survived in almost perfect condition—a statement that cannot be made about any other school of sculpture.

For the pose of standing and seated figures rendered in the round, the Egyptians almost without exception adhered to the anatomical arrangement we know as *the convention of frontality,* also illustrated by Figure 2.10. The expression means that a vertical line drawn from the middle of the forehead to the ground will approximately bisect the statue. It follows that the body must be stiffly erect. It is impossible to maintain this pose and represent any action more complicated than putting one foot slightly forward from the other; by the same token, the expression of content or feeling through physical movement is foreclosed. A certain degree of ceremonial dignity is

nevertheless realized. It is doubtless for that reason that these superb technicians felt it appropriate to continue a feature often unconsciously produced in the sculpture of children and other genuinely primitive artists.

In addition to portrait statues in the round, the Egyptians covered vast areas of wall space with narrative paintings or with relief sculpture to which color might or might not be applied. In all such work, the artist was confronted with the necessity for rendering the human body (a three-dimensional solid) on a flat surface. Some systematic method of projection was required. It is notable that minor and incidental figures, even those in difficult poses, were occasionally drawn with an ease and accuracy that betokens something better than a working knowledge of perspective and foreshortening. But for major art, which is to say wherever the artist became self-conscious about matters like dignity, *the convention of broadest aspect* was applied (Fig. 2.11).

A figure drawn according to this convention exhibits the following peculiarities: The head is seen in profile, but within the profile of the face, the eye is presented in full-face view. The torso is also presented in full-face view. To it are attached the arms and legs, all rendered in profile. All parts are hooked together without any indication of the muscular contortion that would have to take place were the pose attempted by a living model.

Because children often make pictures in much the same way, the notion suggests itself that the convention is childish and that the Egyptian artists

Fig. 2.10 Boston, Museum of Fine Arts. *Mycerinus and His Queen.*

Fig. 2.11 Drawing to illustrate the convention of the broadest aspect.

never grew up. But we can not dispose of it so lightly. Among other things which recommend broadest aspect to the mature mind are such concepts as the following.

Our modern convention of perspective-rendering has important limitations. It permits us only the view of a man as he might appear across our line of sight at a particular and passing instant of time. The merit of our convention inheres in its correspondence with visual experience; but visual experience of an instantaneous kind is often extremely unsatisfactory. When asked to examine a house, a tree, or a statue, we instinctively take more than one look. We walk around the object in an effort to observe each part to the best advantage. We do not remember what we have seen as we saw it at any single moment; we recall, rather, each part of the whole at the time that part impressed us the most. If asked to write a description of what we saw, it is a virtual certainty that we will set down the facts not according to the convention of perspective and foreshortening, but in a manner very close to the convention of broadest aspect.

It will be appreciated, therefore, that the difference between this ancient convention and our own is not a difference between truth and untruth, but merely the question of whether we wish art to correspond with ocular experience or with the procedure we in fact follow when comprehending a set of visual data and remembering them. From the standpoint of completeness, the advantage is with the convention of broadest aspect. It gives emphasis to the significant, disregards the nonessential, and leaves nothing to luck. Outlandish though it may seem until we become accustomed to it, there is no denying that the method is rational, and no escaping the conclusion that it opens up the possibility of a more considered analysis of whatever truth may be communicated by way of the visual arts.

MESOPOTAMIAN ART

Two ethnic groups composed the ancient population of Mesopotamia, the Babylonians and the Assyrians. The greatest cities of the region were Babylon on the Euphrates and Nineveh on the Tigris, the latter being the Assyrian capital. These two peoples remained separate to an unusual degree and hated each other. The political history of the region is an account of shifting ascendancy, first one being on top and then the other. Warfare was developed almost to its logical conclusion. The so-called Palace of Sargon at Khorsabad remains the most imposing fort ever built. It contained about seven hundred rooms, some of them immense, and it rose from the ground on a platform over 50 feet high, about 1,100 feet long, and about 950 wide. The exterior walls were 28 feet thick, and their continuity was broken by a sophisticated arrangement of salient towers designed to permit cross-fire from archers stationed on the battlements. The need for such a structure, and one aspect of the nature of the people, may be inferred from the action of the Babylonians in 612 B.C. In that year they captured Nineveh, killed most of the inhabitants, and did their utmost to destroy the city. Xenophon, who passed that way in 401 B.C. as a member of the ill-fated army of Cyrus the Younger, merely noted (*Anabasis* Bk. III) the existence of a vast and totally uninhabited ruin. He estimated the circuit of the place as about twenty miles, recorded that the walls rose to a hundred feet at some places, and called the site Mespila.

These facts are important because one of Mesopotamia's contributions to later art was a tradition of savagery. The ceremonial portraits of Mesopotamian kings (Fig. 2.12) present an appalling class of humanity. Prodigious strength, described all too unmistakably by the method of broadest aspect, was vested in the monarch whose face, while intelligent, is both fierce and pitiless.

Reliefs with more personal and intimate subject matter have been found in large numbers. Some of them give vignettes of the daily life of the time, but those in which both artist and patron obviously took the most satisfaction are those which show the most sanguinary kind of hunting scene. The king seems always to be in the very act of killing. Some of the animal portraits, if considered merely as demonstrations of representational skill, are rendered with a delicate hand guided by sensitive observation—an impression all but reversed by the cruelty of their content (Fig. 2.13).

Among the various monuments that emphasize the savage aspect of Mesopotamian character, we should make special mention of the imaginary monsters. These exist in various sizes and in the round as well as in relief. Best known, simply because they are immense and therefore conspicuous, are the five-legged beasts, half-bull and half-human, habitually set up to either side of a palace gateway (Fig. 2.14). It is from this general category, including dragons and griffins as well as fanciful combinations of more ordinary anatomy, that we get, by a vague and devious route presently to be explained (page 253), the gargoyles and other grotesques of Western medieval art.

♦ *The Matter of Artistic Style, and the Three Fundamental Styles of European Art* An even more cogent and far-reaching contribution made by Mesopotamia was the invention and perfection of the mode of artistic expression we have come to recognize as the *Style of the Near East,* often loosely and conveniently referred to as "the Oriental Style." Before attempting a definition and analysis, we must digress for a brief account of recent events in art history.

C. R. Morey's most important contribution to scholarship was contained in a short but profound article which appeared in the *Art Bulletin* (Vol. 7, No. 2) for December, 1924. At the time, Morey was attempting to produce an explanation which would bring order out of the chaos in which he found the archeology of the Early Middle Ages. He succeeded in that objective, and in so doing, he wrote down some of the most penetrating, fundamental, and illuminating observations that have ever been put forward by an art historian. He saw that his immediate problem was no local and temporary mix-up. It was, rather, a single instance in the operation of the broad forces which account for the entire history of European art.

His great idea was to realize that the apparent confusion of the Western tradition in art might be explained much as we explain the nature of the several spoken languages, namely, by reference to the history, operation, and amalgamation of only three fundamental styles—each of which had at one time and in its native region existed in a comparatively pure and unadulterated form. The styles Morey recognized were the *Style of the Near East,* the

Fig. 2.12 (top) London, British Museum. *Dying Lioness*. From the Palace of Ashurbanipal at Nineveh. 668–626 B.C. Alabaster. 25 by 39½ inches.

Fig. 2.13 (left) Williamstown, Mass., Lawrence Museum. *Ashurnasirpal the 2nd*. Nimrud.

Fig 2.14 (above) New York, Metropolitan Museum. Five-legged gateway monster from the Palace of Ashurnasirpal the 2nd at Nimrud. First half of the 9th century B.C.

Classical Style which originated in Greece, and the *Northern Style* which was introduced by the barbarian races who destroyed the Roman Empire.

We shall deal immediately with the Style of the Near East, and with the other two in due season. In approaching all three, it is necessary to remember that we are speaking in broad generalizations. As over against the truth of such generalizations, numerous exceptions bear no weight. The reader should neglect them. Still a hypothesis, Morey's theory has so far stood the test of nearly a generation, and when his *Medieval Art* appeared in 1942, the theory was republished virtually as first stated.

Once the main tenor of Morey's thought is accepted, it follows that every later work of art may to a large extent be explained by reference to the crossbreeding that has taken place among the elements that form its heritage. Artists, that is to say, find their personal expression through an artistic language they inherit. They do not invent the language, although a single great career may serve to modify it. They use artistic styles as naturally and unconsciously as we speak English—a native tongue which is a historical accident for each of us, and a tool we turn to our own purpose without complaining that we did not choose it.

It is necessary at this point to give to the word *style* a more formal definition than has hitherto been required. It is a mistake to use the word as a term of praise or to confuse it with passing fashion. We shall be wiser if we reserve it for cases where we discern an established artistic usage. Things that happen only once are not styles. The term becomes appropriate only when we can see a familiar set of visual facts in a familiar coordination.

What facts do we look for, and what coordination?

The first way in which we can distinguish one style from another is by reference to its *favorite medium*. We cannot tell the reason, but we can nevertheless note the fact that whenever and wherever a number of artists may be thought of as a school or related group, all members share the tacit assumption that some particular art is the fundamental art. During the 19th century, it was painting. It was architecture in Gothic France and sculpture in Greece. Modes of expression natural and appropriate for the favorite medium invariably affect everything else and sometimes appear in strange applications.

The stylistic psychology of any artistic school is perhaps even more intimately affected by the *esthetic means* appropriate to its favorite medium. The sculptor thinks always of mass and contour, and the painter who imitates the sculptor will do the same thing. Draftsmen express themselves by using the line, and keep doing so when they paint. The rug-maker and the weaver are inevitably self-conscious about color and texture; if such a man becomes a sculptor, his carving will betray his background.

Subject matter is a third element to which we may refer when defining an artistic style or when contrasting it with another. History shows that the preference for one kind of subject has at times been virtually exclusive—as, for example, the Greek preoccupation with the human figure and the northern genius for the grotesque.

Fourthly and finally, we may know a style by the principles to which it habitually appeals when arranging the component parts of a painting or building into an artistic composition, as, for example, the Greek use of geometry or the dynamics of the Baroque. Once set, the same compositional system will be used innumerable times for works of art which differ radically in scale and purpose, and even in effect upon our sensibilities.

♦ *The Style of the Near East* Keeping in mind the nature of style as such, and the four bare essentials just mentioned, we may now define and characterize the Style of the Near East which, in all essentials, originated in ancient Mesopotamia and was brought to perfection there.

The Near East still produces most of the world's finest rugs; and that was so during antiquity also. Every object of Mesopotamian art bears the imprint of a mind that conceived rug-weaving as the fundamental art. Thus, the Mesopotamian sculptor, when representing a man, dwelt with infinite care upon the rendering of textures in whatever garments made up the costume. Hair and beard were rarely made to look as they doubtless appeared on the living model; the opportunity was taken, rather, to work them into patterns of the kind appropriate to a fine textile. Figure 2.15 shows an example in which the special taste for carpet textures is obvious.

As to subject matter and in spite of the numerous instances during antiquity where outright and descriptive representation took place, the artists of the Near East preferred to use only decorative patterns of the kind still familiar on modern Persian rugs. As time went on, the preference for abstract design grew into something very close to a phobia—if we look ahead to the start of the Christian era, we shall see a Near East which abhorred the representation of humanity and found visual expression only in decorative patterns composed of motives originally derived from plants and flowers and other natural forms, but so conventionalized as to make specific recognition impossible.

We have no rugs from ancient Mesopotamia, but we know what they looked like. The stone slabs of palace pavements (Fig. 2.16) were often carved in very low relief to imitate carpets, and we have some of the slabs. Even better for our purpose are the colored tiles used as exterior finish for walls made from sun-dried brick. An unusually interesting bit of this work is preserved at Berlin; originally it decorated Nebuchadnezzar's palace at Babylon (Fig. 2.17). This single specimen is in itself a demonstration of the Oriental means of expression and of the principles used for composition,

Fig. 2.15 New York, Metropolitan Museum. *A Median Leading Two Horses.* 8th century B.C.

both self-evidently derivative from practices suitable for the design of textiles. The power of the textile tradition may be gauged by the very fact that an esthetic preference of so specialized a type could be deliberately carried over into the manufacture of building materials.

The patterned tile now brought under review exists like a rug as a flat surface. There is no relief of any kind. No gradation of shadow suggests convexity or concavity of form. The technique is a pure case of line and flat tone; and while any skillful artist can manipulate line and flat tone in such a way that contours are suggested but not described, even that expedient was deliberately avoided. Each separate and conventionalized floral motive asserts its visual existence solely as a spot of color in contrast with the background. Contrasts of color, or light and dark, or both together, constituted the ultimate means of esthetic expression to which the Near Eastern artist instinctively turned.

As a whole, the work of art may be described as a succession of spots of light-on-dark, and in understanding the system according to which these are composed, two points need explanation. They are *rhythm* and *indefinite extension.*

Rhythm depends upon the existence of accents. In music, the accented note is struck louder, more sharply, or otherwise given distinction among the rest. The rhythm of poetry depends upon the accented syllable, and the rhythm of dancing depends upon the accentuation of certain motions. But accents alone cannot produce a rhythm; the important thing is to make the accents come according to a system. The system may be utterly simple or unbelievably complex, but without a schedule for the appearance and reappearance of accents, there is no rhythm.

In the visual arts, the rhythmic sensation may be evoked in numerous ways. Undulations of drapery often produce the effect, as do the rise and fall of arches in an arcade. Human figures represented as in rhythmic motion

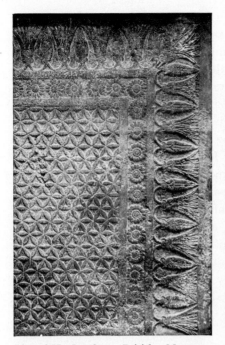

Fig. 2.16 London, British Museum. Fragment of pavement from Nineveh. About 700 B.C.

Fig. 2.17 Berlin. Glazed tiles from the Throne Room of the Palace of Nebuchadnezzar at Babylon. (Stoedtner)

can have a similar influence upon our sensibilities. The essential thing in talking about any particular instance of rhythm is to name the means by which accent is called into being: in the present case we are looking at a rhythm established by spots of light against a dark ground. Each spot gives the eye a kind of shock, and the shocks come at systematic intervals.

Within the field covered by our book plate, we see three different bands of spots across the surface. They differ in the shape and scale of the single motives which are brought out in accent, and they differ in the schedule that governs the arrangement of accents. The phenomenon before us is familiar in music; namely, the experience of comprehending several rhythms simultaneously.

Rhythm, in itself, has no limits. The internal logic of our detail from the brick frieze once at Babylon tells us nothing about where the frieze began or where it will end. It might be a few yards long, or extend from Babylon to Boston without self-contradiction. Conceivably, the composition might spread indefinitely in all four directions until it covered the universe. There is no necessary beginning, middle, or end; no frame and no boundaries.

But what could be better common sense if one is in the business of designing textiles? Can the weaver predict how we will cut up his bolt of cloth, or the rug-maker tell what sections of his rug we may choose to obscure with furniture? Such men are wise if, as in the present case, they restrict themselves to the compositional method studio jargon knows as the "all-over pattern," an expression meaning that every section of the area covered is quite as interesting as every other section, and that our attention is evenly distributed all over the surface. Color, in short, is the means and rhythm is the method for producing the desired result of indefinite extension.

In assessing the value and determining the propriety of the compositional method of the Near East, we must never forget that it was invented for the design of cloth and is useful wherever a more or less indefinite area must be covered with decoration—extensive wall paintings, for example, and continuous friezes of any kind. We must not confuse these peculiar and special advantages with artistic excellence arrived at by other methods and for different purposes. Artistic unity, which we often hear mentioned as an essential element of all esthetic goodness, is absent by the very nature of the Near Eastern method. Unity was, in fact, exactly what they did not want. It is here, we shall find (page 66), that the Oriental mind comes most radically into contrast with the Greek.

Chapter 3

OUR KNOWLEDGE OF GREEK ART—
ITS LIMITS AND ITS IMPORTANCE

OUR KNOWLEDGE of Greek art is more limited than we sometimes permit
ourselves to suppose.

The subject has been under assiduous investigation, almost without
pause, since Winckelmann published his *History of the Art of Ancient Times*
in 1764. It is impossible to exaggerate the amount of scholarly effort expended
upon digging and other forms of archeological activity. It is similarly difficult
to find words to describe in any adequate way the intelligence and the patience brought to focus on every tiniest bit of evidence; everything we possess has been worked to the limit in the hope of shedding all possible light
on problems that still remain unsolved.

As a result of this prolonged effort we have assembled a substantial collection of Greek art, and we have established with something close to certainty the main outlines of its evolution. We can trace its development in
orderly fashion from primitive beginnings to the so-called "Great Age" of the
5th and 4th centuries B.C. Somewhat less neatly but still with reasonable
assurance, we can explain how Greek influence spread with the conquests of
Alexander and how outside influences affected Greece. Next, it is clearly
established that Rome, the political mistress of the Mediterranean world, was
in her art derivative from Greece. Finally, we can describe in a general way
how the Classical Style passed out of existence as antiquity failed and the
Middle Ages began.

With respect to monuments, we are most fortunate in the field of architecture. There are enough well-preserved temple ruins to give us an accurate
knowledge of the best Greek religious buildings. We can also be confident

GREEK ART TO 450 B.C.

with regard to the Greek theater. But we know next to nothing about any other class of Greek building.

We have an excellent collection of originals from the Archaic and Transitional periods of Greek sculpture (about 1100–450 B.C.), and we are well off for monuments from the Hellenistic and Roman periods (323 B.C. to about A.D. 300). For the Great Age (about 450–325 B.C.), our monumental evidence is pitiful: we have only one putative original from the hand of a sculptor who commanded fame and prestige in ancient times. Our picture of Greek sculpture at its best, that is to say, is a mere archeological reconstruction based upon literary evidence, analogies, and monumental evidence of the second, third, and fourth level of excellence. We nevertheless have a clear and probably a very accurate account of what happened.

We know that Greek painting was important. There is some reason to think, indeed, that the Greeks themselves ranked their painters as being greater artists, on the whole, or at least more definitive artists than their sculptors. When writing the *Poetics,* Aristotle mentioned a painter almost every time he wanted to make an analogy with the visual arts, and he hardly referred to sculpture. We may assume that the painters came most easily to mind simply because they had made a greater impression upon him.

But beyond repeating the names he mentioned (Polygnotus, Zeuxis, Pauson, Dionysus) we have almost nothing to say. At times famous paintings were rather freely copied by the commercial artists employed in the decoration of Greek pottery, and we are lucky enough to have inherited a substantial number of their vases. In Greece, even those humbler artists were uncommonly fine, and Greek vase painting constitutes one of the charming byways of art history. It would be unfair to describe it in stronger terms; and as for gaining any satisfactory visualization of the great lost paintings, many of us have studied the vase pictures without success.

In the face of this somewhat discouraging situation, it is undeniable that there is magic in Greek art. It has laid hold on the European imagination as no other art has ever done. It is always there as an influence tending to mold the shape of other modes and manners, and Greek standards are forever asserting themselves as the plane of reference to which other art should be referred.

An important and recurring phenomenon of art history is the likelihood that the Greek style in surprisingly pure form may flare up anywhere. It never completely died out in Italy, even during the Middle Ages. It strongly affected the architecture of the Romanesque cathedral at Autun, and it modified the style of the Gothic sculptors of Reims. Giotto's later compositions are according to the Greek system, and Greece is the underlying ideal of the entire High Renaissance. During the 19th century, David, Ingres, and the other French Neoclassicists sought in the literal sense of the word to bring Greek art back to life—an enterprise that came close to success in the so-called Greek Revival architecture of America. We are correctly reminded of the Greek in many paintings by Picasso.

Nothing else in art history has the same importance.

HISTORICAL CONSIDERATIONS

Our Western civilization, including its artistic tradition, started with Greece, but it is necessary to make it plain what *Greece* means in this connection.

We refer to *Classical Greece,* or to the culture and civilization which achieved its special and definitive character about the time of the poet Homer, who seems to have lived in Ionia (Asia Minor) during the 9th century B.C.

The people we call the Greeks were an amalgam of several races. So far as we can tell, the population of the area sprang from the mixture of its aborigines with the peoples who entered the region in at least three successive waves of invasion and migration, each separated from the last by an interval of centuries. The aborigines appear to have had their centers among the islands called the Cyclades, which stretch like a chain southeasterly from the coast near Athens. Of these people we know nothing more than we can deduce from their art, but even that is significant.

About 3000 B.C. another civilization became dominant. It centered on the island of Crete, with the capital at Knossos. Knossos and other sites on the island have been actively excavated from the first years of the 20th cen-

tury, and the discoveries have been analyzed from time to time in the voluminous reports of Sir Arthur Evans. The ruins of an immense palace have been laid bare at Knossos. Everything points to a civilization notable for refinement of life and justifiable pride of culture. Sea power was evidently the source of its security, for Knossos was without fortification. The Cretan civilization is referred to by various names, most of them intended to be noncommittal. Sir Arthur Evans wisely prefers to call it *Minoan,* a pretty word which has at least the endorsement of later mythology, for King Minos, proprietor of the terrible Minotaur, lived on Crete. *Minotaur* means merely "Minos's bull," and both the frescoes and carvings of this culture show that the bullfight was a favorite sport.

About 1400 B.C. Crete was invaded and Knossos destroyed by fire. We are probably justified in calling the conquerors Achaeans. Their centers were on the mainland at Mycenae and Tiryns, both places being near the head of the Gulf of Argolis. These sites were excavated with astonishing success by Heinrich Schliemann (1822–1890), who worked at Mycenae in 1876 and at Tiryns in 1884.

Schliemann's finds were rich beyond comparison. At Mycenae, he recovered 701 decorated gold discs in one grave alone. The style of the decoration of these, and of pottery and frescoes from the same era, is similar to the style of the material found on Crete, but stiffer and less accomplished. From this and other indications, most scholars draw the conclusion that the Achaeans were culturally more rude than the Minoans, but wise enough to absorb what they could of the earlier civilization.

About 1100 B.C. the Achaeans were overwhelmed by a vigorous people we call the Dorians. Their culture was strong in those elements that make for survival and dominion; they brought the use of iron with them, all earlier inhabitants having been limited to bronze. It now seems that the Dorians were less outrageously barbaric than we used to be told, but it is still obvious that their taste lacked the amenities which were characteristic of both the Minoans and the Achaeans.

The history of the next four hundred years is unusually obscure. The period is often called the Greek Dark Ages, but there must have been some merit in the situation because the classical Greeks emerged at the end of it. Sculpture and painting in the earliest version of the Classical Style begin about 700 B.C. The first full-size statues appear to date about fifty or seventy-five years after that.

It will be noted that Homer's career falls in the middle of the Greek Dark Ages, if dark they actually were. His poems are notably disparaging whenever reference is made to the culture of his own time. Our best guess is that his narratives recount actual events in the heroic Achaean past, which he saw as a bygone age of gold.

Fig. 3.1   (left) Buffalo, Albright Art Gallery. Cycladic idol. About 3000 B.C. 13½ inches high.

Fig. 3.2   (right) Boston, Museum of Fine Arts. *Snake Goddess*. Gold and ivory. 7 inches high.

It would not serve our central purpose to take space for a connected and detailed account of Cycladic, Minoan, Achaean, and Doric art. Certain elements from this past nevertheless survived as the classical heritage, and some aspects of later Greek art are difficult to understand without reference to earlier tastes and customs. A few comments are therefore in order.

ART OF THE GREEK AREA PREVIOUS TO THE CLASSICAL ERA

✦ *The Cycladic Idols* (before 3000 B.C.)   A number of stone statuettes, all fairly consistent in style, have been recovered on the Cyclades from strata which, from other evidence, we can place before 3000 B.C. For lack of a better name, the statuettes are known as the *Cycladic idols*. The British Museum has a number, and there are a good many in the Louvre. A particularly fine example was acquired in 1940 for the collection of the Albright Art Gallery in Buffalo (Fig. 3.1).

The critics of past generations could see nothing but ignorance and crudity in the Cycladic idols. Today we are inclined to be more respectful.

Primitive art used to carry a strong connotation that the artist was unenlightened and knew no better, but that the speaker did. Serious and sympathetic study of earlier civilizations, or those isolated from European influence, has inclined our more recent opinion to caution. Mature reflection very often suggests that the so-called "primitive" peoples were in fact extremely sophisticated, and that their apparent crudity often denotes profound wisdom expressed with devastating directness. In the case of the Cycladic idols, there is much to sustain such a view.

In their original condition, all these little figures were probably painted. The same was true, as a matter of fact, for Greek sculpture of every subsequent period; but neither in this instance nor later is it possible to make any definite statement beyond the fact that color was applied. We do not know what pigments were used, or whether paint was employed to render details now lacking, such as the lips and the eyes. In any event, it is fair to doubt whether the coloration, had it survived, would change the effect to any material degree; and as they stand, the Cycladic idols testify to the existence of a school of sculptors with extraordinary powers of abstraction.

As a critical term for use in discussing the visual arts, we may define *abstraction* as the act of summarizing the appearance of a man, a scene, or an object, as contrasted to attempting a complete and detailed description thereof. All art is to some degree an abstraction simply because the artist's tools and materials cannot accomplish minute visual description no matter how hard the artist tries. But as a useful word, we had best reserve *abstraction* for monuments where the artist declines to employ all the descriptive techniques at hand, and insists upon summarizing so radically that he obviously abbreviates.

Abbreviation, by its very nature, tends to deny us something we might wish to see, but it has the virtue of enabling the artist to select the important and eliminate the extraneous. Obviously, the process can go either a little way or so far that all resemblance to the original subject is lost. The sculptors who did the Cycladic idols abstracted perhaps as much as might be possible without causing us to wonder whether human beings are represented. What is left?

The folded arms and erect pose suggest presence at some solemn ceremony. The thighs, torso, and shoulders are described only enough to tell us that the body is in excellent tone, that the muscles carry it with ease. The head is held high, and even though the face is blank except for the prominent nose, there is a plain statement of racial and family pride. The whole carriage, in fact, suggests an aristocracy and a code of manners where grace might shift instantly into arrogance. However brief his methods, it is difficult to miss the sculptor's intent.

It is an oddity that the art of the Greek area should have commenced

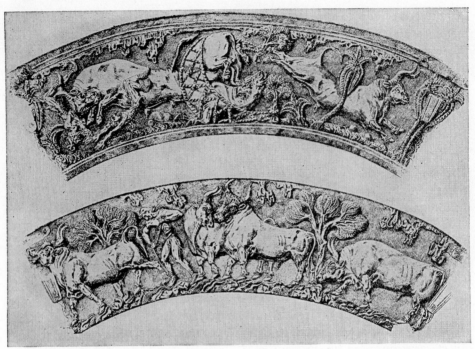

Fig. 3.3 Reliefs from the two gold cups found at Vaphio. Originals in National Museum, Athens. (From an engraving in Sir Arthur Evans, *The Palace of Minos*, Vol. 3, London, 1930.)

with so extreme a style. While it is impossible to make any direct historical connections between the Cycladic idols and later Greek work, it is by no means unreasonable to suggest that the artistic theory behind them formed part of the Greek heritage and left a taste for abstraction capable of coming into the open at any time. It is notable in this connection that the great sculpture of the 5th century, while predominantly naturalistic, nevertheless stands as a substantial simplification of natural fact which partakes strongly of the tendency to abstract.

♦ *Minoan and Mycenaean Art* (About 3000 to 1100 B.C) Minoan art is by no means lacking in abstraction, but exhibits at the same time a direct delight in the actual appearance of people, animals, plants, flowers, fish, and seaweeds. Almost every piece is eloquent of a happy life and a pleasant relation between man and his environment. Among the notable objects from this era, we may cite the following.

Two remarkable gold cups, doubtless of Cretan origin, were found in 1889 at Vaphio, near Sparta (Fig. 3.3). Both cups are decorated with miniature compositions in high relief, executed by the *repoussé* process (that is, the metal being worked or beaten into a mold from behind). The technique is so delicate and yet so vigorous as to belie the scale. Nothing in all art history is more thoroughly lively. One cup shows domesticated bulls enjoying themselves in a pasture. The other shows several Minoans risking life and limb to capture some wild bulls by catching them in nets. The laws of anatomy are blithely defied with consequent gain to the spirit of the occasion.

The Museum of Fine Arts in Boston has a little *Snake Goddess* of gold and ivory, also almost certainly of Minoan workmanship (Fig. 3.2). There is considerable abstraction in the body, particularly about the waist, which duplicates in conventional fashion the waist of many another Minoan figure, but both the posture and the face are eloquent of portraiture. Whoever the young lady may have been, her person and her personality remain herself, never seen before and never duplicated again. The tiny figure can be magnified almost indefinitely without loss of refinement; indeed it rather gains from a substantial increase in size, as on the lecture screen.

Minoan painting and sculpture went dead with the Achaean invasion. Objects associated with the era of Mycenae and Tiryns are obviously derivative from the style which had centered in Crete. They are not lacking in daintiness, but they have nothing like the life typical of the best production of the period before the destruction of Knossos. We may therefore pass over such material.

♦ *The Geometric Style* (About 1100 to 700 B.C.) The art that came in with the Dorians is generally known as the *Geometric style,* and its monuments consist of small bronze statuettes and pictures painted on vases. In general, these are even more radically abstracted than the Cycladic idols. The curves natural to human bodies and to animals are hardened into angular shapes or reduced to circular arcs. Such shapes are connected together to suggest a man or beast as the case may be. Decorative patterns show a similar severity; for the most part they amount to the repetition of the simplest geometric forms like the chevron, the meander, the checkerboard, and simple stripes or hatchings.

It was extremely difficult for the earlier critics to find anything good to say about the Geometric style except that it came to an end in the space of about four hundred years. The modern student has the advantage of broader standards of comparison, and he will reason much as we have already done with respect to the Cycladic Idols.

The best Geometric painting is found on the so-called *Dipylon vases.* These are some very large pieces of pottery used as grave monuments in the Dipylon Cemetery at Athens, from which they take their name. They are not made to hold water and might be called funnels rather than vases—where we put flowers on the grave, it was the humane custom of that time to refresh the deceased by pouring wine down to him (Fig. 3.4).

Fig. 3.4 New York, Metropolitan Museum. Dipylon vase. 8th century B.C.

If we can accept the abstraction, and it is admittedly harsh, some of the scenes on the Dipylon vases are entertaining and even exciting. The funeral procession is a favorite subject, as the purpose of the vase might suggest, but other scenes often appear. Of these, naval battles form a notable category. Some of the vases unmistakably reflect a memory of whole fleets in combat, and tell us that naval warfare was highly developed and that great battles took place in that now forgotten time.

None of the Geometric vase paintings has anything like the quality of the best bronzes from the same era. Of these, a notable example in almost perfect preservation is the miniature horse now in the Metropolitan Museum (Fig. 3.5). Somewhat puzzling to adults who have formed their taste solely upon representation, the merit of the little statue is attested by its great popularity among children. They are almost invariably delighted with it, and they have no difficulty in seeing that the sculptor meant to record the proud stance, the alert ears, the sensitive distension of the nostrils, and the sleek strong thighs. If they worry about the anatomy of the knees, they do not worry long: the artist merely meant to say that the knee is bumpy.

Fig. 3.5 New York, Metropolitan Museum. Horse. Bronze, 6 5/16 inches high. 8th century B.C.

♦ *The 7th Century B.C., or "The Period of Oriental Influence"* During the 7th century B.C., Greek taste seems to have shifted away from the severity of the Geometric style. For reasons that are not entirely clear, but are suggested by the establishment of Greek colonies on the Nile delta and by the spread of Phoenician commerce, the Dorian population had its eyes opened to the art of the Near East, in particular to the art of Persia—which, if we may characterize it in a word, was a richer and much gentler derivative from the Mesopotamian. The entire century is sometimes referred to, therefore, as "the period of Oriental influence." As before, the record of such influence is found almost exclusively in vase painting.

Geometric abstraction did not entirely die out, but the typical vase of the 7th century is decorated with rosettes, confronted birds, grotesque monsters, and various more or less natural but rather schematized animals. Human figures are very rare (Fig. 3.6.).

A strange immobility marks even the most naturalistic items in this catalogue of decoration. Running figures get nowhere. Roaring dragons make no noise. Nothing happens even though action ostensibly is represented.

The reason is not far to seek. The various decorative motives taken up by the Greek workmen come directly from the tradition of the Near East, where since the world began those with artistic inclination have turned most naturally to designing textiles. Textile designers are forced by the nature of their medium to work toward a composition characterized by an even spread

Fig. 3.6 Boston, Museum of Fine Arts. Vase from "the period of Oriental influence." 7th century B.C.

of interest over the entire surface (page 27), and it follows that any bird, flower, or animal appeals to the designer not as a factor in a narrative to be told, but merely as a spot of color against the background. He therefore arranges them without much regard for dramatic content, and his primary purpose is to produce a succession of rhythmic accents.

CHRONOLOGY OF THE CLASSICAL ERA OF GREEK ART

Such was the background when the classical era began in Greece. Each element of the heritage seems to have left something of itself in the Greek genius, and the separate parts of the heredity appear alone or in recognizable combination at odd times and places: the intellectual severity of abstraction, delight in natural fact, a certain love for rich decoration.

At some indefinite time during the latter part of the obscure period we have been covering, a new element came into the artistic philosophy of Greece. There is absolutely no way to explain how or why the decision was made, but it remains one of the most important in European cultural history. The Greeks chose to adopt the human figure as the chief and virtually the exclusive subject of their artistic endeavor. From the 7th century onward, their sculptors made practically nothing else, and their painters seem to have done much the same.

It has long been customary to recognize five periods in the evolution of Greek art during its classical phase. These coincide with significant political and social mutations; but as stylistic divisions, the separate periods correspond most closely with the development of sculpture, and only in a general way with architecture and painting. Greek sculpture therefore stands out as a peculiarly perfect case where the history of art gives a record of the contemporary state of mind.

The earliest statues of large size date somewhere this side of 650 B.C., and the period from that moment until about 480 B.C. is known by the name *Archaic*. Statues from the Archaic period exhibit major technical faults: gross anatomical errors, timid technique, obvious lack of control over facial expression.

The Persian Wars were over by 479 B.C.; and as war so often does, they stimulated the Greek mind and forced rapid development. The first half of the 5th century B.C. is generally called the *Transitional* period, a somewhat unfortunate term, but one which at least suggests progress. The course of the progress was always in the direction of complete technical mastery over both the medium and the subtleties of the human anatomy. Sculpture was still somewhat clumsy at the beginning of the half-century. At the end, the Greek artists had perfect control and were thenceforth limited only by the boundaries of their own imagination. A few lingering minor errors of anatomy (such as failure to overlap the eyelid, or an almost imperceptible stiffness of pose) linger to indicate a date earlier than 450.

The Great Age extends from the Age of Pericles to the death of Alexander, or from about 450 B.C. to 323 B.C. The Great Age is subdivided into the *Greek Fifth Century* (450–400 B.C.) and the *Greek Fourth Century* (400–323 B.C.), and those terms are used in the special sense indicated.

The Great Age is by common consent the period of supreme and definitive accomplishment, not only in art but in philosophy, culture, and ideals. Great civic monuments are the characteristic sculpture of the Fifth Century, usually representing the major gods. The two periods are separated by the tragedy of the Peloponnesian War, from which the political genius of Greece never recovered. Work from the Fourth Century is usually on a smaller, more personal scale. Subject matter is neither so grand nor so stirring, but more gracefully presented. The whole spirit of the century is contemplative and introspective.

Alexander's conquests spread Greek influence eastward and exposed Greece to influences from outside. The results were both inspiring and confusing. Most of the fixed conventions of Greek art went by the board in favor of variety and experiment. Some of the greatest monuments were brought into being and some of the very worst. To distinguish the age from earlier times we call it *Hellenistic* (Greeklike, or cultivating Greek ways) as contrasted to *Hellenic* (true Greek).

The kingdoms established by Alexander's heirs survived more or less independently until the Mediterranean world came under Roman dominion. The year 146 B.C., when Mummius took Corinth and erased the last claim of

Greek independence, is sometimes cited as the end of the Hellenistic period. However significant in political history, the event marks no important cultural or stylistic change. Roman art hardly existed before contact with Greece and constituted a further development of the Hellenistic.

THE ARCHAIC PERIOD (About 650 B.C. to about 480 B.C.)

We may skip lightly over developments during the Archaic period. Its principal contribution was to lay technical foundation for what was to come. Its sculptural output may be classified under four simple types of figures: a nondescript seated type, flying figures, and standing figures both male and female—the male being nude in most examples and the female always draped. Only the two latter categories are of general interest.

Our very earliest statue—at least most of us believe it to be so—is a draped female figure of Naxian marble, now in the National Museum at Athens (Fig. 3.7). An inscription says it was dedicated by Nikandra in honor of Artemis. The statue is shallow and flat, a fact which some have taken to indicate earlier wooden prototypes made from heavy planks. On the whole, it seems more likely that the sculptor, as most beginners still do, merely failed to appreciate how much space he needed for the third dimension.

The Nikandra figure has two features which in all probability reflect some contact with Egyptian work: the hair is spread broadly to either side, as though in a long bob, in an effort to brace the neck against possible breakage; and the pose exhibits the familiar convention of frontality. Both of these features had been habitual in Egypt from the earliest times.

Such crudity did not last long in Greece, and we may next turn our attention to the *Hera from Samos,* of some uncertain later date, now in the Louvre (Fig. 3.8). This statue is almost cylindrical in cross-section, a circumstance which has often been interpreted as indicating technical crudity. One sometimes hears the explanation that the primitive sculptor was translating into stone an early and inarticulate class of figure half-formed from the trunk of a tree. Because we know that naturalism was the coming thing in Greek art, it is deceptively easy to dismiss the *Hera* as an inadequate essay in that direction, but any such notion comes into contradiction with the obvious skill with which certain passages are handled. The differentiation of textures as between the silk of the skirt and the wool of the jacket is a capital instance of unmistakable suggestion without any labored attempt at complete visual description. The same may be said for the truly adequate swell of the bust and the protruding toes. In the end we find it difficult to maintain the thought that ignorance of any kind can be adduced to explain what we see. It is more reasonable to recognize this grandly columnar figure as virtually the final

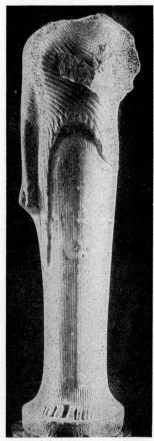

Figs. 3.7–8 Paris, Louvre. (left) Nikandra statue. (right) *Hera from Samos.*
(Alinari; Archives Photographiques)

expression of the strong tradition of abstraction in force when the Archaic period began.

We have a great many standing male figures from the Archaic period. It used to be customary to refer to the lot of them as "the Apollos," but since there is little reason to believe that the god was represented, the somewhat more accurate and noncommittal word *kouros* is becoming popular. It is nothing more than a transliteration of the Greek for *young man* (Fig. 3.9).

As a class, the *kouroi* suggest very strongly that the idea of large sculpture occurred to the Greeks because such art had been popular in Egypt. As though by convention, frontality was maintained almost to the very end of the Archaic era. Another duplication of Egyptian custom was the habit of putting the left foot forward, a nonessential feature that might well have been borrowed more or less unconsciously while trying to emulate a model.

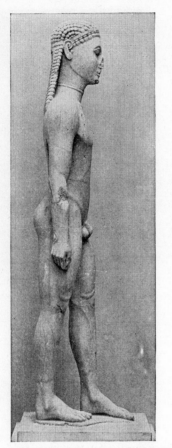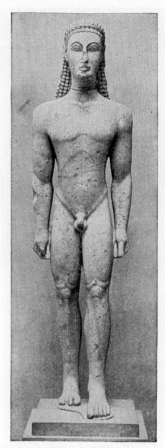

Fig. 3.9 New York, Metropolitan Museum. Statue of a young man.

A great gulf of difference separates the crudest Greek work from the Egyptian, however. The most important change of all is the mere fact that the Greek statues are nude. In the first instance, this custom may have started with nothing more profound than the observation that clothes get in the way when one is exercising, for as a national institution, the Olympic Games appear to date from the first recorded victories of 776 B.C., a year not overly far removed from the class of statue now under review. But however simple its beginnings, the introduction of the nude figure is one of the most important events in the history of art. The simple possibility of using the entire surface of the body opened up broader horizons almost beyond measure.

The artistic worth of the human nude derives from its superiority over the draped figure as a vehicle for communicating content. The state of the emotions and even the state of the soul makes itself manifest not in the face alone, but in the muscles. When the body is concealed by cloth, the artist simply has less area to work with and greater difficulty in making himself plain.

The nude may or may not be erotic. It is an untruth to say it never is, but it is a fair statement that such intention was absent in the overwhelming majority of the many thousand nudes in the history of European art.

During the Archaic period itself, the Greek artists did not get very far with the exploitation of the nude as a vehicle for subtle or important content. Their effort seems to have been consumed in attempting to master the complex mechanics of the human body, and to gain control over pose and expression. They succeeded only indifferently well.

Almost every example of the *kouros* class is much too wide across the shoulders. Evidently, the full width of the block was assigned for the upper part of the body, with the resultant necessity of making the hips too narrow in order to have enough material for the wrists and hands. It was customary to put the ear out of place, usually too high; and to let the eyeballs protrude like marbles from the forehead. Facial expressions usually demonstrate ludicrous lack of control. If serious, they appear to be either stupid or surly; and if a smile is intended, we see the smirk of an idiot.

Toward the end of the Archaic period, say from about 550 B.C. onward, most critics feel the presence of two divergent tendencies of style, the Dorian and the Ionic.

The Dorian is associated with the Peloponnesus where the military and athletic regimen was most rigorously cultivated. Scientific anatomy, or any honest attempt to approach toward it, is identified with this group of sculptors. Their figure style ran to a stocky canon of proportions, a more or less cubical head, grim facial expression, and musculature that imparts a feeling of genuine force even when it is grossly incorrect in detail. The twin *kouroi* in the museum at Delphi illustrate this trend of style in an early form.

The Ionic division of Archaic sculpture was gay. It ran to fancy clothes, elaborate coiffures, and lively faces. The male muscles are often emphasized as much as by the Dorian sculptors, but they seem merely bulky. This light-hearted style, if we may call it that, seems to have centered at Athens and coincides in date with a considerable immigration of artists from Ionia. They fled, it would seem, from the expansion of Persian power—it was in 546 that Cyrus the Great overwhelmed the Greek kingdom of Lydia, captured King Croesus, sacked Sardis, and subdued all the other Ionian cities except Miletus. To the exiled artists, generous hospitality was offered by the court of Pisistratus, then tyrant at Athens.

The Ionizing sculpture of Athens during the next generation has been preserved in good quantity largely because Athens suffered disaster during the

Fig. 3.10 Athens, National Museum. Stele of Aristion. Detail. (Alinari)

campaign of 480. In that year, the Persians, marching south from Thermopylae to their ultimate defeat at Salamis and Plataea, paused to sack and destroy the city. A great many statues stood on the Acropolis. They were all overturned, but not utterly broken. The returning Greeks did not bother to repair them; they simply buried them there. Hence we possess in remarkably fresh condition a considerable number of late Archaic monuments, mostly female figures in richly pleated costumes and with elaborately curled hair.

As a class, these female figures are called the *Acropolis Maidens*. For our purposes the Ionic tendency will be even better illustrated by a male counterpart, the grave monument known as the *Stele of Aristion* (Fig. 3.10). Dated at about 510 B.C. by the type of lettering used for its inscription, this relief shows a Greek dandy dressed to the limit in natty but abbreviated costume. The sculptor appears to have attempted to combine strength and elegance in his rendering of the arms and legs. He did not entirely fail in the latter intention.

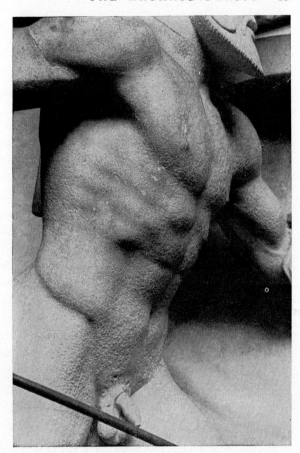

Fig. 3.11 Munich, Glyptothek. Torso of a warrior. From the pedimental sculpture of the Temple of Aphaia at Aegina. (Clarence Kennedy)

Because sobered by its scientific bent, the Dorian tendency was capable of greater discipline and progress along the predetermined line of sculptural development. This fact is splendidly illustrated by the *Aegina Marbles,* the last important sculpture we must classify as Archaic.

The figures come from the pediments (page 80) of the Temple of Aphaia on the island of Aegina, south of Athens. The date of the sculpture hinges upon the style of the architecture, which is Doric just before its final perfection at Olympia and on the Acropolis of Athens. If we make the necessary allowance for a cessation of artistic progress during the period of the Persian Wars (499–479 B.C.), it seems likely that the right moment is somewhere close to 500 B.C. or a little later.

The archeological value of the sculpture from this temple is somewhat discredited by a series of unfortunate manipulations during the 19th century. The site was excavated by a group of young gentlemen, English and German, who had come to Athens as students. They lacked professional qualifications;

but in those easygoing times, they were able to organize an expedition, proceed to the island, and dig. They unearthed the pedimental figures, took them off, and sold them to Ludwig of Bavaria.

Before putting them on exhibition in Munich, Ludwig engaged Bertel Thorwaldsen (1770–1884), then a leader of the neoclassical movement (pages 825 ff.), to repair and refinish the statues.

As the excavators kept no strict records, it is impossible today to be completely certain that we have each statue assigned to its proper place in the pediment, or even to the correct end of the building. As Thorwaldsen did a substantial amount of work and was evasive about what he had done, it is likewise impossible to be sure we are looking at surfaces carved by Greek hands. In spite of the reservations it is necessary to make, however, the figures from Aegina stand out from all other Archaic work with an unmistakably dynamic quality (Fig. 3.11). Minor inaccuracies will strike the eye of the skilled anatomist, and it must be conceded that the sculptor's drive toward expression still outran his technical resources. At the same time, the chunky little bodies have more snap and life than anything ever seen before.

The most important single element of the achievement at Aegina is the fact that the artist depended hardly at all upon the face to carry his meaning. One of the fallen warriors may or may not express pain upon the countenance; it is possible to contend that an accident of lighting produces the effect. Otherwise the case is clear: the faces are nearly neutral, and almost unnecessary.

THE TRANSITIONAL PERIOD
(About 480 B.C. to about 450 B.C.)

The Persian Wars ended with the battle of Plataea in 479 B.C., and the Persian menace became a thing of the past. No other political or military event had anything like the same importance for the history of Europe; it may be said, indeed, that Western civilization acquired by the fact of that victory its best and most distinctive qualities.

The Persian Wars brought spiritual values into issue as no other conflict has ever done. The westward expansion of Persia was politically normal and, within the contemporary frame of reference, ethical. The Greek decision to resist was hardly wise if judged in relation to military probability. The Persian army was the most potent force on earth. It had a record of complete success. The Greeks had no rational evidence for expecting anything but annihilation. To resist under those circumstances amounted to an assertion that certain ideals were more important than all other considerations, including survival.

When the unbelievable happened and it emerged as fact that the Greeks had won the war, ideals as such assumed a new and different aspect. No longer a figment of the imagination, idealism was plainly worthwhile as a basis for practical policy, and the particular ideals of the Greeks seemed obviously more potent than any others. The whole population experienced a driving sense of uplift; no danger on earth could conceivably be worse than the danger so recently faced and conquered.

Under these circumstances, it is not remarkable that the Greeks as a people found themselves looking out upon the universe from a new and more lofty plateau. Their famous tendency to judge all things in terms of man doubtless derived from the consciousness that men seemed for the moment not mere chattels of fate, but intelligent beings capable of controlling the environment. Human dignity, a concept that had scarcely existed before, entered the philosophy of Europe at this point in history—ever to remain as the chief distinction of Western culture.

The progress of Greek sculpture is perhaps our most vivid record of the general state of mind after the Persian Wars.

Returning to find their cities in ruins and their most sacred shrines desecrated and despoiled, the Greeks seem not for a moment to have looked backward. They did not pause to repair even the monuments which might easily have been put back into good order. They simply started on a program of replacing the lot with something new and incomparably better.

Technical advance went forward with incredible rapidity. In the thirty years between the Persian Wars and the middle of the 5th century B.C., more was learned and mastered than during the previous two centuries. By about 450 Greece had the most accomplished school of sculptors, and presumably of painters as well, that the world had ever seen.

♦ *The Ludovisi Throne and the Boston Reliefs* In a period of general advance along a known course of development, we are almost certainly justified in dating monuments on style. Assuming, therefore, that those exhibiting less accurate anatomy come earlier, we may begin the Transitional period with the marble panels of relief known as the *Ludovisi Throne* (Figs. 3.12–13) and the *Boston Reliefs*.

The two are companion pieces. Each consists of three faces of relief, one large and two small. The panels now in Boston have been separated. Originally they probably were in much the same state as those of the *Ludovisi Throne*, which is a single large block of marble hollowed out on one side to form what may have been a bench of some kind.

The main panel of the *Ludovisi Throne* appears to represent the birth of Aphrodite. The main panel of the Boston set seems to show Aphrodite and Persephone with a well-grown Cupid between them holding a set of scales. Probably there is some reference to the story of Adonis.

The four smaller panels have caused considerable puzzlement. Each of the four has a single figure: a nude boy and a nude girl, each playing a musical instrument, an enigmatic young priestess, and an elderly woman with bobbed hair. There is something curiously intimate about the way these four figures are presented; they are not at all in the mood we think of as characteristic of Greek sculpture. Analagous figures may be found in the minor arts, however—vase painting, statuettes, and so forth. The explanation is probably something like this: most of the sculpture we possess is ceremonial sculpture intended for public display, and the monuments now under view are exceptional because commissioned by a private person. Presumably, there were numerous others of the same kind which have not survived.

The "Birth of Aphrodite" is the most important panel of the six. According to the myth, the Goddess was born a full-grown young woman. She emerged from the foam of the Aegean Sea and came ashore on the isle of Cythera, just off the southeastern tip of the Peloponnesus. Apparently we see her being assisted from the water.

Anatomical inaccuracy is evident in the figure of Aphrodite. The breasts are placed too far on either side, and are seen almost in the three-quarter view. Some indication of muscular strain would be necessary for an accurate description of a neck twisted a full ninety degrees; but none is indicated. The eye is also inconsistent with the position of the head; it is insufficiently foreshortened and presents too broad an aspect.

Figs. 3.12–13 Rome, Terme Museum. (opposite) "Birth of Aphrodite," central panel, *Ludovisi Throne*. About 480–470 B.C. (right) "Nude girl playing the pipes," side panel, *Ludovisi Throne*. (Anderson)

Such matters pale into insignificance in view of the radiant look of the goddess as she awakens to life. No praise can be too high, moreover, for the composition; it is still unexcelled.

The arrangement depends upon the interaction of directional impulses from the sides toward the middle, and from the center out toward the sides. The two attendant figures furnish the former; both must have been looking eagerly down toward the face of Aphrodite. The goddess's arms swing outward to right and left; and the relation between middle and side is reinforced by the folds of the sheet of drapery below, and the arms from which it hangs.

The over-all effect is a situation where every part not only fits with the next, but is connected to it by some linear device. Within the composition, coherence is tight and unmistakable, and no frame is needed to declare the integrity and unity of the whole.

If we are correct in feeling that the *Ludovisi Throne* was made during the decade between 480 and 470 B.C., it is evident that a considerable and systematic study of formal composition must have taken place even before the Persian Wars. As restored, the Aegina pediments are arranged on much the same system we find here, but for the reasons stated on page 50, we cannot fairly use them as evidence for the state of Greek composition.

In addition to its excellent composition, the Ludovisi "Birth of Aphrodite" is notable for the subtle linear patterns it presents to the eye. Two kinds of line are used, the zigzag and the graded curve. Angles are played off against swings, and the swings themselves vary in the speed of curvature without departing into another category of curve altogether.

On the principle that the eye will follow the bony structure of any figure down through the spine and supporting leg to the ground, we may for the sake of analysis forget that human females are represented and say that the goddess' two assistants tell abstractly as rather sharp zigzags to either side.

These angular and somewhat staccato boundaries are connected by the swing of easy curves all of which conform fairly closely to the scheme of the parabola. Aphrodite's arms describe such an arc, and the folds of the drapery below show similar arcs, each of parabolic character, but becoming tighter step by step.

By keeping to the parabolic type of curve, the sculptor furnishes us with what we may call a *linear harmony*.

Harmony, as a critical term, is best reserved in the visual arts to indicate the existence of similarity, repetition, or reminiscence. The sense of harmony may be evoked by precise duplication; or, as here, by a more subtle method involving orderly variation upon a theme already familiar. Obviously, artistic harmony is no absolute; it may be definite and emphatic, or suggested by the merest echo of what has gone before.

It is still further necessary to stipulate that any assertion that harmony has been observed must in every instance be accompanied by some statement of the terms in which the harmony is expressed. In the present instance, we have a harmony *of line*. If we were dealing with red repeated here and there, or any other color, we would have a harmony *of hue*. A row of small ivory elephants would confront us with a harmony of hue plus a harmony *of shape*.

In architectural decoration and in the design of cloth, harmony is often built by the repetition of identical motives. White polka dots on a blue ground are a simple example, and the Doric triglyph another. In almost every instance, the idea of harmony goes hand in hand with rhythm as it does in the case of the triglyphs (page 88) or in the colors of a Persian rug.

♦ *The Charioteer of Delphi* The justly famous *Charioteer of Delphi* (Fig. 3.14) is the only full-size bronze we have inherited from Greek antiquity in anything like a good state of preservation. It probably formed part of a complete group that originally included both horses and vehicle; some fragments of the horses' legs were found with it when unearthed in 1896. The style of the statue and some words on its original pedestal appear to settle the date as close to 470 B.C.

The frontal pose seems for an instant to suggest an earlier period, but it

Figs. 3.14–15–16 Delphi, Museum. *The Charioteer of Delphi.* (Above and right, Alinari; below, Clarence Kennedy)

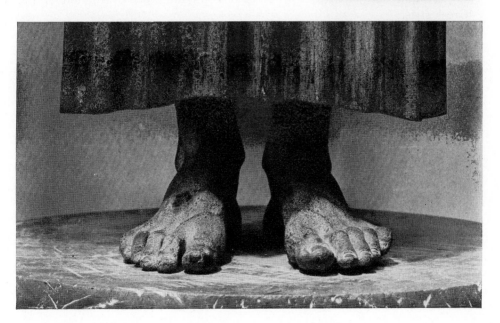

probably reflects nothing more than the military posture assumed when receiving the prize awarded in honor of the victory commemorated by the statue. In most other respects, the anatomy is easy and accurate, and the only significant sign of archaism is seen in the hair.

Except for a few locks about the ears, the hair scarcely exists in any substantial form. Chariot racers presumably would dislike long hair, but the presence of an abstract linear pattern around the upper part of the cranium says quite plainly that the artist wants us to read the texture of hair and not a shaved head.

The explanation of this situation is to be sought in the difficulties of casting bronze. Large statues must of necessity be cast hollow; the weight and the cost of the material preclude any other expedient. As readers of Benvenuto Cellini know from his narrative of casting the *Perseus,* it is a tricky and dangerous process to turn out anything so complicated in its shape as a statue. It should also be mentioned that no industrial castings in general use today put anything like the same demands upon the skill of the men in the foundry. Inasmuch as hair involves multitudinous tiny projections and hollows, it is perhaps the most difficult part of the figure to cast successfully. Complete freedom in modeling the hair was therefore the very last technical problem to be solved.

A further study of the *Charioteer* tends to increase the validity of our recognizing a Transitional period in Greek sculpture. The monument gives evidence of the intense struggle for mastery over the anatomy—the chief artistic effort of the immediate past. It also predicts the future by suggesting the idealism that was presently to become an inflexible convention of the Greek style.

A number of things indicate that the sculptor was, at least in part, committed to the philosophy of objective realism. (See above, page 19.) Without supposing that such details were actually observed in the physique of the young man who posed as model, we find it extremely difficult to explain the wispy sideburns, the peculiar curve of the mouth, and the gathering of the drapery in back—the latter being in adventitious folds of a sort that might be produced by accident in tightening the ribbon which held the gown against the chest and prevented it from ballooning in the wind. The matter is clinched if we examine the feet (Fig. 3.16). Nothing of the kind was ever committed to bronze except by direct study of the living model.

The sculptor's involvement with the coming cult of idealization is manifest in the forehead and nose (Fig. 3.15).

As an artistic philosophy, *idealism* starts, as do most other theories about art, with the appearance of a human being or some other object seen in the natural world. In contrast to the realist, the idealist does not accept visual fact as his artistic law. He does not try to describe what he has observed, but from the very first tries to represent things as they might be rather than as they are.

So understood, *idealism* involves no more than *idea*. A gargoyle may be called idealistic in this strict and simple sense of the term, simply because it departs from natural fact in the direction of the artist's concept of the grotesque and hideous.

Most of the time, however, we find ourselves saying *idealism* with the intention of suggesting that the artist represented things not only as they might be, but also as they should be. The word in his special and somewhat colloquial sense therefore takes on overtones. It suggests beauty greater than we are likely to find on earth. It connotes lofty thoughts, and it involves us in hope and aspiration.

As a practical proposition for us in the studio, the idealistic point of view almost automatically results in a certain degree of abstraction. The artist eliminates the accidental bump or wrinkle which detracts from the beauty of a face. He does not copy the actual outline of the eyelid, but smoothes it into a graceful curve. In the act of beautifying, he tends also to simplify and to regularize. In the end, he usually has something handsomer than his model, but much less personal.

In the Delphi *Charioteer,* the contour of the forehead has been simplified into a shape closely approaching a cylindrical curve. The sinuses are radically abstracted; each is an unbroken flat surface over the eye, and meets the forehead in a sharp and altogether nonnatural edge.

The nose is rather long and its bridge is straight. Seen in profile, there is almost no break in the line where the nose joins the forehead. A straight-edge, that is to say, placed tangent to the bridge of the nose would also be very nearly tangent to the surface of the forehead.

It is this peculiar arrangement of the features that became popular to the exclusion of all others. Only by special exception was any other type of head used at any time between the Transitional period and the Hellenistic age, and it has truly been said that all Greek statues look enough alike to be cousins. It is useful to have a name for so fixed a convention. We may refer to heads with this appearance as having *the classical profile.*

We must emphasize that the classical profile was invented in the studio. It is an artistic abstraction peculiarly appropriate to sculpture—an art that lends itself to expression by means of the simplified mass. The skulls found in Greek burials have no such characteristic, and when by chance such a profile actually occurs in life, it seems hardly so handsome in flesh and blood as in marble or bronze.

♦ *The Olympia Marbles* The most important architectural sculpture of the Transitional period comes from the Temple of Zeus at Olympia, a building known to have been complete before 457 B.C. As usual with Greek temples (see below, pages 77–83), the building itself had but one purpose: to serve as a shrine housing an important cult image, in this instance the seated Zeus of gold and ivory by Phidias himself. It was customary, however, to decorate so important a building with a substantial amount of sculpture designed not so much for its own sake or as an end in itself, but as a subordinate enhancement of the architecture. Both *pediments* (Figs. 3.17–18 and 4.4, page 79) carried full-scale marble statuary rendered in the round and arranged in narrative compositions. The *metopes* (Figs. 3.19 and 4.10, page 85) were also decorated, but in high relief.

As a source of information about the Greek figure-style, the sculptures from Olympia must be appreciated for what they are. The Doric columns of the temple stood a little more than 34 feet high, and the entablature (Fig. 4.4, page 79) must have taken up another ten feet odd. Thus, the pediments were more than 45 feet above the ground. In order to look at them comfortably, one would have to walk to a station some little distance from the temple. This being so, delicacy was hardly appropriate. Simplicity and boldness, even coarse work, was requisite in order to make the statues carry the necessary distance. The sculptors therefore carved out only the main masses. For the hair and other details, it seems certain they relied on the application of color to make the distinction between adjacent contours. Excellent for their intended purpose, these very features make the Olympia Marbles somewhat misleading as examples for close study.

It is also necessary to remember that none of the eminent sculptors of Greece could possibly have found time to work at first hand on statuary intended merely for architectural decoration. Had time been available, the matter of prestige must be reckoned with. It was the Phidian Zeus which shed glory on the site, not the building that contained it.

It seems likely, on the other hand, that a master of exalted standing would take care to exert supervision over the design of architectural decoration, and would then exercise general oversight as the carving proceeded. Pausanias says that Paeonius and Alcamenes were responsible respectively for the eastern and western pediments. Our stylistic evidence, such as it is, makes it likely he was wrong; but in spirit, he probably was right. The *composition* of the pediments and metopes was probably worked out by some great artist. In studying the Olympia Marbles, therefore, it seems wise to concentrate our attention upon the principles of their design. For such a study, they are the most perfect demonstration of Greek art we possess.

The eastern pediment from Olympia (Fig. 3.17) shows us Pelops and Oenomaus at what is apparently the moment before their celebrated chariot race. Oenomaus was king of the southern peninsula of Greece. He had a beautiful daughter named Hippodamia, and her loveliness attracted many suitors for her hand. This, however, did not please the monarch because he had been told by an oracle that he would meet death at the hand of his son-in-law. He therefore undertook to postpone the acquisition of a son-in-law. To the successive candidates, he had formed the habit of making a sporting proposition. "I will race you for it," he would say. "If you win, you get the girl and half the kingdom. If I win, you get executed." Inasmuch as the king maintained the best stables in Greece, he experienced little trouble in deferring his daughter's marriage. Then came the hero Pelops. Realizing he could not possibly beat the king in a fair race, he bribed a groom to remove the pins that held the chariot wheels onto their axles. As Oenomaus swung into the first turn, the wheels came off, the chariot overturned, and the king broke his neck. Pelops married Hippodamia, took the entire kingdom, and gave his name to the area ever since known as the Peloponnesus.

The modern sportsman must look askance at Pelops's methods, but he was remembered among the Greeks as the heroic prototype of all victors in the Olympic games. As such, his story was especially appropriate for the temple before which the Greeks conducted the central and most solemn ceremonies of the Olympic festival.

In handling the narrative, the designers of the pediment were subject to certain limitations. Some of these were physical, some were arbitrarily imposed by the increasingly rigid conventions of Greek art, and some represent universal and permanent artistic problems.

During the Transitional period, Greek taste had found itself, and public opinion was sufficiently definite to govern the mode in which an artist might express himself. The most conspicuous dictate of the sort was the stipulation that subject matter must be restricted to the human figure. This convention was even narrower than it sounds because it also stipulated the kind of human figure that might be used: men and women between 25 and 35, which is to say at full maturity of mind and body and still without blemish from time's attrition. Animals were sometimes permitted if the narrative required it; but in general, no other subject matter was seriously attempted before the Hellenistic period.

One odd result of the exclusively anthropomorphic idiom is the total elimination of setting. Landscape detail and stage properties simply are not there. We see no indication of locality, and we may describe the standard Greek setting as completely neutral if not altogether abstract.

Because narrative subject matter often demanded some statement of the place where the events happened, the Greeks ingeniously adopted the habit of personification. The two young men lolling about at the extreme corners of the eastern pediment are probably meant for the river gods Cladeus and Alpheus, the two streams that run through the town of Olympia. Like every other kind of allegory, personification can become a dangerous habit. We may entertain doubts of its adequacy in the present instance, but it is at least illustrative of the consistency with which the Greeks were willing to follow out their ideas.

Architectural limitations may originally have suggested the idea of the neutral setting. At any rate, they made such a setting seem proper and almost natural. The pedimental space provides a shelf on which the statues may stand. Immediately behind them runs a stone wall. There is room for only one kind of arrangement: the figures must be placed one by one in a single row. Movement, and indeed every sort of directional impulse, must go to the right or left; it obviously cannot go any significant distance inward, outward, or diagonally.

It is historically very important, in this connection, to remember that the pedimental background is *impenetrable*. It does more than curtail movement. It denies the extension of space into the indefinite distance—a point that will assume considerable importance presently.

In addition to the physical restrictions within which he had to compose, and the human figure which formed his only means of expression, the Greek artist was subject also to a convention that governed his presentation of subject matter. We refer to *the unity of time,* which also may be designated as *the instantaneous mode of presentation.*

Because most readers have been brought up with this convention and accept it without thought, it is necessary to emphasize that there are several other ways of communicating visual subject matter, and that the instantaneous mode is actually arrived at not by the operation of natural law, but by conscious selection on the part of the artist. We shall address ourselves to the other modes of presentation in due course (pages 225; 267).

The unity of time, as applied to the visual arts, amounts to the tacit assumption that everything represented in a picture is taking place simultaneously, and that the action presented to the eye shows the position of every figure, the conditions of light, and every other phenomenon in view, just as they were at a special instant in the past.

It follows that a long narrative can be covered only by a series of compositions, one scene to one frame, each adding but one event to the sequence.

The effect of this convention at Olympia (and everywhere else it has been used) is to demand that the designer choose a *point of time,* or a moment when the characters involved in the story would appear in some situation peculiarly vital to the narrative as a whole, or at least characteristic of it. Obviously, much depends upon the right selection. It is a matter of artistic strategy; a mistake can hardly be corrected by any expedient of technique.

The static nature of painting and sculpture compels the artist to assume (or to hope) that the memory and imagination of the observer will function to supply all that the work of art omits. Literature and music have a certain progress in time, but nothing of the sort is available to the man who works under the rule now being reviewed.

Because the sculptors at Olympia could not lay in the atmosphere created by previous events or describe what happened afterward, they were fortunate in being able to feel that everybody knew the story of Pelops. Today we have to repeat it *in extenso* or we do not get the point.

In selecting his point of time, the designer of the eastern pediment, whoever he may have been, was apparently self-conscious with respect to his medium, and much influenced thereby in his choice of the narrative moment.

Speed is the reason for chariot races; they are no good without it. But one may entertain legitimate objections to the direct description of violent movement in a medium which, like stone, is principally characterized by inertia. Marble statues must be heavy. Statues, moreover, cannot move. Some of the most skillful sculptors in history have nevertheless tried to impart the impression of fast movement. It is difficult to name an instance where the result has proven entirely satisfactory—if successful in producing the illusion, the work invariably calls undue attention to the tour de force of technique called up for the special purpose of making a sensation. Many persons therefore take the extreme position of saying that because statues must forever remain static, no sculptor should attempt to represent active figures—also that the best sculpture finds its expression in terms of what can be done with motionless and almost immovable masses.

Without endorsing that view in its literal entirety, one can nevertheless realize that there is much to be said for it whenever sculpture is used to decorate buildings. The architecture being static, an element of harmony results when the statues also are still. Certainly some such consideration must have been in the mind of the artist of the eastern pediment. We therefore find him picking the moment just before the two contestants stepped into their chariots to run the race—a moment, that is, which predicts action but escapes the necessity of describing it.

Having made his decision, the sculptor was then confronted with the necessity of arranging his adult human figures within the frame of the pedimental triangle. This presented a very tricky problem. Adult human beings come in various sizes, to be sure, but there isn't much difference between the big ones and the little ones. The height of the pediment, on the other hand, shows a radical variation from central apex to corners.

The resolution of the problem at Olympia can best be understood by reference to the example itself. The middle portion of the eastern pediment is filled by a group of five persons. They are symmetrically arranged. In the center stands a tall male figure. A nude male, slightly smaller, comes to either side; and beyond each of these males, there comes a clothed female figure. The central statue probably represents Zeus; he is present to oversee the race about to be run off. The others are presumably Pelops and Hippodamia to one side, and Oenomaus and his queen on the other.

The arrangement produces a neat fit in the frame, and the physical fit is achieved in a manner that makes no trespass against one's sense of the plausible. Gods are probably larger than men, and men taller than women. An arrangement of one god, two men, and two women will produce an upper silhouette sloping gently downward to either side from an apex in the middle.

A similar propriety inheres in the fit between the frame and the sloping profile presented by the horses with their chariots behind them. After that, however, the resource of the designer seems to have failed him. There is nothing in the story of Pelops to account for the figures who are made to kneel in front of each team of horses, and there is a similar lack of dramatic motivation for the seated people who fill the difficult space farther on toward the corner. The river gods lying on their stomachs at the extreme ends of the composition may perhaps be explained by reference to the lazy habits of minor deities as a class, but their presence seems gratuitous at best.

It will be necessary to return to the eastern pediment presently in order to discuss the way unity of the whole is achieved; but since that is best illustrated by comparison, let us shift our attention to the arrangement of the western pediment.

The subject of the western pediment (Fig. 3.18) is the battle between the Lapiths (Greeks) and the centaurs. This took place at the wedding party of Perithous. The centaurs, who were cousins of the bride, were invited for the reasons that usually apply in such cases. Like bride's cousins the world over, they took too much to drink, became intoxicated, and became an embarrassment to their hostess. In accordance with the dash of those early and vigorous times, the embarrassment took the form of an organized attempt to abduct all the bridesmaids. A terrific fight ensued, and it is at the height of the battle that the Greek designer has put his point of time.

In the center stands Apollo, a calm, assured figure. To either side of him are figures in violent action. A close look will show that they are arranged in groups of two or three, each group being balanced by its symmetrical counterpart on the opposite side of the center.

On the whole, the triangular space is filled more effectively than that of the eastern pediment. Violent combat makes any posture likely; thus there is rational causation for varying the height of the figures by making some stand, showing some halfway down, and placing still others flat on the floor. The subject is almost a ready-made solution for the problem of putting adult human figures into the pediment.

The coherence between adjacent figures and adjacent groups is surely

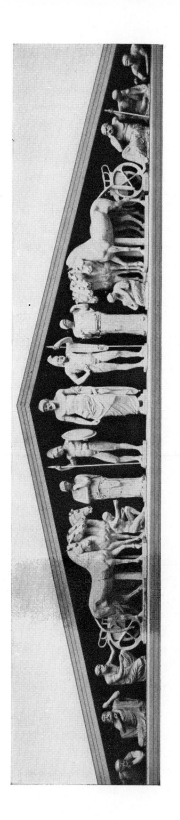

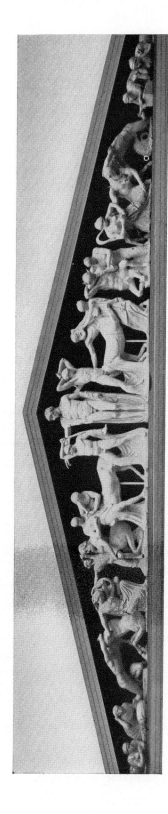

Fig. 3.17-18 The pedimental compositions of the Temple of Zeus at Olympia as reconstructed in the models of the Altes Museum, Berlin. (Above) The moment before the chariot race between Pelops and Oenomaus (east pediment). (Below) The battle between the Greeks and the Centaurs (west pediment). (From photographs by Walter Hege; retouched)

more emphatic than in the eastern pediment, if not absolutely better. The fact of combat furnishes an ideological relationship between figure and figure. As though this were not enough, every motion, every glance, and every gesture directs us to look onward almost immediately to the next figure or next group as the case may be.

It will also be observed that directional impulses of every kind go outward from the middle toward the ends, and inward from either corner toward the middle. The dynamics of the violent narrative are thus brought under discipline and control, and the struggling figures form a tightly knit, intensely coherent, almost aggressively unified whole. By comparison, the arrangement of the other pediment, while unified by much the same system of directional forces, seems a collection of separate statues, each an artistic integer. But both pediments, or either, serve as an emphatic demonstration of the internal logic demanded by the Greek mind, a logic so inexorable that the entire architectural enframement may be dispensed with and still we find each composition almost a universe unto itself.

Excellent though the formal design of the western pediment may be, the reader might be pardoned for harboring a lingering query about the propriety of the subject. Why select so disgraceful an episode for commemoration in the sculpture of a great temple?

The answer is suggested by the difference between the faces of the Greeks and the centaurs. The latter show a complete lack of restraint; almost every countenance is hideous with drink and lust. The Greeks, by contrast, remain calm. This is true even of the girls most violently set upon; all of them maintain a certain serenity of expression.

Obviously, the sculptor did not intend to record a drunken brawl, but to draw a moral from the contrast between the dignity of the Greeks and the bestiality of the centaurs. It was the Greek custom to read into the myths an earlier portent of recent events, and it is probably correct to assume that this particular subject was understood as a prototype for the Persian Wars in which the Greek nation, by superior virtue, had emerged victorious. So long as the Great Age lasted, it remained the fixed custom never to represent current history in the subject matter of public and ceremonial art, pediments or otherwise. Personified abstractions like *Victory* were acceptable to public taste, as were events from the far long ago. The Greek convention inaugurated a habit of the Western imagination; we may name it *the heroic tradition.*

The heroic tradition deals with abstractions and remote events because such material is never subject to the venal pressure of contemporary issues; the more remote, the more that is true. If the person or event is chosen as an instance of virtue or of heroism, it is easy to construe it as inspirational with respect to present conduct. Excellence suggests goodness and heroism begets gallantry. This reasoning continued to govern the major art of antiquity until Rome passed away. It suffered a partial eclipse during the Middle Ages, only to emerge in greater force than ever as the Renaissance reached full flower. Heroic art enjoyed still another period of popularity during the earlier half of the 19th century, when it was revived in an effort to celebrate the advent of democratic government in France and America. No concept is more important in art history, and none has been a more cogent mother of genius: it is to this idea that we owe the very few works of art which in fact arrive at the epic level.

Still more needs to be said about the serene countenance as such. Announced, as it were, at Olympia, it became still another convention governing Greek art, and lasted until the Hellenistic period. Such faces are far from expressionless. In fact, they are highly provocative, but it is difficult to find verbal equivalents for what they tell us. We shall not be far wrong, however, if we take it as the Greek intention to express an aloofness from environment, even a superiority to it—much the same intention that dictated the neutral setting for the pedimental composition as a whole, and indicative of a desire to rise above the particular and incidental toward the kind of truth that is contained in universal principles. These ideas received philosophical expression in Socrates and Plato, but it would appear from the indications of art that they existed in the Greek mind at this comparatively early date.

The metopes of the Temple of Zeus at Olympia were devoted to the labors of Heracles. Some are preserved only in fragments; but the most stirring one of all, *Heracles Taming the Cretan Bull,* is fortunately almost complete in all its vital parts (Fig. 3.19).

The metopes are a subdivision of the frieze of a temple of the Doric Order (see below, Figs. 4.4, 9–10, page 85), and each metope stands between two triglyphs. Because the latter are working members of the fabric, carrying the weight of the roof, all action must be confined within the boundaries delimited by the frame if we are to avoid an apparent threat to the stability of the building. At the same time, violent movement is specially desirable even within so confined a space because the architecture is heavy and static, and needs to be relieved by an element of contrast.

The design of this metope could scarcely be improved upon for the purpose. Heracles yanks one way. The bull pulls the other way. For the moment, the two figures are at a standstill, the momentum of one canceling out the opposite movement of the other. Action was taking place an instant back. Movement will commence an instant hence. But at the precise point of time chosen, there is equilibrium, and no residual forces are left over to endanger the integrity of the frame.

Fig. 3.19 Paris, Louvre. *Heracles Taming the Cretan Bull.* Metope from the Temple of Zeus at Olympia. About 475–465 B.C. (Alinari)

The scheme used here became still another convention of Greek art. It was almost invariably employed whenever strong motion needed to be represented in major sculpture. The theory involved is merely to the picking of a situation when the direction of the motion is about to reverse itself. At such a point in the sequence of any action, there is in fact an instant when things come to a complete stop. For the reasons stated elsewhere (page 61), such an instant gives a pose peculiarly appropriate to full-size sculpture in a ponderous medium, but it is also important to note that no sacrifice of expression is involved. Because the eye sees active figures most plainly at just those brief moments when motion is turned back upon itself, the memory becomes involved. We recall as characteristic of the action itself the poses of the body we saw most clearly.

Over and above its other virtues, the metope of Heracles and the bull furnishes us with a capital example of an interior arrangement in subtle harmony with the shape of its frame.

In this instance, the frame is very nearly a square. The lines defining the circumference come to mind first, whenever a square is mentioned, as being characteristic of the shape. But in thinking of any rectangle whatever, thought of the circumference is promptly followed by consideration of the diagonals. By placing both Heracles and the bull in positions that correspond approximately to the run of the diagonals, the designer has given us what amounts to the theme of the frame expressed in its first variation.

♦ *The Organic Theory of Artistic Composition* The system developed by the Greeks for arranging figures in a pediment is merely an extension of the method used for simpler compositions like the "Birth of Aphrodite" from the *Ludovisi Throne.* There is every reason to believe that this very same system reflects precisely the Greek point of view toward artistic compositions of every kind. It is no accident that the matter was eventually set down in writing, and thus we find it pretty well summed up by Aristotle, who did his work approximately a hundred years after the Transitional period of Greek sculpture.

In the *Nicomachean Ethics* (II. 6), we find him dropping a passing remark (as though repeating something everybody knew already) that in a good work of art "it is not possible either to take away anything or to add anything." And in the *Poetics* (23), he comes out for "a single action, one that is a complete whole in itself with a beginning, middle, and end, so as to enable the work to produce its proper pleasure with all the organic unity of a living creature."

Although he happened to be dealing with poetry and drama at the time, Aristotle might equally well have been referring to the pediments of the Parthenon or those of Olympia. His last allusion springs in part, doubtless, from the circumstance that he was a doctor's son and himself a formidable biologist, but he would never have put the idea forward so easily and confidently had he suspected any one might disagree. Obviously, he had heard it bruited about everywhere that there was an analogy between the structure of an artistic composition and the anatomy of a living thing. By putting the idea so succinctly into words, he succeeded in crystallizing one of the important esthetic theories. We may call it *the organic theory of composition.*

Nothing is more completely characteristic of the Greek mind. *Organic composition* is, in fact, the most cogent and far-reaching contribution of the Greeks to the future history of art. No other theory of composition had any show in the Mediterranean world until northern and Near Eastern influences intruded as Rome declined. The Greek system of composing was revived by Giotto in the early 14th century, was dropped again only to be taken up by Leonardo about 1475. In general, it has been the dominant idea of artistic composition ever since. Something very like it, moreover, constitutes the essence of the structural esthetic which is today the most popular rationale for Gothic architecture.

Certain writers have rather recently formed the habit of using the adjective *architectural* as a term of praise designating a composition in painting or sculpture distinguished by clarity and logical arrangement. They would use that word where we have used *organic,* and there is merit in their idea to the extent that the process of composing involves the painter or sculptor in "building up" his arrangement of figures. *Architectural* in so esoteric a sense has proven, however, a very confusing term. It attributes a false glory to architecture, an art often very badly practiced. The analogy, moreover, between a building and a painting, while perhaps clear enough to the scholar, is likely to impress the layman as unusually farfetched.

THE GREAT SCULPTORS OF GREECE

Six sculptors were celebrated during antiquity as the very greatest who ever practiced the art. They were Myron, Phidias, Polyclitus, Praxiteles, Scopas, and Lysippus. Myron's career falls within the limits of the Transitional period, and the others proceed in the order named until the time of Alexander the Great, for whom Lysippus seems to have been court sculptor.

Time and luck have been devastatingly hard on these famous men. We have nothing whatever from their hands with the possible exception of the *Hermes* of Praxiteles, and even that is suspect in responsible quarters. Scholars have nevertheless expended an incredible amount of ingenuity trying to form some idea of their art. Every resource of historical detection has been exhausted. Over and above direct excavation (which yet may yield epoch-making finds), we have been compelled to rely upon two main sources of information known respectively as *the monumental evidence* and *the literary evidence*. Neither source is in the least satisfactory, but there is nowhere else to turn.

The literary evidence is the testimony of ancient literature. Acting on the assumption that writers who lived before the fall of Rome would in the normal course of life become reasonably well-informed about Greek art, scholars have searched every sentence of every known Greek and Latin text. Every statement about art and every allusion to it has been noted, and its meaning pondered.

From the literary evidence, we have been able to assemble a fragmentary list of the bare names of the statues that once existed, with assignment of each to its author. In many instances, we possess sufficient descriptive material to be able to identify the statues, or copies of them, should they ever be found.

The ideal monumental evidence, of course, would be an original statue of known authorship. In the absence of that, we are compelled to make the best of anything that may in some way or other reflect its appearance. Because the ancients, like ourselves, reproduced famous monuments on coins, in vase paintings, or made small models of them for sale as souvenirs, we can sometimes form a surprisingly satisfactory notion of an otherwise lost masterpiece.

Our corpus of monumental evidence is immensely increased because full-size reproductions of famous Greek statues were long in demand on the Roman market. The more famous the statue, the more likely it was to be copied, and in a few instances we possess a really substantial number of copies after the same Greek masterpiece. By judicious interpretation of these, we can get closer to the original than might otherwise be possible.

MYRON

The period of Myron's activity is closely fixed by unusually reliable evidence. In 446 B.C., his son signed the pedestal of a statue at the entrance to the Propylaea at Athens. The inscription is preserved, but the statue is gone. The son must have had a considerable reputation to have enjoyed so important a commission; presumably he was 35 years old at least. In round numbers, almost any father will be thirty years older than his son; and thus Myron would have been 65 in 446 B.C., and approaching the end of his active career.

The literary sources tell us he was notable as a sculptor of athletes in action and as a sculptor of animals. The latter specialty was presently destined to be squeezed almost out of respectability by the increasing tendency of Greek taste to insist upon expression exclusively in terms of the human figure, but Myron's *Cow* was nevertheless the most popular statue at Athens. Bulls made love to that celebrated bronze beast, calves tried to suckle, and lions tried to eat it up. Or at least so it is said. Whatever else we may conclude, it is evident that technical difficulties were completely under control by the date of Myron's maturity.

Myron's famous statues are impossible of visual recovery on the basis of any evidence we now have, but for his *Discobolus (Discus-thrower)*, a minor work, we are more fortunate. In the eighteenth chapter of the *Philopseudes*, Lucian (2d century A.D.) makes one of his characters say he saw the statue in the entrance hall of the home of "Eucrates the Magnificent." The *Philopseudes* ("The Lover of Lies") is one of Lucian's satirical dialogues, but his allusion to Eucrates' collection of statuary has nothing to do with the satire—the citation is there simply to give an impression of the atmosphere of the great house. As translated by A. M. Harmon, the passage reads:

> "Statue," said I, "what do you mean?"
> "Have you not observed on coming in," said he, "a very fine statue set up in the hall, the work of Demetrius the maker of portrait statues?"
> "Do you mean the discus thrower," said I, "the one bent over in the position of the throw, with his head turned back toward the hand that holds the discus, with one leg slightly bent, looking as if he would spring up all at once with the cast?"
> "Not that one," said he, "for that is one of Myron's works, the discus thrower you speak of. Neither do I mean the one beside it, the one binding his head with the fillet, the handsome lad, for that is Polyclitus' work. Never mind those to the right as you come in, among which stand the tyrant-slayers modeled by Critias and Nesiotes; but if you noticed one beside the fountain,

pot-bellied, bald on the forehead, half bared by the hang of his coat, with some of the hairs of his beard wind-blown, that is the one I mean; he is thought to be Pellichus, the Corinthian general."

It will be seen that Lucian, in this single passage, gives us data about several important statues. We have recognized in Roman copies the *Tyrannicides* of which he speaks, also the *Diadumenus* of Polyclitus, a statue with which we shall presently be concerned. As for the *Discobolus* of Myron, Lucian's description is sufficiently circumstantial to make confusion with any other statue unlikely. More than that, his attribution to Myron is unusually reliable for two important reasons: Lucian lived at Athens where such information was most likely to be available, and he himself had been trained as a sculptor. We rarely get literary evidence from a man who was in the right place to know, and who also had the professional qualifications entitling him to an opinion.

According to a list prepared at Rome in 1951 for inclusion in the catalogue of the *Second National Exhibition of Works of Art Recovered from Germany*, there are no less than seven full-size statues which were certainly made and sold as copies of the *Discobolus*. In addition, there are six statu-

Fig. 3.20 (opposite left) Rome, Borghese Gallery (formerly in the Lancellotti Palace). *The Discobolus*. Marble. 5 feet high. (Gab. Fot. Naz.)

Fig. 3.21 (opposite right) Rome, Terme Museum. *The Discobolus*. Found at Castel Porziano. (Alinari)

Fig. 3.22 (right) *The Discobolus*. Reconstruction combining the features of several Roman copies. (Stoedtner)

ettes, four separate heads, two hands, one arm, and one leg. Over and above these twenty-one items, we can recognize reflections of the statue on engraved gems.

These copies violate the description in matters of detail only. The British Museum *Discobolus* and that in the Vatican now carry heads of a later date wrongly attached to make the athlete look away from the discus, not toward it. An otherwise interesting statuette in Munich is compositionally correct, but shows an attempt to bring Myron up to date by using the softer modeling of a later era. An inspection of the various copies will also reveal substantial differences in quality, doubtless reflecting the standards of the shops from which they came and the price the patron was prepared to pay. Such being the case, it is probably fair to assume that the most subtle and sensitive work is closest to the master so long as we are careful to accept nothing out of line with going custom at the time of Myron's career.

A damaged marble torso found on the shore near Castel Porziano, near Ostia, and now in the Museo delle Terme at Rome is substantially finer than any of the others (Fig. 3.21). The only copy that preserves the head in its proper position is the one formerly in the Lancellotti Palace (Fig. 3.20). By applying the Lancellotti head to the Castel Porziano torso and fitting the latter out with arms and legs, it is obvious we would be closer to the original than before.

But still another step in reconstruction is necessary before we have done the best we can. Like all other marble copies after bronze originals, the Castel Porziano *Discobolus* carries the unpleasant addition of a tree stump intended to reinforce, in this brittle material, the dangerous fragility of the legs. If we eliminate the tree stump and paint the cast with bronze, we arrive at something like Figure 3.22, which is as close as we can get to Myron.

It is rare that the work of archeological detection proceeds in so orderly a fashion to arrive at a positive result. The very neatness with which we have solved our problem is deceptive. It lures us on to the notion we have actually rediscovered Myron himself, but the fact is we have not recovered the work of Myron at all. We merely have a Roman copy thereof which if compared with an original from the hand, say, of Donatello or Michaelangelo, will infallibly impress us as inferior. We do not begin to know Myron, in short, unless we can supply from our knowledge and imagination the snap and life which has escaped the copyist.

Having stated that most necessary word of caution, we need not despond: our composite Roman copy of the *Discobolus* surely preserves much of Myron, and we can form a better idea of his work than we might get of Jefferson's, for example, from the reflection of Monticello on our five-cent piece.

In the matter of technique, the only remaining hint of archaism is in the hair, which is still kept close to the skull. Otherwise, it is abundantly plain that anatomy was completely at the artist's disposal. By using so complex and difficult a pose, he seems in fact almost to parade his accomplishment; and the same may be said for the modeling of the muscles, which are rendered with hard, clean detail as though the master were still conscious of how recently such a performance had become possible. From all of this, and still allowing for the fact that our visual evidence forbids subtle reasoning about matters of surface quality, we may conclude that Myron's style was direct, chaste, and that its appeal came through the beauty of line and contour as contrasted to delicacy of texture and refinements of facial expression.

For analysis of composition, our evidence admits of definite conclusions. All the copies are almost exactly alike with respect to the pose, and are probably very reliable reproductions of Myron's arrangement in all essential particulars. They make it possible to say flatly that the world has never seen a better man when it comes to the manipulation of the single figure.

Very few statues are designed to have an omnifacial composition; and although the *Discobolus* holds up well from almost any angle of view, the effect is best from a station almost directly in front with the eye high enough to see the figure approximately at it appears in Figure 3.21.

In accordance with the over-all Greek theory that the work of art must be complete in itself, Myron took pains to declare an enframement even though none existed in physical fact. By making the eye run around the curve of the two arms, he started it off on an elliptical path, sufficient momentum being accumulated in the process to make it a certainty that we will follow the figure around through space and complete the oval where it would join the farther hand. One of the troubles with the falsely restored copies in London and at the Vatican is the breaking of the suggested ellipse by a head that stares outward and thus destroys the flow of the curve. The original head, on the other hand, tends to reinforce the integrity of the boundary by keeping severely within it.

Having guaranteed the unity of the composition by establishing the concept of an enclosing curve, Myron then ran the body across the oval figure with a strong zigzag movement, and pierced the zigzag, as it were, with the intense straight line suggested by the glance of the eye. Simple enough in principle, the resulting contrast is inexpressibly bold and subtle in execution. There has never been a better artistic demonstration of the famous Greek maxim of neither too much nor too little. After 2,400 years of further experiment with the human figure, the *Discobolus*—which we know only at an archeological remove—must still be listed as one of the greatest statues of all time.

Chapter 4

THE ENTIRE HISTORY of architecture has been influenced by the Greek style. The Greeks lavished almost a hundred percent of their architectural thought upon the temple. They needed houses and public buildings, of course; but none of those were designed to endure. Our knowledge of civil and domestic architecture is therefore limited to what we can infer from evidence that is altogether inadequate; general conclusions of any kind are inappropriate. But the reverse is true of the temple. Its plan and columnar character were established as early as 1600 B.C., if we are correct in our reading of the data unearthed at Tiryns. In the useful list of monuments published as an appendix to his *Greek and Roman Architecture,* D. S. Robertson named no fewer than 133 temple ruins dating from the 10th century B.C. onward to about the year A.D. 150. It is rare to find any single class of monument represented by so many examples, all of which support the flat statement that the Greek temple stands as one of the finest achievements of humanity in any field of endeavor, physical or otherwise.

The fundamental form of the temple seems to have given satisfaction from the very beginning. Its long history is merely an account of increasing refinement. By common consent, the best and most typical temples were those built at Athens during the second half of the 5th century B.C. By concentrating our attention upon those alone, we can learn almost all there is to know about Greek architecture.

♦ *The Acropolis at Athens* The Persian Wars came to an end in 479 B.C., and the Athenians returned to find their city in ruins. Their first efforts were naturally devoted to housing and to military architecture, also to po-

74

GREEK ARCHITECTURE

litical matters such as the organization of the Delian League, an alliance intended to make further aggression impossible. Activities of this kind took the better part of a generation.

In 461 B.C., Pericles emerged as the civic leader of Athens. He held power until his death in 429. After devoting some time to other affairs, he turned his immense abilities to the cultural development of the city, with such brilliant success that the entire era is often and correctly referred to as the Age of Pericles. The principal artistic enterprise undertaken by him was the embellishment of the Acropolis with four new buildings, to replace those destroyed when the Persians occupied the town.

The Acropolis (Fig. 4.1) is a hill rising abruptly from the land around it. Its rocky sides are almost vertical, and access is convenient only at the west end. The place has been fortified since time immemorial, and at the period of which we speak, the top had long ago been leveled off to a more or less even surface about 1,000 feet long by about 500 feet at its widest point. Upon the site thus prepared, Pericles caused four notable buildings to be put up: the *Parthenon* (447–438; lower center), the *Propylaea* (437–432; upper left), the *Temple of Athena Nike* (during the 430's; extreme lower left), and the *Erechtheum* (begun at an uncertain date after 438, finished about 404; upper center). The Parthenon is the only one of the four which might be described as large, and a total of four buildings is a short list. Periclean architecture nevertheless holds its place unchallenged. The reason is quality.

The man personally responsible for the excellence of the work was Pericles' friend Phidias. His reputation had been made as a sculptor; it was for his *Athena Parthenos* that the Parthenon was built. But as general super-

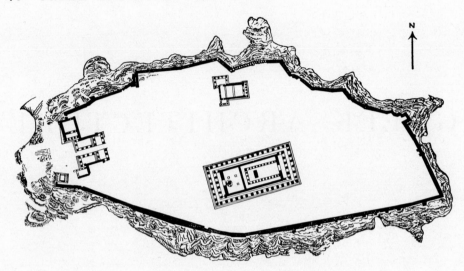

Fig. 4.1   Athens. Acropolis. Plan.

intendent or master of the works, as he might have been called at a later period, Phidias made a contribution that is unique. Artists of the first rank must have assembled at Athens by the score. Over this aggregation of creative persons, unparalleled in world history, Phidias appears to have been able to exert a certain organizing force that was more like inspiration than direction. Every man seems to have outdone himself, and every detail of the vast project finds a common denominator in the Phidian dignity.

The buildings on the Acropolis stood almost undamaged for nearly a thousand years. After the city ceased to have political importance, it remained the intellectual center of the ancient world. A certain amount of material was taken off to Rome in Nero's time, but there appears to have been no systematic spoliation until the 5th century A.D. In the year 426, Theodosius the 2nd issued a decree directing that all pagan temples be destroyed. Apparently the soundness of Periclean masonry proved entirely too hard a nut to crack, for the Parthenon was converted into a Christian church, in which capacity it seems to have served until 1460 when it was again converted, this time into a Turkish mosque. The Erechtheum is thought to have been used for the harem of the resident governor. Even yet, surprisingly little damage of a fundamental kind had been done to the architecture, and had the worst kind of bad luck not intervened, the buildings would be in splendid condition today.

Indeed, everything survived almost intact until about seven o'clock on the evening of Friday, September 26, 1687, when in the course of one of the perennial minor wars between the Venetians and the Turks, an artillery lieutenant succeeded in dropping an explosive shell square in the middle of the Parthenon. The Turks had stored their powder there, and the entire middle portion of the temple was blown to pieces in an instant. Of an inferior building, it is probable nothing whatever would be left today.

Fortunately and by the merest chance, the Marquis de Nointel had visited the city in 1674, and was interested enough in the Parthenon to set his hack artist to work making the so-called "Carrey drawings," preserved today in the Bibliothèque Nationale (Fig. 4.25). These insensitive sketches constitute our only pictorial record of the building as it stood before the explosion.

Our only other pictorial record of early date is contained in *The Antiquities of Athens,* published in London in 1760 by James Stuart and Nicholas Revett. It is a book of plates, with a number of quaint views of the stately classical ruins emerging through and above a hodgepodge of nondescript medieval buildings, domestic and otherwise. Unbelievable though it seems to the modern reader, Stuart and Revett's book had great value as news when it appeared. Athens had all but passed out of the western memory; people were startled to know that important monuments were still there, visible to the naked eye.

It was in 1801 that Lord Elgin succeeded in removing to London most of the remaining sculptures of the Parthenon; they are visible today in the British Museum. But even yet, Greek work was hardly available for study. Photographs dating from the 1890's show the Acropolis still invested with third-rate works of medieval engineering. Only for a very few years has it been possible to see the buildings in proper fashion, or to publish good plates like those which accompany the present chapter.

THE GREEK TEMPLE AS AN ARCHITECTURAL TYPE

The excellence of the Greek temple has so often been celebrated that an effort is required to take a balanced view of the whole subject of Greek architecture. We must attempt to see the building as it is, for what it is, and certainly as no more or less than it is.

The Greek temple is a distinct form or genus in the history of architecture. It illustrates both the strength and the weakness of specialization; it is an extreme type. In order to appreciate what this means, we must understand the purpose for which the building was built. Nothing could be more simple, more direct. The temple was designed to house a single large religious statue (Fig. 4.2). It also served as a setting for ceremonies and sacrifices which took place on the steps, or on altars immediately adjacent. It had no further physical or mechanical function. There was no demand, as there is in a Chris-

Fig. 4.2 Schematic drawing of a typical Greek temple of the Doric Order, showing the cult statue in place. (From J. Durm, *Die Baukunst der Griechen*, Darmstadt, 1881.)

tian church, for a large auditorium where several hundred persons might meet. There was no need to divide the enclosed space into a series of special rooms devoted to one or another of the particular purposes essential to the modern concept of efficiency. If the interior provided a single room (called the *cella*) large enough to house and display the cult statue, the Greeks were satisfied. The most elaborate and expensive temples added to this only one other room, usually called a *treasury* and presumably devoted to the storage of paraphernalia.

One can hardly exaggerate the degree to which this extreme elimination simplified the designer's problems. It was possible for him to avoid hundreds of compromises, each in itself a minor artistic disappointment, and he was saved the vexation of difficult engineering.

Seen in ground plan (Fig. 4.3) the Greek temple is a simple oblong. There was considerable experimentation with the proportions of this oblong. The evolution ran from a comparatively long and narrow shape to the proportion used for the Parthenon, this being not far from the ratio of four-to-nine. The increased width was probably suggested by a desire to gain space for the better display of the statue.

Seen in elevation (Fig. 4.4), the Greek temple rises from a low and horizontal platform which serves as a base or pedestal. Traditionally, the plat-

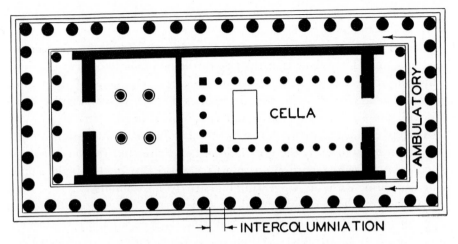

Fig. 4.3   Athens. Parthenon. Plan.

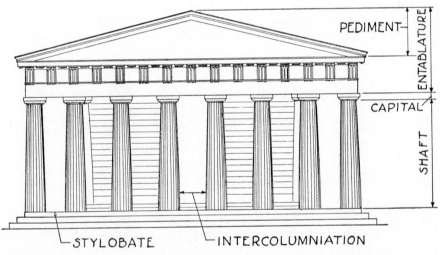

Fig. 4.4   Façade of a typical Greek temple of the Doric Order.

form is made up of three shallow steps; the top step is known as the *stylobate*. Occasionally, we shall find it convenient to extend the meaning of stylobate to suggest the entire upper surface of the platform. It should be noted, also, that the custom of using three steps had to do with the Greek theory of proportion, not with utility. On a large temple, the risers were too high for practical purposes, and a set of smaller steps had to be supplied to let people enter.

Around the outer edge of the stylobate there runs a range of free-standing columns known as the *peristyle*.

Between the peristyle and the cella wall, there is an open passageway known as the *ambulatory* (Fig. 4.3).

Figures 4.5–6 give a good idea of the temple as it appears in three-dimensional actuality. They show that the general shape of the building is defined by the conjunction of two simple geometric solids. The body of the temple is a rectangular oblong solid, and the roof is a solid with triangular cross-section. Figure 4.7 is an attempt to summarize this situation visually.

The appearance of the roof as shown by Figure 4.7 was doubtless complicated in some instances by the installation of skylights; but the general shape (as indicated by representations on coins) remained that of the single, simple triangular form, with the ridge running strictly horizontally.

As seen from either narrow end, or *façade* (Fig. 4.4), the roof makes a triangular gable. The Greek gable is a distinct type in architectural history; we separate it from all others by the special name *pediment*. The most important feature of the pediment is the obtuse angle at the ridge pole. In good Greek work, this ordinarily is on the order of 150°, but in many modern adaptations, a more acute intersection is employed—usually because the Greek temple-front is being applied to a block of utilitarian building out behind, and more height is desirable. The expedient is rarely satisfactory.

We have already dealt at some length with the compositional problems forced upon the sculptors first by the odd shape of the pedimental surface, and secondly by the Greek convention that it must be filled with figures representing adult human beings. (See above, page 58).

Strong boundaries enframe the two solids that compose the Greek temple. They function to give the building a definite, unbroken, completely closed silhouette. Esthetically, the boundaries seem to declare that the composition is altogether self-contained, depends upon its own internal logic, and exists almost as a small universe unto itself. No other type of building asserts a more intense unity. It follows, of course, that all reference to anything outside the boundaries is suppressed, and we must recognize that the unity of the Greek temple involves a certain element of negation. It is something alone and apart, separate from the rest of the world. In general, we find that this is typical of all works of art executed in the Classical Style.

Structurally, the Greek temple is an example of the most elementary kind of engineering. At some very early date and probably as the result of contact with Egyptian customs, the convention became established that all temples should be constructed on the post-and-lintel system. Vertical supports (the posts) were set up at intervals, with horizontal beams (the lintels) making the span across the openings between them. The Greeks were fully informed about the arch; and they surely realized that the post-and-lintel method, while simple enough in theory, is expensive and even dangerous for the construction of good-sized buildings. Once in force, convention seems

Figs. 4.5–6 Athens. Parthenon from the southeast. 447–432 B.C. Approximately 228 by 104 feet. Columns 34 feet high. (Below) View from the east and north. (Both photos: Herman Wagner. Courtesy of the American School of Classical Studies at Athens.)

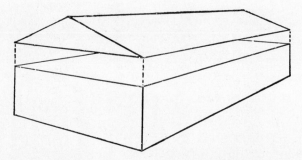

Fig. 4.7 Schematic drawing to demonstrate the shape of
a Greek temple.

never to have been challenged, and the entire history of Greek architecture
amounts to an effort to perfect the post and the lintel. (For structural details,
the reader is referred to Appendix I.)

No temple roof has survived, although some are depicted on coins. The
reason, obviously, is that for this wider span stone was too heavy and too
brittle, and it is certain that the longer lintels were of wood, doubtless
assembled into a framework of the kind known as a *truss* (page 937).

Having committed themselves to it, the Greek architects carried the
post-and-lintel system to an unexcelled level of refinement. The merit of their
work depends, in fact, almost entirely upon perfection of detail, and its
excellence can be understood only by minute study and long familiarity.

For their posts, the Greeks always used the *column,* a word that suggests a circular cross-section whenever used in a technical sense; any other
kind of post is a *pier.* The Greeks developed three different types of column
(the Doric, the Ionic, and the Corinthian), and they developed two kinds of
lintel (one for the Doric and another for the Ionic and Corinthian). Either
kind of Greek lintel is known as an *entablature,* and the complete ensemble
of columns and lintel together is referred to as one of the Greek *orders.*

The three Greek orders are most conveniently told apart by looking at
the *capital,* that part of the column which makes a visual transition from the
vertical of the post to the horizontal of the lintel. The three orders differ
also in matters of detail, and they differ very substantially in their proportions. The Corinthian is lightest, the Ionic a bit heavier, and the Doric much
the heaviest of the three.

It is possible that all three Greek orders were originally worked out in
temples built entirely of wood (Figs. 4.8–9). Often stated as fact, this notion
actually rests upon an ingenious interpretation of slight evidence. There
are those who doubt it, but as an hypothesis, it is admittedly attractive.

In the course of time, the Greek orders tended to become lighter in their

Fig. 4.8 Schematic drawing to illustrate the possibility that the Greek Doric forms had their genesis in wooden construction. (From J. Durm, *Baukunst der Griechen,* Darmstadt, 1910.)

over-all proportions; this was especially true of the Doric. But within the system of whatever proportion happened to be in use at the moment, the parts typical of each order became severely standardized at an early date. The ensemble consists, that is to say, of the same parts in the same number and in the same relative size and placement. An immense amount of trial and error went into the formula so developed; early ruins, it is to be noted, often look clumsy. By the beginning of the 5th century B.C. or thereabouts, further improvement was almost inconceivable.

Because used so often, every part of the Greek temple was given a name. In the recital to follow and in labeling the figures, we have confined ourselves to the more important details and to vocabulary that will prove generally useful.

ELEMENTS OF THE DORIC ORDER

The Doric column is, in comparison to almost all other columns, a very heavy one (Fig. 4.10). Early examples actually show a ratio between height and diameter of close to four-to-one—that is, the greatest diameter multiplied by four will be equal to the total height of the column from the bottom of its base to the upper surface of the capital. The columns of the Parthenon, generally considered to be the happiest proportion ever arrived at for the medium of marble, average about 5.78 diameters to the height.

These proportions were worked out for buildings made of stone; and virtually everyone agrees that, in the Doric Order, any substantial departure

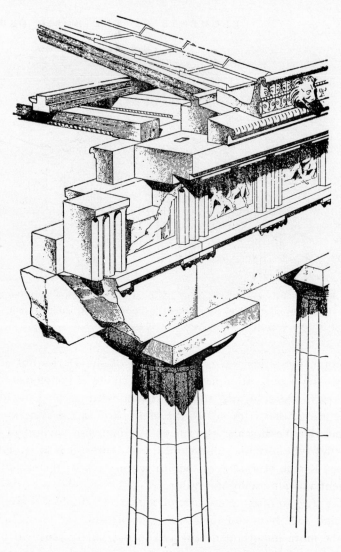

Fig. 4.9 Schematic drawing to illustrate the construction of a typical Greek entablature in the Doric Order. (Drawing by Viollet-le-Duc from *The Five Orders of Architecture According to Giacomo Barozzio of Vignola*. New York, 1891.)

from a proportion so heavy as about five and one-half diameters is unfortunate. The experiment was tried, however, in certain later examples, some of which have columns as tall as 8.5 diameters (Fig. 7.3, page 184). Most people call them "brittle-looking"; and yet the same people have no complaint against the columns in American Colonial architecture, some of which are even lighter. The reason is that the American columns are made of wood, itself a lightweight material of considerable tensile strength. The instance is an illustration of the inseparable relation between medium and design; and

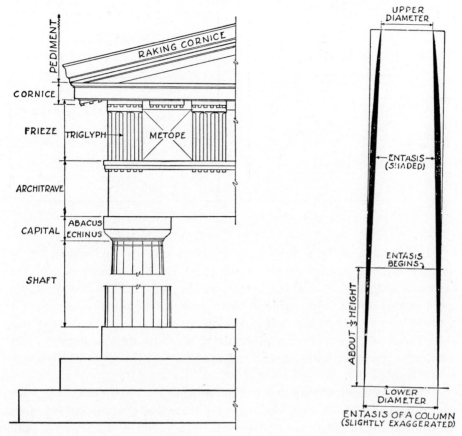

Figs. 4.10–11 (left) Component parts of the Doric Order. (right) Schematic drawing to illustrate the entasis of a Doric shaft.

there is a certain splendid harmony between the ponderous proportion of the Greek Doric and the inertia of stone.

It is notable, however, that people are of one mind in finding these massive columns wonderfully graceful. There is no argument on the point, and it contradicts the ordinary assumption that grace is necessarily associated with delicacy. The beauty of the Doric columns undoubtedly derives in part from the harmony just cited; much of their loveliness must also be ascribed to a list of refinements which will appear in the course of our discussion.

The Doric *shaft* rests flat upon the stylobate. There is no transitional molding, or base. The shaft tapers moderately, being widest at the bottom. In the best Greek examples, the silhouete of the shaft, moreover, is not bounded by straight lines but by curves, giving it a bulge called the *entasis* (Fig. 4.11). The amount of bulge is very slight indeed, and the curves used are of a character more subtle than the arc of a circle.

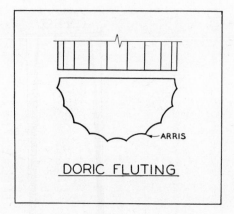

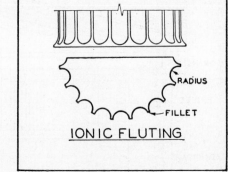

Fig. 4.12 Fluting of a Doric shaft.   Fig. 4.13 Fluting of an Ionic shaft.

It is impossible in a written statement to give an explanation of the delicacy of judgment imposed by the use of entasis. The amount of extension beyond a straight line, the spot chosen for the high-point of the curve, the speed of curvature to either side of this apex, and the pitch of the curve as a whole with respect to the axis of the column—these are some of the variables involved. The difficulty of resolving them is demonstrated by any number of columns, both ancient and modern, which are spoiled by some minor fault of the entasis.

Most Greek columns are *fluted*. The fluting of the Doric Order (Fig. 4.12), which differs somewhat from that used for Ionic and Corinthian (Fig. 4.13), usually consists of some twenty *channels*. The peculiar character of Doric fluting is the result of two things. The adjacent channels meet in sharp edges, each known as an *arris,* and the curvature of each channel is shallow, being a short arc of a circle of long radius. The resulting combination of crisp line and soft shadow is one of the chief beauties of the Doric Order and gives an emphasis to the texture of fine marble not achieved by the slightly different fluting of the other orders.

Over and above the special advantages which pertain to the Doric system of fluting, there are several things that recommend the practice of fluting in general. In the first place, a column is a vertical supporting member. The force it sustains is a force of compression. The axis of each channel of fluting is in line with the direction of that force, and the total effect of some twenty channels is to give emphasis to the fundamental dynamics of the structural forces present.

The arrises extend up and down to form crisp lines, each of which is an unmistakable repeat of the entasis of the shaft. When facing the column, we see one-half its circumference, or ten lines, and thus we observe the entasis

Fig. 4.14 Athens. Acropolis. A Doric capital from the Parthenon. (Walter Hege)

in every aspect from full-face to profile. The difference between the lines as so seen illustrates *variety* as we understand it in art criticism, and the similarity comes close to defining what we mean by artistic *harmony*. The complex elegance of the pattern actually presented to the eye is more evident in Doric than in the other orders because the Doric entasis is ordinarily more pronounced.

It is sometimes suggested that the ample proportions of the shaft combine with the grace of the entasis to produce an impression that the column does its work with ease. This is really equivalent to contending that we experience a feeling of *empathy* (identification of ourselves with what we see in art) when we look at the Doric Order, and it is true that there is a resemblance between the bulge of the entasis and the bulge of muscles bearing weight. While we need not accept the idea as literally true, it offers a profitable train of thought.

The Doric capital (Fig. 4.14) consists of two parts, the *abacus* and the *echinus*. The echinus is the lower part; it is a circular member flaring upward as though to cushion the abacus above. The abacus is a shallow square of stone placed directly underneath the lintel.

This is a very simple capital. It depends for its beauty upon the profile of the echinus and upon the contrast between that curvature of surface and the squared face of the abacus. In good Greek work, the curve used for an echinus is always a *graded curve.* The rate of curvature, that is to say, is not constant as in a circle, but accelerates as the curve goes upward. Careful analysis of a number of examples seems to establish a Greek preference for hyperbolic arcs in Doric echini. Such may have been drawn freehand, but it seems certain the Greeks practiced some sort of analytical geometry. In any case, it is likely that the capitals were turned on a gigantic lathe, probably operated by horsepower.

The complete Greek lintel, or *entablature,* consists of three parts; the three-part division obtains no matter which order is in use. These are the *architrave,* the *frieze,* and the *cornice*—each being a horizontal section stretching the length of the entablature.

The architrave is the lowest of the three. In Doric, it is an undecorated beam of stone resting directly on the abaci.

The cornice is the upper and overhanging member. It extends out from the face of the frieze a distance equal to about one-half the height of the architrave. The cornice may have been invented to keep the drip of the rain away from the joining between roof and wall, but its principal function is esthetic. It tells as a line, and it casts a heavy shadow, thus forming one of the boundaries that close in the silhouette of the temple.

The frieze is the horizontal division between architrave and cornice. In Doric, it is subdivided into *triglyphs* (τρείγλυφος, triple groove) and *metopes* (μετόπαι, interspaces).

The arrangement is best demonstrated by a cutaway drawing showing the construction (Fig. 4.9). The triglyphs, it will be seen, act as short posts, carrying the weight of the roof down to the architrave. The metopes merely fill in the spaces between.

The appearance of the triglyph is important in the total effect of the temple. Each is a block of stone, taller than it is wide, which projects slightly from the surface of the building. The outer edges are beveled, and their surface is cut by two strong grooves of triangular cross-section. The triglyphs, as a result of their form and placement, take the light in a way that gives a vigorous impression of solidity, and produces a pattern of short, strong vertical lines. The triglyphs are placed according to a subtle system to be discussed in detail later. At this point, suffice it to say that there is a triglyph over every column and a triglyph over every *intercolumniation,* or space between adjacent columns—surely the longest word ever invented to signify nothing at all.

The metopes are slightly wider than their height, and they offer a surface that invites decoration. The Parthenon originally had a full set of 92 decorated metopes, each containing an original composition in high relief. Combat subjects were popular for these spaces because they offered a chance of adding movement to the ponderous statics of the temple itself; but as explained above (page 66), the stop-in-action pose was ordinarily adopted to keep the represented action within strict limits, thus avoiding an apparent threat to the stability of the triglyphs and the strucure of he building.

ELEMENTS OF THE IONIC ORDER

Many feaures of the Doric temple are standard, also, in the Ionic Order and need no further explanation. The fundamental shape and arrangement of the building is the same, and yet the general aspect of an Ionic temple differs from the Doric to a surprising degree. The contrast is probably the result of the more delicate proportions which govern individual parts of the building, and of the difference in texture that derives from the generous use of ornamental detail.

All parts of an Ionic temple (Fig. 4.15) are lighter than they would be in Doric buildings of the same over-all dimensions. The proportions of the column will furnish an index to the general scheme of proportions in general. Ionic columns run from about eight to about ten diameters to the height, the individual cases tending to vary more than Doric custom permitted.

The Ionic column always has a base. This consists of an arrangement of concave and convex moldings, there being no rule to govern either the scale, the form, the sequence, or the number of the moldings. Frequently, there is a plinth (a shallow rectangular block like the Doric abacus) underneath the moldings of the base. Occasionally one sees a statement which attempts to read regional or chronological significance into the arrangement of the Ionic base, but it seems safer to assume merely that custom encouraged innovations in this instance and that the bases therefore simply differ from building to building.

The use of entasis is less common than in the Doric order; and if used, entasis is much more delicate. F. C. Penrose (see below) found that the entasis of the Parthenon's Doric shafts measures 0.057 feet. Taking the Ionic shafts of the Erechtheum's North Porch as a standard and adjusting these to the same height, Penrose demonstrated that the maximum entasis for Ionic would, at that moment in Greek history, come to only 0.029 feet—roughly half as much. A great many modern architects have given an Ionic shaft more bulge than this, but always with baleful effect.

Ionic fluting (Fig. 4.13) differs from the Doric (Fig. 4.12). Normally there are 24 channels around the circumference of the shaft, and the adjacent

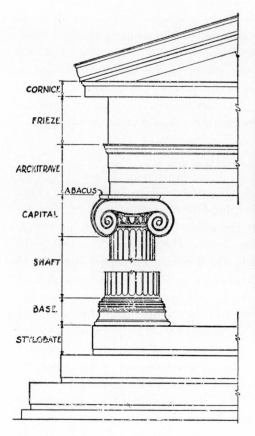

CORNICE

FRIEZE

ARCHITRAVE

ABACUS

CAPITAL

SHAFT

BASE

STYLOBATE

Fig. 4.15 (left) Component parts of the Ionic Order.

Fig. 4.16 (above) Athens. Propylaea. Ionic capital of the passageway. (Walter Hege)

channels are separated by narrow strips, or *fillets,* left from the original sur-face. The channels have a shorter radius of curvature than the Doric, and thus the hollows are narrow and deep. The steeper side of the channel results, of course, in a much darker shadow within: a shadow, moreover, in immediate juxtaposition to the narrow band of full light produced when the direct rays of the sun hit the surface of the fillets. This is different from the way a Doric shaft takes the light, and the sharp alternation of brightness and dark prob-ably accounts more than anything else for the habit we have of describing the Ionic as "more lively" than the Doric.

The distinctive feature of the Ionic Order is its capital (Fig. 4.16). Ap-pearing at first glance to be completely different from the Doric, it is really remarkably similar. A close look will show that the echinus and abacus are still there, with their shape somewhat obscured by decorative carving. The real difference between the two capitals is the addition to the Ionic of the two spiral whirls called *volutes.* Inspection of a series of Ionic capitals (Greek, Roman, and modern) will illustrate better than anything else the difference

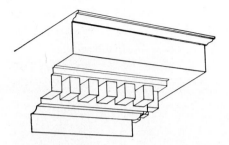

Fig. 4.17 A dentil range.

between curves that are graceful and alive, and those that are not. The merit of an Ionic capital depends almost entirely upon the linear quality of the volutes themselves and the sweep connecting them across the face of the capital. The best examples elicit ready admiration; the inferior examples are very bad indeed.

There was a certain amount of freedom in the design of the entablature for individual Ionic temples. The general spirit of the three-part division into architrave, frieze, and cornice was maintained; but in a number of examples, the frieze proper was omitted and its place taken by ornamental moldings.

One such ornamental molding occurs frequently enough to demand mention as a feature of the Ionic Order. This is the *dentil* range (Fig. 4.17). The dentils are a row of small rectangular blocks placed up under the cornice and sticking out beyond the plane of the architrave about one-half the total overhang of the cornice itself. The name *dentil* comes, it is said, from their resemblance to teeth, and they do indeed look like the teeth of a jack-o'-lantern. In Ionic, when the frieze is included, the dentil range often is omitted.

The Ionic frieze is never subdivided, but runs without a break for its entire length. At times, the Greeks used the frieze to introduce color contrasts; an example is the blue limestone frieze of the Erechtheum (Fig. 4.26). A very fine temple would have its frieze decorated with a continuous composition in relief sculpture—hence the use of the word for any long, narrow, continuous band of decoration.

The only feature of the Ionic entablature which is strictly standard is the architrave. This is not plain as in Doric, but is subdivided into three bands or steps, the projection of each step being very slight indeed, with the result that the shadow it casts is narrow and crisp. In some examples, there is a graduation in the width, or depth, of the three steps, the highest usually being the widest. In other examples, the steps are of uniform height.

A discussion of the Ionic Order would be incomplete without a brief

Fig. 4.18   Athens. Temple of Athena Nike. (Alinari)

reference to the problem presented by the corner capitals of an Ionic peri-style. The Ionic capital lacks an *omnifacial composition*—that is, it cannot like the Doric capital be viewed from all sides with similar satisfaction. The Greek solution is illustrated by the corner capitals of the Nike Temple on the Acropolis at Athens (Fig. 4.18). The capital is given a face on each side of the building, and the volute at the corner is bent out so that its axis bi-sects the right angle made by the front and side coming together. An odd and clumsy shape is made almost necessary at the inside corner opposite the bent volute, but that hardly matters because it is out of sight from any normal station of the observer.

ELEMENTS OF THE CORINTHIAN ORDER

The Corinthian Order scarcely differs from the Ionic except for its capi-tal. The Greeks invented the Corinthian, but used it only a few times. Its ostentatious appearance appealed to the Romans, however, and they used scarcely anything else.

The Corinthian capital is taller than the others, which accounts for the apparent extra delicacy of buildings where it is used. It is simpler than it looks, and its composition follows a rather mechanical routine. There are two fundamental parts: a bell-shaped core, with an abacus on top. The Corinthian abacus is ordinarily concave on the sides, and the profile of its vertical surfaces is often given a delicate reverse curve. The general shape is often called *campaniform,* a Latin derivative meaning no more and no less than bell-shaped.

Foliage in high relief decorates the surface of the bell-shaped core. Leaves of many kinds have been used, first and last, and sometimes more than one variety of leaf appears on a single capital. The Corinthian capital found at the Tholos of Epidaurus (Fig. 4.19) may be taken as a standard example. The leaves there used are a regularized form of the *acanthus,* a free-growing plant familiar in Greece, and they are arranged in systematic fashion. There are two rows of leaves, one above the other. The axis of each leaf is vertical; and the two rows are placed at equal and alternate intervals around the circumference. Usually there are eight leaves to a row.

On each face of the capital, ornaments resembling fern fronds rise from beneath the acanthus to swing up and meet those from the adjacent faces in miniature volutes formed under the four corners of the abacus. Smaller ornaments of the same kind sweep up toward the top and middle of each face of the core, filling in an area that would otherwise remain blank.

GREEK REFINEMENTS:
THE PARTHENON AT ATHENS

The details of Greek architecture instantly impress the layman with their refinement, and years of study tend to reinforce the first impression. It is even more remarkable that a similar and much less obvious perfection is discernible in the design of the temple as a whole. The great fabric was conceived as an entity; and a number of physical facts, some of them demanding the utmost subtlety from the builders, are not to be understood unless we have some grasp of the artistic scheme governing the whole.

The idea of giving an entire building a refinement equal to that of its most delicate part was carried to the limit in the design and construction of the Parthenon. Similar refinements have been noted in other temples, but none compare with the Parthenon in the thoroughness with which perfection was demanded.

There can be no doubt about the facts. The building was measured with minute accuracy by F. C. Penrose, who published his findings as *An Investigation into the Principles of Athenian Architecture,* in 1851. Penrose worked

Fig. 4.19 Athens, National Museum. Corinthian capital from the Tholos at Epidaurus. (Alinari)

with instruments compensated for variations in the temperature, and he rounded off his dimensions at the third decimal place of a foot. His accuracy has never been questioned, and greater precision would obviously be pointless.

While there can be no doubt about the data, there is considerable difference among the theories which attempt to explain the intention of the architects. We had best proceed by reciting the facts first and undertaking to explain them later.

The platform of the Parthenon is not a level plane surface. It rises toward the center in a way D. S. Robertson has neatly compared to the appearance of a carpet nailed down at the four corners only, and suddenly lifted from the floor by a blast of wind. The curvature of the upper surface as a whole produces a curvature in each of the "horizontal" lines that bound the stylobate on its four sides. On the short ends of the Parthenon, the rise amounts to 2 3/5 inches, and to 4¼ inches on the long sides. These curves are repeated in the entablature with slightly less rise.

The columns of the Parthenon are not vertical, but incline inward at a very slight angle. We might compare the building to the base of an extremely tall, narrow pyramid. If we imagine the axes of all the columns projected indefinitely into the air, they would meet at an apex a little more than a mile above the earth. Our statement simplifies the conditions, but only slightly. Readers of Penrose will recall that his measurements proved that the figure varies a trifle from the precisely pyramidal, a fact which need not worry us. Figure 4.20 is an attempt to visualize the situation.

The columns of the Parthenon are not alone in their inclination. The walls of the cella are also made to incline slightly inward while all minor wall surfaces incline the opposite way. The entablature, for instance, has an outward pitch, and the upper edge overhangs the lower slightly but noticeably.

The distance between the Parthenon's columns is not uniform. There is, on the contrary, a clearly discernible difference in their spacing. Those at the corners are slightly more than six feet from their neighbors, while those along the front and sides are just over eight feet apart.

Measurement of the corner columns shows, moreover, that they are slightly heavier than all the others. The increase in diameter amounts to about 1.7 inches, or slightly more than a fortieth part of the diameter of a standard column.

A glance at the building will demonstrate, also, that there is more to the arrangement of the triglyphs than might at first be supposed. As stated earlier, there is one triglyph for every column and one for every intercolumniation. It is perhaps natural to suppose that the axis of each triglyph ought to correspond with the center line of its column or the middle of its intercolumniation, but such is not the case.

Were that system used, mechanical order would of course result, and there would be no trouble if we never arrived at a corner. But the triglyph being shaped as it is, centering one over the corner column would leave at the extreme end of the frieze a blank space which for lack of a better name we may refer to as half-a-metope (Fig. 4.22). The corner of the building would lack weight and apparent force. This would tend to set at nothing the strong boundaries that give the composition its peculiarly intense unity. It would also conflict with other essential elements of the Greek theory of design, some of which remain to be mentioned.

To avoid the situation just outlined, the Greek architects gave up the notion of centering the triglyphs over column and intercolumniation. Instead they brought the pair on adjacent sides of the temple together at the corner (Fig. 4.21). They put the middle triglyph of the frieze centrally over the middle intercolumniation of the peristyle. The others were placed off-center in an amount that increases as we approach the corners of the building.

Such are the most important facts of curvature, position, and inclination which go to make up the so-called refinements of the Parthenen. We must now attempt an explanation. As stated, there is much difference of opinion about the matter. It is worthwhile to summarize the most popular and important theories, after which a new and, it is hoped, a more satisfying idea will be put forward.

It is often suggested that the curves of the Parthenon are a matter of chance. It is pointed out in this connection that irregularities are common in medieval buildings, and we are induced to believe that similar irregularities are inevitable in any fairly large fabric. Other Greek temples, moreover, lack perfect regularity.

This suggestion can hardly be entertained for long. The curves of the Parthenon are symmetrically repeated on opposite sides of the structure. Irregularity might be accepted as the result of chance; systematic and symmetrical correspondence of the strictest kind has never yet happened by coincidence.

A second suggestion, not altogether different from the last, is the supposition that the builders anticipated settling and sinking of the fabric, and that the curves were intended to disappear after a certain period of time. This notion involves two separate presumptions: that the Parthenon has not subsided as expected, and that the Greek builders wanted straight lines. Neither idea will stand analysis.

It is true that many buildings, ancient and modern alike, distort by amounts greater than the curvature of the Parthenon. There are two reasons for it: poor foundations and inferior construction. Unlike the mudbank upon which London lies, the Parthenon rests on bed rock which has not subsided or become compressed by any significant amount during the past 2,500 years. Furthermore, no modern building has anything like the quality of construction put into the Parthenon by builders with something like a thousand years of experience in temple architecture. Greece is wealthy in marble, and the stones used here were of uncommon soundness. The fitting of the masonry is uniquely elegant. No mortar was used. Every joint is the conjunction of two perfectly squared and polished surfaces, and the blocks were brought tight together by methods that need not concern us except to say they virtually preclude the possibility of further movement. It is thus inappropriate to reason by analogy to inferior buildings where, in return for cheap work, we accept as inevitable shrinkage in the materials, squeezing at the joints, and the twisting that comes from a poor substratum, inadequate foundations, or both.

The assumption that the Greek builders wanted straight lines, and intended to get them when the building settled, is similarly out of order. It is true that the modern contractor works on straight lines, but his reason for doing so bears no relaion to esthetic theory. He merely knows that the plumb and level reduce the cost by saving an immense amount of time to make checks and measurements of every imaginable sort. There is no legitimate reason for comparing such work with the work that went into the Parthenon.

The builders of that great temple belonged to quite another guild and class. The nearest modern equivalent is to be sought in the shipyard. Anyone who has worked there will instantly appreciate the curves of the Parthenon. To establish the wonderful lines that were built into the marble and remain, what a world of patient labor in the drafting room and on the lofting floor! What infinite skill and care in cutting the innumerable perfect and subtle bevels that fit so perfectly together and produce the unparalleled loveliness!

More popular than either of these suggestions is the theory endorsed by Penrose, who seems to have elaborated upon a somewhat cryptic passage in Vitruvius.

Vitruvius was a Roman builder of the 1st century A.D. He wrote a treatise on architecture, a copy of which was discovered at Saint Gall in Switzerland by the Florentine humanist Poggio who came that way in 1416. Nothing else survives from the pen of any man who was himself a classical architect, and Vitruvius has therefore occupied a unique position of authority ever since.

In Book III, Chapter IV, M. H. Morgan translates his text as follows:

> The level of the stylobate must be increased along the middle by the *scamilli impares;* for if it is laid perfectly level, it will look to the eye as though it were hollowed a little. At the end of the book a figure will be found, with a description showing how the *scamilli* may be made to suit this purpose.

The drawing Vitruvius mentions did not survive with his text, but the *scamilli impares,* or something very like them, survive in the building trades. As explained in a learned note by H. L. Warren, added as an appendix to Morgan's *Vitruvius,* the *scamilli* are a set of little blocks of varying height. By setting them up at carefully measured intervals and sighting along them, the builder can adjust a stylobate to any curve he wants.

There can be little doubt that Vitruvius knew how to construct such curves, and there can be little doubt, also, that his remarks reflect a general notion bruited about among Roman builders; namely, that a good and proper temple ought to have curvature and inclination something like that of the Parthenon. Further confirmation is supplied by a passing word or two in Cicero (*In Verrem* II, 1, 51) where that famous trial lawyer impeached a witness by suggesting the man was so ignorant as to suppose that pillars should be made to stand exactly plumb.

Building upon such classical tradition and extending its implications in a manner that is admittedly plausible, Penrose asserted that the curves and inclinations of the Parthenon were intended to compensate for optical illusions. Without such adjustments from the plumb and level, he declared that the stylobate would "seem to sag, the entablature would seem to recede, and the angle columns look thin against the sky."

Penrose's suggestion is often illustrated by drawings; a typical set appears among the superb and indispensable set of plates in Sir Bannister Fletcher's *History of Architecture*. Such drawings may not, however, be taken as rational evidence. By no means do they represent the actual conditions obtaining in a view of the Parthenon, but an exaggeration thereof. We must dismiss them as caricature.

In scrutinizing Penrose's theory, we must first of all disabuse ourselves of the prestige it has acquired by a hundred years of repetition. Often stated as fact, it still remains merely a suggestion like any other.

First of all, it is well to examine Penrose's ancient authority.

Any reader of Vitruvius is bound to observe that, Roman builder though he was, Vitruvius was hardly a learned man. His Latin was inelegant, and his powers of expression were poor. The latter undoubtedly reflect something more serious than an absence of ease and grace; the truth is that Vitruvius was neither a well-informed man nor a clear-headed man. Whenever he alluded to anything that demanded close reasoning and subtle knowledge (Polyclitus' canon of proportion for the human figure, for example) he got mixed up and gave us a garbled account. It is plain enough he knew that curvature and inclination were the going custom, and it seems likely he knew a practical method for building them into a temple. It by no means follows that he understood the esthetic theories of the Greek architects who first invented the refinements. In that connection, we must remind ourselves, moreover, that Vitruvius was no contemporary observer. He lived about six hundred years after the Parthenon was built.

Cicero was a person of different stripe. It seems probable that he might have been able to give us a succinct account of the theory involved; but, like Vitruvius, he didn't. He merely referred to it in quite another connection, and passed on.

In sum, we must accept the fact that we have no ancient mandate one way or the other, and the idea that the refinements compensate for optical illusions, if true, must rest on modern deduction.

One way to check Penrose's assertions is to examine modern buildings known to be plumb and level. The examination must be made, of course, under conditions of diffused light and by persons trained in accurate, objective visual inspection—we cannot take a majority vote to decide the matter because the unskilled observer can so easily be persuaded that he sees what he is told to see. When plumb and level buildings are so examined, the optical illusions predicted by Penrose do not appear unless some extraneous factor is introduced. Again, we must beware of the familiar tricky drawings which do in truth deceive the eye, but which bear no fair analogy to conditions at the Parthenon.

Penrose's assertions overlook another fact of importance. They contain the tacit suggestion that the curves are not perceptible with the naked eye, and that the building impresses the observer as being plumb and level. The reverse is true. When a considerable overlay of medieval rubble was removed in 1837, to put the whole stylobate in plain sight for the first time during our era, the curves were at once noted. Three observers actually published the fact, and Penrose's research was undertaken in the first place to verify such statements. Any number of modern observers who have visited the site repeat the testimony of those who first inspected the temple: the curves are there to be seen with the naked eye. Any good-size photograph also shows them up plainly and accurately (Fig. 4.23).

We are thus compelled to believe that compensation for optical illusions offers no satisfactory explanation for the situation we know to obtain. In structures without such adjustments, the optical illusions do not take place, and at the Parthenon the refinements do not produce the plumb and level appearance.

The modern student, accustomed to the best engineering the world has ever seen, will also want to know whether the Parthenon's refinements perform some practical service, but this possibility must also be discarded as unimportant. Drainage is improved by making any floor convex rather than flat, but drainage can be taken care of equally well by some method less heroically expensive and difficult. The increased diameter of the corner columns and the pitch of all columns doubtless tends to increase the stability of the fabric when subjected to shock or vibration of any kind—an earthquake or an explosion, for instance. But in neither case is the adjustment of the right order of magnitude to make any significant difference, and the Doric temple, with its ponderous columns and slight superstructure, is an extremely stable building to begin with.

It would appear that the only avenue offering any hope of explaining the Parthenon's refinements is the assumption that the Greek designers were compelled by some deeply felt esthetic necessity. The idea that esthetic satisfaction might seem so important may not immediately impress the reader as plausible, but the facts point that way.

The artists who assembled at Athens to work under Phidias had the greatest opportunity ever afforded in the entire history of the ancient world. Because Athens controlled the Delian League, unlimited funds were available. It would have been easy to build larger buildings or more buildings. Instead, the money was expended and fabulous labor devoted to the attainment of quality.

Insofar as we can recapture the Greek state of mind and thus understand the exhaustive perfection of the Parthenon, the following considerations are apposite.

As we have seen from our study of Greek pedimental arrangement and other instances of design applied to sculpture and painting (pages 66-67), the Greeks who lived and worked in Periclean Athens were possessed of and committed to a particular and excellent theory of artistic order which we have named *the organic composition*. Of this, the chief elements are the establishment of an intensive and assertive unity for the whole (usually brought about by firm boundaries, either visible or suggested), and, within the frame, the maintenance of coherence between part and part and between part and whole (usually by some logical and unmistakable suggestion). When drawing plans for their greatest temple, would the Greeks suddenly embark upon some new and untried theory of design? That is certainly possible. In one instance, it seems even to have happened (see page 109), but everything combines to indicate that the Parthenon is simply the largest, and also the most subtle, instance of the theory of design so succinctly stated by Aristotle and cited in the last chapter. To understand the building, we merely need apply to architecture what we already know to be true of sculpture. Everything then falls into a reasonable pattern.

All architecture begins with the site. There is perhaps no such thing as a good building as such; we must ask where it is to go and in what surroundings it will come into view. In accordance with classical custom, the site of the Parthenon had been leveled off into a horizontal plane surface.

The upward curve of the stylobate is in physical juxtaposition to the horizontal ground line beneath it. If projected slightly at either end, the curve would have an origin in the ground a short distance from the façade of the building. Thence it would rise to its apex, and swing downward to an ending at a point in the ground an equal and opposite distance beyond the temple's far end.

Given the character of the curve and its reference to the horizontal beneath, any smallest arc of it tells the story. By its own internal logic it says that the middle of the building must come at such and such a point, and that its end must also come at a definite distance farther on. There is no room for doubt. But a straight and horizontal stylobate would make no similar reference to the ground. There is nothing within a straight line to tell us where it begins, ends, or has a middle; it might stop anywhere or go on forever.

The inclination of the columns makes sense by reference to the same theory. The effect is to make the building the base of a pyramidal figure; and as a general proposition, it may be stated that once the notion of symmetry has been evoked in the feelings of the observer, inclination of any sort whatever will demand its equal and opposite.

The increased diameter of the corner columns and their closer spacing both contribute to the same scheme. They strengthen the enframement and emphasize the limits of the composition. The same may be said of the triglyphs which join at the corners of the frieze, but there is more to be discussed before we are through with the so-called "triglyph problem."

5856 FEET
(NOT DRAWN TO SCALE)

101 FEET

Fig. 4.21 (above) Athens. Parthenon. Southwest corner. (S. S. Weinberg)

Fig. 4.20 (left) Schematic drawing to illustrate the inclination of the columns of the Parthenon.

The arrangement of the triglyphs has traditionally been presented as an almost intolerable irregularity of the Doric temple which the Greek designers were clever enough to ameliorate by a kind of artistic counterirritant so subtly applied as to escape attention. Such a view must have had its genesis in the notion that the rhythm of the triglyphs ought to be geared to the rhythm of the columns—a concept that might apply to a machine, but one which is unnecessary when dealing with a work of art.

Because of its projection, its distinctive shape, and the way it takes the

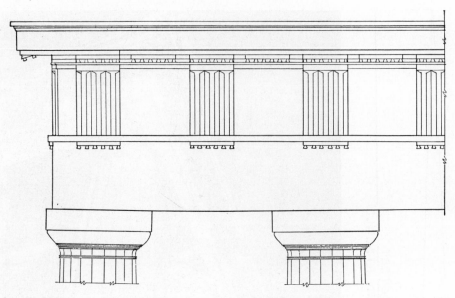

Fig. 4.22 Drawing to demonstrate the result if triglyphs were kept strictly central with columns and intercolumniations.

light, each triglyph is of course an accent. They do not come at precisely even intervals, but that need cause us no more than a moment's difficulty. The spacing changes in a rational manner. There is order, that is to say, in the rate of change. We are perfectly familiar with that type of order in music, and we merely see it here in visual terms. It is probably an excellent thing rather than a fault to have the columns come in one rhythm and the triglyphs in another. The experience of simultaneous rhythm is familiar enough, and we may summarize by saying that the triglyphs constitute an element of variety in the decoration of a building which tends on the whole to be overly regular.

We have been speaking of the composition of the Parthenon as though it were self-evidently a good thing. To an extent, that is true. As the supreme demonstration of organic composition, the great building is unexcelled. It is a celebration of the Greek capacity for formulating clear, consistent ideas and making practical affairs conform to an order directed by the mind. All men must admire such a quality in a people. We must nevertheless be prepared to compare the Greek achievement with others—as, for example, with the Style of the Near East which lacks (but for excellent reasons), the Aristotelian beginning, middle, and end. Before proceeding, it behooves us to pause for a few remarks that may still further explain the character of Greek art.

The various refinements of the Parthenon combine to produce an extraor-

Fig. 4.23 Athens. Parthenon. View in the ambulatory. (S. S. Weinberg)

dinary sense of integration, completeness, and fulfillment. By its very nature, the organic theory of composition seems to proceed toward that result with a beautiful inevitability. It is necessary to appreciate, however, that such a result is achieved at a cost. A work of art which exists in such a state that nothing may be added or taken away is not only static, it is inflexible. Nothing is left to do; indeed nothing more can be done. When they built the Parthenon, the Greeks had arrived at the end of a road. A great many temples were built in later generations, some of them larger and more elaborate. But what is there to be said about them?

Greek excellence was achieved by the method of setting limits. Every one of the refinements of the Parthenon contributes to the establishment of boundaries for the composition. It would appear that the Greek mind sought boundaries because limitation makes it possible to understand, to control, and to excel. But the very same feeling was also a negation: the Greeks may fairly be described as harboring a terror of the indefinite. In art and in all

Fig. 4.24 Athens. Parthenon. View at the west end, showing a portion of the inner frieze. (Walter Hege)

forms of thought, their accomplishment was bought by rigorous restriction of the field of attention, and by stern exclusion of everything beyond the problem in hand.

Thus the Greek temple makes no reference to the universe around it. Its clarity and integration is unparalleled, but it comes at the cost of dealing only with the finite.

♦ *The Sculpture of the Parthenon* Not satisfied with refinement of an architectural nature, the Athenians gave the Parthenon a prodigious wealth of sculpture. In addition to the two pedimental compositions, all 92 metopes were decorated with individual compositions in high relief; and in addition to the metopes, there was an extra and unique feature in the form of an inner frieze in low relief, 3 feet 4 inches high, placed at the very top of the exterior wall of the cella and immediately under the ceiling of the ambulatory. The frieze ran all the way around the cella, and originally measured a full 524 feet long (Fig. 4.24).

In the absence of originals by the great masters of the 5th century, a special importance attaches to the marbles from the Parthenon. As architectural sculpture goes, the work is unusually fine, but can we legitimately associate it with the personal style of Phidias? Opinions vary. Some critics want to believe he designed everything; others contend that he designed nothing. On the whole, the latter contention seems more likely, unwelcome though it is. In view of his immense responsibilities at the time, he must have been compelled to delegate even so important a task as this. From Phidias or some other personality, however, there surely emanated a certain unity both of style and spirit. All the sculpture from the Parthenon is tinged with a lofty sobriety that separates it even from the rest of the Greek output.

The subject matter of the metopes was, as usual, drawn from mythological combat. On the east we might have seen the gods fighting the giants, on the west the Greeks against the Amazons, and on the south the Lapiths and the Centaurs. Only the southern metopes are sufficiently well preserved to make study worthwhile; those from the north side were so badly damaged that even their subject is a matter of debate. On the whole, the metopes are somewhat less satisfactory than the rest of the sculpture. A few of them might even be called crude. The reason is not far to seek: the structural procedure demanded that the metopes be finished early and dropped permanently into place long before it was necessary to carve anything for the pediments or for the inner frieze. Because a very large number of sculptors were required to get the work done in any reasonable time, it is probably a good guess that the carving of the metopes took place at a period of organization during which it was necessary to accept compromises. By the time that first enterprise was complete, the corps of sculptors was capable of working together as a unit, and would by then have become familiar with the conceptions and standards at which Phidias aimed. At any rate, the metopes—taking them as a collection—exhibit unhappy variations in quality.

For its eastern pediment, the Parthenon had the *Birth of Athena,* a subject involving the emergence of that goddess from the forehead of her father Zeus. Inasmuch as she came into the world full-grown and wearing a suit of armor, the delivery was incontestably the greatest obstetrical miracle in history. One would like to know how the sculptors handled it, but except for a very doubtful reflection on a marble well-head in Madrid (showing the situation after it was all over), we have no guidance. The vital central portion of this pediment was destroyed to make room for an apse when the temple was converted into a church during the fifth century A.D. The rest of the composition was memorialized in one of the "Carrey drawings," and the preserved

Fig. 4.25 Paris, Bibliothèque Nationale. The western pediment of the Parthenon as recorded in the "Carrey drawings" made in 1674.

figures are on view in London. The reclining male nude known as "Theseus" has often been suggested as our best source on Phidian figure-style. The rhythmical drapery of the so-called "Three Fates" is something of a tour de force, although much admired. Best of all, however, are the figures which localize the event in the heavens and name the time as dawn: at the left-hand corner, the horses of Helios (the Sun) rise from the sea puffing with energy; and at the right, the tired horses of Selene (the Moon) sink beneath the waves.

The western pediment had the *Contest between Athena and Poseidon for the Land of Attica.* We know the arrangement of the central portion only through the "Carrey drawings" of 1674 (Fig. 4.25). Poseidon's horses were lost in a clumsy attempt to lower them with the object of carrying them off to Venice when the Venetians evacuated the city in 1688—Morosini, their leader, was a descendant of the Morosini who brought home from Constantinople the four bronze horses which now stand over the principal entrance to Saint Mark's.

While it is difficult to reason from so poor a source, the drawing is good enough to suggest that the subtlety of pedimental composition had advanced since Olympia. Instead of posing each figure flat against the background, many of the statues are seen in the three-quarter view, thus calling into operation a very moderate sense of space forward and back in the horizontal plane and producing a more varied pattern of shadow. The chief feature of the design, however, is the elimination of the single standing figure placed on the central axis; at Olympia and probably at Aegina also, the presence of such a figure inevitably suggested a division of the whole into halves. Here at the Parthenon, the middle of the pediment was filled with a criss-cross of diagonals. It is a fair guess that an even more intensive unity was thereby arrived at, but it is admittedly hard to tell from the evidence we are compelled to rely upon.

The Parthenon was first opened to the public on the occasion of the Panathenaic Festival of 438 B.C. Appropriately enough, the subject matter of its lengthy interior frieze was an idealized version of the procession that took place as its final and culminating ceremony. The Panathenaea was originally no more than a local custom. Pisistratus had undertaken to magnify its importance, and by the time of which we speak, the affair had become a national celebration scheduled every fourth year and involving games, musical contests, and oratorical performances. The procession was a great and major spectacle of old men and maidens and a cavalry escort. Forming in the town, it filed up onto the Acropolis. There was performed the focal ceremony of the whole affair: putting a new saffron-colored robe (*peplos*) on a venerable wooden statue of Athena.

The Parthenon is so placed that the visitor approaches it from the southwest corner, and it is there that the design begins. The western section of the frieze still remains in place (Fig. 4.24), and there we see preparations in progress, with some of the horsemen already in motion toward our left. The procession splits, as it were, to follow both sides of the temple; and it comes together again at the middle of the eastern front of the building, where some gods are seated waiting for the arrival of the *peplos*. The arrangement is natural enough, and makes it impossible to inspect the composition backwards.

Although the frieze is ostensibly continuous, the Greek sense of artistic propriety made it necessary that some account be taken of the corners of the temple. Rapid motion was therefore confined to the long sides of the building. Near the corners, we see the movement slowed down, with marshals there to direct the marchers. This is approximately what we might expect in the light of what we already know about Greek art; certain other features, however, require special mention.

Placed up under the roof and shielded by the entablature, the inner frieze received almost all its light by reflection from the ambulatory floor and the ground outside. In comparison to the intensity of the light outside, the frieze existed in comparative gloom. Dark shadows of any kind had to be avoided at all costs; otherwise, it would have been literally impossible to make out what one was looking at. Relief was therefore kept exceedingly low; and the upper parts were modeled out with slightly more depth than the lower. At the top, the relief rises about $2\frac{1}{4}$ inches above the background, and at the bottom, about $1\frac{1}{4}$ inches. In order to avoid greater projection and cast shadows, some radical distortions were introduced: to accommodate the legs of the riders without bringing them out too far from the background, the sculptors simply caved in the rib-cages of the dainty little horses. Still other distortions were employed for similarly rational reasons. Scale was violated, for example, to keep all the heads at the same height, thus repeating the architectural line which forms the upper boundary: men on foot come to the same level as men on horseback, and the horses themselves are on a smaller scale than the men.

In matters of detail, it is probably impossible to find an equally extended design that maintains the same high quality of sensibility. By exception in Greek sculpture, rapid motion is represented; the usual method is to confront the eye with a figure that would be unstable unless we understand that dynamics enter into the situation. Almost every variety of rhythm known to sculpture is to be noted at some place or other in the immense length of the frieze. The manual skill of the sculptors remains unexcelled; where can one find greater brilliance of line, or more sensitive modeling?

It is nevertheless impossible to say whether this inner frieze was a success. There is much to make one doubt it. However excellent in itself, its placement rendered comfortable inspection impossible. Because the eye adjusts to the brightest illumination within the field of vision, not the dimmest, did the frieze attract its fair share of attention in the bright Mediterranean climate? Or was it lost in the dark as details are lost in paintings by Caravaggio and Rembrandt? Now that the roof is gone, it is difficult to guess at these things. As seen on the building, in the British Museum, and in every available photograph, the cast shadows fall downward, which is the reverse of the way they were intended to fall. Even if this were corrected by artificial light within the museum, outdoor circumstances would scarcely be duplicated. In their original condition, moreover, the panels must have been most subtly finished on the surface to take the light in the best manner; but it is hopeless to attempt to restore that surface. In the end we are left in a quandary, with a number of important worries unresolved.

THE ERECHTHEUM

The conventional nature of most Greek architecture is pointed up with emphasis by the very existence of the Erechtheum at Athens (Fig. 4.26). The building was designed by Mnesicles, who must be ranked high among those capable of original acts of genius.

Instead of leveling off the site as classical architects almost invariably did,

Fig. 4.26   Athens. Erechtheum. View from the south. (Clarence Kennedy)

Mnesicles accepted the footing as he found it. He built the structure on two levels that differ by about 10½ feet, and he provided two separate façades, one at the east end and the other at the northwest corner. Doubtless there were religious as well as physical reasons for the arrangement. It is said that Athena's olive tree and Poseidon's salt spring both were to be seen at this very spot; and while nothing has been established with certainty, it is likely that the building was intended to incorporate several shrines, one of which had to do with Erechtheus—hence the name. The interior arrangements have been altogether erased, but it sems most likely that the Erechtheum was a double temple, with a partition at some point separating the east end from the west.

Because the building is asymmetrical, critics have invariably pictured Mnesicles as a much-put-upon man. We are told that he was a clever person, who tried to beguile us away from fundamental imperfection (that is, absence of geometric order) by elegant details and by surprises like the famous Porch of the Maidens attached to the southwest corner on the side facing the Parthenon. On the assumption that no Greek in his right mind would willingly design the building as it stands, we are often asked to excuse Mnesicles on the ground that he hoped to set things right someday by adding an entire wing out toward the west, an expedient which would "balance" the composition by making it symmetrical to an axis through the middle of the Porch of the Maidens.

There is no archeological evidence that compels us to believe Mnesicles intended any such thing. Neither is there any reason to apologize for the Erechtheum as it stands. Everything in view is susceptible of explanation by reference to well-established principles of design.

As always, we must first consider the building in relation to its setting.

It stands about fifty yards north of the Parthenon, and at a slight angle thereto. It is doubtful whether we would think so highly of the Parthenon were it not for its juxtaposition to the irregular and delicate Erechtheum. The two go together, the daintiness of the one setting off the strength of the other. The modern observer, accustomed as he is to the mechanical planning that derives from Rome, might interpret the absence of parallelism as an indication no such relation was intended, but he would be mistaken. By pitching the two axes differently, the Greek designers made certain that the two buildings would take the light differently, and thus avoided the monotonous pattern of shadows which results from putting every surface in line with every other.

The matter becomes even more interesting if we consider the Erechtheum by itself. The south face, toward the Parthenon, is the one that best illustrates the principles in operation (Fig. 4.26). It is necessary, of course, to supply in imagination the missing parts of the entablature, and the vanished roof.

Seen from this point of view, the composition presents us with an extensive area of blank wall stretching to the east and right. At the lower left-hand corner, we see the Porch of the Maidens, which is small in scale but amazing to contemplate—young ladies carrying an entablature on their heads; and still doing it after some 2,400 years! When stated in words, the idea sounds preposterous; but the architect got away with it because his sculptor chose a very adequate canon of proportions and was supremely skillful in posing the figures so that they appear to do their work with ease, even with freedom.

The composition is in perfect balance. It is merely necessary to realize that for the purposes of a work of art, balance is not a mechanical matter but a question of the observer's psychology. We may balance mass off against mass, much as we balance weight against weight when using a simple set of scales. Up to this point, we have found it unnecessary to refer to any other kind of balance, but the Erechtheum demands an extension of our understanding. It confronts us with the phenomenon of the small item which is intensely interesting (the Porch of the Maidens) placed far off center, but establishing by the very fact of its interest an equilibrium as over against a large bulk of comparatively neutral material (the blank wall). In its present condition without either entablature or roof, the composition is out of order because the Porch of the Maidens exerts a disproportionate appeal to one's attention.

Were the Erechtheum the only instance of its kind, we might put it down as a historical eccentricity, and pass on. The arrangement, although most unusual in ancient architecture, is merely an instance of a particular system of composition that must have been used before, and has certainly been used since.

The essential principle is to balance a bulk of inert material against a small item of intense interest. This is some times called *occult balance,* and it is used more often in painting than in architecture. In pictures, the element of intense interest is usually a vista into the distance, most often placed at the upper right-hand corner, or the upper left—an arrangement that became very popular during the High Renaissance (page 634). So long as it does its work, the vista can be put anywhere, and anything else can be used instead of a vista so long as it attracts the proper amount of attention.

We need not be disturbed, therefore, because the Erechtheum does not compose according to the familiar system of bilateral symmetry. On the other hand, its arrangement is so clever and so successful as to increase our admiration for the Greek genius, and to soften somewhat our comments about the limitations of the Greek mind.

THE INFLUENCE OF GREEK ARCHITECTURE UPON LATER STYLES

The influence of the Greek style upon the subsequent history of architecture is a matter of common knowledge. The beauty of the Greek orders has been as cogent, perhaps, as any other single factor in maintaining the cultural prestige of antiquity. As decorative detail, the orders (or reminiscences of them) appear in wholesale quantities on Roman buildings, Byzantine buildings, Renaissance buildings, baroque buildings, rococo buildings, and indeed almost everywhere except in Romanesque and Gothic. This is the literal and mechanical aspect of the Greek influence.

Far more important are the tendencies which derive from the inward spirit of the Greek style. These have to do with the shape and the subtleties of shape given to individual members, and with the way parts combine into an orderly scheme conceived in terms of geometry. In the Greek temple, those impulses combined to produce a building which is, in the last analysis, a gigantic piece of geometric sculpture.

The basic psychology that derives from such a conception of architecture has had a far-reaching effect. It has been the dominant factor in architectural thought since the start of the Renaissance, and it was the dominant factor in the architectural thought of the Romans.

An architect who holds the Greek point of view experiences his first conception of the building in a sculptor's terms. His initial effort to visualize the completed building creates in his mind's eye a picture of the *outside* of the building. He sees a set of masses. Each one will be a familiar geometric solid, pierced perhaps by doors and windows arranged at equal intervals, or according to some other scheme of easily comprehended regularity. The more the mass of the building conforms to the simplicity and unity of the Greek temple, the more closely will it suit the taste of its architect.

Provision has to be made for the human activities that must go on inside the structure and round about it. In point of time, this consideration arrives in the mind of the architect only after he has already formed a preference for an exterior of a particular shape. The truth is that he packs in the practical details much as we pack a suitcase, and the volume of space originally chosen almost always is too much or too little. To use a bit of legitimate jargon, the architect who feels as the Greeks felt "designs from the outside inward."

The process almost invariably produces buildings that yearn for the condition of the Greek temple. Adjustments and additions are difficult to make, and the expense is usually higher than it otherwise might be. Neatness and order are almost sure to be arrived at, however; and no other procedure is so likely to produce formal beauty. As Alberti was so eloquently to point out during the Renaissance, formal beauty is no mere luxury. It has to do with the dignity of man, and is necessary if his soul is to be fed.

Chapter 5

PHIDIAS

THE OPINION OF THE ANCIENTS, as expressed in their literary records, gives the unmistakable impression that Phidias was the greatest artist of Greece. Because we possess so much of it in good condition we are likely to think of the building program on the Acropolis as his greatest achievement, but it would appear that we are mistaken. His fame during antiquity derived from his authorship of the two greatest cult statues of the peninsula: the *Athena Parthenos* for which the Parthenon itself was built, and the seated *Zeus* in the Temple of Zeus at Olympia. For the Greeks these two statues had tremendous religious significance, and as objects of pilgrimage and devotion meant as much or more than the shrine of Santiago at Compostela was destined to mean in the days of medieval Christianity. Phidias's role, in short, was to furnish Greece with its visual imagery for the great gods. The testimony of our literary records is practically unanimous in praising his supreme success in that profoundly difficult and immensely important enterprise.

Both the *Zeus* and the *Athena Parthenos* were of colossal size, standing about forty feet high. Because the *Zeus* was a seated figure, the scale was even larger.

Both were *chryselephantine,* which is to say made of gold and ivory. A complex wooden frame supported the statue. Over this, ivory plates were laid for the flesh surfaces. Precious stones were added here and there. Because of the immense size, areas not ordinarily available for such use (the vertical sides of the soles on Athena's sandals, for example) were employed as fields for subordinate decoration in narrative relief.

It is impossible to say with any certainty which statue was the earlier; and, as a matter of fact, our visual evidence is so slight as to make such a

114

GREEK SCULPTORS
OF THE GREAT AGE

question utterly academic. The only fixed date in the sculptor's entire career is 438 B.C., when the *Athena Parthenos* was dedicated. Either before that or after it, he went to Olympia. There is a record that he got into trouble over an alleged theft of some of the gold used for the *Zeus,* and may even have died in prison. Greek politics being what they were, his association with Pericles may have been the real reason behind the rumor; probably some of his enemies got him after Pericles died in 429. At any rate, we may make the guess Phidias was born about 490, and that his activity extended to 430 or a little longer.

Pausanias, that Baedeker of the Ancient World, was in Greece during the 2nd century A.D., and saw the *Athena Parthenos.* In his *Description of Greece* (I.24.5), he says:

> On the middle of the helmet rests a sphinx and on either side of the helmet griffins are represented. The statue of Athena stands erect and wears a tunic reaching to the feet. On its breast is represented in ivory the head of Medusa, and a *Victory* about four cubits in height stands on one of its hands, while in the other it holds a spear. At its feet rests a shield, and close to the shield is a serpent which no doubt represents Erichthonios. On the base of the statue, the *Birth of Pandora* is represented in relief.

It is from Pliny *(Natural History* XXXVI.18) that we get the further information that "on the shield was wrought in relief the *Battle of the Amazons* on the convex surface, and the *Combat of the Gods and Giants* on the concave side, while on the sandals was represented those of the *Lapiths and Centaurs.*"

115

Fig. 5.1 (left) Athens, National Museum. Varvakeion copy of the *Athena Parthenos*. 39 inches high. (Alinari)

Fig. 5.2 (above) Rome, Terme Museum. Red jasper gem signed by Aspasios. Early 1st century A.D. Believed to reflect the appearance of the *Athena Parthenos* by Phidias. (Sansaini)

Figs. 5.3–4 (above) Coin of Elis. Period of Hadrian (A.D. 117–138). Believed to reflect the appearance of the Olympian *Zeus* by Phidias. Fig. 5.5 (left) Paris, Bibliothèque Nationale. Coin of Olympia. About 360 B.C.

Plutarch (*Pericles* XXXI.4) completes such description as we have with the remark that on the shield Phidias included "a figure of himself as a bald old man lifting up a stone in both hands, and a very fine portrait of Pericles fighting an Amazon." Pericles, he further indicates, was shown with one arm across his face.

Suffering a certain amount of attrition, the original statue still stood in the cella as late as A.D. 375. After that time, accounts vary. There was a fire during the 5th century A.D. in which the *Athena* may have perished; at any rate, it seems to have been gone by about 485. One bit of evidence suggests it was at Constantinople during the 10th century, but we can by no means be certain what actually happened to it. As usual, we are left to do the best we can with what we have.

The *Strangford Shield* in the British Museum is probably a copy after the shield of the *Athena Parthenos,* and seems to show Phidias and Pericles as we might expect to find them from Plutarch's citation. If so, this monument is the nearest thing we have to a self-portrait by any ancient artist, and is in itself evidence for the sculptor's age at the date of the statue.

Other monumental evidence is discouraging to a degree. The so-called "Varvakeion copy" (Fig. 5.1) is the only complete statue that comes anywhere near fitting the stipulations of the literary evidence. One wishes it had never been found; it is lifeless, stupid, vulgar. About all that may properly be deduced from it is a summary notion of Phidias's figure-style as of that particular moment: a stocky canon of proportions and a head characterized by considerable breadth in the region of the mouth and chin. The *Lenormant Statuette* is a bit pleasanter than the "Varvakeion copy," but suffers from poor workmanship and bad condition.

A head in the Staatliche Museum of Berlin is of better quality, as are reflections appearing on Athenian coins. The only reflection of the great Athena which in and of itself has any finesse, however, is a carved gem by Aspasios, now in the Terme Museum at Rome (Fig. 5.2). But even that is florid, and we are forced to the conclusion that visual recovery of the *Athena Parthenos* is today impossible. Unless further evidence comes our way, we must abandon hope of having any adequate idea what it looked like.

For the Olympian Zeus, we are a little better off. The general appearance of the statue we know by following much the same method as before. It was seated on a throne. The upper half of the body was nude. The majesty of the expression was softened by kindness.

The ensemble is reflected on later coins of Elis, the district in which Olympia is situated (Figs. 5.3–5), and in a rather empty fresco of Roman date discovered at Eleusis. A full-size marble head at Boston corresponds generally to the heads appearing on the coins, but its expression overdoes the element of kindness to the complete exclusion of the force for which the original was famous.

If this were all, we would once again have to abandon hope of spiritual or esthetic satisfaction; but among the various coins which presumably reflect the appearance of the *Zeus,* there is one that rings true (Figs. 5.3–4). A mass-produced article in the first place, dulled by usage, preserved by the merest chance, reproduced in the form of a plaster cast, and reproduced again for our book plate, this tiny monument is enough to establish the caliber of its original and the authenticity of the reverence in which it was held.

"When you stand before this statue," said Dion Chrysostomos (*Orat.* XII.14), "you forget every misfortune of our earthly life, even though you have been broken by adversities and grief, and sleep shuns your eyes. . . ." In other places, we hear that the fame of the *Zeus* went through all lands, that it was the unrivaled statue, and stood as the symbol and guardian of Hellas.

Like the *Athena Parthenos,* the *Zeus* remained in position for nearly a thousand years. In A.D. 426 the Emperor Theodosius the 2nd issued his decree calling for the destruction of all remaining pagan temples. That order seems actually to have been carried out at Olympia at least to the extent of putting the torch to the wooden roof and other inflammable parts of the building. It may be that the *Zeus* perished in the fire, but there is a rumor it was taken off to Constantinople, where it burned with the palace in which it stood about A.D. 475.

Left as we are with nothing but a coin and a gem to give us any adequate notion of Phidias's major works, it is tempting to make as much as we can of the architectural sculptures from the Parthenon. Opinions vary as to the extent they may be used as an indication of his personal style. The marbles are certainly unusually fine for the purpose to which they were put, but the whole weight of probability warns us that Phidias can have had very little to do with them at first hand, and perhaps nothing. Any interpretation which connects them with himself must be put forward with the utmost reserve— and is thus useful only for the most general and superficial kind of analysis.

That being so, is there any hope of recovering one of the less celebrated monuments? The wish to do so amounts to strong pressure on every student of archeology, and the hope for a positive result begets a tendency among the best of men to stretch every item of evidence to the limit. Such an instance is Adolf Furtwängler's reconstruction of the *Athena Lemnia,* conducted in 1891 and described in his *Masterpieces of Greek Sculpture* which appeared under the Scribner imprint in 1895.

Figs. 5.6–7 Bologna, Museo Civico. *Athena Lemnia*. Believed to be a Roman copy of unusually fine quality after an original by Phidias. (Clarence Kennedy)

The *Athena Lemnia,* we know from literature, was a bronze statue that stood on the Acropolis. It seems to have been dedicated between 451 and 448 by some Athenians who were leaving their native city to establish a colony on the island of Lemnos. Pausanias (I.28.2) declares to have been Phidias' most remarkable work. His statement might be discounted were it not for the fact that Lucian (*Images,* 4) once said he preferred it to all the other works of Phidias. Lucian was a good critic, and his opinion is repeated by every other critic. The *Lemnia* was preferred by some to Praxiteles's *Aphrodite of Cnidus,* the most famous female nude in history, and there is good reason to believe that the *Lemnia* is the statue habitually referred to as "the Beautiful." If such opinions were entertained by competent men who knew the great chryselephantine cult statues, it is obvious there must have been something exquisite about the *Athena Lemnia.*

We need not take space for a detailed recapitulation of Furtwängler's argument. Suffice it to say that the head shown in our Figures 5.6–8 is of a type known in several marble copies, and on a gem. In several museums there existed some draped bodies recognizable as Athenas because they wore the *aegis,* but all these bodies either had been restored with heads that did not belong or lacked heads altogether.

Two of the bodies were at Dresden. In 1891, it was decided to correct the erroneous modern repairs. In the course of that work, it occurred to Furt-

Fig. 5.8 Bologna, Museo Civico. *Athena Lemnia.* (Clarence Kennedy)

wängler to try the experiment of fitting a cast of the *Bologna Head* into one of the statues at Dresden. "The Bologna bust fitted into the hollowed torso," he says, "as exactly as if it had been made for it, hardly a millimeter of alteration being necessary." He later determined that head and body were carved from the same marble.

The *Bologna Head* had not previously been recognized as an Athena; but under the circumstances just set forth, no other conclusion seemed reasonable. The identification of the newly reconstructed statue as reflective of the *Athena Lemnia* depends upon the oddity that, of all the Athenas famous in antiquity, the *Lemnia* was the only one without a helmet. "Phidias substituted beauty for the helmet" in this instance—or at least so runs one of the epigrams.

The *Bologna Head,* presuming it to be of Roman workmanship, is in a class by itself among marble copies. Nothing we possess so nicely fulfills our hope of Phidias in his gentler, more lyrical moments. Nothing so charming has ever been so chaste, nor anything so strong half so winsome. These circumstances lure us into sympathy with Furtwängler's hypothesis even while sober judgment tells us to hold back. The fact is that the identification rests on descriptive evidence of the very slightest kind, and the mechanical fit of the *Bologna Head* into the torso at Dresden may mean nothing more than the custom of a particular Roman shop. Many another head might, if we pursued the matter to the end, be found to drop quite as neatly into the same cavity.

Whatever else we may think of it, the *Bologna Head of Furtwängler's Athena Lemnia* (as we must call it if we are going to be cautious) is equal to Greek work in quality, and a splendid demonstration of the developed style of the Greek Fifth Century.

The delicacy of the subject and the taste of the workmanship tend to obscure our realization of the stylistic facts. The severity of the classical profile has, it is true, been softened somewhat by subtler contours and by the gentle texture of the lovely marble from which it is carved. The cylindrical forehead is still there, however, and the hard clean edge where the sinuses meet its contour. The hair, while more free than in earlier work, is in fact a sculptor's abstraction intended merely to suggest softness rather than represent it. The contour of every surface, moreover, is made to take a smooth, true curve which necessarily eliminates the lines, convexities, hollows, and innumerable other irregularities inevitably present on the body of any living model. The subdivisions of the head are very nearly in symmetrical balance as well, each curve having its equal and opposite with a precision of balance never seen in nature.

Because most educated adults have been accustomed to Greek sculpture since childhood, these peculiarities of style are usually accepted without comment, or not even noted as peculiarities. It is therefore necessary to give strong emphasis to the fact that the *Athena Lemnia* may not properly be described as realistic, or even by the more general term of *naturalism*. It retains enough resemblance to the human female to preclude our confusing it with anything else, but it is actually at several removes from representative art. Had the process of abstracting and idealizing been carried further along the same line, Fifth Century sculpture would have arrived at something close to modern cubism.

In drawing conclusions from all that has gone before, it is evident that *as an artist* we know almost nothing about Phidias. As an idea, the reverse is true. The Phidian imagery for the great gods continued throughout antiquity. It went on over into the Christian tradition almost without change.

Michelangelo's paintings of the Almighty differ only in detail from the *Olympian Zeus;* no one has ever suggested the conception was unwise or unworthy. In the whole tradition of Western art, we may, in fact, recognize the constant force of a Phidian ideal, for it is he rather than any other artist who best personifies Greece.

POLYCLITUS

Polyclitus flourished at the same time as Phidias. He was a citizen of Argos, and did the great chryselephantine *Hera* for the Temple of Hera at Argos, to replace an earlier cult image destroyed by fire in 422 B.C. For the most part, however, he worked on athletic statues. A number of signed bases were found at Olympia, and we may guess that Polyclitus, true to his southern origin, carried forward into the Great Age the Dorian tradition noted during the Archaic period.

Inadequate reflections of the *Hera* appear on coins. We can also recognize in several Roman copies a reflection of that very *Diadumenus*, or *Athlete with Fillet* (Fig. 5.9) Lucian placed in the collection of Eucrates the Mag-

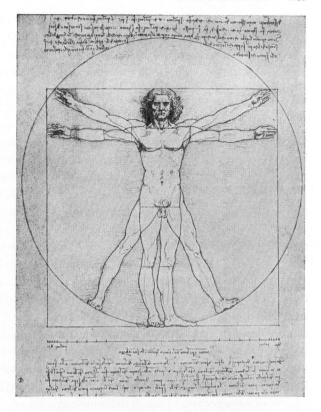

Fig. 5.9 (opposite left) New York, Metropolitan Museum. Terra-cotta statuette believed to reflect the appearance of the *Diadumenus* by Polyclitus.

Fig. 5.10 (opposite right) Naples, National Museum. Roman copy believed to reflect the appearance of the *Doryphorus* by Polyclitus. About 7 feet high. (Alinari)

Fig. 5.11 (right) Venice, Academy. A page from one of Leonardo's notebooks. An attempt to visualize the Polyclitan scheme for human proportions. (Alinari)

nificent. Neither of these monuments have anything like the interest and importance of another which we find reflected in a full-size marble copy at Naples, a fine bronze bust in the same place, and on a grave relief in the National Museum at Athens.

We refer to the so-called *Doryphorus (Spear-bearer;* Fig. 5.10) which Pliny *(Natural History* XXXIV.55) describes as "a boy of manly form bearing a lance, called *The Canon* by artists who draw from it the rudiments of art as from a code, so that Polyclitus is held to be the only man who has embodied art itself in a work of art."

The last part of Pliny's statement gives us the key to Polyclitus's position in the history of art. In addition to being much respected as a sculptor, he was the chief esthetic philosopher of Greece, and from his theories others were eager to learn. Lysippus himself declared that Polyclitus's work had been his "school," and there were others who said the same thing.

Polyclitus evidently made a specialty of Olympic victors (the *Doryphorus* almost certainly falls in that category) because such subject matter gave him an unparalleled opportunity for life-long study of superior human bodies. At the height of his career, he published a theory of proportion as applied to the body. It may or may not be true that the *Doryphorus* is the particular statue executed to demonstrate the rules; but if not, we have small cause for worry. Polyclitus, according to all accounts, worked for refinement along a single theme, and the less discriminating members of the ancient community sometimes complained that all his statues were very much alike.

♦ *Polyclitus's Canon of Proportions*   A number of ancient writers refer more or less definitely to Polyclitus's theory of proportions. "Chrysippus holds beauty to consist in the proportions not of the elements but of the parts," said Galen *(De Plac. Hipp. et Plat. 5)*. "That is to say, of finger to finger and of all the fingers to the palm and the wrist, and of all these to the forearm, and of the forearm to the upper arm, and of all parts to each other, as they are set forth in the canon of Polyclitus." Obviously, he was merely (and probably correctly) attaching Polyclitus's name to the sentiment expressed by Plato in the *Timaeus* (31): "And the fairest bond is that which makes the most complete fusion of itself and the things which it combines; and proportion is best adapted to effect such a union. For whenever in any three numbers, whether cube or square, there is a mean, which is to the last term what the first is to it; and again, when the mean is to the first term as the last term is to the mean—then the mean becoming first and last and the first and last both becoming means, they will all of them of necessity come to the same, and having become the same with one another will all be one."

While suggestive, those statements are difficult; and the reader may be forgiven if he fails to see how they might be applied to art.

He will be happy to turn to Vitruvius, the only extant text that purports to supply the data which might enable an artist to apply such ideas to the practical problems of the studio. In the first chapter of Book III, Vitruvius tried to tell us what fraction of a man's height ought to be allotted to the different parts of the body. The length of the foot should be 1/6 of the height, for example; and 1/10 of the height ought to be the measure of the distance from the wrist to the tip of the middle finger. After mentioning some other proportions, he went on to suggest a more general proposition; namely, that if we take the navel as a center and describe a circle, the extended arms and feet ought to fall on its circumference. That last notion has proven interesting to some of our greatest artists, who have drawn figures to illustrate it (Fig. 5.11). One may doubt whether such drawings are useful, for the truth is that Vitruvius was mixed up. He said just enough, in fact, to drive one crazy.

His garbled statements have nevertheless been sufficient to make the recovery of Polyclitus's system one of the major endeavors of modern scholarship. The research started almost as soon as Vitruvius was rediscovered in 1416 (page 97); and one of the first to work on the problem was no less a genius than Leon Battista Alberti (pages 550–551). Piero della Francesca also thought it worth while to investigate proportion, and the mathematician Luca Pacioli published a *Divina Proportione* in 1509. Similar studies were undertaken at about the same time by both Leonardo da Vinci (Fig. 5.11) and Albrecht Dürer. The quest still goes on. Jay Hambridge's *Dynamic Symmetry* and Irma Richter's *Rhythmic Form* both derive from the Polyclitan tradition. Each author works with what he happens to fancy as *the golden section,* which is the magic-making name for Polyclitus's mathematics, whatever they were.

The several publications mentioned will prove interesting for every reader and fascinating for those adept with figures and diagrams. There is unmistakable merit in every point of view yet put forward, but we must recognize that we are not yet close to Polyclitus. Neither have we yet produced a practical formula for use by the artist. From the general welter of perplexity, a few helpful ideas nevertheless emerge and deserve to be stated.

All the authors seem to agree that beauty—at least as understood by Polyclitus—was no simple quality of an object. It had to do with the fact of relation and interrelation. "Nothing simple and devoid of parts can be beautiful," said Plotinus (*Enneads,* I.IV.i), "only a composite."

Another feature of the theory, and one upon which the ancients set great store, appears to have been the idea of making all magnitudes commensurate. A fundamental unit, or *module,* was chosen. Every dimension of the body then had to be expressible in even multiples of the module. Polyclitus's module remains to be identified. There are those who think it was a unit of volume, not a unit of linear measure. The chief purpose of the module, it also ought to be mentioned, may have been utilitarian rather than esthetic: uniform standards of linear measure were not established as they now are, and it was often necessary to set up a new unit for each job.

It seems clear, also that Polyclitus derived his theory by some sort of statistical procedure. Living models, it seems, were measured one after another for a very long period of time. The measurements were then combined somehow, and the result was set forth as a table. Because Vitruvius, Alberti, and many others have interpreted the process as a systematic effort to determine nature's true and sacred intention (she being visualized as the goddess of art), it is important to appreciate that Polyclitus probably realized as well as we do that nature is impartial as between the beautiful and ugly, producing both with an even hand. In this connection, we might remember the words of an Athenian who was very hard to fool. "When you want to represent beautiful figures," said Socrates to the painter Parrhasius (*Memorabilia,* III.8), "since it is not easy to find one person with every part perfect, do you not select out of many of the most beautiful parts of each, and thus represent figures beautiful in every part?" "We do so," said the painter. Polyclitus's method, in short, aimed at no average result; he stacked the cards in favor of his own intuitive concept of the beautiful.

What started Polyclitus on his research? What keeps the research going? The answer is to be sought in the intellectual atmosphere of 5th-century Greece; and if we look there, it is plain enough. However indirectly, all such thinking derives from the theory of numbers which was the chief contribution of Pythagoras (latter half of the 6th century B.C.). This theory asserted that numbers have a real and objective existence, and are fundamental in the universe. The idea sounds cold and narrow at first, but no utterance of the human mind has proven more profound. Every modern theory of matter and all theories of wave motion relate to it. Even in antiquity, it inspired some transcendent researches.

One of these, and doubtless the one that set Polyclitus on his way, was the Pythagorean theory of music. Pythagoras and his associates investigated the vibration of taut strings and demonstrated that such were lawful: the number of vibrations varies inversely according to the length of the string. With this information in hand, it was possible to define the intervals of the scale.

The concept of universal law was the inspiring part of the discovery— even more inspiring to the Greeks, perhaps, than to ourselves, for we lack their complete faith in conceptual thinking. How wonderfully beautiful must be the supersensory laws by which we can explain music, the primeval art, the most natural and widely felt, the least definite but most connotative! If music be lawful, it ought to be possible for painters, sculptors, and architects to discover analogous laws, principles that have always existed and always have been true. The whole idea still fills the imagination with life, and doubtless was the vision that moved Polyclitus to his great effort.

Not knowing Polyclitus's theory, we cannot say whether he actually produced an analysis of art comparable to the precise definitions and distinctions long established within the field of music. In attempting to appreciate what he was about, it is of the essence to realize that the musical scale analyzed by Pythagoras, and the bodily proportions studied by Polyclitus, were both in general use and giving satisfaction before the researchers began their work. As to whether such matters may or may not be orderly, we do well to remind ourselves of a sage remark once set down by Alberti: "It is a common error of ignorance," said he, "to maintain that what one does not know does not exist."

The proportions of the *Doryphorus* are naturally of special interest, but at first seem strange to the modern observer. The head compares to the height in the ratio of 1 to 6.84, a numeral that has more decimal places than significant figures. The general aspect of the body has often been characterized as "square"; and by all ordinary standards, it is indeed stocky.

At least two reasons may be adduced to account for the popularity of so ponderous a figure-style. Hand-to-hand fighting with the short sword was the fundamental of Greek warfare; when such work was afoot, the *Doryphorus* would be a better man to follow than to face. Sculpture being an art of mass, moreover, weight is the chief means by which the artist can evoke an impression of force and power, and it is notable that heavy proportions have almost always been employed by those sculptors whom we think of as taking a special interest in the theory of sculpture as such.

Whether the modern reader finds Polyclitus's method congenial or not, all the ancient evidence says that the greatest Greek artists found his canon useful. We must therefore take it seriously; and it is a pity that so important a theory should have its chief visual demonstration in the Naples *Doryphorus* (Fig. 5.10), which is admittedly the product of a Roman copy factory of the second or third rank. By making a strong effort of the imagination we can, however, gain some notion of the original.

The Naples copy suffers from being executed in marble. In the original bronze, one would not be annoyed by the adventitious value contrasts resulting from the dark shadows cast by the overhang of every muscular contour. In bronze, these abrupt and almost linear boundaries would be almost necessary as an aid for reading the modeling.

According to all ancient testimony, the work of Polyclitus was distinguished even in that great era for unusual subtlety of technique. His enigmatic remark to the effect that the labor was hardest when the surface came "under the nail" probably refers to the infinite pains he devoted to the modeling of the wax surface of the form from which he cast his bronzes. But beauty of surface, sadly enough, is emphatically absent in the Naples copy, and we can only do our best to imagine what that statue might look like had the copyist been Desiderio or Verrocchio. The bronze bust also in Naples and signed by Appollonius helps in that endeavor, but not much. Unless some new and better copy comes out of the earth, the celebrated refinement of Polyclitus is gone.

In the end we are as usual put into the position of having to be content with general conclusions of the kind we may legitimately draw from the inferior monumental evidence available. Nothing could be harder on Polyclitus. Both the literature and the Roman copies say the same thing; namely, that he was an artist incapable of ostentation. The excellence of his statues was the service of profound convictions in the matter of design. With that in mind, we may perhaps open our eyes to greater beauty in the *Doryphorus* than at first seemed possible.

Knowing it as we must at an archeological remove, the great remaining merit of the statue is in the pose. The *Doryphorus* is presented as walking slowly forward with the poise and rhythm of the athlete who is also a dancer. By comparison, the familiar stop-in-action pose used by Myron and others seems lacking in finesse. Movement is here actually represented, but the overall ease of attitude and the relaxation of the pace cancel out any worry that might be suggested by the inertia of the medium.

The statics of the *Doryphorus* are hardly less interesting. The body is given a slight twist to our left. The supporting leg is on the side of the arm that hangs slack, and the tensed arm above the leg that is eased. The arrangement gives the torso a delicate, sinuous curvature. It also makes it necessary that some muscles be slightly stretched while others are compressed, a situation that produces an infinitely varied modulation of contour.

It is evident the ancients were not mistaken in their estimate of Polyclitus. He had neither Myron's dash nor Phidas's majesty, but his grasp of formal relationships was perhaps deeper and more subtle than theirs. His place in ancient art is comparable to the station later occupied by Verrocchio, the greatest teacher of great masters that the modern world has known.

THE FOURTH CENTURY

Differences of a fundamental nature separate the Greek Fourth Century from the era before it. The whole land had suffered terribly during the Peloponnesian War (431–404 B.C.) and the plagues which accompanied it. The new century thus started with treasuries low and with the population decreased. The effects of the long-drawn-out war were accentuated by prolonged instability in political life. The Spartan hegemony, the Athenian League against Sparta, the period of Theban control, and, finally, the rise of Macedon completed the century.

For art history, the most conspicuous result of these conditions was the abandonment of large public buildings. In Ionia, it is true, several big temples went up—notably that of Artemis at Ephesus (after 356) and the *Didyma* near Miletus (about 330); but on the Greek peninsula, the absence of important buildings seems to reflect a general loss of confidence in civic enterprise.

The Greek genius was by no means asleep, however. With Plato (429–347) and Aristotle (384–321), philosophy attained a new and nobler eminence. The century also produced its great artists, but their art was of a new and more introspective kind.

Because there were no important temples to call great cult statues into being, certain changes took place in the general run of subject matter. The great gods had been the typical subject of the Fifth Century; the Fourth turned appropriately away from these toward material of a more intimate nature. Gods, when they appear in Fourth-century art, are the lesser divinities. Even those were softened, humanized, and presented not at moments from the heroic past, but in activities evocative of charm, grace, and elegance. Epic glory was the business of the Fifth Century; lyrical loveliness belongs to the Fourth.

Personal portraits, earlier conceived and executed as public monuments when done at all, became for the first time an important part of the artist's business. No originals have survived, but it is obvious that considerable realism must have been wanted. Lysippus, for example, is said to have used casts taken from the model as an aid in the studio, but a statement of Aristotle's *(Poetics* 15) shows that idealism was far from being out of fashion. The "good portrait painters," he takes it for granted, "reproduce the distinctive features of a man, and without losing the likeness, make him handsomer than he is." Doubtless those who followed that advice prospered then as now.

Allegory also became a very popular category of subject matter. The mythological narratives used for pedimental sculpture had always been allegorically understood, to be sure; but the pediments, if properly interpreted, had a plain purpose of a social and ethical nature. The new allegories were of another kind.

Lysippus did a famous and typical one, his statue of *Opportunity*. It carried a razor to encourage keenness. It flew on the wings of the wind. The back of the head was kept shaven as smooth as a billiard ball to prevent any grabbing by those who saw it only as it went by. Assuming that our notices are correct, any statue capable of giving so complex an impression was a clever piece of work, but the allegory comes close to feeding on itself. We may infer that the patrons of the Fourth Century were sometimes more interested in refining the process of thought than in drawing important conclusions.

The general tendency of Greek life to change from a heroic to a more humane experience is also well illustrated by the growth of the sanctuary of Asclepius at Epidaurus (near Mycenae). Asclepius was the god of healing. Although his shrine was an old one, it had never been in big business before the Fourth Century, but by 350 or thereabouts, the traffic of patients and visitors justified the construction of a temple to the god, a large gymnasium, a 180-room hotel built around four courtyards, and the finest of all Greek theaters. So far as we can tell, every kind of Greek medicine from the worst to the best was available there; and the place remained a popular resort throughout antiquity.

Such was the atmosphere in which Fourth-century art flourished. Its definitive master was Praxiteles.

PRAXITELES

Pausanias was at Olympia some time during the latter half of the 2nd century A.D. In addition to what he had to say about the important things to be noted there by future visitors, he set down a passing note (V.17.3) which recounts without comment, "In later times other offerings were dedicated in the Heraion. Among these was a *Hermes* of marble, bearing the infant Dionysus, the work of Praxiteles."

On May 8, 1877, a marble statue came to light as the earth was cleared from the floor of the temple (Figs. 5.12–13). It was obviously a Hermes carrying an infant, and the style was in correspondence with everything previously known or inferred about the work of Praxiteles. The piece was immediately

Figs. 5.12–13 (opposite and right) Praxiteles. *Hermes and the Infant Dionysus.* Middle 4th century B.C. Olympia, Museum. Parian marble. About 6 feet, 11 inches high. (Walter Hege)

attributed to him, and remains the only statue which can possibly be an original from the hand of any artist whom the Greeks themselves recognized as a great master.

The remarkable condition of the monument is accountable, paradoxically enough, to the unusually poor construction of the Temple of Hera in which it stood. The Heraion was a very old temple, perhaps the oldest we have, and its cella walls were made from sun-dried brick. After the roof was gone, the rain gradually converted the bricks back into clay. When the statue was overthrown, presumably by the earthquakes of the 6th century A.D., there seems to have been a deep, soft bed of mud ready to receive it. Thus we have it intact except for the two legs below the knee, the right forearm, and both arms of the child.

Hermes is presented as in the act of taking the baby Dionysus to the nymphs of Mount Nysa, by which ladies he was brought up. The god is apparently in no hurry and perhaps even a bit bored with his assignment. He stops for a moment to ease the muscles of the left side by resting his elbow on a convenient tree stump, and he whiles away the time by amusing the youngster with something held high in the right hand, possibly a bunch of grapes.

While very weighty by modern standards, the canon of proportions is more slender than that used by Phidias or Polyclitus. The greater length of the body invited experiment with curvature, and the action of the figure throws the whole form into a pronounced S-curve. The pose is no different in principle from that of the *Doryphorus,* but the desire for elegance is more obvious and certainly far more overt. Curvature of this order of magnitude, it should be noted, was not peculiar to Praxiteles but was characteristic of all Fourth-century masters. The personal factor was the cultivation of grace for its own sake, and the winsome but nostalgic mood.

Aside from the more slender canon of proportions and the pronounced curve of the pose, the most conspicuous element of style has to do with the textures. These are differentiated with a new and almost incredible subtlety. The story is told that the statue was set upright and photographed as soon as found, and copies of the prints went posthaste to Berlin. One of the experts called in to see them complained, it is said, at the stupidity of photographing the *Hermes* in such haste. Someone, said he, should have taken the trouble to remove the cloth from the tree stump.

Unimportant in itself, the anecdote suggests much about Praxiteles. The bold summary modeling of the Fifth Century had been replaced by discrimination carried to its ultimate conclusion. Whereas Fifth-century sculptors had aimed to make a clear, unmistakable, and heroic statement, Praxiteles wanted to miss no least nuance of beauty. The contours of the body were lovingly rendered in modulations so subtle as to defy resolution by the eye alone; the hands must feel the surface if we are to comprehend in any adequate fashion the full measure of the author's skill.

The more detailed modeling and the greater variation between textures has an effect rather startling in comparison to Fifth-century sculpture. One feels a vivid impression of actuality and human warmth. At first this may be mistaken for realism, but it is realism only in a limited and comparative sense. Hermes' hair is modeled freely, for example; and its surface is very different from the areas of flesh. At the same time the hair is abstracted into bunches or locks, as we may care to call them. From a little distance, these take the light rather as hair does, but closely inspected each will be seen to be a small mass defined by orderly contours and twisted in a spiral fashion. The eyes, the lips, and the nostrils show a similar tendency to regularize every curve and make it graceful. The fact is that the *Hermes* is a humanization of an ideal type, not an idealization from the living model.

From the instant of discovery, people have been saying that the *Hermes* was a Praxitelean original. It has all too seldom been made plain that the attribution rests upon what is thought to be the probability (or even what one hopes is probable) and not upon demonstrable certainty.

The only external evidence for Praxiteles' authorship is Pausanias' passing statement. The value of that may be impeached. In the first place Pausanias was not a contemporary critic; he visited Olympia some six centuries after Praxiteles. He was a visitor, moreover, and not a citizen of the place. Like all tourists, he may have got his information about the authorship from some ignorant and irresponsible guide of the sort all too familiar today. Unlike Lucian, Pausanias was hardly enough of a connoisseur to make, or to suspect, attributions on the basis of his own observation.

The style of the *Hermes* fits well with everything we believe to be typical of Praxiteles, but this internal evidence is a bit deceptive also. In the absence of any other original, "what we believe to be typical of Praxiteles" is a very general idea indeed. As compared to the visual data available for the study of most modern masters, we have next to nothing to go on. Connoisseurship in the ordinary sense of minute comparison is impossible.

It means rather little, in any case, to find a statue of Praxitelean style. The great Fourth-century Praxiteles was the most popular artist of the ancient world. His style was imitated for a long time. How are we to know that the *Hermes* is not the work of some very competent later master trained to imitate Praxiteles?

That possibility is rendered more cogent by the fact that the name Praxiteles, while not now common, was more or less frequent in Greece. We know of other artists who were named Praxiteles; some of them may have been descendants. Descendants, indeed, might be counted upon to capitalize on the reputation of the founder of their house by perpetuating his style as long as possible.

Loopholes in the evidence must be conceded to exist. It has even been suggested that the marble *Hermes* Pausanias said he saw was a marble replica put there by way of consolation and penance by some collector lucky enough to have carried off an original *Hermes* of bronze. Had that happened, there is small reason to suppose Pausanias would have known the difference.

Praxiteles' most famous statue was the *Aphrodite of Cnidus*. The goddess was represented as nude, with one hand in front of her. There are reflections on Cnidian coins of Roman date, and these show her standing

Figs. 5.14–15   Boston, Museum of Fine Arts. *Bartlett Aphrodite.* (Clarence Kennedy)

beside a large urn over which she has tossed her drapery—and with the folded surface thereof, her smooth body must have made a vivid contrast.

All the ancient authors united in celebrating her charm. Pliny *(Natural History* XXXVI.20) flatly declared that she was the finest statue in the world. Lucian *(Images* 6) spoke specifically of the "finely pencilled eyebrows" and the "melting gaze of the eyes with their bright and joyous expression."

A good many other pieces of sculpture were accumulated by the citizens of Cnidus, but the *Aphrodite* outshone them all. In 84 B.C., Sulla laid heavy levies upon Cnidus; and King Nicomedes of Bithynia offered to defray the entire public debt, enormous as it was, in return for the statue. But, says Pliny, the Cnidians preferred "to undergo the worst"; and presumably their *Aphrodite* continued to stand there in her open shrine lending fame and loveliness to the island.

No replicas of acceptable quality have been found. The best known is a Roman copy in the Vatican, which reproduces the pose as shown on the coins. After knowing the *Hermes,* it is very hard to reconcile oneself to that coarse statue. The *Von Kaufmann Head* in Berlin is a little better, and casts are sometimes made with this head upon the Vatican body. The resulting statue is still a great disappointment. We must unhappily admit that the wonderful original is still very far off.

The *Bartlett Aphrodite* in the Boston Museum (Figs. 5.14–15) goes far, however, to ameliorate the situation just outlined. It may one day be established as a Praxitelean original. The chief argument against it is the fact that the skull structure is less massive than most Fourth-century work. The chief arguments for it are the workmanship, which is as good as the *Hermes,* and the inexpressible charm which almost spells out the name Praxiteles.

Because the mood is more pensive than joyous, it seems likely that we have here another *Aphrodite,* and not the one from Cnidus. The dreamy loveliness of the gentle face is intensely feminine, not in itself emotional but extending the strongest appeal to emotion.

In producing such an effect, the sculptor must necessarily allow his hand to be guided largely by feeling and intuition, but calculation enters into the method to a very great extent nevertheless. For the general understanding of the Fourth-century style, and its differences from that of Phidias and Polyclitus, the *Bartlett Aphrodite* must be compared in some detail with the *Athena Lemnia.*

The expressive power of the *Athena Lemnia* (Figures 5.6–8) is produced almost exclusively by plastic means. We may define *plastic* as referring to tangible masses, and to the shape thereof. Sculpture is often called "the plastic art" because the sculptor either carves stone or wood into the desired shape, builds up the shape from clay, or casts the shape in bronze. In our own generation (when we are perhaps overly concerned with the internal logic of the various media) we frequently hear it suggested that sculptors should refrain from attempting to get any effect which cannot be produced by masses and contours.

Sculpture of a perfectly plastic kind is susceptible of inspection by touch; ideally, it ought to be intelligible to a blind man. The *Lemnia* comes very close to fulfilling that stipulation, but the *Bartlett Aphrodite* does not.

It is true that the flesh surfaces of the Bartlett head are plastic. Less bold and summary than the *Lemnia,* the contours flow into each other, a veritable study in the nuances of modulation. If we turn our attention to the hair, however, it will become evident that the shape no longer does the work.

The hair of the *Lemnia,* as we were at pains to point out, communicates the idea of texture by an actual modeling of the marble. The hair of the Bartlett head extends deeper into the third dimension, but the very qualities which might be thought to depend on modeling actually derive from the play of light and dark. It is not the stone surface of the hair that gives the impression of soft bulk and texture, but the shadows produced by undercutting the larger locks and roughening the surface in general. The effect depends, in short, upon the existence of reasonably normal light conditions, and we comprehend it by using our eyes.

What is true of the hair is even more true of the facial expression. The sculptor broadened the bridge of the nose near the forehead, and sank the eye abnormally deep in the skull. The eyeballs do not protrude as anatomy says they must, and the lids are reduced in thickness. The result is to lose the eye, as it were, in a dark shadow, and we read the result as expression. The unaided fingertips of the blind man could learn nothing of this by going over the surface; indeed, for him, the face of the *Bartlett Aphrodite* would make little sense.

Some critics have used the word *coloristic* whenever sculpture depends upon light and dark rather than upon modeling. Others would apply the adjective *pictorial* to situations like the one just reviewed, their reason being that pictures also demand the use of our optical equipment. It seems unwise to use either term in such a way. *Coloristic* has always been a tricky word, and *pictorial* is better reserved for reliefs that attempt spatial representation, like those the Romans used to make, and those of Ghiberti.

It is obvious from all that has gone before that Praxiteles was at his best when doing statues of women, and that his finely drawn style was inappropriate for subject matter that demanded heroics. His special gift was to open the eyes of Greece to daintiness, grace, and charm; in fact, he was the first artist in history who made charm a primary aim. The possible weakness of such art is obvious, but if we may judge from the *Bartlett Aphrodite,* no artist has ever offered us a more perfect appreciation of the peculiar loveliness that belongs only to lovely women.

Although we have lost the *Aphrodite of Cnidus,* that statue in itself was enough to give Praxiteles a special place in the history of European art: before it, the female nude was so rare we often say it didn't occur. Ever since, it has been perhaps the most popular subject of all.

SCOPAS

The art of Scopas is still unknown unless we take the liberty of drawing conclusions from sparse evidence of an admittedly shaky kind. Literary sources make the man out to have been a wanderer. He worked in the Peloponnesus and in Ionia. He seems to have been an architect as well as a sculptor, and from the date of the buildings with which the authors associate him, he must have been at the height of his career about the middle of the 4th century B.C.

The only line of inquiry that has led directly to sculpture in what may be the Scopasian manner stems from Pausanias. When noting down his impressions of a visit to the Temple of Athena Alea at Tegea, about 25 miles north of Sparta, Pausanias (VIII.45.4 & 46.1) said, "I was told the architect was Scopas of Paros, who was the sculptor of many statues in different parts of Greece proper and also in Ionia and Caria." It will be noted that Pausanias assumes no responsibility for the fact; he merely says he was told.

The temple at Tegea was a Doric edifice of peculiar beauty, or at least

Figs. 5.16–17 Heads from the pedimental sculptures of the Temple of Athena Alea at Tegea. (left, from a cast in the Metropolitan Museum; right, Alinari)

so it is said. It replaced an older temple that burned in 395 B.C., but the style of the architecture, with columns six diameters high and an echinus profile so tense as to approach a straight line, suggests a dating of about 360 to 350— which would be consistent with Scopas's presence there.

The temple stood for about 700 years and was destroyed by Alaric the Goth during the 4th century A.D. The vandalism must have been unusually savage. Four separate efforts at excavation, beginning in 1879 and extending to 1913, have yielded only fragmentary remains. From the pediments in particular, we have only a few battered heads. The rest of the statuary must have been broken up at considerable effort, possibly for reduction to lime.

Battered as they are, these poor fragments nevertheless exhibit a figure-style that is markedly different from the general run of Greek sculpture. It is necessary to assume the work, or at least the direction, of some powerful personality with ideas of his own. If he was eminent both as sculptor and architect, we may fairly hazard a guess that Scopas would be inclined to exert a more detailed supervision over the sculpture for one of his temples than might be the case with the ordinary run of architects. And if that is so, then probably the original and individual style of these heads is his.

Seen either in full face or in profile, the heads from Tegea (Figs. 5.16–17) make a strangely "square" impression; they would in fact fit neatly into a cubical box. The vertical dimension is relatively less than in any other Greek heads, and the nose is shorter. The Tegean fragments retain enough of the neck to show that the head had a strong twist on the body, and that the gaze was directed slightly upward. The eye is put back into shadow by sinking it deep into the skull, but the method was applied vigorously rather than with finesse: the sinuses overhang the eye-sockets in great rolls of muscle. The nostrils are slightly dilated, and the mouth is opened a little—both features suggesting a strong breathing appropriate to action or excitement.

The subject matter of the eastern pediment was the *Calydonian Boar Hunt*. The hero of that event was Meleager, who had been one of the Argonauts. When Artemis became angry at his father, the King of Calydon, and sent an immense wild boar to ravage the land, Meleager assembled a band of heroes and killed the beast. He gave its head to the virgin huntress Atalanta, whom he loved, and thus set into motion the series of jealous events which resulted in his death.

Now boar hunting always has been and remains the sport of kings. The wild boar is native in Europe and North Africa, and the domestic pig will, if permitted to run wild, revert to type in a few generations. No other European animal is half so dangerous to the hunter, and yet boars may be killed in comparative safety by men who have the nerve and skill. Traditionally, the boars are run with dogs, brought to bay, and dispatched with a heavy spear. The risk comes when a ferocious boar charges, for the hunter then will have no second chance if he fails to drive the spear home.

We have several marble statues of a youth who appears to carry a boar spear; sometimes there is a dog beside him. Meleager was, of course, the heroic prototype of all boar hunters, and the Meleager-subject suggests Scopas. Most of these statues show enough resemblance to the Tegean heads to make an association plausible.

The several statues in European collections have the usual coarseness of the routine Roman copy, but the *Harvard Meleager* (Fig. 5.18) is noticeably better. The modeling is sensitive, the anatomy full of vigor, and the pose dignified. If we are correct in associating the heads from Tegea with Scopas, this statue brings us closer to knowing him than any other we now possess.

The writers say that Scopas went off to Ionia, where he worked on the *Mausoleum* at Halicarnassus and on the Temple of Diana at Ephesus. Both buildings fall approximately in the middle of the 4th century, and both included much sculpture. It is difficult to associate Scopas with the material preserved from these two places, but his influence may be felt in a very general way. Insofar as we have any right to particularize, a train of thought is suggested by the tradition that one of his famous statues was a *Raving Maenad,* possibly reflected in a very battered statue in Dresden. The Maenads were the mad women who accompanied Dionysus, and something can be made of the fact that Scopas was willing to undertake such a work.

The essence of the Maenad-subject is loss of control: the Maenads were traditionally supposed not only to be possessed, but to be habitually in a violent state of intoxication. They flung themselves about in the wildest manner, half in ecstasy and half in torment. Obviously such material could

Fig. 5.18 Cambridge, Massachusetts, Fogg Art Museum. *Harvard Meleager*. Believed to reflect the appearance of a statue by Scopas.

not be handled within the limitations of conventional Greek sculpture. The statics formerly thought appropriate for major statuary necessarily were tossed aside, and the direct representation of fast movement was accepted.

Even more important are the emotional and spiritual implications. Phidias had presented man as a creature of lofty calm for whom environment was a mere abstraction. Praxiteles made man conscious of his surroundings, but easy in his mind about them. Scopas admitted conflict between humanity and the universe; his people feel and struggle.

Whether Scopas's or not, the reliefs from the frieze of the Mausoleum, now preserved in London, are surely in line with the general tendency just suggested. The narrative subject is *The Battle between the Greeks and the Amazons,* and the combat is described in a manner well along the road toward realistic representation. Formal considerations (as, for example, the desirability of putting all the heads on one level to maintain unbroken the architectural lines, as on the Parthenon frieze) were largely cast aside. The figures stand or fall, thrust and parry much as they might in actual hand-to-hand combat. The effect is spirited to a degree, but the older Greek restraints—one might almost say the older Greek dignities—were obviously no longer in force at this date.

LYSIPPUS

The career of Lysippus paralleled that of Alexander the Great. He must have been born about 370 or earlier, because he began making portraits of the conqueror when the latter was a small boy. No other sculptor, it is said, could satisfy Alexander, who in the end declined to permit portraits by any one else. The others emphasized the celebrated and almost effeminate beauty of his person; Lysippus alone was able to combine this with an impression of courage, intelligence, and power.

Of Lysippus' famous allegorical statue, *Opportunity,* we have already spoken. Among his other celebrated works was a *Heracles Epitrapezios,* so called because it was designed as a table decoration—it was a bronze statuette about a foot high, the hero seated on a rock with a wine cup in one hand and his club in the other. By all accounts this tiny object conveyed an extraordinary sense of monumentality. "In how small a space," wrote Statius *(Silvae,* IV.6), "what illusion of great size!" The *Heracles* was a much sought-after collector's item; it is said to have been owned successively by Alexander himself, by Hannibal, and by Sulla. Although we have more than one statuette of Heracles sitting on a rock, both style and details of the composition differ from the descriptions, and it is only on worn coins that we see anything suggestive of the original.

Lysippus apparently made his greatest reputation by doing monumental groups of figures in violent action. In this line, he appears to have anticipated an art form often cited as an innovation of the Hellenistic period. One group showed about twenty-five Macedonians of the king's guard sacrificing themselves in a gallant defensive action. Another showed a troop of Alexander's horse, and still another included several four-horse chariots. Hunting scenes sometimes furnished a pretext for similarly elaborate works of art. Lysippus did a *Lion Hunt* for King Craterus, which was set up at Delphi, and he did at least one hunting scene which included a portrait of Alexander.

It is impossible to say whether Lysippus arranged his grandiose compositions in the form of a frieze, or as free-standing sculpture in omnifacial composition. The latter is more probable, judging by the *Laocöon,* the *Farnese Bull,* and other Hellenistic groups.

A fascinating possibility was opened up, however, when some seventeen marble sarcophagi were discovered in an underground tomb at Sidon in the year 1887. They are now preserved in the Ottoman Museum at Constantinople. One of them, the so-called *Alexander Sarcophagus* (Fig. 5.19), is of peculiar

Fig. 5.19   Constantinople, Ottoman Museum. *Alexander Sarcophagus.* (Sabah)

interest in the present connection. No one doubts that it is Greek work, and there is general agreement that it comes from the last quarter of the 4th century—or within the possible life time of Lysippus. In shape, the Alexander Sarcophagus is like a miniature temple. On one long side and one short side, it shows Alexander hunting the lion and the leopard respectively. The other two sides show Alexander in battle with the Persians.

While no evidence now in our possession would permit a direct attribution to Lysippus, an association with him is almost unavoidable. The reliefs have dash and spirit of the sort required. The rendering of details is very finely executed, another thing the authors describe as characteristic, and more than one of the heads is unmistakably a portrait. If not specifically Lysippic, surely these reliefs are illustrative of the trend of style to which Lysippus himself belonged.

The trend itself is important, regardless of personalities. At this point in their history, it is evident that the Greek artists had made an end of the conventions with which the Great Age began. Their art had not ceased to be heroic, but abstraction of every kind was all but abandoned, and epic events were about to be represented as physical occurrences. Obviously, artistic taste was feeling an ever stronger impulse toward actuality, one aspect of which is vividly illustrated by the sarcophagus under review.

The violent motion was directed in traditional fashion, to be sure; that is to say, to the right and left only, parallel with the background. But the separate figures often overlap each other; and one feels that the sculptor was

Fig. 5.20 Rome, Vatican. Roman copy believed to reflect the appearance of the *Apoxyomenos* by Lysippus. (Alinari)

yearning for an art which would permit the representation of space-in-depth. Such an impression is strongly enhanced by the fact that most of the figures were colored, and still retain some of their color. From a slight distance, the scenes, faded as they are, look very much like painting. Under these circumstances, we find ourselves tending to read the blank marble of the background not as a neutral and impenetrable denial of space (which it had been in the pedimental compositions of the Fifth Century), but as the sky. The author of the *Alexander Sarcophagus* was well along the way, in short, toward an art which would make a direct effort to represent space, to depict scenery, and to show the figure within a natural setting. That result was actually attained during the Hellenistic age.

For Lysippus' figure-style, the evidence is discouraging. By the usual methods, but with something less than the usual weight of probability, two male statues can be associated with his name. They are the *Apoxyomenos* *(Scraper)* in the Vatican (Fig. 5.20) and the portrait of an athlete named Agias, apparently a Greek original of inferior quality, found at Delphi and now in the museum there.

It is hard to accept both statues as originating with the same sculptor. The differences have been rationalized in various ways: that both are portraits and reflect the personal appearance of two men who did not look alike; that the *Agias* is a contemporary derivative (a most unlikely assumption) and differs from the other simply because the *Apoxyomenos* is a later Roman copy; or that the differences exist because one statue was an early Lysippus and the other done late in his career.

On the whole, it seems most likely that neither is within reaching distance of the master's personal work, but that both—to whatever extent they are alike—are "Lysippic" in the sense of reflecting his very great influence upon his sculptural successors for the remainder of antiquity. Standing thus on thin ice, we may be forgiven for attempting to recognize in these two dull statues the elements of a new style.

The first thing to be noted is a new canon of proportions. Pliny (*Natural History*, XXXIV.65) tried to give an account of Lysippus' theory, but his words betray a mixture of fact and hearsay. It is probably a waste of time to attempt making anything of them except in a very approximate way. If we do that, it appears that Lysippus used a more slender figure with a smaller head. It also appears that he was much concerned to give the onlooker a strong impression of the actuality of his figures: ". . . he represented them as they appeared to the eye," said Pliny in an otherwise confusing sentence.

The head of the *Apoxyomenos* measures about one eighth the total height of the figure, a substantial difference from the Polyclitan proportion of one-to-seven or a little less. These measurements, moreover, are inseparably related to certain features of the pose. The longer legs invite more expressive movement of the entire body; and while not active, the figure gives the impression of muscles that have not yet relaxed after exercise. One has a feeling of tense nerves which express their condition in occasional shifts of the body, and the transfer of weight from one leg to the other.

Unquestionably these expedients result in making us feel that the sculptor intended to represent something alive, but much has been sacrificed to gain that end. Lysippus' athletes are neither gods nor heroes. They are simply young men, and tired young men at that. In the face of the *Apoxyomenus* there is a peculiar vulgarity hitherto utterly foreign to Greek art; it seems evident that the statue reflects the appearance of a particular man whose face was no better than it should be.

It is important to realize, in addition to all of this, that Lysippus was giving us an individual person as he appeared at a single instant of time— in contrast to the things we might remember as significant aspects of the sitter's personality or his character. The position taken by the artist was, in effect, a negation of both generalization and idealism. In scenes of action like those on the *Alexander Sarcophagus,* the instantaneous view (probably what Pliny meant by "as they appeared to the eye") is almost necessary and may pass unnoticed; in static figures like these, it thrusts itself forward as an artistic philosophy.

As such, it amounts to the artist's accepting visual experience as equivalent to artistic law. The work of art—within the practical limits of the medium in use—is required to maintain a one-to-one relationship with something the artist saw in nature. This, of course, is the position of the objective realist, and it would appear that Lysippus had gone far in that direction. Because realism of all kinds, objective and otherwise, was destined to flourish during the Hellenistic period, it is evident that the thinking of this last of the great masters had a far-reaching effect.

Chapter 6

INTRODUCTION

IN DEALING WITH the history of art from the death of Alexander until the end of antiquity, we must set aside our habit of outlining by reference to political changes and military events. It has long been customary to recognize a Hellenistic period (323-146 B.C.), a Greco-Roman era (146 B.C. to about A.D. 1), and a Roman period (about A.D. 1 to 476). These divisions correspond approximately to the time of the kingdoms governed by Alexander's heirs, to the period when the Romans were absorbing Greek culture, and to the era of the Roman Empire.

The evidence of the monuments argues against so elaborate a subdivision. It is true that Mummius took Corinth in 146 B.C., and it is fair enough for the historian of politics to use that date as signalizing the end of Greek independence and the beginning of Roman dominion. It is also legitimate to point out that Roman art as such did not start until the reign of Augustus (27 B.C.–A.D. 14); but it is contrary to fact to suppose that these happenings altered the course of cultural history. We should begin our new study, therefore, with the concept that Roman art was not a separate development, that it was merely a continuation of Hellenistic art and part of it, and that both came from the Greek tradition. In other words, this chapter deals with a normal evolution from what went before, a natural extension over a wider area of a familiar artistic philosophy.

Except for Alexander, Greece would be remembered as a historical curiosity. Because of him, Greek modes of thought and Greek values dominate Western civilization. The effect of his conquests was to spread Greek ideas; so many people were favorably impressed that it became a certainty that the Greek spirit would somehow survive. Culturally speaking, Rome was but

146

HELLENISTIC AND ROMAN SCULPTURE AND PAINTING

another Alexander. Without a strong art and literature of their own, the Romans attempted to adopt what they found in Greece. In so doing, they themselves became captured by the tradition they attempted to possess, and they transmitted it to the medieval world and even more directly to the Renaissance.

The latter-day ancients had no feeling that the world had crossed a great divide with the death of Alexander (323 B.C.); the recorded achievements of the following 500 years give the lie to any such notion. In fact, from the outlook of the men then alive, it must have appeared that civilization was constantly and rapidly improving until the Roman polity began to work badly during the 3rd century A.D.

Immediately after the death of Alexander, new cities began to be important. Alexandria, Antioch, Pergamum, and Rhodes were in their heyday larger, richer, and busier than anything ever known before. They totally eclipsed the familiar centers of Greece proper. Commerce became more ramified and sophisticated. Trade went forward over longer routes and in greater bulk, involving practices of credit and banking commonly thought to be very modern indeed. Immense wealth accumulated, permitting those who held it to live more easily, more comfortably, and more beautifully. By comparison, the customs of the 4th and 5th centuries B.C. must have seemed crude and cheerless.

As Benjamin Farrington has so ably set forth in his *Greek Science,* the Hellenistic age saw accomplishments in research on a par with anything that happened in modern Europe prior to the Industrial Revolution. Pure mathe-

147

matics embraced a usable trigonometry which enabled astronomers to observe such refinements of celestial motion as the precession of the equinoxes. Knowing the earth to be a globe, they measured its diameter within 14 percent of the truth; some say much closer. The coordinates of latitude and longitude were established, and the latitude of particular points was measured almost as accurately as we can do it today: the recorded figures put the Pharos (lighthouse) in the harbor of Alexandria out by only 16 minutes of arc, a figure the modern navigator will instantly recognize as the semidiameter of the sun's disc. All sorts of mechanical principles were known, and numerous pieces of machinery were actually built: clocks, water organs, engines for siege and defense. Medicine was within an ace of Harvey's theory of the circulation of the blood. All of this learning, moreover, was organized on a system very much like the system of modern scholarship. Libraries and museums first became important public institutions during the Hellenistic age, and the duty of scholarly publication was widely observed, with the intention of making findings accessible to later generations.

To the modern student, it seems almost incredible that the Industrial Revolution did not start during the Hellenistic period. About the middle of the 2nd century B.C., Ctesibius of Alexandria had already invented a force pump and a pneumatic gun. He knew, that is to say, the principle of the piston and was in approximately the same position of intellectual advantage as James Watt when the latter undertook to invent a practical steam engine. What deterred the sophisticated businessmen of the time from embracing an opportunity to acquire fabulous wealth? The answer is necessarily a matter for speculation, but opinion centers upon two factors, each functioning as a mental block in the psychology of those who controlled society.

The first suggestion is that slaves were altogether too cheap and plentiful; and even at times and in places where this was not true, the ancient imagination was chained to the indispensability of slave labor. In a larger sense, we may say that the absence of modern notions of humanity closed the ancient mind to the desirability of seeking a substitute for the pain and degradation of those persons who were born to bondage. We must not be hasty in our judgment of that narrowness. Saint Augustine (A.D. 354-430) accepted slavery as God's penalty for original sin, and the whole social structure of the medieval world was hampered by the stultifying notion that theory was honorable, but that its application in the form of labor was to be despised even if the laborer happened to be a free man. The artists of the Renaissance, as we shall see, had to fight a battle to prove themselves gentlemen even though they worked with their hands.

Ancient religion also operated to restrain the practical application of science. Heraclides of Pontus knew that the universe was heliocentric as early as 300 B.C., and various astronomers noted the eccentricities of motion which prove that the orbits are not circular. The general adoption of such ideas was foreclosed by the fixed notion that the heavens were sacred, that circles were the only perfect curves, and that the earth was the center of things. It is not surprising that a society committed to such thoughts would, when descending to the lower realms of science, view the whole field of mechanics simply as an opportunity to manufacture artificial miracles for the greater conviction of the ignorant. In fact, except for war machines and a fire engine built by Ctesibius, it is hard to name many useful applications of the data compiled. Ancient research was pure to the extent of being sterile.

The controlling members of society, innocent though they were of concepts which to us seem fundamental, nevertheless had reason to congratulate themselves. Anywhere one looked, there was evidence that the human mind continued to be fertile and productive. In one important area of life, however, there was cause for gloom: in the art of government, the later Greeks have left a ghastly record. Many of their rulers were men of capacity. Brilliance, even genius, occurred about as often as it did during the Italian Renaissance. But from the society as a whole, teeming as it was with thought and possessed of unprecedented potential, there emerged no constitutional scheme capable of producing a decent political order. The polity of the Hellenistic kingdoms defies analysis or description. Each consisted of a hundred different relationships between government and the governed, involving every degree of absolutism and independence. It was truly a world of catch as catch can, and the happiest men of all were mercenary generals, who enjoyed to the limit the luxury of having no loyalties.

The surprising thing is that so much prosperity could exist in an area so badly governed, but even the political troubles of the ancient world were solved by the advent of Rome. The *Pax Romana* was harsh in its original application, but it was the only protracted period of unbroken peace ever enjoyed by the European peoples. It may be said to have lasted from the start of the Christian era to the end of the 2nd century A.D., at which time both economic and governmental regularity began to fail.

Before we are ready to consider Hellenistic and Roman art, we must mention the two new systems of thought which came into being during the Hellenistic period: that of the Stoics and that of Epicurus.

The latter advises us to forget the riddle of existence—the implication being that if an answer to it exists, the human mind lacks the capacity to comprehend it. Such being the case, we had best make the most of the only life we are sure of. Often vulgarized into "the pleasure principle," the recommendations of Epicurus actually make an identity between personal satisfaction and a way of life which, by any standard, is both prudent and praise-worthy. If followed literally and honestly, his philosophy would make a good citizen out of any man.

The Stoics likewise defaulted from wrestling with the ultimates. Our problem, according to them, is to adjust to the world as it is. The chances, moreover, greatly favor our finding the world a bad place to be. Every man's daily routine puts him through toil and often through pain. Whatever plans we make, it is more than likely our hopes will finish in frustration and dis-appointment. No one can or will help another man much. Each person's resource is within himself alone, but by resolute action of the will, the self can be strengthened sufficiently to withstand the worst. No matter what happens, one need not play the part of the coward. A man can learn to face his fate with dignity.

Men capable of these ideas obviously were not the Greeks as they were during the age of Pericles. Both the Stoics and the Epicureans were engaged in finding some way to face a situation too confusing to be understood and circumstances too difficult to be controlled. The relationship between human-ity and the environment had, if we believe what these men said, been changed. The power of events was to be accepted as irresistible. Only blind luck could avert defeat. Fortitude and virtue remained intelligible as concepts; but their practical application could accomplish only a little: in the case of the Epi-cureans, grace; and in the case of the Stoics, dignity. The history of art seems to show that both grace and dignity endured as long as the ancient world, and when we encounter monuments that lack both, we shall know that we have come to the Middle Ages.

Until very recently, it was customary to present Hellenistic art as an art of display, indulgence, and decline. Roman art fared even worse at the hands of the historian; it is still difficult to find an adequate and clearheaded sum-mary of the subject. Admittedly, neither Hellenistic Greece nor Rome pro-duced a single artist of the same order as Phidias or Polyclitus; thus we are denied the special interest of dealing with great personalities. But great as they had been, those personalities were neither perfect nor complete, and we may not perpetuate the notion that every departure from the conventions of the Greek Fifth and Fourth centuries was an offense against artistic ethics.

The obvious differences between the art of later antiquity and that of the Great Age are to be explained in quite another way. The expansion of every other horizon had its counterpart in a great broadening of the artist's horizon. In the following chapters, we shall have occasion to see that the simple Greek temple no longer satisfied the imagination of architects; new structural methods were explored and perfected, new decorative themes were tried, and a great variety of new types—religious, civil, and domestic—

emerged. In sculpture, the most conspicuous development was an immense expansion of the catalogue of subject matter. The Hellenistic and Roman sculptors refused to limit themselves to figures of idealized young adults. Like artists of our own day, they used any subject that pleased or interested them. With respect to style, all artists of this later area depended rather obviously upon Greece, but there is no Hellenistic or Roman style as such. Separate schools and even individal artists determined style to suit themselves, and radically different methods were used in the same place at the same time in accordance with individual preference.

In sum, all of this means that Hellenistic and Roman art present a historical picture more complex and difficult than anything we have yet encountered. At the same time, Hellenistic and Roman archeology are today in far worse case than the archeology of earlier sections of the classical era. We are by no means certain about the location of important centers of production. By chance, we know a few artists by name, but we can make very little of it. Chronology has yet to be worked out; some of the most important monuments are still dated more by opinion than by evidence—and competent men often want to place the same statue a couple of hundred years apart. Except for passing mention of dates, we shall therefore abandon any attempt at chronological arrangement of the text. Instead, we shall endeavor to explain things by reference to the several major artistic tendencies which first made their appearance in history after the death of Alexander.

♦ *The Taste for Colossi* The vigor of Hellenistic life expressed itself in many an overt gesture. Nothing is more typical of the time than the taste for colossal statues, a taste most unrestrainedly asserted by the inhabitants of Rhodes. It is said that no less than a hundred immense figures were once on view there, of which the most famous was the celebrated *Colossus of Rhodes,* put up about 280 B.C. by Chares of Lindus, thought to have been a pupil of Lysippus. Anipater of Sidon (2nd century B.C.), who compiled the earliest known list of "the seven wonders of the world," included the *Colossus* among them. It is a great pity we have no substantial evidence which might help us to visualize so conspicuous a monument, but it is worth making an effort with what we possess. The subject was said to have been Helios, the god of the sun. The statue was of bronze purchased with the money realized from the war machines left behind by Demetrius Poliorcetes when he abandoned his unsuccessful siege of the island. It stood about 105 feet high, or 45 feet less than the Statue of Liberty. There was a winding staircase inside, and "glasses" for looking at distant shores and ships. Contrary to popular legend, the figure did not stand astride the channel leading into the harbor, and the notion that ships sailed between its legs is out of the question except in the case of small boats. As a matter of fact, the exact site of the statue is unknown; we merely know it was adjacent to the harbor. The *Colossus* endured only a short while. An earthquake occurred in 224 B.C., apparently breaking the figure in two. The ruin remained in plain sight until A.D. 672, when the incumbent Saracen governor sold it to a merchant of Edessa. Nine hundred camel-loads of scrap were taken away, it is said; and its value, according to an 18th-century authority, came to the then equivalent of 36,000 pounds sterling.

Another famous colossus was the one Nero set up in the courtyard of his Golden House at Rome, an extravagantly gorgeous palace built after the city burned in A.D. 64. That was also a sun-god, but Nero himself had posed as the model. The statue stood about 118 feet high, and showed the emperor with rays around his head. It was still standing as late as A.D. 354, and was the subject of the baleful prophecy: "While stands the *Colossus*, stands Rome. When falls the *Colossus*, Rome falls; and when Rome falls, with it shall fall the whole world." It is thought the prophecy originated with pilgrims to the Eternal City, and there are versions of it datable back to the 7th century of our era. Because it was near the *Colossus*, everyone has always called the Flavian Amphitheater the *Colosseum*.

Big statues retained their popularity until the very end of the period. The Conservatori Museum at Rome has a bronze head, of good workmanship, about six feet high; it is usually labelled *Constantius*—one of Constantine's sons. A seated statue of Constantine himself (regnal dates A.D. 306–337) was placed in the central apse of the immense Basilica of Constantine at Rome. Some fragments of the arms and lower legs survive in the courtyard of the Conservatori, together with the head (Fig. 6.2), the latter being no less than 8 feet high.

THE REALISTIC TENDENCY

In our study of Lysippus, we had occasion to observe that idealism was already on the wane at the end of the 4th century B.C., and that an increasing consciousness of actuality seemed to be taking its place in the mind of the Greek artist. The process appears to have gone rapidly toward its logical conclusion, and presently the unparalleled resources of Hellenistic technique were devoted to reproducing the appearance of nature—or at least giving a vivid impression thereof. Within the general scope of the realistic movement, we will find it convenient to recognize two divisions. The first has to do with realism as applied to the single figure or to any other object that is best presented in close-up by plastic methods. The second has to do with realism as applied to the representation not of figures and objects, but of entire scenes in broader view, with figures and stage properties placed within the represented space.

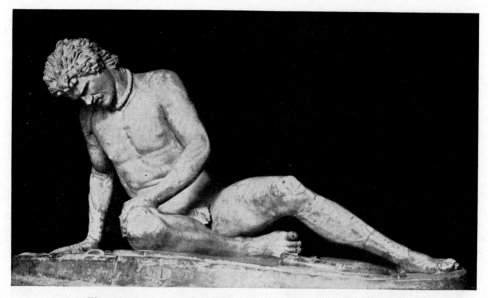

Fig. 6.1   Rome, Capitoline Museum. *Dying Gaul.* (Anderson)

♦ *Representation of Single Figures*   The *Dying Gaul,* now in the Capitoline Museum at Rome (Fig. 6.1), marks the final abandonment of idealistic pretensions and the complete acceptance of objective realism. The figure is a marble replica from a bronze original, one of a set believed to have been dedicated to commemorate the victory over the Gauls of King Attalus the 1st of Pergamum in Asia Minor in 230 B.C. Attalus gained the gratitude of all Greece by soundly defeating the army of these folk who were already forcing their way into the Mediterranean world. It seems extraordinary that an ancient victor should do his enemy so much honor, but Attalus is said to have admired the way the Gauls fought and the way they died.

As evidence of the contemporary belief about the relationship between mankind and the world, the statue is shocking in view of conceptions entertained at an earlier date. The outright expression of terrible pain would have been unthinkable during the Great Age. So would the very idea of making a defeated man, even an enemy, the subject of a public monument. Some vestige of former outlook survives in the dignity with which the man dies, and the *Dying Gaul* may be remembered as an excellent illustration of the then-popular retreat into Stoicism.

Realism is not always severe. Its gentler, more homely applications are known as *genre:* subjects from everyday life, neither beautiful nor inspiring, but presented because they recall familiar experience. The *Boy Struggling with a Goose,* at the Munich Museum, is an example, and the *Old Woman Going to Market* in the Metropolitan Museum (Fig. 6.3) is another. The latter is of special interest as an instance of the expansion of subject matter.

Fig. 6.2 (left) Rome, Conservatori Museum. *Constantine*. 8 feet high. (Anderson) Fig. 6.3 (right) New York, Metropolitan Museum. *Old Woman Going to Market*.

Most of the human beings heretofore seen in Greek art were handsome, healthy, intelligent, and even noble. Even the evildoers (centaurs, for example) had at least been vigorous. But here we see the study of humble humanity at a time of life when the body becomes increasingly frail and unlovely with every passing year. Such a theme might well have invited the sculptor's sense of tragedy; in that case, the statue would have been made the vehicle for expressions of sadness, futility, resentment, and despair. One of the things that makes it genre is the complete absence of connotative overtones; the realism is straightforward, but the feeling is gentle.

Whenever and wherever art tends to be realistic, there is big business in the portrait trade, and personal portraits began to be an important art form with the start of the Hellenistic period. We must distinguish between two types of portrait, both of which we have inherited in quantity. Public men naturally ordered monuments; and this created a demand for such ceremonial portraits as the *Augustus from Prima Porta*, now in the Vatican—a standing figure in the tradition of Polyclitus, with attributes recalling the mythical generation of the Julian line from Venus herself, and surmounted by a flat-

Fig. 6.4 (left) Boston, Museum of Fine Arts. Portrait of a Roman. 1st century B.C. Fig. 6.5 (right) Rome, Torlonia Museum. *King Euthydemus of Bactria.* (Deutschen Archaeolgischen Institut)

tering rendering of the imperial countenance. Much more interesting are the portraits ostensibly ordered for private pleasure; in these, objective realism seems to have reached its logical fulfillment. Portraits of this less pretentious class are usually busts showing head and neck only.

Because so many of them—and their number is legion—stand in plain sight in the museums of Italy, we are all too often told that the realistic portrait is strictly an Italian phenomenon invented by the Romans for their own use, but that is hardly true. Realism of the most uncompromising kind was to be found in later Greek work, long before the Roman market opened up. A particularly striking instance, probably dating from about 230 B.C., is the head of King Euthydemus of Bactria, in the Torlonia Museum of Rome (Fig. 6.5). No Roman face is more incisively and unsparingly rendered; few are so severe. It is true, however, that realism suited the Roman respect for facts; and for that reason, the market for realistic portraits was greatly stimulated as soon as the Romans started to order.

The range of Roman work is well illustrated by the contrast between the Boston terra-cotta head of an unknown Roman (Fig. 6.4) and the head of an equally unknown girl (Fig. 6.6) in the National Museum at Athens. Both show that objective realism at times has the awful finality of an ac-

Fig. 6.6 Athens, National Museum. Portrait of a Roman girl. (Clarence Kennedy)

counting. Nature makes most young girls pretty, but gives them little else. Moderately successful men are bound to think overly well of themselves at sixty. The facts are frozen for all time; the realistic artist, by the logic of his own philosophy, must take them as they come.

The same cast of mind, when turned to the study of flowers and shrubs, produced some of the finest floral sculpture the world has ever seen. From this class of work, a typical and favorite example is the relief known as the *Rose Pillar* from the Tomb of the Haterii, preserved in the Lateran Museum at Rome (Fig. 6.7). Monuments like this give us a new point of view toward realism; one aspect of that philosophy involves a communion between man and nature, a response of the senses to the grandeur of the world and also to the wonder of nature in her more delicate manifestations.

Indeed, if we compare the *Rose Pillar* with the "honeysuckle band" of the Erechtheum (Fig. 6.8), we have before us the difference between sense perception and conceptual thinking. The Greek artist felt compelled to make nature conform to axioms which, to him, seemed luminously true. He therefore idealized his floral ornament. He reduced its forms to the plastic shapes he liked to use, and made them symmetrical. He then arranged the successive items according to the rules of a rhythm selected for the occasion.

The Roman sculptor believed his eyes. Not denying the possible existence of general principles (in terms of which nature may have some ultimate order) he nevertheless declined to discredit the testimony of appearance—

and the appearance of nature is very far from orderly. He therefore gave his rose vine no more regularity than we might expect to see in any well-tended garden, and he included any number of accidental irregularities.

Love of nature is commonplace in the modern world, and the expression of it in Roman floral sculpture is unlikely to impress the reader as historically notable. But the history of art contains no evidence that any one ever loved nature before the Romans did, with the single exception of the Minoans, who had passed out of history leaving little legacy behind them. Belief in the beauty and kindness of nature left European culture, moreover, with the decline of antiquity. Such notions were absent from the medieval temperament until the High Gothic of the 13th century A.D. At that time, nature in its original unspoiled disorder once again rather timidly entered the vocabulary of art—as a modest prelude to the modern passion for natural beauty, the latter not dating any earlier than the 15th century.

♦ *Representation of Space* The realistic enterprise did not stop with the study of the human figure and other objects in nature. It went on to solve the problem of representing landscapes and architectural interiors, which is to say the *setting* in which objects have their existence. Put in even more strict language, this means that artists started to represent *space*.

Every practicing artist, no matter how amateurish, is familiar with the methods for representing space, and with the use of space as an element in a work of art. On the other hand, nothing seems to baffle the layman more; and every teacher of art history can testify that the best explanation is none too good. Starting, therefore, at the beginning:

Our comprehension of space, and our judgment with regard to distance, depends upon two natural phenomena: *linear perspective* and *atmospheric perspective*. The materials and techniques available to the artist enable him to simulate these conditions on the surface of a painting, and somewhat less easily on the surface of a panel of sculpture in relief.

Linear perspective is the studio term for descriptive geometry, or the science of projection. It governs the outline of objects as they appear in drawing and painting, and is easiest to explain when architectural masses—or any other rectangular masses—are projected onto a flat surface like that of the canvas. When that is done, all lines which are parallel on the surface of the mass must, on the surface of the picture, be made to converge in systematic fashion toward one or more *vanishing points*. The same principles apply for the projection of irregular masses (the human body, for example), but the explanation is more tedious and the phenomenon less obvious to the layman's eye. *Foreshortening* is a word used as a near-synonym for linear perspective whenever one wishes to say that some mass (for example, an arm represented as being extended at right angles to the picture-plane, as though directly

Fig. 6.7 Rome, Lateran Museum. *Rose Pillar.* (Gab. Fot. Naz.)

toward the eye of the observer) is presented in bold close-up. From the logic of linear perspective, it follows that more and more distant objects subtend increasingly small arcs across the field of vision; thus small things in the foreground take up more room on the canvas than immense things far off.

If we may judge by the general run of preserved monuments, linear perspective was understood only fairly well by the ancient artists; they used it in a rule-of-thumb way and by no means so scientifically as the masters of the Renaissance. Atmospheric perspective, on the other hand, seems to have been handled very well indeed. In the foreground, where particulars may be discerned, atmospheric perspective results from the shadows which objects cast upon the ground or upon each other. In the distance, the effect is produced by the curtain of dust and vapor which almost always hangs in the air, softening outlines, obscuring details, and neutralizing color. As a means of estimating distance in nature or representing it in art, atmospheric perspective is of greater psychological importance than the geometry of projection. Whenever conditions are abnormal or unfamiliar (as in some parts of

Fig. 6.8 Athens. Erech-
theum. "Honeysuckle
Band," detail. (Walter
Hege)

the American West, where there is little dust and moisture), the ordinary man is prone to make gross errors when he tries to say how far off anything is.

The painter is able to simulate all the conditions of both linear and atmospheric perspective. When carving a relief, the sculptor can of course make use of the principle of the vanishing point. He can also make his relief lower and his modeling less distinct in order to avail himself of atmospheric perspective, but he lacks the ability to "place" objects within the represented space by modulating the color relationships. Offhand, it would sound as though the sculptor had most of the available methods at his command, but the reverse is true. The one technique he lacks is the most important of all. It is by way of the color sensation that we habitually make most of our judgments about distance.

Even when he understands all the above, the layman often has difficulty in appreciating that the space represented within a picture is one of the components the artist manipulates to construct his composition. He arranges space, that is to say, as though it were a thing or material. Perhaps it is here that the difficulty of comprehension arises. People who do not make pictures have had experience with objects. Who has not moved furniture about? Who has not struggled to pack a suitcase? Hence, the habit of thinking of objects as real, and of empty space as nothingness.

But the artist, as he undertakes to visualize his picture, must choose the setting first of all. In what part of the world did the depicted event take place? At what time of year? How far from the eye shall he put the nearest object, and how far into the distance shall he extend the view? And where, within the chosen space, shall he put buildings, trees, rivers, and people?

Obviously, the artist may deal with the problem of space as systematically as with any other aspect of art; and an arrangement of space which has worked for one picture can be used for another. Successful arrangements get imitated; and thus a particular spatial formula has often become characteristic of an individual artist, and even of a group or school of artists.

During Hellenistic and Roman times, there were three such categories which we can distinguish by reference to the kind of space represented and the arrangement of things within it. These are known as the *Neo-Attic,* the *Alexandrian,* and the *Latin*—names which have gained usage although they don't mean precisely what they appear to say. In the discussion to follow, the reader must keep in mind that works of art which differ in almost every other way (and which are susceptible of classification by reference to other factors) can be very much alike with regard to the use of space.

It is also important to point out at this juncture that all three of the spatial formulas mentioned had a long history. Medieval artists took them over for Christian subject matter as naturally as they continued to talk and write the ancient languages. Furthermore, when the artists of the Renaissance turned to classical art for guidance and inspiration, they revived ancient spatial arrangements along with other elements of Greek and Roman art.

The name *Neo-Attic* invites confusion because the same name is at times used with reference to some Greek sculptors who worked in Italy during the 1st century B.C., and who had the habit of signing their work "Athenaios." They had nothing to do with the matter in hand; and the title Neo-Attic as applied to the representation of space merely indicates the probability that such work centered on the Greek peninsula where Athenian prestige lasted the longest.

The Neo-Attic formula was the most conservative of the three; it was, indeed, no more nor less than a continuation of the conventions originally developed for the Greek pediment, a matter dealt with at some length on pages 58–67. For our immediate purpose, the important thing to emphasize is that the designers of the pediments seem to have been reluctant to represent space; and they used as little of it as they conceivably could while still showing anything so solid as the human body. In their formula, the most cogent factor was a blank and impenetrable background immediately behind a single row of figures. The effect of such a background was to create a sense of other-worldliness, an effect enhanced by rigorous avoidance of any landscape or other details which might suggest a particular locality.

This austere formula was relaxed during the Hellenistic period, but it is remarkable how little. The *Alexander Sarcophagus* (Fig. 5.19, page 141) and the frieze from the *Great Altar of Pergamum* (Fig. 6.19), violent though they are in comparison to 5th-century standards, nevertheless maintain the blank background and give the impression that the figures are standing on the narrow pedimental shelf. In Figures 8.11, 8.14, and 8.17, we see an architectural background, an expedient only one short step from the blank stone wall, and just as impenetrable. And if we look several centuries ahead, we can see that the ancient pedimental formula survived in such examples as those shown in Figures 8.17, page 224; 9.12, page 291; and 9.22, page 309. It is worth noting, although not essential to the question of space, that most of these monuments compose in the Greek organic manner.

Typical of the Alexandrian style is the tiny marble panel in Munich showing a peasant leading his bull to market (Fig. 6.9). It belongs to a class of small marble reliefs found in various places, but presumably originating at some common center. The identification of Alexandria as that center is probable, but conjectural. It rests upon two lines of evidence, the first being the likelihood that pictorial reliefs would originate where the study of perspective started. The second reason has to do with subject matter.

With reasonable consistency, the Alexandrian reliefs deal with pastoral and bucolic themes. An analogy therefore suggests itself: there had been no pastoral poetry earlier than the Hellenistic period; it was called into being by the crowded life of the teeming Hellenistic cities, probably as a nostalgic remembrance of simpler days. Theocritus was the father of pastoral poetry. He spent most of his active career at Alexandria, arriving there about 276 B.C. Although there are critics who believe that not one of the reliefs now brought under review may be dated before the Roman era, the affinities with Theocritus and the generally Greek tone make the Alexandrian association far from irrational.

One and all, these pictorial renderings are like the poems of Theocritus in calling up sentimentally lovely Greek figures who people with easy grace an outdoor setting that celebrates, in similarly sentimental mood, the softer and more generous aspects of nature. It is hardly true, however, to say that the figures are *within* their setting. On the contrary, they are brought forward, as though to the edge of a stage. In that position, they loom large, fill

Fig. 6.9 Munich, Glyptothek. *Peasant Taking a Bull to Market.* Marble. 11 inches high. (Kaufman)

up a subsantial proportion of the available area within the frame, and obscure the landscape behind them. The result is to emphasize the human actors and to subordinate the setting. Indeed, the setting is often no more "real" than the painted flats behind a conventional stage, and thus we get the impression that the figures are in front of a backdrop.

We tend, of course, to read the blank upper background as the sky; but almost without exception, compositions of the Alexandrian category seem to have been deliberately arranged to prevent the eye from searching off into the unlimited distance. Nowhere is it possible to enter the scene, as it were, at the foreground and move straight back into space without interruption. Rows of people, landscape details, and stage properties of every kind stand in our way. Apparently, the artists wanted to detain our attention within measurable bounds, and to deter the imagination from soaring off into the infinite.

To sum up: artists of the Alexandrian persuasion were extremely cautious in their use of space. They rarely represented more than ten or twenty yards of it. The reason, obviously, was that they retained the Greek hate for

Fig. 6.10 *Earth, Air, and Water.* "Tellus Panel" from the *Ara Pacis Augustae* (13–9 B.C.). Formerly in the Uffizi Gallery at Florence; now incorporated in the reconstruction of the altar in Rome. (Anderson)

the indefinite and maintained the Greek convention of making humanity the chief vehicle of expression.

Reliefs and pictures of the Alexandrian type had a wide vogue, and seem ultimately to have been produced all over the Mediterranean basin. What we have said of the *Peasant Taking a Bull to Market* is also true, almost word for word, of the so-called "Tellus Panel" (Fig. 6.10) from the *Ara Pacis Augustae,* a great altar erected at Rome between 13 and 9 B.C. Here we see a personified Lady Earth attended by Air and Water, all three celebrating the boost to agriculture when Augustus assumed the purple. Some of the mosaics recently dug up at Antioch also conform to the Alexandrian scheme, notably the splendid *Judgment of Paris* (Fig. 6.11) now in the Louvre. And the same thing may be said of perhaps two thirds of the pictures recovered at Pompeii. Nor did the Alexandrian scheme cease with the decay of ancient civilization. Like the Neo-Attic, it was carried over into Christian art; we shall return to the matter in Chapter 8. And we shall find ourselves referring to it still again in Chapter 16, because many of the smaller Renaissance canvases (notably those of Titian) were inspired by the Alexandrian style.

As the name implies, the Latin style was almost certainly an Italian inno-vation of Roman date. It differed from the Alexandrian in two ways. The definition of detail was impressionistic, and in the vital matter of spatial

Fig. 6.11 Paris, Louvre. *Judgment of Paris*. Mosaic. Found at Antioch. (Archives Photographiques)

manipulation, there was no attempt to curtail or control the represented space: Latin settings carry the eye far off into the unlimited distance. We have a great many panels of relief in the Latin style, but the principles involved are most easily understood by reference to Roman painting.

Figure 6.12 will illustrate what we mean by *impressionism*. Because of the popular application of the same word to denote a school of French painters (Manet, Monet, Degas, Renoir, *et al.*) who flourished during the 19th century, the term may cause momentary confusion here, but impressionism, as such, is as old as painting. It has no necessary connection with spatial representation or with any particular formula for the arrangement of a picture. As an artistic theory, impressionism has to do merely with the handling of the brush.

The laboratory case of the impressionist painter would be a man with only one brush, and that brush a large one. He would find it impractical to work out in minute particularity the arrangement of lights and colors which might, in nature, be noted by the unaided eye on the surface of a single

Fig. 6.12 Rome, Terme Museum. *Putto on a Ladder*. Fresco. 1st century A.D. (Gab. Fot. Naz.)

white button. The impressionist would merely slap down a spot of white, and let it stand as a suggestion for the button. In its purely technical aspect, impressionism is a kind of private conspiracy whereby the painter agrees with himself to describe detail only when it is comparatively large in scale. He has a lower limit of size beyond which he will not go. That lower limit, it must be emphasized, is not set by tools and materials. It is a matter of deliberate choice; the impressionist painter consciously refrains from using the more delicate methods which are available to him.

As compared with a more detailed and plastic rendering, impressionism is closer to the visual experience of the average man. Most of us go through life without ever having occasion to make a minute inspection of anything whatever. We do not examine the human figure, or anything else, with the intense vision of a Greek sculptor. Most of our seeing is hasty. Our visual images are vague and incomplete—in a word, impressions. The impressionist painter therefore has the considerable advantage of offering an artistic experience almost precisely parallel to the visual experience of daily life. The danger is that his art will be no more profound than daily life, but it must enthusiastically be conceded that the good examples of impressionism have a snap and reality more vivid than those of any other kind of painting.

The snap and immediacy to which we refer suffer not at all from the fact that impressionism is superior to any other mode of rendering with respect to the internal logic of a liquid or viscous vehicle applied with the brush. In the nature of the case, impressionism invites strong, racy strokes and demands a certain measure of bold abstraction. When well-handled, impressionistic techniques enhance the life of the painting because the brush

Fig. 6.13 Rome, Vatican. "The Laestrygonians rushing to attack." Detail from the *Odyssey Landscapes*. (Alinari)

strokes furnish a record of the muscular activity of the painter as he worked. One feels the motion and pressure of the brush; and there is a sense of participation denied by smoother and ostensibly more elegant methods.

To all of this, we must add that there is some virtue in the very fact that the impressionist theory forecloses the artist from complete description. The observer's imagination must supply what is lacking—an act sometimes referred to as "the re-creative function," and an experience the value of which is not to be denied.

In the vital matter of spatial manipulation, the inventors of the Latin style, whoever they were, deserve to be remembered as the men who conquered the traditional classical fear of the infinite and opened ancient eyes to the emotional grandeur of vast distances. The pictures that seem most typical of the Latin style are those where the represented space itself assumes the importance of subject matter. None are better than the so-called *Odyssey Landscapes* (Figs. 6.13–14), found about 1850 in a house on the Esquiline, and apparently of the 1st century A.D.

The series of pictures, today incomplete, was conceived as having a continuous landscape. The separate subjects were divided by painted Ionic pilas-

Fig. 6.14 Rome, Vatican. "The Laestrygonians destroying the Greek flotilla." Detail from the *Odyssey Landscapes*. (Alinari)

ters at regular intervals. The narrative comes from Books 10 and 11 of *The Odyssey*, covering the adventures of Odysseus among the Laestrygonians, with Circe, and on his expedition to the lower world. We see his men meeting the stately but immense daughter of King Antiphates, who promptly stirred up a peck of trouble. The savage, gigantic Laestrygonians went into a fury, gathered great rocks (Fig. 6.13), and, rushing to the harbor, dashed to pieces all the ships but one (Fig. 6.14)—also harpooning the men of the crew, whom they carried off for supper. But the wily Odysseus had moored his own vessel outside the cove; he cut the mooring line with his sword, ordered his crew to row for their lives, and got safely out to sea.

In contrast to the shallow stage used as setting for pictures in the Alexandrian manner, the space represented in the *Odyssey Landscapes* opens up from the very edge of the picture. Even the objects in the extreme foreground seem to be emphatically *within* the setting, and not merely in front of it. From there onward, nothing impedes the eye. Figures and other details are placed far enough apart to give one room, so to speak, to go between them; and we can sweep our way into the unlimited distance.

In further contrast with the Alexandrian formula, we see in the *Odyssey Landscapes* human figures which are very small in relation to the total area of the pictures. All the people, moreover, seem to be moving rapidly, and often in directions diagonal to the picture-plane, thus making it necessary for us to postulate the reality of the volume within which motion takes place. But for all the action, the people are mere details in the greater drama of hills, ocean, and air. Not only were these among the first paintings where space itself attained anything that might be called grandeur; they were also among the earliest in which the human actors were given a scale something like the actual proportion of man in relation to the natural world.

Like the Alexandrian, the Latin style survived well into the Middle Ages because pictures so executed were copied along with the classical and biblical texts they happened to illustrate. We shall return to that matter, also, in Chaper 8. It was the Latin style, morever, that sculptors like Ghiberti (Chapter 15) used for their classical source during the generation when the Florentines initiated the great modern research into the principles of representation.

Each of our three categories of spatial arrangement includes its own catalogue of extant works of art; but it nevertheless remains for us to point out that the Neo-Attic, Alexandrian, and Latin formulas were not mutually exclusive. Any well-informed artist working in the Roman world was familiar with all three; and in a particular work of art, he might choose to make a combination.

The painter of Figure 6.15, for example, was obviously a Roman impressionist trying to capture the Alexandrian mood. The subject matter is bucolic, but it will be noted that the figure of Paris is very moderate in scale and is placed well within the represented space rather than in front of it.

Figure 6.16 shows one of the panels of relief which line the passageway of the Arch of Titus in the Forum Romanum. Because the figures are large, in the foreground, and fill up a lot of area, the composition partakes of the Alexandrian form; but a more careful analysis (which entails our making a mental restoration of all the heads that have been knocked off) will show that the sculptor went to great pains to "place" his material within the setting. The missing heads were in the round, and from there on, the relief is graduated by subtle steps until it becomes very low indeed. The effect of atmospheric perspective is unmistakable in spite of the mutilation, and we instinctively accept the blank background not as a barrier, but as the blue sky—which is to say the unlimited distance, and the kind of space characteristic of the Latin style.

THE SECOND SCHOOL OF PERGAMUM AND ASSOCIATED MONUMENTS

At the very start of the Hellenistic period, Greek sculptors—taking them as a class—were in possession of the most accomplished tradition of the human

Fig. 6.15 Naples, National Museum. *Paris on Mount Ida.* Fresco from Pompeii.

figure that the world has ever seen. They also lived in a society still committed to the human figure as its chief, indeed almost its exclusive vehicle for artistic expression. It might not at first be supposed that this combination of circumstances created an artistic problem, but such seems to have been the situation. One of the very few generalizations that applies to every period and school in the history of art is the tendency of the creative mind to seek some enterprise offering the zest of discovery. But what (after Praxiteles, Scopas, and Lysippus) was there to discover about the human figure? Nothing of an essential nature, to be sure. But it was still possible to experiment with the pose, which could be made more complicated, elegant, and stirring than ever before. It was also possible to seek new effects by novel manipulations of the muscles and drapery, with the end result of arriving at more spectacular drama, if not more profound.

From some such ferment as this—and our guess is unlikely to be far from the truth—there emerged one of the distinctive new movements of Hellenistic and Roman art, generally referred to as "The Second School of Pergamum." The most famous single demonstration of the tendency was the *Great Altar of Pergamum* (Fig. 6.19) set up by King Eumenes the 2nd to commemorate his successful repulse (with Roman help) of an invasion threatened by Antiochus of Syria. The *Great Altar* now exists in fragments

Fig. 6.16 Rome. Arch of Titus. A.D. 81. "The spoils of Jerusalem carried in triumphal procession." (Anderson)

which were taken to Berlin and there arranged for exhibition in partial restoration. The work probably began shortly after 188 B.C., which is the only fixed point in the history we are now tracing. For that reason, it is fair to label all associated monuments as belonging to a Pergamene tradition, but some of the most important of them surely date before the 2nd century B.C.

The *Nike (Victory) from Samothrace* (Fig. 6.17) was discovered in 1863. Samothrace is an island situated about forty miles northwest of the entrance to the Dardanelles. From the very earliest times, the place was important as a religious center, and it remained so throughout Greek history. The royal house of Macedon took a special interest in the cult that grew up on this remote, almost inaccessible spot. In the course of time, a number of memorials were set up there, of which this appears to be one.

Because her pedestal consists of the prow of a moving vessel, it is obvious the *Nike* commemorates a naval victory, but we are by no means certain what at Athens and, in 306 B.C., won a smashing naval victory over Ptolemy the 1st victory. Much can be made of the fact that a *Nike* similar in pose and drapery appears on a coin (Fig. 6.18) issued by Demetrius Poliorcetes, one of the most brilliant and dissolute figures of the period, who ruled for a time as tyrant off Cyprus.

Fig. 6.17   Paris, Louvre. *Nike from Samothrace.* (Archives Photographiques)

Fig. 6.18 Paris, Bibliothèque Nationale. Coin of Demetrius Poliorcetes, showing a Nike something like the *Nike from Samothrace*. Shortly after 306 B.C.

The *Victory* on the coin is shown in profile view, riding the prow of a ship and blowing a big horn. The muscles of the statue in Paris seem to require a different position for the arms, but that may perhaps be explained away by the suggestion that the designer of the coin was merely making small changes appropriate to the composition of a metallic disc. He therefore used the profile view to get the broadest aspect, whereas the statue itself composes best from in front or when seen on a moderate diagonal. He also arranged the arms differently in order to adapt the upper silhouette to the circular shape of the coin.

If we are correct in associating the statue with the coin, we have a date of around 300 B.C., but several critics have felt that the differences are sufficient to impeach the evidence offered by the coin. By various arguments, they have persuaded themselves that several other dates are more probable. The chief suggestions have been: the middle of the 3rd century, the latter half of the 2nd, and both the beginning and the end of the 1st century B.C. The reader may judge for himself the truth of our general dictum that Hellenistic archeology is confused.

As to the statue itself, there can be no question that it is, and probably always will remain, the supreme example of personification. The ample and magnificent figure alights in perfect poise on the forepeak of the fast moving galley. Common sense simply fails to register against the inspiration of the imagery; it seems thrillingly true that Victory is a goddess who brings fortune to her own.

The concept, in itself, is an index to Hellenistic taste. The extraordinary success of this particular statue must not be permitted to obscure its author's purpose. He was indulging in outright theatricals of a kind hitherto not indulged in by Greek artists engaged in the production of public monuments. No one can quarrel with the effect when it is so fine as we see it here, but hell beckons for the artist, musician, or author who makes a business of providing thrills.

It is doubtful whether any ancient statue evokes a stronger sense of reality, and it is therefore necessary to give some emphasis to abstract methods the sculptor used. The drapery, for example, is a superb instance of rhythmic line and contour. It is utterly unlike the folds into which actual cloth might fall. It is impossible, in fact, to arrange cloth in such a fashion unless the stuff is made into a sculptor's material by the addition of paste or glue. The impression created by the plastic manipulation of the drapery is an impression of actual forward movement of the body through the resistant air. Or, in more general terms, we are compelled to postulate the physical materials of the environment in order to make sense of what we see.

It is interesting in that connection to recall that the statue was first set up in the Louvre without the base. It enjoyed small popularity, but when the base was unearthed in 1875 and added to the ensemble, the *Nike* almost immediately became celebrated as one of the chief treasures of that great museum. The setting, in short, is not an accessory but an indispensable element—a situation not to be complained of, but one that signifies a considerable alteration in the Greek philosophy of art.

The figure style is typical of the entire Pergamene tradition. Vigorous monumentality was the aim. The canon of proportions approaches the gigantic. Youth, daintiness, even grace are sacrificed, and the compensation is an amplitude of adult beauty which in itself conveys a sense of adequacy and permanence. For public monuments of a patriotic sort, there have been worse conceptions.

The pose is understandable as a derivation from the tradition begun by Polyclitus and continued by Praxiteles and Scopas, but every tendency to be noted in the work of those earlier men was carried very far indeed by the master who did the *Nike*. The legs are stretched wide apart. The great torso twists at the waist with a compound rotary movement to throw the bust forward and bring one shoulder lower than the other. The muscular conformation thus was made into an indescribable complexity of surfaces, some flat, some tense, some soft and bulging. Nothing so intricate and involved had ever been undertaken during the Great Age, and the technique required for such a performance, while superb, inevitably attracts attention to itself for that very reason. We may list parade of skill as another feature new with the times.

The *Great Altar of Pergamum* was a grandiose architectural rectangle surrounding the altar proper. A monumental staircase opened on one side. Around the other three sides, there ran a roofed colonnade raised high on a basement story, and around the entire outer surface of the basement story,

Fig. 6.19 Berlin, Pergamum Museum. "Athena killing a giant." Detail from the frieze of the *Great Altar of Pergamum*. (Deutscher Kunstverlag)

there ran a continuous frieze in high relief almost 8 feet high and no less than 400 feet long. The subject was the battle between the gods and the giants (Figs. 6.19–20).

No earlier display of sculpture could compare with this one for sheer dazzling extent, and the magnitude of the work was matched by an unequaled parade of technique. As though that were not enough, the enormous number of figures demanded that every ramification of the subject be worked to the limit. Giants are there in every known form, including some with legs like snakes. There are monsters, also, of an altogether original kind, to say nothing of lesser deities who had almost never before appeared in art because no one else had the room to put them in. As a display of erudition, the composition may be compared with Raphael's later frescoes (Chapter 16). Unlike Raphael, the Pergamene sculptors helped us by inscribing the name of every figure.

In point of style, the Second School of Pergamum falls in line with the tendencies already described, except that all of them were vigorously exaggerated. The figure canon recalls the *Nike from Samothrace,* but the bodies are not only big, they are bigger. The poses are more than complicated; they are bizarre. Where sculptors of the Greek Fifth Century had eliminated and simplified, those of Pergamum stressed every detail. Each twisting torso

Fig. 6.20 Berlin, Pergamum Museum. "Head of a Giant." Detail from the frieze of the *Great Altar of Pergamum*. (Stoedtner)

seems to confine living tissue under intense compression; the muscles bulge as though they would burst the skin. Such treatment is not realistic; indeed, it reflects a new and differently directed idealism.

Philosophically, the Pergamene frieze is a disturbing monument. What are we to make of the religion of an age capable of visualizing, for the purposes of a public monument, its major gods as involved in mortal combat and having a very bad time of it? The display seems, when considered in the light of such implications, to be evidence of spiritual insecurity well-nigh incurable.

The *Laocoön Group* (Fig. 6.21) was discovered at Rome in 1506 on the site of the Baths of Trajan. In 1531, a restoration was undertaken by a sculptor named Montorsoli, who in all likelihood restored Laocoön's right arm with insufficient curvature back toward the head. The unfortunate Laocoön was a Trojan priest who tried to warn his fellow citizens against the wooden horse. He met his death at some later time while walking on the beach with his sons; savage serpents appeared, attacked the three men, and strangled them.

Because of its early discovery and because the Roman Renaissance was at that very moment in full flower, the group attracted immediate attention and

Fig. 6.21 Rome, Vatican. *Laocoön Group.* About 50 B.C. (Anderson)

extravagant praise—a circumstance which may be assigned, in some degree at least, to the unusual size of the piece as well as to the contemporary habit of praising everything of classical origin. In much the same mood, Lessing wrote his famous essay called *Laocoön* (1766), in which he compared the sculptor's handling of the Laocoön theme with the rendering of the same subject matter by Vergil—attempting therefrom to deduce general principles about the nature and limitations of both poetry and the visual arts.

Not one modern critic would agree with the high estimates just cited. Undeniably a superb technical demonstration, the *Laocoön* seems, by comparison with more sober statuary, to be offensive for that very reason: the sculptors (there were three of them) tried to overwhelm us with a display of their skill. The group remains a morbid thriller, a roller-coaster terror, about which one refuses to be distressed.

The monument nevertheless stands as a kind of historical milestone. It is the first instance (among preserved statuary) where a major work of art was devoted to the subject of despair. Where is human dignity when such a thing can happen? And yet, if we are right in accepting the now-popular but by no means certain dating of about 50 B.C., antiquity had a long course yet to run.

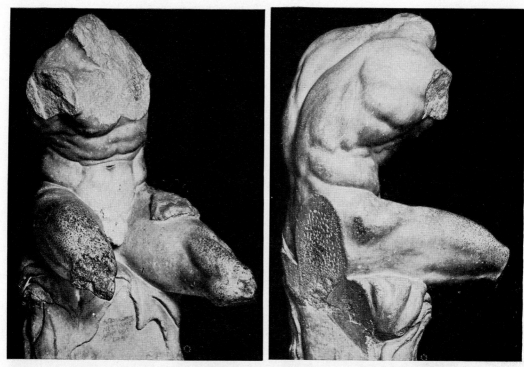

Figs. 6.22–23   Rome, Vatican. *Belvedere Torso*. (Anderson)

The *Belvedere Torso* (Figs. 6.22–23) is known to have belonged to the Colonna family at Rome as early as 1430 or thereabouts; it came to the Vatican with Clement the 7th (regnal dates 1523–1534), who set it up in the court called the Belvedere—hence its name. If the paw attached to the skin on which the figure sits were that of a lion, we might call it a Hercules, but because the paw is almost surely that of a panther, we probably have the fragments of a faun. Considerably less spectacular than some other monuments of the Pergamene tradition, the torso has a special place in history: Michelangelo derived his later figure style from it, as any student of the ceiling of the Sistine Chapel can verify by inspection. That greatest of all modern sculptors even went so far as to refer to the battered figure as his "school."

The *Aphrodite from Melos,* or *Venus de Milo* (Fig. 6.24), was found by a peasant on that island in 1820, and sold to the French ambassador at Constantinople. The statue therefore went to Paris at a psychologically advantageous moment. The Greek War for Independence (1821–1830) was just under way, and had stirred up an immense amount of sympathy in western Europe. The citizenry, especially the French, was also in precisely the right mood to rejoice over the acquisition of a notable antiquity—neoclassicism had recently established itself as the most fashionable form of esthetics, and the Romantic Revolt had not yet begun to do its work. It is therefore no

Figs. 6.24–25   (left) Paris, Louvre. *Aphrodite from Melos*. (Archives Photographiques) (right) Rome, Vatican. *Apollo Belvedere*. (Anderson)

wonder that the statue soon became famous, and it has remained so ever since by virtue of its central placement in the principal museum of the greatest tourist center in the modern world.

Although the serious student is bound to feel some annoyance over extravagant praise in any form, the public has made no error in thinking highly of the *Aphrodite;* the only mistake is the supposition that it is better than some less-advertised pieces of Greek work which happen to be just as good. Any sober view of the thing itself is sure to give it a top rank among Hellenistic monuments.

There has been a great deal of debate over the dating, some of it motivated by a desire to enhance the prestige of the work by putting it in the

Greek Fifth or Fourth Century. A pedestal found nearby carried an inscription which might settle the affair, but the pedestal cannot be firmly associated with the statue. Thus the date must rest upon one's deductions from the style, and on that basis, most of the recent authorities are agreed in putting the figure about 100 B.C.

The chief arguments for that date have to do with the content and with the pose. The content seems to be an attempt to combine the sensual charm of Praxiteles with the cold serenity of the Fifth Century. On an opulent torso, we find a strangely Phidian head which is nevertheless modeled to give some sort of expression, one hardly knows what. The pose, while less overtly vigorous than some others in the general tradition of Pergamum, is extravagantly manipulated. Head and shoulders are given a strong lift up and to the statue's left. The right hip swings outward to the right so far that the word contortion may legitimately be applied, and the left thigh thrusts strongly out in front. The upsurge of the torso at the top is offset by the droop of the drapery below. The precarious hang of the drapery, moreover, is in itself a theatrical touch, combining with everything else to suggest a period of much sophistication and a rather academic inclination to sample every kind of taste at once.

THE CULT OF ELEGANCE

The coexistence during the Hellenistic age of every kind of taste is well pointed up, in fact, by the contrast between the tradition that stemmed from Pergamum and the cult of elegance now to be discussed. Of the latter, the prime and central monument is the famous *Apollo Belvedere* (Figs. 6.25–26), so called because it has always stood in the Belvedere at the Vatican. Discovered at some early date, it has been viewed by visitors to Rome from the 15th century onward. The notion persists that the marble statue now in Rome is a copy, itself from the 1st century B.C., after a Greek bronze by Leochares, a sculptor of the late 4th century. Because we have no adequate way to form any notion of Leochares' style and because the *Apollo* is an extreme demonstration by any standards, it seems wiser to accept it as predominantly an original creation from its own period.

The artistic philosophy of its author may be inferred from the incongruity between the subject and its style. A certain lady named Niobe had seven sons and seven daughters. She was careless enough to boast of her many children to Leto, a lady who had only two, and Leto's feelings were hurt. But Leto's two were Apollo and Artemis, who took immediate action to put Niobe in her place. They took their hunting bows, sought out the prolific family, and shot all fourteen children full of arrows while their helpless mother looked on. The myth is one of the most brutal in the history of Greek litera-

Fig. 6.26 Rome, Vatican. Detail from the *Apollo Belvedere*. (Anderson)

ture; were it to be committed to sculpture at all, one would think it might have attracted the interest of some morbid realist capable of rendering the heartless brother and sister as the dangerous animals they had for the moment become.

Instead of that, we see Apollo in the very act of letting off an arrow, his pose as self-consciously graceful as a dancing master, his face vacant of expression, his hair and drapery a definition of the careful carelessness that has ever been the special province of the dandy. The rendering of the nude anatomy is even more important. The stylistic intention appears to be almost opposite to the musculature cultivated by the Pergamene tradition. Instead of emphasizing and exaggerating the bulge and number of the muscles, a systematic effort seems to have been made to simplify the surface into the smallest feasible number of contours. Each contour was then polished to a smooth, gentle curvature. That elegance and even grace result, no one can deny; but a certain weakness—especially inappropriate for so robustly callous an action—is all too apparent.

Like the *Belvedere Torso,* the *Apollo Belvedere* had historical influence thrust upon it. When, during the period of the French Revolution and the days that followed, it fell to the painter David (Chapter 16) to bring neo-classical art into being, he and other members of the movement fastened upon the figure style represented by the Apollo and made it their own. They believed they were working from Greek sculpture at its purest and best, an archeological error made possible only by the lack of better examples from the classical period—most of the good ones, as set forth above, having become accessible only after it was already too late to change the temper of neoclassicism.

Chapter 7

THE HISTORY of architecture during the Hellenistic age and under the Roman Empire bears a striking resemblance to developments during the latter part of the Gothic era, and also to what happened as the Renaissance moved on into its baroque and rococo phase. In all three instances, even the ordinary architect was erudite in the manipulation of the current style. Professional opportunities, moreover, were many and generous, but nothing had happened to change the world enough to create a demand for the discard of the style to which people were then accustomed, and the invention of a new one. Every problem presented by the inner logic of the incumbent style had been solved long ago; there was no great or fundamental challenge to the imagination. In its absence, designers tried to get what satisfaction they might from sophisticated variations on familiar themes. It is all too easy for the historian to dismiss such work with a passing word; some of it is very fine indeed, and all of it is entertaining. It is true, however, that the reader is already well equipped to understand the architecture of late antiquity, and we may legitimately save space by confining ourselves to a few broad generalizations.

TRENDS AND VARIATIONS

The first of these is the existence of an obvious parallel between the architecture of late antiquity and its contemporary sculpture, the latter already reviewed in Chapter 6. Amid the confusion of many separate tendencies of style, we may discern at least three distinct trends of architectural thought. Most conspicuous and most fertile was the tendency to complicate

182

HELLENISTIC AND ROMAN ARCHITECTURE

design and proliferate ornament, as exemplified by the round temple at Baalbek (Fig. 7.1) and by the rock-cut tomb façades of Petra (Fig. 7.2). Keeping always within the classical idiom and yet contorting it, such architecture arrived at compositions so spectacular as to be hardly classical at all—the natural counterpart of sculpture in the Pergamene tradition.

Over against this strident urge for display, we may note a certain lesser number of designs which, like sculpture in the class of the *Apollo Belvedere,* are distinguished by overt chastity. Among them the small **Doric** temple at Cori (Fig. 7.3), about 35 miles southeast of Rome, is a conspicuous example. Its shafts are no less than 8⅔ diameters in height, its abaci virtually straight-sided, and its total effect so neat and sanitary that the Parthenon seems by comparison somewhat immodest.

In addition to the two trends of taste just cited, the realistic point of view, so productive in the field of sculpture, made itself felt in architecture also. Its operation was manifest in the appearance of a great variety of specialized buildings, some frankly and completely utilitarian: markets, law courts, theater and amphitheaters, race courses and grandstands, fora, aqueducts, libraries, lighthouses, sidewalks protected by roofs and colonnades, gateways, bathing establishments, and so on. We are dealing, in short, with the architecture of an increasingly refined civilization, with complexities disturbingly like our own.

Like contemporary sculptors, Hellenistic architects believed in colossal dimensions. The tendency was well under way, as a matter of fact almost before the Hellenistic period began. The two greatest temples of the 4th century B.C.—that of Artemis at Ephesus (begun in 356) and that of Apollo

Fig. 7.1 Baalbek. Round temple. (After an engraving from Melchiore de Vogué, *Architecture civile et religieuse Syrie central*, Paris, 1866.)

Fig. 7.2 Petra. Khazna. (Julian Huxley)   Fig. 7.3 Cori. Doric temple. (Alinari)

Fig. 7.4 Nîmes. Pont du Gard. 175 feet high. (Richard W. Dwight)

Didymaeus at Miletus (335-320)—have linear measurements approximately twice those of the Parthenon. On the basis of cubic measurement, which is a better criterion for size, they were eight times as big. It must be emphasized that there was no practical necessity for immense buildings; the motives were esthetic. Scale counts!

But even the Hellenistic Greeks must take a place far behind the Romans whenever scale enters our calculations. The Colosseum is an oval some 620 feet long, 500 feet wide, and a little more than 157 feet high; it seated about 40,000 persons. The Pont du Gard at Nîmes (Fig. 7.4) rises 157 feet above the stream it spans. The rotunda of the Pantheon at Rome (Fig. 7.5) is 142 feet in diameter and 142 feet high. The main hall of the Basilica of Constantine (Fig. I.27, page 959) was 226 feet long by 82 feet wide, and its cross vaults swung 114 feet above the floor. These measurements were approximately duplicated in the so-called *tepidaria* (literally, "warm rooms;" actually, the main concourses) of the Baths of Caracalla and those of Diocletian. These immense rooms, in size and appearance almost exactly like the main concourse of the Pennsylvania Station in New York, were all but lost in the ground plan of the entire establishment (Fig. 7.6) which, as a whole, amounted to a veritable district set up on a platform 1,080 feet on a side.

In assessing the cumulative effect of the architecture of later antiquity, we must never forget these enormous dimensions; and in so doing, we must prod ourselves with the realization that our own sensitivity to scale has become somewhat jaded by the performances of the 20th century. To the medieval man, even the Gothic man, the size of Roman buildings represented something quite out of the question by reference to any techniques he knew or could imagine as practical. His topography was marked with Roman ruins, and he could explain their colossal dimensions only by assuming that Roman

Fig. 7.5 Rome. Pantheon. From an engraving. (Anderson)

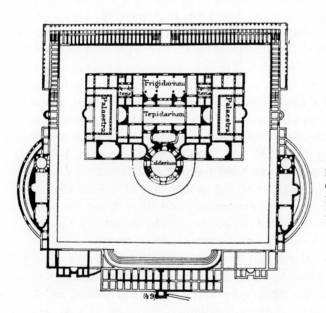

Fig. 7.6 Rome. Baths of Caracalla. Plan. (From J. Durm, *Die Baukunst der Römer*, Stuttgart, 1905.)

times were grander than his own. To the man of the Renaissance, Roman scale stood as a challenge, a test of whether he was worthy to recapture the power and scope of the ancient world. It is significant the test was met only two or three times: the Cathedral of Florence, Saint Peter's at Rome, and Saint Paul's in London. Otherwise, for scale like the Roman, the world had to wait for the Industrial Revolution, and it is no wonder the uniquely beautiful buildings at Athens tended to become forgotten amid a wealth of larger and more assertively gorgeous monuments.

In a world teeming with builders hard at work, it was inevitable that a certain amount of progress should take place even though no fundamental change of view came to the architectural philosophy established during the Great Age of Greece. A few important experiments were tried. Some of these proved successful; and in the ensuing discussion, we shall confine ourselves to Hellenistic and Roman developments important enough to have exerted a substantial influence on the future.

◆ *Standards of Construction during Late Antiquity* It is possible to read in a hundred books that standards of construction became inferior as soon as the Great Age of Greek art passed into memory. The judgment is hardly fair. It rests upon the presumption that the marble of Periclean Athens may be taken as typical of "Greek work," in comparison to which we may in the same breath express our scorn for the masonry of the average workaday Roman contractors. The buildings on the Acropolis are of course a special case, uniquely fine and typical of nothing; the Greeks did a great deal of work that is worse, some of it even worse than the dead average of later antiquity.

However inevitable, such comparisons furnish a poor start toward an appreciation of Hellenistic and Roman construction. We should commence, rather, by attempting to visualize the problems that opened up for the architect as the Greek horizon expanded after the death of Alexander and again as Rome organized the civilization of the whole European world. The assignment, if we may call it that, was bigger than the task of lending beauty and dignity to a single part of a single city. It amounted to nothing less than the construction of entire cities in all kinds of places, some with building materials in good supply near at hand and others remote from essential resources. The explanation for the Hellenistic and Roman outlook lies waiting for the reader if he will turn to one of the several translations of Vitruvius.

A mere perusal of the headings will suffice to indicate what is meant. Vitruvius felt under the necessity of writing a section giving people advice about the selection of a site for a city. Throughout his text, he returns again and again to consequences of the choice. Streets, he warned, ought to have their direction determined by that of the prevailing winds. He wrote at some length about finding water, storing water, and distributing water around the town. He pointed out that domestic architecture must vary in style with the climate, and had something to say about the exposure desirable for rooms of one kind and another. He also put forward suggestions for adapting one's house to the site available, and he cited considerations to be kept in mind when selecting a place to build the various public buildings considered necessary in that age of ramified economy and government.

His statement of general desiderata is accompanied throughout with rather specific instructions for the handling of materials. Brick, sand, lime, stone, stucco, timber, and paints found their place in his book at one point or another. Before he let himself go with respect to architecture as a cultural manifestation, he took time, moreover, to write down a few home truths about foundations and substructures. Indeed, it is only when he forsook the practical and ventured into the history, philosophy, and psychology of art that he got beyond his depth and ceases to carry conviction.

Space prevents our trespassing further upon what the reader may find for himself in Vitruvius, but it is important to give special emphasis to the great single development in the materials of architecture, a development that first became important in Hellenistic days and emerged in Roman times as supremely important. We refer to concrete.

Even the best cement is less attractive than good cut stone; less attractive, even, than good bricks. At the same time, no rational person can overlook the tremendous advantages offered by the material. Because concrete can be mixed by unskilled workmen from ingredients obtainable almost everywhere, and poured by them, it is feasible for a few educated architects to direct the labor of an immense number of men—and thus construct buildings more cheaply than would otherwise be possible. Concrete may be used clear, adulterated with nondescript rubble, or reinforced. In good Roman work, the latter was most often used. As in the dome of the Pantheon, the cement would fill the interstices of a logical lacework of brick arches. The strength and endurance of a wall or vault so constructed is beyond calculation; suffice it to say that if permanence is all we have in mind, Roman concrete is the best building material the world has yet seen. The Roman dominion made its excellence a matter of common knowledge, with the result that concrete remained the builder's chief reliance throughout the Middle Ages and Renaissance. Today when machinery has replaced the unskilled labor of earlier centuries and iron is available for reinforcement, concrete has more than ever come into its own. Its introduction during late antiquity must be classed as a major event in the history of architecture.

ROMAN ARCHITECTURE

♦ *The Roman Temple* There is no important Roman architecture from the republican period. Augustus himself is quoted as saying, "I found Rome a city of bricks, and I shall leave it a city of marble." He got the idea from contact with the architecture of Hellenistic Greece, and his policy is but an illustration of the extraordinary capacity of Rome to assimilate good things wherever they might be found. At that time, the Greek architectural tradition was the most accomplished the world had yet seen, and the Romans felt no impulse to invent another. Their temples, therefore, conform to the Greek type with certain historically significant changes.

One of the very best is the so-called *Maison Carrée* (Square House) at Nîmes (Fig. 7.7), originally dedicated to two grandsons of Augustus and dating from the very first years of the Christian era. As compared to the Greek temple, the most important difference is the introduction of a pedestal, or *podium,* which raises the entire building half a story above the ground. The podium provides useful space below the floor of the cella and, by increasing the total height, tends to increase the temple's value as a landmark. The podium makes it necessary to provide a staircase by which one may climb up to the cella level, and we see such a staircase attached to one short end of the building, which thus attains a certain emphasis as the principal front or façade. It is important to note that the capacity of the stairway is far greater than that of the door to which it leads; it can accommodate more people than we can imagine wanting to enter or leave the building at any one moment. The purpose of such a stairway is not functional, but esthetic: it is a grandiose piece of geometric sculpture, worthwhile for its varied mass, for the play of line it provides, and for the way it takes the light at different times of day. If of practical dimensions, it would have no such merit of appearance.

The Romans rarely used the free-standing peristyle of the Greek temple because they disliked the waste of interior space inevitable whenever an ambulatory was included on the plan. They therefore brought the cella walls out to the edge of the podium, and ran a peristyle of *engaged columns* (that is, columns in contact with the wall) around. As a further means of dignifying the main front, it was customary to keep the cella fairly short, leaving several columns free-standing to form an entrance porch at the top of the stairway.

It is the Roman adaptation of the Greek temple, and not the Greek temple itself, which has dictated the design of so much modern building in

Fig. 7.7 Nîmes. Maison Carrée. Early 1st century A.D. 87 by 45 feet, columns 29 feet high. (Archives Photographiques)

the several classicizing styles. The deep portico at the entrance end is the "temple front" we find attached to innumerable blocks of utilitarian construction. The elevation of the Roman temple has also proven historically important. It established a sequence of elements: podium, order, entablature, roof—which we may find repeated in all proportions on thousands of exteriors all over the world.

The Maison Carrée, like most other Roman columnar buildings, was built in the Corinthian Order. The entablature is much the same as the Greek Ionic except for the addition of small scroll-like brackets under the cornice. These are called *modillions*. They have a historical importance because they were borrowed in later times by Renaissance and baroque designers, who used them (often in exaggerated sizes) to soften the linear transition presented to the eye when two parts of a building must come together at a right angle. It will also be observed that the Roman pediment is commonly built with an angle slightly more acute than the Greek. The change may be good to whatever extent it tends to balance the podium, but most critics dislike the proportions it dictates for the pedimental triangle.

♦ *The Question of Etruscan Influence on Roman Art* A great many scholars feel dissatisfied with any historical treatment of Roman art that does not include some allusion to Etruscan influence. The Etruscans, it will be remembered, were the strongest contenders against Rome in the early days when Rome was still attempting to establish her rule over the peninsula. They lived in the district we now call Tuscany, and in the end they were so thoroughly chastened and absorbed by the Romans as to render Etruscan archeology a most difficult subject.

According to Vitruvius, the standard Roman temple, as described in the last section, conformed in the details of its arrangement to Etruscan temples. Having got the general idea of the temple shape from the Greeks, the Etruscans supposedly modified the type to the extent of making the cella wider, as

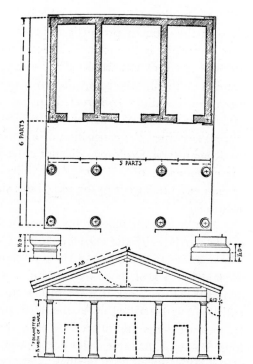

Fig. 7.8 Plans of a typical Etruscan temple. Drawn according to the description given by Vitruvius.

just described, and adding the entrance porch. As drawn by Vitruvius, a typical Etruscan temple was almost square in plan (Fig. 7.8). Undoubtedly, Vitruvius correctly reflected the current belief among Roman architects that these features were of Etruscan origin, and there is no reason to challenge his archeology. On the other hand, there is small cause to magnify the importance of an artistic influence which resulted in so simple and superficial an effect.

There is some reason to feel, even though we cannot begin to prove it, that Etruscan precedent affected the whole history of art in Italy in a more subtle and profound way. We refer to the perennial and otherwise inexplicable recurrence in Italy of a predilection for ponderous proportions. This is first seen in Roman architecture. A Roman structure of given over-all dimensions will contain a greater bulk of masonry than a building in any other style except the Egyptian. The Colosseum has, in all probability, more openings than any other building ever put up by the Romans; and yet in any view of the exterior, the eye is met mostly by solids. In the Arch of Titus, where the designer's sense of form was in no way constrained by the problem of permitting crowds to circulate, a much greater proportion of the cubic volume was assigned to masonry.

It is difficult to find a practical reason for such exaggerated weight and solidity. The ideal of permanence—that common possession of all great builders—might at first seem to be indicated, but it is really very doubtful whether the Roman proportions produced a superior factor of safety. To increase weight is to increase the load on every working part of the fabric, and the safety of the whole may be expressed by the relation between the strength of the members and the stress to which they are subjected. The very inertia of buildings constructed in the Roman manner may at times be dangerous: during World War II, Gothic buildings (lightly built but logically braced) sustained the concussion of bombing better than heavier buildings of the Roman type. Explosives did not enter into Roman calculations, of course; but earthquakes did. We may certainly question whether the sophisticated Roman engineers went in for great bulk simply because they thought it might be stronger.

The love of the massive for its own sake is pretty well established as their motive, in fact, by the extremes to which the Romans went upon occasion. The quarries at Baalbek in Syria yield a dense and somewhat crystalline stone notable for lack of flaws. About half a mile south of the modern town, one may still see the block that establishes an all-time world's record. Called "the trilithon," it lies tilted up as though ready for dragging to the building site. Its measurements are 70 feet, by 14 and 13. The weight is over a thousand tons. Stones of the same order of magnitude were actually built into the walls of the great ensemble at Baalbek. Three of them, with a cross section 14 feet by 11, measure 64, 63, and 62½ feet long. Such blocks present a herculean problem for the builder, and there is no special good in them if we are merely interested in sound construction. Split into smaller pieces, any one of them would furnish material for a house 60 feet by 60 on ground plan, 40 feet high, and with walls a foot thick. For such a performance, some reason other than the structural must be sought.

The heavy Roman proportions seem much more likely to have had their genesis in the plastic sense which so strongly dominated all classical taste. A strong tactile interest begets a feeling for mass. An interest in mass breeds a desire for greater mass, which is to say for ponderous proportions. In view of the fact that the Romans carried this process much further than the Greeks and, unlike the Greeks, failed to work out an elegant system of proportional relations, we must call the tendency Roman or find some other source for it.

If a source existed, it was probably Etruscan. There are two main reasons for believing this. Still standing in the ancient city walls of Perugia is an Etruscan arch known as the Arch of Augustus because part of the frieze above dates from that reign. It is a semicircular arch and terrifically, even inchoately heavy.

The same may be said of other remains of Etruscan work, few though they are. Some Etruscan paintings survive. The figure style is bulky to a degree. Are we therefore to believe that Etruscan precedent established a

Fig. 7.9   Termessus. Façade of the temple. (From Lanckoronski, Nieman, & Petersen, *Städte Pampyliens u. Pisidiens,* Vienna. 1892.)

love for pure bulk, and passed it on to the Romans and everybody else who has since lived in Tuscany? If so, the Etruscan temperament demonstrated an extraordinary power for survival.

There are even those who believe it lay dormant in the Italian population for an incredible number of centuries, coming sporadically out into the open to produce the ponderous figure style of such artists as Giotto, Signorelli, and Michelangelo. Were some other suggestion conveniently at hand to explain these phenomena, the notion of recurrent Etruscan taste would be preposterous, but nothing else seems so satisfactory as a probable cause for otherwise capricious happenings.

Pending findings of a very substantial kind, however, the whole question of Etruscan influence must be labeled a possibility, not a fact; and suggestions like these must be accepted as inferential.

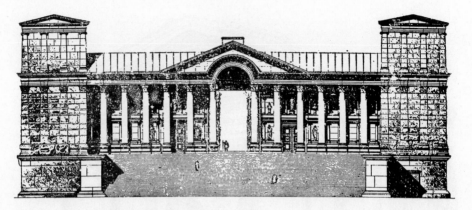

Fig. 7.10   Baalbek. Entrance portico. (From Weigand, *Baalbek,* Berlin & Leipzig, 1921.)

♦ *Combinations of the Arch and the Orders*   The Greek prejudice against the arch was strong enough to last a very long time, and seems to have relaxed only under the Roman Empire.* As soon, however, as the arch became artistically acceptable, designers began to work with compositions in which it was combined with the orders. Arches were made to spring from columns in the justly famous colonnaded streets of Palmyra, in certain parts of the small town known as Diocletian's Palace at Spalato, and elsewhere. Experiments of various sorts and kinds were tried, and two particular ensembles of arch and order achieved historical importance.

The first is well illustrated by the façade of the temple at Termessus (Fig. 7.9), a place on the banks of the Catarractes River in southern Asia Minor about 23 miles from the coast. It was this very same arrangement that Brunelleschi borrowed for the façade of the Pazzi Chapel (Fig. 13.22, page 513) when, as one of the leaders of the then-new Italian Renaissance, he conceived a revival of classical architecture. The point of the arrangement was to dignify the central intercolumniation which leads to the cella door; and with that purpose in mind, the entablature was broken in the middle and a handsome arch swung up into the pediment above. Once the theme became established, variations on it were tried. Of these, a significant one is that illustrated by the entrance portico at Baalbek (Fig. 7.10). There the entablature was broken, to be sure, but less abruptly. Conceived as a great molding, the ensemble of architrave, frieze, and cornice was carried clear around the curve of the arch, to continue in its usual horizontal form on the far side. Much the same use was made of the curved entablature for the entranceway

* Appendix I, pp. 932ff, gives a discussion of the physical principles of the arch and vault. A working knowledge of these is requisite to the discussion which follows.

leading from the forecourt of Diocletian's Palace at Spalato, but in that application, the arched opening is central in an ensemble of only three inter-columniations. To either side of it, there is a square-headed opening of the usual Greek kind. Taken together, the three amount to the architectural motive which became famous during the High Renaissance under the name *Palladian window* (p. 644).

For the combinations of arch and order just cited, there is no generally accepted name, probably because each instance differs slightly from the last. The so-called *Roman Arch Order*, however, became sufficiently standardized to become a recognized item in Europe's architectural vocabulary. The motive is seen in its simplest form on the numerous triumphal arches of Rome, each a memorial gateway put up in honor of some military conquest or other impor-tant event in political history. The Arch of Titus is a good example. It was erected in A.D. 81 to commemorate the capture of Jerusalem, an event that had taken place a decade earlier. The structural parts consist of two substan-tial piers with an arch spanning the opening between them. Above the arch there rises a block of masonry half a story high, technically known as an *attic*, and offering a useful field for inscriptions. The Greek orders are applied to the surface of the structure just described; they do no work and have no value except that they are handsome. As distinguished from other combina-tions of the same elements, the Roman Arch Order puts the columns to either side of the arch, and runs the entablature *above* its crown. Once established, this simple motive may be repeated any number of times. It was used three times on each face of the Arch of Constantine (Fig. 7.11), for example, and the designers of the Colosseum repeated it continuously on each of the three lower stories, all the way round the circumference of that immense pile.

As used on the arches of Titus, Constantine, and Septimius Severus, the applied entablature shows a characteristic that has become a standard resource of the architect. We refer to the use of *ressaults*—a ressault being a block or chunk of entablature that rests directly on the capital of a column. As seen on the Arch of Constantine, there is a ressault over each column, but between the columns, the entablature is made to recede almost to the surface of the wall. The columns and their separate ressaults, to put it another way, are in the round, while the rest of the entablature is in low relief. The purpose of the expedient is to eliminate the cast shadow which would fall from an entablature of normal projection, still retaining the strong vertical that results from a column in the round. The ressaults cast shadows, but they are small shadows, located where they do not trespass against the curvature of the arch.

By combining the arch with the orders, the Romans were able to produce compositions that are undeniably good-looking. The combination of square

Fig. 7.11 Rome. Arch of Constantine. A.D. 312. (Alinari)

and curved openings is the opposite of harmony as we have defined it, but contrast and variety are often equally to be sought. There are strong arguments, nevertheless, against this and other Roman habits of design; they are summarized in a later section.

♦ *The Roman Conception of Architectural Space* Space is part of the architectural medium. The painter can represent space, and thus make some use of it in his art. A few modern sculptors have attempted to make reference to space by devices calculated to direct the attention of the observer toward it, but for the most part, sculpture as we have usually known it must resist space. Only the architect has an actual volume of air at his disposal.

It was the greatest single achievement of Roman architecture to have arrived at this conception, and to explore in a particular way its esthetic possibilities. The Egyptian notion of interior design had approached absolute zero; the most sacred part of their temples was a cramped sanctuary notable for darkness. The Greek cella was better than that, but we may wonder whether it offered an amplitude in keeping with the dignity of the statues housed therein. The majestic volume enclosed by the dome of the Pantheon (Fig. 7.5) may not be mentioned in the same breath.

The Roman interior, vast though it may be, represents a logical extension of the principles laid down for all classical art. It is, in its fundamental character, as plastic as any Greek statue—an apparent paradox we must make haste to explain. Taking the Pantheon as an example, it is fair to say we are dealing with a work of art where the solids are more important than the voids. The masonry of the dome dominates a large portion of our conscious-ness. It is the act of less than an instant to recognize its shape as hemispherical, and we remain permanently impressed with the shape. The hollow squares (*coffering*) sunk into its surface serve not only to enhance the texture, but to make more keen one's feeling for the thickness of the ceiling—and hence its tangible solidity. The interior of the Pantheon is, in short, as truly a piece of geometric sculpture as the exterior of a Greek temple. There is no difference in principle; we have merely exchanged the convex for the con-cave, and are inside the sculpture rather than outside.

The same interior demonstrates also that unity-through-separation which characterizes all classical art. No windows permit us to discern or recall any-thing outside the building; wherever the eye may look, so long as the line of sight is kept within normal limits, the vista is closed. To enter is to enter the world-that-is-the-Pantheon. No other extant interior separates the occu-pant from the rest of the universe in the same degree, and it is interesting to see that the oculus left open at the crown militates not at all against that impression. It opens at a remote and inaccessible spot upon a void foreign to our experience. It is doubtful whether the high-set windows of other Roman interiors functioned differently.

It would be incorrect to conclude from this that the Roman version of interior design constitutes a negation of space. The designers of the Pan-theon were far from negligent with respect to the emotional implications of the magnificent cubic-footage enclosed by their building, but like all classical artists, they assigned to the tactile sense a reality more vital and essential than that of any other sense. This led them to feel that air itself was a sculptor's material, to be sequestered and molded into a predetermined contour—in this instance, that of a cylinder surmounted by half a sphere. Their position on the matter was by no means untenable. Indeed, there is perhaps no better way to deal with the problem of interior design, and certainly none more appropriate to the disciplines of the Classical Style. As a matter of historical fact, moreover, the Roman and plastic conception of enclosed space remains one of the two (and only two) approaches to the matter yet to appear in the whole history of architecture—the other being most perfectly realized in the French Gothic of the 13th century A.D. and in some of our most modern buildings of steel and glass.

◆ *Roman Symmetrical Planning* A great many Roman architectural designs involve more than one building. Artistic order, that is to say, was imposed upon an extensive area, with single buildings conceived as mere parts in a grander composition. The idea did not originate with the Romans; but when they undertook to organize the civilized world, examples of such design multiplied and their scale became grander than ever before. It is the Roman system of composition rather than any other which has, for better or worse, set the pattern for the greater number of similar enterprises ever since.

Excellent examples of Roman practice in the layout of such group-design are the Forum of Trajan at Rome, the ensemble of temple and forum at Baalbek in Syria, and the gigantic baths built at Rome by Caracalla and Diocletian (Fig. 7.6). In each of these instances, a certain amount of reconstruction is necessary in matters of detail, but the evidence is sufficient to make our generalizations reliable.

The Roman procedure in arranging such a composition was as follows: First, the surface of the site was leveled off to a plane. Second, through the center of the available area, or through some other convenient point, two axes were drawn at right angles to each other. At this juncture the governing conditions of the plan were set. All subsequent designing, whatever its apparent variety and complexity, proceeded with direct and simple reference to the plane and level surface, and to the axes drawn across it. The third step was to lay out in ground plan the various buildings to be included in the ensemble; and the fourth to arrange the subdivisions within the plan of each building. The plan of the Baths of Caracalla gives an instantaneous summary of the Roman mental machine and its functioning in work of this kind.

In designing of this type, symmetry is of the essence; but because it is often impractical to maintain absolute symmetry to both axes, one is chosen as the "main axis." To it, symmetry is strict and perfect, while to the "subordinate axis," symmetry is maintained only so far as feasible. The main axis is sometimes the long one, sometimes the short one; that is a mere detail.

Symmetrical planning, especially when the plan embraces an extended area, requires explanation. Its reason for existence is far from obvious. Symmetry has no relation whatever to practical considerations. Such plans demand the plane and level site beneath them; otherwise the symmetry is rendered less intelligible. The duplication of rooms at equal and opposite distances either side of an axis often makes it necessary to tolerate a substantial increase in the cubic bulk of the building. Both these features of the symmetrical system represent cost over and above provision for daily use—an oval room is often a pleasant change from the rectangular, but what conceivable human need can be adduced to suggest an economic justification for oval rooms in symmetrical pairs, as seen in the Baths of Caracalla? Neither economy nor efficiency entered into the account, and we must accept the fact that Roman symmetrical planning took place in response to some deeply felt psychological need.

The need was not for beauty. Most Roman plans make pretty drawings when seen in India ink on white paper. But the niceties of arrangement thus revealed were destined to be concealed by the roof; and, in the absence of airplanes, were never contemplated by anybody once the building was complete. We ordinarily see architecture in elevation, along a horizontal line of sight; and the materials of the draftsman differ from those of the builder. For the Romans, symmetry appears to have had an almost religious power, nevertheless. They served it with devotion worthy of a better cause. Their true reason? *Order!* We cannot repeat too often that symmetry is not a principle of beauty, but a way of imposing regularity. As such, it appealed to a race of military men and administrators, but as compared to the disorder with which the buildings on the Acropolis are arranged, symmetry is a tedious business.

♦ *Outstanding Reservations about Roman Architecture*   Every serious critic feels some sense of reservation with respect to Roman architecture; and in addition to the matters already covered, it is important to mention certain further and broader implications of Roman practice—because, on the whole, most modern builders have approached their problems with the same attitude as the Romans. Some of the time-honored objections to Roman work are cogent; some will not bear analysis—but in the end, material for a negative critique exists.

Something is always said about the Roman habit of using the Greek orders decoratively, applying them as surface embellishment to buildings engineered on the principle of the arch. The column, so this argument goes, had been invented as a structural member. In the average Greek temple, it was not otherwise used; every column actually carried considerable compression from the weight above it. As applied decoratively by the Romans, the orders carry no load, or so little it doesn't matter. At this point in the usual statement of the argument, a tacit appeal is made to the supposed dignity of labor as contrasted with idleness, the latter by plain implication being an evil. The upshot is to assign the structural act a value higher than the decorative act.

Before the reader knows it, he finds himself entertaining the notion that diverting into decoration a member hitherto put to work is a form of prostitution. Without entering the difficult question of the respective influence of labor and idleness upon human character, it is possible for us to see that structure is not work in the human sense. Even more emphatically, it is plain that decoration bears no resemblance to idleness. Its artistic value is of the highest; those who insist upon disapproving of it must sternly turn their back upon the Elgin Marbles and all the statuary of Reims and Amiens. It may also be pointed out that the Greek column, while used structurally by the Greeks, is in effect a piece of abstract sculpture; as a mechanical device, it leaves much to be desired.

The real complaint against the Roman use of the orders has nothing to do with their alleged structural chastity or violation thereof. It has to do with the confusion of the Roman mind with respect to architecture and engineering. They evidently separated the two arts as we moderns have so often and so disastrously done. After the engineers left, the decorators arrived to conceal Roman concrete with a surface overlay (that is, a *veneer*) of marble and to apply the orders, statues, or whatever. The separation of the two arts naturally resulted in a failure to integrate structural parts and decorative parts, and it may be said that Roman work in this respect is inferior both to the Greek and to the best we have from the Middle Ages.

The point is strongly brought home by the contrast between the more elaborate examples of the triumphal arch and the several great aqueducts which still survive: the Claudian, that at Segovia in Spain, and the famous Pont du Gard near Nîmes (Fig. 7.4). Because the aqueducts were considered purely utilitarian, they were left altogether without decoration. But while decoration may enhance beauty, it never makes it. The unadorned structure must depend upon its fundamental shape and line. The Roman aqueducts are universally admired for their scale and for the powerful rhythmic swing of their great arches. It would appear, however, that these virtues were arrived at almost by chance. What did the Romans do to find handsome curves for the arches, to adjust proportions nicely, to arrive at a good surface texture? Let the reader compare the Pont du Gard with the nave arcade of Amiens (Fig. 11.13, page 374), with the arcades designed by Brunelleschi (Fig. 13.21, page 511), and with the Ponte Santa Trinità at Florence. The difference is hardly one of more or less decoration, but of greater sensitivity. As Roebling was to demonstrate so conclusively at the end of the 19th century, the elementary parts of an utterly plain bridge can have the highest elegance.

We have no right to complain, however, because the Roman builders failed to exploit the esthetic pattern existing in the interplay of structural forces in the fabric of a great building—a realization which forms an essential part of the Gothic genius. All classical art, Roman architecture included, was an art of form, and the genius of Roman engineers was devoted to the production of handsome shapes and pleasing surfaces. If well done, there can be no objection to architecture of that kind, but the false separation of structure from beauty seems often to have lured the Romans into shoddy applications of their own philosophy. Decoration is detestable unless very fine indeed, and the general run of Roman decoration is poor stuff. Roman moldings resolve themselves into dull circular arcs, as contrasted with the tense curves typical of good Greek work. Roman capitals are often poorly shaped and coarsely carved, with the Corinthian the predominant choice. Luxuriance and display are the result, rather than beauty, and it was not for nothing that Edgar Allan Poe wrote *glory* when he thought of Greece, and *grandeur* for Rome.

Chapter 8

INTRODUCTION: A STATEMENT OF COVERAGE

No period in European history is more confusing than the span of years that started with Rome's decline; and no part of that history is more confused than the history of art. We deal with the physical legacy of a world in flux. Military operations, large and small, succeeded and failed. Races corroded each other by contact, or merged imperceptibly. A major religious change was in progress; and other cultural and social changes succeeded each other rapidly, or existed side by side, leaving the historian baffled to know what was cause and what effect. Political and economic conditions were bad, as everyone knows; and that fact contributes heavily to the burdens of the art historian—for in bad times the artist is usually forced to confine himself to small enterprises. A small enterprise ordinarily means a portable work of art; and thus, a manuscript found today in the library of a castle in Carinthia may have originated at Reims or in Syria—and no one knows when, for meticulous accession records were unheard of before the 19th century.

No other period challenges the art historian as this one does; but the very difficulty of the problems, many of them permanently insoluble, has served to attract the vigorous interest of some of the best scholars in Europe and America. Their findings are still largely hypothetical, and depend upon archeological argument of the most abstruse kind. Insofar as such can be reduced to an over-all statement, the attempt will be made herewith; but at best, our chapter cannot be more orderly than the data it tries to set forth. Let us begin by making a statement of the coverage at which we shall aim.

In point of time, we begin at an indefinite moment: with the decline of Rome and the advent of Christianity. We terminate with the start of the Romanesque period, in round numbers about A.D. 1000; and we shall use

THE ART OF THE
EARLY MIDDLE AGES
IN WESTERN EUROPE

the term *Early Middle Ages* to denote the whole of this era and to make a distinction between this period and the *High Middle Age* (1000–1400) which produced the Romanesque and the Gothic styles.

Geographically, we have several areas to consider. The Roman world was artistically more or less of a unit until the 6th century A.D., the approximate time when the separation between Rome and Constantinople became artistically apparent with the maturing of the so-called *Byzantine style*. After the 6th century, we deal—in regions that were formerly classical—with Italy alone. We shall use the name *Early Christian* to denote the art of the entire Mediterranean world prior to the 6th century, and that of Italy until the year 1000.

We must then proceed to consider certain artistic movements widely separated from each other and connected to Italy only by the common tie of Christianity. First and most important is the art of the barbarian peoples who destroyed the Roman Empire. The *Barbarian*, or *Northern*, Style is the third of the fundamental styles recognized by C. R. Morey (see above, pages 24–27); and it flourished only where the Romans had never been: in Ireland and in Scandinavia. The art of the so-called "Carolingian Renaissance," the period of the empire established by Charles the Great, requires attention even though space prohibits any substantial consideration of its archeological problems. Finally, the pre-Norman monuments of England, obscure though they are, may not be omitted if the later art of England is to be understood. And last of all, there must be a word or two about the incomparable Bayeux Tapestry, the greatest secular monument of the earlier Middle Ages. For reasons already made plain, the reader must not expect a smooth or even a connected narrative, but he may look forward to making the acquaintance of some very great works of art.

THE END OF ANTIQUITY

Most of us learn in school that the Roman Empire ended in A.D. 476. That date is significant only in the barest legal sense. It was the year in which Romulus Augustulus, the last man holding a *pro forma* claim to the imperium by right of succession from the Caesars, resigned. He did so at the request of Odoacer, a Goth, who thereupon established a kingdom in Italy.

Things did not happen so suddenly. The event of 476 merely symbolized the reality of a disintegration that had long been in the making. The *Pax Romana* had lasted for about 200 years, or from the reign of Augustus to the end of the first generation of the 3rd century A.D. By that time, barbarian pressure (always a fact of Roman life) had ceased to be geographically remote. Actual invasions of Italy were in prospect, and began to take place on a substantial scale by the middle of the century. The state, in short, had proved unable to perform the first office of government; namely, the physical protection of its citizens.

Under such conditions, no arm of society has anything like the importance of the army. No individual compares in prestige with the man who controls the soldiers. It was only natural to find that the office of emperor became synonymous with military authority, and eventually one of its perquisites. It is conceivable, of course, that a great personality might have saved the situation by combining in himself soldierly skill, statesmanship, and a magnanimous philosophy. No such personality appeared at the time of the emergency; and there were, between 235 and 285, twenty-six so-called "soldier emperors," none of them able to hold office for long, and each of them gaining it in the first place by intrigue. It has been suggested that such a situation was inevitable because the Roman army had become almost entirely professional (that is, mercenary), and was largely recruited from border populations with no special loyalty to Italy. Other hypotheses have been put forward: as, for example, the suggestion that Christianity, with its emphasis on the spirit rather than the world, and on gentleness rather than power, proved corrosive to the imperial ideal of military dictatorship. Whatever the reason (and no one is satisfied that he knows it), this fact is evident: by the close of the 3rd century A.D., Roman civilization was in an advanced stage of decay.

Toward the end of the 3rd century, two leaders emerged who, however unsuccessful their efforts may have been, had sufficient courage and imagination to take steps of a nature as radical as the situation itself. In 286, the Emperor Diocletian relinquished the theory that central government could be maintained. He partitioned the Empire and divided the imperial authority with colleagues. He also built himself a palace (so-called, but actually a small town) at Spalato, or Split, on the Dalmatian coast. Its decorative details are among the most original from late antiquity; but the important thing to appreciate is that the design of the whole was governed by considerations of defense. High walls and salient towers surrounded the entire area. Diocletian's estimate of public order may be inferred.

In 330, Diocletian's successor, Constantine, made an even more pessimistic decision. He defaulted from the attempt to maintain physical control over the entire Roman territory, abandoned the western half of the empire, and moved his capital to the city of Byzantium, known afterwards as Constantinople, and now called Istanbul.

That expedient resulted in a political and cultural separation between East and West which has lasted over 1,600 years. It was successful from Constantine's point of view because it enabled him to retain the eastern empire intact. Popularly known as the Byzantine Empire, the government established by him in 330 endured until the Turkish conquest of 1453. Its history and art, largely separate from the western tradition, do not concern us here. We deal with them at length in Chapter 9 below.

Political events of the first magnitude, stated so briefly, seem as abstract as the planetary motions. Nor do we help ourselves greatly by remarking that "ruinous" taxation was required to keep up the military machine, with resulting disaster to "agriculture" and "commerce." Suicide, we hear, was on the increase, but the idea has a certain sanitary distance from our own sensibilities. It is necessary, indeed, to make a special effort to comprehend the devastation that took place.

In 410, the Visigoths under Alaric sacked Rome itself; and in 452, Attila the Hun came to the gates of Rome and then retired—traditionally because rebuked by Pope Leo the 1st, but probably because well paid. In 455, Gaiseric and his Vandals sacked the city; the wanton thoroughness of their destruction accounts for the stigma ever since attached to the word *vandal*.

These events were no more than significant instances in a general process. According to one estimate, the population of metropolitan Rome amounted to about 1,500,000 at the start of the 2nd century A.D. By about 400, the population was somewhere around 500,000, and after the events just described, not more than 5,000. On several occasions and for various short periods, it is believed, the entire population fled, leaving the Eternal City totally vacant.

A spiritual pall descended, it would seem; and the Campagna, that vast and fertile plain which surrounds Rome and originally gave it prosperity, remained almost uninhabited and little cultivated until the end of the 19th century. Even today, the city is less extensive than it was, and truck gardening goes on amid the ruins in areas once densely populated. It must be emphasized, moreover, that outrages decidedly did not cease with the 5th century.

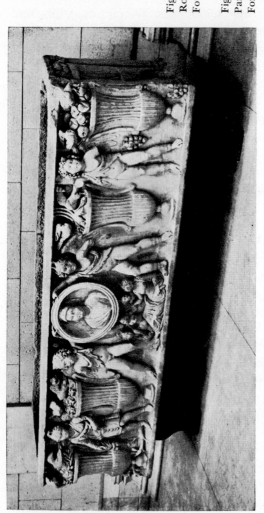

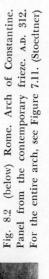

Fig. 8.1 (left) Buffalo, Albright Art Gallery. Roman sarcophagus with putti personifying the Four Seasons. About A.D. 200.

Fig. 8.2 (below) Rome. Arch of Constantine. Panel from the contemporary frieze. A.D. 312. For the entire arch, see Figure 7.11. (Stoedtner)

They continued throughout the earlier Middle Ages and later. Rome was sacked again by Totila the Ostrogoth in 546; and once again by the Saracens in 846—they by that time having made the Mediterranean into a Moslem lake.

While the colossal decay went inexorably on, what of the population? Unable to find a solution in fact, they sought surcease in games and celebrabrations, a condition commemorated by a class of ivory carvings known as the *consular diptychs* (Fig. 8.16), of which many are preserved from the end of the 5th century and later. Upon assuming the somewhat hollow title of consul, the politicians of this distressing period were accustomed to order a number of ivories, each with the donor's portrait, and hand them around as gifts to important friends. Almost invariably the newly appointed public figure was shown in the act of tossing out a money bag as the signal for the start of a horse race. As Karl Federn quotes a certain Roman of the time, "It is as though the Roman people had eaten the herbs of Sardinia and were forced to break out in a disease of laughter. *Moritur et ridet*—it laughs and dies!"

No chapter in history is better illustrated by art than the disastrous and fateful decline of the only world-order the genius of mankind has yet produced. It takes no technical knowledge to read the course of events in any series of dated monuments; one has only to look, and he sees antiquity fade before his eyes.

The most obvious sign of decadence is in technique. Signs of weakness were apparent at the end of the 2nd century; and by the middle of the 3rd, most monuments were conspicuously poor by comparison to earlier standards. Many were manifestly incompetent, but we must always remember that something produced at the very same moment by an artist more fortunately situated might, upon occasion, be excellently well done. The good work was sporadic, however; and the passage of time generally spelled out a further loss of skill. The trend is well illustrated by the following comparison.

A marble sarcophagus now in Buffalo (Fig. 8.1) is thought to have been produced in Italy about A.D. 200. Neglecting the portrait medallion which was done over in a later style, we see across the front four *putti* who, reading from the left, personify the seasons: Winter, Spring, Summer, and Autumn. The sculptor of these figures appears, on the whole, to have been as competent as contemporary portrait artists; but it is patent he knew his business none too well. His carving of fruit and flowers lacks the snap and life characteristic of Augustan ornament; and his handling of anatomy and drapery is somewhat less than knowledgeable. But a strange and haunting loveliness still emanates from the monument; one is reminded of the fragrance of a dying flower. In such tombs, as C. R. Morey once remarked, the latter-day Romans buried the last of Greek beauty along with themselves.

If we pass on to the beginning of the 4th century, it becomes impossible to maintain that the classical spirit was still alive. The Arch of Constantine (Fig. 7.11, page 196) was erected to commemorate his victory over Maxen-tius in A.D. 312. It is generously decorated with sculpture, and would appear at first glance to testify that good artists were still working at Rome. Scholarly inspection of the various reliefs has proved that the reverse was true. Almost all the sculpture was secondhand. The only work surely of Constantinian date is found in the two narrow friezes at a level just above the crowns of the smaller archways (Fig. 8.2). Of considerable interest to historians because they furnish us with an early instance of the impingement of Orientalism upon classical art (see below pages 215–227), there can be no question that the sculptor of these panels was grievously short on skill. The dumpy little figures are inarticulate, almost dead. Workmanship is perfunctory in general, and occasionally the work was scamped. Because an observer looking up from the ground level would find his view partially obscured by the molding below, the man neglected to carve feet on a great many of his figures. Other examples might be cited, but this one is enough evidence for the conclusion we must necessarily draw. Conditions were bad indeed if Constantine, with all the facilities of imperial authority at his command, felt compelled to borrow sculpture, and for new work could find no one better than the author of this mean and niggardly frieze.

More poignant than the decadence of technique is the course of the decline as we see it reflected in the faces of individual Romans whom we know through their portraits. Had we no other source on Roman history, its general outline might be surmised from this evidence alone. Until the end of the 2nd century, Roman portraiture depicts a vigorous and competent popu-lation. Vespasian, who ruled from A.D. 69 to 79, had the countenance of a man who might today be at the head of a great and prosperous industry—an appearance entirely consistent with his magnificent capacity and substantial success in the business of government. Marcus Aurelius (A.D. 161–180) had a face so confident that it was completely composed, as though pressure and hurry had been civilized out of existence—which is remarkable in view of the facts of his reign: earthquakes, pestilence, military campaigns of the most tedious and uninspiring kind. It is no wonder his *Meditations* betray a great weariness, and it is natural that Stoicism (a philosophy calculated to make patient endurance tolerable, as contrasted with the production of positive good) should have appealed to him with religious power. The important thing is to realize that (for the ostensible purposes of portraiture, at any rate) Marcus Aurelius felt able to maintain the theory that man still had within himself the capacity to rise above the confusion and mischance of environ-ment.

Fig. 8.3 Naples, National Museum. *Caracalla* (regnal dates: A.D. 211–217). (Alinari)

The downward trend commenced, perhaps, with Caracalla (regnal dates 211–217). That monarch, as we know him in the familiar bust portrait now in Naples (Fig. 8.3), seems almost the type of man who succeeds by expending energy faster than he can ever take it in. His face has power and intelligence, but his nervous pose betrays him. As the 3rd century went on, outright neurosis becomes evident even to the casual observer (Fig 8.4).

To illustrate the end of the appalling story, we have two imperial portraits, both of great size. One is the immense head of Constantine, already mentioned in another connection (Fig. 6.2, page 153). Its eight feet of height, and its grim exposure to the weather in the courtyard of the Conservatori, make it all the more devastating as a document of bad times—for the face is the face of a man who has seen a ghost.

In Barletta, a town on the Adriatic coast of southern Italy, there exists a baleful standing figure 14 feet high (Fig. 8.5). People say that it came from the wreck of a Venetian ship which met disaster there in 1204, presumably on the way home from Constantinople. After lying neglected on the shore for 250 years, it was set up in its present position with restorations to the legs and hands. Sometimes it is called a portrait of Valentinian the 1st (late 4th century), but the truth is that no one knows just who is represented. The

Fig. 8.4 (above) Rome, Capitoline Museum. Maximinus (regnal dates: A.D. 235–238). (Alinari) Fig. 8.5 (right) Barletta. An unidentified emperor. Early 5th century A.D.? Bronze. 14 feet high. (Anderson)

costume is that of a Roman general; and the exhausted eyes look out at us from features that show a certain strength of character, but betoken even more clearly coarseness and vulgarity—a devastating revelation of an insensitive personality broken by circumstances more brutal than itself.

Horrible as must have been the state of mind those who watched the end approaching, there is tragedy also in the popular viewpoint. The man in the street saw much to indicate that civilization was strong. Diocletian, the very monarch who provided himself with a personal fort, also dedicated a bathing establishment as big and as elaborate as Caracalla's. Maxentius, the man who competed with Constantine and lost, raised the great basilica (Fig. I.27, page 959) which his rival took over and renamed for himself just as he was about to abandon Rome to its fate. These are among the largest and most grandiose of Roman buildings, demanding for their construction the highest order of engineering and organization. Such things illustrate the paradoxical nature of human affairs. Like a floating ice cake in the spring, the Roman polity retained much of its outward form and some of its strength, but it was ready to melt away faster than seems possible.

EARLY CHRISTIAN ART

◆ *Christianity and Its Effect upon Classical Sculpture and Painting*
Amid the tragic decadence of late antiquity, Christianity gained momentum because it offered hope—making sense out of a world in confusion by stating that the world itself was temporary and possessed of significance only by reference to the higher reality of heaven.

Such a view of life was in substantial contrast to the imperial ideal. As a result, Christianity was unpopular with the Roman government—never more so, in fact, than during the reign of Marcus Aurelius. Noted as a humanitarian, this man is also remembered as a philosopher. It was therefore plain to him that the Christian allegiance to a God beyond and above the empire could not, either in theory or in practice, be reconciled with what he considered the political necessities. He therefore undertook to suppress the new religion by methods today considered inhuman. Few Roman emperors had the same grasp of philosophical implications, however; and for the most part, Christianity was tolerated if the Christians themselves eschewed any action calculated to attract attention or to acquire power for themselves.

By the end of the 3rd century, the new faith had become so important in the Roman polity that it was no longer feasible to restrict it. In the year 313, Constantine therefore promulgated the Edict of Milan, which removed the legal restraints hitherto curtailing Christian activity. Subsequently, he embraced the new faith himself, and it presently emerged as the official religion of the entire empire.

There is ample evidence to prove that Christian art was produced prior to the Edict of Milan. Certain paintings in the catacombs at Rome almost certainly were executed earlier than 313; but for all practical purposes, it may be assumed that any important or conspicuous monument of Christian art necessarily came later. It seems equally probable that the Edict of Milan was the signal for a prolific output of Christian art of all kinds. Much of this was probably the direct result of Constantine's personal interest. He himself caused many a church to be founded, of which few survive except in name.

The acceptance of Christianity had almost no immediate effect upon artistic style. Just as Christian authors wrote in the classical languages, the first Christian artists used the idiom of late classical art. The earliest depictions of Christ, to cite the most conspicuous subject of all, show him in the

Figs. 8.6–7 Rome, Lateran Museum. *Good Shepherd*. 3rd century A.D.? Marble. 37½ inches high. (Sansaini)

guise of a young and rather handsome Greek youth; and thus we see him in the justly famous statue of the *Good Shepherd* (Figs. 8.6–7) in the Lateran collection at Rome. This is very nearly a duplicate of numerous pagan statues of Hermes carrying a ram or some other sacrificial animal, the most famous being the *Calf-Bearer,* one of the Archaic monuments recovered from the Persian debris on the Acropolis at Athens. As contrasted with the Roman statues from which it derived, the Lateran *Good Shepherd* seems pathetically to aim at spiritual content far beyond the technical skill of its sculptor; there is perhaps no nobler example of meaning that seeks expression through crass material.

In similar fashion, and for subjects which required a setting, the Christian artists found it convenient to use the spatial formulas which had been popular during late antiquity; and thus the Alexandrian, the Latin, and the Neo-Attic kinds of setting were given a prolongation of usefulness.

The familiar *Christ as Good Shepherd* in the Mausoleum of Galla Placidia at Ravenna conforms to the Alexandrian arrangement; and the same may be said of the miniatures of the *Paris Psalter* and the *Joshua Roll* (Figs. 8.8–9). The two latter introduce us to the art of manuscript illumination, an enterprise peculiarly important during the earlier Middle Ages. In considering these manuscripts, or any to be cited later, the reader needs to keep certain general considerations in mind.

The Christian religion has its foundation in the written word; and the Church could not function without books. The arrival of a universal church called into being, therefore, a bookmaking industry which spread all over Christendom. Fortunately for the history of art, there was a demand not only for texts but for pictures to illustrate them.

Now, in the nature of the case, every Christian text (and every classical text, for that matter) was necessarily a copy; and the very desire for a copy involved the sense of authenticity. It was the duty of the scribe to copy the words set before him. By the same token, the artists felt compelled to copy the pictures faithfully.

But what was a scribe to do if the text was illegible, or included words and abbreviations he could not understand? Similarly, what if a picture had been damaged? And what if an artist lacked the skill to reproduce a set of illustrations? That situation occurred any number of times; and in such cases, the "copies" bear a tenuous and even bizarre relation to their originals. But whenever a skillful artist was put to work, a style which might be centuries out of date enjoyed a precise if momentary revival.

To some such circumstances, we must assign the complex pedigree of the miniatures just cited. *David Playing the Harp* might easily be mistaken for a pagan picture of the Alexandrian sort. Indeed, it may be said that the composition is amusingly innocent of anything necessarily Christian. The lady Melody, who sits beside David, does not figure in the Christian narrative; and neither does Echo, who pokes her head in at the upper right. The label "Bethlehem," moreover, is scarcely sufficient to certify the respectability of the lazy god who localizes the scene by the time-honored method of personification. Obviously, what we have is a reasonably competent copy of something much earlier. The best guess is that the copy itself was executed about A.D. 700, probably at Constantinople. As to the date of the archetype, the word "early" is as far as most scholars care to go.

Much the same thing goes for the illustrations in *The Joshua Roll*: it seems to be a 7th- or 8th-century copy after an early original; but in this instance, the original must have been very good, and the copyist considerably less than first class. The numerous pictures (the roll extends to about

Fig. 8.8 (left) Paris, Bibliothèque Nationale. Grec. 139. Folio 1 verso. *David Playing the Harp.* (Giraudon)

Fig. 8.9 (opposite) Rome, Vatican. Pal. Grec. 431–IV. *Joshua Roll.* Illustration for Joshua 5:13-15.

35 feet in length) seem slick and even elegant at first glance. A moderate amount of study tends to destroy that impression. Anatomical details are often incorrect or slurred. Spatial relationships, while perhaps recognizable as conforming to an Alexandrian model, are by no means easy to read and understand.

The best of the miniatures from the so-called "First Vatican Vergil" illustrate in similar fashion what could happen when a copyist, doubtless sincere but of no more than moderate ability, undertook to deal with an archetype in the Latin style. Figure 8.10 shows a typical example. The impressionistic handling of detail is unmistakable; and it seems plain that we are meant to understand that the space is deep, and the figures within it. The impressionism is not bold, however. It is merely vague; and the lack of definition fails to obscure the artist's limited command of anatomy. It will be noted, also, that the figures do not overlap each other; neither do they overlap the building and the trees in the background. By carefully isolating each separate object in this manner, the artist obviously was able to dodge the more subtle problems of "placing" things within the represented space. We can not know whether the same was true of the model he had before him; but it is scarcely harsh to infer that he lacked confidence in his own ability to control the tones, and thus to render spatial relationships by atmospheric perspective alone.

Once in a while, however, the task of copying a manuscript happened to fall into the hands of an artist who was himself a great master. Such was the case during the 9th century when some now vanished Book of Psalms, il-

lustrated with pictures in the Latin style, was sent for copying to a man greatly accomplished in the linear technique, which had come into European art with the barbarian invaders of the Roman world. The result was the *Utrecht Psalter* (Figs. 8.41–42), perhaps the greatest of medieval manuscripts, and one to which we shall return in another connection.

In so far as any sweeping generalization can be useful, it is fair to say that the main trend of Christian pictorial art was away from both the Latin style and the Alexandrian. Both, we may surmise, were excessively specific with regard to time and place, and neither lent itself conveniently to the other-worldliness which is the essence of the Christian narrative. The Greek pedimental setting, usually called Neo-Attic, offered precisely that quality. With its blank and neutral background, it provided a setting localized nowhere on earth, and thus rather easily construed as heavenly. It is the business of the section below to deal with the further evolution of the Neo-Attic formula.

♦ *The Influence of Oriental Art upon the Classical Style: Flattening and Loss of Plasticity* The evolution just referred to was gradual, and the resulting change of style substantial. The whole process reflected the fact that Christianity was a religion that came from the Near East. It not only started there, but flourished there to an extent unknown in the West until much later.

A church building at Edessa in northern Syria was referred to as "old"

Fig. 8.10 Rome, Vatican. Lat. 3225. Folio 7 verso. The "First Vatican Vergil." An illustration for the *Fourth Georgic*, verses 125 ff. Apparently showing the old gardener from Corycus giving instruction to his servants. Probably 4th century A.D.

in the year 202. One at Arbela in Mesopotamia is said to have been built in 123. Of the church polities still surviving, the oldest of all is the Armenian. It will be recalled that the Epistles of Paul were addressed to Christian communities in the Near East. The most splendid churches of the early centuries stand in parts of Syria which today are inaccessible. They were abandoned as a result of the Arab conquest of the 7th century; but even in ruins, they are architecturally superior to any pre-Romanesque church in Italy or Western Europe.

The importance of the Near East is still further emphasized by the choice Constantine made: unable to keep all, he chose the more valuable half of his empire and moved his government eastward. It must still further be remembered that Christianity was not the only Eastern religion in vogue during late antiquity; the Olympian gods were competing also with Mithras, with Atys and Cybele, and with Osiris. As religions, the others suffer by comparison with Christianity and were destined to drop out of sight; but at the time, all channels were effective in converting the Roman mind to Eastern culture. The general absorption of Eastern points of view had its effect upon art, and, as time went on, made an end to classical art.

It is difficult to imagine two styles more different than the Greek and the Oriental. A crossbreed between the two was and is irrational, but that is precisely what happened. We can review the evolution by considering a series of monuments which, if not dated exactly, are dated well enough to fall into

Fig. 8.11 Constantinople, Ottoman Museum. Sarcophagus from Sidamara. About A.D. 150.

sequence. The general effect, as we shall see, was to "flatten" classical art until, ultimately, its plastic character was destroyed and all but forgotten. The end product was the *Byzantine style,* which arrived at its permanent peculiarities about the middle of the 6th century A.D.

Let us start with the *Sarcophagus from Sidamara* (Figs. 8.11–12). It was found at the place of that name in western Asia Minor; and because of its great weight, may be presumed to have been made there. At first glance, one might assume it to be something from the Greek Fourth Century, and the mistake would be a natural one. The figures, considered individually, are not unlike those of Praxiteles and Lysippus. They are worked in the full round, and it should specially be noted that they bend gracefully toward us and away— the pose thus being used to emphasize the existence of the third dimension and the spatial displacement required for the statute. Better on the whole than most of the Roman copies which so greatly influence our visualization of Greek work, the actual date of these figures is probably about A.D. 150; and they constitute a vivid demonstration of the extraordinary power of Greek art to survive in places where survival was favored by tradition and circumstance.

The setting is also reminiscent of the Greek. The statues stand on a shallow platform. The background is immediately behind them. It is embellished with architectural detail, but it shares with the Greek pediment the

Fig. 8.12 Constantinople, Ottoman Museum. Detail from the Sarcophagus from Sidamara.

quality of being solid and impenetrable. Every suggestion of motion is necessarily to the right or left, and never to any significant extent in or out.

The Oriental influence which hardly affected the figure-style of the Sidamara statues made itself more than manifest in the architectural detail. A comparison with any typical piece of Greek or Roman ornament will show that a change had taken place. Greek and Roman detail tends to be plastic, but the Sidamara designer was working toward expression on a flat surface. Every smallest item of floral ornament tends to be brought forward into the same plane as all the others, and every detail is silhouetted sharply by deep undercutting of its edges. Such work takes the light very differently from its classical counterpart. Graded shadows are almost absent, and the total effect resolves itself into a pattern of bright whites sharply juxtaposed to black darks. A rhythmic alternation of light and dark results, and it is the rhythm which attracts and hold one's attention. Shapes, outlines, and other visual facts which, under other circumstances, might exert an appeal tend here to be overlooked altogether.

Architectural detail of the sort just described constitutes the closest approach that can be made in marble, and with sculptor's tools, to the color rhythms so characteristic of Oriental textiles. In good examples, the effect is rich and excellent, something new under the sun. It was destined to become extremely popular in Early Christian, Byzantine, and Moslem decoration.

Fig. 8.13 Berlin, Staatliche Museum. Detail from the Frieze from Mschatta. (Marburg)

Because of their ability to annoy, the desert tribes who lived in the Arabian desert east of the district of Moab, which itself is the land east of the Dead Sea, were able to extract subsidies and other concessions from the Romans, the Persians, and everyone else who ever wished to live quietly in Syria proper. Where the grazing was good, the leaders of these tribes were accustomed to spend a great part of the year at the edge of the desert; and when they became wealthy from the sources just cited, some of them built elaborate stone palaces there. Mschatta was such a palace, and its ruins are still in view. One feature of the palace was a gorgeous enclosing wall about fifteen feet high decorated with a lacelike frieze of ornament. Parts of the frieze are now in Berlin, and our Figure 8.13 illustrates a detail thereof but fails to demonstrate the strong rhythm established by repeats in chevron-pattern of the great V's, and fails also to bring out in proper emphasis the large rosettes which also recur as strong accents.

It would be hard to name a monument which more perfectly demonstrates the merging of classical and Oriental taste during the period when antiquity was on the wane and the Middle Ages were beginning. There is enough plasticity in the moldings, and even in the representative forms, to make us remember Greece, and yet the subject matter itself and the dominant glitter of black and white are plainly from the Near East. The date has never been settled. Some authorities want to put it earlier, but most are noncommittal and set limits at the 4th and 7th centuries A.D.

With respect to architectural ornament, the result of the Orientalizing process may be illustrated by the decorative carving of capitals and other surfaces in Hagia Sophia (Fig. 9.4, page 280). As seen there, classical forms amount to a faint memory. Insofar as possible, the carving had achieved the condition of surface decoration on the flat, with two dimensions only. When we have arrived at this point in the evolution, we have the mature Byzantine style before us.

We return now to the flattening process as applied to the human figure —which, as stated, was more resistant than ornament to the Oriental influence. Among preserved monuments, the one which illustrates the next step after the figures on the Sidamara sarcophagus is a splendid ivory of the Archangel Michael, now in the British Museum (Fig. 8.14). Its extraordinary size (about 16 inches high) would make it notable in any case, but the great dignity of the figure lends truth to the often repeated comment that no other ivory carving compares with this—it is rare that we may call small things noble. Probably executed somewhere in the Christian East, probably in some region where Greek art remained unusually vital, and probably not later than the 4th century of our era, it gives a first impression of roundness and plasticity. Closer inspection reveals that the expression takes place only in part through the manipulation of contours. The pose approaches the frontal, with both legs brought almost into the same plane as the torso. Only the head retains any vigorous suggestion of roundness, and it will be noted that the feet hang down over the steps as though the sculptor no longer cared about foreshortening and even less about giving expression to the mechanical action of carrying weight. The format is a typical instance of the Neo-Attic, and it has been suggested that the archway with steps derives from the proscenium of the Roman theater which had similar doorways for the entrance of actors onto the stage.

In Berlin, there is a fragment from a fine sarcophagus of the Sidamara type, also probably of about A.D. 400, with an interesting figure of Christ, represented, as usual in early monuments, without the beard (Fig. 8.15). The statue is carved very nearly in the round, but in no sense was the sculptor sympathetic to statues in the round. The figure faces square front; and, as compared to the *Angel* of the British Museum, a peculiar importance has been given to what we may call its front face, or façade. The operative carving of both anatomy and drapery is confined to a near-plane surface roughly parallel to the background. We feel no impulse to investigate how the figure

Fig. 8.14 London, British Museum. *The Archangel Michael.* Ivory. 4th century A.D. About 16 inches high.

might appear from one side or the other; it is perfectly certain there is nothing interesting around the corner. All of this is antithetical to the nature of true classical art, and the effect arrived at here is approximately what we might expect to see were a Greek statue compressed from behind against a sheet of plate glass.

The next and very nearly the last step in the evolution toward flatness is to be seen in the consular diptychs (Fig. 8.16), a class of ivory carving already cited in another connection. Some of the earlier diptychs have truly plastic qualities, but those that date after 500 impart little sense of contour— an effect, it must be pointed out, that has nothing to do with the fact that the relief is low. Even the lowest relief can be skillfully manipulated to excite the tactile sense, but at this point in the history of art, the desire to do so was absent. It is characteristic of the consular diptychs to show feet that collapse downward like the flappers of a duck. Even the floor beneath the feet was often tipped upward for its better functioning as an item of flat pattern. The Roman toga, moreover, had by this generation given way to vestments heavy with Oriental embroidery, vestments that were necessarily stiff and flat, thus contributing to the general impression.

Fig. 8.15 (opposite) Berlin, Staatliche Museum. Fragment of a sarcophagus from Sulu Monastir in Constantinople, showing Christ with two Apostles. About A.D. 400.

Fig. 8.16 (right) Paris, Bibliothèque Nationale. Diptych of the Consul Anastasius. A.D. 517.

In point of date, the consular diptychs have brought us into the 6th century. Well along the road toward the Byzantine style, they nevertheless lack some of its essential features. More had to happen before that style emerged in its own name and right. It is reasonably clear that the critical changes took place at Constantinople during the first half of the 6th century, but it is difficult and perhaps impossible to trace the development in detail. An immense destruction of art took place all over the Byzantine Empire during the period of Iconoclasm (726–843; see page 283). A number of frescoes and mosaics are still obscured by Turkish whitewash. Because almost nothing remains at the capital, we are forced to depend upon examples in the provinces. Supposedly, such examples are inferior to those that once existed at Constantinople.

Insofar as we may safely describe what happened, the following narrative, inferential though it is, probably does not distort history much.

Both the Alexandrian formula and its derivative, the Latin style, passed virtually out of use except for occasional copies in manuscript illustration. In view of the instinct of the Oriental artist to seek expression on the flat surface, spatial representation of any kind had a very doubtful chance for survival in the art of a society increasingly Near Eastern in its culture and

Fig. 8.17 Ravenna, San Vitale. *Emperor Justinian and His Courtiers*. Mosaic. About A.D. 547. (Anderson)

outlook. But since Christian narrative demanded human actors, an altogether abstract art was out of the question. The Neo-Attic formula was the only thing in sight which offered an acceptable compromise. Its indefinite settings were especially attractive, we may assume, to a population given over to a mystic and nonmaterial religion, and it is noteworthy that most Byzantine artists tried to make the setting more abstract than ever before. The architectural backgrounds common in earlier works executed according to the Neo-Attic scheme were generally discontinued in favor of blank areas of gold. Even the ground line at the bottom of a scene was commonly omitted, probably with deliberate intent to deny or forget the physical truth of gravitation. To these statements a few exceptions must necessarily be made. Certain subjects—the Nativity, for example—would be unintelligible without a few stage properties. Although such were of course included in the pictures, their number was reduced to a minimum; and the rendering was brought so close to line and flat tone as to deny the observer any significant suggestion of spatial displacement beyond and behind the plane of the picture-surface.

Fig. 8.18   Ravenna, San Vitale. Detail from *Justinian and His Courtiers*. (Alinari)

The process just described produced works of art like the mosaic picture of *Justinian and His Courtiers* in the choir of San Vitale at Ravenna (Figs. 8.17–18). The church was dedicated in 547. Presumably the mosaic dates from about the same time. It is one of a pair, the other showing Theodora and her ladies. For all practical purposes, we may remember these pictures as the first major-scale monuments which illustrate Byzantine art in the sense of a new style centering at Constantinople and radiating into Italy and Sicily.

As a derivative from the Neo-Attic formula (and ultimately from the Greek pedimental compositions) the general format of the picture has already been sufficiently discussed: we look up at a single row of figures silhouetted against a blank ground of gold.

Changes in the figure style and rendering now need to be described. Let us begin with the distortion of the human figure. Because important political personages were represented—people who wished to be recognized by name whenever anyone looked at the picture—the heads remain in normal proportion, except for a considerable enlargement of the eyes (Fig. 8.18). Legs and torso, however, have been elongated, and the effect of their abnormal length has been enhanced by the repetition of verticals in the drapery. By actual measurement, the average Byzantine head comes out at one-ninth, one-tenth, or an even smaller fraction of the total height; it is often impossible to be definite, because, as here, we commonly lack a firm ground line to take as a base. It seems likely that the vertical distortion had to do with ideas of dignity; it is merely an exaggeration of the erect posture considered appropriate on ceremonial occasions. If our memories of classical art and our modern habits of thought make it difficult to accept the distortion, we must sharply remind ourselves that we are dealing with the Middle Ages and with the work of men who had no such reverence for the body as we do. As a matter of fact, the extra length of the Byzantine figure is moderate by comparison to the slenderness of the ladies who appear in fashion magazines.

The emperor and his men are clad in rich vestments which stretch from neck to ankle and totally conceal the mechanism of the body. These clothes are so stiff and heavy that only one pose is possible: the static figure standing erect. Movement, if attempted at all, must be very slight indeed. As a vehicle for artistic communication the human body—that essential of all classical art —was necessarily made almost useless; and it is important to appreciate that Byzantine artists rarely relied upon the body to carry any substantial part of their content.

Instead, they relied on the broad flat areas of color made possible by applying the Near Eastern temperament to what once had been the undulating folds of Greek drapery. The robes seen here are modeled, to be sure, in light, half light, and dark, but that old and familiar sequence of tones is no longer gradual. Instead, the eye is confronted by abrupt shifts (white, gray, black) which amount almost to stripes. The representative function of the stripes is easy enough to understand in the present example; in many later Byzantine pictures, drapery is in fact reduced to a completely flat pattern.

We may sum up by saying that the Byzantine style is a hybrid. Its Greek heritage remained in the form of human actors in a narrative and in the formula according to which the picture was composed. But so far as such a thing was physically possible, Greek art had been converted into Oriental pattern: Justinian and his companions tells as a near-approach to color accents on the flat surface, arranged in a simple rhythm.

The virtues of the new style may at first escape the reader. Its aim was hieratic solemnity, an atmosphere perhaps uncongenial to the modern American. It is nevertheless a pictorial record of a very considerable area in our history. From the 6th century to the 15th, Constantinople was the center of the Western world. Its court and its church presented a spectacle of opulence almost impossible to imagine. Contemporary descriptions of its stately ceremonies seem to be hyperbole, but are probably factual. No city in history has left a more resplendent memory.

We must also remember the placement for which such mosaic pictures were designed and the circumstances under which people looked at them. As a relief from the generous sunlight, most churches in the Mediterranean area have small windows. Some are dark enough to make candles appropriate at noon. In dim light, the reflective quality of mosaic makes it the best of all media. Mosaic pictures have the power to carry with undiminished clarity over distances impossible for paintings in any other medium.

With the arrival of the Byzantine style we have something new, and an art capable of effects which, if no better than those possible in either of the styles from which it had derived, were certainly different. The long and further history of this style concerns us no more in the present chapter; we shall summarize it in Chapter 9. Enough has been said, however, to inform the reader about the evolution that was going on during the Early Christian centuries, and to prepare him for monuments in any stage of transition.

♦ *Early Christian Asceticism and the Negation of Classical Beauty* An idealized and excellent anatomy had since the Greek Fifth Century retained its standing as an artistic desideratum. Beauty of that particular kind had a value, it would seem, as self-evident as one of Euclid's luminous axioms. It continued to have the same value in certain parts of the Empire. These regions are geographically vague, but are presumed to be localities in the Greek area more or less insulated from the general course of change, thus permitting the Greek formulas for physical loveliness to survive as Elizabethan English survives in the mountain communities of Tennessee and Kentucky. The British Museum's ivory carving of the *Archangel Michael* (Fig. 8.14) may be presumed to have come from some such place.

But in other places, and probably most, physical beauty in general, and the Greek formula for it in particular, got themselves into bad company. It was inevitable, perhaps, that Greek art would be associated with paganism in much the same way that the Rococo was associated with the decapitated French aristocracy in 1789 and later. It was natural that there would be a tendency to discard and dislike any art tending to remind people of distasteful things.

There was, however, a more positive reason for the negation of Greek beauty. It was more common in the earlier centuries than it is now to translate into extreme action those aspects of the Christian theory which have to do with a contempt for the world, for material things, and for the flesh. Chrisianity is in part a religion of renunciation, and one way to renounce the world was to become a hermit. Hermitage of one sort or another was common enough in the early centuries to be described as popular. It was often indulged in with spectacular austerity. Saint Simeon Stylites, who died about 460 after spending 35 years on top of a tall column, was no isolated example of religious athleticism. He had many colleagues. The modern reader must thoroughly understand that such men were not considered eccentric. They were considered holy, and their holiness received tribute in the most tangible and expensive fashion. One of the noblest Syrian ruins is the monastery of Saint Simeon Stylites at Kalat Seman, about halfway between Antioch and Aleppo. An octagonal enclosure was erected around the base of his column, and four large churches stretched out from that octagon like the arms of a Greek cross.

People who treat their bodies as Saint Simeon treated his rarely conform in their appearance to the norm of Greek statuary, but Simeon and others like him constituted the closest possible approach to the Christian ideal. It is no wonder, therefore, that people began to read spiritual significance into the ravagement characteristic of their bodies. Some such feelings must account for the advent of what amounts to a cult of emaciation. A good instance would be the male figures (Fig. 8.19) across the front of the elaborate ivory cathedra (bishop's throne) traditionally, but probably not correctly, known as the *Throne of Maximianus*. The throne has been at Ravenna from a very early date, and doubtless originated somewhere in the Christian East before the end of the 5th century.

♦ *The Subject Matter of Early Christian Art* In handling the Christian themes, the early artists used two different methods: allegory and symbol, and historical narrative represented in the usual way. The use of symbolism suggests secrecy, but it is hard to know what the motive for secrecy may have been. We must not be too ready to accept the usual suggestion that the Christians communicated with each other in cryptic ways because they dared not be open during the three centuries when their religion existed under the ban of the law. The Roman police were entirely too competent to have been fooled by so simple a ruse. As a criterion for date, symbolism in itself indicates little; we cannot say there were no historical subjects before A.D. 313; and there were innumerable symbolic subjects later than that.

A good example of allegory is the subject of the sheep. Whenever we see a sheep in Early Christian art, we must depend upon the context to tell us whether we are to read it as a symbol for Christ himself, or one of the Christians. "Behold the Lamb of God," said John the Baptist (John 1:29), and the word has ever since been a synonym for Jesus. But there are also a great many passages in the Bible which refer to members of the Christian community as sheep (Matthew 15:24; John 10:1–27 and 21:15–1).

Fig. 8.19 Ravenna, Palace of the Archbishop. Detail from the so-called *Throne of Maximianus*, showing four Apostles. Ivory panels on a wooden frame. About A.D. 500. (Anderson)

If Christians are sheep, Christ is their shepherd—as so beautifully set forth in the 23rd Psalm and in the *Good Shepherd* statue of the Lateran (Figs. 8.6–7). The name *Good Shepherd* must be of very early origin; at any rate, Walter Lowrie (*Monuments of the Early Church*, page 218) found it in an early prayer for the dead: "Let us pray God that the deceased carried on the shoulders of the Good Shepherd, may enjoy the fellowship of the Saints." The prayer comes from the Sacramentary associated with Saint Gelasius, who was Pope from 492 to 496.

The prime case of outright symbolism is furnished by the frequent appearance of a fish more or less realistically depicted. If juxtaposed to loaves of bread, the fish may merely refer to the miracle of the loaves and fishes; and by extension, that event may be construed as a prefigurement in cryptic form of the Last Supper. More often, however, the fish appears all alone. If so, we are to read *Christ*. The association depends upon an acrostic pun. The Greek word for fish is ἰχθύς (ICHTHUS); and the five letters of ἰχθύς may be arranged as the initials of an expression as follows:

Ἰησοῦς	Χρίστος	Θέου	ὑιος	Σώτηρ
Jesus	Christ	of God	the Son	Savior

Fig. 8.20 Ravenna, Sant'Apollinare in Classe. Sarcophagus of the Archbishop Theodore. 5th century A.D. (Alinari)

The vine was another popular symbol for Christ, being derived from the expression "I am the vine and you are the branches" (John 15:5). If associated directly with wine-making, as it is in some of the mosaics of Santa Costanza at Rome, a reference to the Last Supper may be assumed. Very frequently several symbolic subjects appear together in a single composition. That is true of the well-known *Sarcophagus of the Archbishop Theodore,* preserved at Ravenna, where we find the vine and the grapes intimately juxtaposed to a medallion and two peacocks (Fig. 8.20).

The peacocks symbolize immortality. Apparently they had carried some such connotation even in pagan art. The association seems to have been threefold. In the first place, the peacock was confused with the phoenix bird, which was reborn every 500 years after consuming itself in a bonfire. Secondly, the periodic renewal of the peacock's splendid feathers came to be associated with the idea of resurrection; but even more convincing than these notions was the belief, shared by so great an authority as Saint Augustine himself, that the flesh of this bird would never putrefy no matter how long it might be kept.

The medallions which occur on the main face of the Sarcophagus of Theodore and three times on the cover are the medallions of Jesus Christ. The Greek letters X (chi) and P (rho) for the *Chr* of *Christos* are combined with the intial and terminal letters of the Greek alphabet, the A (alpha) and W (omega) of Revelations 1:8, "I am Alpha and Omega, the beginning and the ending, saith the Lord. . . ." The circular shield upon which the letters are inscribed may be a mere carry-over from the art of coinage. Or it may reflect the religious confusion of Constantine, who is said to have confounded Christianity in some way with the worship of the sun. It is also likely that the monogram was thought of as a sign of triumph; for that reason it was rarely used after the Gothic invasions of Italy during the 5th century.

The monogram of Christ seems to have been construed as a near-symbol for the cross, to which it bears a far-fetched resemblance. However that may

Fig. 8.21   Rome. Santa Sabina. "The Crucifixion." Panel from the cypress doors. A.D. 432 or shortly after. (Anderson)

be, it is notable that the earliest Christian art contains no reference to the Crucifixion, for the very good reason for Christ's death on the cross was highly disadvantageous to the missionary effort of the new religion. In late antiquity, crucifixion was the punishment meted out to criminals of a loathsome and contemptible kind, who were thus put to death slowly and in a manner dreadful enough to reduce the fortitude of the most stoical victim, leaving him at the last an example of complete degradation.

It took generations to bring about a reversal in the significance of the Crucifixion; and we may make a shrewd guess that it required Constantine's famous vision of the Cross in the Sky to give the symbol any honor with the Roman world at large. He used the cross, mostly in monogram form, on coins and on military standards. The earliest extant instance of its appearance, in its modern symbolic meaning, in a work of major art is the cross which rises grandly against the background sky in the mosaic picture filling the apse of Santa Pudenziana (Fig. 8.28), an important monument to which we shall return presently.

At about the same time, it seems that actual pictures of the Crucifixion became common—representations, that is to say, describing the event itself in some detail. One of the earliest of these (Fig. 8.21) is on a panel of the cypress doors of Santa Sabina in Rome, a church dedicated in 432. Here we see the three crucified figures against the background of a city wall, apparently to tell us the execution took place outside Jerusalem. The rendering is curious, because the position of the figures is not at all as we are accustomed to seeing it. They do not hang suspended from the arms, but stand with the arms held sidewise.

Their attitude corresponds with the position then customary for prayer. In Early Christian art, a figure standing erect and praying is technically known as an *orant,* or *orans.* The imagery derives from the classical posture for prayer, which was still in use during the early centuries. In Homer, men "lift up their hands and pray aloud" (*Iliad* III.275), and they were so shown by pagan artists—for example, the *Praying Boy* of the Lateran. But in Mark 14:35, we are told that Jesus went forward a little, and *fell on the ground* to pray. His action resembled the etiquette of a subject abasing himself before an Eastern potentate. It is interesting that modern custom follows the latter form; and the shift in manners is merely another illustration of the way in which Oriental taste was gradually superseding the classical.

But it is one thing to suggest a derivation for the orant, and another to tell its precise meaning as understood by the Early Christians. It seems likely that several significations were current, none of them necessarily excluding the others.

The simplest explanation is that the orant represents the soul of the deceased who, having arrived in the realm of blessedness, prays for his loved ones left on earth. By playing up the connotations of this spirit-portrait, it is possible to contend that the orant might upon occasion mean much more. Prayer postulates *faith,* a virtue upon which Christianity hinges. In the absence of any other specific symbol for faith, the orant may have that meaning. And since faith, when construed generically, is the amalgam giving unity to the Church, we often find ourselves referring almost interchangeably to "the Faith" and "the Church." By the same token, the orant may stand for "the Church." On some of the catacomb ceilings, this is very probably the true interpretation, because the orant appears there in complete separation from the idea of individual portraiture and often in compositional relationship to the Good Shepherd. The likelihood of this meaning is enhanced by the fact that such orants are female, a custom in grammatical agreement with *ecclesia,* a feminine noun.

For an example of narrative subject matter, we may turn to the well-known *Jonah Sarcophagus,* now in the Lateran Museum, and so-called not from its occupant but from the subject that takes up most of the space (Fig. 8.22). We see Jonah thrown overboard into the mouth of the whale, spewed up on shore, and finally taking his ease under a tree. Other scenes are there

Fig. 8.22   Rome, Lateran Museum. Jonah Sarcophagus. (Anderson)

also: the raising of Lazarus, Moses striking water from the rock, and a jack-in-the-box who stands for Noah in his ark. It will be noted that a single train of thought is dominant in the choice of these subjects. Each one amounts to an instance in which the faithful escaped destruction through the direct and physical intervention of God himself. In Early Christian days, preoccupation with deliverance was not confined to art; it is reflected also in many early prayers, a parallel noted by several scholars. One prayer quoted by Walter Lowrie (*Monuments of the Early Church,* pages 198–199) is sometimes still used to commend the soul to God in the hour of death. It reads:

> Receive, O Lord, thy servant into the place of salvation which he may hope of thy mercy. Deliver, O Lord, thy servant from the pains of Hell. . . . Deliver, O Lord, his soul as thou didst deliver Enoch and Elijah from the common death of the world. Deliver, O Lord, his soul as thou didst deliver Noah from the deluge. Deliver, O Lord, his soul as thou didst deliver Isaac from sacrifice at the hand of his father Abraham.

And in this and other prayers, we find much the same formula repeated to cite the precedents established by the delivery of Daniel from the lions, the three children from the fiery furnace, Abraham from Ur of the Chaldees, Job from his sufferings, Moses from Pharaoh, Susanna from false accusation, David from Saul and from Goliath, Peter and Paul from prison, Thecla from torture, and Jonah from the belly of the whale.

The intent behind such a prayer is pathetically clear. Helpless in the disaster of Roman disintegration, these people could not, in any worldly terms, imagine a solution for their troubles. God alone might help them. Indeed the hope of His help was the only hope available, and the citation of precedent the only reassurance.

Such, then, were the themes of Early Christian sculpture and painting. It is remarkable how, at this remote date, we can feel their meaning. As communicators of content, no artists have ever been more successful—a fact that emerges with ever greater clarity as we pursue the history of religious art from century to century. Some of the best technicians in the world, working under conditions infinitely more propitious to success, have aimed at the sublime and have arrived at bombast. But in these early monuments, often badly executed, where do we find a real failure?

♦ *The Early Christian Basilica*   The great architectural achievement of the Early Christian period was the invention of the *basilican church*.

This set the type for all subsequent church architecture. A great many changes of style have since taken place, but their effect upon design has been restricted to construction and surface appearance. With the exception of odd and experimental buildings, the standard Christian church has retained the plan, the orientation, the parts, and the arrangement of parts much as they were first established in the basilicas built in the days of Constantine.

Basilican churches existed at one time all over the Roman world. Fragmentary ruins may be seen to this day as far afield as England and Armenia. For basilicas still in good repair, the modern student must turn to Rome and Ravenna; in these two cities, numerous very early churches are in daily use.

But most of those are unfortunately not in anything like their original condition. Renaissance and baroque additions in the form of altars, ceilings, and murals mar the interiors. Out of doors, pretentious portals, if not entire façades, belie the character of the buildings. It is not so much that these later embellishments are gorgeous; the disharmony has to do with a gross incongruence of style. Appreciating that fact, the authorities at Ravenna have been conducting, within the last few years, a scholarly campaign of restoration, removing many of the additions and revealing once again the directness and simplicity which distinguish Early Christian architecture at its best. The High Renaissance and the Baroque have their own virtues, but not these.

No one knows why the early Christian churches are called *basilicas*. The same word was familiar, of course, in Latin usage, where it meant a courthouse. A similar mystery surrounds the derivation of the building. Transitional and experimental monuments are usually at hand to explain the evolution of a new and original type, but not in the case of the basilican church. The ruins of some pagan basilicas (notably the Basilica Julia in the Roman Forum) demonstrate a certain analogy to the basilican churches. But the parallel features are features that do not count. The things that make the Christian basilicas worthwhile seem absent from the Roman ruins.

No other great architects ever worked under handicaps comparable with those which impeded the Early Christian builders. The modern reader can only marvel at the momentum of a civilization which enabled them, in such a situation, to construct not only numerous churches but some of the largest and noblest ever built.

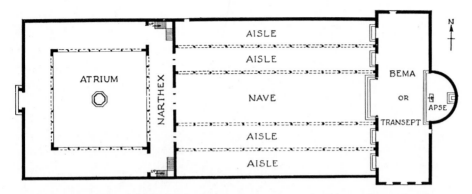

Fig. 8.23 Plan of a typical Early Christian basilica. Smaller churches usually had only three aisles instead of the five shown here. The salient bema is shown because it was the architectural ancestor of the fully developed transept. In Early Christian times, most of the smaller churches had no bema. Note that north is at the top of the drawing.

One aspect of the decline of Rome must be listed, however, as a substantial asset to Early Christian architecture. The subsidence of paganism proved more than a spiritual blessing. Pagan temples were on the market, and fine building materials could be had secondhand and ready-made. Almost every range of columns built into an Early Christian church once decorated some heathen shrine, now dismantled. Indeed, cases exist where columns, lintels, and other parts must have originated at several different Roman temples— and we find them all put together in more or less informal fashion to make one Christian church.

It is hard to know what the Early Christian builders might have done had this classical material not been at hand. Inevitably, Roman columns and capitals (usually tending to err on the side of display) seem incongruous and flamboyant in buildings distinguished chiefly by virtues of a more transcendental kind. The reader must attempt to discount this mischance of history.

As seen in ground plan (Fig. 8.23) the Early Christian basilica has the general shape of an oblong. By convention, the long axis is oriented east and west. The altar is placed at the eastern end, and the entrance doors and façade at the west end. Local conditions occasionally make the usual orientation undesirable (as at St. Peter's itself), but in speaking of any church it is common to say "west end" when we mean the entrance front, and "east end" when we mean the rear of the building, regardless of what the actual directions may be.

Proceeding from west to east, and using the bird's-eye view of the church (Fig. 8.24) as a supplement to the ground plan, we find that the structure is divided into the following parts:

An open courtyard (called the *atrium*) precedes the church building, or

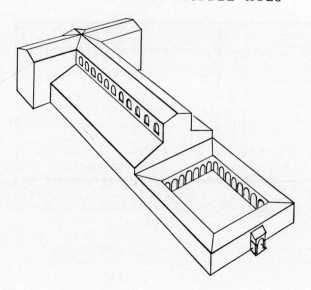

Fig. 8.24 Schematic drawing of an Early Christian basilica.
(Drawing by Henry Tisdall)

basilica proper. This is surrounded by an arcaded walk. The effect is similar to that of the cloister, so familiar in the later Middle Ages, and the Early Christian atrium is undoubtedly the architectural ancestor of the cloister. Most extant basilicas have lost their atria—an unfortunate deletion, especially in a teeming city like Rome, for the atrium provided a most desirable transition from the activity of the street to the quiet of the church. The baptismal font was usually placed in the middle of the atrium. There is some reason to believe that noncommunicants were excluded from the church itself, but were permitted to enter the atrium. However that may be, it is certainly plain that the designers conceived the building as becoming progressively more sanctified from west to east.

At the east end of the atrium is the *narthex*. The arrangement of the narthex differs in different buildings. For our purposes, it is enough to say that the narthex is the vestibule of the church, and usually consists of an aisle or corridor running in the north-and-south direction.

The main body of the church—and here the reader should use the perspective cross-section (Fig. 8.25) in conjunction with the other drawings—is divided into *aisles*. In the example shown, there are five aisles; but smaller churches ordinarily had only three. In either case, the middle aisle, known as the *nave*, is substantially the widest. The division of the plan into nave and side aisles became an almost inflexible convention of church design. The Early Christian decision to use this particular arrangement was one of the crucial decisions in the history of architecture.

In a large church, side aisles make it possible to have a number of chapels, each with its own altar. The chapels are extremely useful for the smaller and more intimate services: weddings, baptisms, funerals, and others attended by a gathering that would be utterly lost in the vast space of the nave—and for whom it is nevertheless a comfort to participate in the associations which cluster around an old and famous building. It is entirely practical to hold several such services simultaneously in different chapels.

The modern reader, accustomed to a great variety of specialized buildings, needs to be reminded that churches did not exist during the Middle Ages for the performance of services only. The buildings were in constant use for various community purposes, and even served as shelters for pilgrims. The separation of nave and aisles had obvious advantages in such a situation.

Returning to the plan, we find that nave and aisles open, at their eastern end, into a *transept*. In effect, the transept is still another aisle, running north and south, and extending outward from the east-to-west walls of the building. In height, the transept often rises, as it did at Old St. Peter's, to the full elevation of the nave, and maintains that level for its entire length. As a result, it becomes a conspicuous feature of the exterior, as seen in the bird's-eye view. The word *transept* is often used in the plural (*transepts*) if the context suggests it. If small and inconspicuous, as it often is, the transept is occasionally referred to as a *bema*. Occasionally, it was omitted altogether.

At the extreme eastern end of the basilica, and centered on its long axis, is the *apse*. This is a recess, semicircular in plan, and usually covered with a semi-dome. The high altar was ordinarily placed just in front of it, and the bishop, in cathedral churches, had his cathedra centered against the eastern wall of the apse.

Turning now with greater particularity to the vertical cross section of the basilica (Fig. 8.25) we find that the roofing is divided into three parts, each of which may be considered as a unit.

Over the columns of the nave arcade, vertical walls are built. These rise to a considerable height, and are topped off by a gabled roof.

Each side aisle is covered by a roof of the lean-to type. At their highest, these aisle roofs reach a level that is considerably higher than the top of the nave arcade and considerably lower than the spring of the gabled roof over the nave.

The vertical wall rising over the nave arcade is thus subdivided into two parts. These are (1) the *triforium area,* extending from the top of the nave arcade to the level at which the aisle roof abuts the side of the building; and (2) the *clearstory* (sometimes spelled *clerestory*), which rises from this point to the spring of the gabled roof over the nave.

Almost every clearstory in history, and the device is as old as Egypt, has been pierced by windows. Excellent lighting results. So much light is ad-

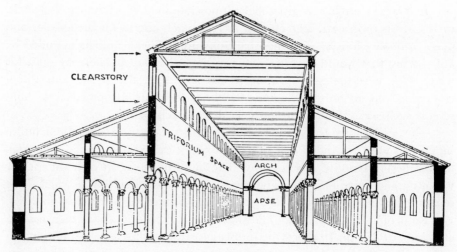

Fig. 8.25 Perspective cross section of an Early Christian basilica, with component parts labeled. (Drawing by Dorothy Shea)

mitted, in fact, that clear glass is undesirable. Stained glass was the natural answer; and various other expedients, all tending to reduce the glare, have been used.

The division of the plan into nave and side aisles had obvious advantages for the operation of the church, as we have seen, and clearstory lighting was indeed a great merit for a building so arranged. Unhappily, the clearstory came at a price.

A designer who wants to use that feature is confronted with structural difficulties of the most serious kind. How is he to support the roof? If he chooses to carry it on a set of wooden trusses, he will have a strong, light roof; but he will also have one that invites both rot and fire. The second choice, and the only other choice available in Early Christian times, was to build some kind of vault. But how is one to provide abutment for a vault springing from a very great height?

From that second choice, the Early Christian builders were foreclosed by economic conditions; but the Church has always, and properly, taken a long-term view. The Church wanted buildings which would survive not for generations but for centuries; and as a result, architects wrestled for more than seven hundred years before, by Gothic methods, they were able to produce at reasonable cost a fireproof building with clearstory lighting and the traditional basilican floor plan.

Such are the physical features of the Early Christian basilica. It would be a mistake to round off the discussion at this point, leaving the reader with the impression that those early monuments are of interest only for historical and sentimental reasons, and represent, as works of art, the mere best that might be expected under bad conditions. The reverse is true. No excuse is needed. Properly interpreted, the Early Christian basilica is a radical advance over any previous building. It symbolizes, in fact, the advent of a broader concept of architecture. For sheer originality, it is unexcelled.

In the design of the basilica, the Early Christian architect focused his attention upon the interior. In this, he continued what had become almost standard practice among the Romans. But in his treatment of the interior the Early Christian designer worked toward new ends. These are (a) progression and focus, and (b) an architecture conceived in terms of voids rather than solids. It is possible, even though delicate argument is involved, to read into each of these ideas a peculiarly Christian meaning.

The idea of progression and focus is best appreciated as one enters the church from the west end and faces the altar. The effect of progression derives from the sequence of the columns. One sees a column beyond a column beyond a column. Ultimately, the eye arrives at the altar. There is no impulse to think of the columns as individual objects; one does not count them. The thing comprehended is the process of moving step by step toward a destination.

The effect of focus is a function of the architectural horizontals. It is most easily explained by reference to a drawing or photograph, but operates as plainly in the actual building. If in a photograph of any basilican interior, a straight edge is placed along any horizontal (for example, the line formed by the bases of the nave colonnade, or the line formed where the clearstory meets the ceiling), it will be found that these lines intersect at a vanishing point which is very close to the position of the altar.

These two arrangements acting in unison make it almost impossible for one to avoid a concentration of attention toward the east end of the church in general and the altar in particular. The effect of such concentration, naturally, is to suggest that the east end of the church symbolizes a goal, result, or condition of peculiar sanctity, toward which it behooves one to move. No earlier architecture provided so meaningful an interior.

It is interesting to see that the pictorial decoration of the church was arranged in general consistency with this idea. The available monuments show considerable variety, making it difficult to suggest that any fixed scheme of arrangement was ever arrived at in Early Christian times. It nevertheless appears that the subject matter ordinarily chosen for the triforium and clearstory was historical and that the subject matter chosen for the apse was transcendental. For the *arch* (that is, the wall space between the walls and ceiling of the nave, and the actual arch of the apse-opening), it seems to have been customary to choose scenes midway between the two—historical and yet divine. Thus, in Santa Maria Maggiore at Rome, we find the available wall

Fig. 8.26 Ravenna, Sant'Apollinare Nuovo. Diagonal view from aisle, showing mosaics in the triforium. About A.D. 510-56. (Alinari)

spaces of the nave decorated with mosaic pictures depicting events in the careers of Abraham, Jacob, Moses, and Joshua.

Even better known, perhaps, are the nave mosaics of Sant' Apollinare Nuovo at Ravenna (Fig. 8.26). There are three series of pictures, each at a different level: (*a*) at the very top, above the clearstory windows, there are scenes from the life and passion of Our Lord; (*b*) between the windows there appear single male figures, probably representing prophets and apostles; (*c*) below these, on the walls of the triforium proper, there are two long processions of crown-bearing martyrs. The female martyrs are represented as proceeding from the town of Classis toward an enthroned Madonna and Child. The male martyrs proceed from Ravenna toward an enthroned figure of Christ.

A good example of an elaborately decorated arch is that of Santa Maria Maggiore at Rome. Unfortunately, the pictures do not show up at all well in the best available photographs, but a list of the subjects will perhaps suffice to illustrate our point.

Across the crown of the arch is the Throne of the Apocalypse; to either side of it are Peter and Paul and the symbols of the Evangelists (see below, page 241); below it, is the signature of Pope Sixtus the 3rd, who had to do with a remodeling of the basilica about the middle of the 5th century.

On the left side of the arch, reading downward, we may see *The Annunciation,* including an angel who reassures Joseph with respect to the miraculous pregnancy of Mary; *The Adoration of the Magi; The Massacre of the Innocents;* and *Jerusalem.*

On the right hand side of the arch, also reading down, there are *The Presentation of Christ in the Temple;* a scene sometimes identified as Christ disputing with the doctors, and again as the arrival of the Holy Family at the court of King Aphrodisius of Egypt—whose idols fell down when they approach; *The Magi before Herod;* and *Bethlehem.*

Most of the material, it will be observed, involves the operation of divine

Fig. 8.27 Ravenna. Sant'Apollinare in Classe. Mosaics of the apse and arch. On the arch: Christ with the Signs of the Evangelists, and the twelve Apostles in the guise of lambs. In the apse: the Transfiguration on Mount Tabor (above) and Saint Apollinaris in paradise (below). Second quarter of the 6th century. (Anderson)

forces in events which are historical in the sense that they happened on earth, thus fulfilling the stipulation that the arch suggests a transition from worldly to heavenly things.

The arch of Sant'Apollinare in Classe (Fig. 8.27) is far less pretentious. In the lower register, around the extrados of the apse, are the twelve apostles symbolized as sheep. Above, we see a bust portrait of Christ; and to either side of him, four strange creatures rise in half length from the clouds. These are the symbols of the Evangelists, destined to have a long history in the art of Europe. They also appear in the apse of Santa Pudenziana at Rome (Fig. 8.28), and we must do our best to explain them without further delay— merely noting, as we pass on, that by symbolic means, this arch also conforms to the general principle of subject matter from the lifetime of Jesus.

The man stands for Matthew, the lion for Mark, the ox for Luke, and the eagle for John. It is not at all certain how or why these monsters came to be associated with the Evangelists, but the symbolism is generally thought to derive from Ezekiel's vision as set forth in his first chapter. In their present meaning, the symbols appear to date from Jerome's commentary on Ezekiel (end of the 4th century), but other interpretations were current in the early days.

The story usually told to account for the individual assignment of the symbols is this one: The man goes to Matthew because he dwells on the human generation of Jesus Christ, and sets considerable store upon the fact of his incarnation. The lion goes to Mark for several reasons. The lion is the king of beasts, and Mark is held to stress the royal dignity of Christ. Baby lions, according to a myth, were born dead. After three days, they came to life when the sire roared—a procedure construed as an allegory for the Resurrection, of which Mark is the principal historian. Mark's Gospel, moreover, begins with "the voice of one crying in the wilderness" and ends with "he that believeth not shall be damned." Roaring and cursing, it was said, tend to be habitual with the lion. Luke has the ox because he dwelt upon the priesthood and sacrifice of the Savior, the ox having for centuries been the typical sacrificial animal. The eagle belongs to John, we are told, because his imagination soared upward like the vertical flight of the eagle to arrive at an actual contemplation of the divinity of Christ.

For the apse, it was apparently considered appropriate to select a scene that demanded a setting beyond and above the time and circumstance that curtail all earthly activity. It is probable that some such intention dominated the thought of the now unknown architect of the noblest apse of all, that of Santa Pudenziana (Fig. 8.28). Various suggestions have been put forward with regard to the date, ranging from the 2nd to the 8th century, and the question remains vexed. The majority opinion would put the picture at about A.D. 400.

The theme is probably that of Christ and the Apostolic College, but there has been considerable argument over the identification of the setting and over the reason for the presence in the picture of two ladies.

If we are correct in believing that a heavenly setting was usually wanted for the apse mosaic of a basilican church, we would be required to read this as the Heavenly City. In that case, the two ladies conveniently become the *Ecclesia ex Circumcisione* and the *Ecclesia ex Gentibus,* an interpretation suggested by the identity of the male figures over whose heads they hold wreaths. Peter, who was conceived as head of the Jewish element in the church, is always depicted as wearing a square-cut white beard. Paul, the Apostle of the Gentiles, is always a lanky, bald-headed man with a long, pointed brown beard. The uniformity of the iconography makes it likely that this is how the men actually looked in life.

A much less lofty but no less imaginative idea of the matter denies all holy content whatever. The setting, we are told, is Rome, and the district the part

Fig. 8.28 Rome. Santa Pudenziana. Mosaic in the apse. Christ enthroned with the twelve Apostles. About A.D. 400. (Anderson)

of Rome where Pudens, the donor of the church, lived. The persons represented become, in this interpretation, nothing but Pudens and his family engaged in the ceremony of foundation; and the two ladies are his daughters Praxed and Pudenziana.

A third suggestion, spiritually midway between the other two, says that the city is Jerusalem. Thus the mound on which the cross is set becomes Golgotha. The small domed building to left of center becomes the Holy Sepulcher, and the immediate foreground would be the atrium of the Constantinian basilica of the same name where, on Good Fridays, the bishop was accustomed to set his throne before a cross, reading passages from the Gospel while surrounded by his presbyters. Unfortunately, the buildings needed to make this identification positive have long since vanished; they went, so far as we know, during the Arab invasion of the 7th century.

Various other things about the picture are notable. As pointed out above, this is probably the first monument of major importance where the cross appears in its modern connotation as a symbol for sacrifice and glory. If we are correct in calling the central figure Christ, we have also the earliest instance of the now-familiar Syrian and bearded Jesus of modern imagery. In addition, we must remember this mosaic when the time comes to study the great ceremonial pictures of the High Renaissance (Chapter 15). Lacking the historical perspective which we of today so conveniently acquire, the men of the 15th and 16th centuries often made the mistake of thinking that the Early Christian basilicas were classical temples converted to Christian use, or at least were "Roman churches." Mosaics like the one now under discussion were therefore construed as examples of classical art, and played a formative role in the great effort of that period to make the world over again on ancient models.

So many associations seldom cluster around a single work of art; and it is a tragedy that the apse of Santa Pudenziana has been badly handled in the course of history. There is reason to believe it was modified somewhat during the 8th century. We know it was cut down at the sides in the 16th century, and at the bottom during the baroque era. Finally, in 1831–1832, considerable restoration took place on the right-hand side. The monument is nevertheless archeologically reliable for conclusions of the sort mentioned above.

The apse mosaic of Sant'Apollinare in Classe (Fig. 8.27) lacks the same grandeur, but is infinitely more quaint and charming. Two subjects merge together in the picture, and an explanation is required before it can be understood.

At the crown of the arch, the hand of the Almighty is seen to issue from the clouds. The central and upper field beneath is filled by a jeweled cross enclosed in a circular glory studded with stars. A small bust portrait of Christ is at the center of the cross. To either side, half-length male figures rise from the clouds.

The lower part of the picture seems to be the ground beneath the very same sky in which the cross is seen. It is a garden setting, and a bearded saint stands in the center foreground, his arms uplifted in the position of the orant. A dozen sheep stand on the same level as the saint, and there are three more sheep in the middle distance. These latter seem to be giving their attention to the cross in the sky.

The probable explanation of this obscure composition is as follows:

The upper section is to be understood as a symbolic rendering of the Transfiguration on Mount Tabor (Matthew 17; Mark 9; Luke 9). We are to read the cross as *Christ,* an interpretation driven home by the juxtaposition of the cross to the words ΙΧΘΥΣ and *Salus Mundi,* and to the letters Alpha and Omega. The half-length male figures to either side are Moses and Elijah, who came into view upon that occasion. The three lambs immediately below stand for Peter, James, and John, the witnesses to the event.

It is doubtful whether the lower part of the picture has any narrative content whatever. The saint is labeled as Apollinaris himself. The twelve lambs are the apostles. The setting is probably paradise—the word being construed in its original Greco-Persian sense: a park, or a garden.

The total effect of the two-part composition comes closer to unity, in the emotional sense, than one might at first suppose. The Transfiguration amounts to an occasion when persons resident on earth were given, in physical fact, a glimpse of heaven; while in the lower scene, we find heaven actually represented. It was visualized, apparently, as a permanent state of salubrious climate where Apollinaris, the apostle of Ravenna, enjoys an appropriate reward.

The date of the mosaic is fixed with fair assurance in the second quarter of the 6th century, and the style is a good instance of a halfway station between classical and Byzantine art. The author was of two minds. He still loved the bucolic charm of the outdoor setting as it was habitually made to appear in Hellenistic and Roman painting. On the other hand, he felt impelled toward the consideration of objects for their value as flat areas of color, adaptable to rhythmic arrangements like those seen in Oriental textiles. Unable to do one thing or the other, he handled the figures of Moses and Elijah in plastic fashion, and he preserved to a moderate degree the conventions of spatial relationship: it is at least clear that we are supposed to understand that the lower edge of the picture is nearer than the upper edge, but it is notable that there is no overlapping of silhouettes, every object standing clear from every other. Each item, moreover, is taken in broadest aspect and laid flat, as it were, against a comparatively blank and neutral ground.

The meaning of *an architecture conceived in terms of voids rather than solids* can best be comprehended if one takes up a station in the outer aisle of any large basilica, and looks diagonally across the building (Fig. 8.29). From this point of view, the basilica confronts us with an arch beyond an arch beyond an arch. The area of the openings is greater out of all proportion than the area of the solids. The thing that counts is the existence of the openings. The columns and arches signify only because they outline the openings, defining them, as it were, for our visual apprehension. In such architecture, any comment is almost necessarily directed to the character of the opening, and rarely to the solid members performing the act of enframement.

The psychological effect of the basilican interior is, as a result of the preponderance of voids, almost opposite to the effect produced by a Roman interior like that of the Pantheon, where, as set forth above (pages 196–197), the solids mean much and the voids little.

Openings have a certain suggestive power. It is possible in physical fact to walk through an opening. This possibility is noted and felt even though

Fig. 8.29 Rome. San Paolo fuori le Mura. Founded A.D. 386. Rebuilt during the 19th century. Diagonal view across the nave. (Alinari)

we have no immediate intention of doing it. The result may be described as a *sense of exit,* or of potential exit. Roman interiors, and the innumerable modern interiors deriving more or less directly from Rome, achieve their unity and completeness by denying the sense of exit. They exist, as it were, each as a small universe unto itself.

In a building like the basilica, however, there is unity of an entirely different kind. The sense of exit is unintelligible unless we understand that there is somewhere for us to go, which is the same thing as saying that the universe is not contained by the building in which one happens to be. Thus, as we look through the nearest archway, we see another beyond it, and another still beyond that—until, whether it happens to be in view or not, we are bound to arrive at an opening which will reveal the world. There is, in a word, a chain of suggestion connecting the interior to the outdoors. The train of thought thus set into motion is likely to lead one on toward consideration of the world as a whole, and finally of the infinite. The artistic "unity" of the Early Christian church results, in short, from its integration with all else. This is in radical contrast to the unity of classical buildings, which, excellent though they are, depend for artistic oneness upon separation from all else.

Our interpretation of the basilican church is one that invites direct association with Christianity. Such an association makes of the church building an analogue for the world as conceived by the Christian.

A casual inspection of either the world or the basilica is likely to result in a sense of confusion. Details make sense only when construed as steps in a progress that leads to where we would be. Motivation is lacking unless one focuses his attention and directs his movement toward an ideal—of which the altar is the visible and earthly symbol.

The unity of the immediate and particular with the general and infinite has always been a central concept in Christian teaching, which in this respect appears to go somewhat beyond Plato in asserting not only that the fact and the principle are connected, but that the two are one. The basilican designers, in their use of openings, appear to have acted in correspondence with that idea.

Such suggestions are derived from a reading of the buildings themselves. Documentary proof is lacking. In its absence, it is possible to construe the intentions of the designers differently. It is difficult to believe, however, that those men were not conversant with the implications of Christian thought, or that they did not desire to design buildings which (within the inevitable limitations of the architectural medium) would correspond to Christian ideas. More than one modern architect has, by his own say-so, been motivated by considerations equally abstract and perhaps less worthy, and we probably take no liberty in assuming that the earliest Christian churches were meant to have meaning as well as utility.

The exterior appearance of the basilica—as illustrated by the few examples we are lucky enough to have on view today—was nondescript (Fig. 8.30). This fact has long been a puzzle to critics. In the absence of definitive evidence, several interpretations are equally attractive.

There may be symbolic meaning in the radical contrast between the glowing interior and the ascetically chaste exterior view. Is this an architectural parallel for the character of the ideal Christian? Have we here a cryptic but eloquent statement that what counts is inner and spiritual beauty, and that alone? Such an explanation is anything but farfetched, and it has satisfied some very learned scholars.

Another contention, based upon the subsequent history of architecture and upon compositional facts, must also be entertained. The nondescript character of the basilican exterior results to some extent from the absence of decorative detail, but it could not be corrected by supplying that lack. The buildings look like great sheds because the shape of the building-mass is that of a shed. The ridgepole of the nave roof lies gaunt against the sky. Its axial

Fig. 8.30 Ravenna. Sant'Apollinare in Classe. View from the east. The tower is later, probably from the 8th century. Note that there is no bema. (Alinari)

power has the same force out of doors as inside, but it does not make the same sense: there is no altar to which the eye is guided. Similarly, on purely compositional grounds, it may be said that the length of the church has no rational beginning, middle, or end.

It is entirely possible that the Early Christian builders, either through necessity or by a conscious rejection of classical formalism, adopted a theory of architecture almost identical to 20th-century functionalism. They surely focused their attention almost exclusively upon the interior arrangements which, in a purely functional sense, remain unexcelled for the performance of Christian services. They conceived the walls and roof to be no more than an envelope enclosing the desired facilities, and let them assume whatever shape they might.

If so, the parallel to modern times is enlightening, especially in view of what happened in the centuries to follow. It seems obvious that people were dissatisfied with the basilican exterior, and that neither the symbolic argument nor the functional argument sufficed to explain away the evidence of the eyes. Byzantine architecture is, among other things, an attempt to combine the basilican nave and aisles with a good external composition. Similarly, the many towers of the Romanesque and Gothic, integrated by a great variety

Fig. 8.31 Cross section and plan of a typical Early Christian church of the central type. (Drawing by Dorothy Shea)

of stratagems with the basilican mass, were hardly undertaken merely to ring bells.

Imperfect though it is, the Early Christian basilica is nevertheless a mighty landmark in the cultural history of Europe. No other type of building has had anything like the same influence upon the history of architecture. No other building advanced, with reference to its immediate past, further ahead into realms as yet unexplored by the architect. And yet no architects ever received less from the economy and polity within which they found themselves. Thus, in terms of absolute achievement, it is difficult indeed to cite a parallel.

♦ *The Central Church*   The Early Christians did possess a type of building not subject to the particular criticism just leveled against the basilica. This is the *central type* (Fig. 8.31), a term deriving from the symmetry of the structure to its central vertical axis. Such buildings were sometimes built with a Greek Cross (arms of equal length) for the ground plan, like the Mausoleum of Galla Placidia at Ravenna. More commonly, however, they were either circular or octagonal, as respectively illustrated by Santa Costanza at Rome and San Vitale at Ravenna.

In all central buildings, the symmetrical emphasis upon the vertical axis produces a powerful focus upon a point in the middle of the floor. Appropriate for a tomb or baptistery (where font or sarcophagus, as the case may be, can be put at that precise point), such a focus is ill adapted to the great majority of Christian ceremonies. In a word, the interior of a central church is impractical.

But the clearstory of a central building, whether covered by a dome or not, rises like a squat tower in the middle of the mass. It gives unity to the exterior design much as the hub of a wheel provides a point of common reference for the spokes and rim. The exterior composition of a central church is omnifacial, and looks equally well from any point of view. Such buildings are naturally better landmarks than the basilicas, with more artistic interest and dignity. Nevertheless, the fundamental fault just cited foreclosed the central type from any great popularity. It was used for a few rather small, rather specialized buildings.

THE BARBARIANS AND THEIR ART

♦ *The Sources of the Barbarian Style*   For the early history of the barbarians, we have nothing like the comparatively systematic sources that enable us to make a reasonably connected narrative of Greek and Roman history. Thus the origin of the Barbarian Style in art is a matter for debate and falls within the province of the anthropologist rather than the historian. Insofar as a definite statement can be made, the evidence seems to permit the following.

At the time when the Romans penetrated into the regions north and west of Italy, those areas were populated by tribes who had come from somewhere else, presumably from an easterly direction, and for reasons at present unknown. The general tendency to migrate from east to west continued well into the classical period, a notable instance thereof being the Gallic pressure upon Pergamum during the 3rd century B.C.—which resulted, as we have seen in the erection by Attalus the 1st of a commemorative monument to which the *Dying Gaul* (Fig. 6.1, page 154) belonged. It is surprising how little the Gaul resembles typical members of the modern Latin races, and how very like he is to many an Irishman or Scandinavian.

In their effort to trace the Barbarian Style in art, scholars tend to reason in this way: A conspicuous feature of all art that is barbarian or derives therefrom is the frequent and habitual use of animal subject matter, usually grotesque and more often than not demonstrating a fondness for the invention of plausible but highly imaginary monsters. Now animals had been very common in the art of ancient Mesopotamia, and the Persian empire had, in due course, fallen heir to the artistic tradition originally centered in the region of the Tigris and Euphrates. From Persia, the same tradition was transmitted to the region north and east of the Black Sea. It seems to have been brought there by some people called the Scyths, and the whole region, indefinite in area, has ever since been referred to as Scythia. Whether the Scyths were wandering barbarians who merely came in contact with Persia or were

Fig. 8.32 Oxford, Ashmolean Museum. Greco-Persian gem. 5th century B.C.

related to the Persians, no one cares to state in any arbitrary fashion. There is merely a tradition that they had been there and left, presumably because driven out, and probably about the 7th century B.C. As so many other barbarian nations did, the Scythians gradually lost their ethnic identity; at the start of the Christian era, their name no longer meant anything. But the art they once practiced had spread far to the west and far to the east as well.

The narrative as given above appears to be corroborated by the history of language, and the monumental evidence for it is a great collection of small objects found in barbarian burials. There is an unmistakable resemblance between objects found at widely separated points. Two examples may be cited, merely as an illustration of the method.

A Greek gem now in the Ashmolean Museum at Oxford (Fig. 8.32) shows the figure of a prancing hybrid monster best described as a lion-griffin. He belongs to the genealogy of the fantastic five-legged beasts that once frowned down from either side of certain Mesopotamian gateways (compare Fig. 2.14, page 25), but the workmanship is probably Greek. The object belongs to a class of gem known as the Greco-Persian, and it is supposed that such things were made by Greek artists resident in Persia, or made in Greece for export to markets in Persia.

A belt buckle found in Siberia also has a lion-griffin on it (Fig. 8.33). The beast is not a duplicate of the other, but the resemblance is so close that a connection must be assumed. The object belongs to a recognizable category of Siberian finds, of which it is an unusually definitive example. As compared

Fig. 8.33 Leningrad, Hermitage Museum. Gold belt buckle found in Siberia. About 5¼ inches long. (From G. Borovka, *Scythian Art*, London, Bouverie House, 1928.)

with the beast on the gem at Oxford, this one illustrates even more convincingly the survival of the cult of savagery which formed so notable an aspect of ancient Mesopotamian art.

Some very important stylistic innovations are also to be noted. The Siberian buckles reflect a self-conscious cultivation of the asymmetrical: most of them are substantially higher and heavier on one side than the other. There is no suggestion of a governing enframement; the animals themselves form the silhouette, which is irregular and complicated. In handling the bodies of beasts, the author of this design, whoever he may have been, was like all other barbarian artists in caring nothing whatever for anatomical fact. He twisted and contorted things in a strange way, as though driven by an inward force to seek an elusive pattern that remained forever beyond him. At this stage, the animals retain much plastic quality; but if their bodies were elongated, made thin, and abstracted into a linear interlace, this very subject might appear in one of the Irish manuscripts (compare Figs. 8.34, 35, 36).

If we knew more about the objects found in Siberian burials, the genealogy just set forth would be more dependable, or would be corrected, as the case might be. But almost nothing is certainly known about that class of material beyond the fact that its style must derive from Scythia and its date must fall within the period covered by the present chapter. We may rest the matter by saying that such art was widely dispersed in northern and western Europe by the time the Roman empire began to expand into those regions. It was temporarily submerged wherever the Roman role was imposed, but it remained latent in the population as an artistic instinct nevertheless—ultimately to spring to life once more at the start of the Gothic period. Only two parts of Europe escaped the Roman and classical culture: Ireland and Scandinavia. In both of those regions, the Barbarian Style flourished in the period between the fall of Rome and the start of the Romanesque.

♦ *Irish Art* (Early 5th century to about A.D. 900)   In 431, Saint Patrick, then at Auxerre, was consecrated bishop and at once set forth for Ireland. His success as a missionary was phenomenal; and within the space of a generation, Ireland was a Christian land. His career set into motion a cultural development which stands out like a light in the general rudeness of the Early Middle Ages. It was from Ireland that missionaries went forth to Scotland, to Northumbria, to France, and even into Italy itself. Indeed, it is scarcely an exaggeration to say that for a brief period Irish Christianity bade fair to wrest the primacy from Rome.

The church in Ireland was largely monastic. Its principal art was the illuminated manuscript. With respect to art, its development came to full flower about A.D. 650, and maintained a high level during the 8th century.

Disaster then struck. The Vikings came. Their first recorded raid was in 795. A veritable tempest of destruction ensued, destruction so unbelievably thorough that in most places where monasteries once stood, there is literally nothing left to see. By 880, or thereabouts, Ireland was ruined as an artistically important center.

The very few manuscripts we are lucky enough to possess stand, however, as paridigms of the Barbarian Style.

♦ *Essential Features of the Barbarian Style*   The dominating characteristic of the Barbarian Style is the fact that it is dynamic. Because dynamism can take many forms, it is hard to find one or two examples which sum up in themselves all the important qualities of barbarian art. There can be no more typical monuments, however than the "Cross Page" from the *Book of Lindesfarne* (Fig. 8.34) and the "Monogram Page" from the *Book of Kells* (Fig. 8.35). The two manuscripts take their names from the monasteries with which they were once associated. Lindesfarne was an Irish foundation in Northumbria. Kells is in County Meath, about forty miles northwest of Dublin.

The observer's first impression of either is one of complexity, and he is right. Unlike classical art which finds expression through compositions involving only a few large parts, the northern and barbarian instinct was to use a myriad of tiny details. The sense of infinite number is never absent from our feeling about its monuments.

Because humanity lacks the power to comprehend infinite number in any

Fig. 8.34 London, British Museum. *Book of Lindesfarne.* Folio 26 verso. "Cross Page." First quarter of the 8th century.

sudden or rapid fashion, it is impossible for barbarian work to take effect upon the sensibilities except with the passage of time. Comprehension is gained by repeated acts of partial inspection, each added to each, until we begin to assimilate what we see. Complete familiarity, even with the single composition, arrives only after a series of separate visual experiences until in the end we possess ourselves of the whole.

Northern art follows a procedure of visual communication fundamentally different from the classical. Classical compositions, as we have seen (pages 65–67), tend for the most part to have their effect as a single, instantaneous vision of the whole. We therefore found it convenient to name the classical system *the instantaneous,* or *simultaneous, mode of presentation.* We shall

Fig. 8.35 Dublin, Trinity College. *Book of Kells*. Folio 34 recto. "Monogram Page." Shortly after A.D. 800.

Fig. 8.36 Line drawing after an animal in the *Book of Lindesfarne*. Irish. Early 8th century A.D. (From Françoise Henry, *Irish Art*, London, Methuen, 2nd ed., 1947.)

refer to the northern method—in which time and memory play so large a part—as *the cumulative mode of presentation.*

The force of what has just been said is much enhanced by the northern habit of defining every detail, however minute, with a precision so intense as to be passionate. The component parts of any full page of Irish illumination are as the sands of the sea. It is nevertheless self-evident that every minute element received in its turn the fierce focus of the master's complete concentration—which lives forever in the surpassing clarity of every line and boundary. We often hear it suggested that too much attention to detail is dangerous; it may militate against unity of the whole—and in other artistic styles, details may legitimately be suppressed or slurred over for that very purpose. Northern art neither sought nor wanted unity of that particular kind, as we shall see when we get further on.

Imaginary monsters were the only subject matter natural to barbarian art; nothing else was ever represented except through necessity or under outside influence—the human anatomy and plant forms were specially foreign to the instinct of the style. Even the monsters were abstracted in an extreme degree (Fig. 8.36); otherwise they are not typical.

The nature of the abstraction is plain enough from our illustrations: regardless of what he started with, the northern artist invariably reduced it to pure line. Pure line was his chief esthetic reliance, and so far as possible the only system of expression he used. The line served him in two ways.)

The "Cross Page" of the *Book of Lindesfarne* (Fig. 8.34) shows us the first of the two. Whenever the barbarian artist wanted to fill up a space, he resorted to patterns of linear interlace. Confronted for the first time with an example, one is likely to dismiss it as nothing but another braid, but that is an error. Frequently, the interlacing conforms to a geometric system or something like it; but just as we make up our minds that we understand the rhythm of over-and-under, the line will suddenly take a twist or curve that

Fig. 8.37 The letter *Chi* from the Monogram Page of the *Book of Kells.* (Tracing by Stephen Dwornik)

could not possibly have been predicted by all the logic of what has gone before. In small matters, we may describe the habit as capricious; in important affairs, the qualities indicated are invention and a certain fundamental flexibility and adaptability of which both classical and Near Eastern art are completely incapable.

The three large letters on the "Monogram Page" of the *Book of Kells* (Fig. 8.35) are the Greek *chi, rho,* and *iota* which transliterate as the *Chri* of Christ. If from the rest of the decoration we take out the great *chi* and let it stand alone as in Figure 8.37, we have a good illustration of the other way in which the northern artists put line to use. The letter starts from a point of origin at the intersection of its several legs. Thence, the four legs sweep away in powerful, moving curves to dissolve in sharp points at the end. Except for using a center from which to start, the arrangement contains not a single element that can be understood, described, or discussed in the vocabulary of geometry. The four parts of the letter are uneven in length and weight. They are unlike in curvature. Symmetry is not only absent; it evidently was disliked and eschewed. There is no balance whatever; in fact, the Barbarian style feels no need for the "repose" so often praised in classical art.

As one looks at this magnificent monogram, the eye moves fast, with an urgent force. Gathering momentum as it goes, the glance sweeps through the curves and off into space at the end—to move still further along a path predicated by the curvature. Presently, one recovers, and returns again to the composition. So vital is the experience that we begin to read the movement into the work of art, thus endowing the line with life.

As distinguished from the organic compositions of the Greeks and the rhythmic compositions of the Near East, we may call the barbarian organization *eccentric*. It will be observed that the eccentric theory begets asymmetry. It also brings about the silhouette characteristic of and peculiar to northern art. Instead of the plainly defined boundaries and compact unity of the Greek temple, any northern design will have what we may call the *dissolving silhouette*, characterized in initial letters by a multiplication of small projections pointing outward in all directions, and in the architecture which presently came from the barbarian tradition by towers and spires pointing up into the air to produce the broken skyline typical of most medieval buildings.

THE ART OF THE CAROLINGIAN ERA

For convenience, we shall use the adjective *Carolingian* to indicate the cultural movement set into motion by the career of Charles the Great (regnal dates 771–814). A more detailed survey would demand our making a distinction between the lifetime and immediate influence of Charles, and the separate movements that took place in France and Germany after his death. It will be sufficient for our purposes, however, to think of the whole affair as one, and we shall use Carolingian as though it included the art sometimes catalogued under the headings *West Frankish* and *Ottonian*. In point of time, the period under review stretches forward at least as far as the reign in Germany of Henry the 2nd, who died in 1024.

Charles was the only monarch of the earlier Middle Ages who proved able to organize a central government in Western Europe. His power depended to an unfortunate extent upon his personal capacity rather than upon well-conceived and durable institutions of government, but at the height of his success he held, in name at least, everything from the Pyrenees to a line drawn between Denmark and Dalmatia, including Italy as far south as Rome.

On Christmas Day of the year 800, Charles attended services in the old basilican church of St. Peter at Rome. On that occasion the Pope, under circumstances that have never been entirely clear, crowned him Roman emperor. The papal act raised serious questions of jurisdiction, and proved in future a perennial subject of friction between church and state. There can be no question, however, that Charles conceived himself as heir to the Caesars, and his imperial program as an effort to restore Roman order.

Personally preoccupied with military enterprises and with political organization, Charles nevertheless did an immense amount to initiate and foster cultural revival. He delegated authority to various able men, of whom the most important was Alcuin of York (735–804). There is a tradition that Alcuin's handwriting became the model for the script used all over Europe. However that may be, the "schools" organized by Alcuin at Aachen, Tours,

Reims, and elsewhere actually produced a monumental amount of learning, with the result that we often hear the whole era described as "the Carolingian Renaissance"—an exaggerated term, but an indicative one nevertheless.

Had Charlemagne's empire been kept intact after his death, the effect upon both history and art would probably have been beneficial to an extent appreciable only in our own time. But imperial unity apparently appealed to the 9th-century mind as a principle far less important than the right of the individual heir to inherit his proportional share of a decedent's estate. At the Treaty of Verdun in 843, the empire was divided among the claimants. The division took cognizance—probably for administrative convenience at the moment—of language differences and other situations conducive to separatism rather than unity. Louis the German took everything east of the Rhine. Charles the Bald took the west. Lothair took what was then called "the middle kingdom," part of which still bears the name Lorraine, a softening of Lotharii Regnum. What has become modern France and modern Germany, indeed nationalism itself, started with this division—and with it the turmoil of the 20th century.

It is extremely hard to interpret the artistic monuments we have inherited from the Carolingian era. Indeed it would be an error to build our picture of those times on the basis of the physical relics still in existence: a considerable corpus of illuminated manuscripts, a number of statuettes, a certain amount of jewelry, and some rather discouraging architecture. Fortunately, there is reasonably adequate information about material we no longer have.

♦ *Carolingian Architecture* At Ingelheim and at Aachen, it is possible to discern the general outline of palaces built by Charlemagne himself. The gates of the palace at Aachen were standing, it is said, as late as the 14th century. Literary evidence supplements the meager remains, and we read of terraced gardens, banqueting halls, and river views commanded by upper windows and balconies. Obviously such facilities were not constructed except in response to a certain standard of dignity and refinement in the life of the court, but all the palaces were built of wood and other impermanent materials—a fact we modern historians are likely to weigh too heavily. We also hear of a fort at Merliacum that literally towered over the plain, and had a moat and drawbridge. It would appear that the design of defensive fortification improved greatly during this era for the simple reason that the central government could not protect its citizens from the Viking raiders. The strong tower intended as a place of refuge probably dates from Carolingian days; it was good enough to serve against the Vikings because they usually went away promptly and long before the garrison could be starved out.

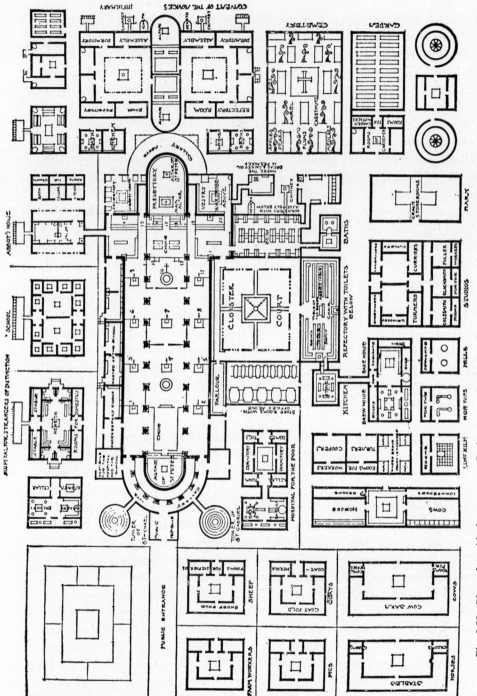

Fig. 8.38 Plan of an ideal monastery. Redrawn on the basis of a manuscript of Carolingian date found at Saint-Gall. (From A. K. Porter, *Medieval Architecture*, New Haven, Yale University Press, 1909, Vol. I.)

Fig. 8.39 Lorsch. The Basilican Gate. About A.D. 800 (Marburg)

Perhaps the most interesting single bit of evidence is a plan found at Saint-Gall (Fig. 8.38), showing the arrangement of a monastic establishment. Often presented as reflecting actual construction, it is now generally conceded to be an imaginative layout for an ideal monastery. The geometric regularity of the composition suggests that the monks had studied the precious copy of Vitruvius which lay waiting in their library for another 500 years before its existence was announced to the modern world (see above, page 97). The plan is proof enough that men of this era thought in terms of a complex and highly developed community. It would be difficult for the production manager of a modern factory to arrange better for the various functions and services requisite to a self-contained and self-sustaining community. In addition to a church and dormitories, barns, stables, storage cellars, and workshops, there is provision for a hospital, a guest house, and a library.

The standard type of church in Carolingian days was the basilica. In the absence of classical columns in ready supply as in Italy, most of the Carolingian basilicas carried their wooden roofs on coarse piers capped by clumsy capitals. Among existing examples, the small, severe *Basse-Oeuvre* at Beauvais, (the nave to which the great Gothic transepts, choir, and apse are now attached) is as illustrative as any. At the little town of Lorsch near Worms, however, there still stands a set of three arches (Fig. 8.39) known as *The Basilican Gate.* Traditionally, and probably correctly, the monument is supposed to be all that is left from the narthex of a substantial basilican church. The date falls at the end of the 8th century, or during the first half of the 9th. With its high peaked modern roof and the addition of a couple of apses, nothing at first gives an impression of being less classical. It will be noted, however, that the arches and columns of the lower story fit the scheme of the Roman Arch Order even if the proportions and spacing differ. The ten pilasters of the upper story are patently Corinthian by intent, however provincial their execution. The chevron ornament above them and the polychromed masonry are typical incongruities of the sort that lend quaintness to monuments from the whole era covered by the present chapter.

For his personal church at the Aachen capital, the great Charles was determined to have something more pretentious than the standard basilica. His *Palace Chapel* (now the rotunda of the cathedral) was started in 796, and dedicated in 804 by Pope Leo the 3rd, who had wintered at Aachen in order to be there for the ceremony. It is doubtful if we can name a building that ever inspired its contemporaries to congratulate themselves more heartily. The remarks of some of these men are worth quoting; we take our excerpts from the admirable documentation included by Kingsley Porter as part of his *Medieval Architecture* (Yale University Press, 1909. Vol. I, pages 170 ff.). Various writers mention the deluxe ecclesiastical furniture provided: gold and silver candelabra, bronze choir screens, bronze doors, and such—to execute which, workmen were imported from far places. On this general theme, Einhardt *(Life of Charlemagne)* added for emphasis that "since he could not obtain elsewhere columns and marbles for this building, he had them sent from Rome and Ravenna." In another passage, the same author credited the builders with "wonderful art"; but he was moderate in his praise by comparison to Angilbert *(Carmen de Carolo Magno* iii, 94) who declared: "Where the second Rome, in her mighty new flower rises great aloft . . . some build well the temple lovely with its mighty mass, the temple of the Eternal King."

Resounding even in translation, Angilbert's periods earned him the contemporary nickname of "Homer"; but the church he praised is very much out of keeping with the hyperbole. Solid and adequate, the Palace Chapel at Aachen is a medium-size building of the central type, covered by a dome a little over 47 feet in diameter. The design appears to have been borrowed direct, and without intelligent analysis, from that of San Vitale at Ravenna— a fact of more than passing interest because Justinian's portrait appears at San Vitale (Fig. 8.18) and the church was peculiarly associated with his name and reputation. Charlemagne's choice of that particular model betokens something approaching a servile admiration for the Byzantine empire and illustrates as well as anything the manner in which all Western Europe, throughout the entire Middle Ages, looked toward Constantinople as modern men look to Paris, London, and New York. It was the great and gilded metropolis, the center of the world. Conditions in the West may be inferred from the fact that Charlemagne had to import his skilled workmen, had to get his classical columns second-hand, and astonished his contemporaries with what amounts to a coarse and modest church. It is nevertheless the sober truth that his chapel was the most important building constructed in northern Europe between the fall of Rome and the late 11th century.

♦ *Carolingian Manuscripts* Books were the great preoccupation of the Carolingian era. The brains and energies of its best men were directed to the acquisition and preservation of books and to the production of copies. A great number of illuminated manuscripts survive from the period. Stylistically, they furnish us with a bewildering tangle of problems. There were apparently a number of centers at which the work went on. Within the limits of human patience and with occasional interpolations by the scribe, the copies were turned out with reasonable strictness insofar as the written text was concerned. With respect to the illustrations, it was apparently customary to copy more freely. Sometimes, indeed, the Carolingian illuminator lacked the skill to copy any other way. Thus any particular miniature may demonstrate a style and composition of very complicated genealogy. In every instance, one must attempt to visualize the pictures in the manuscript used as a model— pictures which themselves may have had an involved derivation. One then must interpret what he sees with reference to the technical training of the illuminator who did the work. Of great historical interest, the detailed pursuit of such questions is hardly appropriate to the present section. Suffice it to say that the questions exist, and that there is to date no general agreement on such fundamentals as the number and location of the various Carolingian centers.

The dead average of Carolingian illumination is artistically inferior. The illuminators, or most of them at any rate, worked under conditions scarcely conducive to originality. Their business was to reproduce, not to create; but even under that system—closer to the factory than the studio—some of them rose to greatness. The occasional excellence of a single figure was now and again surpassed by an equally brilliant imagery embracing an entire scene. For an instance, we may turn our attention to a justly celebrated miniature from the *Codex Aureus* from St. Emmeram at Regensburg, now in the Staatsbibliothek in Munich (Fig. 8.40).

The narrative comes from the Apocalypse (Revelation 4:10–11), where the four and twenty elders cast their crowns before the throne, saying, "Thou art worthy, O Lord, to receive glory and honor and power, for thou hast created all things, and for thy pleasure they are and were created." Christ is symbolized by the Lamb, and we see the elders grouped before him in a great hemicycle. Stylistically, the work is made understandable by supposing that the artist was in the habit of working from models that put figures in front of a neutral background; but it is impossible to explain the content by any conceivable derivation from the classical. The imagery itself is transcendental, and the surcharge of feeling is as wild and exalted as the Apocalypse itself. This is perhaps the first monument we have reviewed which indicates that the medieval temperament—as distinct from the classical and

Fig. 8.40 Munich, Staatsbibliothek. *Codex Aureus* from St. Emmeram at Regensburg. "The Four and Twenty Elders before the Throne." (Stoedtner)

the modern—was at long last beginning to find itself and means for its expression.

Every other Carolingian monument, or all of them together, may be dismissed as insignificant by comparison to the *Utrecht Psalter* (Figs. 8.41–42). That incomparable manuscript fortunately lends itself to reproduction, and it is now available in Ernest DeWald's monograph *(The Utrecht Psalter,* Princeton University Press, 1932). The book consists of 108 vellum leaves. The miniatures are line drawings in brown ink, and there is a picture to illustrate every bit of the text that lends itself to visual expression. In addition to this terrific volume of material, the artist had the energy to include an

Fig. 8.41 Utrecht, University Library. *Utrecht Psalter.* Folio 1 verso. Illustration for the 1st Psalm. The upper register shows the righteous man opposite the ungodly man, who appears to the right as a prince accompanied by soldiers. An angel stands behind the righteous man, who has the law book of the Lord on the lectern before him; he meditates thereon day and night, as indicated by the sun and moon in the sky above. In the middle, two persons are seen discussing these men. The lower register shows, at the left, the tree planted beside the river of waters, with the river emerging from an urn held by a reclining demigod. In the middle, the face of the wind appears, blowing at a group of the ungodly. At the right, demons are casting more of the ungodly into the pit of hell. (C. B. Van Weelderen)

LAUDENTNOMENEIUSIN
CHORO·INTYMPANO
EITPSALTERIOPSALLANTEI
QUIABENEPLACITUMEST

CHORO·INTYMPANO
TURREORUM·ETGLADII
ANCIPITESINMANIB:EORU
ADFACIENDAMUINDICTA

EXSULTATIONESDIEINGUT
UTFACIANTINEISIUDICIU
CONSCRIPTUM·GLORIA
HAECESTOMNIBUSSCIS
EIUS

Fig. 8.42 *Utrecht Psalter.* Folio 83 recto. Illustration for the 150th Psalm. (C. B. Van Weelderen)

enormous amount of contemporary detail: birds, animals, tools and apparatus, men at work, landscape, and virtually everything else that came under his eye.

The whole history of art hardly contains a parallel example of freedom on the part of an artist. We have to make an effort to appreciate that the miniatures preserve some resemblance to an earlier model. In fact, it can be said the book is "a copy" only by pointing out that most of the drawings seem to adhere to an original border; and that the trees, the hills, and the half-hidden buildings here and there recall similar items in the Joshua Roll and Paris Psalter. The model must, however, have contained pictures less like the Alexandrian and more like the *Odyssey Landscapes* (Figs. 6.14–15, pages 166–167), because we see little figures moving fast within the represented space of great landscapes of infinite extension out into the distance. As an equivalent for the impressionism of Roman painting, the artist avoided the cursive outline and drew his figures by making the pen zig-zag in a brilliant but nervous fashion. All of these phenomena are best explained by the assumption that the master, whoever he was, was an accomplished manipulator of the Celtic linear technique, and of sufficient prestige to adapt the style of his model as he chose. Such a man was rare indeed during the Carolingian era.

The northern temperament is made manifest by matters more important than a mere preference for line. In response to his classicizing model, the artist gave many of his pictures a certain measure of geometric order, but he obviously cared little for it. The schemes that came most naturally to him eschewed both rhythm and balance. The compositions hold together and make sense only through the fact of an all-pervading animation and vitality. The narration is according to the so-called "continuous method" familiar in much Roman work (the reliefs on the Column of Trajan, for example). Episodes which happened at different moments, that is to say, are included within the same picture without separation by frames or any other visual barriers. So strong is the common bond of action, however, that one does not care even if he bothers to know. The psychology of the observer's comprehension, it is still further to be noted, is not instantaneous as in classical art, but cumulative. The total impression is built up by the successive impact of innumerable visual experiences, each intense—a fact which makes the manuscript belong to the north even though its original came from the Mediterranean.

Details are better studied by reference to the captions under our book plates. Certain general conclusions of an extremely significant kind can be drawn from what we may call the pictorial policy of the artist. When he read in the first Psalm that the righteous man delights in the law of the Lord and meditates upon it day and night, this formidably imaginative master felt compelled to visualize the event as physical fact. In like fashion, the illustration that goes with Psalm 150 actually shows us the musical instruments which the psalm requires, including a pipe organ, even to the detail of a musician raging at the organ boys to give him more wind.

We may pass over the naïveté that permitted so profound a mind to visualize in 9th-century French terms events described by a Jewish writer of a remote epoch. The crucial realization is this: the artist conceived the Scriptures as a record of human experience within the confines of this earth—for even his deities differ from men only by having the power to neglect gravitation. Unusual in its own day, this is the philosophy which was destined to dominate European thought, and to produce the so-called "representative convention" of modern art. (See below, Chapter 13.)

There is no voice to challenge the assertion that the *Utrecht Psalter* belongs among the very greatest monuments of pictorial art, or that its unknown author deserves to have his name mentioned in any company. There was no man of equal caliber to carry the style forward, however, and found a school. There are of course a good many items which are obvious derivatives, but they all make the same impression as a watered drink.

To the last statement, there is a single notable exception which, if we wish to be strict about it, falls in the Ottonian period as distinct from the Carolingian.

In 1019, when Saint Bernward was bishop at Hildesheim, a set of bronze doors were installed at the Church of Saint Michael (Fig. 8.43). The doors have since been removed to the cathedral. They consist of sixteen panels of relief, embracing selected scenes from Genesis and from the life of Christ. Most of the scenes have a single row of figures against the background, but it is more than plain that the master strenuously intended to represent actual distance as distinguished from the backdrop of a stage. His little figures move with the same nervous vitality as those in the *Utrecht Psalter;* most of them break loose, as it were, from the panel behind. Unskillful and unscientific in the matter of anatomy, this artist was magnificent in the department of vigorous gesture; small though they are, his people move with an epic finality. Their extraordinary power is not in the least diminished by the harsh and masterly realism of the faces.

With the doors of Hildesheim, spatial representation ceased for some time to play an important part in painting and sculpture. By the logic of their subject matter, a number of popular scenes required some kind of setting, but anything so adequate and convincing as this demonstration remained all but unheard of until the realistic movement of the 15th century had done its work.

♦ *The Bayeux Tapestry* The Bayeux Tapestry (Figs. 8.44–45) has often been presented as a historical curiosity, largely because modern eyes have long been habituated to "correct" drawing and "accurate" anatomy. The truth is

Fig. 8.43 Hildesheim. Cathedral. Bronze doors, lower half. A.D. 1007–1015. Left side, reading down: Expulsion from the Garden of Eden, Labors of Adam and Eve, Offerings of Cain and Abel, Murder of Abel. Right side, reading up: The Annunciation, The Nativity, Adoration of the Magi, Presentation in the Temple. (Stoedtner)

that no other monument from the period of the Norman Conquest is half so important as a work of art. The tapestry is in fact an embroidery in eight colors of wool on a ground of coarse linen. Originally there were 76 scenes, of which we retain 72. The narrative begins with the decision of Edward the Confessor to assign the English succession to Duke William, and with his dispatch of Harold to make the arrangements. Considerable space is assigned to Harold's exploits and adventures in France, and the story concludes with

Figs. 8.44–45 Bayeux, Cathedral Museum. The Bayeux Tapestry. (above) The Norman fleet crossing the Channel. (below) The Battle of Hastings. (Giraudon)

William's amphibious expedition and the battle at Hastings. The width is 20 inches, and the length 231 feet—in the space of which we see over 600 human figures, more than 500 animals, 37 ships, and a great deal of scenery. A gallant but incorrect tradition says that the work was done by the Norman queen and her ladies, hence the name "La Tapisserie de la Reine Mathilde" —a designation that seems to have originated during the early 19th century. The weight of evidence suggests that the actual patron was Odo, Bishop of Bayeux and half-brother to the Conqueror.

It is easy to make the mistake of associating the tapestry with manuscript illumination, but the true analogies are with mural painting—of which we have much from the 12th century and rather little from this period. The designer obviously carried over into his drawings the habits and techniques he was accustomed to use for the execution of big frescoes intended to be seen from a considerable remove. There is no laboring of detail. Eyes, noses, and mouths are rendered by broad harsh lines. There is a minimum of modeling; most of the representation is in line and flat tone, with strong contrast of hue. In physical fact, there is a resemblance to the cultivated boldness characteristic of some 20th century painters, but the master of the Bayeux Tapestry was able to carry conviction as none of the modern primitivists can do: he was himself a member of a violent society with rough ways, and his coarse methods were as natural and authentic as breathing.

The power and brutality of combat, and the undeniable fascination of war, have perhaps never been dealt with so well in the history of the visual arts. Not one of the combat artists of World War II was able to achieve a like power. Meissonier's painfully descriptive paintings of Napoleon's army are worthless by comparison, and even Goya must take second place. Where can one find a better picture of a well-organized fleet at sea? Is there anywhere on earth another battle scene with even a fraction of the same clash and rhythm? As visual description, the pictures are grossly incomplete, but nothing important has been left out. Every single thing is unquestionably true, and the total effect is literally vested with authority.

Like so many other monuments from the earlier Middle Ages, the Bayeux Tapestry seems hardly to have started the artistic tradition which its excellent qualities justified. The prestige of miniature pictures in manuscripts appears to have been too great; and the power of both Romanesque sculpture and Romanesque painting (see Chapter 10), if any criticism of it is appropriate, was unfortunately diluted by complexities and refinements more in keeping with the work of the master penman. The grand simplicity of the tapestry was hardly ever arrived at again.

GENERAL CONCLUSIONS

In view of the evidence cited in this chapter alone, it is hardly possible to maintain the old-fashioned view that we may properly use the words "Dark Ages" when referring to the period of history between Rome and the 12th century. The development of the basilican church, the perfection of the Irish manuscripts, the *Utrecht Psalter,* and the Bayeux Tapestry require no defense. They simply take their own place among the great artistic monuments. It is thus plain that we may not dispose lightly of the culture of the Early Middle Ages. Indeed, what other era witnessed so many decisions which were to prove historically determinative and perhaps final?

We may not, on the other hand, indulge in overestimate. Most of the time, the art historian cites his examples from plenty. He mentions one work by Donatello, or writes about the Parthenon. The reader is supposed to assume that the citations are typical of a class—which is to say that there are many others of the same kind, and what he learns will prove useful when he sees them. During the period covered by the present chapter, that is not so. The examples that have been cited hardly amount to the total, but the chapter is still no survey. Almost every work of the first rank has been referred to at least by allusion. It is altogether plain that the 500 years, more or less, which have passed under review did not compare in rate of production with various other areas of art history.

From this we may learn much about the life of the time. Conditions obviously militated against a superior level of culture. The preserved physical remains are inexpensive except for the small amount of jeweler's work that still exists. The artifacts most characteristic of the time are small to the point of being conveniently portable. The remarkable, indeed the amazing thing is that so poor an era produced so much—and, even more incredible, that so many of the survivals remain among the memorable instances of human achievement.

Chapter 9

Byzantine art is the art of the East Roman Empire, centering at Constantinople. It is an oddity of history that the name is taken from the original title for the city, for Byzantium was a word already 200 years out of date by the middle of the 6th century when the style became clearly defined. (See above, pages 215–227.)

Byzantine art is one of the most important cultural phenomena in European history. It lasted longer than any other European style. Its geographical coverage was immense, and it long furnished innumerable persons with the idiom of their visual imagery. Strange and foreign to the American eye, often carelessly explained and misunderstood, the Byzantine is by no means to be thought of as an exotic taste. It has a peculiar beauty and grandeur. It appeals to emotions which are different, and therefore new. It offers satisfactions not to be found elsewhere.

As compared to other areas of art history, Byzantine archeology remains in a formative stage. A reliable synthesis is probably impossible at this date. The literature of the subject is still dispersed in the files of learned periodicals, in occasional monographs, and in several languages. In spite of the immense efforts of Strzygowski, Millet, and Dalton, and with all honor for the valuable papers that occasionally emerge from Dumbarton Oaks, the only comprehensive and comprehensible summary that exists today is Charles Diehl's *Manuel d'art byzantin*—which bears the date 1925, was largely compiled about fifteen years earlier, and has long been out of print and hard to buy. It is extraordinarily difficult, in fact, even to accumulate a reasonable number of photographs of Byzantine monuments.

The reason for all this is not far to seek. Byzantine territory began to

BYZANTINE AND
ITALO-BYZANTINE ART

fall into Moslem hands as early as the 7th century, and the capture of Constantinople by the Turks in 1453 merely concluded the process. Innumerable examples of pictorial art have vanished forever, and perhaps as many more remain obscured by Turkish whitewash. Travel in the more remote parts of what was once the Christian East has been slow and difficult, often unsafe. There are a great many towns that have not seen a visitor from Western Europe within the memory of the oldest inhabitant.

It is entirely likely, however, that the next twenty to thirty years may resolve the confused situation. Relations between Turkey and the West have become increasingly cordial. The attitude of the incumbent Turkish government is liberal and enlightened—as evidenced by the secularization of Hagia Sophia and the program for cleaning its mosaics. Warning the reader, therefore, that a much better and more adequate chapter will doubtless be possible before this book is many years old, we shall content ourselves with the conventional outline and confine our statements to a brevity altogether out of keeping with the importance of the field.

The Byzantine style has three chronological divisions, each commonly referred to as a *Golden Age*. The First Golden Age commenced with the reign of Justinian (527–565), and lasted until the outbreak of *Iconoclasm* in 726. The Second Golden Age is dated from the end of Iconoclasm in 843 to the year 1204 when the Fourth Crusade was diverted to the capture of Constantinople. The Third Golden Age covered the period from the end of the Latin Monarchy established by the Crusaders to the final fall of the city, or from 1261 to 1453. These dates refer, of course, to eras of substantial produc-

Fig. 9.1 Constantinople. Hagia Sophia. A.D. 532–537. Minarets: 15th–16th centuries. 247 feet long, 231 feet wide, 184 feet high. (Marburg)

tion of art in what we may properly call Byzantine territory. They do not apply with the same accuracy to the various provincial schools in Sicily, Russia, and elsewhere. To the latter, we shall have occasion to make passing reference as the historical connections come up.

THE FIRST GOLDEN AGE

The most important enterprise of the First Golden Age was the design and construction of Hagia Sophia at Constantinople (Fig. 9.1). The present edifice is the fourth church of the same name on the same site, the third having been destroyed in the course of the so-called Nika riots of 532. Work appears to have commenced at once on the new building, and it was dedicated by Justinian himself in December of 537. The name *Hagia Sophia* is a transliteration from the Greek; it means "Holy Wisdom."

Hagia Sophia is an immense building; it is also a fabric so brilliant in design that it remains today one of the wonders of the world. The architects were Anthemius of Tralles and Isidorus of Miletus. Where did they learn to build so well? Because both of them came from Asia Minor, some scholars have maintained that the most advanced architectural thinking must, at that time, have been going on in the Near East.

Other scholars have contended that Hagia Sophia is very nearly unthinkable unless we assume that the men who built it were inspired by the numerous domed monuments in and near Rome. The argument has been one of the most polemical on record; but neither side has been able, as yet, to adduce a dated series of experimental buildings which form anything like an acceptable genealogical chain culminating in the great church at Constantinople.

Are we, then, to entertain the idea that Hagia Sophia itself was an experimental fabric? Certain imperfections in the engineering, and the occurrence of serious accidents during and after construction, lend color to that notion; and if we ever learn the facts, it may well appear that Anthemius and Isodorus were the boldest architects in history.

The purpose of the design is best discerned in the plan (Fig. 9.2). It was an attempt to combine, in a major building, the advantages of the basilican nave, the well-composed exterior of the central church, and the great merit of a fireproof roof. The result was immensely successful; much more so, in fact, than other famous domed buildings like St. Peter's at Rome and St. Paul's in London. Every aspect and vista of Hagia Sophia, inside or out, reinforces the conviction that there is nothing like it in the whole world.

As seen in ground outline, the church is an oblong, and considerably wider for its length than the average. The peculiar interest of the building is

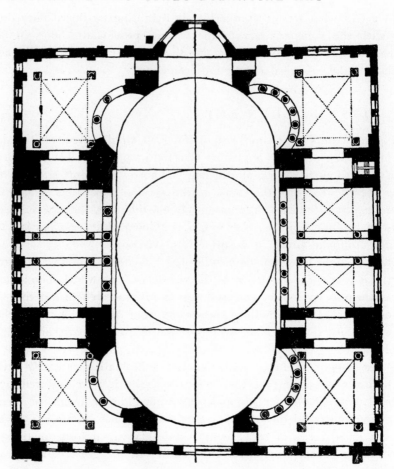

Fig. 9.2 Constantinople. Hagia Sophia. Plan. Left half at ground-story level. Right half at gallery level. (From A. K. Porter, *Medieval Architecture*, New Haven, Yale University Press, 1909, Vol. I.)

the method adopted for roofing over the nave. That was accomplished by centering a large dome (107 feet in diameter and rising 180 feet above the floor) over the middle of the nave. Half domes of the same diameter adjoin to east and west, but at a lower elevation, and there are four fractional domes still lower down at the four corners.

From four gigantic piers, pendentives rise to form a ring of masonry about 130 feet above the floor, from which the great central dome springs. It is this feature of the engineering—the mature and perfect solution for a dome over a rectangular floor plan (see Appendix I, pages 950–953)—that makes Hagia Sophia so great a puzzle to historians. The pendentive itself had been known for some time. Rudimentary applications can be found both in Italy and in the East at a much earlier date; the earliest known, if its date is really of the 2nd century, exists at Gerasia in Palestine. The remarkable thing, therefore, is not the mere fact that the pendentives were used at Hagia Sophia, but the fact that they were used, perhaps for the first time, in an immense building, to great advantage, and with advanced if not complete understanding for the possibilities of the form.

No other great interior presents anything like the same number of varied vistas (Fig. 9.3), and none has ever been more perfectly integrated (Fig. 9.4). Much of the power and fascination of the building derives from the sense of magnificent space—very like in effect to the sense of nobility, and enhanced by the use of innumerable columns and other members of the normal size. The wonderful dome, pierced by forty windows around its base, rests as lightly as a cloud above the floor. The eye sweeps upward through the subordinate vaults into the dome, and down again toward the apse. It would be a mistake to say the curves flow into one another, for they do not. As contrasted with modern streamlining, where the individual contour means nothing and the flow of the whole means everything, each vault retains its own shape and identity. We can see and feel it for itself, that is to say, and also with reference to the entirety.

Most of this the reader must regrettably accept on faith, for reasons of psychology rather than optics. A great many photographs are available which purport to show the interior as a whole; and it is geometrically true that they do so. But no single negative embracing everything from top to bottom can be satisfactory even though the exposure be made through the best of lenses. The human eye embraces an angle of vision of about 120 degrees, of which a central cone of perhaps 65 degrees is alone in good focus. Visual inspection of such an interior demands, therefore, a succession of acts. The attention is first directed here, then there—an experience difficult or impossible to reproduce on paper.

Color, moreover—rich, deep, and glowing—was an essential feature of the design. The walls and arches were constructed of brick and mortar, but the entire Mediterranean world was ransacked for columns and marbles of unheard-of variety. There is Phrygian white marble with rose-colored stripes, green marble from Laconia, blue from Libya, black Celtic marble with white veins, and white marble from the Bosporus region with black veins, Egyptian starred granite, and Saitic porphyry. Eight immense purple columns were brought from Rome, having come originally from Baalbek, and there are eight green ones that once were thought to have come from Ephesus. To this display, we must add the superb mosaic pictures which have been out of view since the 15th century; originally, they covered every important wall surface, the most important being a Madonna in the apse, an Apocalyptic Christ in the dome, and four seraphim on the pendentives. We can only imagine the church as it will be when the cleaning begun in 1934 is complete.

Figs. 9.3–4 Constantinople. Hagia Sophia. (left) Diagonal view from the south aisle. (opposite) General view of the nave from the west. (Marburg)

The inexhaustible excellencies of the interior are scarcely equaled by the exterior view—which is, nevertheless, one of the most interesting in history. As seen from a distance, the great church is a landmark never to be forgotten: superb, serene, modest. Its imperfections become apparent only in comparative close-up and upon analysis.

We must discount, of course, the nondescript buildings which cluster around the base; they are an accretion of the years and no part of the original plan. The same thing may be said of the varicolored striping which mars the exterior. The four minarets are a Turkish addition.

The extreme haste of the construction was unfortunate. Trouble seems to have been experienced before the building was half done. Piers sank in differential fashion, splayed out of vertical, and allowed arches to drop between. The foundations and substructure of the fabric have, in fact, been a constant worry from the beginning. The present dome is the second, or even the third, to cover the nave. The first collapsed completely in 558. Rebuilding

proceeded under the direction of Isidorus the Younger, a nephew of one of the original designers; and it is believed he used a steeper pitch for the new dome, an expedient that somewhat marred the unity of the interior ceilings, but produced less thrust. An ambiguous record seems to say that the dome fell again in 567, but whether partially or completely, one cannot be sure. Part of it certainly fell in during the year 987. To this catalogue of disaster, we must add the fact that the four great supporting piers, as originally designed, proved too light; they were strengthened by Isidorus the Younger, and apparently remain as he left them—their greater bulk choking the aisles.

The abutment of the vaults, all too often explained in sentences more systematic than the facts, was surely more daring than prudent. Piercing the main dome with forty windows at its very spring was an esthetic inspiration of the first order, but no one can call the expedient cautious. There is a certain merit in the placement of the two large semidomes to the east and west of the main dome. In that position, they tend to contain its thrust, but it must be conceded that they are hardly high enough to act as efficient buttresses. To the north and south, there seems originally to have been no equivalent provision for the containment of the great central dome. The unsightly masses of masonry which inefficiently perform that office today were added entire, or at least greatly increased in size, as late as the 13th century. For the diagonal thrust of the four immense pendentives, there seems never to have been any well-conceived scheme of abutment.

It would be a mistake, therefore, to suggest that the abutment of Hagia Sophia depends upon a system of thrust and counterthrust comparable to the scheme later developed in France for the Gothic cathedrals. On the face of it, we are justified in making the guess that neither Anthemius nor Isodorus had anything of the sort in mind. We know, for example, that they went to great pains to reduce the weight of their vaults by using hollow tile and other very light material, and also, that they attempted to cement everything together. As contrasted to a logical system of buttresses, the aim seems to have been to eliminate thrust altogether by producing homogeneous and even monolithic vaults which would exert no more thrust than a teacup once the mortar had set hard. That, it would appear, is the reason the domes stand today.

Admitting all these faults, it is nevertheless impossible not to feel deeply that an important theory of exterior design is implicit in the appearance of Hagia Sophia. Except for the architecture of the First Golden Age and its derivatives, the builder's art has traditionally been an art of angles and flat surfaces. Here the design was governed by the nature of the convex curve—as seen in the contour of the main dome and in the swing of the subordinate domes which build up toward it. While different from modern streamlining as already set forth above, the effect is closer to that recent theory of design than anything which has come and gone between the 6th century and our own era. Modern ferroconcrete lends itself to such manipulation. Materials available before the Industrial Revolution do not. One might well hazard the guess that the true modern architecture, when it arrives, will be an art of curves, and more like the Byzantine than we have perhaps supposed.

Because they are larger and more conspicuous than the later Byzantine churches, the monuments of the First Golden Age—of which Hagia Sophia is merely the prime example—are the monuments which were emulated elsewhere. San Vitale at Ravenna, almost precisely contemporary to Hagia Sophia, was an attempt to imitate, in a region at that time provincial, the style of the metropolis. Charlemagne's Palace Chapel at Aachen (see above, page 262) was an imitation of San Vitale in a part of the world more provincial yet. St. Mark's at Venice (begun 1063; disregard the addition of the conspicuous false domes) took its Greek cross plan and its five domes on pendentives direct from Justinian's Church of the Holy Apostles which stood at Constantinople until torn down in 1463. Exactly the same plan was popular in the 12th-century Romanesque of Aquitaine. St. Front at Perigueux is the prime example, and there are others much like it in the same district. Even more important than these West Christian borrowings is the little-appreciated fact that the domed architecture of the Moslem world, indeed much of the architecture of the whole Orient, came into being only after contact with the buildings at Constantinople. The Taj Mahal at Agra is a plain case in point.

♦ *The Period of Iconoclasm* The First Golden Age of Byzantine art was brought to a disastrous end by the Iconoclastic Controversy. In a technical sense, the period of the controversy began with a decree against images issued in 726 by the Emperor Leo the Isaurian. It ended with the restoration of images by a later Theodora in the year 843. In bitterness of feeling and ruthless action, the entire affair must be ranged as the greatest and longest of the many altercations that shook the foundations of early Christendom. Ostensibly having its genesis in a difference of view about modes of worship, the struggle came to involve issues of almost every other kind: geographical, racial, social, political, and military—a web so complex and interwoven as to tax the re-creative powers of the best historians, and to render a true picture of the situation quite beyond the scope of our present purpose. It is important, however, to take note of the fact that Iconoclasm was coincident in date with the beginning of the split that has since separated the Eastern and Orthodox communion from the Roman and Catholic.

With respect to the history of art, Iconoclasm (literally, the smashing of icons, or images) stands as a matter of major importance because it almost completely eliminated any chance we might have had of studying the best Byzantine painting and mosaic of the First Golden Age. The religious issue involved was the age-old conflict between monotheism and polytheism, and the fear of idolatry. The complaint of the Iconoclasts was that the various saints had become, through the agency of idols (that is, representative art), objects of worship roughly analogous to the numerous minor gods of the pagan hierarchy. They alleged still further that works of art on display in churches (pictures and statues in their capacity as mere objects) were often worshiped for themselves, as distinguished from worship of the person or ideal the picture was intended to recall or symbolize.

The Iconoclasts held political control at the capital for more than a hundred years. Their purpose, however deeply felt, was ruthless, and their actions efficient and devastating. Religious art of all kinds was systematically destroyed in wholesale fashion. Of the wealth of material that once existed at the capital, we have virtually nothing. It is possible, of course, that something of importance may still appear at Hagia Sophia and elsewhere, but we

Fig. 9.5 London, Victoria and Albert Museum. Ivory casket from Veroli. Panel showing Rape of Europa. Middle 9th century.

shall be fortunate if much turns up that dates from the First Golden Age.

For the reasons just cited, we shall omit any attempt to survey the subject. Indeed, insofar as any conception of 6th-, 7th-, and 8th-century work may be reconstructed, the reader cannot do better than refer back to our citation of mosaics at Ravenna (pages 222–227), or refer ahead to the section within the present chapter where we deal with the Italo-Byzantine school (pages 301–310).

While Iconoclasm must be regarded as a cultural tragedy for which there is no repair, the darkness of its effect is mitigated by one pale ray of happy light. The Iconoclasts focused their animosity upon religious art. They did not have the same objection to secular art. It is therefore generally supposed that artists sought employment in the production of objects of a nonreligious kind; and for models, they turned to the two rich sources available to them: classical sculpture and Oriental textiles.

A typical product of that tendency is a small ivory casket, formerly in the cathedral at Veroli, a place about fifty miles to the east and south of Rome, and now in the Victoria and Albert Museum of London (Fig. 9.5). The general aspect of the principal panel of relief cannot fail to evoke a sense of reminiscence in persons who are familiar with later classical art. At the same time, the heavy borders consist of scrolls and rosettes deriving from motives familiar in Near Eastern work, these items alternating with bust-portraits that recall Roman coins and gems. In itself a distinctly minor work, the Veroli casket illustrates a healthy tendency: it comes from a new inspiration even if its sources are old, and it is lively. As such, it helps us to see how Iconoclasm, however accidentally and unintentionally, brought about a desirable relaxation of the hieratic standards at which Byzantine art—if we may judge from such instances as the mosaics at San Vitale—had evidently arrived. The effect upon the art of the Second Golden Age was excellent, as we shall presently note.

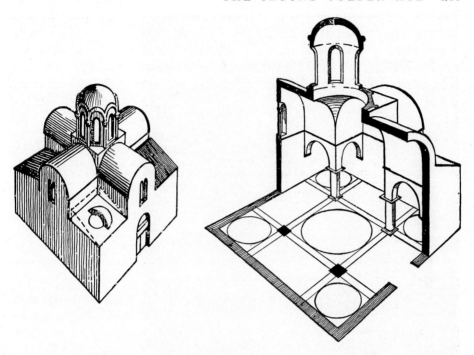

Figs. 9.6–7 Schematic drawings illustrating a typical four-column church of the Second Golden Age. (left) Exterior composition. (right) Component parts. (Drawings by Henry Tisdall)

THE SECOND GOLDEN AGE

♦ *The Four-column Church* The churches of the Second Golden Age are distinguished not by size but by smallness. The largest of them are very modest in dimension, and the little ones are tiny. The architects of the period nevertheless displayed a remarkable sense for three-dimensional composition, and they developed a distinctive type of building that is without a peer in that respect.

All too often obscured by ill-arranged additions to the fabric of the church proper, the elements of the new type are best studied by reference to schematic drawings such as our Figures 9.6 and 9.7. Three levels, or stories, are involved. The ground outline is a square, from which walls rise vertically for some distance to form what we may call the first story. The second story consists of four short sections of tunnel vaulting arranged symmetrically around the central dome to form the arms of a Greek cross. The tiny dome, set high on a drum, rises from the center of the cross to form the third level of the composition.

The typical system of construction is indicated by Fig. 9.7. Well within the larger square of the ground plan, four piers are set up to define the

Fig. 9.8 Athens. Little Metropolis. About 1150. 38 by 25½ feet. Interior height to crown of dome: 36 feet. (Nellys)

corners of a smaller and interior square. The piers carry the inner ends of the second-story vaulting, and the dome above. As indicated by the circles in the corners of Figure 9.7, and at the lower corner of Figure 9.6, small saucer-shaped domes were often added over the otherwise vacant corners of the ground story. During the period now under review, these four extra and subordinate domes were usually very low indeed, and concealed under lean-to roofing. During the Third Golden Age, they were emphasized by conspicuous cupolas (Fig. 9.15).

As a new and distinct architectural type, such churches deserve a name; we might call them *the four-column churches of the Second Golden Age*. Experiments with the several elements of the form can be traced in the early architecture of Armenia and Asia Minor, but the scheme in its entirety seems first to have been worked out in the so-called "new church" of Basil the 1st, usually called *La Nea*. It must have been complete when that emperor died in 886; and, although long since vanished, it ought to be remembered as the pilot model for the entire era.

At Constantinople, perhaps the best extant example of the new type is the building now called the *Kilissé Djami* (formerly Saint Theodore Trio), a structure extremely difficult to illustrate photographically. For a free-standing building, we may turn to the Little Metropolis at Athens (Fig. 9.8).

Fig. 9.9   Mistra. St. Theodore. Late 13th century. (Marburg)

It differs in some details from the typical, but the differences are not in view on the exterior. Most churches of the period were varied in their mass by salient apses, and their texture was enriched by elaborately patterned brick-work. A capital example is the church of Saint Theodore at Mistra (Fig. 9.9), that remarkable ruined town a few miles west of Sparta.

Interior views of the four-column churches are difficult to obtain. Figure 9.10 is probably the best available. It shows the interior of the smaller of the two churches at the monastery of Hosios Loukas, dedicated to Saint Luke Stirites who died there in 946, and located a short way to the east of the modern hamlet of Stiris, which lies near the sea on the north shore of the Gulf of Corinth. The walls and ceilings have rather recently been done over in a delicate rococo fashion, a fact we may disregard because of the good light and because the usual clutter of ecclesiastical furniture is absent.

In summarizing our remarks about the churches of the Second Golden Age, we may pass over such matters as the homely and comfortable excellence of their texture (a considerable relief at times from the slick surface of classical marble). We may also defer attention to the special refinement of door and window openings: the period was approximately contemporary with the Romanesque of western Europe, and we may save space by referring the reader ahead to Chapter 10, where he will find that similar openings were the common property of East and West at this moment in history. The great

Fig. 9.10　Hosios Loukas. Small church. Early 11th century. (Marburg)

and special distinction of the four-column church resides in the almost infallible excellence of their exterior composition.

They compose in masses. We may think of the ground story as a great square solid. Each arm of the Greek cross above is, in broad terms, a mass something like a Greek temple if it happens to have gables, or a cylindrical shape if the roofing corresponds to the vault below. The dome and its drum ordinarily amount to an octagon surmounted by a hemisphere. The composition is an arrangement of no less than seven masses which vary in shape and in scale. Masses, moreover, juxtapose to one another in such a way that the smallest is on top, acting as the hub of the system, and the biggest at the bottom. Such a design gives a powerful effect of solidity and stability. The build-up to the dome proceeds as though by inevitability, and the order is sure. The words necessary to describe such a composition, it will have been noted, have a curious familiarity for the modern reader: they sound very like the several aphorisms from Cézanne which only yesterday were cited as the sanction for cubism and today furnish the chief authority for abstract art of every kind.

The churches of the Second Golden Age have a monumentality quite beyond anything that might be predicted for little buildings. It seems impossible that the Little Metropolis measures only 25 feet across the façade; and that its dome has a diameter of no more than nine. As though to emphasize its distinction as the smallest cathedral in the world, the blocks of masonry—most of them from classical ruins—were not reduced in proportion, but remain of normal size. And yet where can we find a design that betokens a broader view of architecture or is more strong and competent?

◆ *Mosaics and Ivories* As early as the 8th century, the idea seems to have been prevalent among the Eastern clergy that the church building was to be understood as a symbol of heaven on earth—a conception that found its best expression in the pictorial decoration of the interior. In the dome, it was customary to put a mosaic picture of Christ, the Lord and Master of the universe. On the pendentives or squinches, the four Evangelists appeared; they were the men who had revealed Christ to the world. In the apse, Mary found her place, with a communion of apostles often below her; these were the persons who formed the link between God and man. Such a system seems to have governed the arrangement of pictures in Basil the 1st's famous La Nea; and by the 11th century, it had apparently become a fairly strict convention. Among the monuments that are accessible and well-preserved, the most complete mosaic cycles are to be found in the larger church of the monastery at Hosios Loukas and in the Monastery Church at Daphni, a site on the ancient Sacred Way between Athens and Eleusis. From the standpoint of quality, it may be said that no other Byzantine pictures are equal to those at Daphni; they reflect the Greek style, and recall the spiritual elegance of Hellenic idealism. We may select only two of the best for comment.

A view upward into the dome (Fig. 9.11) shows a bust-length portrait of Christ enclosed within a circle. Of an awful solemnity, this majestic represen-

Fig. 9.11 Daphni. Monastery Church. Late 11th century. View into the dome, showing mosaic picture of Christ as Pantocrator. (Prof. Cesare Fasola)

tation of Our Lord presents him in an aspect unfamiliar to the average citizen of the Western world. His strength approaches the brutal. His expression is harsh. How can we reconcile such a rendering with the gentle Savior?

The answer has to do with the various functions for which Christ may be imagined to be responsible in the operation of the religious polity. We see him here in the role of *Pantokrator* (literally, "all-ruler"), which means in his executive and judicial capacity as governor of the universe, whose inhabitants he will one day bring to the ultimate reckoning of the Last Judgment. It is in this guise that most Christians thought of him and visualized him until the popular imagery was revised by the movement of sentiment and affection— which we can see reflected in art not much earlier than the West Porch at Chartres (Fig. 12.3, page 416), and of which the prime exemplar was Saint Francis.

It is in the *Crucifixion* at Daphni (Fig. 9.12) that we may see most clearly the influence from classical Greece. Neglecting the figure-style for the moment, the formula for the picture might be described as follows.

Against a neutral and impenetrable background, human figures appear in a single row as though on a shallow stage. The people are rather large and are presented in comparative close-up. The composition is arranged on the principle of bilateral symmetry, the figure of Mary balancing that of Saint John at an equal and opposite distance from the central vertical axis. Mary and John, furthermore, direct their gestures inward and upward; their action serves to close the composition on either side, and to establish the triangularity of the arrangement.

Fig. 9.12 Daphni, Monastery Church. *Crucifixion.* Mosaic. (Alinari)

All of these points might with equal accuracy be cited as characteristic of the formula used for the Greek pediments (see above, pages 58–67), and there can be no question that we see here an instance—in a different medium and very different in superficial appearance—of the traditional organic composition first developed by the ancient Greeks. Indeed, the only departure from an almost Phidian restraint is the inclusion of a mere indication of setting. At the foot of the cross, we see a small mound of earth and a skull; these signify Golgotha.

The figure of Saint John is Hellenic to a degree. The vertical dimension of the body is scarcely exaggerated. The pose has the chiastic twist familiar in Greek art from Polyclitus onward. The head has the classical profile, and the expression is more than reminiscent of Praxiteles' melting sweetness. The

drapery also is very Greek. Indeed it is only when we look closely at the anatomical details that we can find a substantial divergence from ancient standards, but it is true that the chest is sunken, and lacks that athletic convexity
which was a Greek convention. The hands are exaggerated and their structure
neglected; likewise the toes. The mechanical action of wrists and ankles is
misunderstood.

Further evidence of Greek feeling is to be noted in the graded curves
into which the artist has abstracted the Savior's torso, and the graceful bend
given the spurt of blood from his side. Otherwise the figure is a good example
of the small store set upon anatomical accuracy during the Middle Ages.

Such matters are not even remembered, however, when one considers
the content. As a historical narrative, a sequence of physical events, the
death of Christ on the cross could be contemplated in detail only by persons
having a legitimate interest in its medical aspects, by morbid persons, or by
people without sensibilities. A colored motion picture of the Crucifixion would
be beyond endurance. No subject can be named which better illustrates the
limited usefulness of art that aims merely to represent.

The reality of Christ's death has its existence in the realm of ideas and
the emotions. It is important as the prime symbol for the very essence of
generosity and personal sacrifice—in the name of which it exerts an ennobling
influence upon human motivation. The subject presents the artist, in short,
not with a narrative problem, but with a demand for interpretive power of
a high order. It is fortunate, therefore, that the Byzantine artist working at
Daphni had the benefit of the renewed classical inspiration brought about
by Iconoclasm, also that he lived within walking distance of Athens. In all
history, the Greeks were pre-eminent for their ability to extract from sordid
and physical facts lessons that are divine; that capacity was the great legacy
of the Greek genius to the Christian world. Upon the artist of the Daphni
Crucifixion it induced order, clarity, elegance, and restraint.

He therefore kept his picture completely free from distracting details.
The three persons who appear are the three most intimately connected with
the tragedy; no others are necessary to convey its meaning. The fact of the
Savior's passing is indicated only by the pathetic relaxation of his body; the
agony is over. Mary's erect pose betokens a state of shock; but even in shock,
she holds herself with dignity. It is her figure, indeed, which carries most of
the meaning, for her entire attitude is one of comprehension rather than
panic. Our view of the Madonna is at once touching and heroic, both intimate and royal.

In accordance with its Eastern heritage, Constantinople never produced
any significant amount of large statuary, but there was no prejudice against

ivory carvings, and such were never more exquisite than during the Second Golden Age.

For our immediate purposes, the best example for special attention is the single figure of the Madonna (Fig. 9.13) now in the Archepiscopal Museum of Utrecht. There is no more typical instance of what we may call the standard Byzantine Madonna—an artistic type which became virtually a convention, and is important because it furnished all Europe with its visual imagery for Mary over a period totaling nearly 700 years.

The proportions are elongated. Precise measurements always involve a certain amount of interpretation with regard to the limits between which we measure, but it may be said that the figure now under review is at least ten heads to the height. The impression of tallness is greatly enhanced by unusually narrow shoulders and by an extraordinary and abnormal length of calf and thigh—putting the waistline very far above the usual.

The child is customarily held on the left arm. It is rather difficult to understand the mechanics of the costume, but it seems we may infer the existence of two garments: a dress or gown gathered up at the waist; and a loose mantle or jacket worn over this, swung up over the head to form the familiar female headdress. The skirt falls to the ground; one knee pokes slightly forward to make a convexity; and on the other side, the folds are arranged in a radiating pattern reminiscent of a partly opened fan.

The head and its covering demand special attention. The upper silhouette of the cranium is rounded like a bullet, and the distance between the eyes and the extreme top of the figure is so great that there must be a special reason. Little as the Byzantines cared for anatomy, the likeliest guess seems to be that some form of stiff hat was worn under the mantle to give this appearance. Seen in full-face or in profile, the shape of the head is a delicate oval. The mouth is small, the nose long, and the eyes large and almond-shaped. The length of the cheek, from mouth to eye, is peculiarly great, and the total effect of the face is strange in the sense that an overbred animal is exotically attractive. Often loosely described as "Oriental," this type of head is merely a refined exaggeration of a shape that occurs rather often among the populations of the eastern Mediterranean. The purpose of so finely drawn a figure was to suggest not nature and ordinary life, but an ethereal state of being from which the holy persons look out upon us, their own thoughts turned inward and their eyes demanding a recognition of their significance.

The standard Byzantine type for the Madonna remained constant in East Christian art for a very long time. With minor variations, it is the same as the Madonna who appears in the art of western Europe also. The peculiar fixity of a particular visualization requires a word of explanation.

In recent centuries, it has been more or less taken for granted that artists

Fig. 9.13 (left) Utrecht, Archiepiscopal Museum. Ivory Madonna. 11th century. (C. B. Van Weelderen)

Fig. 9.14 (opposite) New York, Metropolitan Museum. Ivory Crucifixion. 11th century.

should have almost unlimited freedom to invent imagery for whatever subject they might undertake to deal with. The physical appearance of the Madonna, that is to say—or the arrangement of figures and stage properties for a Nativity—are commonly thought to be within the jurisdiction of the individual. We even compare modern artists by reference to their fertility of imagination in this respect. Without suggesting that we are wrong in doing so, it is necessary to understand that medieval custom was different.

The imagery for any sacred character and the iconography for any narrative scene became established at a very early date; thereafter, the arrangement was governed by strict and specific rules. The authority of such rules, indeed their very existence, has often been denounced by recent writers as an intolerable repression of the creative imagination. There can be no doubt that it often was, but there was more reason for the rules than one might at first suppose.

The rules were intended to make pictures correspond to historical truth. Saint Peter, as we have already mentioned, always appeared with a square-cut white beard because people believed he wore one. Similarly, Saint Paul was always shown as a lanky man with a bald pate and a long, pointed brown beard. For the imagery of the Madonna, there was similar circumstantial evidence.

According to a persistent tradition, Saint Luke himself had painted a portrait of the Virgin. During the 5th century, the Empress Eudocia acquired a panel at Antioch and brought it home to Constantinople; she believed, and others believed, that the picture was the very same one painted from life by the Evangelist. It was set up at a crossroad, doubtless enclosed in some kind of shrine, and it acquired the nickname *Hodegetria,* loosely "she who points the way."

It is impossible for us to know exactly what the *Hodegetria* looked like.

Much less can we assert that the contemporary connoisseurs were correct in identifying the hand of the painter Luke. But the facts make less difference than what was accepted as truth in 5th-century Constantinople, and it is a fair guess that the standard Byzantine Madonna does not differ radically from the *Hodegetria*. That being understood, it is easy to see why public opinion would compel every artist to stick very close to the original type, and would consider any meddling an impious outrage.

In histories of Italian painting, the word *Byzantine* has so often been used in an unfortunate sense that it behooves us to correct the impression—an impression gained from provincial and more or less inadequate work in Italy, and one which is altogether erroneous when applied to the production of the best Byzantine masters. The excellence of the latter was never better demonstrated than in a series of miniature ivory altar pieces, some of them literally of pocket size, related in style and coming mostly from the 11th century. The most elaborate of the class is the well-known *Harbaville Triptych* in the Louvre. On the main face, it shows an enthroned Christ with more than a dozen other figures; and on the reverse we see still other saints flanking a central panel of uncommon beauty which perhaps represents the Triumph of the Cross in the Garden of Eden. While heavily vested in the usual stiff costumes, the figures of the saints are obviously studied from nature and vigorously individualized.

Even more exquisite, if such a thing is possible, is a tiny *Crucifixion* in the Metropolitan Museum of Art (Fig. 9.14). The quaint iconography is explained thus: the cross springs from the body of Adam (according to a widely held belief it had actually done so), while above are the soldiers who cast lots for the Savior's clothing.

♦ *The End of the Second Golden Age* The Second Golden Age of Byzantine art was brought to an end by the Fourth Crusade. In the entire history of Christendom, no other scandal compares with this crusade. Assembling at Venice with the intention of going to the Holy Land in Venetian ships, the Crusaders were persuaded to act as mercenaries in the service of Venice. In that capacity, they captured and sacked Zara in Dalmatia. Encouraged still further by the Venetians, they next proceeded against Constantinople. In 1204, they entered the city. There they behaved in a manner shocking even to the sensibilities of a world that took excess for granted as the inevitable privilege of conquerors. Dividing the spoils with the Venetians, the Crusaders gave up any idea of fighting the infidel. They simply settled down in the region of the Bosporus, establishing a loose feudal government known as the Latin Monarchy. Never accepted as *de jure* by the population, the actual power of that government was maintained always on a most adventurous basis. Except for the capital and a few strong points here and there along the coast, it was no government at all. In the year 1261, under the leadership of the distinguished Paleologus family, the western rulers were expelled, and the Byzantine Empire re-established.

During the period of the Latin Monarchy, Constantinople was rendered sterile as a market for art. Architects and artists left the city. Many of them found employment in the Balkans and in Russia, regions already well disposed toward the Byzantine style. The dispersion of artists at this particular juncture in history is probably the reason why Byzantine art, elsewhere given up long since, survives to this day as the ecclesiastical style of Russia.

Seen against the broader canvas of world history, the Fourth Crusade and Latin Monarchy mark the final, and as yet irreparable, schism between Greek and Roman Christianity. The differences of doctrine are of course important to the respective clergy, but the popular basis for the separation springs from a lingering resentment against the brutality and debauchery of the Crusaders, of which the best that can be said is to pronounce it a blasphemy. This sadly natural reaction of the Byzantine population also had the effect of making Moslem civilization seem on the whole better than that of the Christian West, thus tending to diminish the will to resist the Arab invasion when it finally came.

THE THIRD GOLDEN AGE

The best examples of Third Golden Age architecture are to be found in the Balkans rather than in the region of Constantinople. Excellent monuments to illustrate the character of the style are the Church of the Holy Apostles at Salonika (1315), and the Serbian churches of Ravanitsa (1381) and Manassia (Fig. 9.15), which dates from 1407.

In plan the usual church of the Third Golden Age does not differ from the four-column buildings of the previous era: there are the same Greek cross inscribed within a square, the same central dome, and the same subordinate domes in the corners. In elevation, however, there is a substantial change. The proportions of the lower square, or first story, are exaggerated vertically; and the vertical dimension is often emphasized by attaching slender engaged shafts to the exterior wall surface. The four corner and subordinate domes, usually concealed entirely during the Second Golden Age, were commonly raised high on drums. They act as towers, and complicate the sky line. The over-all effect has often been characterized as "Byzantine Gothic"— a term that undoubtedly has historical validity because the western Gothic was at its height just as the Third Golden Age began.

Fig. 9.15 Manassia. Church. 1407. (From P. Pokryskin, *Church Architecture in Serbia*, Leningrad, 1906. By permission of Am-Rus Literary & Music Agency, New York.)

For the purpose of understanding the changes that gave new flavor to the pictures of the Third Golden Age, it is wise to begin with an example which dates considerably earlier than the Fourth Crusade, but one which nevertheless signalizes the trend of the future. The painting referred to is the celebrated *Ikon of Vladimir,* a half-length panel picture of the Madonna and Child (Fig. 9.16). It almost certainly was painted at Constantinople before the end of the 11th century, and it was exported thence to Russia. It there acquired an immense reputation as a picture with almost miraculous religious power. In 1395, for instance, it was brought to Moscow with the idea that it might help in repelling the armies of Tamerlane.

Generally similar to the standard Madonna in figure style and costume, the Madonna here is nevertheless strikingly different from the stately empress familiar in earlier work. The contrast has little to do with style; it is a matter of content. In the Vladimir Madonna, the baby has his arm around his mother's neck; he pulls himself toward her in a warm embrace. Mary inclines her head downward, holding her cheek against his, and she pulls the child to her in a gesture like his own. The picture is full of maternal desire. It has the tone of personal experience—experience, moreover, in which the observer

Fig. 9.16 Moscow, Historical Museum. *Ikon of Vladimir.* 11th century. (Courtesy Mr. Alfred Barr)

shares because no man alive has failed to participate in similar acts and feelings at some time.

Such qualities are the very ones that have long been cited as the special contribution of the humanistic philosophy which we conventionally suppose to have been unknown in Europe earlier than the Italian Renaissance. (See below, pages 469–475.) As knowledge of later Byzantine art becomes more complete and more accessible, it is obvious that many notions may have to be revised.

A number of important frescoes and mosaics are preserved from the Third Golden Age. Of these, perhaps the most notable are the mosaics of Kahrié Djami at Constantinople, from which we reproduce only one (Fig. 9.17). In comparison to the general run of modern representative painting, these pictures of the very early 14th century may very well make the impression of being stiff and conventional. But in comparison to the mosaics at

Fig. 9.17 Constantinople. Kahrié Djami. *Magi Following the Star* and *Magi before Herod.* Mosaic. Early 14th century. (Sabah)

Daphni, they reflect a fundamental change in point of view. The artist of Daphni was a mystic. His purpose was devotional. His pictures stand as symbols for values of a transcendental kind. The artists of the Third Golden Age, on the other hand, seem to have thought of themselves as dramatists. Their purpose was to tell the sacred narrative in such a way that it would carry conviction; and in their view, there was nothing more convincing than a sense of actuality.

The most obvious index to this new conception may be discerned in the setting. Buildings and landscape appear in an intelligible relationship with the human actors. As for the latter, no one can doubt that the artist intended to show something that was alive, moving, and surrounded by air and space.

Here again, we find that East Christian artists appear to have anticipated those of the West. Techniques of accurate representation, in particular, have long been claimed as artistic evidence for the superiority of the Western view of life and the world. The truth is that the mosaic painter of Kahrié Djami had little to apologize for in this respect, even to his great Florentine contemporary Giotto.

THE END OF THE BYZANTINE EMPIRE

In 1439, the Emperor John Paleologus journeyed to Italy to participate in the Council of Florence, the purpose of which was to reconcile the Roman church with the Greek. The concessions he was willing to make might actually have done so had they proven acceptable in the East; but the reverse was true—the attempt simply infuriated the population, and is reckoned actually to have facilitated the Turkish conquest which was about to come.

The intelligent face of John Paleologus is commemorated on a medal by Pisanello (Fig. 12.9, page 437). His visit to Italy did a great cultural service even though his prime objective was not realized. In his train, he brought several distinguished Greek scholars. The bearing of these men in public debate and private conversation fascinated the Italians, and it was at this date that the study of Greek in addition to Latin achieved its traditional importance in Western education. In particular, the Greeks knew Plato, a philosopher almost forgotten in the West since the time of Saint Augustine. According to the testimony of contemporaries, the great Cosimo de' Medici, head of the famous Florentine house, immediately determined to set up at Florence an academy for Platonic studies. Thus commenced the so-called Neoplatonic movement which so profoundly affected art history by molding the spirit of Botticelli and by furnishing the philosophy by which Michelangelo lived. (See below, pages 529ff.)

The emperor's progress from town to town was marked by an inflated bombast of elaborate and expensive ceremonies. At that moment, such were probably mistaken for grandeur; it seems doubtful whether anyone appreciated that the empire had only fifteen years more to live.

In February 1453, Mohammed the Conqueror laid siege to the city of Constantinople. The defenders were able to hold out some time because of the excellent system of defensive walls; but on May 29, the Turks forced an entrance, and the Byzantine empire came to an end after more than a thousand years of existence.

ITALO-BYZANTINE ART

From the time of Justinian in the 6th century to the time of Giotto at the beginning of the 14th, Italy was an artistic province of Byzantium. To this statment, we must make only the exception of the great Nicola Pisano (see below, pages 447–449), who dedicated his famous classical pulpit at Pisa in 1260. In the previous chapter (pages 222–227), we have already dealt with the mosaics of Ravenna, a place where there was little production subsequent to the 6th century. In other regions, however, work in the Byzantine style

Fig. 9.18 Torcello. Cathedral. Mosaics of the apse and arch. 11th century. (Anderson)

continued to be turned out in quantity until the end of the 14th century and later. The chief centers were at Venice and on the island of Sicily.

Always more than half eastern in its taste and culture, Venice kept to the Byzantine style longer than any other Italian city. The mosaic decoration of St. Mark's began as soon as the walls were ready, and the building is today a museum of every change in style that has come since. Like so much provincial work, the work at St. Mark's lacks the elegance and refinement to be expected at the artistic capital. Occasionally, however, the Italo-Byzantine artists rose to a very high level; this we may see in the stately Madonna which occupies the semidome of the apse at Torcello, an island near Venice (Fig. 9.18). With the usual row of apostles beneath her and sustained, as it were, by a flood of glowing and somber color, she seems in her person to embody the most solemn and majestic concepts of religion.

Fig. 9.19 Monreale. Cathedral. Interior, choir. *King William the 2nd Offering a Church to the Madonna.* Mosaic. 12th century. (Alinari)

During the 12th century, an immense amount of Byzantine art was produced in Sicily. Accessible to the modern traveler and surviving in lavish quantity, the Sicilian mosaics furnish our best opportunity to experience the Byzantine interior as the Byzantine designers wished it to be. Indeed, if we may judge by the frequency of inscriptions written in Greek, many of the artists who worked on the island must have come from the Near East.

The chief monuments are the Palace Chapel and the Martorana Chapel at Palermo, and the great cathedral churches of Monreale and Cefalù. Virtually every square foot of the vast interior at Monreale is covered with pictures in mosaic; every surface confronts the eye with rich, somber, jewel-like tones. Superb though the general effect may be, the quality of individual pictures is inferior to those at Cefalù, where much less survives.

Figure 9.19 shows an example typical of the work at Monreale and typical, also, the general run of later Italo-Byzantine art. Any one familiar with this mosaic in the original will feel inclined to say that its color is so wonderful as to render any criticism invidious; and yet it is a fact that Giotto (Chapter 12) turned his back on just such art as this and thus made himself celebrated as the father of modern painting. Why? Among other obvious defects, we may cite the drapery of the Madonna. Neither the major convolutions nor the minor folds preserve any reasonable relationship to the human form; and yet we are asked to read humanity into the figure. It is indeed difficult to do so; and it is not unfair to contend that the Byzantine manner, at least as manipulated by artists who worked in the provinces, had been feeding too long on its own conventions. The only remedy for such an art was to have artists return to the direct study of nature.

♦ *The School of Siena*   By bold steps and leaving much unsaid, we have brought ourselves to a point where it is appropriate to consider the artistic situation in Italy at the end of the 13th century—the period which witnessed the self-assertion of numerous new and vital city schools of painting, and, through the agency of the 14th-century School of Siena, a new and (as it was to turn out) final flowering of Byzantine art.

The force and prestige of the Byzantine conventions had been considerably weakened by the attrition of time and the advent of new ideas. The art that began about 1300 differed from that of earlier periods principally in the fact that the artist enjoyed a much wider margin of choice than before. At Rome, Pietro Cavallini at first cautiously departed from Byzantine models, and then attempted to recover some measure of Roman naturalism. At Florence, as we shall see in Chapter 12, the great Giotto struck out for himself along untried lines. But at Siena, the most conservative city in the world, it seemed natural to attempt to pump new life into the time-honored formulas.

Duccio (active 1279; died 1319) was the founder of the new Sienese school. In 1311, he finished an immense altarpiece for the cathedral of that city. The main face showed a large Byzantine Madonna enthroned among saints. The reverse of the great panel carried 26 small rectangular panels of narrative painting, covering significant events from the Passion of Christ. In addition to these 26, there were still more subordinate panels in the *predella* (the lower border) and in the Gothic pinnacles across the top. In all, it has been reckoned that there were originally no fewer than 91 compositions in addition to the *Madonna in Majesty* of the main front. Long since dismantled and removed from its place in the cathedral, most of the preserved material is on view today in the cathedral museum nearby. A few panels have wandered into other hands; one of them is the *Temptation on the Mountain* in the Frick Collection of New York.

The head of Saint Agnes (Fig. 9.20), one of the saints standing to the right of the Madonna on the main face, is in itself an epitome of Duccio's painting. The physical type is already familiar; the painter's special contribution has been to infuse the old formula with a warmer life, even with per-

Fig. 9.20 Duccio. "Head of Saint Agnes." Detail from the *Madonna in Majesty*. 1308–1311. Siena, Cathedral Museum. (Anderson)

sonality. Much of the meaning, moreover, is carried by the slow winding of the infinitely graceful lines, some of them brought out in pure gold against a darker ground. As the eye follows these curves, the mood of the painting is induced.

Duccio's line requires special comment. There is no other line just like it in western Europe, even in Gothic France which was contemporary and where linear calligraphy had been carried to a high level of accomplishment. The nearest true parallel is to be found no closer than China, where the Sung painters had used pure line with similar purpose and effect. We must either postulate an alchemy of circumstances which somehow caused Duccio to develop the same esthetic means, or we must suppose that he had seen some Chinese painting. The latter hypothesis is more likely. It has long been entertained by scholars, almost all of whom have failed to summon the courage to make an actual assertion in the absence of objective evidence. The likelihood that Chinese paintings were now and then on view at Siena puts no strain on the imagination, however.

We know that Vasco da Gama rounded the Cape, went to the Orient, and returned on his great voyage of 1497–1499. We hear that Columbus discovered America by mistake, having intended to reach the Far East. We forget, or we never hear, that the Middle East was not actually sealed off until the end of the 14th century, at which time the western Tartars embraced Islam, the Seljuk Turks advanced, and the Mongol dynasty was overthrown in China. Until then, the routes were open. Marco Polo (about 1254–1324) had been to China and back. A Roman Catholic bishop established a diocese at Peking at the end of the 13th century. During the 14th, Francesco Pegolotti, a member of the Bardi bank at Florence, was enough impressed with the traffic to write a set of directions covering the route to Peking. It was safe all the way, he said, if one merely took reasonable precautions.

One commodity that came westward over these trade routes was lapis lazuli which, when powdered, provided painters with their ultramarine blue— at Siena, virtually the standard pigment for the Madonna's robe. If painter's materials were thus imported, it would have been remarkable if a few Chinese paintings failed to find their way west. Doubly so, indeed, if we stop to remember that the favorite pictorial form in China was the roll, the most conveniently portable kind of art and the kind least likely to be damaged in transit. The real puzzle is not that Duccio showed certain Oriental affinities, but why he and other Sienese artists were the only western painters who did.

Duccio stayed continuously at home, where he had the reputation of getting into trouble with his friends and neighbors. The other great Sienese painter of the 14th century, Simone Martini (1285?–1344), was not only a widely traveled man of the world, but a distinguished gentleman. Well-born and himself a knight, he associated on terms of personal friendship with the highest in the land. He was, in fact, one of the very first artists to do so— a matter to which we shall allude at some length in a later chapter (see below, pages 429–430). After important commissions all over Italy, he was called in 1339 to the Papal Court, then resident at Avignon. He died there in 1344. Petrarch, also at Avignon, knew him well; in two of his sonnets, he speaks appreciatively of Simone's portrait of Laura, a picture unhappily lost. The presence of this eminent Sienese painter at Avignon had wide repercussions upon the history of art, for Avignon proved to be the focus of origin for the so-called International Style (pages 429–441), a type of Late Gothic painting of unusual charm.

Like Duccio, Simone turned out a number of altarpieces of the kind that were virtually standard with the Sienese painters. The painting was done in tempera on prepared wooden panels. The background was invariably blank and of pure gold. The central subject was always a Madonna (for Siena considered herself to be under the special protection of the Virgin). Customarily, the Madonna was dressed in a gown and headdress of the usual Byzantine mode, the color being ultramarine blue. Such paintings were sumptuous and expensive; the blue pigment alone often cost a staggering sum and a good deal more than the gold, which cost enough. The Isabella Stewart Gardner Museum of Boston has a fine altarpiece by Simone, a Madonna with four saints. While there one should look, also, at the little single Madonna by Lippo Memmi, Simone's closest follower; it is in the better condition of the two. The museum visitor must remember, also, that Sienese paintings suffer when taken out of context. They were designed to carry the length of the nave in dark churches, lit only by candles on the altar. Very few of them remain in position, a rare exception being Pietro Lorenzetti's panel on the high altar of the Pieve at Arezzo.

The pictures for which Simone is best remembered, however, are those in which to some extent he broke away from the Byzantine manner and became a man of modern times. Like all members of the upper orders during the High Middle Age, he was literally fascinated with the theory of social hierarchy. Anyone who inspects with a sharp eye his frescoes of the life of Saint Martin, in the church of St. Francis at Assisi, will receive a lesson in stratification that scarcely seems possible. As a native son who had acquired a broader horizon, he looked with good-natured satire upon the provincial solemnities of his own small city, an attitude we can see plainly demonstrated in his portrait of Guidoriccio Fogliani (Fig. 9.2), mercenary general whose small services were thus commemorated on the wall of a principal chamber in the Palazzo Pubblico. Across a grand landscape panorama, dotted with hill towns and showing a military encampment over which flies the incomparable black and white banner of Siena, the silly little fat man rides his magnificent horse, taking himself seriously.

The drapery of the general's horse has been hailed as the most gorgeous linear symphony in European art. Certainly a notable demonstration, it suffers by comparison with Duccio. Duccio's quiet conceals his daring; he often relied upon a single strand of gold to carry an entire field. For a full understanding of the multiplication and complexity in which Simone indulged here and elsewhere, we must refer the reader ahead to the most florid of the Late Gothic, a movement in which he was actually an early participant.

The Gothic affinities just suggested come out even more plainly in the famous *Sant'Ansano Annunciation* of 1333 (Fig. 9.21). All too often cited as the quintessence of both Simone and the entire Sienese school, it is better de-

Fig. 9.21 Simone Martini. *Sant'Ansano Annunciation*. 1333. Florence, Uffizi. (Anderson)

scribed as half Byzantine and half French; the Madonna's gown, for instance, duplicates French costumes of the very same date. It doubtless came from Paris, which even then occupied its familiar position as the fashion center of the West.

The workmanship is consummately fine, but Simone's *Annunciation* remains a curiously shallow picture. He participated, like Duccio, in Oriental methods, and here attempted to characterize persons and describe their emotions by the use of line. Every curve of Gabriel's body, wings, and drapery is suave, flowing, and urbanely pressing forward. By contrast, Mary shrinks back, startled and even annoyed, this being indicated by her receding silhouette and by the sharper twists and angular junctions within the drapery.

When Simone left for Avignon, the leadership of the Sienese school passed into the hands of the brothers Pietro and Ambrogio Lorenzetti, both of whom seem to have died in the Black Death of 1348. In spite of the important commissions entrusted to them by an enthusiastic clientele, neither brother had

Fig. 9.22 (above) Simone Martini. *Guido-riccio Fogliani.* 1328. Siena, Palazzo Púb-blico. (Anderson)

Fig. 9.23 (left) Pietro Lorenzetti. *Madonna with Saint John and Saint Francis.* Assisi, Church of St. Frances. (Anderson)

anything like the distinction of Duccio or Simone. Ambrogio's large frescoes of *Good and Bad Government,* executed for the Palazzo Pubblico between 1337 and 1339, are a tedious imitation of Giotto (who had by that time made his reputation. On one occasion, however, Pietro outdid the ordinary stand-ards of the firm. We refer to his *Madonna with Saint John and Saint Francis* in the left transept of the lower church at Assisi (Fig. 9.23). The Mary is a poignantly appealing figure; mystic yearning survives in sufficient force to guarantee dignity, yet the effect is emotional to a degree beyond anything yet cited in the present chapter. The painting may be described, in fact, as very forward-looking for its date in the 1330's; it actually foreshadowed the famous Madonnas of Donatello. (See below, page 488.)

The later history of the Sienese school is of general importance only in broad outline. Excellent paintings continued to be produced well into the 15th century, but no new masters of significant originality appeared. True to the extreme conservatism of the city, each successive man did his best to pro-vide sensitive but minor variations upon the formulas of Duccio or Simone Martini. In a remarkable way, all of these masters kept alive the essential and peculiar spirit of Siena long after the rest of the world had gone modern. For special students and connoisseurs, the field is a paradise, but we must pass on.

Chapter 10

T HE NAME *Romanesque* refers to the new style of art which appeared in Western Europe about the year A.D. 1000 and went out of use with the great sweep of Gothic taste that took place during the second half of the 12th century.

The word itself requires explanation. Its denotation is the same as *romance*—that is, from the Roman. It was originally applied to this art because it flourished in territory which had once been Roman, and because Romanesque architecture, like that of Rome, made extensive use of the round arch, the engaged shaft, and ponderous proportions. The resemblances are superficial, however, and by no means prove that the later style evolved from the earlier. In fact, the better one knows the Romanesque, the less Roman it seems.

THE DIRECT CAUSES OF THE
ROMANESQUE STYLE

The emergence of the Romanesque style was visible evidence that Europe had at last recovered from the collapse of ancient civilization. Insofar as the development may be connected with any system of politics, it seems to have been made possible by the relative safety and prosperity provided by the feudal system, then fully developed. The movement coincided, also, with the growth of social self-consciousness in the numerous cities and towns which were gradually replacing the village-economy of the earlier Middle Ages. But above all, the Romanesque was an expression of the Catholic Church, and especially of its monastic element.

312

ROMANESQUE ART

In theory, the feudal system provided a central government, with all officials deriving their authority by delegation from the king. In practice, effective power fell into the hands of the men best able to make their strength felt by those around them. In view of the economy, which was agricultural and based upon the theory of small, self-sufficient units, and also in view of the unbelievably bad roads and consequent delays and dangers in communication, the largest region which could be administered efficiently corresponded in size to the modern county. The count or duke thereof could get around fast enough to keep track of affairs and make his will felt; he paid only lip service to the king whom he rarely saw. Europe, in other words, was then divided into much smaller units than the nations of today. The words England, France, Germany, Italy, and Spain signified little. In attempting to understand the Romanesque, one must think, rather, in terms of Normandy, Burgundy, Aquitaine, the Auvergne, Languedoc, Provence, Lombardy, Tuscany, and so on, words which survive today mainly as a link with long ago. Each of the regions named had a local variation of the Romanesque style; and each corresponds with the sometime existence of a *grand seigneur* who governed in the manner described.

The political subdivision of Europe accounted for the teeming variety embraced within the Romanesque style; but the style remained essentially the same wherever found. The reason is to be sought in the organization of the Roman Catholic Church.

For the modern reader, who lives in a secular world, an effort of the imagination is required even to conceive the situation as it then existed. The separation between the spiritual and the temporal, which we take for granted,

313

had hardly come into the European mind even as a theory. It was impossible then for any man to go through life without coming into contact, and repeatedly so, with the authority of the Church. Not only did the Church collect taxes (tithes) in its own name and right; the Church courts had jurisdiction over more than half the matters in which the normal citizen might sooner or later be involved. They ruled on everything of which clerics might complain or be accused, and on certain subjects, by virtue of their impingement upon religion or ceremony, the Church ruled no matter who was involved: marriage, affairs of widows and orphans, wills and inheritance.

The Catholic polity was something more, it will be appreciated, than an organization offering religious ceremonies at stated intervals. It was an engine of government. People were more frequently and more keenly conscious of it than of the civil authority. The humblest person could not follow his obscure way of life except in relation to the clergy. The most powerful prince ruled in fear of ecclesiastical rebuke.

In visualizing the Church as it then existed, the modern reader must still further adjust his ideas to the scale of monasticism. Today, we have only casual contact with monks and nuns; but during the Middle Ages, the secular clergy (those who do the work of the church among the people) comprised only part, and at times the weaker part of the hierarchy. The regular clergy (from the Latin *regula,* for "rule," and applied to monks and nuns because they lived according to rules laid down by their order) were numerous, rich, well organized, and powerful. Cluny, founded in 910, was the greatest abbey of all, but only one among many. In its heyday, Cluny owned and controlled no less than 390 major establishments in various parts of Europe—a statistic which makes it obvious that the monasteries had absorbed an immense section of the population.

It is evident there was cause enough for the exclusively religious cast of Romanesque art. A certain number of civil, domestic, and military buildings survive from the era; and there are a few instances of secular painting and sculpture. By comparison, however, those exceptions weigh little. Even so, the reader must not imagine that the government of the church had yet reached its ultimate perfection; that was delayed until the 13th century, and will concern us in the next chapter.

Each of the causes so far cited, and all of them together, were of gradual application. Something further is required to explain the rather sudden start of what amounted to a pan-European building effort, for churches dating before 1000 are scarce, while almost every locality has one or more Romanesque buildings still in good repair and daily use. The missing bit of motivation, the final impulse which brought action, was very probably the safe passage of the year 1000 itself.

Although a great many scholars have been at pains to scout the whole notion, and although the Church often warned against it during the 10th century, there is undeniably much evidence that any number of people expected the end of the world in that year. In attempting to comprehend such a belief, the reader must appreciate that it never entered the medieval mind to construe the words of the Bible as plain language. Far from meaning what they said, the sacred writings were generally thought to be guarded and cryptic, their true purport to be fathomed only by a great effort of interpretation. So approached, and digested and redigested with devious intelligence, passages and combinations of passages often attained, in the imagination of medieval readers, some surprising implications.

Briefly, the idea of the Sabbath (Genesis 2:3) was combined with the "thousand years in Thy sight" of Psalm 90:4 to create the notion that world history must proceed according to units of a thousand years, vaguely as the day of the week. The "wars and rumors of wars" mentioned in Matthew 24:6 and Mark 13:7 would (according to a parallel passage in Luke 21:11) be announced to the world by earthquakes, pestilences, and "fearful sights and great signs . . . from heaven." To these passages, we may add the twentieth chapter of Revelation; for an imagination already whetted to expect the worst, its wild metaphor could easily seem to announce the end. It is obvious that a certain proportion of the learned were by no means easy in their minds; and the ignorant and superstitious were of course prepared to despair wholeheartedly. People were seeing things all the time and everywhere, and identifying them as portents.

During the decade 990–1000, a great many worrisome events happened. There were five successive years of crop failure. Fires, the perennial curse of medieval life, were unusually frequent in both France and Italy. The plague known as Saint Anthony's Fire became epidemic. Serious heresies arose in several parts of the continent. Vesuvius, as though to predict the whole course of events, erupted in 993 with a hideous emission of noxious gases.

We are lucky enough to have a chronicle of those years, the work of Raoul Glaber, a monk who died at Cluny in 1044. Glaber took special note of the year 1000, and in an often-quoted passage, he noted that ". . . it befell almost throughout the world but especially in Italy and Gaul, that the fabrics of churches were rebuilt, although many were seemly and needed no such care; but every nation of Christendom rivaled with the other, which should worship in the seemliest buildings. So it was as though the very world had shaken herself and cast off her old age, and were clothing herself in a white garment of churches."

It is unnecessary to exaggerate Glaber's testimony to draw the conclusion that he himself believed the year 1000 to have been a signal for the commencement of building activity. As a matter of statistical fact, however, the greater number of important Romanesque monuments seem to have been started somewhat later. The elements of the style were worked out during the 11th century. The greatest production took place in the 12th.

THE ELEMENTS OF THE ROMANESQUE STYLE IN ARCHITECTURE

The Romanesque was the most diverse style in history. No two examples are alike; every building seems to reflect in some measure a novel conception. It is nevertheless possible to draw up a list of features which, by their repeated appearance all over Europe, furnish a kind of common denominator for all monuments. The diversity explains itself largely by reference to geography, each region having its peculiar type of church, built of the local materials and with an arrangement of towers, apses, and transepts found nowhere else. The features possessed in common by all regions are a series of special motives (doors, windows, moldings, piers, capitals, and so on) scarcely predicted by any earlier style and for all practical purposes the contribution of the Romanesque. To these we shall now turn our attention, leaving a brief treatment of the regional differences for another section.

Before we proceed, it is necessary to warn the reader what to expect. Familiarity with classical art may be a positive handicap in attempting to comprehend the Romanesque. No abstractions governed the designers of the 11th and 12th centuries. Geometric order, either in plan or elevation, did not preoccupy them for a moment; they used such order or left it alone as they chose at the time. There is no system of proportions to which they adhered; their style encompasses some of the most delicate and some of the most ponderous building known in Europe. Because bulk transport over long distances passed beyond the realm of feasibility when Rome fell, we may expect to see any of the typical Romanesque motives executed in cheap brick, local limestone, exquisite marble, or whatever else may have been at hand. Almost every color available in masonry occurs at one place or another, and the textures may be as slick as silk or of a homely coarseness like tweed. The thing that counts, if we are to grasp the essential unity of the style as a whole, is to be able to recognize the typical motives no matter how they may be varied or on what part of the building they may appear.

♦ *Towers* It is difficult for us even to imagine a time when towers and steeples were rare; and we are thus likely to overlook the fact that the Romanesque was the first architectural style to make consistent use of the tower as an integral element in church design. We think of a church tower as a place to hang a bell; and it is true that the association of churches and bells must be at least as old as the traditional "invention" of the church bell by Saint Paulinus of Nola (died 431). It is difficult, however, to account for all the

Romanesque towers by that simple and practical consideration. A certain symbolical intention may also have operated to increase their popularity.

Towers over the crossing, for example, may have evolved from the domes of *martyria* (tombs raised over the graves of martyrs), a more or less familiar type of building in the Near East. Towers incorporated into the western façade (very rare in Italy, common elsewhere) may have been suggested by the notion that the emperor, God's vicar on earth for secular affairs, ought to be honored by a conspicuous feature—balancing the sacred apse—on the part of the church that faced the world. Either of these ideas might have suggested the construction of a single tower; but both together hardly account for the multiplication of towers which was so evidently the Romanesque ideal.

The notion of the tower obviously struck a sympathetic chord in the esthetic sensibilities of the people. In other words, they felt a powerful stylistic impulse; and whatever else they may accomplish, towers tend to give a building the broken and "dissolving" silhouette typical of the Northern and Barbarian Style; and we may assume that the Romanesque builders, whatever they may have thought about the iconographical significance of their towers, were inclined to use them because they instinctively liked them.

However that may be, it has been habitual, ever since the Romanesque period, to think of the tower as a Christian symbol. For many persons, a church without a tower is no church. The vertical momentum imparted by a tower is intimately expressive; it is impossible to challenge the propriety of an association with the aspiring element in Christianity. But before people could make the association, they had to have towers to look at—and the introduction of towers would seem to have antedated the modern symbolism.

◆ *Doors and Windows*   In every architectural style, much and sometimes everything depends upon the particular kind of door or window which may be characteristic of the style as a whole. The standard Romanesque opening, as already indicated, was the round arch, but the round arch was rarely used in a plain and simple form. The Romanesque produced many combinations and manipulations of the round arch, of which five are the most important: the splayed opening, the Lombard porch, the Tuscan door, the compound arch, and the wheel window.

Figures 10.1 to 3 illustrate the *splayed opening*. As the name implies, the splayed door is beveled in the plan view, and flares out toward one through the thickness of the wall. No other kind of door fulfills its purpose so well. In a crude and mechanical sense, a door is merely a device that permits circulation in and out, at the same time protecting the interior from the weather. Artistically, a door is far more important than that. It is a barrier which can invite or forbid. The splayed doorway brings the actual opening

Fig. 10.1 Aulnay. St. Pierre. South transept portal. 12th century. (Marburg)

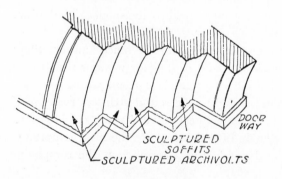

SCULPTURED SOFFITS
SCULPTURED ARCHIVOLTS
DOOR WAY

Fig. 10.2 Perspective cross section through the four orders of a typical Romanesque splayed arch.

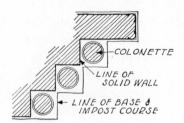

COLONETTE
LINE OF SOLID WALL
LINE OF BASE & IMPOST COURSE

Fig. 10.3 Cross section through the compound supports beneath a typical Romanesque splayed arch of four orders.

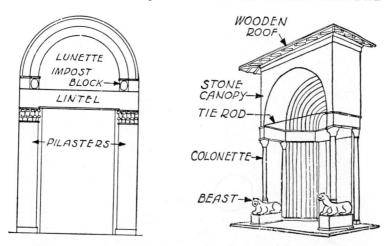

Figs. 10.4–5 (left) Schematic drawing to illustrate the principal parts of a typical Tuscan portal. (right) Schematic drawing to show the principal parts of a typical Lombard porch.

into focus; and by walking under its overhang, one finds himself halfway in while still outside. Without further effort of the will, he may pass into the building.

Both in the Romanesque and later in the Gothic style, the splayed doorway was made up of several concentric arches, at Aulnay four of them. Each of the four arches that make up the doorway at Aulnay may be described as an *order;* and the ensemble is conveniently referred to as a *splayed arch in four orders.* It is important to note, in order to get the flavor of the Romanesque, that each of the four orders has a simple cross section (Fig. 10.2) and remains clear and distinct from its neighbors. It is the comparative simplicity of the Romanesque which must be kept in mind; Gothic, as we shall see, worked toward elegant complication.

The *Lombard porch,* indicated schematically by Figure 10.5, and well illustrated by the main portal of the cathedral at Modena in Lombardy (Fig. 10.25) is made up of the following elements. The builder starts with two stone beasts sitting on pedestals. Lions were the most common; but there was no rule about it, and those who preferred griffins or elephants made free to use them instead. From the back of each beast, there springs a slender colonnette, and from the colonnettes, the arches of a delicate canopy. At Modena, a second story was provided; most Lombard porches have only one.

The *Tuscan door* appears in Figure 10.4, and in a somewhat unusual form on the main front of the cathedral at Pisa (Fig. 10.23). In typical exam-

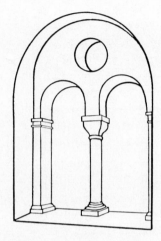

Figs. 10.6–7 (left) A typical Romanesque wheel window. (right) The compound arch. (Drawing by Dorothy Shea)

ples, two fat Corinthian pilasters form the door jambs; a lintel spans the opening, and there is a relieving arch above the lintel. Lions' heads, or other grotesques, were often used to mark the impost of the arch; and within the *lunette* (sometimes called *tympanum)* one often finds a panel of relief, or perhaps a painting now protected by glass.

The *compound arch,* in its simplest essentials, is shown in Figure 10.7. It amounts to a side-by-side arrangement of little arches which spring from a colonnette and are enclosed within the frame of a big arch. Never used as a door, it was often employed for windows, for the openings of a triforium gallery, and for exterior galleries in the thickness of a wall, as we see it at Modena. The compound arch was common in Byzantine architecture of the Second Golden Age. It passed on from the Romanesque into the Gothic, pointed arches being substituted for the round. It also occurs in a few examples of Early Renaissance work, in which case classical mouldings and classical columns take the place of the medieval. Surprisingly simple in its form, the compound arch enriches any building with an intricate play of line and surface, and an ever-changing pattern of light and shadow.

The conspicuous circular window above the central entrance at Modena is still another typically Romanesque motive usually known as a *wheel window*. The complex of stone mullions within it is called *tracery*. As it happens, the tracery at Modena appears to have been restored during the Gothic era, as one can tell from the pointing of the arches. A more usual form during the Romanesque would be like Figure 10.6. A wheel window is often called a *rose window*. If the tracery impresses one as the spoke of a wheel, use the former term; if as the petals of a flower, use the latter.

♦ *Motives for Decorating the Surface of Walls* Whatever their practical utility, the several Romanesque motives so far cited served the esthetic purpose of lending an extraordinary interest to the wall surface of the Romanesque church. In that particular department of architecture, it is a fair statement that no other designers were ever so clever and inventive as those of the 11th and 12th centuries. Among the many minor and decorative devices developed to aid in the same purpose, the following need mention.

In innumerable instances, an otherwise blank wall was subdivided by delicate horizontal moldings which project but slightly and cast a narrow, crisp shadow. These are known as *string courses.* A string course was often strengthened in its effect by the addition of *corbels,* and the combination is called *corbel table.* Two kinds are shown in Figure 10.8. The Lombard corbels are tiny arches hanging in mid-air. The French are little brackets projecting at right angles from the wall, and sometimes decorated with gargoyles.

The *blind arcade* (Fig. 10.9) is found on the grand scale at Pisa (Fig. 10.23), where it stands the full height of the aisle walls and runs completely around the building. With components of every imaginable proportion and in every conceivable size, the same motive can be seen wherever Romanesque was built, both indoors and out.

Geometric shapes formed still another resource of the Romanesque architect. At Pisa, we see them used as hollow coffers sunk into the wall. Elsewhere, and especially in Lombardy, crosses, diamonds, triangles, and other simple forms were used whenever the builders felt inclined to have an odd sort of window.

♦ *The Eccentricity of the Style* To the list of typical Romanesque motives so far cited, we must add another element which is underlying and fundamental, but by no means susceptible of easy definition. We refer to what may be called the eccentricity of the Romanesque—a factor which was in part spontaneous and in part the product of calculated intention.

Any persual of a dozen or more measured drawings that accurately reflect the physical facts of as many Romanesque monuments will surprise if not shock the modern reader. Walls are often out of parallel. Bays of vaulting are defined by "squares" which are not strictly rectangular. The arches of an arcade (Fig. 10.24) rise to different levels at the crown and differ somewhat in curvature and span.

Such irregularities reflect easygoing building methods. Medieval society was simply incapable of the discipline familiar in Roman times and today. Its armies, for all the romance we read about them, were probably the most inefficient and ineffective in history, size for size; and its armies of builders were similarly loose in their organization. Plans, in the modern sense of a

FRENCH TYPE   LOMBARD TYPE

Fig. 10.8   Corbel tables. (Drawings by Dorothy Shea)

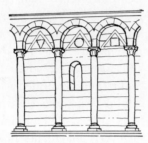

Fig. 10.9 A typical blind arcade of the Romanesque period.

complete set of drawings done to scale, were unknown, although it is likely that a master builder often made a small model to illustrate essential details of the intended fabric. As a result, there was nothing like the modern regularity of procedure. Much was left to the improvisation of the moment or to the whim of the individual foreman.

Such methods—and they obtained throughout the entire Middle Ages, not applying to the Romanesque alone—were anything but economical. A great many churches fell down, altogether or in part. On the other hand, who would trade medieval irregularity for the sterile precision of Roman and modern methods? In an informal way, and often capriciously, the effect arrived at was similar to that of the refinements of the Parthenon. There is life in the stones. The buildings are quaint, picturesque, lovable.

Deliberate eccentricity often formed part of the Romanesque intention. In the open arcade running around the apse of the Pieve at Arezzo, the fifth column from the left was given a dog-leg twist, not by accident but obviously by design. Another instance of whimsy let loose in architecture is the famous Leaning Tower at Pisa (Fig. 10.23). Proof of the designer's intention is not absolute; but the weight of the evidence attests that the lean was planned from the beginning. In that connection, it is important to realize that there were other leaning towers, including two at Bologna and one at Ravenna.

For Romanesque eccentricity, the reader must not look for a rational explanation; the thing itself is not of the mind. Let him instead turn back and review the pages where we first dealt with the northern temperament as expressed in art. The leaning towers and other deliberate violations of common sense are to be explained as the Irishman explained jumping through the plate glass window: he couldn't say why, but he could say it seemed a good idea at the time.

♦ *The Theory of Structural Logic: "Organic Architecture"*   Each of the three outer orders of the splayed arch at Aulnay (Fig. 10.1) comes down on its separate colonnette, with a section of wall acting as support for the fourth order. Such an articulation of supports was the essence of the new theory of structural logic which first captured the imagination of Europe during the Romanesque period.

Much earlier architecture had been structurally logical in the sense that it stood, and has endured. We refer here not to the mere capacity to oppose the force of gravity, but to a theory of design which had its genesis in the forces brought into play by the mechanism of a building, and in the work done by each component part. There are four parts to the arch at Aulnay; there are four parts in the support beneath. A one-to-one correspondence exists between the work being done and the shape of the members that do it. Thought of collectively, the assembly of supports under either side of this arch would be referred to as a *compound support*.

The compounding of supports was probably invented in the first place in an attempt to eliminate (more strictly, to omit) unnecessary masonry. The idea was to make the least material do the maximum amount of work. Structures so designed depend for their safety upon an accurate analysis of forces, and precision in the placement of parts. It follows that designers, as they become more and more familiar with a particular structural problem, will begin to give every part a shape best adapted to the work it must do. Beauty may or may not result.

The structural esthetic was more or less perfectly understood in different parts of Europe; but wherever it operated, major inspiration took place. Indeed, it was this theory of building which enabled the Romanesque architects to put up the first vaulted buildings Europe had seen for centuries. It was reserved for the Gothic period to solve in final fashion the age-old problem of ecclesiastical architecture; namely, how to design a well-lighted fireproof building of the traditional basilican form. The Romanesque experiments which prepared the way for the Gothic were, however, clever, vital, fascinating, and various.

During any period of experiment, many things are tried only to be discarded. Such was the case with eccentric vault forms like those of St. Ours at Loches (Fig. 10.12) and St. Philibert at Tournus (Fig. 10.10). Domes on pendentives (several of them in a row, covering the nave) were popular for a

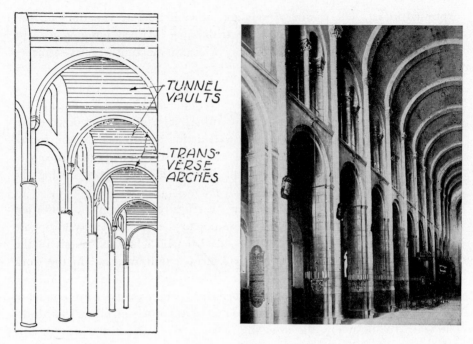

Figs. 10.10–11 (left) Tournus. St. Philibert. Drawing to illustrate the method of vaulting: a series of small tunnel vaults at right angles to the axis of the nave. (right) Toulouse. St. Sernin. View in the nave. (Archives Photographiques)

while in Aquitaine, but never took hold elsewhere. In the main, it can be said that the Romanesque builders experimented with the tunnel vault, and ultimately gave it up in favor of the cross vault.

The best of the tunnel vaults were ribbed, as in Figure 10.11. For all practical purposes, the thrusts of such a vault may be assumed to be concentrated on the ribs, and may conveniently be contained by salient pier buttresses like those shown in Figure 10.14.

When integration is wanted for an interior, no other vault compares with the tunnel vault. It is a natural unit rather than a juxtaposition of separate parts; and its axial force is so great that visible ribs do it no harm. There is no telling what might have happened had the Romanesque builders chosen to refine this excellent form; but they abandoned it half developed. Most Romanesque tunnel vaults, ribbed or plain, have an abutment system of the kind shown by Figure 10.13, with a gallery vault at high level opposing the nave thrusts. Such construction was clumsy, expensive, and guaranteed to make the church gloomy.

Because the cross vault made it convenient to place big windows all along both sides of the nave, experimental cross vaults were common in Roman-

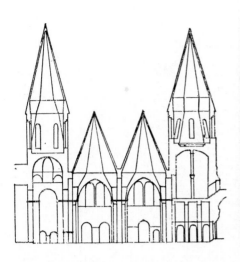

Figs. 10.12–13 (left) Loches. St. Ours. Schematic drawings to illustrate the peculiar vaulting which consists of a series of hollow pyramids. (right) The abutment of a tunnel vault by means of two continuous half-tunnel vaults. From a model of Notre Dame du Port at Clermont-Ferrand. (Archives Photographiques)

esque architecture. Usually, the nature of the form was imperfectly under-stood, and its special advantage exploited only in part. Even so, the Roman-esque builders produced a number of buildings which were undeniably in advance—and far in advance—of anything earlier.

The earliest logical and mature use of the cross vault occurred when the present nave of Sant'Ambrogio at Milan was designed (Figs. 10.15–16). The precise date remains to be established. Some parts of the church may be as early as the 9th century; but there are records of building (or rebuilding?) between 1046 and 1071, again about 1129, and still again in 1196. The best guess is that the vaults date from the middle or late 11th century.

Fig. 10.14 Salient pier buttresses arranged to take the thrust of a ribbed tunnel vault. From a restoration of the Abbey Church at Cluny, built in the 12th century and de-molished during the 18th. (Stoedtner)

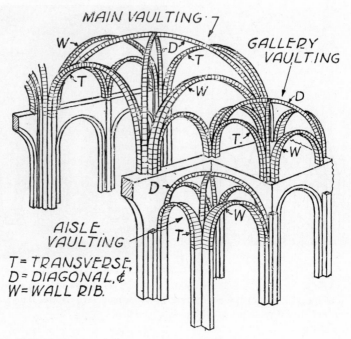

Figs. 10.15–16 Milan. Sant'Ambrogio. (top) Schematic drawing to illustrate the arrangement of the more important parts of the fabric. (Drawing by Dorothy Shea). (bottom) A detail from the plan, showing the relationship between the nave and aisle bays, and the reason for an alternating system of supports.

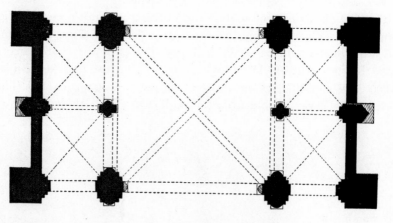

Figure 10.15 is an attempt to show in schematic fashion the complicated skeleton of ribs which forms the fabric of Sant'Ambrogio. The great vaults, it will be seen, were buttressed in adequate if not elegant fashion by smaller cross vaulting at the triforium level. A study of this drawing, in connection with Figures 10.16 to 21, will make plain better than words the extent to which the entire design, from its first conception, was governed by a pene-

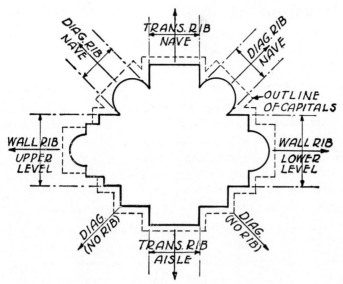

Fig. 10.17 Milan. Sant'Ambrogio. Cross section through one of the larger compound piers.

Fig. 10.18 Longitudinal cross section to demonstrate the rise of the domical vaults.

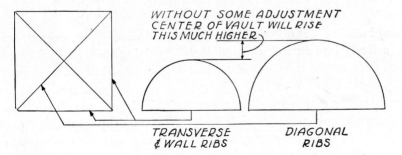

Fig. 10.19 Schematic drawing to demonstrate why the cross vaults are domical.

trating sensitivity for structural fact; and the reader should take care to note that many questions ordinarily decided by artistic intuition (and for the sake of appearance only) were here settled by reference to structural logic. Every capital, for example, was placed at a level determined by the impost of the arch it carries. Capitals bearing diagonal ribs have a diagonal orientation. The shafts from which the great nave ribs rise are unbroken verticals; they cut boldly throughly all subordinate material.

It will be noted that not all the piers are the same size. For some reason best known to themselves (there being no advantage one way or the other), Italian architects have traditionally preferred to use square bays of vaulting; and at Sant'Ambrogio and elsewhere, the aisles were therefore made half as wide as the nave (Fig. 10.16), with the result that two small bays exist in the aisle beside each big bay in the nave. Because a pier was needed to take the spring of every transverse rib in the aisles, the total number of piers was determined not by the nave vaulting, but by the number of bays in the aisles. But since some piers carried many shafts and others few, the size and shape of any particular pier was adjusted accordingly. Any church with such a system of supports is said to have "the alternating system," as contrasted with "the uniform system" common in France.

The intimate and functional relationship between part and part, as seen at Sant'Ambrogio, bears some analogy to the skeletal structure of a living thing. The attractiveness of the analogy is increased by the notion that there is life in the arches. Subjected to compression and exerting thrust, they seem to be undergoing an experience of a muscular kind.

The remarks just made will suggest a train of thought that has been popular among critics for at least three generations. It has been usual to refer to a fabric like that of Sant'Ambrogio as *organic,* a term which entered the American vocabulary through the eloquent teaching and persuasive writing of the late Charles H. Moore. We have used the same word to name the system of composition invented and perfected by the Greeks (page 65). There is no reason why the term may not prove useful and perhaps helpful in both applications, but a word of caution is requisite. *Organic* seems to say alive. *Inorganic,* a word Moore used too often, suggests lack of life. Moore applied it to any building that did not happen to be vaulted and, moreover, to demonstrate a lively interest in structural logic. By doing that, he invited people to close their eyes to the merit of all buildings possessed of a timber roof.

By any standard, Sant'Ambrogio was a notable design and a highly articulate expression of what was then a new esthetic theory, one which has since proved wonderfully productive. It seems a shame to call attention to some serious faults. The abutment was very far from a neat or final solution to the problem; the high gallery condemned the nave to near darkness. The doctrinaire application of structural logic to the piers (one part in the pier

Figs. 10.20–21 Milan. Sant' Ambrogio. 11th century? (top) Diagonal view across the nave and (right) detail showing one bay of the nave arcade. Length of nave: about 210 feet. Width betwen main piers: about 37 feet. Height to underside of vault: about 62 feet. (Alinari)

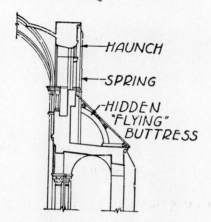

HAUNCH

SPRING

HIDDEN
"FLYING"
BUTTRESS

Fig. 10.22 Caen. La Trinité (Abbaye aux Dames). Drawing to illustrate the placement of the buttresses.

for every part in the vault) made it necessary to accept a pier of great bulk and tedious complexity (Fig. 10.21).

The chief and major defect of the building is indicated by Figures 10.18 and 19. It appears never to have occurred to the builders to stilt the ribs of their vaults (as the Gothic designers were later to do) in order to govern the height to which the crown of each rib might rise. They simply used a half circle for the shape of every arch they built. The bays being square, it followed that that diagonals had to rise higher than the other ribs; and because of that, each bay of vaulting was forced into a shape much closer to the dome than we might at first suppose. The ceiling, therefore, confronts the eye with a series of great gloomy and separate hollows; it is almost the opposite of an artistic unit.

Of all the faults found at Sant'Ambrogio, clumsy abutment is perhaps the worst. In other words, the designers failed to recognize and exploit the concentration of thrusts (Appendix I, pages 955–958) which literally invited the invention of a new and neater system of buttresses. That step, so far as we know, was taken by the man who designed the vaults for the church of the Trinity at Caen (Figs. 10.22, 10.31).

The church has no gallery. Instead, the triforium space is occupied by a frieze of blind arcading. There is a lean-to roof behind the triforium and over the aisles. Under that roof and opposite each impost where the ribs of the vaulting gather to concentrate the thrusts, we find a series of segmental arches pitched steeply downward to meet the outer walls. Too low to do their work efficiently, these are nevertheless *flying buttresses* except that they were not permitted to fly. To arrive at the system which became standard for the Gothic, it was merely necessary to bring such buttresses out of doors and raise them to where they belonged.

THE REGIONAL STYLES OF THE ROMANESQUE

Limitations of space permit only the briefest passing description of the more conspicuous features which differentiate the various local styles of the Romanesque; and we must, moreover, restrict ourselves to the regions that succeeded in producing styles which were not only autochthonous, but distinct. So rapid a summary is bound to be bare; even so, it may serve to suggest the richness of local culture which still survives in Europe.

The simplest classification that is free from misleading implications is as follows: In Italy, the Romanesque of Tuscany and that of Lombardy attained a definite character. In France, no less than six regions must be cited as having produced distinct types of architecture; they are Provence, Auvergne, Languedoc, Aquitaine, Burgundy, and Normandy. Other regions in general failed to arrive at an explicit style; they tended to borrow and combine from the Romanesque of the districts cited and from other sources as well. Thus, in southern Italy and Sicily, Norman and Saracen influences merged with Italian elements to produce an architecture which was then decorated with Byzantine mosaics. Spain, during this era, tended to borrow from France and, as always, was affected by the presence of Moorish art. Germany was strongly Lombard, and England was an artistic province of Normandy.

The churches of Tuscany are beyond compare the loveliest and most graceful of all. Often built almost entirely from the superb local marble and unique in their attempt to make every part delicate rather than ponderous, these buildings have an effect which has often been compared to that of a ship under sail. The cathedral at Pisa (Figs. 10.23–24) is only the largest and most famous monument of the district. Smaller churches at Lucca, Florence, Arezzo, and Toscanella are equally worth knowing.

In a period notable for structural ingenuity, the Tuscan architects were distinguished for a complete lack of interest in the progress of engineering. One might mistake Pisa for an Early Christian basilica were it not for its Romanesque detail; and in the matter of detail, the most striking feature of the Tuscan style is the profusion of open galleries, always in the form of miniature arcades over slender colonnettes. Ideally, an entire building would be enveloped by such arcading, a result actually achieved in the Leaning Tower. Where open galleries were not wanted, the Tuscan builders used blind arcades on delicate pilasters, or at times engaged columns.

The Lombards were the first to give mature expression to the structural esthetic (as at Sant'Ambrogio), and unquestionably that was their greatest contribution to the history of architecture. We must not, however, overlook the remarkable decorative value of their churches. Modena (Fig. 10.25) is a

Figs. 10.23–24 Pisa. Cathedral (1063–1100) and Leaning Tower (1174–1350). Cathedral: 312 feet long. Tower: 179 feet high. (below) Detail of the blind arcade on the south side, showing irregularity in the height and span of the arches. (Both photos: Brogi)

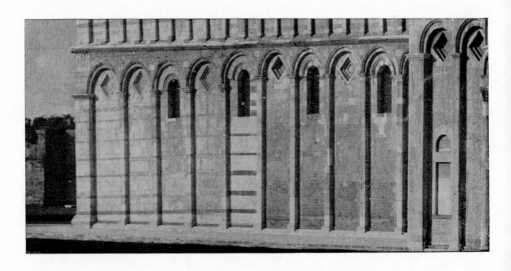

Fig. 10.25   Modena. Cathedral. 1099–1106. (Anderson)

good example. Built of darker stone and less dazzling than Pisa, its masonry has nevertheless a quiet elegance. It was customary in Lombardy to unify the composition of the façade by strong verticals, usually in the form of pilaster strips, as here; but only about half the Lombard façades have Modena's basilican cross section. More typical, perhaps, was a screen façade like that of San Michele at Pavia, with a single very broad gable across the top. Open galleries were very common, and for those, the Lombard designers preferred to use compound arches rather than simple arcades. The standard doorway was of course the Lombard porch; and Lombard corbels were used profusely to decorate horizontals.

The two most important churches of the Provençal Romanesque are St. Trophîme at Arles (Fig. 10.26) and St. Gilles nearby. The special feature of these is the splendor of their western portals. Distinctively Romanesque in

Fig. 10.26 Arles. St. Trophîme. Main portal. (Archives Photographiques)

detail, both emanate a monumental calm not always associated with the style. Because both date later than 1150, that characteristic may reflect the advent of the Gothic point of view; but to an even greater degree, the atmosphere of weighty quiet probably derived from the unparalleled wealth of classical material which still stands in Provence. Because of the difference in proportion, the resemblance may not at first be noticed; but both these portals reflect the standard scheme for a Roman triumphal arch: the podium at the bottom, and then the familiar sequence of order and entablature. The capitals, furthermore, do not deviate much from the Corinthian silhouette, and the larger statues possess a dignity aptly described as "senatorial."

The churches of Auvergne are, as a group, the oldest of the French Romanesque; and to the builders of Auvergne goes the credit for inventing the system of abutment illustrated by Figure 10.13. Excellent as an insurance of structural stability, nothing could have been much worse when it came to providing light for the interior. Hence a bold adjustment to the elevation (Fig. 10.27). Over the crossing, we find a rectangular attic with a north and south dimension the width of the nave; and above the attic, we see a squat tower. Windows were thus provided at an ideal height, but hardly in an ideal relation to the axis of the nave.

The Auvergnat churches were peculiar, also, for an unusual complication at the eastern end. Six or eight columns were ordinarily arranged to form a

Fig. 10.27 Saint-Nectaire. Church. 11th century. View from the southeast. (Archives Photographiques)

kind of open apse with an ambulatory behind it. Opening off the ambulatory, we often see a series of miniature chapels, circular in form, and arranged radially like the petals of a flower. These are called *absidioles*. Seen in ground outline, the arrangement is strikingly similar to the High Gothic; and seen in elevation from the east, the various masses present the eye with picturesque harmonies and constrasts of size and shape. Absidioles, apse, attic, and tower arrange themselves in a graduated and ascending sequence. The effect is both solid and lively, and there are analogies to the best examples of modern abstract painting and sculpture.

Toulouse is the principal city of Languedoc, and its central monument is the church of St. Sernin (Fig. 10.12). The Romanesque churches of the region—to be visualized roughly as the southwest corner of France—are much like those of Auvergne. While the western front of St. Sernin is without special distinction, the view from the east is imposing. The apse is flanked by absidioles radially arranged, the transepts extended; and while the attic familiar in Auvergne was here omitted, there was an unmistakable attempt to build the masses up into a composition culminating in an octagonal tower.

A special interest attaches to Saint Sernin because at Compostela, at the extreme northwest corner of Spain, there stands the church of Santiago which is—except in matters of mere detail—a duplicate of St. Sernin. The resemblance is almost certainly to be explained by reference to the medieval habit of going on pilgrimages. Tradition has it that the body of Saint James, after transportation from the Near East by ship, was laid to rest at Compostela. Presently that remote spot eclipsed all others as a destination for pilgrims. While details remain obscure, it is believed the church maintained a considerable organization to provide for their safety and welfare. Inasmuch as Toulouse was an important stopping point on "the way of St. James," the virtual identity of the churches is probably thus to be explained.

Figure I.21 (page 953) was taken from a Romanesque church in Aquitaine. Because they vaulted their churches with multiple domes carried on pendentives, and because they occasionally made use of the Greek cross plan, the 12th-century builders of Aquitaine, it has long been assumed, enjoyed some more or less direct contact with Byzantium. St. Front at Périgueux is usually cited as the most important monument in the area. It is surely unexcelled in the unique and delicate complexity of its skyline; but it is a special rather than a typical building. The cathedral at Angoulême and Notre Dame at Poitiers (Fig. 10.28) are more in the usual run. Both have the façade peculiar to Aquitaine: roughly basilican in cross section, flanked by towers with the characteristic pine cone spire, and enriched with sculpture and carving. Perhaps no façades better illustrate the rough and kindly texture of the Romanesque, improved rather than harmed by centuries of weathering.

The Abbey Church at Cluny (Fig. 10.14) was the central monument of Burgundy, and unquestionably the greatest of all Romanesque churches. The church proper had a double set of transepts and no less than fifteen absidioles opening off transepts and ambulatory. Its length approached 500 feet, to which we must add the length of a monumental narthex, itself another nave, extending westward five bays more. Largely the work of the middle 12th century, the magnificent building survived until the time of the French Revolution. By then neglected and in disrepair, it was destroyed with blasting powder, and the rubble sold for building stone—a succinct illustration of the extreme modernity of what we may call the historical sense. The architecture of Cluny is known through the archeological reconstruction conducted by Kenneth Conant. A few pieces of the sculpture have survived, and their quality establishes the presumption that the excellence of the immense fabric was as notable as its size.

Cluny being gone, we must form our impression of the Burgundian Romanesque by reference to smaller monuments such as the Abbey Church (La Madeleine) at Vézelay and the cathedral (St. Lazare) at Autun (Figs. 10.36 and 10.29). The distinctively Burgundian contribution had little to do with the major components of the buildings; indeed, the architectural features

Fig. 10.28 Poitiers. Notre Dame la Grande. (Archives Photographiques)

remind one of Auvergne and Languedoc. The local flavor inheres in a special precision and finesse, even a richness and a luxury, notable in every detail. Not only is there much more sculpture than elsewhere, but every bit of carving, even the smallest molding, is of unequaled delicacy. In addition, an imponderable aura from the antique imbues everything Burgundian: the fluted pilasters at Autun seem spiritually more classical than many a bit of work from the Italian Renaissance. That circumstance may be less surprising when we remind ourselves that fragments of a temple to Apollo may still be seen at Autun, and that the Porte Saint André once formed part of the Roman walls.

It will be noted that the arches at Autun are not round, as usual in the Romanesque, but pointed, a form usually thought of as Gothic. While by no means common, pointed arches were occasionally used during this period; no confusion is possible if one compares the large simplicity of the orders to the elegant complexity of the Gothic.

Fig. 10.29 Autun. St. Lazare.
(Marburg)

Because of its connection with England, and because it made so direct a contribution to the French Gothic, the Norman Romanesque seems in many ways to have been the culmination of the style. No church is more Norman than the gaunt and ruined Abbey at Jumièges (Fig. 10.30) which, at the date of its consecration in 1067, was the grandest building produced in the west since Early Christian times. Jumièges might be called a basilica transformed by the Romanesque. In plan and general disposition of parts, it conforms to that model, and it carried a timber roof; but in every aspect of appearance and atmosphere it was a new thing. It is important as one of the very earliest major buildings where a frank attempt was made to emphasize the vertical dimension; and its façade embodied, as became standard practice in Normandy, twin towers integral with the central section. At the crossing, still another tower soared into the air; of that, only a fragment remains.

The two abbey churches at Caen, La Trinité (Abbaye aux Dames) and Saint Étienne (Abbaye aux Hommes), were founded by William the Con-

Fig. 10.30 Jumièges. Abbey church. 1067. (Archives Photographiques)

queror and his queen. Students of the period differ as to whether these churches were intended from the first to carry vaults. Certainly the present vaulting is clumsy, and hardly in harmony with the refinement of the parts beneath—even though it is probably a fact that the designer of the vaults at La Trinité invented the flying buttress (Fig. 10.22). By comparison to the Burgundian, and indeed by comparison to almost all other Romanesque, the Norman churches were austere; there is a little sculpture but not much, and few other decorative details. It was the Norman façade (Fig. 10.31) that went directly into the Gothic, and became the formula for the western front of all the great Cathedrals of France.

ROMANESQUE SCULPTURE AND PAINTING

The Romanesque period witnessed the revival of monumental sculpture and painting. Since Early Christian times, the art of painting had been largely

Fig. 10.31 Caen. La Trinité (Abbaye aux Dames). Width of façade: 79 feet. (Archives Photographiques)

limited to the production of miniature illustrations designed to be bound up in books. Of full-scale sculpture, Europe had seen almost none since pagan antiquity.

It is not easy to account for the revival at this particular moment in history; but whatever the cause, it is clear that the strengh had gone out of the distaste for sculpture which Europe had imported from the Near East along with Christianity. Once under way, the artists of the 11th and 12th centuries produced a prodigious harvest of material; so much, indeed, that a whole lifetime of study would hardly be enough to make one intimately familiar with all the monuments. To save space, we shall confine our attention to Romanesque sculpture alone, and to certain French monuments which, by common consent, may fairly be called the definitive examples of the style as a whole. Of Romanesque painting, we must content ourselves with the mere remark that its stylistic features are similar, and that its study has of late years occupied the attention of some excellent scholars. A few examples are on view in American museums, notably the paintings that originally decorated the apse of Santa Maria de Mur, now in Boston.

The best way to approach Romanesque sculpture is by attempting to visualize the practical problems faced by the sculptors themselves and by the bishops and priests from whom all the orders came. Confronted with the necessity of reviving an art that had been out of use for about 500 years, what were the sculptors to do? How were the churchmen to describe what they wanted?

It is probably no exaggeration to say that the complete catalogue of Romanesque sculpture reflects somewhere the appearance of almost everything that might have been on view in the medieval world. Direct observation of nature, that is to say, occurred. Most of the time, however, the Romanesque sculptor found his model in the works of art his ecclesiastical patrons already owned, and were used to: the illustrations of Christian manuscripts. These models account for much that is complex and strange. Not only were the available manuscripts of a great many kinds; the sculptors, with little tradition in their own craft, were deriving their art from an extremely sophisticated tradition in another medium.

In a very few instances, it has been possible to identify the particular miniature which served as a model. Usually, we have to study the style of the sculpture, and thus make a fairly good guess about the class of manuscript from which the sculptor worked. Within the great variety of styles brought into the total catalogue of the period, it is fair to say that most work in the main current of the Romanesque derived from manuscripts of two kinds.

For animals, grotesques, and devils, the whole northern tradition furnished sources of incomparable virtuosity. We may imagine frequent reference to such manuscripts as the *Book of Kells;* but in order to account for the plausible but fantastic creatures seen on the face of the outer order of the splayed arch at Aulnay (Fig. 10.1), we must refer also to the *bestiaries,* a peculiar kind of book which had become immensely popular.

A bestiary purported to furnish information about the appearance and nature of living creatures. A large one might include descriptions of as many as 200 animals, from whose habits the text would draw religious lessons. As a class, the bestiaries may be traced back into pagan times, and some of the entries reflect classical fables. The zoological metaphor in which the Bible abounds also stimulated the medieval imagination, and if we look for them we may see lambs of God, lions of the House of Judah, and even the deaf adder that stoppeth up her ears. The influence of the bestiaries did much to make Romanesque sculpture into an art "splendidly free from the fetters of realism"—for most of the beasts in the bestiaries are imaginary.

Fig. 10.32 Vézelay, Museum. A Romanesque capital. (Archives Photographiques)

Drawing upon the northern tradition as expanded by the bestiaries, Romanesque artists brought into being a class of sculpture in which the wildest and strangest visions of the mind were reduced to tangible representation and made permanent in stone. The entire society of the period was peculiarly congenial to such material. No account could possibly be long enough to describe in detail the manifold variations of the Romanesque excursion into the supernatural, and we must be content with only an instance or two to illustrate the temper and trend of the time.

The story of the Devil's endeavor to tempt Christ seems, for example, to have furnished a precedent for innumerable personal appearances by the Black Master and his demons to humbler Christians. Raoul Glaber, quoted above (page 315) in quite another connection, says that the Devil bothered him on at least three occasions. "He was of small stature. He had a protruding belly, and a low forehead. His large mouth revealed a denture like that of a dog. His hair stood on end, and his movements were convulsive." It is one of the innumerable contributions of Emile Mâle to have recognized that Glaber's description conforms very closely with the devil who appears several times on the capitals of Vézelay (Fig. 10.32).

For subject matter demanding the presence of the human figure, the leading Romanesque sculptors (in France, at any rate) seem to have relied for their models upon manuscripts either produced by the Carolingian school

Fig. 10.33 Souillac, Notre Dame. *The Prophet Isaiah.* (Archives Photographiques)

from which the Utrecht Psalter had come or deriving from one of the traditions set in motion by that school. Their preference is profoundly indicative of the direction in which European taste was moving, for it had been the great achievement of those artists to have adapted northern line to the rendering of the human figure. In suggesting their work as a favorite source during the period covered by the present chapter, it is necessary to stipulate that we refer to figure style only; the spatial representation so competently handled by the illuminators formed no part of the Romanesque borrowing.

The Romanesque handling of the single figure is epitomized by *The Prophet Isaiah* on the Abbey Church at Souillac (Fig. 10.33). The slender canon of proportions, the extravagant pose, the action of the body in the region of the hips, and the surcharge of feeling all remind us of the

Utrecht Psalter. With incredible skill, the sculptor has rendered in stone the swirling curves of some master penman. In several places, he resorted to undercutting in order to produce shadows which recall the darker areas of paintings; and it will be noticed that the meander pattern beneath the figure was rendered in perspective. It would be difficult to cite another example so completely in defiance of the theory which tries to govern design by reference to the medium (see above, pages 61, 159); but it would be a rash critic who attempted, for that reason, to say this figure was bad.

For the modern student, to whom the beauty and dignity of the body seem axiomatic, this and other Romanesque figures nevertheless require considerable apology and explanation. The anatomy of the *Isaiah* is emaciated, unhealthy, unlovely, and incorrect. The author of this figure lived, however, in a world where the scientific point of view had not yet intruded; he probably never heard it suggested that statues should conform to the mechanical facts of living models. His religion, moreover, told him to hold the body not in respect, but in contempt. Its creation in the divine image was minimized, and its capacity as an instrument of temptation and evil was reinforced by constant warning. The point was not to celebrate humanity, but to visualize states of the spirit. So appreciated, the Romanesque figure style becomes not only comprehensible but fascinating.

Still another consideration must be understood before one is ready to study Romanesque sculpture. We refer to the fact that the society of that era considered sculptors as workmen who embellished churches. There was no cavil about artistic independence; sculpture was kept in the service of architecture, and was subordinate to it.

The very same thing was true during most of the Gothic period; but there was a substantial difference in the kind and degree of cooperation between architects and sculptors. Niches and pedestals of the right sort were integral with the design of Gothic churches, and sculpture has never been better shown (see below, pages 368–371). By contrast, it must be conceded that Romanesque architects were almost invariably arbitrary and often rather stupid when it came to making provision for the work of sculptors. Major compositions had to be crowded into spaces that appear, at times, merely to have been left over. Narrative subject matter of a briefer kind was often ordered as a replacement for acanthus leaves on the capitals of piers and columns. Single figures of the greatest saints were specified at points where no one would now dream of putting them.

All of these things combined to produce an art at first extremely confusing to the modern student. Distortions are commonplace, often simply for the purpose of adjusting things to the space assigned. Miniature figures are juxtaposed with oversize figures, in defiance of normal relations of scale. Compositions teem with item after item, as though a tempestuous spirit were

Fig. 10.34 Moissac. St. Pierre. Tympanum: *Christ Enthroned among the Four-and-twenty Elders*. From a cast. (Archives Photographiques)

being cramped within the containment of the frame. Such things being true, it is no wonder that critics of the Renaissance and later—their thinking curtailed by classical standards—damned Romanesque sculpture as barbarous whenever compelled to notice it at all.

Turning our attention to the major monuments of Romanesque sculpture, we find ourselves embarrassed by a wealth of material, and any choice we make is bound to disappoint almost everybody. For considerations of space alone, however, we must restrict our text to considering the three great tympana: that of Moissac, that of Vézelay, and that of Autun.

The subject of the tympanum at Moissac (Fig. 10.34) is taken from the fourth chapter of Revelation, where Saint John describes his vision of God's throne. A gate opened into heaven, revealing the Almighty surrounded by four-and-twenty elders who wore crowns of gold, and by the four beasts we know as the symbols of the Evangelists (see above, pages 241–242). In his hand, God held a book sealed with seven seals, and there was "a strong angel proclaiming in a loud voice, 'Who is worthy to open the book, and to loose the seals thereof?' " The artist has supplied a second angel, but that is no liberty, since many of them were there, continuously singing.

Crowded and confusing at first glance, the composition becomes vivid and clear as one gathers familiarity: like all other art related in any way with

Fig. 10.35 Vézelay. Church of the Madeleine. Tympanum: *Pentecost*. From a cast. (Archives Photographiques)

the Northern Style, the total effect arrives only after a cumulative process of comprehension. Once one knows the tympanum well, the realization emerges that no style bound by the rules of natural fact could possibly compete with the Romanesque in the field of Apocalyptic imagery. Transcendental visions demand an art that surges beyond the limits of all possible experience on earth.

For the student who becomes interested in problems of stylistic derivation, the Moissac tympanum offers an added interest. Professor Mâle (*L'art religieux en France du XIIe siècle,* Chapter I) believes that he has identified the very manuscripts (or some so like them it makes no difference) which were usel as models by the Moissac sculptor. The four-and-twenty elders with their peculiar musical instruments appear in an illustration preserved in the Bibliothèque Nationale, in a copy of the commentary on the Apocalypse written by Beatus of Liebana, a Spanish monk. For the figure of Christ, Mâle found a likely source in a miniature now in the library of the cathedral at Auxerre.

Although other explanations have been suggested, it seems almost certain that the tympanum of Vézelay (Fig. 10.35) was intended to represent Pentecost. The bare description of the event as given in the second chapter of Acts has been considerably elaborated and built upon by the imagination of the artist. In the middle, there is a Christ enclosed in an elliptical glory (a full-length halo). To either side of him, a bit of cloud serves as an indication of his heavenly location. We are intended to suppose that his body is the radiating center through which the heavenly spirit passes, thence being transmitted to the Apostles below by means of rays emanating from his fingertips. The agitated draperies indicate the sculptor's attempt to depict the "rushing mighty wind" that swept down from heaven and filled the house.

Different scholars have advanced different views about the identity of the numerous figures across the lintel below the main scene, and those contained in the compartments which run above and around it. While it is far from easy to decide the matter, a probable explanation is as follows:

During the Middle Ages, Pentecost was understood to signify more than the gift of tongues; it was a mandate to carry the Gospel to all humanity. That idea furnishes a reason for the otherwise incomprehensible variety of people who crowd every available space. A detailed study will reveal many of the wonders of the 12th-century ethnography. Many of the figures, it seems, were intended to represent the various heathen to whom the word would be taken. Of special interest are the Cynocephaloi, a dog-headed tribe believed to live in India; and the Panotii, with immense ears, who were then to be found in South Russia—or at least so it was said. In the semicircle around the whole, in little circular compartments, are the Signs of the Zodiac and the Labors of the Months, subjects which remained in high favor as long as the Middle Age lasted. Over and above their interest as genre, it seems plausible to suppose that the monthly cycle of activities would suggest the passage of time on earth. The astronomical symbols seem similarly related to the vaster concept of the universe, and of eternity.

The tympanum of St. Lazare at Autun is a *Last Judgment* (Fig. 10.36). It is signed by the sculptor Giselbertus, who stated his purposes plainly: *Terreat quos terreus alligat error*—"Let this horror appall those bound by earthly sin!"

In the lower register, the dead are rising from their graves. Two of them, just to left of center, carry musette bags, one with the mark of the cross and the other with a conch shell, the badge of pilgrims to Jerusalem and Compostela respectively. In the middle of the lunette above is a gigantic figure of Christ. The inscription around the border of his glory announces the business of the occasion: to the blessed he will award crowns; the evil he will send to perdition. The tympanum, judged barbarous by the canons of the church, was covered with a brick facing in 1766—a mistake which probably saved it from complete destruction during the revolution, but one that accounts for the mutilation of the Christ and other figures. The head of the Christ was identified, however, in 1949; and it is back in place today.

To the Savior's right, in the top register, we see the Virgin; and to his left, Saint John the Evangelist. Both are there to act as intercessors for the souls who come to judgment. Beyond them, and in several other places, are angels with trumpets, blowing the blast that will one day announce the end

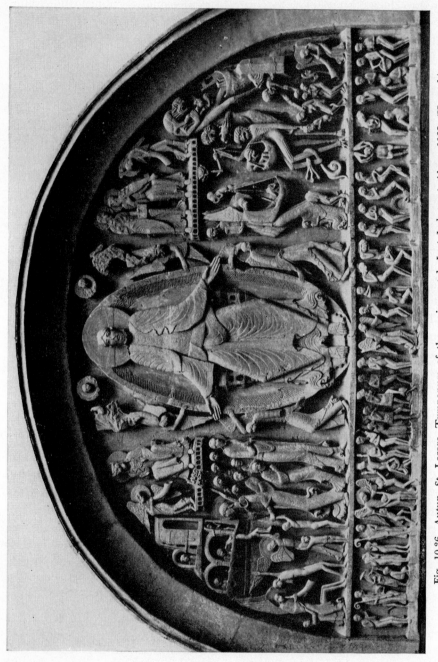

Fig. 10.36 Autun. St. Lazare. Tympanum of the main portal: *Last Judgment.* About 1132. (Hurault)

of the world. To Christ's right and a bit below, Saint Peter stands with his immense key; he is surrounded by angels who help him chaperon the souls of the blessed into the heavenly city. On the other side, Saint Michael superintends the weighing of the souls. The ethics of the Devil and his minions may be inferred by their eagerness to pull the scales down on their side. Those who have failed the test are tossed into the flaming mouth of hell, which opens like a hopper at the extreme right.

Living long after the Greeks and long before the Italian Renaissance, Giselbertus was not bothered by artistic theories which inevitably influence our thought today. Among those theories, we must make special mention of the notion that there is an inevitable association of art with beauty—an idea that we inherit from the Italian artists, who in turn had inherited it from antiquity. Creation of beauty was obviously quite the opposite of Giselbertus's intention when he executed his famous *Last Judgment*—which is probably the most terrible and hideous work of art on record. It is immensely important to appreciate, however, that his philosophy was different from the Greek idealists' not in kind, but in direction. Where the Greeks picked, chose, elided, and in general corrected the works of nature to fit their peculiar ideas of the noble and beautiful, this 12th-century sculptor (also starting from things he had seen in the world) used his imagination to produce the worst devils in history. His point of view was not far different from that of the modern surrealists. They derive their subject matter from the little-known reaches of the mind, often with shocking effect. He drew his from the visualizations evoked by the more extreme and terrible suggestions contained within the Bible, and he arrived at the most extreme and radical art the world has yet to see.

Chapter 11

THE GOTHIC ERA

G OTHIC ART began to assume its characteristic forms during the first generation of the 12th century. As though by manifesto, the existence of a new style was announced in the year 1140, when the Abbot Suger approved the plans and caused work to commence upon a new church for the royal abbey at Saint Denis, about 2½ miles outside the northern walls of Paris, and on the site where the martyred first bishop of the city had been buried—after walking, it is said, all the way from his decapitation on Montmartre, carrying his head in his hands. Unfortunately, Suger's church was almost completely obliterated by a reconstruction undertaken in 1231, the new work being done in the then dominant High Gothic style. From what is left and from what may legitimately be inferred, St. Denis was the first large and important church in which all parts were fully articulated to produce the skeletal structure henceforth typical of the Gothic.

It would be a mistake to suggest that the design of Suger's St. Denis was created by a single act of inspiration. The truth is that every essential of the new system had been in plain sight somewhere or other among the manifold variations of the Romanesque. The novelty lay in an original synthesis of well-tried features; and for the synthesis itself, earlier and humbler churches in the vicinity had pioneered the way.

St. Denis is to be remembered not only as the signal for the arrival of the Gothic style, but also as the monument which marks the assumption by France of the cultural leadership of the whole Western world. The France to which we refer is not the extensive modern political unit, but the medieval France, more exactly known as the *Île de France,* which was the traditional name in feudal times for the district reserved by the king as his personal do-

GOTHIC ARCHITECTURE

main. The name is often rather loosely applied, and the area designated differed from time to time. For our purposes, we may visualize it as the region around Paris. Chartres, Amiens, Reims, and Bourges may be thought of as suggesting its artistic if not its political boundaries.

Once the internal logic of the new style had been made manifest at St. Denis, development went on apace within the Île de France. Perfection succeeded development, and refinement perfection. Word of the new advances went outward from the Île de France to all parts of Christendom, attracting ready interest. As the 13th century opened, almost every region was prepared to abandon its local Romanesque for the novel French manner—which was more or less perfectly understood, as later pages will demonstrate. And as he reads the text below, let the reader often remind himself that where the Gothic went, everything else that was French went with it. French books, French clothes and manners, French schools and procedures, French customs and institutions—all were a pattern for the rest of the Christian world. It is a simple statement of fact to say that the heart of Gothic Europe lay in Paris.

♦ *Reasons for the Cultural Primacy of France during the Gothic Era* The primacy of France depended upon more than the presence in that area of the cleverest architects; it derived from a great combination of things. In the first place, the power of the French kings, hitherto nominal, had been strengthened into the best centralized and best administered civil authority in Europe. Philip Augustus (reigned 1180–1223) was the creative genius who performed the final act of solidifying the royal power; superb in both diplomacy and force, he looms as a personality of brutal grandeur.

351

A much more attractive figure was Philip's grandson, Louis the 9th, who came to the throne in 1226. With the Pope, he had a *modus vivendi* which was positively cordial by contrast to the relations between the pontiff and other rulers. While both Germany and England were disrupted by civil wars, he managed to maintain comparative peace in France. He understood very well the value of court display as an adjunct to the royal dignity; but at the same time, and with the insight of an artist, he discerned the meaning of restraint in dress, and of gentleness and consideration in relations with others. His lifetime coincides with the general acceptance of the ennobling code of chivalry, which has ever since remained the European philosophy of manners. The contrast, indeed, between his court and that of his mighty grandfather has caused more than one historian to declare that there were absolutely no gentlemen in western Europe before the 13th century. Profoundly religious, Louis injured his health by ascetic practices. An accomplished knight, he went on two Crusades; he died in North Africa on the second, in the year 1270. All the virtues of medieval society seem to have been concentrated in the person of this king. He was canonized in 1297, and he is usually known as Saint Louis.

In addition to being the seat of a monarchy both strong and good, the Île de France had certain material reasons to aid its assumption of leadership. A glance at the map will show that the area was uncommonly well situated to participate in the general expansion of trade which took place all over Europe during the Gothic era. The celebrated and circulating Fairs of Champagne, the most highly developed system of marketing since Rome, were conveniently at hand. The district was also ideally placed to profit by the traffic along several great river highways. Prosperity ensued, and must not be forgotten as a necessary precondition for the construction of great cathedrals.

By comparison to the rest of Europe, the Île de France had, when considered as a likely center for a new era in human culture, the immense additional advantage of being the seat of the greatest of medieval universities. After existing informally for a generation and more, the University of Paris assumed its corporate identity shortly after 1150. It set a new standard for all the others, and it remains one of the best. No other institution has ever had teachers remotely comparable to the series of great men who taught there. Abelard and Peter Lombard were among its earlier professors, to be followed by Albertus Magnus and Saint Thomas Aquinas.

The university had started as a place where advanced students might receive instruction in the art of dialectic; and the earliest curriculum, if it may be called that, set the pattern for future policy. By importation from Spain and the Near East, Western scholars had gradually come into possession of better and more complete texts of Aristotle. They put their improved knowledge to work in a full-scale attempt to create a distinctively Christian philosophy which has ever since been known as the *Scholastic*—the name is not an attempt to describe their ideas; it merely means they taught in schools. The great single monument of Scholasticism is the *Summa Theologica* of Saint Thomas, a work that concerns us deeply because it bears intimate analogies to Gothic art.

Saint Thomas's great idea was to prove the truth of the Christian dogma by reference to data we see about us in the world. His ultimate aim was to present a consistent picture of the universe by showing that every item and object fitted into the divine scheme. The final conclusion to which his thinking leads us is the concept that there is no conflict between the finite and the infinite, but that one is simply an extension of the other.

So brief a summary does severe injustice to a work almost as large in bulk as it is in intellectual grandeur; let the reader seek the original for himself. We have said enough, however, to make our present point, namely, that the colossal scale of Thomas's inquiry made brilliant powers of arrangement necessary. Thousands of ideas had to be marshaled in an effective system of heading and subheading. His success may be judged by the numerous ways in which one may hear it said that everything in the *Summa* fits into a place. Its minute parts fit not only one another, but make sense in relation to the general scheme. Word for word, the same statement is precisely true of the French Gothic cathedral.

It is not suggested that all the master builders were philosophers with university training, but it would not be surprising to find proof one day that some of them were. The important thing to appreciate is the certainty that Scholasticism had a much broader and more popular base than we might at first imagine. The artists of that period breathed in a deep respect for sustained intellectual activity. That, without doubt, was the reason why everything Gothic—over and above its other excellencies—had to stand logical analysis and satisfy the rational faculty. In comprehending the force and color of what has just been said, we must attempt to see that the Gothic mind felt no need to separate the idea of divinity from the physical world. To the builder of the period, it probably seemed plain common sense to regard the stones of his church as details in God's universal order. Thrust and abutment, for one in such a state of mind, were less brute forces, and more a department of celestial physics. Building (so viewed) became more than a skill; to understand it was to possess an essential constituent of the knowledge by which men might come to a Christian understanding of their world.

Such seem to have been the reasons for the superior ingenuity which distinguishes the Gothic of northern France from all the rest of Gothic, making it at once more scientific, more elegant, and more abstract. But still another reason—a final item to remind us that history does not always proceed along avenues laid out on the grand scale—must be adduced to show why the Île de France became the birthplace of the new day. The region had not been prosperous during the Romanesque period. Its monuments from that time are small and few. There thus existed the plainest possible reason for architectural activity: in Paris and the towns around it, there was a lack of adequate churches.

♦ *The Name "Gothic"*   Before attempting to deal with the monuments, it is requisite that we pause to explain how the new French style came to be called Gothic. The word is a misnomer, and in general use today only through habit. The first persons to use it were men of the later Renaissance who wanted to give trenchant expression to their contempt for everything medieval. There were, of course, no Goths left in Europe during the 12th century; as an ethnic group, they had been absorbed at least 600 years earlier, but the memory of their barbarism persisted.

Gothic retained its opprobrious connotation until the latter part of the 18th century. Its use in any kindly sense was probably unknown until the time of Horace Walpole. During the 19th century, medieval studies began to vie with the classical; in the field of art history, the most important product of that movement was the still indispensable *Dictionnaire raisonné de l'archi- tecture française du XIe au XVIe siècle*. The author was Viollet-le-Duc, and his ten volumes constitute a gold mine of lucid architectural drawings, some of which we reproduce here. The publication date was 1868. Thus, Viollet-le- Duc, although scarcely a member of the Romantic movement (see below, pages 838–852) coincided with it in time and lent prestige to its interest in medieval values. The result was that *Gothic* began to emerge as a term of praise.

Once so established, it followed inevitably that an attempt would be made to refine its meaning. One of the most cogent thinkers along that line was Charles H. Moore, the first curator of the Fogg Museum at Harvard. With respect to the name Gothic, Moore's intention was to award it as a kind of accolade to buildings which corresponded closely with his organic theory of architecture (page 328). Moore asserted, that is to say, that the essence of the Gothic style, and therefore the honor of the name, was to be found in a peculiar structural system which depended for stability not upon inert mass ". . . but upon a logical adjustment of parts, whose opposing forces neutralize each other and produce a perfect equilibrium." All other buildings, however much they looked like Gothic, Moore relegated to the category of "pointed" architecture.

Moore derived his theory from Viollet-le-Duc, but his central position at the oldest university in America lent his words a special influence which still continues. His assertions always had an unusual power to convince; and as a teacher of teachers, he has probably been more precisely remembered and more explicitly quoted than any other critic of art.

Moore was correct, perhaps, in what he asserted, but gravely wrong in what he denied. His strictures would deny the name Gothic to everything from the era except the architecture of northern France. In construing Gothic solely as architecture, he forgot the sculpture, the stained glass, the manuscripts, the furniture, the jewelry, and all the other arts that are truly Gothic—and to which, actually, he alluded often. In presenting Gothic as a mechanical evolution brought about by a gradual refinement of engineering, he left out the crucial truth that there would have been no Gothic except for the presence in Europe of the Northern and Barbarian Style, of which Gothic was demonstrably the mature and ultimate expression.

♦ *Gothic as a Product of the Northern and Barbarian Style*   As set forth in the last chapter, the Romanesque period signalized the emergence of the medieval mind from a keen and helpless sense of inferiority to Rome. The Gothic period marks the arrival of the European population upon a new plateau of existence: they were then ready to express themselves in terms of their own. They respected Rome, but they did not feel inferior. Dante's choice of the vernacular was one result of the new cast of mind. Gothic art was another.

It would be extreme to say that Roman influence was completely absent from the Gothic. Its presence in matters of detail is often plain enough; and it may be argued that Gothic engineering derived from a logical power ulti-mately traceable to the Romans. But however casual the inspection, it is mani-festly clear that the effect of any work of art in the Gothic style is completely different from anything classical. The intention was not in the least the same, and the artistic idiom is impossible to explain by reference to the antique.

Gothic is linear. At Ulm or Amiens or Toledo, wherever the eye falls, it finds itself on a line along which it is impelled to move. Gothic architects went to an immense amount of trouble to produce such an effect. In one way or another, almost everything they did had some relation to the production and multiplication of lines. They reduced the bulk of working members to the limit of safety—an excellent structural expedient, to be sure, but also a process which reduces the possibility that a pier or a buttress might impress us as a mass. The narrower and thinner anything becomes, the greater the likelihood that it will tell as a line.

The linear predilection is specially conspicuous in Gothic moldings. If the splayed doorways of Amiens (Fig. 11.1) are compared with the Roman-esque door at Aulnay (Fig. 10.1, page 318), the increased complexity of line will be instantly apparent. The cross section of any Gothic molding, to put it another way, is exceedingly subdivided in comparison to its Romanesque

Fig. 11.1   Amiens. Cathedral. Western doors. Width across façade: about 130 feet. (Clarence Ward)

counterpart. Compare the moldings shown in Figure 10.29, page 338, with those that appear in Figures 11.1, 13, 18, and 24. Indeed, it seems that the ultimate ideal of every Gothic architect was to reduce his esthetic means to unadulterated line, and in a few examples of the Late Gothic (Figs. 11.29 and 11.31) that ideal was very nearly arrived at. Nothing built of stone could be less plastic; and to achieve more linearity, one would have to resort to structural steel and wire rope.

The instinct of every Gothic artist to multiply lines was part and parcel of a general stylistic desire to multiply parts. Every Gothic object, whether a manuscript page (Fig. 12.10, page 425) or a cathedral (Fig. 11.2) consists of an infinite number of small details, each intensively defined. Standing in the nave of Amiens (Fig. 11.13), who can count the parts? But when we walk into the Pantheon at Rome (Fig. 7.5, page 186), we see only two things: the cylindrical rotunda below and the dome above.

In their methods of composition, the Gothic artists felt no need of geometric order. Symmetry like that of the western front of the cathedral at Paris is rare rather than common, and even there is far from strict. The situation at Chartres (Fig. 11.2) is much closer to the normal for Gothic. The two western

Fig. 11.2 Chartres. Cathedral. The three western doorways, together with their sculpture, originally formed part of an earlier church and date from about 1145. Most of the fabric, including the south tower, is of the first half of the 13th century. The spire on the north tower was added in 1510. (Roubier; courtesy French Government Tourist Office)

Fig. 11.3 Schematic drawing by Viollet-le-Duc to show how a Gothic church might look with its complete set of spires.

towers are radically different; the eccentric arrangement is not only more interesting, but more true to the nature of the style.

By contrast to the classical artist whose instinct was to enclose his compositions within actual frames of a simple geometric outline, or to suggest in some subtle but unmistakable way the existence of an unseen but very present boundary line (see above, pages 66, 73, 80), the Gothic artist invariably attempted to produce a silhouette distinguished by innumerable sharp projections and innumerable deep indentations. His smallest punctuation mark (Fig. 12.9, page 423) thrusts its little spiny points out into the space around it. Wherever statues were comparatively free from the restrictions ordinarily imposed by architecture, they were given a very complicated outline (Fig. 12.13, page 428). In architecture, a broken outline was feasible only at the top—which suggests the genesis of the vertical emphasis for which the Gothic church is noted. It being impossible to throw the eye off in all four directions, the decision was made to emphasize the easiest and most practical direction: upward. All lines lead up until they converge at the tip of a spire. Momentum then carries the eye out into the sky (Fig. 11.3).

But even on the skyline, a dissolving silhouette was by no means easy to provide. A few odd situations made such an outline almost natural if not automatic; Mont Saint Michel was perhaps the most fortunate site of all from that special point of view. Otherwise, it was requisite to build unusually tall steeples, as at Salisbury (Fig. 11.27), or to multiply miniature finials in prodigal fashion as at Milan (Fig. 11.37).

Such are the major elements of a more abstract kind that go to make up the Gothic style: the linear idiom, the myriad detail, the dynamic and eccentric composition which demands the broken silhouette. To these we must add a minor element that has to do with content: whenever the Gothic artist undertook representation, he demonstrated a powerful taste for the grotesque. When rendering the human body, he did not hesitate to distort whenever it helped or convenienced him.

All of these factors in combination can signify only one thing: Gothic was a product of the Northern and Barbarian Style. (See above, pages 250–258.) No other artistic source can possibly explain it. By comparison with earlier monuments in the same style, Gothic was disciplined by civilization and inspired by Christianity, but it was nevertheless the product of a deep and long-dormant yearning for an authentically northern art which made itself manifest just before the middle of the 12th century, swept all before it, and came forward in full force in 13th-century France.

♦ *Chronology* We shall find it convenient to recognize three subdivisions within the Gothic style of architecture: the Early Gothic (second half of the 12th century), the High Gothic (13th century), and the Late Gothic (everything after the 13th century).

The Early Gothic churches are a distinct departure from the Romanesque, but differ from those of the next century in the matter of proportions. They are heavier and give a quieter effect. The great Gothic century was the 13th. Both Paris and Chartres retain parts preserved from Early Gothic churches on the same site, but in both cases, the bulk of the fabric dates from the 13th century. Amiens was started in 1220, Beauvais five years later. During the same period, an immense number of churches went up all over Europe: the cathedrals at Salisbury, Burgos, Toledo, León, and Siena; St. Francis at Assisi, St. Elizabeth at Marburg, and so on. There has not been so much church building in one era since.

Many a critic has been rather harsh in his remarks about Late Gothic architecture. It is true that the social and religious causes of Gothic did not survive the 13th century. It is equally true that the later architects put most of their energy into the decorative aspects of the style, and felt no inspiration from the engineering which had for some time been generally understood. It is still further true that history had left the Gothic behind by about 1450, by which date the Renaissance was well under way in Italy. It is nevertheless undeniable that some of the finest Gothic is very late indeed. The best examples are in England and Spain, both regions where the population was reluctant to accept the taste of Italy.

Fig. 11.4 Laon. Cathedral. Started about 1165. Over-all length: 397 feet; 178 feet across transepts. Towers: 187 feet high. (Clarence Ward)

THE EARLY GOTHIC

The cathedrals at Sens, Noyon, and Senlis must have been, in their original condition, very like Suger's St. Denis. As they stand today, altered and changed, they present perplexities of style and date which foreclose adequate treatment in a general work.

The latest monument which could properly be called Early Gothic is the cathedral at Laon (Figs. 11.4–5).* Work appears to have commenced in 1165, and to have continued until about 1225. The ground plan of the church is unusual among the large cathedrals of France. The transepts extend further from the nave than was customary, and the east end is square. Both features

* Laon (Aisne); by road, 34 kilometers northeast of Soissons; in a direct line, 75 miles north-east of Paris. Inevitably, there is confusion with the city of León, in the middle of northern Spain, about 70 miles south from the Bay of Biscay; capital of the ancient kingdom of the same name; site of another Gothic cathedral mentioned several times below.

Fig. 11.5 Laon. Cathedral. Width across nave: 67 feet. Height of vaults: 78 feet. (Clarence Ward)

occur in other churches of the same diocese, and both are typical of England. Perhaps the matter is to be explained by the fact that an Englishman held the see during the early part of the 12th century.

Laon is also distinctive in elevation. It has five towers: two for the western façade, as in Norman Romanesque; two flanking the nave westward of the transepts; and another over the crossing. It was intended that there should be two more, or seven in all. The remarkable thing is not the number of towers, for the Gothic went even further than the Romanesque in the matter of the broken skyline, but that as many as five were actually put up; few churches, indeed, ever received the full complement of towers originally visualized by the builder. The towers themselves are magnificent. Poking their heads out at different levels are statues of oxen, in memory of the beasts who hauled the stone up the precipitous hill on which the town and its cathedral stand. "I have been in many countries," wrote Villard of Honne-

Fig. 11.6 Salamanca. Old Cathe dral. Drawing of two bays of the nave. (From C. H. Moore, *Gothic Architecture*, 2nd ed., New York, The Macmillan Company, 1906.)

court, the only Gothic architect from whom we inherit a word, "but I have never seen such other towers." Aside from the special magic of Laon, what are the differences that separate the Early Gothic from the Romanesque? The façade of the church of the Trinity at Caen (Fig. 10.31, page 340) will give us a closely analogous composition in the earlier style, and comparison will bring out the following differences.

The Romanesque building, for all its splayed doors and blind arcades, is fundamentally a plastic expression. One is impressed with the stone: its weight, its shape, and the solidity of the masses into which it is built. It can hardly be said that Laon is without plastic interest, but something has been added. One is first impressed, perhaps, with the play of surfaces in and out. The splayed doors are much deeper. The wheel window is set well into the thickness of the wall. Going higher, we find that the western towers are not simple units of shape as they were at Caen, but consist of many smaller parts cleverly coordinated with each other to make an integral whole. There is so

much openwork that the voids begin to have as much effect upon our sensibilities as do the solids.

Whatever else it may be, the total effect of Laon is considerably more complicated than that of any Romanesque building. There is a greater articulation of parts, and there are more parts. Perhaps the most important aspect
of the result is the creation of spatial relationships more subtle and ramified
than any to be found in all the earlier styles of architecture. Space penetrates the masonry in numerous places and at new and unexpected angles.

The spatial expectations raised by the exterior are not belied indoors (Fig.
11.5). The actual area of openwork has been made relatively much greater
than ever before, and the masonry correspondingly reduced in bulk. The
difference from Romanesque will be made plain if we once again avail ourselves of a comparison. Figure 11.6 shows the nave arcade, the clearstory, and
part of the cross vaulting of the Old Cathedral at Salamanca, a design that
is Gothic in every sense except that the hand and heart of its architect remained Romanesque.

Turning with more particularity to the fabric of Laon, it will be noted
that there are four horizontal divisions in the nave system. The triforium
space, that is to say, is subdivided; over a high gallery of compound arches,
there is a smaller and shallower gallery in bays of three simple arches carried
on colonnettes. The four-part arrangement had the advantage of gaining
height, a dimension that was put to very good use on the exterior of the
church. The same four-part system was characteristic of all Early Gothic
churches.

The cross vaults of the nave are of the six-part type. An extra transverse
rib was run across the nave through the intersection of each pair of diagonals,
thus dividing each bay of vaulting into six cells rather than the usual four.
Six-part vaulting was popular in France both during the Romanesque period
and for the Early Gothic. It is difficult to say why. The extra rib helps very
little in the matter of reducing thrusts at the fundamental points of concentration, and the extra cells of the vault complicate an overly complicated
form still further. But as compared with the best Romanesque vaulting, the
vaults at Laon reflect a major advance. For a detailed discussion, we refer the
reader ahead to pages 377–386. At this point, it will suffice to say that a more
thorough understanding of the cross vault had made excellent clearstory
lighting both safe and convenient, and that the age-old problems of church
architecture were very close to a final solution at this time.

One cannot look at Laon or any other Gothic building without being
impressed by an elegance heretofore unknown in the history of medieval
architecture. Simple in comparison to later Gothic, the moldings used at Laon
are delicate and subtle in comparison to the Romanesque. Not only has the

absolute bulk of each part been cut down; there was also evidently a serious preoccupation with proportions and relative proportions. One instance is the graduation in the weight and thickness of parts as the fabric rises; the nave arcade is heavy, the triforium light, and the clearstory lighter still. Still another indication of the new esthetic sense is to be seen in the clever equilibrium between horizontal and vertical lines, both dimensions being emphasized and both equally so. Finally, it is significant that structural logic had been tempered with a nice feeling for form. The engaged shafts which correspond to the ribs of the vaulting come down only to the nave capitals, and there they stop, permitting the lower piers to be unencumbered and neat.

THE HIGH GOTHIC

♦ *The Cathedral at Amiens* It is customary to think of the 13th-century cathedrals of northern France as representing the Gothic in its best and most typical form. Considerations of chronological priority do not enter into the verdict, because the French churches are almost exactly contemporary to those of other lands. The pre-eminence of the Gothic of the île de France rests, rather, upon considerations of design. As a group, the churches of that region are more uniform in appearance than those of any other region. In their construction, they conform more thoroughly to what we may call the disciplines of the style. In matters of detail, they show a richness and polish—and yet a harmonious simplicity—not duplicated elsewhere or at any other time.

Among the French churches, Amiens (Fig. 11.7) demonstrates the greatest over-all elegance and coherence. In the evolution of Gothic, it came at the perfect moment when all the subtleties of the style were understood and before any tendency toward elaboration had started to assert itself.

Like most other cathedral churches in France, Amiens was dedicated to the Virgin Mary. Dedications to the Virgin had been frequent enough in other times, but during the 13th century there were so many that we almost forget all the other saints. The reason is not far to seek: it demonstrates the degree to which the chivalric code had transformed French society. In sum, chivalry assigned to the female the staggering responsibility for maintaining on earth almost every kind of idealism. Her task began with personal loveliness and ended only with the attainment of transcendent virtue. Her person was sacred, and her mere presence was enough to enforce better behavior than men considered suitable between themselves. The thought of her was an ethical power extending outward to the ends of the earth; in distant lands, it inspired her true knight to valor altogether beyond his ordinary capacity. Only the Madonna might conceivably fulfill every detail of so amazing an obligation; hence the cult of the Madonna in Gothic art, the innumerable churches dedicated to her, the countless pictures and statues. She was the ultimate fulfill-

Fig. 11.7 Amiens. Cathedral. Started 1220. Height of north tower: 216 feet. (Clarence Ward)

ment of womanhood, and a queen who owned the hearts as well as the allegiance of all mankind.

Amiens owes much of its excellence to the fortunate circumstance of having been built to a single set of plans and by a single continuous effort long enough to complete most of the fabric. The present edifice replaces an earlier church which had been struck by lightning in 1218 and badly damaged by fire. Work on the new cathedral apparently commenced immediately.

It appears that the choir of the old church was still usable. Therefore, the builders started their work with the façade, a reversal of the usual custom. By 1228, they had raised the nave to the clearstory level, and the nave was vaulted over by 1236. The façade was by then complete up to the level of the stringcourse just above the rose window. Sixteen years had sufficed for an immense amount of construction.

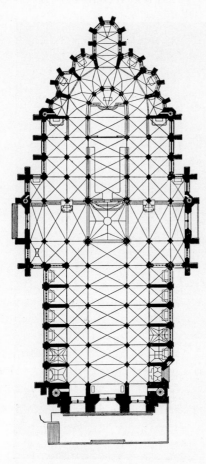

Fig. 11.8 Amiens. Cathedral. Plan. (From B. Winkler, *French Cathedrals*. London, Charles Tilt, 1837. From plate facing page 6.)

From that point on, things progressed more slowly. A fire damaged the east end of the building in 1258, and the ceremony of dedication (which presumably signalized the completion of the sanctuary) was delayed until 1279. The two western towers were carried to their present height between 1366 and 1402. There is no knowing whether they were meant to be left square-headed or to have spires. The *flèche* (literally "arrow"), the delicate tower over the crossing, dates from 1529, and the gallery between the two western towers was added by Viollet-le-Duc during the 19th century. Thus, Amiens, like most other Gothic churches, became venerable but never complete.

The Plan. An outline drawing of the plan of Amiens (Fig. 11.8) has a deceptively stubby appearance which is altogether obliterated in the building itself by the articulation of the elevation. Such a drawing shows us a cruciform church with transepts of moderate projection and a very long choir. The three western doorways open directly into the nave and side aisles. West of the crossing, the space which might have been used for a second set of aisles is subdivided by lateral partitions to form chapels. The transepts have three aisles, and a five-aisled arrangement was used for the length of the choir. An ambulatory of one aisle runs round the semicircle of the apse, opening into a set of seven radial chapels.

But there is more to be discerned in the plan of Amiens than this. A great many persons testify that French Gothic plans bring up memories of lace. The impression is far from superficial; it is just another way of saying that we must expect to understand Gothic in terms of lines and spaces. Of that general condition, there is more than a suggestion in the ground plan. As indicated by the inked-in sections, the total area of masonry is minute by comparison to the space enclosed by the boundaries of the building. It may be said, indeed, that the Gothic church has no walls. In the traditional sense of the wall as a structural member under compression, that is literally true. In Gothic, the weight of the superstructure is carried by a framework of arches which spring from a series of isolated supports. The delicacy of each separate support testifies to the perfection of the abutment of the vaults above, for such supports have little strength against any load other than a directly vertical one. The interior is protected from the weather by immense windows.

By contrast to the square bays which were popular in some Romanesque schools, the main vaults of Amiens are arranged in a series of narrow oblongs, with the long axis of each oblong at right angles to that of the nave. Such was the usual scheme for Gothic. By adjusting the proportions of the oblongs, it was perfectly convenient to make them correspond with any desired inter-columniation and to any rational arrangement of the aisle vaults. The need for an alternating system of supports was thus eliminated. In order to achieve this new freedom in plan, it was necessary for the Gothic designers to invent a radically ingenious arrangement of the vault ribs, a matter to which we shall return in due course.

The Elevation. Most of the French cathedrals are city churches. Most of them face on city squares. For that reason and in some contrast to the Gothic of England and Germany, the French churches were designed on the assumption that the western façade—considered as a composition in its own right— was more important than the appearance of the whole building as seen from some other angle. The façades of Chartres and Amiens (Figs. 11.2 and 7) give a good idea of the grace and power with which such churches loom above their surroundings. Of the two, Amiens is the more typical, for Chartres had a checkered history.

As the prime illustration of a special type in the history of architecture, the façade of Amiens deserves detailed attention. The fundamentals of the composition come directly from the Norman Romanesque (see above, pages

338–340), but during the 13th century certain Gothic features became standard. Upon occasion, these latter might be large or small, and placed high or low, but there seems to have been a feeling that all ought to be there.

The façade is divided into three parts both vertically and horizontally. The two towers and their smaller doors correspond to the side aisles. The large central door opens into the nave. Strong vertical buttresses which, though continuous, exhibit an extraordinary variety of form at different levels, mark these three vertical divisions. The verticals have enough relief so that they always take the sun, and stand out as axial elements unifying the façade. Most photographs have been taken in a diffused light, but the French façade is at its best when bold dark shadows are cast to the right or left.

The horizontal boundary lines are plainly visible, though considerably less vigorous. An elaborate molding runs across the façade at the height of the gable over the central doorway. The next horizontal division is itself subdivided. It consists of an open gallery of delicate, pointed compound arches, and a "row of kings"—a series of male statues in niches. The notion that they represent either kings of France or kings of Judah may have a basis in fact, but probably has an even stronger basis in fancy. Above the row of kings, we find the rose window with its curvilinear tracery, and the two towers which, at this level, are pierced with arches.

The thing that counts about the tripartite horizontal division is not the mere fact of its existence, but the relation maintained between solids and voids. In the lowest section, there is scarcely any open work at all. In the middle section, the voids and the solids are approximately equal. In the upper part, the openings occupy more area than the masonry. There is reason behind such a graduation. The lowest and heaviest part of the façade corresponds closely in height to the nave arcade, the heaviest section within. The middle part of the façade fits with the triforium level, and the more open upper section has its interior counterpart in the clearstory. The designers, we may guess, felt driven to prove the unity of the whole building by demonstrating in this way the intimate coherence of its parts. It is by such insistence upon relationships that they showed themselves as working with artistic problems in very much the same way that the Scholastic philosophers worked with religion.

A similar instinct for order and relationship made itself felt in the disposition of the numerous statues on the façade and throughout the church. Because each cathedral was in this respect an individual proposition, we must avoid any suggestion that the Gothic designers followed a book of rules. It is true, however, that they recognized certain general principles of hierarchy, and arranged their sculpture with a nice sense for precedence. It will be understood in what follows that we are concerned here not with the statues as

Fig. 11.9 Amiens. Cathedral. Trumeau of the central door, with "Le Beau Dieu." (Roubier)

such (which is the business of the next chapter), but only with the architectural implications of the sculpture.

On the *trumeau* of the central doorway (the place of highest honor) we usually find, as at Amiens (Fig. 11.9), a statue of Christ. In a similar position on the trumeaux of the lateral doorways, are statues of the Virgin and of Saint Firmin, the first bishop of Amiens who died a martyr's death in the year 289. In the central tympanum over the Savior, we find the event for which the universal church had engaged to prepare mankind: the Last Judgment. In that position it catches the final glow of the setting sun which one day will set on the last evening of the world. In the splay of the central doorway, statues of the Apostles flank that of the Christ. Saint Firmin is accompanied by other saints of whom the cathedral possessed relics, and Mary is accompanied by figures recalling the story of her life.

The principal statues of the façade thus took account of sacred personages and events of both general and local importance; and, in a similar manner of having a reason for everything, it was more or less customary to put Old Testament subject matter on the façade of the northern transept because the northern dark and cold seemed analogous to unenlightenment. New Testament material was common for the southern façade, facing the region of warmth and light.

In controlling the style of their statues, the Gothic architects were less unreasonable than the Romanesque (see above, page 344), but they were rigorous. No matter how sacred the subject, the statue was thought of as an embellishment of the building and subject to architectural rules. Because Gothic was fundamentally a linear art, that general proposition was construed as meaning that statues should be used to lend variety and interest to architectural lines. On the façade of Amiens, we find them used for almost nothing else.

A straightedge placed along the axis of one of the great verticals bisects not only the buttress it follows, but several statues as well. The little statuettes that decorate the separate orders of the splayed doors are arranged to conform with the curvature of the arch, not with the rules of representation, for some of them appear to be in the act of defying gravity. It will be further observed that each of the large statues in the door jambs below is placed in such a way that its axis, if projected, carries into the curve of an order in the archway above.

The relationship between architecture and sculpture, as just described, seems to have been well-understood as early as St. Denis. Like many another logical system, it was more rigidly and literally applied when new. Thus, the statues on the west porch at Chartres (Fig. 12.3, page 416), which dates from about 1145 and formed part of the Early Gothic church replaced by the present one, are uncompromising in their architectural reference. In order to make certain that each figure would tell as a line, the vertical dimension was radically exaggerated, and the poses were made to conform with the principle of frontality.

The 13th century was slightly less doctrinaire. The *Beau Dieu* of Amiens was designed with a primary regard for its architectural purpose. The proportions of the body were governed by the dimensions of the trumeau to which it was to be attached. The pose is strictly vertical, and the elbows are held in contact with the sides. The right hand, raised in benediction, projects straight up. Only in the drapery is there a suggestion of the diagonal. But as Figure 11.9 indicates, there is much naturalism in the anatomy and much plasticity in the modeling.

If we study the façade still further, it will be unmistakably clear that its designer went to a great deal of trouble to provide a proper place for every statue. A great many figures stand in niches. For others, corbels project from the wall, and there are canopies overhead. The design of the building, it

Fig. 11.10   Chartres. Cathedral. (Aéro-Photo)

may even be said, demands a statue wherever we see one: sculpture is literally incorporated into the surface of the walls.

So quickly stated and reviewed, the Gothic theory of sculptural decoration sounds mechanistic and unfeeling, but no such impression can be entertained when we judge by the results. An amazing number of statues were accommodated by these methods. Reims is said to have about 2,000 in all, of which 530 appear on the western front alone.

A Gothic artist would doubtless have declared that the purpose of decoration was to increase the beauty of the thing decorated—the meaning of which we may comprehend by walking away from a Gothic church until we reach the distance where the eye can no longer resolve small details. The statuary then begins to tell as a flicker of light and dark enlivening the fundamental lines of the church. At a very great distance when even that much may not be accurately discerned, one is still conscious of an opulence of texture never to be observed where sculpture is lacking.

The transepts, which scarcely show up at all in the ground plan, were given during the 13th century a development only less imposing than the western front. They rise as high as the nave (Fig. 11.10), and each has a considerable façade of its own.

It must be confessed, however, that the French architects never arrived at an adequate handling of the great volumes imposed by the dimensions of the interior. This fault becomes distinctly and disturbingly apparent whenever one takes a station to the north or south, and sees the cathedral in full broad-side (Fig. 11.11). The western towers, so imposing from the front, seem to shrink and lose their power. The elaborate transepts lack the strength, and the flèche lacks the scale to adjust the composition. The long, level ridge of the roof obtrudes itself as the most conspicuous feature in sight; and the dissolving silhouette—that essential of all northern art—is destroyed.

The eastern aspect of a French Gothic church is, however, almost as grand as the façade. From that point of view, the flying buttresses show up to the best advantage. They meet the vault ribs at points of concentration, and swing through the air carrying the thrusts to the vertical pier buttresses which are placed at intervals around the semicircle of the apse. The entire assembly (apse, radial chapels, and buttresses) is known as the *chevet*. The chevet of Amiens is not the best, so we substitute for it that of Le Mans (Fig. 11.12), perhaps the most powerful and ascending composition of them all.

The Interior. The nave of Amiens (Fig. 11.13) has long been recognized as the supreme achievement of 13th-century architecture. Its excellence depends not so much on any fundamental advance over immediately previous church design as upon a perfect fulfillment of everything good in the Gothic style. In a period noted for grace, the details stand nearly alone in their elegance. Every line and contour has a modest beauty, and in no other Gothic church was so nice a standard maintained throughout the entire fabric. But perfection of detail would not be enough to justify the assertion that Amiens is the best of the Gothic cathedrals. The building is even more notable for the success with which the possibilities of scale and proportion were realized; and it is, moreover, perhaps our best illustration of the Gothic concept of spatial composition.

Amiens is a very large building. The apse is about 125 yards from a man who has just come in through the western doors, and the vaulting is approximately 135 feet above his eyes. In making esthetic use of such scale, the architect was helped by the nature of the style he worked in; as in all Gothic buildings, the whole is an ensemble of small parts, a northern infinity of detail. In exaggerated form, the effect is similar to that of Hagia Sophia (page 279). We construct our concept of the size of the whole by adding up, as it were, the sum of the parts. Impressive today, this effect must have been even more so originally, when all the windows were presumably of stained glass. The dim and colored light must have increased, as though by atmospheric perspective, the sense of distance and size.

Scale counts; but in addition to the effect of absolute size, both the vertical and the horizontal dimensions received direct and unmistakable emphasis. It is easy to stress one dimension at the expense of another; the interior of Amiens is remarkable for the reconcilement of length and height. The verticality of the nave would be plain from its proportions alone, for

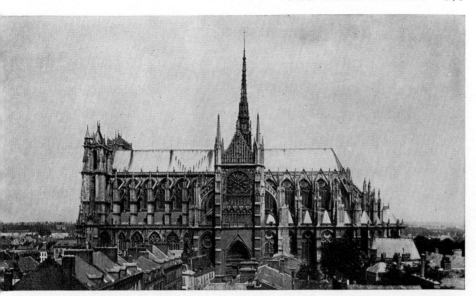

Fig. 11.11 Amiens. Cathedral. View from the south. Height to ridge of roof: 200 feet. To tip of flêche: 370 feet. Length: about 475 feet. (Giraudon)

Fig. 11.12 Le Mans. Cathedral. The chevet. End of the 13th century. (Archives Photographiques)

Fig. 11.13 Amiens. Cathedral. View of the nave from the gallery of the south transept. Width of nave: about 46 feet. Extreme width of church from wall to wall: about 150 feet. Height to underside of vaulting: 139 feet. (Clarence Ward)

it is more than three times as high as it is wide. In addition, the arches point up, and there are literally innumerable vertical lines.

But a good many things are simultaneously at work to give power to the long axis. First, there is the rhythmic repeat of the bays, which produces a sense of progression toward apse and altar. Then there are three linear horizontals which lead the eye to the far end of the church: the successive capitals of the nave arcade form one such line, the floral molding at the lower boundary of the triforium is another, and the string course along the base of the clearstory is a third.

To a great extent, the wonderful harmony of height and length was made possible by a relaxation of the theory of structural logic. Although the excellence of the French cathedrals has often been cited as prima-facie proof of the organic dogma, the fact is that detail for detail Amiens is less precise than Sant'Ambrogio at Milan (page 328) when it comes to furnishing us with an illustration of form governed by structural principles. At Amiens, the shafts that correspond to the wall ribs were radically reduced in diameter, and are carried down only to the triforium level. The shafts corresponding to the diagonals are only slightly larger, and they terminate on the abaci of the nave capitals. The only verticals of any substantial size are those under the transverse arches. They alone go to the floor, and only they are permitted to cross over a horizontal line.

It is important to point out in passing that there is no mechanical basis for the diameter assigned to each of the clustered vertical ribs. Their size is not in proportion to what they carry; if the wall rib is adequate to bear the weight upon it, the shaft under the transverse arch is altogether too big. The dainty order of the graduated sizes simply softens the boundary between the wall surface and the verticals engaged upon it. They rise gently from their background, and blend gently back into it.

A sober succession of declarative sentences may with good luck describe all the details we have mentioned, but more poetical language is needed if we are to give any hint of their effect when brought into complete and simultaneous view. Almost every writer who has commented upon the nave of Amiens has resorted to the vocabulary of flight, for no other physical sensation so well combines the vertical and the horizontal as we see them architecturally combined at Amiens. When we speak of the "soaring effect" of this interior, we are telling the truth, but it is important to understand also that we are recognizing a new quality in the linear idiom of northern art. Celtic line had by this date, risen above its original impetuous movement, and come to maturity. The jerk and yank of Romanesque sculpture had likewise given way to a serenity of motion. Amiens is dynamic art at its best, full of poise and elegance, full of grace and dignity.

The Gothic builders invented no new theory of interior space; they merely had the techniques which made it possible to follow out the implications of the Early Christian system (pages 245–247). Many of the items mentioned in the paragraphs above contributed to the Gothic spatial composition. The innumerable small details, each a unit of measure, perform their function as readily with reference to the enclosed volume as with reference to length and height. The soaring effect produced by the various linear elements may also be thought of as a spatial concept: to suggest flight is to suggested an unlimited volume of air expanding from the foreground into the remote distance. But most important of all, Gothic engineering (see next section) opened up the interior in a manner hitherto impossible, and gave the voids an emphasis never seen before.

A diagonal view across the nave of Amiens (Fig. 11.13) gives us in a more perfect and refined form the same experience noted when one takes up a similar station in one of the Early Christian basilicas (Figure 8.29, page 246). Beyond one archway in the immediate foreground, there is another, and beyond that openings succeed each other until we come to a door or window. As an approximate statement, it is fair to say that every line of sight ends in an accessible opening, and that no other kind of terminal was permitted if the architect could possibly help it. Hence the great rose which "opens up" the long axis on the west, and the windows of the apse at the eastern end.

Both the size and the accessibility of Gothic windows are important in the effect. The interior is not shut away from the outdoors (compare the Pantheon, pages 195–196). Light and air interpenetrate the architecture.

Similarly, the windows provide no barrier for the mind. Either in thought or in action, it is easy to make the transition from indoors to the immense universe outside. It may be said, indeed, that Gothic space is a continuation of universal space, and part of it, differing from the Early Christian only in the greater degree of artistic success with which it is handled.

These facts, it must be added, contribute powerfully to the truth of the idea that Gothic architecture forms a physical record of Christian aspiration. Through the medium of space, it is made clear that nothing exists alone; even the mighty fabric of the cathedral relates itself to the divine order, and occupies an appointed place.

The experience of Gothic space is one of the most profound the visual arts provide; but for the fullness of its effect, another element, not so far mentioned, must be present. That is the stained glass, which still exists in anything like the original amount and condition only at Chartres in France and at León in Spain.

As a major art, stained glass painting became feasible as soon as Gothic engineering eliminated the structural handicaps which in every earlier style had curtailed the size of window openings. From the standpoint of adequate illumination only, most Gothic windows are in fact too large; and unless the glass is colored, the interior is likely to suffer on bright days from an unpleasant glare. But by flooding the whole church with colored light, the Gothic artists introduced a new element.

While it is possible to prepare a useful rationale for color (See Appendix II) it was true in the 13th century and it is true today that the effect of color upon us is one of the great emotional mysteries. Upon entering Chartres, all persons experience a surge of feeling that goes altogether beyond understanding. It is easy, and certainly very appropriate, to associate that experience with the supernatural or transcendental component of religion. Color, it might be said, is the physical attribute of mysticism. By comparison with churches that lack stained glass, Chartres calls up an experience which is much more intimate: no other monument brings one so close to fulfillment, or so nearly satisfies the soul's yearning for union with the infinite.

♦ *Gothic Engineering* The stylistic and spiritual intentions of the Gothic era would have been impossible of accomplishment except for the fact that the builders of that time were engineers of the highest order. Engineering has been correctly defined as the art of making the findings of pure science available for human use; but when we apply the word to anything medieval, the reader must understand the difference between the *ad hoc* experiments of the 11th and 12th centuries, and modern methods. In all the medieval world, there was no mathematics capable of dealing with mechanical problems; indeed, there never was until the development of the calculus during the 17th century. On the other hand, when Robert de Lusarches took the responsibility for designing Amiens, he had at his command an immense and certain knowledge about the construction of vaulted churches. He could calculate not at all, but he carried in his memory a tremendous record of reckless trial and disastrous error—and he knew how to build. His outlook was not stultified, moreover, by any distinction between art and engineering. Indeed, one of the chief glories of Gothic architecture is the truth that for once in all history, structure and beauty were everywhere and always the same, to be separated only for purposes of discussion, and even then with apologies.

In attempting to understand the superb mechanics of Amiens and other cathedrals, it is well to begin with a brief list of fixed considerations.

The basilican type of church was as firmly established as Catholicism itself. Conceivably, another type of building might have been invented to serve the ritual as well and might have been easier to build. But probably nobody gave a moment's thought to the matter. The ribbed cross vault was, by 1220, almost as firmly established as the basilican church; the master builders knew it would work and knew they had men who could construct it.

Masonry was the only fire-resistant material available. One can not help wondering what the Gothic builders might have done with structural steel. In considering their masonry, there are several points to remember. A good deal of cement went into the fabric of every Gothic building; but the use of concrete as a fundamental material (as the Romans had done) seems to have gone out with antiquity. Although one occasionally comes upon an ingenious application of mortar and rubble, it is evident from their structural system that the Gothic architects thought in terms of cut stone under compression, and provided for its action.

Gothic architecture, moreover, was an architecture of small stones; much of the atmosphere of the style derives from it. Most of the stones laid during the period were small enough to be hoisted and put in place by a gang of men. It is rare to see a block that could not have been pulled along a country lane on a sledge drawn by oxen. The miserable facilities at hand, it seems, provided the necessity which was the mother of Gothic invention.

Referring to the several structural drawings (Figs. 11.14 ff.) it will be evident at a glance that the designers were keenly alive to the esthetic difficulties imposed by the thrust of arches. Most of what they did may be interpreted as an attempt to reduce the absolute thrust of every arch in the fabric, and at the same time to prevent the abutment from spoiling the beauty of the church.

Of the various stratagems resorted to, none has anything like the importance of the extreme delicacy of construction characteristic of the High Gothic. Every component was reduced in scale to a proportion approaching the danger point. The result was an architecture which made the most efficient use of materials on record, with the possible exception of the best (but not all) of the bridges designed by Roebling. No architecture ever used less masonry in relation to the cubic content enclosed. But above all, the reduction in the weight of every part categorically reduced the thrust of the arches and vaults.

The daring of Gothic construction is no figure of speech. Consider what happened at Beauvais. Started only five years later than Amiens, with vaults only a few feet higher and with parts only a little lighter, the choir was completed and put to use in 1272. In 1284, the vaults came crashing down; and the present vaulting, in six parts, is a rather unsatisfactory correction of the original mistake.

The pointed arch was a second innovation that helped to control thrust. As set forth on pages 944–945, its advantage is not that its thrust, measured

Fig. 11.14 Amiens. Cathedral. Perspective cross section.

in pounds, is less; but simply that the thrust is directed at a steeper angle toward the ground—a consideration of the utmost importance in view of the lofty placement and delicate proportions of the fully perfected flying buttresses. It should be noted, however, that round arches occur in Gothic, especially in Italy.

As for the flying buttress, it was made necessary by the basilican form of the church. It was almost never used unless a clearstory rose above side

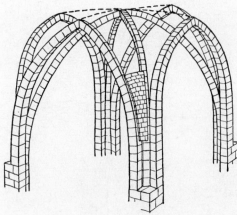

Fig. 11.15 Drawing of the developed Gothic vault.

DEVELOPED GOTHIC VAULT
POINTED & STILTED ARCHES
ALMOST LEVEL CROWNS
A SECTION OF THE THIN WEB
SHOWN IN PLACE

aisles. Sainte Chapelle at Paris, for example, needed no aisles because of its special purpose, and its abutment is by pier buttresses only. But where vaults were high and clearstory windows large, it was imperative to find a buttress that would cast the least possible shadow across the windows, hence the segmental arches we call flying buttresses (Figs. 11.13, 19, 20), which meet the nave vaults at points where thrusts are concentrated, take the compression, and swing it over to pier buttresses arranged along the outer borders of the church.

The flying buttresses of the High Gothic are extraordinarily slight for the work they do, but were used with confidence all over northern France. No such performance would have been possible except for the development of a new and special form of vault—a vault with a peculiar shape which brought the thrusts of all ribs into a single force focused upon a very narrow area at

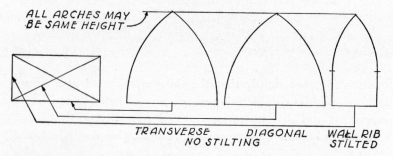

ALL ARCHES MAY
BE SAME HEIGHT

TRANSVERSE   DIAGONAL   WALL RIB
NO STILTING   STILTED

Fig. 11.16 Schematic drawing to illustrate the Gothic method for bringing all arches of the vault frame to the same height regardless of their great or short span.

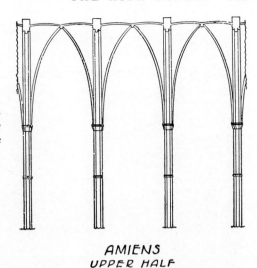

Fig. 11.17 Amiens. Cathedral. Longitudinal cross section to illustrate the very
moderate undulation of the vault surface
along the axis of the ceiling.

AMIENS
UPPER HALF

either side of the church. Only because the precise direction of that force was
known was it possible to counteract it by putting a flying buttress in exactly
the right place and pitched at exactly the right angle.

Ordinarily, one can gain an adequate comprehension of the thrust pattern
of cross vaulting by reference to the plan view only. When, however, we deal
with the more subtle elements of Gothic vaulting, we must be prepared to
give simultaneous consideration to the grouping of arches and shafts as they
appear in vertical elevation.

Figure 11.15 shows a single bay of Gothic vaulting as it would appear in
frame; and Figure 11.16 shows in schematic fashion the arches which make
up the assembly. Because of the oblong shape of the bay, the span of these
several arches varies considerably, the diagonals being much the widest.
However, by giving the transverse ribs a steeper pitch, and by stilting the
wall ribs, the crowns of all six arches were brought to much the same height.

One excellent result is illustrated by Figure 11.17. Instead of rising up in
great concaves, as at Sant'Ambrogio (Fig. 10.18, page 327), the vaulting of
Amiens undulates only slightly. The bays have a fairly "level crown." The
advantage of the level crown is apparent in any view of the nave. Although
the nature of cross vaulting tends to make each bay a separate artistic unit,
the level crown provided a reasonable coherence between each bay and the
next and a reasonable continuity in the long axis of the ceiling.

About the stilting of the wall rib, there is more to be said; that expedient,
indeed, was the inspired detail upon which everything else depended. A glance
at Figure 11.18 will show that the transverse arches which designate the boundary between adjacent bays belong to each bay equally. Because we know that

Fig. 11.18 Amiens. Cathedral. View into the vaults of the choir and apse. Height to underside of vaulting: about 139 feet. (Clarence Ward)

they thrust at right angles to the nave and directly in line with the buttresses, we may dismiss them from further discussion. Let us instead concentrate attention upon the diamond-shaped areas of vaulting which spread upward from each pier, being bounded and defined by the diagonals.

Figures 11.14, 19, and 20, show these from various angles; and it will

Figs. 11.19–20 (left) Schematic drawing to illustrate the concentration of thrusts achieved by the special system of cross vaulting developed in France during the High Gothic era. (right) Schematic drawing to illustrate the impingement of flying buttresses against the double plowshare solids of French vaulting. The proportions are approximately standard for the period of the High Gothic. (Both drawings by Henry Tisdall.)

be observed that we are dealing with a three-dimensional solid of masonry, a solid of peculiar shape. We need a name for it. Sometimes referred to as the *Gothic vault conoid,* it might better be called the *double plowshare solid* of Gothic vaulting.

If we imagine one of these solids to be cut by a horizontal plane at a level near the haunch, its cross section will be approximately as shown by Figure 11.21. Such a cross section graphically illustrates the tremendous advantage (from the standpoint of focusing all thrusts upon a narrow area) obtained by stilting the wall rib. Figure 11.22 indicates what the situation

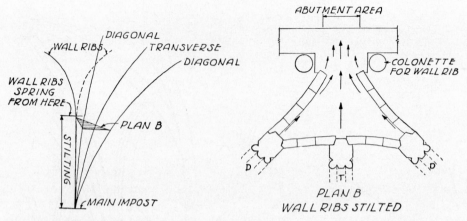

Fig. 11.21 Schematic drawing to illustrate the focus of thrusts made possible by the stilted wall ribs and the double plowshare solid. Left: The various ribs seen in perspective. Right: A cross section through the double plowshare solid at the level of the haunch of the diagonal ribs.

would be were the wall ribs not stilted. It is an imaginary cross section, similar to Figure 11.21, but drawn on the assumption that the wall ribs were made to spring from the same level as the others. In rising, such wall ribs would spread apart as fast as they rose; and the further they spread apart, the wider would be the area between them. In other words, the compressive force of the vault thrusts would be dispersed over a broad surface—a surface that could not possibly be covered by the narrow face of a flying buttress. Ponderous and unshapely buttresses would be required. Too, the window area would be considerably reduced.

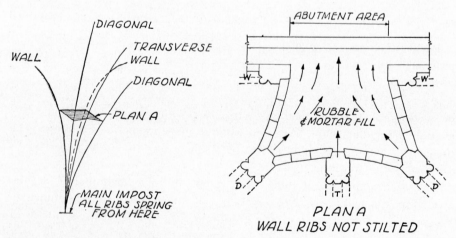

Fig. 11.22 Schematic drawing to be compared with Figure 11.21: the thrust pattern of a ribbed cross vault without stilted wall ribs.

Fig. 11.23 Amiens. Cathedral. One of the flying buttresses of the nave. (From C. H. Moore, *Gothic Architecture,* 2nd ed., New York, The Macmillan Company, 1906.)

The description just completed will give the reader an introduction to the major achievements of Gothic engineering. Detailed inspection of the monuments will reward him with an almost infinite number of structural refinements in which the builders themselves obviously took the keenest pleasure. Wall ribs, for example, usually have capitals at the level of their own springing. The tiny spires placed as finials for the pier buttresses (Fig. 11.23) almost always appear at the outside edge of the buttress, where their small weight aids the abutment by squeezing the outer joints of the masonry more tightly together. Once generally understood, moreover, the flying buttress itself was used in a great variety of dispositions; no two churches have them arranged in just the same way.

Another sidelight on Gothic engineering is the fact that those great designers refused to be enslaved by their own structural theory. For example, the upper tier of flying buttresses at Reims ostensibly impinges upon the vaulting at the haunch, but when the roof burned off after the bombardment of 1914, it was revealed (to the great surprise of people not intimately familiar with the church) that those buttresses came nowhere near the haunch. They were too high, and they had been pushing against each other through horizontal beams for nearly 700 years. From that instance alone, we may observe that the Gothic architects, although more concerned than any earlier school with mechanical excellence, were not immune to the charm of form.

◆ *The 13th-century Church and the Spread of the Gothic Style*   The 13th century was a heyday of church building, and everywhere the style was Gothic. Over and above the unique prestige of the Île de France, there must have been other strong reasons for the adoption of a single and universal style—a considerable contrast with the previous diversity. The strongest reason of all is doubtless to be sought in the character of the 13th-century Church.

The difference between Gothic Christianity and Romanesque Christianity was not a matter of the comparative level of individual piety. It had to do, rather, with church government. The relative separatism of the ecclesiastical polity during the two Romanesque centuries is well evidenced by the numerous local subdivisions we are compelled to recognize within that style. The centralization of authority at Rome was reflected by the general use of the Gothic.

A detailed description of the events and methods by which the Bishop of Rome extended his power and perfected his administration would be beyond the scope of our immediate subject, but the reader will require a bold outline of the papal situation if he is to comprehend the motivation behind the transmission of the Gothic to all Western Europe.

The Popes had, in the first place, made good use of the feudal system. They held lands personally; and over a considerable part of central Italy, the authority of the Pope was the government. They had vassals, as other monarchs did; and while the *de facto* authority of the pontiff must have seemed remote in some of the regions of which he was technically the overlord, an immense prestige attached to the fact that whoever held the Vatican also was acknowledged feudal lord of Sicily, Aragon, England, Ireland, and the Latin monarchy established after 1204 at Constantinople. At any moment and upon any pretext of his own choosing, the Pope could and did assert his right to interfere in the practical affairs of the populations mentioned.

In addition to the powers just cited, which belonged to the Pope in his capacity as a property holder, there were other recognized powers which derived from the moral and spiritual status of the Vatican; often these proved even more cogent when the Church wished to sway the imagination and, in some measure, direct the impulses of men. From the moment when Leo the 3rd crowned Charlemagne, the Popes had claimed the right to crown, or not to crown, the elected successors of Charlemagne. Endless friction and conflict ensued; but in the period immediately before the 13th century, the papacy had enjoyed better than average success in asserting the superiority of the spiritual leadership over the temporal. The Popes thus started the Gothic period in a position of great political influence.

Upon the daily affairs of all persons, the Church continued, as before, to exercise an ever-present effect unknown today; more and more, policy and even specific direction tended to come from Rome. The collection of church revenues was perfected into a complex system of taxation which gave the Church a share in almost every profitable enterprise, and fetched into the Vatican treasury an enormous sum annually. Canon law, which previously had lacked unity and system, was brought into uniformity, largely as the result of Gratian's *Decretum*—a compilation of documents, plus a treatise in which the learned author attempted to solve their contradictions and arrive at a coherent judicial system. Brought together about 1148, Gratian's work, although not a set of statutes, presently began to acquire the effective authority we recognize today in the writings of Blackstone and Coke.

In addition to the jurisdiction the Church claimed as its own, its function in the medieval world was made even more effective and indispensable by conditions which, for the time, played into its hands. The feudal monarchies, even that of France, were quite loose and ineffective; they simply did not perform many of the duties necessary for the operation of society. Into the vacuum stepped the Church with an organization so perfect it may rightly be compared with that of the Roman Empire. The papal prerogative to appoint bishops, long disputed, had become absolute early in the 12th century. By the start of the 13th, its technique had been refined into a system of patronage and discipline rarely equaled in the history of human institutions. In every community of the Western world, the Roman authority was thereby represented by direct appointees of the Pope, most of them able and much-respected men. It was the exception rather than the rule for promising young churchmen to remain in one place; almost all of them had served the Church in many lands before they could be called mature or became prominent. With them, they took their medieval Latin, in which language all church business was conducted. Inelegant by comparison with the classical, it was nevertheless the closest thing to the gift of Pentecost yet seen on earth. It furnished a channel for the passage of information and ideas the like of which had not been seen before the perfection of the Catholic polity, and unknown since. Where there is unity of tongue, there is likely to be unity of taste, and the Gothic style in art seems to have traveled the obvious route.

But none of these things nor all of them together furnish us with an adequate explanation either for the imposing powers of the 13th-century Church or for the completeness with which Gothic art was devoted to the service of religion. Lusty and often barbariously cruel, Gothic society was genuinely religious in a sense for which history has no parallel. The people believed what the Church taught. Their membership in a common religion was everywhere symbolized by the building of churches in a common style.

♦ *The High Gothic in Spain, Italy, Germany, and England* The largest and most famous French cathedrals are not earlier than, but approximately contemporary with those of the rest of Europe. Salisbury was begun the same year as Amiens. The cathedrals at Burgos and Toledo were started in 1221 and 1227 respectively. The church of St. Francis at Assisi dates from 1228, and that of St. Elizabeth at Marburg from 1223. The figures make it unmistakable that the actual transmission of the style from the Île de France outward must have taken place before 1200. In trying to understand the operation of the French influence, it would therefore be a mistake to give a great deal of weight to the highly perfected work of the 13th century. While no simple statement can be entirely true, it appears generally that the foreign architects, insofar as they depended directly upon French models, remembered as they worked, not the High Gothic of Amiens, but the Early Gothic—and often in a less developed state than at Laon.

Few of the foreign churches carry out the logic of the style as it was understood in northern France at the time Amiens was designed. As machines, most of them lack the precision and polish common in French work. Flying buttresses, if used at all, tend to have a clumsy shape, and often are neither placed nor pitched ideally. Moldings are simpler. Most parts tend to be heavier.

Spain. During the 13th century, Spain was an artistic province of France. It is possible to recognize a bit of authentic local flavor in the tracery of the rose and in the cusped arches of the triforium openings at Burgos, but much of the surface embellishment that gives character to the interior is, like the lantern and western spires, Late Gothic. The moldings and piers of Toledo are very French. The western façade of León derives directly from the unique lateral porches of Chartres; León is, in fact, a watered version of a French church.

Italy. Italian Gothic is one of the anomalies of art history. It is like a bird that cannot fly. Nothing but the overwhelming prestige of France could have brought a northern style into the very dooryard of classical art, and the out-land manner was never fully understood or accepted. The vaulted cathedrals at Florence and Siena are the most famous, perhaps, but they give a false impression of the typical form taken by Gothic architecture in Italy. For that purpose, Santa Croce at Florence (Fig. 11.24) will serve us better.

It may be described as a wooden-roofed basilica built with pointed arches. The piers, capitals, and moldings betray in their form an extreme reluctance

Fig. 11.24   Florence. Santa Croce. Started 1294. (Anderson)

Fig. 11.25   Florence. Santa Croce. Plan.

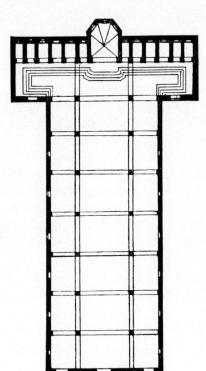

Fig. 11.26 Marburg. St. Elizabeth's. Started 1235. Interior from the west. (Marburg)

to render more than lip service to the prevailing French fashion, a condition in general true everywhere on the peninsula. The plan of Santa Croce (Fig. 11.25) is peculiar to Italy and typical of the average Italian Gothic church. The apse and choir amount to a separate chapel, narrower than the nave. To the north and south, a series of smaller chapels open through the eastern wall; in two of them on the south side, Giotto did cycles of frescoes, and the church contains an amazing collection of monuments by famous artists of the Renaissance.

Germany. It has often been said that the Romanesque style was more congenial to the German temperament than was the Gothic, and that buildings like the cathedral of Cologne (a direct derivative from Amiens) reflect no more than a temporary affectation for something French. Such statements are half true, to be sure, but they overlook at least two excellent contributions to the Gothic which appear to have originated in Germany.

In the arrangement of the interior, the Germans made an interesting departure from the traditional cross section of the basilica. St. Elizabeth's at Marburg (Fig. 11.26) is an example. The nave and the side aisles are of equal height, eliminating the conventional triforium and clearstory. The effect is to open up the interior from wall to wall and to unify rather than subdivide

Fig. 11.27 Salisbury. Cathedral. Started 1220. (National Buildings Record)

the space it contains. As a type such buildings are known as *hall churches*. Instead of a chevet, St. Elizabeth's has a trefoil arrangement at the east end.

In the composition of the exterior, the Germans also proved inventive. The cathedral at Freiburg in Breisgau will illustrate their contribution in this department. Instead of the twin towers characteristic of France and common all over Europe, the western front was given a single tower of monumental dimensions. Because the German nave was usually much lower than that of a comparable French church (the interior height at Freiburg is about 89 feet, and the tower stands a full 380 feet high) such towers dominate the composition and make a diagonal view of the building as good as its eastern or western aspect. The principle involved was carried to its logical conclusion in the Late Gothic cathedral at Ulm (Fig. 11.36).

England. The cathedral at Salisbury (Fig. 11.27) is stylistically the most consistent of the High Gothic churches of England. Work began in 1220 (the same year as Amiens), and the building was substantially complete forty years later. No other great English minster ever went up in so prompt and straightforward a fashion.

In plan, Salisbury conforms to the shape of an archiepiscopal cross, the length of the choir being exaggerated to accommodate the second set of transepts. Like most other English churches, the apse is square, maintaining the local tradition dating from the very earliest years of the Middle Ages. Compared to Amiens, the plan seems long and rambling, with far greater extension of the transepts; but in terms of feet and inches, the church is no longer. The effect of length depends, rather, upon a nave that is both narrow and low. Salisbury measures only 32 or 33 feet between the piers, and the vaults swing only 82 feet above the floor, compared to 139 feet at Amiens.

An interior view of Salisbury can hardly be expected to please people who have learned their taste at Amiens and Laon. The English were never much interested in the organic theory of architectural design; and there is neither the refinement, the logic, nor the coherence between part and part which so distinguishes the French cathedrals.

All of that is forgiven if not forgotten when one goes outdoors. Like most other English churches, Salisbury stands in a park. The lawns and trees around it have received competent and sensitive care for generation after generation; and the church, taken together with its setting, forms a picture incomparably better than anything to be seen on the Continent—where noble buildings are usually in immediate juxtaposition to all the bustle and squalor of commercial life within a crowded city. It is no accident that the medieval architecture of England has formed one of the traditional subjects for painting, as the reader may see for himself in the numerous portraits of this very cathedral by no less a master than John Constable.

The church itself could hardly be better designed for the situation in which we find it. From any and every angle of view, its silhouette is rich and various. The grand central tower, 404 feet high and the loftiest in England, dominates and centralizes the composition, and gives the mass of the building an omnifacial organization in sharp contrast to the unfortunate appearance of Amiens when seen from the side.

The façade of Salisbury is modest in comparison with the west front of either Lincoln or Peterborough, but it conforms to a general English custom of designing the entrance front as though it were an independent screen without any necessary or essential relationship to the building behind. The artistic philosophy involved is not far different from that which became popular during the Italian Renaissance; both then and now, most critics feel some sense of reservation about it—especially when the screen, as a screen, leaves something to be desired in harmony and coherence of line and texture.

As the reader may have reflected when considering the comparatively

Captivity was followed by the Great Schism. In legal technicality, the schism moderate height of the nave, the design of Salisbury is but one instance indicating that the Gothic architects of England remained ultra-conservative in matters of structure. By 1220, anyone who cared to learn might have acquired without great trouble an adequate knowledge of abutment by means of the flying buttress, but such buttresses are absent from Salisbury and most other English churches. The walls are thick; and with the addition of small pier buttresses at appropriate points, enough inertia is provided to contain the thrusts. It may be questioned whether Salisbury is thereby rendered safer against earthquake, bomb concussion, or other destructive accidents: during World War II, it was the delicate but well-braced Gothic of France that stood punishment best of all.

LATE GOTHIC ARCHITECTURE

The forces which had made Gothic did not outlast the 13th century. After that inspired era, the 14th century is horrible to contemplate.

It was the century of the Hundred Years' War. Northern and western France were subjected to pillage and ruin. From the standpoint of the population, it made little difference whether French or English armies passed over the land; the result was the same. As the creative center of European life, France was through.

The so-called Babylonian Captivity of the papacy began in 1305. The Popes removed to Avignon, where they remained until 1378. The Babylonian came to an end in 1415 when the Council of Constance elected Martin the 5th, deposed one of the competing Popes, and persuaded the other to resign. But the harm was done. The whole of Europe had resented the sojourn at Avignon, and the general state of mind was not in the least mollified by the sumptuous court maintained there by the pontiffs. The position of the Pope was forever compromised. Church government ceased to be what it had been. Discipline was difficult, and in some places impossible to enforce. Many of the clergy became notorious for their corruption.

Certain controversies in the matter of doctrine tended to undermine still further the unity of Christendom. Bitter differences of opinion, it must be remembered, had been perennial within the Catholic Church, but those who lost the argument never got away with it before the 14th century. During the 13th century, for example, Roger Bacon had been silenced, Emperor Frederick the 2nd of Sicily and all his line had been eliminated, and the Albigensian heresy had been crushed out of existence with a ferocity as sincere as it was terrible. But during this new era, John Wycliffe rose up in England to claim that the Bishop of Rome had usurped his extraordinary powers, thus paving the way for the ultimate secession of the English church. Unlike earlier heretics, Wycliffe died in his bed, the papacy being without power to get at him. Some of Wycliffe's students at Oxford returned to their native Bohemia with the ideas they had learned in England. The upshot was the heresy of John Huss, at whom the Church could get. Huss was burned at the stake, but under circumstances that impressed innumerable persons as grossly unjust. An irresistible ground swell of feeling began to make itself felt—presently to become a tidal wave sweeping on toward the Renaissance, the Reformation, and modern times.

Heart-rending enough to this point, the narrative of the 14th century is still incomplete. In 1348, all Europe was swept by the plague. Known in England as the Black Death, that epidemic was the worst on record. It is difficult to make a sound guess as to the mortality, but most authorities feel that about half the population of Europe died of it.

In the face of such a historical summary, it is difficult to see how cultural progress of any kind was possible, and it must be conceded that unified Christendom suffered a blow that has proven as yet irreparable. At the same time, the current of tragedy did not sweep with equal force everywhere. It left islands where humane accomplishment remained feasible: this is the century that produced Chaucer, Dante, Petrarch, Giotto, and the Late Gothic.

Modern art history has yet to do its work on the Late Gothic. Historians may perhaps be forgiven for taking more interest in the origin of styles than in their maturity, but it is unfortunate that the variations of the Late Gothic have not been competently classified. Hence a plethora of semi-official names, bound to be confusing. Some of these names refer to chronology, others to locale, and still others merely attempt to be descriptive. It is fair to hazard a guess that the confusion reflects a general condition during the whole Late Gothic episode. Rather little, that is to say, depended upon the precise state of a centralized style, and much upon the improvisation of the individual architect. For convenience, therefore, we shall simply group our examples according to the modern national divisions.

◆ *England* For the reasons cited, building almost ceased in France during the 14th century, but in England churches went up at regular intervals, and seem to show a more orderly movement toward the later stages of development. Indeed, it is possible to follow a kind of evolution in the tracery of windows and in the increasingly elaborate patterns assumed by the ribs of the vaulting. Starting with the "Early English" of 13th-century Salisbury, there was a "Geometrical Decorated" stage, a "Curvilinear Decorated," the "Perpendicular," which was popular during the 15th century, and the "Tudor" of the 16th. Easy enough to set down on paper, this classification, although more reliable than most during the later Gothic, is very, very hard to apply to individual monuments with any real assurance.

Fig. 11.28 Exeter. Cathedral. Vaulting of the nave. 14th century. (Crossley; National Buildings Record)

The cathedral at Exeter, like most English churches, had a protracted and heterodox history. The towers adjacent to the transepts are Norman, and a few fragments of masonry may date from Saxon times. The vaulting of the nave (Fig. 11.28) is our best example of the English Late Gothic in its early stage. The crown is level, and a ridge rib runs the length of it. From each main impost on either side, no fewer than eleven ribs spring upward and outward in a radial pattern. Some of these meet at the ridge rib; others meet their opposites at various points along the transverse arches. The traditional appearance of cross vaulting is done away with.

The addition of subordinate ribs makes it necessary to introduce two new terms. An extra rib that springs from a pier is a *tierceron*. Tiercerons are to be distinguished from *liernes,* which run between two main ribs, springing from one and terminating on the other without coming into any contact with a pier.

The esthetic purpose of the new rib system at Exeter can hardly be explained in terms of a simple and single intention. It certainly indicates a desire to produce an interior more opulent than that of any High Gothic church. In addition, it seems to have been an attempt, and a good one, to pull the ceiling into better axial unity by burying the familiar and confusing contours of ordinary cross vaulting under a new complexity of line and texture.

The tracery of the windows at Exeter would fall into the category of "Curvilinear Decorated," and there is a distinct difference between the Late Gothic as we find it there, and the ultimate or "Perpendicular" stage of the style. Insofar as the transition was orderly, it may be studied at Winchester and Gloucester, both originally Norman churches and both remodeled during the 14th century to fit contemporary fashion. For the Perpendicular in full flower, we must turn to King's College Chapel at Cambridge (Fig. 11.29) and to the Chapel of Henry 7th, attached to Westminster Abbey at its extreme east end (Figs. 11.30–31).

The exterior of King's College Chapel is unimpressive; it amounts to a rectangular framework of piers and arches, with the skyline rather weakly broken by a number of small spires. The interior, however, is surely one of the best ever designed. The walls, if we may still call them that, consist of 25 immense stained glass windows. The windows are so big, in fact, that the supremely delicate stonework functions, in an almost literal sense, as a mere frame of reference for the light and color that flood the space within. The arches used for the window heads and the transverse ribs are good examples of the four-centered "Tudor" arch (see also Fig. I.4, page 939); they are "pointed" only in a very strict sense of the term. The name *Perpendicular* comes from the tracery of the windows. Curvilinear work is restricted to the extreme upper part; and about halfway up, the vertical mullions are inter-

Fig. 11.29 Cambridge. King's College Chapel. 1446 to about 1535. (Country Life)

sected by a horizontal mullion, or *transom bar*. These particular windows are unusual in having but one transom bar; others of the same class have many.

A geometrical description of the so-called "fan vaulting" of the chapel would be tediously long and artistically insignificant. Those familiar with the double plowshare solid of the High Gothic will have no trouble in recognizing the heredity, but it is worth remarking that these plowshare solids are true conoids with a semicircular cross section. The vaults were built of cut stone voussoirs; they do not depend upon the ribs for support. Because the latter—once "working members"—now became a mere enrichment of the surface texture, fan vaulting has been unpopular with those who attach moral significance to the revelation of structure.

The circular nature of the fans made it awkward to adapt such vaulting to a rectangular plan because an empty space inevitably appeared in the middle of each bay. At Cambridge, those spaces were glossed over by carved pendants decorated with heraldry. In successive bays, the Beaufort portcullis alternates with the Tudor rose.

The Chapel of Henry the 7th (Figs. 11.30–31) represents the Late Gothic in an extreme form. Built at the time architectural stonecutting had reached its quintessential perfection all over Europe, the vaulting is a tour de force of daring. The voussoirs are a triumph of applied geometry; depending on their bevel alone, the architect suspended in mid-air large pendants of stone.

The exterior is only less remarkable. It was one of the very few instances where the nature and logic of perpendicular tracery had full rein. The pattern of window lights, transom bars, and mullions was carried in low relief right around the vertical piers and other areas of masonry. Even through the soot of innumerable London winters, this supremely neat working of the surface carries unhindered; in the deepest and most smoke-laden fog, to see this building is to see something chaste and gay.

All Gothic, early or late, was predominantly a vaulted architecture, but we must not omit to mention certain notable developments in wood. Because English society was and remains (all London notwithstanding) rural and agricultural by preference, and because the climate is favorable for it, that country has always raised trees and entertained an uncommon liking for wood. During the Late Gothic era, when elaboration was the order of the day, the taste came out in a great number of superb wooden ceilings of different kinds. Among them the most famous type was the *hammer-beam roof,* evolved at the end of the 14th century.

A hammer beam (Fig. 11.32) is a bracket designed to carry a vertical strut at its upper and outer end. The strut, in turn, connects with an inclined rafter, and stiffens it. The rafters may therefore be longer than otherwise feasible, and the span between wall and wall (and hence the area of free floor) greater. The hammer-beam roof of Westminster Hall (Fig. 11.33), one of the very widest wooden spans ever attempted prior to the invention of new methods during World War II, is a notable example. But before we let our enthusiasm for the marvelous craftsmanship carry us away, it should be mentioned that the hammer-beam roof is scarcely admirable as a structural device. As a consequence of its shape, such a roof exerts thrust. Fortunately, a wooden

Figs. 11.30–31   London. Westminster Abbey. Chapel of Henry the 7th. 1502–1520. View from the southeast (above) and view of the vaulting (below). (National Buildings Record; Crown Copyright)

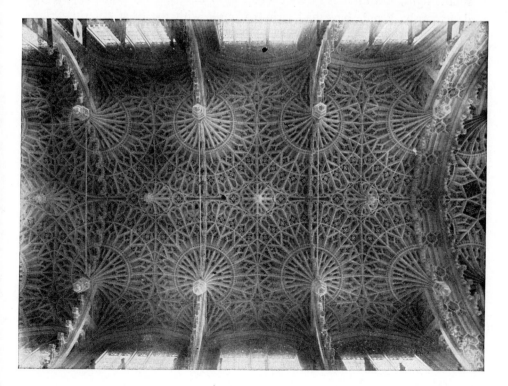

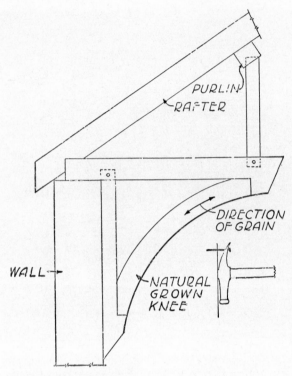

Fig. 11.32 Schematic drawing of hammer-beam support.

roof is light, and there is rarely enough snow in England to increase the load dangerously. People have had serious trouble with the form elsewhere, however.

Every man who reads or speaks English has a special place in his heart for the domestic architecture of the Tudor period. These are the houses in which the English raised country life to the artistic level. These are the rooms

Fig. 11.33 London. Westminster Hall. Hammer-beam roof. 1398. Span: 68 feet. (Tuck; National Buildings Record)

Fig. 11.34 Middlesex, England. Cottage at Kingsbury Green. (From M. S. Briggs, *The Homes of the Pilgrim Fathers in England and America*, Oxford, Oxford University Press, 1932.)

where the poets and the wits did their thinking, their writing, and their talking. The stupendous adventurers who went to the New World remembered Tudor villages when they thought of home.

It is generally conceded that English homes of the Late Gothic era represent a considerable improvement over anything earlier in date. From Hampton Court Palace to the smallest house in the Cotswolds, the design of such buildings proceeded on much the same theory. The required rooms were laid out as seemed best by owner and builder. Many plans conform roughly to the shape of a square, an H, or an L, but geometry did not in the least detain or preoccupy the men who put up these houses. They concerned themselves with the means and the practical needs of the family, with the conformation of the site, the direction of prevailing winds, and the view from the windows. Then they enclosed their rooms with walls and roofing. The method, it will be seen, is identical to the procedure advocated by our most advanced architects today. It is true that "modern" houses look different from Tudor houses, but the resemblance would be surprising if a gabled roof were added to many a "radical" 20th-century dwelling.

A small Tudor cottage (Fig. 11.34) is sometimes deceptively reminiscent of the temple form; but the resemblance is of no consequence. Because the span between walls was difficult to handle, such houses were always narrow from front to back. Their gables had the steep Gothic pitch, and the sky line was broken by chimneys and chimney pots arranged in an apparently haphazard and antigeometric fashion—merely to conform with the placement of fireplaces indoors. The second story was often given an overhang which added slightly to the floor area above and invited the attachment of decorative pendants similar in nature to the pendants which hang from the vaulting of Henry the 7th's Chapel. Narrow clapboards were common in England, but just as common and much more conspicuous was the construction known as *half-timbered*. The timbers of the framework, that is to say, were left in plain

Fig. 11.35 Topsfield, Massachusetts. Parson Capen House. 1683. (Wayne Andrews)

sight, and the interstices filled in with plaster. Timbers or clapboards, which-
ever was used, the result was a Gothic complexity of line.

The cubical unity of the smaller Tudor cottages reflected the simplicity
of the life lived by those with modest means. As soon as any family bettered
itself, additional rooms, of any size and shape and running in any convenient
direction, were simply added on. Thus any old or large Tudor dwelling is
likely to be long, low, irregular, and rambling.

♦ *America* The High Renaissance was almost over in Italy before any
important change took place in the architectural taste of the English people.
It has often been a matter for remark that England has always remained
Gothic. Where else, as a matter of fact, is the central government conducted
in buildings of that style? The very same point may be illustrated by reference
to the earliest permanent dwellings in the British colonies in North America.

Few of the earliest colonists had any claim to aristocracy. For that reason,
few of them had any personal taste for the Italianate detail modestly added
to great houses in England from the time of Henry the 8th onward. It was
reserved for their descendants, men like Jefferson, to look seriously at the
work of Palladio, Inigo Jones, and John Webb, and to imitate it in America.
Naturally and without self-consciousness, the 17th-century colonists put up
homes of the kind they knew (Fig. 11.35).

Thus while Italy and France were baroque, America was still in the
Gothic stage; for that fact, no apology is necessary. Only a few of the earliest
houses survive, but there is much to be said for those that do. Unaffected by

Fig. 11.36 Ulm. Cathedral. Started 1337. Restored 1880-1890, at which time the upper stories of the tower and the spire were completed in accordance with a design dating from the late 15th century. (Deutscher Kunstverlag)

the sociological influence of the Renaissance (pages 563–565), our 17th-century houses were designed for a domestic economy that did not contemplate servants. The kitchen fireplace was the center of the home, and the kitchen was identical with the living room and the nursery. By that simple arrangement, to which American architecture is now returning, the colonial housewife was saved many a step.

♦ *Germany, Spain, and Italy* The cathedral at Ulm (Fig. 11.36) carried to a conclusion the principle of the single western tower. At ground level, the over-all length of the church is a little more than 400 feet. The great tower soars to an apex 528 feet from the ground (Washington Monument: 555 feet. Woolworth Building: 750 feet) making it the highest church in the world.

Notable though it is, Ulm is scarcely typical of the later Gothic in Germany. Indeed, many would contend that Germany's special contribution to the period was the brick Gothic. Innumerable churches were so constructed;

Fig. 11.37 Milan. Cathedral. 1386–1500. (Brogi)

the Frauenkirche of Munich is an unusually large example located in a favorite tourist city.

It is little appreciated, moreover, that the civil and domestic architecture of Late Gothic Germany had a pronounced effect upon the appearance of many an American city. In order to understand why, one must recall the years before 1914, when Germany was as much admired in America as Hitler's Reich was later despised. One thinks of the old houses at Nuremberg, and of the great city squares so common in Germany. Congestion combined with prosperity to produce multistoried houses with immense gabled roofs high enough to accommodate within themselves an extra story or two.

The Cathedral at Milan (Fig. 11.37) was started in 1386. Except for matters of detail, it was complete by 1500. There being no architects in Italy of sufficient reputation, masters were summoned from France and Germany. Two of the latter had worked at Ulm. No one can say that these men were negligent in their attempt to dazzle the world. The church is immensely big. The masonry is fine marble, in itself an elegance and a luxury almost unknown in

Gothic architecture. There are said to be 2,300 statues (mostly modern). The nave capitals themselves were transformed into pedestals for statuary. The vaulting is not vaulting at all, but a dreamy lacework of open tracery.

One's first impression of Milan is the best. Closer inspection reveals that the carving lacks sensitivity, the statues are empty of content, the innumerable little pinnacles individually dull, and the interior, which seems grand when one first enters, merely grandiose—for it does not show the proportions and the spatial understanding of Amiens. As though to complete the disillusionment, the engineering was bad; tie rods had to be added in order to control thrusts not properly handled by the buttresses.

Italy is full of civil and domestic architecture from the Late Gothic period, much of it in good repair and in daily use: at Venice, the Doges' Palace; at Florence, the Palazzo Vecchio and the Bargello; at Siena, numerous private palaces still occupied by the families that built them. Such buildings are Gothic only in the sense that the pointed arch was used for openings. Deriving as they did from military architecture and marked by the expediency always associated with such a source, it would not be overly harsh to say that many of them have no "style" at all. Even so, they have the patina of age and use, which combines with richness of historical association to soften the sentiments of the sternest critics. In sober truth, however, the only great and definitive work of architecture produced in Italy during the period now under review was the so-called "Mangia Tower" rising over the east end of the Palazzo Pubblico at Siena (Fig. 11.38).

The general form of the Mangia upsets all the ordinary proprieties of tower designing. It is slender and delicate at the bottom, heavy and wide at the top. Presented with a table of dimensions, almost any one would feel inclined to make a flat statement that the design was certain to prove a failure; yet the truth is that no other tower so perfectly fulfills the Gothic ideal of flight, and by implication the Gothic ideal of infinite space. The eye runs rapidly upward along the plain shaft, much as it runs up the stem of a flower to the elongated and attenuated corbels which spread outward like a blossom. But no flower was ever large enough or grand enough to impart the sensation of soaring to which all observers testify.

Spain presents us with the phenomenon of a population which might with equal reason have expressed itself artistically in the idiom of the Near East or in the northern and linear style which flowered in the Gothic. The earlier history of Spanish architecture demonstrated a tendency to do one or the other, with provincial dependence upon the French or the Moorish source as the case might be. But during the 15th century, the Near Eastern heritage amalgamated with the northern for the first time in the so-called "Plateresque" style. The name is from *platero* (silversmith), and the style was characterized

Fig. 11.38 Siena. Palazzo Pubblico. 1287–1305. Tower. 1338–1405. (Alinari)

by opulence of decoration and exquisite precision of details. San Gregorio at
Valladolid (Figs. 11.39–40) is an excellent example. The immediate impact
is more Oriental than Gothic. The Gothic component comes out, however,
in the arrangement of the sculpture, its subject matter, in the continuous
buttresses and the broken skyline, and in the elaborate variety of novel
inventions on the theme of the pointed arch.

◆ *France* During most of the Late Gothic era, Frenchmen were compelled to limit their architecture to comparatively small buildings, or to finishing touches on churches of earlier date. Most of the Late Gothic monuments of France are of the latter class: towers, porches, choir screens, rose

Figs. 11.39–40 Valladolid. College of San Gregorio. 1488. (Richard W. Dwight)

windows, tombs (Fig. 11.41), and similar items. By a kind of tacit understanding, the original plans (if they still existed) were cast aside, and the
work to be done was freely designed to fit the fashion of its own date. Thus
we find that the transept façades of Beauvais do not correspond with the
Gothic of the choir, but to the Gothic as it was in the early 16th century.
The same thing may be said of the new western front of Rouen, and the
façade of Troyes. In every instance, it would seem, when new work was added
to old, the junction between the two was handled cleverly. Now that several
centuries of weathering have intervened to blend all the masonry into a
common color, it is often difficult to recognize the precise place where the
later additions begin. Such being the case, the casual observer may be forgiven for thinking that everything in view comes from the same period; if
so, he forms the mistaken notion that the High Gothic—really a rather chaste
style—was very fancy indeed. The northern and later spire of Chartres is an
instance in point (Fig. 11.2).

About the middle of the 15th century, conditions became more propitious
in France, and some notable work was done. The Late Gothic choir and apse
of Mont St. Michel were begun in 1450. Hard and perhaps impossible to

Fig. 11.41 Bourg. Church of Brou. Tomb of Marguerite of Austria (died 1530). (Archives Photographiques)

photograph in any adequate fashion, nothing could better illustrate the Late Gothic at its flamboyant and exquisite best. The so-called "Butter Tower" at Rouen dates from 1487. One may have a preference for something less elaborate or a good reason for wanting something more simple, but it would be a stubborn purist indeed who dared level any serious argument against it.

As the 16th century drew near, there was a reaction in France against the extremes at which the Late Gothic had arrived. A certain number of buildings, therefore, were designed with the idea of using flamboyant carving not as an over-all investiture of architectural form, but as a foil played off against plain and neutral surfaces. The nave of St. Pierre at Coutances (Fig. 11.42) is a case in point, and the church of Brou, put up at Bourg by Margaret of Austria, is another. It would not be hard to contend that both represent the best, not of the Late Gothic alone, but of all Gothic. Wonderfully gentle and lovely, this final flower of the medieval style seems to sum up all the inde-

Fig. 11.42 Coutances. St. Pierre. Nave. Finished 1494. (Marburg)

finable qualities of France. At no other time has there been so perfect a combination of chastity and finesse.

♦ *Transition from the Gothic to the Renaissance: the Châteaux*   Readers with a sense for the schedule of history must have realized long ago that a great many of the Late Gothic monuments fall much beyond the date we ordinarily use to mark the beginning of the Renaissance, but the Renaissance (in the simple sense of a style consciously derived from the classical) was at least a hundred years old in Italy before it had much influence north of the Alps. It first attracted the attention of influential Frenchmen in the course of the Italian campaigns of Charles the 9th and Louis the 12th, who invaded Italy twice during the decade 1494 to 1504. Those monarchs were so charmed by the new Italian style, especially its northern variation, that they undertook to import it when they returned home. The first effect of the foreign taste and

Fig. 11.43   Chambord. Château. 1526–1544. View from the air. (French Government Tourist Office)

the transition from one style to another is marked by the existence of a number of monumental residences, mostly in the Loire Valley, where, for a span, the aristocracy made a vogue of elegant country life in the charming countryside of Touraine.

For our immediate purpose, the best example to study is the château at Chambord (Fig. 11.43). The general conception was borrowed from military architecture, and conforms fairly well to the type known as a *concentric castle*. The essential feature of such a castle is that it shall have one wall within another, permitting the outer defenses to be sacrificed gradually while the garrison retreats in good order to an impregnable central unit variously known as the tower, the donjon, or the keep. The main block of building at Chambord, containing the important halls and chambers, is a reminiscence of the donjon. The turrets are circular because that shape more easily resisted the impact of the battering ram, and they project from the wall in the manner of towers intended to restrain an enemy from scaling by permitting cross-fire from above. But as a military building, Chambord was out of date: during the 15th century it had been made abundantly plain that any commander who understood the crude artillery of the era might expect to take the strongest castle in a matter of days. Reflection upon these points will suggest a certain artificiality in the design of all the châteaux. For perhaps the first time in our study we encounter a sentimental harking back to forms that had once been useful, but at the date of building had little to offer beyond atmosphere.

While all its elements are medieval, even to the broken skyline, a Roman spirit governed the disposition of parts at Chambord (pages 197–199). The plan was kept perfectly symmetrical to its short axis, and approaches symmetry to the long. In elevation, mass was made to balance mass according to the classical, and not the Gothic rule. The windows, moreover, were made square-headed, and strong horizontals predict the coming revival of entablatures. Such things also meant that the Gothic was about to end.

Chapter 12

THE BUSINESS of the present chapter is twofold. It is in the first place an
attempt to make the reader acquainted with the nature and quality of
statuary and painting produced during the Gothic period; to make him individually acquainted with all its important monuments would demand a book
much larger than this one. But over and above their worth as art, those
same monuments offer us perspective on the manner and process by which the
Middle Ages came to an end and the world of the Renaissance began. The
second aim of this chapter is to open up that perspective for the reader.

In the north of Europe, there was no precise break between medieval
and Renaissance culture. The Renaissance art of France, Flanders, and Germany came into being by a gradual and even orderly transition from the
Gothic. Things were different in Italy, where the population had never entirely
accepted the Gothic nor forgotten the classical. Ideas and expressions in the
key of the Renaissance were more overt in Italy, but it is impossible to maintain the conventional notion that the entire movement originated there.
Indeed, the very earliest examples of northern Gothic sculpture contain within
themselves a prediction of the future, which is to say, a hint of the values which
have governed European motivation from the 15th century onward into our
own time.

The medieval mind had seen life as an equation between man and God.
If the notion of personal worth asserted itself at all, it was submerged in the
need for grace. We all know, of course, that innumerable persons during the
Middle Ages failed to live up to such idealism, but we must distinguish
between ideals and behavior. Insofar as the accepted dogma of society gov-

412

GOTHIC SCULPTURE
AND PAINTING

erned, the suggestion that either a good or a complete life might be possible on earth had been outlawed. All hope had been fastened on heaven.

Such was the philosophy that produced the great cathedrals and gave to Gothic sculpture and painting an elevated religious tone. But neither the philosophy nor the art was destined to last forever. New ideas and new feelings began to assert themselves almost before the old had full expression; and if we were able to name the moment when Western civilization passed into the Renaissance, it would be the instant when a majority accepted in their hearts the idea that this world was respectable.

It was during the 14th and 15th centuries, and all over Europe, that the human individual began to put himself forward and insist upon himself as the essential element in society. *Humanism* became the faith of the world; it has furnished the basis for virtually all philosophical speculation these past 500 years. Of both individualism and humanism, we shall have much to say. For our immediate purpose, the following will suffice.

The word *humanism* has been used in a variety of senses, some of them entirely arbitrary. We use it here to designate the philosophy that starts from the concept that the individual has dignity—worth in and of himself and during his brief and mortal life. Such a view conduces to a picture of reality as an equation between the race and the environment, and such was in fact the outlook that became general as the Renaissance arrived.

Consciously or unconsciously, artists were sensitive to these ideas. As the chapter proceeds (and the dates get later) the reader will note how art history finds its frame of reference less and less in the great ecclesiastical tradition and the immense cathedrals which survive as the principal monuments of the

413

medieval church. More and more, we shall find our attention directed toward single pictures and single statues—works of comparatively small size, executed by individual artists. By a natural transition, we will find ourselves considering each work of art as a single and personal expression of its author.

Humanism and individualism made it necessary that artists should deal with the human figure. We shall presently realize that the single human being became the prime factor, the irreducible unit in all art, competing for attention only with the setting necessary to explain human action.

Similarly, acceptance of the world made it necessary that art should become expressive of satisfaction not in supernatural things, but in extant things. For such expression, the more florid aspects of the Gothic style were readily adaptable, and were so employed, but it is obvious that the more intelligent members of the population were dissatisfied with the best Gothic could do. Keener and more forward-looking, they appreciated that acceptance of the world did not at all comport with the existing and general ignorance about natural fact. Hence the start of modern science, one concomitant of which was a categorical demand that art became more realistic—that artists were compelled and felt compelled to undertake a massive research program directed toward the achievement of complete competence in anatomy, perspective, and all other representative techniques.

In studying Gothic sculpture and painting, we must take account, therefore, of two classes of patronage and two kinds of artists. The work of the *Gothic Realists* is exemplified by vivid studies like the *Jonas* at Bamberg (Fig. 12.1), obviously the work of a master who literally believed that the appearance of things, including all the unlovely accidents in nature, amounted to the law of art. It is history that realism was the art of the future. Its theory became so generally accepted that it virtually governed European art from the end of the Middle Ages to the end of the 19th century.

In substantial contrast with the Gothic Realists were the artists whom we may call the *Gothic Mannerists*. The figure of the personified *Synagogue* at Strasbourg (Fig. 12.2) is typical of their output. Such men were comparatively indifferent to accuracy of representation, although most of them knew enough about it to avoid the obvious mistakes which would label their work as out of date. Their central purpose was to emphasize grace and elegance in the figure and to capitalize on fine clothes for people, fine trappings for animals, and the lovelier aspects of scenery and the climate. Their art was the perfect counterpart for the more luxurious kind of Late Gothic architecture.

Gothic Mannerism had nothing like so long a history nor so important an influence as Gothic Realism. It continued as a strong style only while the feudal aristocracy was able to conduct a life of gorgeous pageantry vaguely based on the code of chivalry. The last flower of Gothic Mannerism was the

Fig. 12.1 (left) Bamberg. Cathedral. Detail from the screen of Saint George's Choir. *Jonas.* About 1230. (Marburg)

Fig. 12.2 (right) Strasbourg. Cathedral. *The Synagogue.* About 1250. (Marburg)

so-called "International style" which dominated much of European art from about 1350 to 1450, after which only the most conservative artists showed elements of mannerism, and the whole movement passed away.

GOTHIC SCULPTURE

♦ *Early Period: The West Porch of Chartres* The three western doorways of the present Cathedral of Chartres were preserved from an earlier fabric. The statues probably date shortly before 1150, at which time they were the last word in modernity. We usually cite them as the earliest preserved examples in an authentically Gothic style, but the reader should make a mental note that the work at Chartres was probably derivative from slightly earlier and similar statuary executed for Suger's Saint Denis.

The statues at Chartres (Fig. 12.3) were the work of men to whom the Gothic theory of architectural sculpture (see above, pages 368–371) was a new

Fig. 12.3 Chartres. Cathedral. Central doorway of the West Porch. About 1145. (Archives Photographiques)

thing, to be implemented in the most exact and dogmatic manner. Because Gothic is linear, the figures were radically distorted in the vertical direction. Each statue is so tall that its plastic values are all but lost in its function as an enriched architectural line; and for the same reason, all the poses were kept frontal and stiff.

And yet there is much here that will please the most ardent humanist. Each face is unique and personal. Hundreds of visitors have demanded to know the names of the sitters. The old folk are characters and the young people are charming. Only one or two of the girls and women are pretty, but all are winsome and dainty—an emphasis upon femininity new in European art at this time, and reflecting, no doubt, the arrival of the chivalric code of manners.

♦ *High Gothic: Paris, the Later Work at Chartres, Amiens, Reims* During the 13th century, architectural dictates were forced upon the sculptor,

Fig. 12.4   Paris. Cathedral. North door of the west front. Detail of the tympanum, showing six Royal Prophets. About 1230. (Tel)

but much less severely. When a given figure was meant to run with an architectural line, it was incumbent upon the sculptor to minimize diagonal impulses of the sort produced by extended arms and crosswise drapery, but no one asked him to make the figure itself into a kind of line. Excellent niches and brackets were designed as an integral part of the architecture, with the result that statuary has never been more advantageously displayed. Within reasonable limits of cooperation, the sculptors could thus do about as they pleased. With a nice sense for the implications of their own medium, the best men conceived and executed all the larger statues as free-standing figures rendered plastically and in the round, and the "architectural restrictions" may be written off as having done no harm. There was, for instance, no particular reason for distortion; and while less precise than the laboriously accurate anatomy of the 15th century, most 13th-century work is approximately correct.

The content of 13th-century sculpture was, like the style, both restricted and free. There seems to have been a common understanding that all religious art should aim at a lofty and spiritual tone, but within that policy considerable variation was permitted. Thus, we find that High Gothic sculpture, while recognizably uniform in style, presents a great range of content. Each city, in fact, seems to have given its statues something of its own special character.

Of the *Beau Dieu* at Amiens (Fig. 11.9, page 369) we have already

Fig. 12.5 (left) Chartres. Cathedral. Statue of Melchizedek, on trumeau of the central door of the North Porch. (Tel)

Fig. 12.6 (opposite) Reims. West front. The *Annunciation* and the *Visitation*. (Roubier)

spoken in another connection; perhaps there is no statue more typically or perfectly Gothic. Neither is there any other work of art which so graciously combines reverence with a sense for the matter-of-fact. Indeed, there is something of that latter quality in the *Madonna* to the south, and a great deal of it in the *Saint Firmin* on the other side. Who is he if not a rather faithful portrait of one of the solid men of the town, a monument to all the people who do the world's work?

In some contrast are the six royal prophets who sit across the lower register of the north or *Virgin Portal* on the west front of Paris (Fig. 12.4). A continuous scroll runs across their knees; probably it signifies philosophical agreement. In their faces, as befitted a university town, we see the plain but indefinable mark of the scholar.

Or we may go again to Chartres, where the statues of the two transept porches were gradually assembled from around 1210 to as late as 1275 (Fig. 12.5). Easier in pose and more plastically realized than those of the west

porch, these later figures maintain the same lyric and even mystic charm. One tends to think of them as transfigured rustic types; the male countenances, in particular, have a gentleness almost never seen except in the country.

Two of the best-known and best-loved statues at Reims are the Mary and Elizabeth of the *Visitation* (Luke 1:39-45), to the right of the central doorway (Fig. 12.6). Where can we go for a more perfect rendering of Elizabeth's mature tenderness for Mary? Of for Mary's joy in her approaching motherhood, made solemn by the knowledge of her holy mission?

The monuments just mentioned are typical of the High Gothic at its best. As statues in their own right: above criticism. As architectural decoration: unexcelled in the whole history of art. As an expression of the Gothic ideal: a gracious moderation of earlier severity in the direction of human warmth. To such remarks, a more complete demonstration than we can undertake in the present text would add a staggering variety of lesser sculpture including in its subject matter an exhaustive survey of almost every creature on earth or imagined—an encyclopedic catalogue of all things included within the divine scheme.

But at a very early date, High Gothic statues began to exhibit certain qualities which predicted the decline of the medieval synthesis to the same degree that they predicted the future course of art. Shortly after the middle of the 13th century, for example, the two transept portals of the Cathedral of Paris were finished, complete with sculpture. It would not be hard to contend that the doorway of the northern transept with its beautiful Madonna on the trumeau (Fig. 12.7) is the most perfect bit of Gothic that we have. It is strong without being coarse, delicate without a hint of weakness, mature but not yet overblown, and the very definition of elegance. But if we take a closer look at the figure of the Madonna, we may sense all that was good in the 13th century, and yet feel a certain departure from its religious motivation.

The model chosen for the Madonna was a woman of about 35. Her body was heavier and more robust than a girl's, but her pose was lithe and fluent. She stood with the weight on the left foot. The right leg was held slack, with the foot slightly back and the knee gently forward to make a convexity in the drapery. The baby (now lost) was originally present to balance the composition. The costume is of peculiar interest, for it was during the 13th century that Paris became the world capital for female fashions. The waist is high, and the upper parts of the dress, including the sleeves, are closely fitted around shoulders and bust. The skirt, by contrast, contains a voluminous amount of cloth which necessarily falls in great undulating folds. In order to walk, or merely to free the feet for an easy standing posture, such a skirt must be caught up (as here) by a hand—a gesture that produces a diagonal cascade of drapery to one side or the other.

There is no possibility of a contention against the statement that this Madonna is utterly charming; but at the same time, she signalizes the discard of Gothic conventions. The curvilinear pose and diagonal drapery, although moderate at this point in the evolution, announce the intention of sculptors to break completely away from the subordination of sculpture to architecture. What was to be gained in freedom for their own art was, in equal measure, to be a sacrifice of integration for all the arts. In the matter of content, we may be happy to welcome the arrival of that peculiar department of charm—something both less and more than beauty—which makes the Frenchwoman an adornment of the race, but at the same moment we embrace standards that are more worldly and less spiritual than those of a generation earlier.

In the last instance, the loss may with equal truth be described as a gain; but it is difficult to take the same view about statues where elegance became the actual subject matter, virtually to the exclusion of sacred content. That rather strong statement is hardly unjust when applied to the work of a

Fig. 12.7 (left) Paris. Cathedral. Madonna on the trumeau of the north transept portal. Shortly after 1250. (Alinari)

Fig. 12.8 (right) Amiens. Cathedral. Madonna on the trumeau of the south transept portal. *La Vierge Dorée*. 1280–1300. From a cast. (Bulloz)

master who appeared at Reims about 1260 and produced two very popular angels, one of whom is now placed as the Gabriel of the Annunciation (Luke 1:26–35) in Figure 12.6. For the bodies, he used a very tall, slender proportion. For the pose, he used a strong S-curve. The combination produced sinuous and even serpentine figures, an impression fortified by the exaggerated grace with which the head is poised. The inner lines of the drapery and the silhouette of the wings have a similarly self-conscious refinement. On the face, there is a smile that has gained a notoriety almost equal to that of the *Mona Lisa*. Doubtless the sculptor intended it for the sublime; if so, he failed, as innumerable others have failed in the same endeavor.

Useful as they are for purposes of explanation, it will be obvious that the categories of Gothic Realism and Gothic Mannerism were not mutually exclusive. Both tendencies were often operating within the same work of art. As an instance, we may cite the well known *Vierge Dorée* of Amiens (Fig. 12.8), so-called because the figure was originally gilded. The statue is realistic because the model, if there was one, must have been a bourgeois woman of 35 or 40. But feeling that the subject called for elegance as well as actuality, the sculptor posed the figure in the curvilinear, hip-shot manner then in fashion, dressed her in an extreme gown in which diagonal lines predominate, and made her smile at the baby—a smile which seems more than a little calculated for its effect upon whoever might be watching.

The popularity of this figure is perhaps enough to prove it not without merit; but coming as it did toward the end of the 13th century, it unquestionably furnishes us with an illustration of the extent to which earlier standards (admittedly severe) had been relaxed. The pose and the drapery make it virtually anti-architectural; it might actually be better if removed from the cathedral. The process of humanization, which was in so many ways a good thing, seems in this case to have come close to vulgarizing the content.

FRENCH MANUSCRIPT ILLUMINATION

An immense number of books survive from the Gothic period, but they have not been given their proper place in art history. All too often, we find such material dismissed with a mere allusion which seems to hint that serious authors have no time for pretty little things. The truth is that book designing reached its high point during the 13th century, and has never been so good since. As to the art of decorating pages, there has never been anything finer, and the little pictures which are worked in here and there are, except for their tiny size, as worthy as any other class of painting. In addition to their absolute value as works of art, the Gothic manuscripts have a peculiar importance historically. During the 13th century, the art of bookmaking became more and more closely centered at Paris until it approached a near-monopoly, and was referred to as such by Dante. The influence of French taste upon the rest of Europe may in large measure be accounted for by the continuous export of those portable works of art.

For a typical piece of work corresponding in date and spirit to the great cathedrals, we may turn to a page from a Gospel lectionary (book of readings) now in the library of the British Museum (Fig. 12.9). It has often been said that every element and quality of the Gothic style shows up somewhere on every page of Gothic illumination, and the statement is scarcely an exaggeration. This particular page, for example, has a composition closely analogous to that of the cathedrals. There is the same absence of symmetry, the same dynamic use of line to achieve an eccentric type of unity, the same intimate organization of details into a complex whole. The text and the pictures and

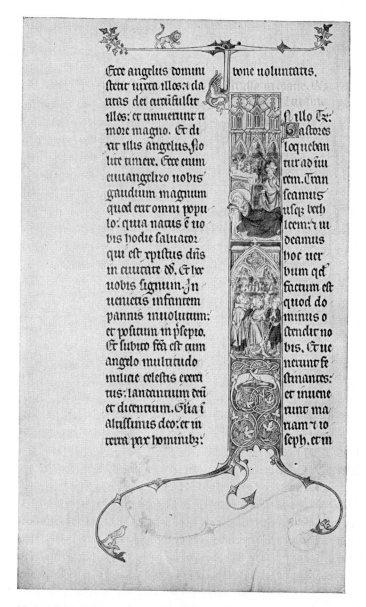

Fig. 12.9 London, British Museum. Additional Manuscript No. 17341. Folio 10 verso. A French Gospel Lectionary of the 13th century. *The Adoration of the Magi.*

the decorations all form essential parts of a single and coherent visual scheme. Just as the Gothic architect designed suitable niches for the accommodation of statuary, the Gothic book designer provided an enframement of much the same sort for the pictures. His choice of architectural forms for the purpose was no matter of chance, it appears to have been a uniform custom by which we are reminded of the cathedral, and reminded, also, that no work of Gothic art ever exists alone. It will be noted still further that every letter and punctuation mark was given the intense definition typical of all northern detail; also, that each one is in itself a miniature demonstration of Gothic composition and outline. There could be no more thoroughgoing manifesto of the universal nature of the Gothic style, or of the determination of every Gothic artist, whatever his medium, to make his work a reflection of the idea that the universe is complicated, and can be made intelligible only by a supreme act of logical organization.

Certain other features peculiar to Gothic illumination and more or less constant in its practice are worth mentioning. The space below the lower picture is filled with a 13th-century version of the Irish interlace. The floral spray sweeping across the top and bottom of the page also takes a Celtic swing; and it will be noted that its upper branch is, by all the laws of anatomy, the foliate double tail of a little dragon. But the vocabulary of these artists was not limited to the grotesque. At the top of the page, there is a very good lion; and at the bottom, an excellent bird.

All of these items tend to attract our attention one by one, and to delay comprehension of the fact that the two little paintings, taking them as a pair, depict the Adoration of the Magi. Here again we see how very Gothic is the work of the Gothic illuminator. The effect of the page is not instantaneous, as in classical and Renaissance art. We proceed cumulatively, noticing one thing at a time, and ultimately construct for ourselves an organic whole.

In strict logic, we should probably reserve the word *illumination* to describe pages like the one just reviewed, and to signify that the painter accepted a scheme of subordination in which the picture (a part) was made intelligible by its decorative relation to the page (a whole). So understood, the little *Adoration* bears the same relation to the entire composition as the *Beau Dieu* (Fig. 11.9, page 369) bears to the Cathedral of Amiens. Such a conception of the function of pictures continued until about the middle of the 13th century, up to which time the full-page *illustrations* (that is, separate pictures that belong to books merely because they are bound in) were rare even in very handsome manuscripts.

It was only natural, however, that the Gothic painters would, like the sculptors, find themselves working away from standards which, while excellent, tended to curtail the independence of individual artists. The first stage in the process is well illustrated in the work of Jean Pucelle (Fig. 12.10), an artist who attained special prominence as early as 1320, and ran the best shop in Paris for about 25 years. The word *pucelle* was then used for a dragon-fly, and the master used to sign with that insect. His assistant Chevrier, for a similar reason, signed with the bagpiper.

In the matter of style, Pucelle maintained an approximation to the

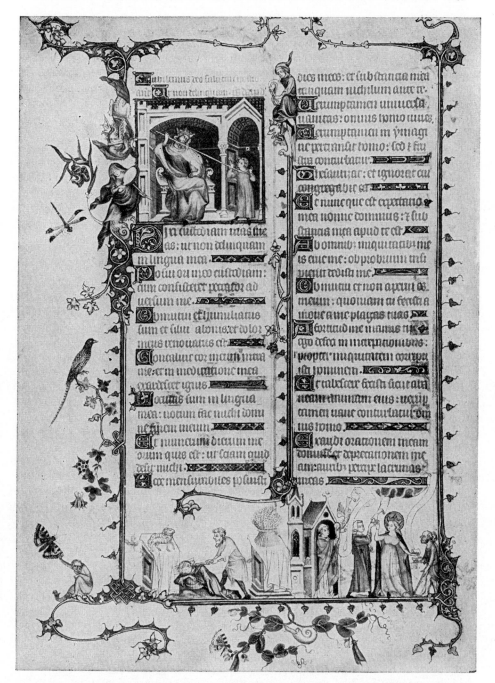

Fig. 12.10 Paris, Bibliothèque Nationale. Lat. 10483. *Breviary of Belleville*. Folio 24 verso. Saul throwing a spear at David (upper left), the murder of Abel (lower left), and figures symbolizing the Eucharist and Charity. From the shop of Jean Pucelle.

Gothic ideal of page composition, but he gave the pictures much more room and prominence. He and his men devoted their delicate technique to butterflies, squirrels, birds, plants, grasses—all of which appear like embroidery in the margins. The tiny things in nature have never seemed more joyous, nor more joyously drawn; and the demonstration, if florid, is altogether beguiling. Before we pass on, however, it is worth remarking that Pucelle's realism only went half of the way. His birds and insects vibrate with life; they reflect not only keen joy in nature, but keen study of it. Presented to us on the blank background of the page, the very same creatures seem to have an existence much like specimens in the museum or laboratory, which is to say that Pucelle took no account of the environment and did not attempt to represent it.

As time went on, the internal logic of painting asserted itself more and more. Pictures tended to break away from the text, and the end result was to make the full-page illustration the standard thing rather than the exception. That state of affairs was achieved by the end of the 14th century, at which time easel pictures (ever since the most popular and prevalent European art form) began to appear in ever larger numbers. To illustrate the transition at its halfway mark, we cannot do better than inspect the illustrations of the *Pontifical of Metz,* one of which we reproduce in Fig. 12.11. The book is a volume of services to be read by a bishop, or pontiff, and we find it open at the page which gives the order for the dedication of a church. In comparison to our earlier examples, the size of the main picture has been considerably enlarged. A proportional enlargement of the lettering enables the latter to keep its visual importance in the composition, but the spray and other details necessarily remain about their former size. The art of painting had, in short, stolen the show, and illumination no longer existed in its 13th-century sense. A notable minor feature of this and innumerable other Gothic pages is the addition of an element of humor. In the present instance, it amounts to no more than a caprice of the imagination; but on other pages of the same manuscript, there are examples of impudent grotesques who indulge in outright satires of the principal scene.

While the figures in the dedication scene are, if considered singly, good examples of moderate mannerism, the scene in which they appear shows an effort at realism when taken as a whole. There seems to have been some intention of representing space and indicating the relative placement of different persons within it. At the date when this work was done, there was probably not a single master in France who could have carried off the enterprise successfully. The requisite techniques of drawing and of tone relations were not yet understood; but the die had been cast, and the next great effort in the history of painting was destined to gain mastery of those very skills.

Fig.12.11 Cambridge, England, Fitzwilliam Museum. *Pontifical of Metz.* First half of the 14th century. A bishop sprinkling holy water during the ceremony of dedicating a church; parody of David and Goliath.

GOTHIC MANNERISM
AND THE ARRIVAL OF THE
INTERNATIONAL STYLE

The first half of the 14th century witnessed the complete divorce of sculpture from its previous inseparable relation to architecture. Free-standing statues became common. The most popular subject was the Madonna and Child, and the new fashion seems to have appeared at about the same time in both France and Italy (see below, page 450). Of the numerous French examples, the most famous is the so-called "Notre Dame de Paris" (Fig. 12.12), a figure set up in the choir of the cathedral in the year 1330. Its sobriquet explains the content: the statue has always been rather loosely construed as a symbol for the city, the more superficial aspects of which it so perfectly per-

Figs. 12.12–13 (left) Paris, Cathedral. "Notre Dame de Paris." 1330. (right) Paris, Louvre. Silver statuette of the Madonna. 1339. (Alinari; Archives Photographiques)

sonifies. No one ever thought of it as being religious except in the most technical way; and it survived intact the wholesale destruction of religious art that took place during the French Revolution. It is notable that the costume is almost identical with the gown of the Virgin Annunciate painted three years later by Simone Martini (Fig. 9.21, page 308), and the exaggerated pose and canon of proportions are likewise much the same—illustrating once again how literally French taste was accepted all over Europe.

Although there are a great many of them, full-size stone statues were not the typical product of 14th-century mannerism. The Madonnas that best sum up the spirit of the period are the exquisite little statuettes done in gold, silver, or ivory (Fig. 12.13). Such objects, it is important to mention, were never intended for public exhibition. They were made for private patrons— a class of person hitherto rare, but beginning in the 14th century to assume a controlling position in relation to art of all kinds. Because the little figures were intended for private devotions, the artists who did them worked away from the solemnity typical of High Gothic cathedral sculpture. They sought to establish between onlooker and statue a relationship more personal and intimate than might be appropriate for public monuments. In that endeavor, they enjoyed varying degrees of success. Some statuettes are no better than cute; others seem lovely beyond description.

The Popes came to Avignon in 1305, and the papal court soon became a cultural center. Artists and men of letters came there from all points, sojourned, and returned home stimulated and refreshed by intercourse with their peers from other lands. Petrarch, the reputed inventor of the sonnet, made his first trip to Avignon in 1326. In 1339, his friend Simone Martini (see above, pages 305–306) also came. Giotto having died three years before (see below, pages 453–466), Simone was at that moment the most prominent Italian artist alive, but his special ability to influence the style of other artists rested upon grounds that were not altogether artistic.

Siena, from which he came, was and still remains the most self-consciously aristocratic city in Europe. Simone, who was himself a knight, appears to have moved in the upper circles of Sienese society. No northern artist earlier than Jan van Eyck (died 1440) had anything like the same social position. In order to assess the importance of that fact, certain medieval prejudices must be recalled.

Medieval society was obsessed with the notion of propriety. Some functions and activities were honorable. Others were venal. In the former, an aristocrat was proud to engage; the latter he would not touch. As applied to our special interest and the matter of Simone's influence at Avignon, we must deal with a particular ramification of such conventions.

The *liberal arts,* in their original Greek meaning, had been the arts open to free men who were free in the sense that they might depend upon the work of slaves to provide them with all the necessities of life. During the Middle Ages, the list of liberal arts was frozen; only seven studies were so recognized: grammar, logic, rhetoric, arithmetic, geometry, music, and astronomy. Those arts were "liberal" because the mind of the student was "free" to go where it would in the realm of pure reason, without being impeded by the recalcitrance of matter. Carpentry, by contrast, was not liberal; it was *adulterine* because the thoughts of the carpenter were adulterated by the necessity of using his hands to force his tools against the stubborn wood. Artists, because they worked with their hands and used tools, had traditionally been classed as laborers. There was serious discrimination against them for that reason long after the period now under consideration. Michelangelo himself (died 1564) once felt compelled, for example, to ask a correspondent to address him by his surname Buonarroti—letters sent to Michelangelo the Sculptor might suggest to careless people that he belonged with the brick-layers.

During the early 14th century, the prejudice against artists had commenced to diminish in Italy, although it obviously was still there. Fortunately situated individuals like Simone probably suffered comparatively little inconvenience; we may remember him as the man who introduced northern Europe to the concept of the artist as a gentleman, and we can scarcely exaggerate the added effect it gave his influence.

Simone stayed at Avignon five years, and died there. He did a good deal of painting, almost all of it irrevocably lost. He brought to Avignon the peculiar linear genius of Siena, and he found in France a Gothic linear predilection almost as accomplished as his own. As to whether he was the teacher or the collaborator, we need not argue; the fact is that the style of Sienese painting combined at Avignon to produce a new version of the Late Gothic which was enthusiastically received by every lord and lady in Europe. From Avignon, artists returned home. The result was that schools sprang up in numerous places and that the style was much the same everywhere. Hence the name *International style* for the delicate art of the people who move through the pages of Sir John Froissart—the society that crossed the great divide at Agincourt in 1415.

The greatest monument of the International style is the manuscript known as the *Très Riches Heures* (Figs. 12.14–15). For a reasonable comprehension of that sumptuous book, the reader is referred to the good colored plates published as a separate monograph in *Verve* for April–July 1940 (Vol. 2, No. 7). The work was done for John, Duke of Berry, the younger brother of Charles the 5th of France. The political and social theories of the Duke of Berry are shocking by modern standards; no one was more savage in reducing those who opposed him or more merciless in bleeding those whom he had in his grip. But the fabulous wealth thus accumulated made it possible for him to spend most of his 76 years in unceasing patronage of the arts. Toward the end of his life, he conceived the project of making himself the owner of the handsomest book ever produced by the hand of man.

He first commissioned a Book of Hours known today by the popular name of the *Très Belles Heures de Notre Dame,* but he became dissatisfied before the work was complete; and about 1412, he disposed of some of the pages, as we shall recount in the next section. The reason for his change of plan seems to have been his discovery of some artists known today as The Brothers Limbourg, who had come to France from Gelderland, south of the

Zuider Zee. He set them to work on a new manuscript, the *Très Riches Heures;* and they ceased work when the Duke died in 1416. By that time the Limbourgs had completed 39 of the larger pictures, two of medium size, and 34 little ones. Between 1485 and 1489, the manuscript was completed with the addition of 61 more pictures by an artist named Jean Colombe.

It will be evident that the *Très Riches Heures* is not a monument in the ordinary sense; it is a major museum in portable form, and a treasure trove for anyone who wants a glimpse of the world as it was 500 years ago. The name *book of hours* derives from the *hours canonical,* the schedule used by monasteries for the daily routine of religious exercises. As ordinarily used, the phrase describes a book of readings intended for a similar round of private devotions on the part of a lay owner. For his convenience, extra material was often bound up with the religious sections: a calendar, for example, and tables for finding the date of Easter. Because services devoted to the Virgin were popular, the illustrations often included some very lovely Late Gothic Madonnas.

In the *Très Riches Heures,* the most interesting pictures are the full-page illustrations for the calendar, each arranged with a semicircular tabulation of dates immediately above a rectangular picture showing a scene typical of that time of year. In each instance, the vista includes a castle owned by the Duke, or one of his favorite views. A great favorite is the page devoted to February (Fig. 12.14) which represents a farmyard in winter. Nothing could be more quaint or pleasing, but the work is almost as clumsy from a representational point of view as the execution is delicate. The artists had only the vaguest knowledge of either anatomy or perspective, and their attempt at genre has often been characterized as "realism without any science."

If we turn to the miniature for August (Fig. 12.15), the chill of winter is long forgotten, and so is the damp green of early summer. The grass has reached its honey-colored stage; and in the middle distance before the castle of Étampes, peasants are busy haying. Some of them have taken time off to go swimming. Across the foreground, a cavalcade of ladies and gentlemen come by, bound for a leisurely afternoon of hawking; and lest the jewellike elegance of the rendering beguile us, it would be well to inspect the anatomy with a critical eye. The figures of the nobility have been elongated to fit contemporary notions of grace, in the name of which some preposterous distortion has been indulged. The lady riding pillion on the darker horse to the right furnishes a conspicuous instance. Her head and neck are within the realm of possibility, but her bust, waist, abdomen, and thighs are bizarre—an excellent lesson in the extremes to which the Mannerists were prepared to go.

It is important to remember that the illustrations of the *Très Riches Heures*—to us quaint and naïve—were more than up to date in 1416. The novelty at that time lay not so much in the degree of representative accuracy

attained as in the content. In the first place, these are among the earliest pictures which completely exclude religious subject matter or ecclesiastical overtones of any kind. In the second, they are evidence of an awakening: people had opened their eyes to the face of nature, they found the earth surpassing full of wonder and delight, and they felt no need to interpret or analyze. What landscapes make a more direct appeal to the senses than these? Where can one find pictures more adequate to evoke the feeling of temperature and the seasonal differences in the texture of the air? The smell of the ground at different times of year is also called to mind, and the experience of muscular activity.

The International style appealed to the families favored by the feudal system, and there is much nostalgia as we look back on the lords and ladies

Figs. 12.14-15 The Brothers Limbourg. Two miniatures from the *Très Riches Heures du Duc de Berry*. *February* (opposite); and *August*, with the château of Étampes in the background. Chantilly, Musée Condé. (Giraudon)

who moved through daily life as though participating in a pageant. But in the light of events, they shine with the luster of an overblown rose. Their manners were but a sublimation of the coarse realities of the past. The sun of chivalry had already set, and the color of their display was the iridescence of the afterglow. We cannot survey in detail the numerous local schools of the International movement, and must be content with a few remarks which will prove useful in other applications.

At Cologne, the greatest Internationalist was Stefan Lochner (1400–1451), who made a specialty of painting ingénue Madonnas with corn-colored hair (Fig. 12.16), usually in a setting of roses or violets. Pure sentiment has never been done better. The slightest reservation seems invidious; nevertheless, by making Mary into a sweet child asking our love and protection, Lochner opened the door to a reduction of her status.

Fig. 12.16 (left) Stefan Lochner. *Madonna with a Violet*. Cologne, Archiepiscopal Palace.

Fig. 12.17 (opposite) Bernardo Martorell (The Master of Saint George). *Saint George and the Dragon*. Tempera on panel. 38 x 56 inches. Chicago, Art Institute.

At Barcelona, a certain Master of Saint George (he may have been named Martorell) was at work from about 1430 to about 1450. His title is taken from a big altarpiece (Fig. 12.17) showing Saint George and the dragon, which combines within itself all the good and all the weakness of the movement. As representation, it is insistently naïve. As danger, bravery, combat, and deliverance, it is closer to the dance floor than to the blood and guts of war. And yet there is much that brings back to life for a moment the authentic beauty attached to the profession of arms. The saint swings his horse and poises the lance with a wonderful inevitability, the superb motion of a connoisseur of dynamics to whom violence itself was subject matter for artistic cadence and timing.

In Italy, the International movement was somewhat more strongly affected by local conditions. During the 14th and 15th centuries, Italian paint-

ing tended to form itself on the basis of local schools identified with one of the provinces of the peninsula or with a single city. Each of the Italian schools started with painting of the International kind, and rapidly matured as the Renaissance itself went forward. The painters cited here might well find a more comfortable place in Chapter 13, but it is important to point out the extent to which Late Gothic Mannerism survived in spirit for a very long time even in Italy.

In Lombardy, Pisanello of Verona was the most important master, his activity extending from about 1430 to about 1455. As a painter and draftsman, Pisanello (in keeping with his somewhat later date and his residence in Italy) was an immensely competent technician, but his outlook remained as direct and enjoyable as the Limbourgs. His most notable drawings form a series of animal studies in which Gothic Mannerism was strengthened by an acute

Fig. 12.18 Pisanello. *Saint Eustace's Vision of Christ in the Form of a Stag.* 1436. London, National Gallery.

observation. It was his custom to combine such single studies into paintings, a good example of which is seen in Figure 12.18.

Pisanello occupies a special place in art history because he was the greatest medalist who ever lived. His medals were not intended to be worn at the end of a ribbon, but were conceived as relief sculpture in portable size. Most of them are discs about four inches in diameter, with an extreme thickness of a quarter of an inch or so. The obverse usually has a profile portrait in bust length; and on the reverse, there is ordinarily a symbolical, historical, or mythological scene related in some way to the sitter (Fig. 12.19). Pisanello did not strike his medals from a die. He preferred to cast them, a process which permitted him to bring out all the gentler qualities of the bronze, including the marvelous lettering which is so soft and yet so sharp.

Gentile da Fabriano (about 1360–1427), the first notable painter of Umbria, was an artist of much greater importance than one might suppose. Luck has been unkind to him, and most of his bigger commissions have perished. The pictures that remain are distinguished by gentleness and sweet

Fig. 12.19 Pisanello. Medal of John Paleologus, commemorating that Emperor's visit to Italy in 1438–1439. Florence. Obverse: portrait of the Emperor. Reverse: the Emperor stopping at a roadside shrine while on his way to the Council of Florence. (Anderson)

reverence, a quality which endeared him to Michelangelo and gave that most unsparing of critics an affectionate appreciation of Gentile's art.

Most people remember Gentile for the large *Adoration of the Magi* now in the Uffizi, finished in 1423, but the picture is, as a matter of fact, one of his few failures because the composition was ruined by an unsuccessful attempt to swing interest to the left. As an artistic avhievement, there is much more to excite serious interest in a little panel from the predella of the same *Adoration,* showing the barnyard of the inn at Bethlehem (Fig. 12.20). There is reason to believe it may be the first nocturne in modern painting. It establishes Gentile, conservative though his idiom may have been, as one of the leading experimental artists of his generation.

We ordinarily associate influence with extroversion, and we may therefore tend to overlook the far-reaching effect of Gentile's career. He was a man of reputation, and his work was in demand all over Italy. About 1409, he went to Venice, where he spent five years doing some frescoes in the Ducal Palace. He then worked at Florence and at Orvieto and was subsequently called to Rome by Pope Martin the 5th, who was anxious to restore the dignity of that city after the interim of Avignon. Fire destroyed the frescoes at Venice, also those in Saint John Lateran at Rome; but we can nevertheless make an excellent guess that Gentile's Venetian sojourn accounts in large measure for the atmosphere maintained throughout the history of that school. Jacopo Bellini (1400–1474) was the first Venetian master of consequence; his half-length Madonnas are surprisingly like Gentile's (Fig. 12.21). Giovanni Bellini, his son, might be described as a High Renaissance Gentile (Fig. 14.34, page 627). And so it went: stray as they might into other channels,

Figs. 12.20–21 Gentile da Fabriano. (above) *Nativity*. Predella panel to the *Adoration of the Magi*. 1423. Florence, Uffizi. (left) *Madonna*. New Haven, Yale University Art Gallery. (above: Anderson)

the great Venetians habitually returned to the soft tempo, the lyric gentleness, and the sublimated femininity suggested by this early master.

The sculptor Ghiberti (pages 517–522) stands in history as one of the research artists who discovered our modern methods for representing infinite vistas of space, but his figure style and spirit are the most elegant kind of Gothic. Ghiberti's assistant Benozzo Gozzoli (1420–1497), also a superb technician, is notable largely because neither his taste nor his ideas had advanced in the least beyond the light and easy content we associate with painters like the Master of Saint George. His *Journey of the Magi* (Fig. 12.22) seems, in fact, to be nothing more profound than an excellent record of one of the pageants that took place in Medici Florence. Fra Angelico (1387–1455) belongs more thoroughly to the Renaissance, and thus finds a place in our treatment of that era. It should be realized, however, that the Gabriel of his celebrated

Annunciation (Fig. 13.29, page 525), might actually replace one of the smiling angels of Reims without attracting any comment whatever.

Paolo Uccello (1397–1475), a painter whom nobody entirely understands, has often and carelessly been dismissed with the comment that his place in history was earned by his investigation of the geometry of sight and the principles of linear perspective. Such a view is not wrong, but surely it is incomplete. Uccello's battle pieces of the Uffizi and in London (Fig. 12.23) are among the most vigorously decorative paintings ever executed. In every particular, however, they fit the art which started at Avignon, with the simple but profound difference that sure technical knowledge and a certain classical monumentality had brought the International style up to an entirely new plateau. Uccello used perspective to simplify contours in a manner which comes close to the strong abstraction of analytical cubism. A fair and final estimate of this fascinating artist must, it would seem, make him both a conservative and a radical—and certainly an immense success.

GOTHIC REALISM AND THE ESTABLISHMENT OF THE REPRESENTATIVE CONVENTION

While Late Gothic Mannerism was running its course as outlined above, the artists who were interested in realism continued their work. By 1350 or thereabouts, they had set in motion the convention which was destined to govern European art, almost with the force of law, from the beginning of the 15th century to our own day. We refer to the *representative convention*, by which we mean that something very close to the philosophy of objective realism (page 18) became the fixed and only theory of art acceptable to the public.

The representative convention has amounted to a tacit understanding by all parties that the human figure, when it appears in painting and sculpture, must conform closely to the proportions that are normal for the average living model. The convention assumes also that details of anatomy will be scientifically accurate within very narrow limits of tolerance. It further assumes that linear perspective must approximate very closely the actual geometry of sight, and it assumes in addition that the tonal relations employed for atmospheric perspective ought similarly to correspond with the colors observed in nature.

Every artist has trespassed against the rules of the representative convention, and every careful student knows it. The truth is that strict adherence to the convention is not only impractical, but impossible: the materials and techniques of art can not and do not reproduce nature.

Figs. 12.22–23 (above) Benozzo Gozzoli. *Journey of the Magi*. Detail. 1459. Florence, Medici Palace chapel. (below) Uccello. *The Battle of San Romano*. 1432. Tempera on panel. 6 feet high. London, National Gallery. (above: Alinari)

But the liberties taken have almost always been cautious minor infringements calculated to escape casual attention. And it is notable that critics, when explaining substantial differences in style, have been remarkably careful to hint that accurate representation is the proper thing. Thus, we hear that Giotto emphasized one aspect of "reality," and Monet another.

The experts, in a word, have conspired to cheat the system, always with the sure knowledge that the public would get angry if confronted with anything in art not recognizable as "true to life." The widespread distaste for 20th-century abstraction has had its genesis in the fact that the leading artists have refused any longer to be governed by representation. The public, on the other hand, continues to insist that the convention be respected.

The advent of the representative convention may be associated with the person of King Charles the 5th of France (1337–1380), sometimes called Charles the Wise. With greater particularity, it may even be thought of as having to do with that monarch's nose, a large one with a distinctive shape. Hardly a handsome feature, the royal proboscis might have been altered a bit in the interest of Gothic grace; but with the arrival of the then-new convention which has now lasted so long, every fact of appearance put an obligation on the conscience of the artist even if it happened to be an unfortunate accident. For that reason, the various portraits of Charles (Figs. 12.24–25) were handled with a realism literally unmerciful.

It is interesting that the very words *portrait* and *representation* seem first to have come into general use during the 14th century. The two were used as near-synonyms and were most often applied to the tomb monuments which became increasingly popular at the time. The purpose of these portraits was to give people a more personal and physical immortality than had hitherto been asked, a hope which by its very existence betokened the waning of the Middle Ages. To illustrate the severe enthusiasm with which realistic truth was insisted upon, we may turn to the tomb of Bertrand du Guesclin (Figs. 12.26–27). The 14th century had produced no greater hero, no finer gentleman. In his long and brilliant military career, he gained the respect of his foes as much for his character as for his valor. He spent the last decade of his life as Constable of France. But his tomb portrait is true to life in the sense of telling us that his person was insignificant.

With respect to the representation of anatomy, it is likely that the credit for the earliest achievement of complete competence must go to the sculptors of Burgundy, and probably to Claus Sluter, who died in 1406. His greatest monument was the so-called *Moses Well* in the Carthusian monastery of Champmol near Dijon. More accurately described as a well-head, the composition originally consisted of a hollow pedestal surmounted by a Crucifix. The general conformation of the pedestal itself (Fig. 12.28) appears to be a

Figs. 12.24–25 (left) Paris, Louvre. Portrait of Charles the 5th. Detail of the *Parement de Narbonne*. 1374–1378. (right) Paris, Louvre. Statue of Charles the 5th. About 1378. (Giraudon; Archives Photographiques)

Figs. 12.26–27 Saint Denis. Tomb of Bertrand du Guesclin. Died 1380. (Archives Photographiques)

conscious reflection of the classical Corinthian capital. Around a hexagonal core, six male statues are arranged under an overhanging abacus, with angels bending out under its corners in place of the familiar volutes. The larger statues all depict elderly gentlemen; they are prophets (Fig. 12.29), and supposedly they are engaged in explaining the necessity of atonement for the sacrifice of Jesus. All of them are notable figures, but the Moses is the most impressive of all—hence the name of the well. As Michelangelo was later to do (page 608), Sluter followed an incorrect translation of the Bible which describes Moses as having horns on his head after his long sojourn with God on Mount Sinai.

Earlier realists had been quite as unsparing as Sluter in the matter of anatomy. The extra power of his work derives from a more incisive rendering of momentary poses. The most trivial and even the most ill-advised gestures and expressions were made permanent in his sculpture, as the unlovely little angels under the abacus amply demonstrate. The accuracy of such figures is precise; no artist needs to know any more about anatomy than Sluter did. In only one particular was he still the prisoner of medieval conventions: he still conceived sculpture to be an art of drapery, and he lost the action of torso and legs (and hence the expressive power of the body's complete surface) beneath a superfluity of cloth. Voluminous drapery became, in fact, a special feature of Burgundian sculpture, and it was destined, as we shall see, to have an overly long history in all northern painting as well.

For the establishment of the representative convention in painting, we must return to the manuscript called the *Très Belles Heures,* discontinued by the magnificent Duke of Berry in 1412, as mentioned on page 430. The scribes had done their work, and a number of miniatures had been completed in the going Franco-Flemish-Mannerist style when the Duke made up his mind to start again with the Limbourgs. Some of the finished pages were bound up as a book and ultimately found their way into the Rothschild collection. Often called the "Hours of Paris," these recently came to the Metropolitan Museum of Art in New York.

Some of the unfinished pages, complete only as to text and foliate borders, were bought by William of Bavaria, Count of Holland, who was the Duke's nephew. Part of them ended up in the library at Turin, where they were lost in the fire of 1903. Fortunately, photographs had been made, and a handsome monograph was published by the French scholar Paul Durrieux, under the title *Heures de Turin.* Other pages from Duke William's part of the book eventually arrived in the library of Prince Trivulzio at Milan. Those latter leaves are usually referred to as the "Hours of Milan." Rather recently, they passed to the library at Turin, a destination that hardly simplifies a nomenclature already vexing enough.

Why did William want to buy the unfinished leaves of the manuscript?

The best guess seems to be that he wanted to commission a piece of work by a particular artist. If so, his judgment was more than good. The small number of miniatures done before his death in 1417 rank among the chief wonders of European art.

One of the pictures shows Duke William landing on the beach at Veere in Holland (Fig. 12.30). The date was June 1416. The Duke had been to England to assist in making peace after the campaign of Agincourt, and he had sailed home in the remarkable time of twenty hours. The picture shows his happy daughter Jacqueline there to meet him. She was then seventeen years old, but was destined to lose both her father and her husband within a year and to spend the rest of her life in an unequal struggle with betrayal and intrigue.

On another page Duke William had his artist paint a *Birth of Saint John*

Figs. 12.28–29 (opposite and above) Claus Sluter. *Moses Well*. 1395–1406. Height 10½ feet. Dijon, Chartreuse de Champmol. (above) Detail: Isaiah. (Archives Photographiques)

the Baptist at the top; and across the bottom, he had a river view put in (Fig. 12.31). The stream is placid; it goes past a castle in the middle distance, and curves off around a tree-grown bluff. Far away, we can see some magnificent hills. In the immediate foreground, Saint John is performing the baptism, a ceremony that goes almost unnoticed against such scenery.

When the historian looks at these tiny pictures and reflects that they were done before 1417, he loses his breath. He loses it every time, no matter how often he has seen them. It takes no expert to see at once that they are the work of a man who knew things completely beyond the imagination of the Limbourgs. This artist diminished the size of distant objects systematically and he did it with marvelous precision. He handled shadows and atmosphere with a similar ease. He understood, moreover, how to make his space convincing by providing a linear continuity from the foreground into the dis-

manus sue proterit me possint me

Figs. 12.30–31 Two miniatures painted on leaves of the manuscript originally known as the *Très Belles Heures*. (above) William of Bavaria landing at Veere, from the so-called "Turin Hours" lost in 1903. (below) Baptism of Christ from the so-called "Milan Hours," now in the Museo Civico, Turin.

tance. In the *Baptism,* for example, the eye picks up the shore line at the lower left-hand corner, and follows the river bank into the far away. A similar device was used for the beach at Veere.

The effect of all this was to produce pictures where the space, air, and light strike one with the force of physical experience. One feels the puffy northwest breeze blowing over the Dutch estuary; and in the *Baptism,* one almost expects to hear the sounds that carry so far in the still air of a perfect day at sunset. By comparison, the landscapes of the Limbourgs seem reduced to mere backdrops. Duke William's painter knew how to put things *in* the space he represented.

We need to remind ourselves that his work was done at the very moment when the Limbourgs were considered the best artists in northern Europe, and were enjoying the most lucrative commission; but the contrast between their work and his is the difference between ingenuous experiment and the ease of learned mastery. We are confronted, then, with the arrival of a phenomenal genius who was able, in one act of creation, to lift medieval painting to the Renaissance level. His name has naturally been sought with every resource of scholarship, but conclusive proof of his identity is sadly lacking. Without entering into argument about the evidence, let us simply say that the master was probably Hubert van Eyck, who died at Ghent in 1426. His younger brother Jan van Eyck (pages 475–481) was the first major painter of Flanders and the founder of the northern Renaissance.

ITALY DURING THE GOTHIC ERA: THE PROTO-RENAISSANCE

Italian Gothic was always a reluctantly imported fashion; and like the architecture of the same period, Italy's sculpture and painting was often Gothic more in date than in style. The classic tradition never entirely died out, and neither did the Byzantine. Humanism did not appear earlier in Italy than in the north; but it hit harder and moved faster. It filled the familiar Byzantine and Gothic figures with life, and made them vibrate in a new key. Individualism—if we can conceive it as separate from humanism—was more pronounced among the Italian population, and became overt at an early date. Most French and Flemish artists retained the outlook and attitude of craftsmen until well after 1400; but Nicola Pisano's marble pulpit (page 449), the very first work of art conceived as the personal expression of a great man, dates from the year 1260. It begins, moreover, a section of art history destined to last more than four centuries, the whole of it being for the most part an account of the activities of single artists as distinct from schools and movements. All of these considerations have led certain writers to designate the art of Italy during the era about to be reviewed as *Proto-Renaissance,* by which they mean that the style might still be Byzantine or Gothic, but that the content was often distinctly modern.

As his name suggests, Nicola Pisano (about 1205–1278) made his home at Pisa during the period of his important achievements, but he was not born there. He came from southern Italy, and some writers prefer to call him Nicola d'Apulia. The point is worth mentioning because it accounts for his use of an extremely classical style at a time when most Italian art was Byzantine in nature, with more or less admixture from the French Gothic.

During Nicola's formative years, South Italian artists had been producing a great many pieces of sculpture which the casual observer might easily mistake for Roman work. It was remarkable that any one then alive had the independence to create anything so contrary to the spirit of the time; and the reader will not be surprised to hear that the phenomenon was connected with the personality of the genius and emperor Frederick the 2nd (died 1250), and remains as but one of the numerous developments in which he demonstrated the qualities that earned him the popular title of *stupor mundi*.

Nicola's greatest monument is the marble pulpit still in use in the Baptistery at Pisa. The pulpit is a hexagonal box carried on Corinthian columns, with a stairway up from the floor. Five panels of high relief form its walls, of which we reproduce the one illustrating Luke 3:22–28, ordinarily called *The Presentation of Christ in the Temple,* and sometimes *The Circumcision* (Fig. 12.32). Certain defects impress themselves immediately. In the first place, no photographs at present available convey an adequate impression of the superb surface of the marble; the reader must defer judgment until he can study the original. As in so many other reliefs of medieval date, the composition is painfully crowded, and the excellence of the artist makes itself manifest only in the single figure, or in a couple of figures seen together— which the observer must separate out by making a special effort, much as one isolates an aphorism from the text around it. If we make that compromise with Nicola Pisano, he emerges as a sculptor of unexcelled power.

The figure of Saint Simeon will serve to illustrate the point. Like several other figures on the pulpit, its classical source has been specifically identified. It is an adaptation of the Bacchus on an ancient marble vase decorated with a scene showing that god in company with the Maenads. Perhaps no character in art history ever received an equal adjustment of spiritual status in the upward direction; Nicola's Simeon differs from its classical source as the alpha of civilization contrasts with its omega. The personal force of the artist seems to have entered with explosive pressure into the marble, and the figure inspires an admiration not untinged by fear. The same epic and even wrathful quality was destined to occur again in Italian art; Jacopo della Quercia had it, and so did Michelangelo. To neither sculptor was Nicola inferior, and

Fig. 12.32 Nicola Pisano. *The Presentation in the Temple* (Luke 2:25–35). 1260. One panel from the pulpit of the Baptistery of Pisa. In the center is Simeon holding the Christ child. (Alinari)

we may confidently give this early master a place in that select company of artists who have in fact achieved the heroic.

Nicola Pisano started a tradition in sculpture which lasted until the beginning of the 15th century, at which time it was rather suddenly replaced by the style associated with Donatello. Historians have formed the habit of referring to all such sculpture as *Pisanesque,* but the designation is somewhat misleading. Except in a very general way, few of the sculptors involved followed Nicola's style.

The most important of them was Giovanni Pisano (about 1250–after 1317), Nicola's son, who for a time was unquestionably the leading artist of Italy. He designed the Campo Santo at Pisa, and the façade of the cathedral at Siena, perhaps the finest bits of Gothic in Italy. In 1305, he was called upon to furnish a Madonna for the altar of the Arena Chapel at Padua (page 459), a commission which virtually labels him as the best sculptor then available.

In the course of history, Giovanni's special importance is the fact that he nipped his father's classical Renaissance in the bud. He had in all probability sojourned in France between 1266 and 1277, which is to say at the

Fig. 12.33 Giovanni Pisano. *Madonna and Child*. Pisa, Campo Santo. (Anderson)

moment when elegant statues like the north portal Madonna of Paris (Fig. 12.7) were the very latest thing. Giovanni was so impressed with the type that he took it back to Italy with him—standing Madonnas having been rare on the peninsula up to that time. Of his many versions of the subject, one of which is shown in Figure 12.33, it may be said that he avoided the linear virtuosity of the French models, and made the expression more plastic. He eschewed, also, the *chic* of Paris, substiuting for it a serenity both human and classical. It should also be noted before we pass on that these sweet and stately figures are among the earliest modern statues conceived as semiportable sculpture, each piece complete in itself and without necessary reference to an architectural composition.

Like his father, Giovanni Pisano was fond of marble pulpits, and did several. The most elaborate was done for the cathedral at Pisa, and completed in 1310. Damaged by fire in the late 16th century, it is no longer in use, but part of the sculpture is preserved at Pisa, and part at Berlin. The *Crucifixion* panel (Fig. 12.34) illustrates exceedingly well Giovanni's departure from the style and spirit of his father. He seems to have been affected not only by the French Gothic, but by such Romanesque monuments as the tympanum at Autun (Fig. 10.36, page 348), where the figure style is different but the surcharge of feeling the same. It is impossible, in fact, to cite a more emotional and unrestrained *Crucifixion* than this one. In order to carry the import of religious passion at fever heat, the artist resorted to startling

Fig. 12.34 Giovanni Pisano. *Crucifixion*. From the pulpit completed in 1310 for the Cathedral of Pisa. (Anderson)

devices: pathological emaciation, distortion, hysterical gestures. The total effect can scarcely be called tragedy; it is closer to despair. Highly subjective on the part of the sculptor, and demanding the intimate participation of the observer, it establishes its author as an exponent of the philosophy of expressionism; when brought into contrast with the serene Madonnas by the same hand, it certifies Giovanni as an artist of unusual range.

♦ *The Career of Saint Francis*   The start of the superb Italian tradition in painting was closely connected with the great and modern religious impulse inspired by Saint Francis of Assisi (about 1182–1226). Biographies of that wonderful man are available everywhere, varying in tone from careful history to sloppy appreciation; but one and all, they tell of a personality full of love for God, for nature, and for humanity, and loved by all people in return. It is necessary to point out that Francis looked out upon nature with eyes different from those of the later humanists. He enjoyed it because it was related to God; they enjoyed it more directly, and because it was beautiful. Even so, Francis was the first man of definitive influence to declare an identity between the worship of God and joy on earth. "Praised be my Lord and God," he sang in his glorious *Canticle of the Sun*, "for Mother Earth who governs and sustains us, who gives birth to all the many fruits and colored flowers."

While every modern citizen is familiar with the concept of the Deity as an object of affection, the idea was a new one when Francis began his work. We need not pause to debate whether Francis was the prime mover or merely a conspicuous participant; the important fact is that a fundamental reorientation between man and God was then in progress. The *Pantocrators* of Byzantine art and the *Last Judgments* so popular in Romanesque and Gothic had reflected a harsh church. Such art had been spiritually elevating in the sense of stating the just claims of religion and the consequences of delinquency. Saint Francis's method was different. He asked people to serve the Lord because the Lord loved them, and they could learn to love Him. Our entire concept of the fatherhood and kindness of the Almighty seems to have been extraordinarily rare if not altogether unknown before this balance was swung. It is obvious that God and man would be brought closer together by such thinking; but in order to understand the practical effort on art, we must say more.

One tendency of the Franciscan doctrine was to increase the respectability of representative art by endorsing the legitimacy of joy in the natural world. That was immensely important at the time, but the new idea of love for God proved even more important. Francis established the belief that the love of man for God, and of God for man, was similar to the affection felt by one person for another. More profound and important, to be sure, but the identical emotion in different degree. The important point to grasp is the assertion that God himself has feelings like our own; it is the essential concept in the humanizing process by which art was about to be transformed, and the saints to become better understood.

What was accepted as true of love, it seemed to follow, might be true of the other emotions. Granting that much, people found the Holy Family and all the saints endowed with sensibilities like their own. It began to be possible to understand the sacred narrative as a series of events illustrative, in principle at least, of certain types of experience, both exalted and terrible. What had happened before was bound to happen again and again; the great men of the Church became important not because they were unique and remote, but because they too were human. While susceptible of cheap misunderstanding, the effect of such concepts was on the whole good: one had some chance of emulating persons like himself, and none of following in the footsteps of those who were supernatural.

It is the presence of such ideas that makes the great difference between northern art of the later Middle Ages and the Italian. Homely realism was incipient in the north at the very period we are discussing, but neither the French nor the Flemish artists were capable of revealing the grander mysteries of faith in the language of common feeling. They possessed accuracy of representation, but they lacked the emotional authenticity which made it possible for certain Italians to express all the power of religious conviction with the warmth of an event occurring at home.

"Let the brethren have care," wrote Francis in one of his colloquies, "not on any account to accept churches or dwellings that may be built for them unless they are in accordance with the rule of Holy Poverty." In another place, he visualized the proper Franciscan buildings as poor little churches, preferably abandoned by others. The negation of property was central to his rule, and he must have been aware that great monastic orders had, more than once in the past, made architectural and artistic investments during periods of spiritual laxity. But the admonitions of the founder were destined to have only a moderate effect upon the policy of the order.

The grandiose double church of St. Francis at Assisi, really two Gothic naves built one over the other on the side of a hill, was started in 1228. Because of the generous Italian sunlight, the builders walled up most of the space available for windows, leaving only a moderate area for glass. By the same act, they provided an excellent field for fresco painting. Toward the end of the 13th century, painters began to come to Assisi to decorate those walls. In the course of time, virtually every important master had a commission there, until there was no space left.

There was extra reason for hurrying such work along during the final years of the 13th century. The year 1300 was a Jubilee year; and the monks wanted to make their church attractive to the pilgrims who would inevitably stream through the town on their way to and from Rome. About 1295, therefore, a cycle of 28 frescoes from the life of Francis was commissioned for the Upper Church. The series runs all the way around the nave, constituting its lowest and most advantageously placed tier of pictorial decoration. The incidents depicted were apparently drawn from Saint Bonaventura's life of Francis, a book dating from 1261. The handling of the subject matter is completely different from anything of earlier date; plainly, a number of the pictures reflect the operation of a mind with an exceedingly forward-looking approach to human problems. Although no one cares to assign all 28 frescoes to him, although no impeccable evidence even places him at Assisi at the time, and although certain prominent modern critics are convinced he was never there, tradition is probably correct that the painter was Giotto.

♦ *Giotto* Giotto was probably born in 1266. Vasari, whose *Lives of the Most Eminent Painters, Sculptors, and Architects* first came out in 1550, wrote the date ten years later, but he was almost certainly wrong. Giotto, according to tradition, was apprenticed to Cimabue, a strong master in the

Italo-Byzantine style and the leading painter at Florence. Assuming that the boy went into the shop when he was about twelve or thirteen, and served his seven years, he would have left Cimabue's employment in 1285 or 1286. It would then have been customary for him to spend several years as a journeyman. It is more than probable that he did, and that explains why we have no notices of him until he appeared at Assisi: journeymen were the graduate students of art, and graduate students leave no mark in the places they sojourn.

Journeymen went from town to town doing odd jobs. When a journeyman-painter walked into a place, he called upon the first master painter whose shop he saw. The master was under obligation to give him work if he had it, to help him get work with someone else, or to furnish him with food and lodging and money enough for the trip to the next town. After several years of such profitable wandering, the young man would settle down somewhere, but he was not permitted to do business in his own name and right until he had gained admission to the local guild. Admission was granted upon the presentation of a painting or statue which the masters of the guild were willing to endorse as sound work; hence the word *masterpiece,* which now has a different meaning. After acceptance of the masterpiece, the new member had his name recorded in the archives of the guild, and he was ready to accept commissions.

Giotto's style was a complete negation of the Italo-Byzantine manner which had dominated Italian painting for 700 years and in which he must have been educated by Cimabue. Obviously, Giotto was a man of superior independence; it is equally plain that the experience gained during his *Wanderjahre* must have changed his outlook and provided him with new convictions. It is a pity that we do not know where he went, what he saw, or what he did during those eight or ten years; but it is possible to make a shrewd guess or two.

Giotto painted pictures peopled by heavy, thick-set figures dressed in the extremely simple costumes worn by common folk all over the medieval world. The principal feature of his technique was a vivid and meticulous definition of mass—a declaration, as it were, that no fact of the visual world is more important than the existence of solid objects. One way to explain the statuesque nature of this figure style is to suggest that Giotto, a painter, was imitating statues.

He probably was. In order to get the effect desired, Giotto had to paint as though his figures existed in ample but diffused light. By grading his shadows with precision as they modeled from light into dark, he described the surface of every contour accurately. So exact are the specifications of convexity and concavity that a competent sculptor might with ease translate one of Giotto's people into stone; there would never be any doubt how the carving should be done.

In 1896, when he published the first edition of his *Florentine Painters*, Bernhard Berenson coined a phrase which explains much about the intensely plastic nature of Giotto's art. Berenson said that Giotto painted in such a way that retinal impressions attained *tactile values*. Although inspected with the eyes, that is to say, Giotto's pictures cause one to experience a powerful excitement of the sense of touch. Berenson contended that any representative painter is always wisest when he concentrates on tactile imagery. If the observer can be convinced that the painted figure has tangibility, his imagination will supply all other necessary phenomena: space within which to stand, ground to stand on, the action of gravity, air to breathe, and light to see with.

There is no doubt that Berenson was on the right track, even though he concentrated his argument too exclusively upon the plastic element in Giotto's painting. A more adequate explanation of Giotto's methods is the one furnished by Denman Ross and Arthur Pope. They said that Giotto painted in *the mode of relief,* for an explanation of which we refer the reader ahead to pages 498–501. It is odd that neither Berenson, nor Ross, nor Pope—while saying so much that suggests Giotto learned his style from the sculptors— gave emphasis to the historical probability that he actually did so.

During the 1280's, the best place to see sculpture in quantity was France. France, moreover, was still the unchallenged leader of Europe in every cultural matter, including art. France, therefore, was an obvious destination for an ambitious young artist out to see the world; and while proof is lacking, it seems more than likely that Giotto, like Giovanni Pisano, went there. While there, he would naturally have been interested in what was then the latest French sculpture, which included narrative scenes in very high relief, one of which appears in Figure 12.35. It is not farfetched to suppose that Giotto, when he returned home, undertook to adapt such compositions to the ample wall spaces so rare in France and so plentiful and then so empty in Italy.

By comparison with any painting by Giotto, the actors in Figure 12.35 are without the spark of life; indeed, the most remarkable feature of Giotto's art was his ability to endow not the face, the hands, or the pose, but the absolute totality of the figure with meaning. Where did he learn how to do that? In part, we may assign his rare capacity to the operation of genius, but it has all too often been explained by reference to his "direct study from nature."

Without any doubt, Giotto did study from nature, but he must have been rather discriminating about it. The anatomy of the average human being is not an expressive vehicle. Giotto might have watched ordinary citizens move

Fig. 12.35 Paris, Cathedral. Tympanum over the so-called "Red Door." *Coronation of the Virgin*. About 1270. (Archives Photographiques)

and gesture for years without learning a single useful thing. It is necessary to suppose that he studied the more lucid action of experts. Had he studied dancers, he might have learned to represent motion much better than he ever did. Thus the theater—of which there was a great deal in both France and Italy—remains the obvious place where he learned how to paint human beings utterly perfect for the parts they play, and to compose them into pictures which strike home with a truth and vitality not only beyond the capacity of any earlier artist, but beyond that of all other artists to date.

To the hypothesis of a long experience in acting and producing, we may add a minor point or two of corroboration. How else explain the curious miniature architecture in so many of Giotto's pictures, so odd and impractical in design, so unreasonably out of scale with the people? Such constructions were ordinary stage properties in the medieval theater. They had to be portable, and they were intended merely to symbolize the presence of buildings.

With respect to Giotto's settings, it has often been remarked that he reduced them to the bare essentials, including nothing that would distract from the content and nothing not necessary to it. Greatly to be praised for many reasons, this particular economy of means is part and parcel of the art of the stage designer.

The best-known picture at Assisi is *Saint Francis Preaching to the Birds* (Fig. 12.36). Francis was one of those persons to whom all sorts of animals respond with complete trust. The tale is told that one Sunday morning he called some birds to him, and they sat quite still while he preached them a sermon. Delicate sentiment is somewhat outside the realm of Giotto's usual interest; but it is significant to see that when he undertook it, he produced a painting not only popular but worthwhile. The daring of the performance can hardly be overstated. Success depended upon the willingness of the public to accept the picture in the spirit of a little child. In such matters, there is no middle ground; success is absolute, or failure is maudlin—and there can be no excuse for the artist.

The *Saint Francis Renouncing His Father* (Fig. 12.37) shows Giotto in the field where he stands alone. The narrative behind the painting runs as follows: After he had returned home from military imprisonment at Perugia, Francis practiced an evangelical religion. His acts and utterances seemed in bad taste, and proved embarrassing to his parents—especially his newly formed theories against property. Presently an open break occurred. Relations went from bad to worse, culminating in the shocking incident chosen by Giotto for his point of time. The enraged father has undertaken to beat his grown son. The son has run for sanctuary to the cathedral, only to be overtaken and publicly denounced on the steps outside. The father has just issued a demand for obedience by virtue of the material support hitherto provided by his money, including the very clothes on Francis's back. In response to that reasoning, Francis immediately stripped himself naked, and made a statement of renunciation covering both his earthly father and the clothing.

The picture is remarkable for the states of mind and shades of emotion contained within a single frame. The father, a much put-upon man according to the best of his own judgment, may even be said to be pleading in the best interests of his son. Most youthful evangelists are merely disturbed and unstable young men; who could then have predicted that Francis would be remembered as a saint in glory? As Giotto understood him, this parent was to blame for nothing.

Another kind of feeling is being experienced by the Bishop of Assisi, who covers the boy's middle with his own robe and mutters instructions to an assistant. As all bishops must, he had to compromise with Mammon so that the work of God on earth might proceed. An intransigent rebuke to an influential citizen can at times be the only course; but as an administrative technique, it has always been strong medicine. Bishops ever hope to find another way first; but at the same time, could this bishop on this occasion deny his protection to a church member coming hotfoot to claim it as a right, and declaring in a loud voice the precise sentiments the Church publicly recom-

Figs. 12.36–37 Giotto. (left) *Saint Francis Preaching to the Birds.* (opposite) *Saint Francis Renouncing His Father.* Frescoes in the nave of the Upper Church of St. Francis at Assisi. About 1296. (both photos: Anderson)

mends to all? Surely there has never been a more expressive picture of a man who wishes he could be somewhere else.

As a foil to the important figures, Giotto provided us with the minor actors so typically present at embarrassing moments. We see the tensely impassive faces of those who dare not commit themselves one way or the other. There is also the fool who thinks his whisper can't be overheard and who passes a snide remark. There are the inevitable children who don't know whether it would be safe and interesting to throw stones or better to seek a less dangerous situation.

Almost every critic has commented adversely upon the composition, which is divided. It is of course fair to contend that the division corresponds with the gulf of misunderstanding between the parties represented, and may therefore be justified on dramatic grounds. Still another guess, and one that seems most likely of all, is simply that Giotto came to Assisi comparatively fresh from the theater. Scenes of confrontation are common on the stage, and very forceful. But the play moves on, as pictures do not, and what is ap-

propriate on the boards may be less so in the more static and permanent art of wall painting.

Giotto's greatest surviving monument is the fresco cycle in the Arena Chapel at Padua. The name comes from the ruins of a Roman arena, still visible on the site. The donor was Enrico Scrovegno, who had been anxious to atone in some measure for the evil memory of his father, a notorious usurer whom Dante (*Purgatorio,* Canto 17) placed in the seventh circle of hell. It is probable that Giotto himself designed the building. Architecturally, it is a mere brick shed about 95 feet long, but the tunnel-vaulted interior, with a perfectly flat expanse of wall surface and carefully placed windows, provided an excellent field for frescoes. Work began in 1303, and the consecration took place on March 16, 1305. It is evident that Giotto had made himself head of an exceedingly well-organized shop.

Both side walls are covered with narrative pictures which rise in three registers over a lower row of personified Virtues and Vices. Color (bright

Fig. 12.38 Giotto. *Meeting at the Golden Gate*. 1303–1305. Fresco. Padua, Arena Chapel. (Anderson)

and springlike, and by no means suggested by our black-and-white plates) pulls everything together, and serves to synthesize the great diversity.

A guiding thought runs through the subject matter of all the pictures. Giotto's purpose was to give us a meditative exposition of the mysteries of Incarnation and Redemption as demonstrated by events in the lives of Mary and Jesus. The narrative commences with the experiences of Joachim and Anne, the parents of Mary, largely as set forth in the *Protevangelion,* or *Book of James,* from the *New Testament Apocrypha,* with the help of which the student may follow the earlier part of the history. The series then carries on through the earthly career of Mary and the Savior, and culminates in the *Last Judgment.*

An unbroken flow of narrative was no more available to Giotto than to any other painter. Narrative painting must of necessity be episodic unless one is willing to abandon the simultaneous mode of representation (page 60). The significance of the episodes chosen thus becomes the first test of artistic judgment, and the matter was one in which Giotto did not demonstrate uniform success. A full-scale study of the chapel would perforce include a number of rather dull, superfluous pictures, but if we restrict our attention to a

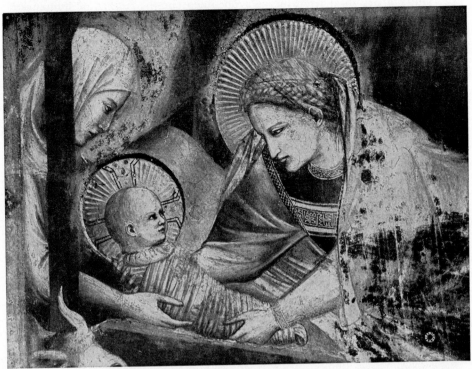

Fig. 12.39   Giotto. *Nativity*, detail. 1303–1305. Fresco. Padua, Arena Chapel. (Anderson)

few of the best, we shall find ourselves dealing with drama of supreme range and penetration.

It is hard, for example, to see how the dignity and beauty of faith might be better expressed than we find it in the *Meeting at the Golden Gate* (Fig. 12.38). Joachim and Anne had been weighed down with grief because they had arrived at old age without children. Some days before the event depicted, Joachim had taken himself off on a lonely trip to visit his shepherds in the mountains. An angel came to both the elderly husband and his wife, to say that a child would be born. Joachim hurried home, and Anne went out to meet him. Half a dozen bystanders appear with the principal actors; they gossip as they pass along, giving only a casual glance at the old couple who kiss as they meet. But Giotto's power to tell a tale with the briefest means is summed up in those two crucial figures. They move with the deliberation of age. Their stance remains unchanged, and their embrace is a bending from the waist only. The whole tempo of the scene reflects the peaceful masculine and feminine of the long married. Transfigured by the divine grace and lost in the privacy of their special knowledge, they express their joy not overtly as children might, but in quiet confidence.

Quite apart from its value as a document in the history of humanism, this picture has a special bearing on doctrine: it is the closest thing we have to a representation of the Immaculate Conception. Often carelessly confused with the Virgin Birth (the birth of Christ), the Immaculate Conception was the conception of the Virgin by Saint Anne, by virtue of which Mary was born, lived, and died free from original sin. No part of the sacred narrative was more bitterly debated, pro and con. In fact, the whole story of Joachim and Anna had been condemned by writers no less redoubtable than Augustine, Jerome, Innocent the 1st, and Bernard—without, however, undermining popular belief. In the generation immediately before Giotto's, the theme had been gaining support, and was included in *The Golden Legend* of Jacobus de Voragine (about 1280). In 1348, the papacy gave formal approval to the worship of Anne. As men repeated the tale, it was natural that they should ask artists to visualize it. The iconography we see in Figure 12.38 was not original with Giotto; his version is merely the best rendering of the subject. But because artsts did furnish the imagery (and in spite of all admonition to the contrary) there was widespread belief that Mary had been conceived at the instant Joachim kissed Anna at the Golden Gate.

It is important to distinguish between this picture, which shows the actual event, and devotional pictures of Mary as the beneficiary of the Immaculate Conception. The latter were very popular during the 17th century (page 638).

The *Nativity* is likewise a picture where Giotto made supreme use of the single figure. Most of the surface is occupied by inert material intended merely to supply the necessary quiet of midnight: the sleepy donkeys, a somnolent Saint Joseph, the quiet shepherds with their sheep, and some angels flying with muted wings in the sky above. At the extreme left (Fig. 12.39) we see the Virgin. She rises slightly on her elbows, and obviously with some pain, to receive her baby from a gentle nurse. It is doubtful whether an equal force of passion has ever been communicated to the world by so small an area of painting. The imagery is painfully vivid—so real, indeed, as to banish from memory every other version of this popular subject. Not only did Giotto paint the *Nativity;* he painted maternity itself.

For the *Flight into Egypt* (Fig. 12.40) Giotto chose to set the event in a rocky pass of the mountains. Cliffs hem the Holy Family in. Movement is curtailed in every direction except forward, and the urgency of the situation is heightened by the impenetrable, massive, material limits to action. An angel in the sky gestures angrily for more speed. Mary sits stiff, erect, tense on the back of the donkey; she can only hold her child and await the outcome, now beyond remedy, for nothing more can be done. More in frustration than hope, Joseph turns to urge the driver to go faster, and the man pulls forward on the halter. But it does no good. The donkey merely cocks his ears

Fig. 12.40   Giotto. *Flight into Egypt*. 1303–1305. Fresco. Padua, Arena Chapel. (Anderson)

the other way. Thus in a picture that strains the human spirit with anxiety, we are given to understand that the fate of Christendom once hinged upon the intractable temperament of an ass.

If space permitted a detailed account of every picture in the chapel, it would be plain that good compositions are often juxtaposed with careless and even perfunctory arrangements. It would also be plain that the *Flight into Egypt*, considered as an essay in formal design, is one of the very best paintings there—and, indeed, one of the best to antedate the High Renaissance. Pictorial means were used to integrate the picture. It needs no frame to define its beginning, middle, and end. The limits are established by the three persons entering from the left, and by Joseph's inward and backward gesture on the right. The Madonna fits into a stable and lucid triangular space, and provides a powerful central axis. The rocks behind have a pyramidal shape, harmonious to the triangle just mentioned.

Arrangements so subtle and complex do not occur by chance. We must assume that Giotto had turned his attention to the problem of composition, and in the process had come across enough classical work to have deduced, once again, the method of Greek organic composition (page 66).

The world has produced an immense amount of painting since 1305, but Giotto's work at the Arena Chapel remains unsurpassed by any subsequent monument of Western civilization. During the 14th century, there was nothing with which it might even be compared. Giotto was a famous man, a first citizen. Opportunities beckoned wherever he looked. In addition to records which place him, off and on, in his native Florence, we know that he worked on important commissions in Rome, Rimini, Verona, Ferrera, and perhaps also Avignon. About 1318, he was again working at Florence, doing the wall paintings in the Bardi and Peruzzi chapels of Santa Croce.

Pictures from both chapels are often reproduced with the label "Giotto," but we can accept them as his only in a very restricted sense. At some unknown date, the frescoes were covered with whitewash and virtually forgotten. In 1841, they were rediscovered, but the date was still too early. The pictures were of course dilapidated, and a painter named Bianchi was engaged to renovate them. He did more harm than the whitewash. His over-painting looks more like a 19th-century German greeting card than it does like Giotto; but even if the hand is no longer Giotto's, the compositions must be.

Restored as they are, the paintings are still adequate to justify several statements about the course of Giotto's thought and art during the period of his full maturity. In comparison to the work at Padua, the psychological climate is less intense, the tempo grander, the intention less actual and more majestic. There is a breadth of view and a dignity of arrangement hitherto not observed. All of these qualities are at their best in the justly celebrated *Death of Saint Francis* (Fig. 12.41). To students familiar with the later history of Italian painting, no picture could be more full of suggestion; at this point in his career, and in the early 14th century, Giotto had already made himself master of almost every worthwhile element in the so-called "Grand Style" of the High Renaissance.

The point of time is the moment of death. Across the middle of the picture, the ponderous corpse of the saint lies in utter stillness. All eyes are directed toward the dead man except for those of one brother who is granted a vision of the soul's ascension. In wonder too sudden for ecstasy, he looks upward toward the sky, where angels may be seen lifting the immortal element heavenward. Dramatically speaking, the picture compares the static incubus of death with the freedom and transcendency of the eternal.

The formal means used by Giotto to present this stately spectacle depend fundamentally upon a slow harmony of ponderous verticals and horizontals, upon the contrast of these with diagonals, and upon the dynamic and directional power inherent in the glance of the eye.

Fig. 12.41 Giotto. *Death of Saint Francis*. Between 1318 and 1322. Florence, Santa Croce. (Anderson)

The composition is framed in on either hand by several figures who stand like statues, all of them motionless but intent upon the dead man. The verticality of those figures is echoed in the paneling of the wall behind; but even that emphasis is insufficient to overbear the predominating motive of stability and the horizontal.

The grouping opens up in the middle to bring the bier into full view. It is notable that the recumbent figure is very large, and the bier very long. Across the top of the enclosing wall runs the most powerful linear device in the picture, likewise horizontal.

Across the rectilinear elements just outlined, we may discern the existence of a superimposed triangular figure. To the right, one leg thereof is established by the inclined shaft of the cross and banner. To the left, by following the line of sight of the monk who sees the vision, we construct the other side of the figure. Both lead the eye to the celestial incident above and thus serve to integrate an arrangement which otherwise would exist in separate registers.

Bare statements like those just made must not be construed by the reader as an adequate description of Giotto's composition. At best, plain language can only suggest the visual activity by which one comprehends pictorial form, and it is legitimate for an author to point up his meaning by occasional resort to superlatives. The *Death of Francis*, repainted as it is, remains one of the very greatest essays in formal design. It is as lucid as any known composition by the Greeks, and there is no extant Greek work of the same complexity. It is free from the erudition which so often lured even the best painters of the High Renaissance into sophisticated display. At the date when Giotto finished it, there had been no one since the fall of Rome who could even have attempted a similar performance; and after his death, there was, for about a hundred years, no one who so much as comprehended the secrets of his method.

Giotto died in January, 1337. He had been once more to Assisi after finishing his work at Santa Croce. He had executed a fresco commission in the Bargello at Florence, which contains the familiar portrait of Dante, restored by an insensitive hand after having been damaged in a fire. Giotto did work also at Milan, and he spent three years at Naples, where in 1330 he was named a "familiar" of the court of King Robert—an incident of some significance because it illustrates the comparatively early date when Italians began to feel disposed to accord artists high social standing by virtue of their achievements in art. In 1334, Giotto was named chief architect to the city of Florence; and in that capacity, he made plans for the bell tower of the Cathedral which is still called "Giotto's tower."

Such were the honors heaped upon a man whose merit and scope give him status as a world figure. It would not be difficult to contend that Giotto had the most profound intelligence yet to express itself in art. His work was marked throughout by robust good sense. Everything he did demonstrates a determination to realize the objects of faith as facts. Subtleties and details did not delay him, even the detail of beauty. His people are without physical or intellectual distinction; often they are unlovely, and some times vulgar. His choice of such types must have been deliberate; doubtless it had to do with humanism. He wanted to present the great events as events typical of universal human experience, the very same sort of joy and sorrow that inevitably comes to the ordinary man and woman.

After Giotto's death, Italy produced no artist of the first rank until the 15th century. Every year continued to produce a substantial amount of painting, however; and to fill in the history, a paragraph or two may be justified.

The school of Siena (pages 304–310) continued to maintain a good overall level of quality and kept its special character throughout the 14th century. At Florence, painting took two different directions. One group of men, of whom Bernardo Daddi and Spinello Aretino were exemplars, tried to combine the style of Giotto with that of Siena. They painted mostly on panel, and their formula was to clothe one of Giotto's large and plastic figures in ultramarine blue and silhouette it against a blank ground of gold. The other group at Florence made an attempt to extend to panoramic proportions the narrative techniques that had made Giotto famous. The *Allegory of Church and State,* in the Spanish Chapel at Santa Maria Novella in Florence, is a good instance of their work. As wall decoration, such frescoes delight the eye with color, but not one of the Giotteschi appears to have had the slightest notion of the elements that made Giotto great. In particular, none of them could compose very well; and with a certain bland realism, they presented things in all their original disorder and without a bit of the lucidity which had enabled the master to tell the truth. Unpopular for centuries, Giottesque painting nevertheless had enough merit to serve as the principal source for the style of the modern Mexican artists Rivera and Orozco.

Chapter 13

THE START of the Renaissance marked the beginning of modern civilization. The new era may be said to have arrived by 1400, or shortly thereafter; and we shall find it convenient to recognize two subdivisions: the 15th century is appropriately known as the *Early Renaissance,* and the 16th as the *High Renaissance.*

The cause of the Renaissance was not the revival of classical studies; the ferment of classical enthusiasm which so dominated the imagination of several generations did not, as a matter of fact, commence until all the decisive philosophical decisions had been made and all the modern values generally accepted. The Renaissance, in short, was not what the name seems to say: a mere rebirth of classical culture. It was a fundamental change in human nature. All society joined in the belief that certain specific things were worth working for, worth having, and worth defending. The very same things have been central in our motivation ever since, and give a specious validity to the old saw that "human nature is the same everywhere." Grossly wrong if applied to all humanity and all history, the notion is approximately accurate if we limit its application to the inhabitants of Western Europe during the past 500 years.

As demonstrated in Chapter 12, the new point of view did not come as a sudden burst of light; there were signs of it as early as the West Porch at Chartres (page 415). Signs and predictions are not actualities, however; and the Renaissance never became a reality until its fundamental concepts had been universally accepted as self-evidently true. The ideas to which we refer are summed up in the words *humanism* and *individualism,* and by the phrase *belief in the value of the world.* Because all the art we are yet to survey

468

THE EARLY
RENAISSANCE

amounts, in spite of its great variety, to a single celebration of the beliefs just named, it is time to explore the philosophy of the Renaissance more thoroughly than we have yet done.

THE ADVENT OF HUMANISM

The emergence of human nature in its modern form coincided with the period when the medieval church was declining from its position of dominance in European society. While outright paganism was conspicuous in the behavior of certain individuals, it would be a mistake to infer that religion lost all its meaning, or even most of its meaning. Many of the brilliant leaders of the period, the very men whom we remember as actual builders of the modern world, were profoundly sincere in their faith: Pico della Mirandola, for example, and Marsilio Ficino. The change should be thought of less in terms of a negation of the religious values and more as an awakening to the worth of things of which the medieval mind had been comparatively unconscious, or of which medieval society had been taught to be ashamed.

More was involved than the mere act we attempt to describe as the opening of eyes to the wonder and beauty of the world. Even more was involved than the actual placement of hope and belief in our life here as mortals. The Western world crossed the great divide, it would seem, when people began to feel confidence in the possibility of human achievement. The thing that best characterizes the attitude typical of the Renaissance is the feeling that one holds a map in his hand which shows the road to fulfillment of the heart's desire. Seeing life as an equation between himself and the environment, Western man undertook to subdue nature and make it work for him. The geographic exploration of the globe coincides with the period we now study. So does the start of modern science, which may be thought of as exploration in greater detail. Since the 15th century, the resources of the planet have been located, mapped, and are today all but catalogued. The physical laws of nature had been codified by methods increasingly and stupendously precise and refined, and the forces of nature have been harnessed and put to use.

The artistic counterpart to the age of exploration was an increased realism. With respect to the human anatomy, the realists of the Renaissance cast off every vestige of medieval prejudice. Nudity lost its connotation of shame. Anatomical investigation of the entire body became a routine part of artistic training. Dissection presently extended the knowledge of artists beyond the limits of surface examination. As an artistic vehicle, the nude regained something like its ancient usefulness; but as distinguished both from the classical nude and from Gothic realism, the anatomy in the average Renaissance statue or picture is more intensive in its correctness. More than adequate for their immediate purpose of carrying content, such figures might often be mistaken for biological studies—which in fact they often were.

With respect to the representation of space, a working knowledge of perspective and foreshortening was replaced by stricter standards. The convergence of lines to a vanishing point, and consistency therein with regard to every object in the picture, was insisted upon with the utmost severity. The result was to call into being draftsmanship the like of which the world had never seen before. Even the lesser and minor artists of the Renaissance, if we judge them only by their capacity to represent, had a technique beyond praise. As for the great men, we need merely recall that Michelangelo sneered at Titian because "Venetians can not draw."

Atmospheric perspective was hardly susceptible of the same reduction to rules; conditions of light and atmosphere permit too many variations. Although often disregarded as superfluous by artists who preferred to paint in the mode of relief (pages 498–501), the subject nevertheless received thorough investigation. When precise linear perspective was combined with a scheme of tones calculated to induce the sensation of space and distance, representative painting attained an unprecedented power to convince. Pictures began to assume a verisimilitude that is startling even today when the world has had a long time to get used to it.

The convention of exact representation was only one way by which art reflected an acceptance of the world. The cognate idea of man's place within the environment found an outlet in various manifestations which, in one way or another and from this angle and that, expressed and recorded a new consciousness of the self. We have summed up that new consciousness with the phrase *human dignity,* which is an abstraction. Without denying that the grand abstractions run the show at all times, what of the particular notions which served during the Renaissance as impulses to govern action—including the creation of the works of art which stand as monuments to the hope and belief of that time?

Power was one of the values which came in with the Renaissance. Beginning with the 15th century, a certain measure of personal power (which is to say, independence and freedom) began to be looked upon as a human right. In the nature of the case, power could not be evenly distributed; it often came into direct conflict with the human dignity of the less powerful. Hence the forces of public order which have compelled most individuals to seek power in the milder form we call wealth, and to use it with varying degrees of moderation. But the forces of public order have never in themselves reflected a disbelief in the value of power, no matter how much they have restrained it. They have stood, rather, as the collective effort of individuals, each wanting to protect his own sphere of anarchy; to moderate individualism, that is, in the interest of human dignity.

In order to live as befits his dignity, the individual must have enough power to regulate the circumstances of his daily routine. During the Renaissance, countless persons began to ask for more than mere protection from the elements and a diet sufficient to keep them alive. They felt entitled to comfort and to health. Having that, it was taken for granted that a man would strive for still further improvement of his lot on earth: for a house that provided beauty in addition to comfort; for food that was pleasurable as well as nourishing; for clothes that were handsome over and above being adequate; for tools, utensils, and weapons which were articles of choice; and for a code of behavior that lent ceremony to the conduct of business both at home and abroad. Carried to an extreme, the process described results in display, a vice all too often illustrated in the history of art. In a more genial form, the combination of power and dignity has demonstrated elements of nobility, and has certainly affected art for the better.

In order to understand the art we are to study, we must appreciate that it most often expresses the feelings of persons who believed that man can realize his highest good by being true to himself. That, essentially, is an artistic concept. Everything hinges upon the individual's confidence that his body, his mind, and his personality constitute an artistic medium, potentially responsive to the creative imagination. The activities of his life are, by extension, a work of art also. His home and possessions logically become a setting. As a doctrine consciously held, the concept of life as a work of art awaited overt expression until the High Renaissance, when it was stated in words as

plainly as we state it here (page 551). The incipient force of the thought may
be discerned, however, much earlier. How else are we to account for the vital
quality of personality, as imponderable and as actual as an electric shock,
which literally stares out at us from even the slightest objects of Renaissance
art (Fig. 13.1)?

Success in the humanistic endeavor, as just described, has never been
universal; but whenever a man of special powers extended himself to the full
potential of his personality, the event was conspicuous and the man became
famous. Because fame, coming soon or late, almost always arrived for those
who approached the common ideal, humanity leaped to the assumption, perhaps an illogical one, that fame itself was a reward and a fulfillment. Even
power came to be thought of as a mere steppingstone to the higher good of
fame; few men have been content with the reality of the former if denied
the prominence that ordinarily goes with it.

Fig. 13.1 (opposite and right) Desiderio da Settignano. *A Princess of Urbino*. Berlin, Staatliche Museum. (Clarence Kennedy)

Fame has probably been the closest thing to an absolute known in the workaday world. "In my mind's eye," once wrote Lord Nelson, "I ever saw a radiant orb suspended which beckoned me onward to renown!" The same statement might have been made by any other successful man during the past five centuries; and in saying what he did, the great admiral gave expression to the point of view the modern world has substituted for the medieval beatitude of salvation. Unable to live very long, people have projected themselves toward eternity by doing something to get remembered by. As death approached, how many a man has laid down with comparative equanimity all that he ever had in the comfortable thought of leaving a reputation behind him!

The general acceptance of fame as a desideratum has been amply reflected in the history of art. The remarkable thing to contemplate is the complete success enjoyed by those wise enough to employ first-rate artists for the purpose of making their names and personalities immortal. The reader needs merely to page through the illustrations of this book to find numerous examples of men and women who would be totally forgotten except for the existence of statues and pictures; and in the periods to be covered below, let him note the increasing incidence of personal monuments. We refer not only to portraits, but to the identification of great enterprises with personalities— culminating in the colossal extravagance of Versailles (Fig. 15.2) built by Louis the 14th because his minister Colbert shrewdly propounded the policy that "a king is known by his monuments."

Another aspect of the belief in fame was the way in which works of art gradually became something more than a reflection of the desires of the patron, however great he might be. Giotto's frescoes are not remembered in the name of the donor Scrovegno; we think of them as the personal monument of the artist. Giotto was an early instance of what has been commonplace since. In this chapter, we embark upon an era when artists insisted upon signing, recording, and even boasting of their artistic achievements. Recognition was necessary or they could not breathe.

In that latter connection, it is important for the reader to understand that most of the good artists got prompt and generous recogntion. Giotto and Simone Martini, we have already mentioned; both lived and died as esteemed citizens of Italy and the world. Fra Angelico (1387–1455) found it difficult to keep free from the unsought honors and responsibilities which were thrust upon him. When Raphael died in 1520 and when Michelangelo died in 1564, the whole world mourned and the bodies lay in state like those of emperors. Rubens (1577–1640), remembered by us as a painter, was esteemed in his own time almost as much for his sagacity as a diplomat. Sir Joshua Reynolds (1723–1792) associated on terms of friendship with royalty and with the intellectual élite around Dr. Johnson. He also accumulated a very large fortune.

For something over 400 years, the profession of artist held out to ambitious young men a glittering hope for the future. The artists cited in the paragraph above were typical; any number of others might be named to draw the same illustration. It is important to appreciate that in every instance, the foundation of fame and fortune was neither birth nor luck, but good art; and it is specially important before we turn to specific matters to realize that the situation just summarized changed radically for the worse during the 19th century. Not until then did any good artist find himself compelled to sacrifice a single comfort or decency of life as the cost of doing the work he wanted to do. Not until a hundred years ago, more or less, did any great artist lack for money and friends. Because neither the present author, the present reader, nor any living artist has witnessed anything like the conditions of art during the Renaissance and later, the human tendency to judge from our own experience must be sternly governed.

As he considers what we have set forth above, the reader must be forcefully reminded that wherever we have referred to *man* we have meant not the human race, but the population of Western Europe and its derivatives in North and South America. The philosophy of humanism was peculiarly a European product. It was often debased into materialism, and has been in that form a sanction for the worst kind of behavior. In innumerable instances, however, humanism has brought about the results visualized by its most ardent advocates.

During the past few centuries, European culture has been permitted to maintain an autochthonous growth. The products and the customs of Europe have often moved outward to affect other regions; but there has been little influence, and until World War II certainly no impact, from the other direction. The present indications, if we may be permitted a guess, are that the Renaissance ended in 1914. Certainly 20th-century art betokens a change in the standards described above; but to that matter, we must return in Chapter 17.

THE FLEMISH SCHOOL OF THE 15TH CENTURY

Realism was the most important feature of all European art during the 15th century. There were two main centers of production, Flanders and Italy. Donatello (page 487) was the dominant figure at Florence, and that city was by far the most important center on the peninsula. Almost exactly contemporary with him was Jan van Eyck (about 1380–1441), who with his brother Hubert (page 447) founded the Flemish School and set the style for all the art north of the Alps. Because his work continues without a break the tradition of Late Gothic realism, we shall deal with it first.

The most famous monument connected with the name Van Eyck is the altarpiece of *The Adoration of the Lamb,* colloquially known as the Ghent Altarpiece, set in place in the church of St. John (now St. Bavon's) at Ghent during the month of May, 1432. The work is a very large triptych, with two side panels hinged to open out in panoramic fashion, or to close from either hand and thus cover the middle section. Paintings appear on both sides; and depending on how we count them, some twenty subjects or more are depicted. It will be seen that the monument is not a picture, but a collection of pictures. For that reason, and because the handling of detail is meticulous and minute, the illustrations so often published in books of normal size probably do more harm than good in showing the reader what this work looks like. Rather than

Fig. 13.2   The brothers Van Eyck. The Ghent Altarpiece. 1432. Ghent, St. Bavon's. (Paul Bijtebier)

attempt inadequate illustration here, we refer the reader to several places where he can find good colored plates, fairly large in scale.*

As we find it today, the main face of the Altarpiece has two registers (Fig. 13.2). The upper consists of seven separate panels, of which five are tightly filled, each by a large figure seen in close-up. There are five panels in the lower tier; and in considerable stylistic contrast to the upper, these panels show a deep landscape, continuous across the five, peopled by numerous small figures seen rather far away. The bearded Christ in the middle panel above

---

* Leo van Puyvelde, *The Holy Lamb*. Paris & Brussels, Marion Press, 1947.
  Emile Renders, *Jean van Eyck*. Brussels, 1950.
  Ludwig Baldass, *Jan van Eyck*. Phaidon Press, 1952.
  Life Magazine, Vol. 26, No. 16 (April 18, 1949) has a short explanatory article accompanied by colored plates.

is on axis with the lamb below; thus it is possible to construe the upper register as heavenly.

There is no denying, however, that the juxtaposition is anything but comfortable, and the reason is a simple one. Namely, the numerous panels which form the present Ghent Altarpiece were probably never intended to go together. According to an inscription on the frame, the work was commenced by Hubert van Eyck, and finished by his brother Jan. Hubert died at Ghent in September, 1426, at which time Jan was in Spain on a mission for the Duke of Burgundy. The supposition is that Jan, when he returned, was pressed by the donor to complete the commission, but was also very much occupied with his official duties. The guess, therefore, is that Jan finished up the pictures he found in his brother's shop, and assembled them into an arrangement of which the best we can say is that it offers a certain iconographical coherence.

The iconography of the picture in the lower register is of special interest, and requires explanation. There is no agreement among scholars as to particulars; but the imagery certainly has something to do with the following sources. Some of it apparently reflects John I:29, and the 7th, 14th, and 19th chapters of the Book of Revelation. It seems also to have been influenced by Jacobus de Voragine's *Golden Legend;* and the reader will do well to peruse his chapter on the Feast of All Saints, where he describes a vision seen by the sacristan of St. Peter's. Certain details thereof appear to be reflected in the picture.

Insofar as the meaning may be summed up briefly, the theme has to do with the idea of redemption through the Blood of the Lamb. An altar and a fountain are placed on the central axis of the main panel. The Lamb stands on the altar. From his breast, a stream of blood flows into a chalice; this, presumably, becomes (by a mystic process) the water issuing from the fountain below, upon the base of which we find an inscription adapted from the 22nd chapter of Revelation: "This is the water of the river of life proceeding out of the throne of God and of the Lamb."

Angels kneel on the grass around the altar; some swing censers and others carry the instruments of the Passion. Four processions converge toward the sacred area. From the left come Prophets and Gentiles, followed by Knights of Christ and Just Judges. From the right, Apostles and Confessors, followed by Hermits and Pilgrims. A group of Virgin Martyrs is seen approaching from the right-hand middle distance; and a group of male martyrs from the left. Out behind, a superb landscape opens up into the vastness of the sky, the horizon line being broken by fanciful buildings in the Late Gothic style.

Among the seven pictures of the upper register, the *Adam* and *Eve* are

Figs. 13.3–4 (left and above) Jan van Eyck. *Madonna with Chancellor Rolin*. About 1436. Paris, Louvre. (Giraudon)

the most important. Neither is in the least a pleasant figure, but either or both may be said to constitute a historical landmark of the greatest importance. For the first time since antiquity, the public found itself confronted with two human nudes rendered on a large scale with meticulous accuracy by an artist who was technically competent to do it. It may be contended that neither figure demonstrates any significant use of the revealed muscles as a vehicle for the communication of an emotion or state of being (as the Greeks had done, and as the Italians were almost immediately to do), but no one can quarrel with Sir Martin Conway's passing remark that the work literally bristles with intelligence.

The special flavor of Jan van Eyck's work is best discerned in his single panels of simpler iconography, of which the *Madonna with Chancellor Rolin* (Figs. 13.3–4) may be taken as typical. The figure of the Madonna is somewhat heavier than average, but is otherwise of the type that remained popular in Flanders for a hundred years thereafter. The peculiar arrangement of the hair (tight across the head and caught back from the ears, but hanging free in a long bob over the shoulders) remained constant for a very long time, as did the high-waisted costume, with a voluminous over-mantle which spreads out over the floor and gives the whole figure a more or less triangular silhouette.

Two important features of the Flemish style are well illustrated by Figures 13.3 and 13.4. It was a matter of pride with these artists to describe every detail with the utmost intensity. The smallest wrinkle in the skin, even the stubble of the beard, received an analysis reserved by most painters for the tonal modulations of an entire mountain. The work most have been done with the aid of a lens, and we may therefore name the Flemish convention in that respect as *microscopic*. For the equally meticulous description of distant landscape, *telescopic* is more expressive. As technical terms, both words are useful whenever we want an antonym for *impressionism* (page 164). Call it microscopic or telescopic as the case demands, the more closely we examine Flemish paintings, the more we see.

For the rendering of space, the Van Eycks originated a color convention that remained standard in northern painting for a century and more. Natural boundaries of one kind and another were usually contrived in order to divide the setting into a well defined foreground, middle ground, and distance. Warm tones and strong contrasts of hue were reserved for the foreground. The middle ground ordinarily contained a mixture of warm and cool tones, neutralized somewhat in order to reduce the contrasts. In the distance, warm tones were avoided altogether, and everything was pulled into a common tonality of rather strong blue-green.

The sequence corresponds with natural fact to the extent that contrasts diminish in the distance, but this particular arrangement of colors is rarely observed in actuality. Special conditions, however, occasionally produce it. When the air has been cleaned by a recent rain storm, and while the sun is still obscured by white clouds and the light highly diffused, the distance often takes on the same intense blue-green we see in Flemish painting. The phenomenon is unlikely to occur unless the trees are in leaf.

No on can say whether the tradition is correct which names the brothers Van Eyck as the inventors of oil painting, but they were surely the first important masters to use that vehicle extensively and explore its possibilities to the full. The precise nature of their medium still defies analysis, although several modern researchers have arrived at similar results. The process was nothing like the linseed oil painting in common use today, for which reason a brief summary of the method will prove illuminating.

Most Flemish paintings are on wooden panels. First, the surface of the panel was covered with a ground of fine cement (called *gesso*), which gave

Fig. 13.5 Jan van Eyck. *Saint Barbara.* Brush drawing on white ground. Monochrome. Blue glaze on sky probably added later. Antwerp, Musée des Beaux Arts.

a smooth surface. The entire picture was then drawn in ink, and the modeling carried out in neutral monotone. The appearance at that stage would be very much as we see it in the little *Saint Barbara* (Fig. 13.5).

The next step was to apply color. Most of the Flemish paints were transparent; properly, they should be referred to as *varnishes,* or *glazes.* They were apparently used not in a liquid state, but thick and stiff like glue. After each field had received its glaze, the viscosity of the latter permitted prolonged work with the brush. The glaze could be made thinner here and thicker there simply by stroking it with the bristles, and the result would be to refine the tonal modulations already established by the monotone painting below.

The system was very long drawn out. Today, when there has been so much emphasis upon the value of spontaneity, the Flemish oil technique seems unbelievably tedious, but it had certain virtues that deserve emphasis. It produced pictures which still gleam like jewels; the problem of preserving them is not a problem of preserving the paint, but a problem of maintaining the wooden panels. Correction, which is so easy and so much abused when painters use opaque pigments and linseed oil, was so difficult as to be impractical; that fact made it necessary for the painter to visualize the completed picture in minute detail before he began. As compared with methods which permit the artist to be more easygoing, the Flemish procedure was admittedly rigid, but it induced a thoroughness and maturity of consideration which make the pictures seem "right" in a way that is all too rare. For those technically interested, moreover, there is a special beauty in the precision with which every surface, however small, is intimately expressive of the master's intention.

♦ *Painting in the Mode of the Total Visual Effect* Flemish oil offered still another quality of interest to painters and patrons who were literally inspired by the ideal of representation. With respect to making strong intensities of hue available at low levels of value, the new vehicle was and remains second only to mosaic and enamel. In other words, oil lacked the limitations inherent in both fresco and tempera paintings; and its qualities seem to have invited painting in *the mode of the total visual effect*. Jan van Eyck, if not the inventor of that mode, was the first master to make good use of it. The picture which most perfectly exemplifies his accomplishment is the portrait of John Arnolfini and his wife (Fig. 13.6).*

The phrase mode of the total visual effect was added to our terminology by the researches of Denman W. Ross and Arthur Pope.† Ross and Pope conducted a general exploration into the theory behind European painting. They gave learned attention to the properties of the different media which had been available to painters of different schools and periods, and they inquired in the most meticulous fashion into the relation between the painter and the facts of the visual world. They came to the conclusion that virtually every picture in the immense catalogue conformed in its technique to one of four fundamental systems designated by them as the modes of painting. Sweeping though their findings were, their validity has been attested by a significant absence of challenge.

The modes they recognized were: (1) *the mode of line and flat tone,* (2) *the mode of relief,* (3) *the mode of the total visual effect,* and (4) *the Venetian mode.* The mode of line and flat tone was mentioned in connection with Paleolithic painting and needs no additional explanation here. We shall deal with the mode of the total visual effect at once, and refer the reader ahead for material about the other two modes (pages 498 and 621).

With respect to tonal relations, any painter who uses the mode of the total visual effect puts himself in the position of the objective realist (page 18). As the name of the mode indicates, he accepts the light and color of

* The terminology used in the paragraphs below is explained in Appendix II.
† The latest and most complete exposition will be found in Mr. Pope's *The Language of Drawing and Painting,* Harvard University Press, 1949.

nature in the same spirit which makes the realistic sculptor accept the structure of the human body. Whatever he sees, he construes as an artistic rule, and the first thing to look for in pictures that conform to this mode is a specific indication of the source or direction from which the light comes. Something of the kind is almost always included, as though to tell us the painter has obeyed the rules.

Objects and parts of objects are made to cast their shadows in a fashion that is orderly and consistent with the light source indicated, but a word of caution is necessary lest the reader apply that criterion too literally. Reflected light sometimes plays hob with what seems at first to be the simple logic of illumination, often reversing the shadow pattern that might be predicted for a particular field. The principle involved is nevertheless as stated.

Fig. 13.6 (opposite and above) Jan van Eyck. *John Arnolfini and His Wife.* 1434. London, National Gallery.

Examination of the human form, or any other object of complex shape, when seen in a good light, will reveal that the normal eye under normal conditions does not, and indeed cannot, see everything that is there. It is difficult or impossible to follow the contours within the areas of shadow; and if we are honest with ourselves, we must admit that our knowledge of shape within the darks rests more upon inference than upon perception. The effect just mentioned is somewhat enhanced by the instinctive tendency of the eye to accommodate itself not to the darkest areas in view, but to the brightest. Pictures executed in the mode of the total visual effect usually take account of the phenomenon just described. In the darker areas, detail is made increasingly vague, and sometimes blacked out altogether.

Because of the pitifully short value range available in paint, it is obvious

that there had to be discovered some rational way to render the tonal relations of nature on the surface of the canvas or panel. Those painters who have
made best use of the mode of the total visual effect seem to have looked upon
the contrast between the natural value scale and the painter's not as a disaster,
but as a proportion. Unable to make direct use of the former, they could
nevertheless transpose it into paint by an act of just and systematic compression. Thus, the pigments in the pictures do not and cannot contrast with
each other as the local tones do in nature, but it is possible to maintain their
lesser contrasts in much the same relation.

It will be noticed that painters using this mode did not, when modeling
a field of white, allow themselves the full range of values. They kept the
darker shadows in the white field up as high as the middle value, or thereabouts. Conversely, when modeling a black drapery, the convexities of the
folds (which receive the strongest and most direct illumination) hardly go
above the middle value unless, in a special situation, it was requisite to
indicate a bright highlight reflecting from an otherwise dark surface.

With respect to the modulation of hue, pictures in the mode of the total
visual effect are consistent with the action of colors as observed in nature.
The paints are brought to strongest intensity where the illumination is
strongest, and the shadows are gradually made more neutral as they become
darker. This particular detail of technique has a representational usefulness
more important than might be supposed. One hears a great deal, especially
in the art schools, about colors that "come forward" and colors that "recede."
It is true that certain tones are more useful than others for indicating spatial
displacement forward and back, but it is suggested that intensity, as such, has
received too little recognition as an operative factor in the representational
scheme.

It will be seen that the mode of the total visual effect depends upon an
unbroken chain of logic through which the mechanics of a painting may be
traced back to the data of visual experience. It was in the order of events
that such a method was worked out during the 15th century when representation challenged artists because so few of them could do it.

There is certainly no earlier and there is still no more remarkable
demonstration of the mode than the Arnolfini portrait. The subject was extensive. Many fields were involved, each with its local tone and its special
relation to the source of light. The play of light was greatly complicated by
reflections, and by the capacity of different surfaces to reflect. The technical
problem was, in fact, too ramified and difficult to permit adequate description
in words; but even in our small book plates, it is immediately plain that the
subtlest variations of value and hue were rendered with an unbelievable
consistency and precision. The figures and objects in the picture give no

suggestion of colored sculpture. There is also no suggestion of light controlled in some unnatural way. Thus, Arnolfini and his wife (unimportant people that they were) gained a measure of immortality by their presence in a painting which stands as one of the first instances in history where an artist was able to arrive at a complete realization of existence in air and space.

The merits of the mode of the total visual effect are plain enough. It is the one and only straightforwardly "natural" way to paint, and the only kind of painting which even attempts to maintain a one-to-one relationship between the picture and what the eye actually sees in nature. Such being the case, it will perhaps surprise the reader to be told there has been very little of it. Jan van Eyck's followers used the mode, but less consistently than he; and it was popular again in 17th-century Holland (pages 740ff). Most other painters have preferred to work in a different manner; and the reason is not far to seek. Any attempt to render the total visual effect necessarily binds the artist to a number of rules which, if true of the actual world, need not be true of painting. Emphasis, suppression, and every other technique of emotional expression may be foreclosed if one insists that the painted scene be kept in strict correspondence with the very same scene as it might appear to the eye in the real world. Hence the popularity of other modes which proved accurate enough to satisfy the demand for representation, but were more flexible.

♦ *Followers of the Van Eycks*   The work of the Van Eycks started a tradition that lasted a hundred years, and their influence extended over an immense territory. In fact, their style dominated the taste of all Europe until the end of the 15th century, and in some places even longer. Only in Italy was there enough independence of mind to produce artists who did not attempt to imitate the Flemish manner.

The most important master in the period immediately following the Van Eycks was Rogier van der Weyden (about 1400–1464), sometimes called Roger de La Pasture. A more introspective painter than the Van Eycks, he was peculiarly concerned with the element of tragedy in the Christian story, and with interpretive portraiture.

Hans Memling (about 1433–1494) and Hugo van der Goes (about 1430–1482) stood out as leaders in the next generation. The latter has a special distinction because he was the author of the *Portinari Altarpiece,* a large panel depicting the Adoration of the Shepherds, now in the Uffizi. As the name implies, it was done for an Italian patron. He shipped it to Florence, probably about 1477. One sometimes hears it said that its arrival introduced the Italians to oil painting, a statement which is untrue by about one generation. It is no exaggeration, however, to mention that the wonderful Flemish colors, to say nothing of the magnificent way in which space was represented, made a sensation in the town which was then the cultural capital of the world. For the next two generations, the student-painters in Italy studied Hugo van der Goes with almost the same care they accorded the work of their own Masaccio.

The latest Flemish master who can be described as a Van Eyck derivative was Gerard David (about 1460–1523). If we take any earlier Madonna from the Flemish School and compare it with his *Rest on the Flight into Egypt,* now in the National Gallery at Washington, it will be easy to draw up a long list of similarities. There are a few differences, but they are not immediately obvious.

It was not until the arrival of Hieronymus Bosch (about 1462–1516) that the North produced a master of sufficient force to make a significant change in the style set by the Van Eycks. His work is dealt with in the next chapter.

Between the art of 15th-century Flanders and that of Germany, there existed the most obvious parallels. The sculptors Veit Stoss, Adam Kraft, and Tilman Riemenschneider all used a figure style similar to the Flemish painters. The same thing may be said of Conrad Witz, a remarkable painter of light and space, who worked at Geneva and Basel. Because there is some doubt about direct contact between Switzerland and Flanders, Witz's career serves to strengthen the probability that 15th-century realism rose like the tide, being caused by no man. Martin Schongauer, who did his best work in black and white prints, continued the Van Eyck tradition until the very end of the 15th century. He spent most of his life at Colmar.

France during the 15th century was likewise an artistic province of Flanders. Nicholas Froment, Enguerrand Charenton, and the unknown Master of Moulins can be distinguished by the expert as French; but the learned often overlook the obvious: in all essentials, those masters were provincial Flemings. The anonymous artist who painted the famous *Pietà of Villeneuve-les-Avignon,* now in the Louvre, and the painter Jean Fouquet were men of a different stripe. Their Flemish affinities are evident, but both were capable of strong abstraction in a startlingly modern manner.

The recent researches of Chandler Post have furnished the world for the first time with an authoritative and reasonably complete catalogue of Spanish painting of the 15th century. From that great effort of scholarship, the most important conclusion to be drawn is that Spain, like France and Germany, was largely dependent upon Flanders for the style of its painting. Jan van Eyck had been there in 1428–1429. He came not to paint, but to negotiate for a royal marriage; but his visit established the prestige of Flemish art in Spain. Paintings and tapestries from the Low Countries were continuously imported; and even Isabella, an enthusiastic collector of Rogier van der

Fig. 13.7   Donatello. Details from *Lo Zuccone* ("the pumpkin head"). Probably intended for a Job or a Habakkuk. Florence, Giotto's Tower. (Brogi)

Weyden, preferred to hire Flemings rather than Spaniards. It was no accident, therefore, that native masters like Fernando Gallego and Bartolommeo Bermejo, both active toward the middle of the century, imitated the Northern style.

THE EARLY RENAISSANCE IN ITALY

♦ *Donatello and the Style of the Early Renaissance*   Realism was as strong in Italy as in the North during the 15th century. To a surprising degree, any attempt to characterize Italian realism tends to evoke the same words and phrases already used in our treatment of the Flemish masters, but every person of ordinary sensibility knows there was a great difference between Jan van Eyck and the Italians. The difference is not easy to locate or describe, but it will be felt the moment one makes a comparison between the figure of Arnolfini (Fig. 13.6) and *Lo Zuccone,* shown in Figure 13.7. The comparison has to do with content. The *Zuccone* seems far less to be the chattel, and much less the victim of the world. Every muscle is instinct with power, and if the

Fig. 13.8 Donatello. Detail from a Madonna in the Victoria and Albert Museum, London.

face is wrinkled with the struggle of an intense life, one feels that the effort still goes on and that there is strength to make the effort. The difference between the Italians and the Northerners seems to be that the Italians expected to get somewhere. It is evident that humanism and individualism were more vital in Italy.

In the matter of style—and let us consider it for the moment merely in its physical and mechanical aspect—there was considerable difference between Italy and Flanders. Flemish realism originated with painters. The leading Italian realists were sculptors, pre-eminently the sculptor Donatello (about 1385–1466). More than any other man of his generation, he had the peculiar power of impressing himself upon his contemporaries. Where he led, other artists followed. With the significant exception of Masaccio (page 502), the style of almost every 15th-century Italian, sculptors and painters alike, resembled the style of Donatello.

The style of Italy during the Early Renaissance is epitomized in the numerous half-length Madonnas by Donatello. Introduced by him at an early date in his long career, the conception became a formula repeated with minor variations by almost every artist in Italy. Figure 13.8 shows a detail from one of Donatello's own Madonnas; but in order to illustrate his influence upon others and because Professor Clarence Kennedy's peculiarly sensitive photograph is available, we choose to summarize the features of the type from Figure 13.9, a Madonna in similar style by Donatello's close follower, Desiderio da Settignano.

Whether we find it in sculpture or painting (and we shall presently see that the same thing was also true of architecture), the style of the Early Renaissance was always conceived as low relief. We possess, of course, many free-standing busts and statues; but even upon those, details of every kind were rendered with a minimum of projection and often by what amounts to a linear method (Figs. 13.1–2). The work, that is to say, was felt as an interplay of line and surface, with very little movement in and out, and with a careful avoidance of broad, dark shadows. As expressed in sculpture, the modeling characteristic of the period often became a tour de force of slightness. In Desiderio's Madonna and in some of Donatello's pictorial relief (Fig. 13.10) the subtlety of surface is prodigious. Ideal conditions of light are requisite, indeed, for the simple reading of such modeling, a truth indicated by the extreme rarity of satisfactory photographs thereof.

The world was young in Italy during the 15th century, and there is no better proof of it than the figure style used by painters and sculptors whenever left to their own devices. The typical Madonna of the period was always a girl. Some times, she was as young as seventeen; and until the time of Leonardo (page 571), it is surely hard to cite a Mary who might be older than twenty-five. The canon of proportions was tall and slender. Such women might stand 5 feet, 6 inches tall, and weigh 110 pounds. Lithe rather than thin, the type is an active one; flesh and muscles were always shown in good training, and the texture of the skin, while often delicate, suggests the natural bloom of youth rather than an effort to idealize.

Donatello and his followers gave these youthful Madonnas contemporary costumes. It is evident that 15th-century realism governed even the sweetest subject, for the artists were mechanically accurate in the representation of clothing. One can always tell what garments were being worn, how they were made, and where they buttoned or tied. This is worth mentioning for later contrast with the costumes of the High Renaissance, when clothing of the ordinary kind gave place to generalized undulations of drapery.

It is notable, also, that the favorite costumes of the 15th century seem to have been of rather light, soft material. Most artists rendered them with innumerable small hollows and ridges, much as lighter and looser stuffs tend to wrinkle. Perhaps a concession to realistic accuracy, the effect is often far from rhythmic and in some instances unpleasantly busy.

Such were the physical conventions of the style of the Early Renaissance. With remarkable uniformity, a long series of artists adhered to the formula; but within its limits, a great variety of personal expression was possible.

Fig. 13.9 Desiderio da Settignano. *Madonna and Child*. Turin, Pinacoteca. (Clarence Kennedy)

Fig. 13.10 Donatello. Detail from *Saint Peter Receiving the Keys from Christ*. Marble relief. London, Victoria and Albert Museum.

The high intellectuality of Donatello's Madonnas was peculiar to him. So was the intensity with which he so often imbued them, as though the whole tragic narrative were foreknown and too distressful to bear. Other artists, while producing Madonnas substantially the same in every physical particular, ran through an immense range of spiritual content, or lack of it. Filippo Lippi (page 534) made the Virgin a lyrically pretty girl who turns out, upon long acquaintance with the pictures, to be nothing else. Mino da Fiesole virtually defined the word *dainty,* and Desiderio the word *winsome*. The learned and introspective Botticelli (page 535) penetrated to the truth like Donatello, but made it a holy mystery rather than a human tragedy.

It is necessary to add a word about a common quality of content which remained constant in Italian art during the entire Early Renaissance, regardless of the shallowness or profundity of the individual master. Fifteenth-century Italian art was *intimate*. Pictures, statues, and reliefs were almost never above life-size; most of them are comparatively small. Almost all were designed to be shown at the eye level. When looking at them, the natural impulse is to walk up within three or four feet, and often to come closer for the inspection of special areas. The persons seen in painting and relief were brought forward in the frame, as it were, and the statues are similarly easy to construe as persons in the same room with us. Attitudes, postures, costumes, and facial expressions lack self-consciousness; the guarded dignity of a cere-monial appearance is absent. The cumulative effect of all these things is the impression that one has come into personal relation, and has been permitted to share the private feelings of the sitter for a portrait, the Madonna, a saint, or anyone else who appeared in the art of the period. Such an experience is peculiarly endearing, and it is no wonder that the Early Renaissance in Italy is specially popular with American students, themselves born with a taste for informality. As a historical phenomenon, the quality just reviewed should be kept in mind as an element of contrast between the work of the Early and that of the High Renaissance.

It took a great man to have so large an influence in the brilliant period of the Italian 15th century. Perhaps the key to Donatello's stature is suggested by the range and variety of his art. He was in the forefront of the general investigation into the techniques of representation; indeed, he was often the first to conquer a particular problem. He handled almost every type of content. No other artist so taxes our capacity to feel, for to know Donatello is to have experienced almost every different emotion in the catalogue. His accomplishment, in a word, was greater than that of any other 15th-century artist; and leaving much to the future studies of the reader, we shall have to content ourselves with a few examples selected to illustrate the numerous ramifications of his work.

Realism runs like a guiding theme through all his production, but it would appear that classical inspiration of a special kind, absent in the north of Europe, helped him on his way. As a youngster, he took a trip to Rome with Brunelleschi (page 509); and there, at a formative period of his life, he was confronted with the achievements of Roman realism. There is no doubt that the inspiration received was cogent. There is equally no doubt that ancient Rome never produced a sculptor of Donatello's caliber. The penetrating glance of the *Zuccone* (Fig. 13.7), the terrific arms, and the muscles tensed in readiness for the mind's next order—all these things separate it from the workaday output of the Roman portrait factories. Physically speaking, the representation is unsparing; but a concern with spiritual mean-ing (frequent in all Florentine art) permits the most unlovely body to par-ticipate in God's image.

There are a number of other works equally scientific with regard to anatomy, but completely different in content. The well-known *Saint George,* in a niche on Or San Michele, is still an unsurpassed exposition of man in his twenties, the time maturity asserts itself just as the body is strongest and

Figs. 13.11–12 Donatello. (left) Detail from the *Annunciation*. About 1433. Florence, Santa Croce. (right) *Feast of Herod*. 1421–1427. Siena, Baptistery. (Brogi; Anderson)

most responsive. The Mary of the sandstone *Annunciation* in Santa Croce is a feminine counterpart for the *Saint George,* but even more particular attention should be directed to the infants who stand as acroteria above the pedimental frame (Fig. 13.11). They were among the very first since antiquity to be accurately rendered. They are devastating when compared with the sublimated children of some other artists—Sir Joshua Reynolds, for example—which fact suggests that the truth can charm as cogently as it sometimes chides. The architectural frame of the *Annunciation* is notable in itself. All the details are of classical origin, but their relative size and combination is original and free.

Not satisfied with studies of the single figure, Donatello extended his researches to embrace the entire field of pictorial sculpture. An early and now sadly weathered example is the *Saint George and the Dragon,* originally the predella for the statue of Saint George; it was done in 1416, a date which invites comparisons. Even better for study is the *Feast of Herod* (Fig. 13.12), a relief specially interesting as an example of representative strategy. The displacement of things into the distance is rendered by four stages in the lowering of the relief, each stage being assigned a particular remove from the foreground. Architectural barriers separate the several vertical planes suggested by the arrangement, making the spatial relationships not only legible, but almost inevitable convincing. *Saint Peter Receiving the Keys from Christ* (Fig. 13.10) may be cited as typical of the master's more mature and

Figs. 13.13–14 (left and opposite) Donatello. *Gattamelata*. 1446–1453. Height of horse and rider: about 9 feet. Padua, Piazza Sant'Antonio. (Brogi; Anderson)

confident productions in the field of spatial representation; but, as stated, the modulations of surface are so elaborately cunning that the work is a failure unless given the benefit of special lighting.

Monumental works of art were rare during the 15th century, but there were a few. It was natural that Donatello should have received the commission for the most ambitious undertaking of the entire period. We refer to the *Gattamelata* (Figs. 13.13–14), the first full-scale bronze equestrian statue since Roman antiquity, and still the greatest on earth.

The *Gattamelata* is at first a puzzling work of art. It lacks the great crashing drama with which the High Renaissance and the Baroque attempted to lift us toward the sublime. Although it is a very large statue indeed, the whole method and purpose fit the wonderful, intimate perception of the 15th century, and contrast with the heroics of the so-called "Grand Style."

It may be said that the *Gattamelata*, when seen for the first time, is not even impressive. Everybody begins by wondering why a man on so high a horse cannot put on a better show; but by that erroneous first impression, we gain an insight into the mind of the author. It presently becomes evident that the significance hinges upon the incongruity of scale between horse and rider; and that the apparent absence of any performance by either is in fact the meaningful situation with which we are presented. The general sits his mount

with a stiff grace, a lifetime of military horsemanship behind him. Obviously his pose was merely habitual, and he himself unconscious of it. The bridle rein lies slack from the left hand, while the right raises the baton in a quiet, conventional gesture. The great horse underneath is tense with nervous power, a volcano of energy ready to explode into action at any instant.

By what authority does the man sit so calmly in the saddle, directing, controlling, and containing strength so much greater than his own? A look at the face will give the answer. It is full of rational intelligence: the memory, the experience, and the judgment the horse lacks and no animal can have. In general terms, the statue may be described as a profound demonstration of humanism; but with greater particularity, we should point out that the content is neither formal, idealized, nor ceremonial. It would be hard to find a more public place than the Paduan square where the pedestal is raised; but even so, almost as doctors are admitted into the affairs of their patients, we are shown the private, inward character of a man.

The works so far considered will give the reader a sample of Donatello's realism in its more judicial and naturalistic aspect. Differing as they do in detail, all the examples cited above show us the artist more or less governed by the normal manifestations of anatomy and scenery. But from time to time throughout his extended career, Donatello projected his theories far beyond

Fig. 13.15 Donatello. *Repentant Magdalen*. Florence, Baptistery. (Brogi)

the ordinary limitations. In a number of his most powerful productions, he extended realism well past anything that may be construed as objective analysis either of character or of form. As distinct from his rational faculty and his judgment, he permitted his feelings to enter into the act of creation. He crossed, that is to say, the vague boundary line which separates realism from expressionism.

The emaciated statue of the youthful Saint John, now in the Bargello, is a case in point. How are we to reconcile such things with the fact that it was Donatello himself, and nobody else, who started the Renaissance tradition of the human body emerging in glory from its medieval mortification? And yet the *Saint John* was but a way station on the road Donatello traveled.

At some indefinite date toward the end of his life, he carved the *Repentant Magdalen* (Fig. 13.15), a wooden statue in the Baptistery at Florence. It is impossible to deal with that piece of work in moderate terms. Beauty, in any ordinary denotation, is a word quite out of place. For the casual observer who usually associates art with relaxation and entertainment, a view of the *Magdalen* is equivalent to the whip of an insult. Even the serious student is likely to find the imagery shocking. The work is not genre. The intention is foreign to the grotesque. All the familiar formulas fail to explain it, including the one which makes realism a research enterprise. Try as we will to escape facing the question, the savage fascination of the statue forces us to account for the legitimacy of the hideous in art. Without suggesting that the following words solve so vexed a question, they may at least be helpful.

An artist of Donatello's experience must have been conversant with the nature of his medium. He would appreciate, for instance, that the poet asks the reader to supply most of the images, and that the reader may escape the poet by choosing his own psychical distance when threatened with shock and offense. It is, on the other hand, the privilege of the sculptor to choose his own imagery, and his medium delivers it to the eye of the public in the most tangible manner available. For that very reason, Lessing urged in the *Laocoön* that sculptors apply the whip gently and discreetly, with a courtly regard for the sensibilities of human beings.

Why then did Donatello smash down all the standards of artistic decorum? Successful, honored, and admired—and knowing we cannot escape—what vengeance did he seek? Why does he make us look, holding us there with all his power, disgusted as we are and in pain? For it is evident that the model for the *Magdalen* was a female cadaver, and that with a technique few sculptors could equal, Donatello chose to confront us with a walking death apparently capable of question, answer, and ethical responsibility.

In searching for the truth within the revolting spectacle, we may make something of the fact that the *Magdalen* was chosen for placement in the Baptistery. It was there that infants were first admitted to society, to begin the career inevitably ending in physical decadence and death, and quite as surely including the crucifixion of sin and repentance. There was a certain propriety in predicting the end at the beginning, and a spiritual realism in so grim a reminder at the ceremony where all is innocence and joy.

But the desperate extreme of the *Magdalen* was not unique in Donatello's later work, and some more general motive must be sought for what amounted to a policy of getting after us to inflict upon hearts and nerves a ruthless exacerbation. If a satisfactory explanation is ever forthcoming, the reasons will probably be found in the subconsciousness only now being revealed by psychological research. Among those findings is the proposition that the will to die, like the more familiar will to survive, is latent in the population. Suicide, it has been suggested, results not from impulse but from a pattern of desires traceable far back into the childhood and heredity of an unfortunate minority. Viewed in the light of such ideas, it becomes evident, pending a definite explanation, that Donatello's *Magdalen* may be assigned to needs more profound than morbid. Once again, it would appear that we have an example of artistic insight penetrating centuries ahead of science, and finding an expression beyond present understanding.

After such a citation of major achievement, short though it is in relation to the subject, a summary of Donatello's standing in history would seem redundant. It is nevertheless true that certain important aspects of his genius are inconspicuous and need to be remarked upon.

First, our sense for dates must be kept unusually on the alert or we shall forget that, in point of historical fact, Donatello was a "primitive" artist. His original efforts, that is to say, had to begin with technical problems. To appreciate the state of Florentine sculpture during Donatello's youth, the reader will have to investigate archeological byways ordinarily entered only by specialists in the field. Suffice it to say that ignorance is hardly too strong a word for describing Donatello's starting point. In the presence of supreme skill, as shown in the incomparable *Gattamelata,* it is almost impossible to believe that the competence before us commenced with primary research into such elementary matters as anatomy.

We expect a certain amount of crudity in the work of pioneers, but it is absent in Donatello. Even that is hardly so great a wonder as the variety of his output. He worked on every scale. He used almost every material in which sculpture can be made, and virtually every technique ever used. In the usual sense of the term, he had no style. Most artists, however good, tend to rely upon habitual formulae and modes of expression; Donatello changed his to suit almost every new work of art. Similarly, there is no particular tone or content to which we can tie him down, unless it be the intelligence that is always there, and the modesty that made him avoid parade.

♦ *Painting in the Mode of Relief* During the 15th century most Italian painters thought of their pictures as performing much the same function as a panel of low relief by Donatello or Desiderio. They had very little interest in the mode of the total visual effect. As we have seen (page 455) Giotto had not painted that way, and with the interesting exception of Antonello da Messina (1430–1479), scarcely any Italian ever did. Almost every Italian picture was executed in the technique recognized by Ross and Pope as the *mode of relief.*

The word *relief,* as just used, is not completely descriptive. We ordinarily think of it as indicating projection from a background. In order to understand what we are driving at, the reader must extend the application of the term. Painters who used the mode of relief followed in the footsteps of Giotto. They assigned philosophical priority to the tactile values. They considered painting and sculpture to be more or less interchangeable. Many of them were, in fact, consciously imitating sculptors. Some painters used a manner analogous to sculpture in low relief. Other works find their counterpart in high relief, and still others with sculpture in the full round.

The availability of pigment materials played a very important part in establishing and maintaining this particular way of painting. The oil vehicle was not available anywhere until invented in Flanders about 1400, and it remained almost unknown and unused in Italy for about seventy-five years thereafter. Before oil came into general use, wall paintings were executed in fresco, and panels in tempera. Both vehicles are subject to a sharp loss of intensity whenever darkened in the least. Any attempt to neutralize the shadows as the Van Eycks had done was bound to result in broad areas of gray. The darker the local tones, the greater the proportion of neutral— which is to say that the picture would be virtually without the appeal of color.

It became habitual, therefore, with workers in the mode of relief to put the full strength of the pigment wherever a dark tone was required. From there, they modeled up toward white. Sometimes they merely added more and more white to the original pigment. Sometimes they shifted first to a lighter hue, and then to one still more light, finally arriving somewhere near white at the very end of the gradation. Value-wise, the sequence conforms to the arrangement of tones in nature by putting the tints on the convexities of the drapery, and the shades down in the hollows. But with respect to intensities, the system quite reverses the order we observe in the world around us. For in nature (except for the "high lights"), hues are invariably most intense where the illumination is strongest.

The system of modeling just described has some advantages. With vehicles incapable of producing vivid color at low values, it made possible the production of pictures which, if not opulent in hue, are at least blond and gleaming. A more subtle matter has to do with the spatial implications of intense and neutral tones. In paintings of the sort we now discuss, the drawing of drapery and other details demands that we read certain parts as being further away than others, but the intense hues are in just those places. Our habit of feeling that intense colors "come forward" tends to soften the indications given by the drawing. But what seems to be a method of design at war with itself turns out to provide an added charm. The net result is to emphasize the flat surface of the painting, an effect in distinct harmony with the truth that all pictures exist in fact upon a vertical plane.

The mode of relief involved an almost complete disregard for natural conditions with respect to the action of light. An extreme instance is seen in a *Last Supper* (Fig. 13.16) by the Florentine painter Andrea Castagno. Ostensibly, the light in the picture comes from two windows pierced through the wall to our right. If so, the persons nearest the windows ought (by natural logic) to be more strongly illuminated than the figures remote from the win-

Fig. 13.16 Andrea del Castagno. *Last Supper*. 1445–1450. An interior painted in the mode of relief. Florence, Sant'Apollonia. (Alinari)

dows. Similarly, the figures located toward the source of light should cast shadows on those next removed. A general darkness, moreover, would necessarily obscure everything underneath the table.

But none of these things are true of the painting. The lower extremities of the figures, which we might expect to be lost in a great shadow, are revealed beneath the table in exactly as much light as everything else. There are no cast shadows anywhere; and all the way across the scene, each person is illuminated as generously as those right next the windows. In a word, the light is the same everywhere, a condition impossible in nature even when all the circumstances favor diffusion.

Such a painting can not be a transcription of a scene the painter saw, for it is impossible to see anything of the kind. What we have, rather, is a synthesis of many separate observations, each detail and each field of drapery having been studied under selected conditions of light. It goes without saying that the principle of selection depended upon the accurate revelation of shape. The light that suited best was the light that made most definite the contour of the convexities and hollows which give us a positive sensation of mass. The system is abstract and arbitrary, but it does emphasize the tactile values.

In their desire to realize objects as entities displacing space, many Italian painters deliberately overlooked the effect of atmosphere, which even on a clear day and even over moderate distances tends to soften outlines and reduce contrasts of hue. A glance at Figure 13.17 will illustrate the point. Distant buildings are diminished in size according to the rules of linear perspective, but each and every one is modelled with almost the same vigor and precision as figures in the immediate foreground. The affinities between such painting and contemporary sculpture will be made evident by comparing Benozzo's frescoes with the bronze panels of relief done by the sculptor Ghiberti (Fig. 13.25). It is worth remembering that Benozzo was for some time an assistant in Ghiberti's shop.

Figure 13.18 will demonstrate in similar fashion the rather literal way in which so many 15th-century paintings virtually duplicated the style of Donatello. It is the work of Carlo Crivelli (about 1430–1495), a somewhat unenlightened artist with faultless technique. Instead of darkening the shadows according to the way shadows act in nature, Crivelli maintained the lighting at a level sufficient to reveal every contour he happened to be interested in. No amount of rationalization will explain, in terms of natural cause and effect, lighting of this kind. It is obvious the artist cared nothing for the laws of the visual world, and everything for the expressive power of shape. As thought to emphasize his method, Crivelli often rendered details in actual low relief—as here, the Madonna's crown and necklace. No one feels any sense of incongruity; in fact, most people do not even notice it.

Fig.13.17 Benozzo Gozzoli. *Journey of the Magi*. Detail. 1459. A landscape painted in the mode of relief. Florence, Medici Palace chapel. (Alinari)

♦ *Masaccio* Masaccio, the first great painter of the Renaissance in Italy, was one of the most remarkable characters in history. Born in 1401, he was killed at the age of twenty-seven. As a master in his own right, he painted for approximately five years. On technical grounds, it is possible to associate his hand with about twenty pictures, but there are critics who will challenge some of those. In any case, only three or four are useful in their entirety as a demonstration of the powers that make Masaccio significant.

An infinite number of men have left a larger corpus of material behind them, only to pass into oblivion as soon as they died, but Masaccio instantly became a historical figure. His present reputation is greater than ever, having been enhanced by the sober methods of modern history. The reason for all of this is that his painting contained within it the germ of almost everything realized by the full tide of the High Renaissance. Masaccio, to put it colloquially, was virtually the inventor of the "Grand Style." Inasmuch as the "Grand Style" has remained the tacitly accepted ideal and criterion of all European art, regardless of excursions in other directions, until the advent of postimpressionism, it may be said that Masaccio's ideas remained implicit in European taste until 1900 or thereabouts. But the reader must not confuse such long-term influence upon history with an immediate effect like that achieved by Donatello. It was the latter, as explained above, who set the pace for most 15th-century work; but the personality of Masaccio was always brooding over Florence, waiting for the day when the humane and intelligent art

Fig. 13.18 Carlo Crivelli. Detail from a Madonna in the National Gallery, London. 1476. The human figure painted in the mode of relief.

of the Early Renaissance should give way to conceptions more Godlike and sublime.

Masaccio's greatest work was done during the period of his association with the fresco decoration of the Brancacci Chapel at the Church of the Carmine in Florence. There is an unfortunate amount of confusion about the authorship of the pictures there. The original contract was set in motion by

Fig. 13.19 (left and opposite) Masaccio. *Expulsion of Adam and Eve from the Garden of Eden* and a detail: "Head of Eve." About 1427. Florence, Church of the Carmine. (Alinari)

Brancacci's will in the year 1422. The commission was apparently awarded to Masolino, a master who painted in a late version of the International style. Probably he was the head of the shop in which the youthful Masaccio worked. Before the work at Florence can possibly have been completed, Masolino was at Buda in Hungary, working on another contract. Was Masaccio left in charge at Florence? Did he take the contract over in his own name? How much work had been completed when the direction shifted? Who did what? What are we to look for in the pictures? When he visits Florence, the reader can spend a profitable day attempting to answer those questions for himself by studying the originals. What we want here is the mature work of Masaccio, uninhibited and undiluted. We very probably have it in two frescoes: the *Expulsion of Adam and Eve from the Garden of Eden* and the *Tribute Money.*

The *Expulsion* (Fig. 13.19) is ostensibly a simple picture, but one can exhaust his knowledge and judgment before he really understands it. Tradi-

tionally, the subject had been popular because it gave artists a socially acceptable reason for studying the nude. Masaccio, as we shall see, examined
the visual reality of the figures, but his primary purpose had little to do with
facts. His overwhelming concern was with the initial act of original sin. Hopeless remorse is personified by his Adam. The convulsive Eve sums up every
cry of shame and despair utterable by a woman. Over earth's disillusionment,
the severe and pitying angel flies on sublime wings. The picture embodies a
higher drama than any other work of art we have had occasion to survey
since the chapters on Greece. The event itself was crucial in the moral history
of the race; and the action, as shown, has heroic overtones. It was such a
subject, and such a treatment of the subject that separated Masaccio from
his contemporaries of the Early Renaissance. When successful, the "Grand
Style" at which he aimed achieved epic status.

Having perhaps gained some entrance into the august and gloomy spirit
of the painter, we must turn to a list of technical matters of importance to

the serious student. Masaccio originated his own theory of art, which produced pictures seemingly less attractive than those we think of as typically Florentine and of the period. There are no pretty costumes, no jewels, no pleasant furniture. There is none of the linear calligraphy we love to see in the hair, and none of the smooth, youthful contours of the body. The pretty white light that so softly and so certainly illuminates everything has given way to broad, dark shadows; and the shadows in turn have taken away the bright colors, so that a somber tonality dominates the whole.

Masaccio, as all these things indicate, turned away from the contemporary Florentine version of the mode of relief, with all its affinities to the subtle sculpture of Donatello. When we move close to his paintings, to examine them minutely (Fig. 13.19), we find none of the usual finesse. Details are absent. The construction of the bodies is declared largely by an arrangement of shadows; and as shadows, those painted by Masaccio lack the elegant gradations other artists cultivated. One may be forgiven, at first, for thinking him a slovenly painter.

The matter is to be explained by reference to the way in which the eye receives visual data. Unlike his contemporaries, Masaccio refused to employ a contrived lighting. He also declined the use of the telescope to reveal the distance and the microscope to bring up local details. He appears to have accepted, as artistically valid, a process of seeing that is in some ways less satisfactory, but one which is correct with reference to most human experience: his paintings correspond closely to the fuzzy imperfection of the single view, as it is actually available to the unaided eye, from a single station at a specified remove from the object of sight.

But the shapes and masses are nevertheless forcefully described. They are what he wanted us to see through the screen. The comparative difficulty with which we perceive them does not militate against the artist's belief in their special validity. In other words, when he chose to take the human optical powers, limited as they are, as the first frame of reference for his art, Masaccio did not, by that act, turn his back on the fundamental philosophy of the mode of relief, nor did he abandon tactile values as such. He merely complicated the matter by adding a new element, the physiology of sight. It is that which seems to have made him blend the forms insensibly into one another, fogging the definition of contours and denying linear edges to the silhouettes.

Still another important difference separates Masaccio's style from that of his Italian contemporaries. Most of the latter took their idiom from the delicate low relief of Donatello. Masaccio's painting, with its more ample range of shadow, finds its natural counterpart with sculpture in the round. The particular kind of sculpture called to mind, moreover, is to be sought among the larger and more solemn monuments of ancient art. The question

Fig. 13.20 Masaccio. *Tribute Money*. About 1427. Figures are life-size. Florence, Church of the Carmine. (Anderson)

suggests itself: was there in Masaccio's background some antique statue, or some series of statues, as yet unidentified, which inspired him as the *Belvedere Torso* was later to inspire Michelangelo?

Years ago, when the history of Italian painting was all too often presented as an evolution in representative technique, Masaccio was labeled as the man who invented atmospheric perspective. No one takes so limited a view today, but it is still necessary to point out that he used that device more obviously and with greater effect than did any other Italian painter of the 15th century. By dimming the tones and outlines of the angel in the upper background of the *Expulsion,* he succeeded in making us read that figure as behind the Adam and Eve. It is worth noting that the ordinary effect of atmosphere was exaggerated for the purpose; only a bad London fog can curtain details to such a degree within the space of two or three yards. The boldness of the manipulation suggests not mere representation, but drama. Adam and Eve attract attention because they alone are rendered in something like a full range of values; the focus upon them seems to suggest an intention to contrast the all too present nature of worldly pain against the dim way in which we discern the divine justice of events.

The *Tribute Money* (Fig. 13.20) was a much more ambitious undertaking. Immediately recognized as Masaccio's testament, it received the minute study of every young artist who lived or sojourned at Florence for the next hundred years and more.

The subject comes from Matthew 17:24–27. Having arrived at Capernaum, the Holy Company was asked to pay a small tax; but they were without funds. Acting on instructions from Jesus, Peter went to the shore, caught a fish, found a coin in its mouth, and handed the coin over to the collector. The Gospel gives that narrative, together with a certain amount of dialogue between Jesus and Peter. The meaning and intent of the talk is extraordinarily vague, however, and it is difficult to make anything important from it. As for specific information, Masaccio's picture adds little to what we can read in the Bible.

Perhaps under the influence of some Roman monument, he arranged the picture according to the continuous method of narration. Three successive events are combined within the same composition. In the middle, we see the collector accosting the Holy Company. At the extreme left, Peter takes the coin from the fish's mouth. At the extreme right, he hands it over to the same collector. Obviously, the impressive monumentality of the painting can scarcely derive from so trivial a set of events; to explain it, we must venture boldly forward into the mysterious realm of the imponderables.

It would seem that Masaccio here took up the problem of mural painting where Giotto left off at San Croce in the 1320's (pages 464–466). Large figures are accommodated in an ample setting, in juxtaposition with architecture in scale with themselves. The governing principles of the composition are the same as Giotto's, and the atmosphere is one that seems to be reaching out toward grandeur.

Masaccio's use of space is probably the most important single element contributory to the majesty and solemnity of the conception. Prodigious mountains loom up in the distance, more cogent in their venerable dignity because far away. In that setting, we find a race of men equally prodigious. Their bodies are Herculean, their strength gigantic. Their faces betoken vast intellect, and their mood is fierce with righteous purpose. Even their clothing has the heave of the mountains in every fold. No one else even attempted such pictures at the same date. Although many have tried to do so since, Masaccio's is one of the very few authentically heroic styles in the history of art. Who else can so convince us that he deals not with people, but with men whom God intends shall subdue and possess the earth?

Had Masaccio been able to continue his career, the High Renaissance would very probably have arrived earlier, with consequent changes in the schedule of Italian painting and the entire history of European art. But in 1428, he abandoned the unfinished commission at the Carmine. The work was brought to an inconclusive completion fifty years later by the younger Lippi. Masaccio went off to Rome, probably as much to escape creditors as to seek glory. He got into trouble there. He died either from poison, or from a knife wound received in a drunken brawl; there is gossip both ways. He left no school behind him to establish a tradition. He simply stepped off the stage, having achieved eminence in the space of a single scene. No other artist so overwhelms the observer. His power is unadorned, uncomplicated, sheer.

♦ *Brunelleschi* Daring was the outstanding characteristic in the personality of Brunelleschi, the first great architect of the Italian Renaissance. But that impetuous virtue was remarkably combined with a capacity for precise calculation, and with austerity of taste rarely associated with an unbridled imagination.

Brunelleschi at first intended to be a sculptor; and he achieved sufficient proficiency in that line to be Ghiberti's closest competitor in the famous contest of 1401, which resulted in Ghiberti's getting the commission for a set of new bronze doors for the Baptistery of Florence (page 517). Disgusted with his failure to excel, Brunelleschi took himself off to Rome in company with the youthful Donatello, and never thereafter engaged seriously in the sculptor's art.

In 1418, he was back in Florence; and in that year, he won a competition —this time, the commission for the design and construction of the great dome over the crossing of the Cathedral at Florence. He had no reputation as an architect at that date, and certainly none as an engineer. His temerity in entering the contest was exceeded only by the courage of those who put the project in his hands. The situation was one where both parties to the bargain overreached themselves: famous monument that it is, Brunelleschi's dome leaves much to be desired. For details, we may refer the reader to W. B. Parsons's excellent work,* commenting here only as follows.

The city of Florence had voted the new cathedral as early as 1294. The original plans are said to have been made by Arnolfo di Cambio, who died in 1302. The church as it now stands is one of the biggest in Europe. Not satisfied with scale alone, the citizens projected an architectural novelty. Instead of using the conventional Gothic east end, they decided to open up the crossing into an immense octagon. Presumably, a dome was visualized from the beginning to cover that area. There was some conference about details in 1366, and the present walls of the octagon must have been approximately complete by 1405 or so.

It is here that the modern reader must pause in wide-eyed amazement: no one on earth had any definite idea how to build the required dome. The span measured about 150 feet. The last dome of that scale had been the dome of Hagia Sophia (page 278). Brunelleschi was thus undertaking a task unparalleled for eight centuries, and from that we may judge the spirit of the times and the temper of the man.

The winning design got the prize, it is said, because Brunelleschi had figured out a way to build the dome with a minimum of centering: he made the pitch so steep that the sides approach the vertical.

Historically speaking, the design is important because it amounted to

* W. B. Parsons, *Engineers and Engineering in the Renaissance*, Baltimore, Williams & Wilkins. 1939.

something like a manifesto of the philosophy of Renaissance architecture. In order to get the most benefit from the shape, the architect abandoned inert abutment and made the dome spring from the top of a high drum. The thrust is contained by chains under tension, as described in Appendix I. Practically every dome built during the Renaissance, and since, has conformed to the same general type, the popularity of which signifies a belief in the value of pure form even at the expense of risky construction.

The construction decided upon was Gothic rather than classical in method. Eight large segmental arches were raised like ribs, converging at the oculus. The eight main ribs formed the guiding lines for a network of smaller ribs and connecting arches, very much in the manner of Gothic tracery but in a different application. The smooth surfaces visible within and without are superficial covering. They exist to serve the Renaissance ideal of form, and it will be noted that Brunelleschi, when he decided to conceal the working framework beneath, indulged thereby in a complete negation of the Gothic theory that structural fact might be made to suggest esthetic design.

The dome soars 308 feet into the air; it is a mighty landmark. The curve of the exterior silhouette, however, is weak and uninteresting. The interior appearance amounts to a most unfortunate hole in the ceiling, something that harms rather than aids the effect of the nave. For such reasons as those, we may turn with some relief to the smaller buildings in the design of which Brunelleschi established himself among the immortals.

The façade of the Foundling Hospital (Fig. 13.21) was probably designed in 1418. Its most conspicuous feature was an open loggia of nine delicate arches springing from slender Corinthian columns and approached by a broad flight of shallow steps, also nine in number. Above the arcade, we see a subtle entablature, and above that, a second story pierced at intervals by windows, each centered over an arch. Circular medallions in terra cotta, the work of the Della Robbia shop, fill the spandrels.

How rare it is that a notable work of art can be described in so few words! But the hand of this designer was sure. His brief expression was perfect. Everything fits everything else, but still remains pure and separate. The entire composition is like springtime, a new life, an indication that the world was young.

Of the styles antedating the 15th century, one instinctively recalls the Greek as the closest to Brunelleschi's work, but there is almost no chance he had ever looked at anything we would call Greek today. His inspiration probably came from a combination of sources. He had, of course, been to Rome; and the separate parts of his architecture are classical in form but a great deal lighter in proportion. He also retained much of the feeling of the Romanesque of Tuscany, as exemplified by San Miniato, a church in plain sight on a hill over Florence, and by the grander buildings at Pisa (Figs.

Fig. 13.21 Florence. Foundling Hospital. Designed by Brunelleschi. Started 1421. (Anderson)

11.1–2, page 332). And yet there seems to be more in the superb elegance of his style than we may account for by referring to Roman and Romanesque inspiration. We cannot prove that he had visited Paris and Amiens; neither can we prove he did not. It seems likely, however, that in some way he formed a taste for the High Gothic of France, and if we are to characterize his work in a phrase, we would not be far wrong to call it Latin handled with a French accent.

In blending and fusing those disparate elements, Brunelleschi was evidently extremely conscious of the taste for low relief by which contemporary painters and sculptors were governed. His architectural style was primarily an expression in terms of line and surface. The entablature, the window frames, and the moldings might well be described as more drawn than modeled. Their relief is slight; were it less, the individual parts would be indistinct. It is obvious that the designer was deliberately avoiding the plastic mass characteristic of Roman work; at the same time, by keeping every projection close in, he narrowed the cast shadows and prevented them from interfering with the flow of artistically invaluable lines.

But over against all the specific and physical sources he so marvelously made into a new style, it is plain that Brunelleschi understood and accepted

certain classical principles of design. Viewed as a whole, the façade of the Foundling Hospital is a horizontal rectangle enclosed by substantial architectural boundaries. Symmetry governs the arrangement of parts, even though the symmetry is not paraded as it was in most Roman composition. Each part, moreover, is an artistic unit, a small composition which conceivably might stand alone. The system in use is plainly the organic scheme of composition, which originated with the Greeks (page 66).

While we must repeat again that it seems very unlikely that Brunelleschi had ever studied any Greek art, his work has one virtue common in Greek design and almost invariably absent from the Roman. We refer to the employment of blank spaces (often called "functional voids") in the composition. His interest in that device seems to have invited its use with daring liberality. The proportion of empty wall is altogether out of the ordinary. Each fastidious motive is widely set off from its neighbor, compelled to stand on its own chaste merits like a theme stated by one instrument. It is the ostensibly vacant areas which give the whole façade its unexcelled gentleness, its perfect grace and quiet tempo. We ordinarily do not associate risk and daring with tranquillity, but the extreme simplicity of the design was almost preposterously bold. A single error, even a hint of imperfection in the smallest detail, would have been enough to ruin the whole.

Fig. 13.22 (opposite and right) Florence. Pazzi Chapel. Designed by Brunelleschi. About 1430. (Alinari)

The Pazzi Chapel (Fig. 13.22) seems to have been started in 1429. The date of completion is less definite; it is generally believed that some of the work, at least, went on after Brunelleschi's death in 1446. For that reason, some scholars have worried as to whether the present edifice is purely his, or not. Dodging such argument and assuming that the original architect dictated the major dispositions, the little building is of peculiar interest because it gave the designer an opportunity to demonstrate whatever theories he may have entertained. The functional need was uncomplicated. The scale was miniature. There were, in short, almost none of the usual considerations which interfere with impulses that are purely artistic.

The little church has only three component parts: a handsome tunnel-vaulted loggia across the western and entrance front; a nave chamber running parallel to that, with its long axis north and south; and a dome centered over the nave. The type seems to have been borrowed in a free way, as was to be the case with many another Renaissance church, from the four-column central churches of the Byzantine Second Golden Age (pages 285–287).

For the entrance front, Brunelleschi seems to have wanted a monumental façade on the miniature scale. He drew up what amounts to a screen of low-relief architecture carried by six columns with an entablature over them. He broke the entablature in the middle to raise an arch over the entranceway, much in the manner of certain Hellenistic and Roman temples (Fig. 7.9, page 194). To the right and left of the central arch, he put sections of paneling enframed by paired pilasters. The entire composition was closed in at the top by a second entablature.

Having thus completed the composition for the façade—and, in effect, it amounts to one classical temple on top of another—Brunelleschi seems to have felt no need to relate the western screen to the mass of the building behind. As we see it today, the front elevation of the chapel seems, artistically speaking, to break in two. Behind and above the exquisite screen, there rises the dome over the nave. The latter was made high, in order to produce the proportions desired for the interior. The screen could not conveniently be made higher because the horizontal nature of classical architecture had already been strained to the limit. Thus, there was no good way to make a connection between the façade in front and the building behind it. With his usual boldness, Brunelleschi simply accepted that fact. He made the exterior of the dome as plain and inconspicuous as possible, and he put a stilted lean-to roof over the vault of the loggia, where it hardly fills the gap very well.

It is unreasonable to suppose that what we see was the result of carelessness or improvisation; Brunelleschi was the last man to be easygoing. The lack of coherence between part and part, to say nothing of an absence of definite relation between every part and the whole, must have had its genesis in a philosophy of design. It seems evident that Brunelleschi considered it sufficient to make each element, taken by itself, a perfect thing in terms of its own internal logic. As to making every part fit the next, and as for maintaining throughout all parts a consistent sense for the entirety, we must assume he thought it not worthwhile. It is difficult to accept his point of view, especially when one considers the innumerable buildings since constructed, as the wag said, "with a Queen Anne front and a Mary Anne behind."

As to the interior of the Pazzi Chapel, the walls and ceiling admirably carry out the principles of expression by line and surface already characterized above. The atmosphere is therefore much less ponderous than that of a Roman interior, but it will be noted that the world is shut away as definitely as it was in the Pantheon (Fig. 7.5, page 186). Brunelleschi had discarded, that is to say, the Gothic theory of interior design (pages 375–377), and he had returned to the modeling of air and space which had been popular during classical antiquity (pages 195–197). The choice was of course but another instance of the resurgence of Roman taste in Italy at the time. It is also important because the taste reflected has, on the whole, been dominant in the design of interiors from that moment until steel and glass became available during the latter half of the 19th century.

Brunelleschi was one of the men who searched for the secret of classical art, and who believed they would find it by mathematical analysis. Although remembered as an architect, it was he—or so many scholars are coming to think—who was largely responsible for working out the theory of perspective which so greatly advanced the art of representation. He also researched into the mystery of proportion, having doubtless been influenced by the cryptic remarks of the recently recovered Vitruvius (page 97). In his later work, he seems to have made an attempt to apply such conclusions as he was able to draw.

He had occasion to design two basilican churches at Florence, San Lorenzo in 1419 and Santo Spirito in 1435. The choice of the basilican type was in itself significant, because the Early Christian basilicas (page 234) were then thought of as classical churches. Both the buildings mentioned show Brunelleschi's free classical detail at its superb best, but we need not reiterate praise already given. Our chief concern here is with the serene spatial expression at which he arrived, particularly in the interior design of Santo Spirito. Difficult to comprehend by way of drawings and photographs, the effect is almost tangible when one enters the building. If not able to reproduce the experience by describing it, we can at least suggest in part the method the architect himself seems to have followed. Like the Greek sculptor Polyclitus, he evidently believed there was magic in the use of a *module,* or unit of measure which would divide evenly into every important dimension of the whole.

As Santo Spirito now stands (Fig. 13.23), the ground outline is incomplete. Brunelleschi intended to continue westward a little further; it was his purpose to run the aisle entirely around the building without a break at the façade, thus providing a narthex at the entrance and a western range of interior columns reminiscent of certain pagan basilicas, like the Basilica Julia in the Forum Romanum.

The design of the east end was also an innovation. Discarding the time-honored semicircular apse, he opened up the crossing into what we may call three arms of a Greek Cross. The arrangement seems to yearn for the condition of the central church, one of which Brunelleschi had actually designed in 1434. It was to have been known as Santa Maria degli Angeli, but construction was abandoned before the building was halfway up. We know it today from the ground outline and some apparently reliable engravings. The central church may be associated in a curious way with humanism (page 560); and as a type, it was destined to have a strong span of popularity later in the Renaissance. Indeed, it looked for a time as though the basilica would pass out of use altogether.

With the unaided eye, it is easy to see that the plan of Santo Spirito depends upon a harmony of commensurate elements. The apse duplicates either transept. The open floor inside the columns is a square, and the nave consists of four and a half such squares—or an even five had the designer's

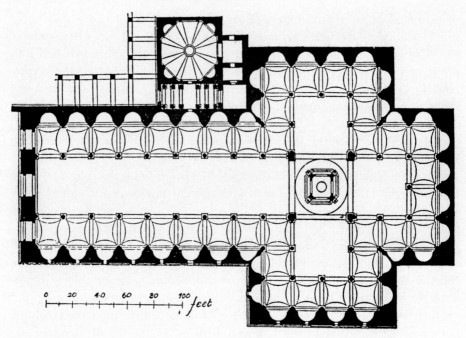

Fig. 13.23   Florence. Santo Spirito. Plan. (From N. Pevsner, *European Architecture*, Scribner, 1948.)

intention been carried out. All the items mentioned are in turn reducible to multiples of the intercolumniation, as one may prove with dividers.

Were drawings of the elevation available, it would be possible to show that the principle of commensuration was applied in similar fashion to the vertical dimensions; and if one appreciates that the linear dimensions merely define cubic modules of space, it seems plain that some rather complex and definite formula was being applied. While serious doubts must assail the man who cares to assert that strict multiples of the same unit make good proportions, or indeed that any proportion is inevitably better than any other, there can be little question that Brunelleschi was experimenting along such lines. Let the reader decide for himself whether the great architect thereby explained the secret of his own success.

Brunelleschi's style established the norm for the Early Renaissance architecture of Italy. At Florence, other architects used detail similar to his, especially for the arcaded courtyards in the great palace-forts, each a hollow square, which they built for the powerful families of the city. In Florentine painting, especially in the work of Fra Angelico (Fig. 13.27), we find buildings of a similar type. The remarkable truth of the matter is, however, that not one other architect was able to rival the spiritual authority of the man who originated the style. The Palazzo del Consiglio at Verona might at first seem a brilliant exception to that statement, but familiarity will soon settle the question. The distinction of Brunelleschi's gifts may also be estimated by the caution with which his manner has been used in modern times. Even in America during the 19th century, when every kind of historical imitation was being drawn up helter-skelter, most firms steered clear. Only McKim, Mead, and White—an office peculiarly anxious to establish its artistic superiority over all others—made any serious attempt to emulate Brunelleschi. They had comparative success with the Morgan Library in New York, and with the Art Museum at Bowdoin College. Both structures are graceful enough, but no one wants a watered drink from the fountain of youth. As yet, Brunelleschi stands alone.

♦ *Ghiberti* Ghiberti first became famous when he won the competition held in 1401 to select the sculptor for a new and second set of bronze doors for the venerable Baptistery at Florence. It is important to understand that the Baptistery already had the finest bronze doors in the world, the work of Andrea Pisano, a sculptor strongly influenced by Giotto. The building had three entrances, so perhaps three sets of doors were in order, but also it was typical of the time and place to want something better than the best, to expect to get it, and to be willing to pay for it.

Some interesting rules governed the competition. It was stipulated that the competing works of art should be in relief, and that they should conform in size and shape with the Gothic medallions that made up Andrea Pisano's doors. The subject was likewise specified. It was the sacrifice of Isaac, a story demanding the use of landscape, animals, and human figures both clothed and nude.

Ghiberti's nearest competitor was Brunelleschi (page 509), and the two competing panels are preserved (Figs. 13.24–25). Few modern critics disagree with the verdict. Ghiberti was obviously much more at home in the third (and represented) dimension. As though to declare the existence of air and room, he made his foreground figures overlap those further removed, and he gave the anatomy an elegant *contrapposto,* so that each pair of shoulders became, in effect, an axis diagonal to the plane of the background.

It would be hard, furthermore, to overstate the extent to which Ghiberti's composition coming at the very beginning of the 15th century, was forward-looking, although a similar interest in the formalities of arrangement became common enough during the High Renaissance. The operative group of Abraham and Isaac, he placed high and to the right, its intensity being balanced by a bulk of more quiet material filling the remaining (and larger) area of the frame. Attention was directed toward the crucial action by directional impulses from the left.

Figs. 13.24–25 Brunelleschi (left) and Ghiberti. Panels submitted in the competition of 1401. Florence, National Museum. (Alinari)

As already mentioned in another connection (page 438) Ghiberti's figure style, although scientifically correct with respect to anatomical structure, continued the physical types and the costumes of Late Gothic Mannerism. Therefore, one tends to think of him as a conservative, even a reactionary, artist, forgetting that his urbane performance embodied profound—and at that time new—mastery of representative science. It also embodied an equally profound and equally new grasp of the Antique. Ghiberti's nude Isaac was taken directly from a classical torso then in his personal possession and today preserved in the Uffizi. Taken by itself, the Isaac might well be confused with Hellenistic work of unusually high quality, and it was perhaps the first figure in modern art to demonstrate an obvious honor for the body.

Having received the commission for the new doors, Ghiberti devoted twenty-one years to the project. The general character of those doors is well suggested by the competition panel. They consist of small scenes in pictorial relief, enclosed in the same Gothic medallions.

In his autobiographical *Commentaries,* Ghiberti mentioned that the doors cost the city 22,000 florins. Vasari, in his life of Ghiberti, gave the same figure. Any attempt to convert 15th-century money into modern buying power is subject to interpretation, but curiosity dictates that the attempt should be made. It is possible to calculate by reference to the value of land, by reference to the known income of families of known standing in the community, and by other methods. Scholars have tried it various ways, and their conclusions are remarkably similar. Namely, these doors cost not less than two million dollars, and probably a little more. The sum is significant. It indicates the social climate in which Renaissance art flourished, and it points up our earlier remarks about the attractions of an artistic career.

There was no complaint about the cost. On the contrary, the citizens at once commissioned Ghiberti to do a second set of doors. When these latter were finally hung in the main portal of the Baptistery, the date was 1452. The doors of 1403–1424 went to one of the lateral entrances, where they still are, with Andrea Pisano's doors filling the third portal opposite.

Ghiberti's second doors fulfill in rich measure the promise of his earlier career. He abandoned the scheme of Gothic medallions and laid out a plan consisting of ten large rectangular panels surrounded by an elaborate border of foliate ornament interspersed with tiny human busts and exquisite statuettes in niches. The panels contain stories from the Old Testament, presented according to the continuous mode of narration (page 217). The little busts and statuettes ostensibly comprise sibyls, Hebrew worthies, and other historical notables; but from the sharply individualized faces, we may guess that contemporary portraiture was involved.

The ten large panels of which one is shown in Figure 13.26 present the sacred narrative at a tempered pace that is still not without dramatic moments. The figure-style, as seen in the detail given by Figure 13.27, is more wonderful than ever before; it combines the acme of Gothic grace with an ease of anatomical science most uncommon at an earlier period. Over all and everything, we feel the magic spell of an unequivocal desire for beauty which was in part the gift of the classical revival, in part a heritage from the Late Gothic, and in part Ghiberti's own. But none of those excellencies, nor all of them together, constitute the central interest of the work; at that time and in history, Ghiberti's great accomplishment was the sculptural conquest of space.

In his earlier sculpture he had, to be sure, undertaken to represent depth, but he had been cautious about it. An inspection of the competition panel and of the earlier doors will show that he generally brought his figures up front, with a setting behind them, more or less in the manner of the Alexandrian division of ancient pictorial art (page 161). Displacement out into the beyond was indicated clearly enough in such earlier work, but the vistas were often closed by architecture or landscape, and successive steps further away were commonly marked by some barrier or hurdle of setting. The infinite and unlimited sky rarely was permitted to occupy any substantial part of the available area.

The reliefs of 1425–1452 were incomparably more bold. There is no further suggestion of action near the front of the stage. The represented

space does not begin, in fact, at the lower border of the panels; it seems to start some yards this side of it. The nearest figures stand, that is to say, in the middle ground; and the atmosphere sweeps out into the furthest limits of the firmament. In several panels, architecture was required to fulfill the requirements of a setting within city limits; but even then, one has no sensation of masonry presented broadside to announce definite vertical planes of spatial removal. The perspective is both precise and elegant, making the buildings fade off gradually. The living air, moreover, seems to pass freely in and out the windows and doors. There are, in truth, no conventions or rules we need keep in mind to understand the sculptor's purpose; it is emphatically plain he meant to furnish us with an illusion so perfect that we would read the scenes as real.

The inspiration for so magnificent a performance is probably to be sought in a number of places. Maitani's reliefs on the façade of the Cathedral at Orvieto, dating about a hundred years earlier, come to mind at once

Figs. 13.26–27 Ghiberti. East doors of the Baptistery at Florence. 1425–1452. (opposite) Panel with the *Sacrifice of Isaac*. (right) Detail showing the *Creation of Eve*. (Both photos: Brogi)

as predicting what Ghiberti achieved with the aid of science unknown to Maitani. In addition, it seems probable that he had studied some examples of Roman painting, and the cognate relief, of the general type we have elsewhere named the Latin style (page 163); a general description of one of the Odyssey Landscapes will duplicate in circumstantial fashion a general description of one of Ghiberti's panels.

Ghiberti's reliefs, if we had nothing else to prove it, are evidence enough to demonstrate that the Italian artists of the Early Renaissance wasted very little energy over certain questions with which modern criticism has been strenuously concerned. We refer in particular to the idea that there is an intimate relationship between medium and design. The tools and the stuff with which the artist works, that is to say, are held to possess a special nature, distinct from the nature of other tools and other raw materials. It follows, if we choose to accept such a theory, that whenever a man decides to become a sculptor, he should reconcile himself to the internal logic of sculpture. He should strive only for the kind of expression of which sculpture is capable, and he should eschew any attempt to cultivate effects that are not directly in line with the nature of his chosen medium.

On the basis of such thinking, Ghiberti has been made the target for some of the best-calculated derogatory comment in the annals of art criticism. The contention against him is that he endeavored to accomplish with sculpture that representation of distance which painting, with its modulations of tone (page 159), represents so easily, so directly, and so adequately. That Ghiberti had superb technique, no one dares to deny; but technique, or so says the argument, is beside the point. Or, if not beside the point, is there not an actual complaint that Ghiberti had to make a parade of his skill in order to succeed, thus attracting more attention to the manipulation than to his meaning?

The cogency of these contentions will manifest itself only in the presence of the originals. Any photograph after Ghiberti, especially if it be a good one, is itself a picture. The spatial relationships it seems to show depend rather little upon qualities in Ghiberti's sculpture, and much upon the light and dark which belong solely to the picture.

In other words, we may be certain that any photograph clear enough to get published was taken under special conditions of light. Indeed, it is to be assumed that the photographer set up apparatus for lighting the relief to the best advantage. At any other time of the day, or on another kind of day, the pictorial qualities of the bronze panels might not show up nearly so well. Actually, they usually do not. Cast shadows fall the wrong way. Value relationships become confused. Textures are more obtrusive. All too often, it must be confessed that in spite of our admiration, we find ourselves looking at solid plate metal where Ghiberti intended us to read the soft blue sky.

♦ *Fra Angelico* "Fra Angelico" was a nickname. The painter universally so called was christened Guido, and took the religious name Fra Giovanni of Fiesole when he entered the Dominican order at the age of twenty. He came to be called Angelico in affectionate recognition of the pretty angelic types (Fig. 13.28) that fill his earlier pictures.

As a painter and a personality, he has been secure in the esteem of scholar and public alike for several centuries. It therefore requires an act of stern historical self-discipline to say that he was an artist of the second rank, separated from the Donatellos and the Masaccios by a demonstrable difference. Theirs was stupendous genius, big enough to open up a new era. Angelico's gifts and capacities may be summed up by saying that he combined the best of the old with a sound grasp of the new, and originated neither. But even in a century opulent with greatness, that was enough to make him a considerable figure.

In order to round out the contemporary picture, it is necessary to appreciate that Donatello and Masaccio represented the speculative wing of the profession. Their work was of interest to forward-looking patrons who were willing to take a chance. Our hindsight assures us that those were the patrons who judged correctly; but in any given year, the volume of established business did not go to the great innovators, but to the artists who were popular in the sense of not being too far ahead of public taste. The reader will note that Angelico's formative period coincided with the late maturity of Gentile da Fabriano, who died in 1427. At Florence, moreover, there was still a great deal of painting in the same Late Gothic and International style of which Gentile was merely the most famous Italian exemplar.

One of the most prosperous establishments at Florence was, for example, that of Lorenzo Monaco (about 1370–1425). Angelico surely knew him, and may have worked for him. Monaco's art was intelligently eclectic. Probably born at Siena and trained by some enthusiastic follower of Simone Martini, he had picked up a thing or two from the later Giotteschi; and he had an International style tinged with Florentine monumentality. Florid and poetical in about equal measure, his pictures were notable for prodigies of linear calligraphy.

Everything we know about Angelico makes him out as a thoughtful, intelligent man. As a young artist, it must have appealed to him that art like Monaco's (on the basis of proven performance, general popularity, and financial record) was safer than originality; but the thoughts that crossed his mind were certainly not entirely mundane. In an age distinguished for the decline of the religious sanctions and the onset of actual corruption in the Catholic polity, Angelico was a sincere Christian. He did not enter the monastery by chance or under duress, but freely as a young man who must already have been able to support himself well in his profession. When he made his choice of a style, he probably felt that Gothic art, which had scarcely ever been used for anything but Christian subject matter, was the art of the church. He accepted it as loyally as he embraced the dogma.

The Death and Assumption of the Virgin, of which Figure 13.28 shows a detail, is ample illustration of Angelico's earlier style. It is one of four panels done for the account of a single patron; the other three are in the Angelico collection now housed at San Marco in Florence. The casual observer might be forgiving for dating such pictures a hundred years before their actual time.

The frames are florid Gothic. The figure style and costume are about the same as those seen in Gothic manuscripts. The average angel painted by Angelico at this period of his career looks, indeed, like a miniature rendition of one of the smiling angels at Reims (Fig. 12.6, page 419). There is much gold, and the colors are dainty and glitter like jewelry. Everything at first seems like a mystic's view of heaven, but a closer examination shows that the world had been discovered. The anatomy is too well constructed to date earlier than the 15th century, and there are other indications that the painter understood very well the disciplines of the new representative science.

Fig. 13.28 Fra Angelico. Detail from *The Death and Assumption of the Virgin.* Before 1430. Boston, Isabella Stewart Gardner Museum. (Anderson)

From that point on, the general development of Angelico's art shows a judicious absorption of the findings of his contemporaries at Florence. The *Madonna of the Linen Guild,* dating from 1433, was given no Gothic frame, but one in the form of a simple round arch, and the gentle Mary was more plastically described than before. Two pictures of the *Coronation of the Virgin* also come from the middle 1430's. The one in the Uffizi has its setting in a blaze of glory, and the one at the Louvre provides a raised dais of solid steps. Both of them, however, demonstrate a regard for the mechanical realities familiar on earth: gravitation, the displacement of bodies in space, anatomical construction, and so on. And yet none of this may properly be construed as an acceptance by Angelico of the worldly values discovered in his time and accepted as governing principles by so many artists of his era. We probably come close to the truth when we say that he attempted to harness realism to religious expression, and that from his point of view accurate representation was worthwhile only as a technique for demonstrating the reality of Christian truth mystically apprehended.

The suggestions set down above are well borne out by the greatest commission of the painter's career, which we are lucky enough to possess almost in its entirety. We refer to the extensive fresco decoration of the convent of San Marco at Florence. The monks went into residence there in 1436. Most of Angelico's painting dates between 1439 and 1445. The property had been given to the order by Cosimo de' Medici. The architecture is a hodgepodge of Italian Gothic, but extensive rebuilding, alteration, and some additions were put in progress. The architect in charge was Michelozzo, a man who collab-

Fig. 13.29 Fra Angelico. *Annunciation.* About 1440. Fresco. 7½ by 9¾ feet. Florence, San Marco Museum.

orated for a period with Donatello and who ranks second only to Brunelleschi as a designer in the style of the Early Renaissance. Within the convent, Angelico and his shop executed nearly half a hundred frescoes. Some were very large, and others were as small as panel pictures, being painted on the walls of the individual cells. With notable exceptions such as the badly repainted *Crucifixion,* one of the largest of them all and once a great painting, the general state of preservation is excellent.

Among the larger pictures is the familiar *Annunciation* (Fig. 13.29) which for generations has been a favorite monument of Italian art. It came as the culmination of a long period of rehearsal. Angelico had made a specialty of the subject. He always used the same figures in approximately the same costumes and poses. We must point to his cautious development of a single theme as one of the differences separating him from the prime movers of the Renaissance; but at the same time, few paintings embody so many elements of diverse interest. It is all but impossible to put down everything that the reader might legitimately demand to be told.

In response to the nature of wall painting, Angelico changed his style substantially. The tiny glittering details so appropriate for little panels (which presume an intimate inspection by eyes only a foot or two away) are absent. Instead, we see wider, simpler, stronger areas of tone. Linear calligraphy is still much in evidence, but it is disposed in big swings of line, as contrasted with the elegant complexity of the painter's earlier rhythms. The composition as a whole has been opened up; there is more distance between the figures, more room everywhere, and a convincing amplitude of air. All of those measures combine to produce a painting suitably viewed from a station across the room; and one capable of giving the broader effect generally wanted for architectural decoration.

Certain aspects of the setting have a special significance. The garden, as such, was in the direct tradition of the International style; but there is good reason to believe that Angelico meant it to refer to the imagery of the 4th Chapter in the Song of Solomon, where a lady is metaphorically referred to as "a garden enclosed . . . a spring shut up, a fountain sealed." The passage was peculiarly appropriate in association with the Annunciation because it had often been construed as a symbolic prediction of Mary's perpetual virginity.

The patch of ground opening up to the left is of course a mere detail in a more important subject; but a closer view will reveal a side of Angelico's personality for which the reader is unlikely to be prepared. We might expect a gentle, lovable painter to excel at painting flowers; but exactly where, at this date, can we find blossoms, leaves, and grasses like these? The representation is incisive, penetrating, authentic—in the strictest sense, the work of a scientist. Botany has never been served by a higher talent.

The little loggia is another feature we might dismiss as nothing remarkable, a standard bit of setting unconsciously included by the painter. The reverse is actually the case. At the moment of painting, such an arcade was the last word in Renaissance architecture. In fact, it would be more accurate to call it the prediction of the next move; a study published some years ago by Langton Douglas makes it seem likely that the architects learned more from Angelico than he from them. Only a man with a professional interest would experiment with capitals as he did here. The demonstration as a whole would have been quite beyond the capacity of any naïve and casual artist. It compels us to believe that the painter, old-fashioned though he was in some respects, was learnedly familiar with every detail of the classical revival.

The figure style is yet another thing that becomes more profound than we expect. Ostensibly a mere reliance on old formulas and repeated by Angelico rather monotonously from picture to picture, it nevertheless was something unique. He actually produced a Madonna both holy and humane. The ethereal face is at once actual and ideal; the personality that of a saint, but a saint possessed of personality. It is obvious that neither humanism nor individualism had passed this painter by; and once again, we are made to realize that hardly any man of the era was more completely informed about the progress of the times.

The literal sense in which the last statement is true makes it necessary to pass on from the *Annunciation* to an accomplishment not demonstrable within the limits of a closed garden. Angelico was a magnificently competent landscape painter, conversant in every detail with the skills developed by Masaccio, Donatello, and Ghiberti. A great many of the pictures have deep landscape backgrounds, of which the *Deposition from the Cross* at San Marco (probably finished in 1440) may serve as an instance. It is doubtful whether any other painter except the dead Masaccio could have equaled the performance at the same date.

The work at San Marco was a great success, and Angelico found himself pressed with important commissions thereafter. Two of them took him to Rome, once in 1445 and again in 1447. The second, a series of scenes from the life of Saints Stephen and Lawrence, done for Nicholas the 5th, survives. For the settings, Angelico painted rich complexities of heavier Renaissance architecture, and he filled them with dignified figures solidly rendered. No one who has felt the sweetness of his earlier painting can be happy about the change, but the change itself is interesting because it predicted an important transition in Italian art. First, it may be remembered as the complete end of anything that even looked back to the Gothic. Secondly, although dating only in the middle of the century, the pictures looked forward to the ceremonial art of the High Renaissance.

♦ *Jacopo della Quercia* Circumstances have conspired to cloud our estimate of Jacopo della Quercia (about 1374–1438); but even though we have little from his hand, it is plain that his contemporary reputation was well founded.

The *Tomb of Ilaria del Carretto,* in the Cathedral at Lucca, has long been attributed to him by word of mouth tradition. Unquestionably it is one of the loveliest monuments from the entire Renaissance. No other work of art so perfectly demonstrates the capacity of the Italian temperament to understand everything in terms of beauty; death seems merely to have given that exquisite lady a more perfect sleep. Because the poetic quality there expressed seems very different from the tone and content of Quercia's documented works, serious doubt has been cast upon the authenticity of the attribution, but the inconsistency involved in accepting it is hardly so great as the contrasts included within the sure work of Donatello. Without attempting to settle the question, it may be observed that the burden of proof is upon those who doubt.

Fig. 13.30 Jacopo della Quercia. *Creation of Eve*. 1425–1438. Portal relief. Bologna, San Petronio. (Brogi)

Quercia's most important commission was for the *Fonte Gaia* at Siena, a sculptural ensemble involving numerous figures in the round, and some panels of narrative relief. Only battered fragments remain, now stored for safe keeping in the Palazzo Pubblico.

We are fortunate enough to have one important commission in a good state of preservation. In 1425, Quercia began a series of reliefs for the jambs of the main portal at San Petronio in Bologna. They go together with some statues of the Virgin and the Saints, and comprise subject matter from Genesis and from the infancy of Christ. From the standpoint of style, the panels (Fig. 13.30) fulfill almost to the letter the recommendations of those who would quarrel with Ghiberti. Landscape settings were used; but where Ghiberti tried to include everything, Quercia could hardly eliminate another detail without canceling the pictorial effect entirely. With a similar severity of purpose, he handled the narrative with only two or three figures to a panel.

Quercia modeled his figures in very bold relief, and they fill the foreground. In other words, it is the figures that do the work in his compositions, and not the setting. The formula corresponds closely with the Alexandrian division of Hellenistic art (page 161). Without much doubt, the derivation was direct and intentional, but the figure style incorporated within that familiar scheme could hardly be more different from the elegant weaklings who people those bucolic yearnings from waning antiquity. Quercia's people belong to a recurrent tradition of central Italy, a taste which appears to stretch back into the remote Etruscan past, accounting for the repeated appearance —without proximate cause—of an anatomy heavy enough to be called gigantic. Giotto and Masaccio belonged to the same tradition, which passed on from the earlier Renaissance into the work of Signorelli and Michelangelo.

There is much in Quercia, also, to recall numerous sources closer in date. The hip-shot poses remind one of the S-curve which had been popular in French Gothic art of the mannerist persuasion, but he used the device as an expression of heaving force rather than of grace. The burning actuality of his narrative finds its closest resemblance in the passion with which Nicola Pisano had imbued his figures; but in the case of Quercia, the passion became a fierce power, potentially dangerous and devastating. It was this special and personal feature of his art that was destined to prove the strongest single influence upon Michelangelo.

While there were good artists in every Italian town during the first half of the 15th century, Quercia was unique among the great originators in not being a Florentine. Incongruously, he was a citizen of Siena. His monumentally plastic art was the direct opposite of the local tradition; and it is interesting to note that Francesco di Giorgio, who projected Siena's mystic and delicate painting right through the 15th century, was not born until a year after Quercia died. In view of these facts, it is legitimate to understand Quercia's art as an early and conspicuous instance of self-expression. That his personal choices and purposes were generally respected even by the extremely conservative society of his native city is a circumstance indicating the degree to which individualism had become an accepted philosophy in Italy.

♦ *Florentine Neoplatonism and Its Influence upon Renaissance Art*
When, in a general way, we want to contrast the art of the Early Renaissance with that of the High, we find ourselves saying that the 15th century was a century of realism, and the 16th one of idealism. The distinction is coarsely made and too briefly stated to be true, but the statement is on the right track. The cause of the change is to be sought in the intellectual life of Florence, and it can be localized in the thought of a circle of erudite and powerful men. We refer to the members of the so-called "Florentine Academy," sometimes called the *Platonic Academy,* and more strictly described as the *Neoplatonic Academy.*

The Academy was considerably less institutional than its name might suggest. Actually it amounted to a circle of intellectuals under Medici sponsorship. At the period of our present interest, the group was more or less dependent upon the philosopher Marsilio Ficino (1433–99). The organization, if we may call it that, had grown up rather naturally as the result of Cosimo de' Medici's personal interest in Plato.

That avocation, so far as we know, dated from the Council of Florence and Ferrara (1438–39), to which John Paleologus (page 301) had come from Constantinople, bringing in his train a number of distinguished Greek scholars. In their arguments at the Council and in private discourse, those latter opened the eyes of Italy to the importance of Plato, a philosopher who had been out of use in the West since the time of Saint Augustine.

According to the testimony of younger contemporaries, Cosimo soon conceived the idea of a Florentine academy devoted to Platonic studies. An obvious part of the program was to make Plato accessible to Italian readers. Because only a small portion of the material existed in any language an Italian could easily handle, a full-scale effort at translation was requisite. For that, Cosimo made some long-headed plans. He apparently picked at once Marsilio Ficino, then seven years old, and arranged for his education. In 1462, he set the young man up in a villa at Careggi, a spot in the hills a couple of miles north of town. From that event, we may date the only formal organization the Academy ever had.

For the next generation, the villa at Careggi was the spiritual home of the most brilliant men alive. Ficino had a most endearing personality. His greatest pleasure was to call his friends around him, and they would sit listening while the master expounded the dialogues. In addition to direct contact with every leader of thought who lived at Florence or might pass through, Ficino maintained a large correspondence. His letters, friendly in tone but prepared as though for publication, circulated all over Europe; a few we know about were received in France, Germany, Poland, Hungary, and the Low Countries, to say nothing of all the cities in Italy.

As a translator, Ficino finished his work with Plato in 1477, and committed it to print in 1482. Hardly comparable to our modern renderings, his text nevertheless remained in wide use until superseded during the past century. He then turned his attention to Plotinus, and finished a translation of the *Enneads* in 1492. That second effort of scholarship proved to be immensely important. It colored Ficino's interpretation of Plato; and thus, it slanted his influence upon art and poetry. Plato died in 347 B.C. Plotinus was born about A.D. 205. The dates give modern students a signal to look for differences, but Ficino got no such signal. Thus the distinction between Platonism as of Plato and the Neoplatonism represented by Plotinus largely escaped him. Having recorded that circumstance, which will explain why the academy should be called Neoplatonic, we need pursue the matter no further at the moment. Our concern is with the influence of the Academy upon the history of art, especially as it is reflected in the work of Botticelli (pages 534–545) and Michelangelo (pages 598–611). We shall try, that is, to recapture the environment and to understand art by reference to the spiritual food of the artist. That will involve us in much that may at first seem far removed from painting and sculpture, but we shall connect it up in the end.

As the central figure of the Florentine Academy and the acknowledged first philosopher of the century, Ficino put his mark on every educated Italian for a hundred years. By so doing, he placed himself at the focus of the immense influence Italy exerted upon world culture. The Platonism of Spenser and Goethe came to them by way of Florence; and we can follow the effect right on into the 19th century in the writings of Wordsworth, Emerson, and Thoreau—to mention only a few names at random. Every student of history must pause in reverence at so bountiful a harvest, but every student of ideas must at the same time feel a strong sense of paradox in the phenomenon. Ficino, if we compare him with the great men of philosophy, makes a poor showing.* Of original and creative material, he gave us little that is first-class. His energy seems to have been consumed trying to understand and explain ancient ideas, and even those were modified more than he knew by the society of which he was a member. The world, however, was hungry for the kind of food he had to offer; and he was there in the act of offering it. Because of that historical chance, a thinker of the second order opened the eyes of great artists and set them on their way.

Among the various theories developed by the Florentine Academy, two had a direct and unmistakable effect upon art. The first was the theory of creation, by reference to which the work of Michelangelo becomes intelligible; and the second was the theory of love and beauty, which tends to explain certain artistic developments which first became important in the painting of Botticelli.

The Florentine theory of creation had perforce to take account of the existence of the Christian Church. Ficino's central purpose, indeed, was to reconcile the traditional European religion with the classics. He himself became a priest in 1473, and canon of the Cathedral in 1487. Appalled by the irresistible tide of the new civilization, he hoped that Plato would prove a means, as Aristotle had for Saint Thomas, of saving the world for the Church. For a time, he even sympathized with Savonarola when that great and bigoted preacher took over Florence in the name of ideas that damned Ficino's Medici sponsors, and would have done his own work to death had they permanently prevailed.

Ficino's confusion with Plotinus helped him to reconcile Christianity with the ancient standards, for much of that philosopher's thinking had already been absorbed into our dogma by such early fathers as Augustine. Plotinus followed Plato in his general conception of the creation, and man's present situation. The difference may perhaps be summarized as a greater readiness to invoke the supernatural.

According to the narrative as understood by Ficino, mankind had originally lived in glory. In some primeval disaster, man got separated from the

* See P. O. Kristeller, *The Philosophy of Marsilio Ficino*, New York, Columbia University Press, 1943.

divine. We need not investigate how such a thing happened; the significant fact is that people now find themselves in a condition somewhere between the unhappy and the intolerable. Obviously, the strongest human instinct must be to seek reunion with the glory from which we have been banished; to do otherwise would be to declare one's self insane.

A course of self-purification was recommended as the best procedure, and it was part of the psychology of the Renaissance to assume that much might be accomplished even during a mortal lifetime. It will be seen that the idea is cognate to what we have elsewhere (page 471) referred to as the artistic concept of life, and the effect was to add a Christian sanction to the ideals of humanism and individualism. By directing and refining the impulses already within themselves, men might hope, even during life, for temporary reunion, a state defined as *ecstasy*—literally to stand outside one's self. Perhaps Thoreau meant somewhat the same thing when he spoke of drifting on Walden Pond, and experiencing moments when he "ceased to live and began to be."

We may now turn to the idea of beauty as it came to be understood at Florence under the spell of the Neoplatonic studies. Beauty, as those men conceived it, was a component of creation. When men had lived in glory, they also had lived in beauty. For that reason, the notion became current that people knew beauty whenever they saw it. They simply remembered it. The yearning for beauty, it will be seen, was thus given a meaning closely equivalent to the soul's yearning for reunion with the divine. Not only did the idea make it a permissible thing to want beauty; it virtually labeled the desire as a religious impulse.

The reader may also have observed that the definition of beauty, as given above, was more noble than distinct. It assigned to beauty a function that had to do with the elevated and spiritual impulses of mankind, but it made beauty a matter of intuition nevertheless. At the practical level of ordinary life, the definition furnished small guidance. In fact, it invited men to settle such questions their own way, and to name as beautiful anything they happened to fancy. To the particular kind of beauty which in fact proved favorite among the men of the Renaissance, we shall presently turn our attention. The matter was inseparable from the Neoplatonic theory of love, which we must now review.

Love had been made necessary by man's fall from grace. It was understood to be the instinct which impelled him to seek reunion with the divine. In instances where that had actually been accomplished (the saints in heaven, for example) love had served its purpose. There could be no more desire, nor any intelligible reason for desire. The state of glory would presumably be the state of complete fulfillment and continuous satisfaction into eternity.

In order to make such ideas useful, it was necessary to place love and beauty on earth. That was done by saying that beauty emanates from its locus in heaven, permeating nature and dwelling in many places. It was therefore made reasonable to find beauty in trees, rocks, bodies, and for pictures and statues to be beautiful. They all got their beauty from above. Much, indeed, as the lines of force from a mighty magnet give life to iron filings, and pull them toward itself.

As Plotinus put it in the 5th part of the 3rd *Ennead*, "Everyone recognizes that the emotional state for which we make love responsible rises in souls aspiring to be knit in closest union with some beautiful object; and it is sound, I think, to find the primal source of love in a tendency toward pure beauty, in a recognition of it, and a kinship with it." On a cognate theme, Ficino himself wrote, "Love unites the mind more quickly, more closely, and more stably with God than does knowledge, because the force of knowledge consists more in distinction, that of love more in union." In plain words, the Florentines believed that love started to operate whenever beauty was noted, and that love, when it came, was to be welcomed because it moved one toward God.

The Neoplatonic theory of both love and beauty was wonderfully popular with the Italians. Ficino's friends were doubtless competent philosophers, and as such they would be interested in following out the Platonic machinery into the more and more abstract levels of idealism. The citizenry at large wasted no energy on so impersonal and impractical an endeavor. They thought they knew what Ficino's words meant, and they thought they knew what to do about them. With chivalry in the immediate background and still a living thing, it seemed obvious that nobody would have been crazy enough to put forward at Florence a philosophy suggesting that ladies step down from their pedestal. The Florentines were delighted to have all kinds of beauty made thoroughly respectable, but the kind that came most often to mind was the beauty of women. Ficino was understood to say that the experience of this beauty, and the consequent onset of love, amounted to a discipline for the soul, virtually an act of worship. His conscientious attempts to distinguish between higher and lower forms of love, and beauties greater and less, were construed in gallant applications. Men saw visions of fair women, but fair women now symbolized the yearning of the soul toward eternity, and the pathos of man's separation from the divine.

As we look back upon what happened, it is evident that Florentine Neoplatonism opened every eye to the complexity of the human emotional system, and to the advisability of its refinement. First in Italy and then elsewhere, a considerable literature of love and beauty came into being. Ridiculous popularizations of course occurred, but it is remarkable how strongly

Ficino's subtle and elevated teaching resisted the intrusion of vulgarity. Even the publications intended to guide ladies in beauty culture at least suggested that beauty was a subject not to be understood without a reasonable effort at discrimination. For some of the more important documents, no praise can be too high. There is no more eloquent discourse than the speech of the Cardinal Bembo, to be found toward the end of Baldassare Castiglione's *The Courtier* (1528), where the reader will find the tradition of chivalry most gracefully combined with the sentiments of Plato's *Symposium*. The same might be said for Spenser's *An Hymne in Honour of Love* and his *An Hymne in Honour of Beautie,* both marvels of much in small compass, and both derivative from Ficino.

♦ *Botticelli* The painter Botticelli (1444–1510) was the first important artist to be deeply affected by Neoplatonism. His profound and baffling nature may not immediately make itself apparent. No artist ever made sentiment more lyric in its soft loveliness. He appeals by being winsome and wistful at the same time. It is easy to think one loves his pictures; but after some little acquaintance with them, there comes a consciousness of the conflict and frustration that existed within him.

We must understand at the outset that the inner beauties of Botticelli's art are not for everybody. Even in 15th-century Florence, he was not a popular artist in the sense of appealing to the public at large. He worked for a small circle of erudite persons who had the knowledge and taste to appreciate his exotic genius. Most of them were directly associated with the Florentine Academy, as indeed the painter himself may have been. It was his special role in history to create the visual imagery that expressed and commemorated the idealism newly introduced to Italy by the Neoplatonic movement. His career also included an episode connected with the conflict between the life of the Renaissance and the views of the Church; of that, we shall say a word at the end.

With respect to style, Botticelli need cause us no problems. To the day of his death, and long after the manner of the High Renaissance had been introduced to the world by Leonardo and others (pages 579–586), he continued to paint in the low relief manner inaugurated by Donatello at the very beginning of the 15th century. He got his fundamental training in the shop of Filippo Lippi (1406–1469). A comparison between Figures 13.31 and 13.32 will show how much the pupil owed to the master. It will also indicate the difference between the natures of the two men.

Lippi, like many another man of strong appetites and coarse behavior, maintained throughout his spectacular career an almost reverent taste for the daintier, more virginal aspects of feminine beauty. In his picture, we get little

Figs. 13.31–32 (left) Fra Filippo Lippi. *Madonna Adoring the Child*. About 1455. Tempera on panel 25 by 36¼ inches. Florence, Uffizi. (right) Botticelli. *Madonna of the Eucharist*. 1470–1474. Tempera on panel 24¾ by 33 inches. Boston, Isabella Stewart Gardner Museum. (Anderson; Alinari)

else; but in Botticelli's version of the same subject, we instantly feel overtones and connotations. The sentiment is of the same kind, but of loftier order. The faces are more finely drawn. The youthful muscles of cheek, eye, and mouth have already been stretched and modeled by thought and feeling. The grapes and the wheat, symbols of the Last Supper, drive the meaning home. Botticelli's picture is both an idyl and a tragedy.

As a young man, Botticelli also worked for a time with the sculptor and painter Antonio Pollaiuolo (1429–1498). Pollaiuolo was a famous anatomist; and as an artist, he made a specialty of putting the human body into unusual and even contorted positions. What he liked best was a powerful figure in violent action (Fig. 13.33). His studies were at times academic; but in all cases, they were saved by the zest of the man. Everything he touched is vital. In his detailed demonstrations of nature's complex and ingenious machinery, one feels the intellectual joy of fruitful research; and at the same time, there is an animal fulfillment of action for its own sake.

Violence in any form, even the harmless vigor of athletics, was foreign to Botticelli's temperament, but his art nevertheless owed much to Pollaiuolo. It was that second master from whom he learned how to make his figures

Fig. 13.33 Antonio Pollaiuolo. *Hercules and the Hydra*. 4¾ by 6 11/16 inches. Florence, Uffizi. (Anderson)

move, something which many artists of the time could do passably well but not with the same superb authenticity.

Botticelli's two most famous pictures are the *Primavera* of 1478 (Fig. 13.34) and the *Birth of Venus* of some six or seven years later (Fig. 13.35). It is certain that both were done for Medici patronage, but there is a minor confusion as to which Medici gave the order. In 1503, the two were in a villa at Castello, a house owned by the illegitimate branch of the family. It seems likely, therefore, that the original owner was Lorenzo di Pier Francesco Medici, natural second cousin to Lorenzo the Magnificent.

In part, both paintings constitute a direct attempt to bring antiquity back to life. As we shall see, the painter knew that certain Greek artists had painted similar subject matter, and that certain classical poets had used similar imagery. A more proximate cause, however, was the Neoplatonic theory of love and beauty, which was enough in itself to account for the choice of Venus as the central figure and for the ethereal idealization of the feminine which forms so striking a feature of both works.

The *Primavera* consists of nine figures seen against the background of an orange grove, with Venus herself in the center. As a demonstration of formal design, the composition is notable. One is at first conscious of the color, now

Fig. 13.34 Botticelli. *Primavera* or *Allegory of Spring*. About 1478. Tempera on panel 6 feet, 8 inches high. Florence, Uffizi. (Alinari)

sadly dimmed by time and by treatment of the panel to rid it of worms. If less bold than they were, the tones are still exciting. The effect may be compared to tapestry, except that where tapestry is rich the painting is keen and dainty. Warm spots vie with cool for possession of our feelings, and tints with shades. As between one category and another, there is little to choose. The principle in use is that of tonal balance, and the result is to spread color interest almost evenly over the whole surface. In the matter of using intense hues to re-establish the flatness of the panel (page 499), Botticelli was an expert. Although space is represented to the depth of thirty feet or more, the picture surface gives one a peculiar sense of smoothness, a characteristic extremely attractive in paintings intended (as this one probably was) for permanent incorporation in the paneling of a wall.

As to the content, the spirit is Platonic, but the details of iconography have proven elusive. A small literature exists on the subject, from which we shall draw only a few of the more obvious bits of analysis. The picture appears to be a great mixture of allusions, all of which were undoubtedly instantly recognizable by the learned gentlemen for whom the painting was intended.

The general theme seems to come from the *De Rerum Natura* of Lucretius (1st century B.C.). Venus, in the ancient world, had also been goddess of gardens; and in his opening invocation, Lucretius hailed her as the great generative force of the world. Such a notion was carried out by Botticelli in almost every detail of his painting. The earth produces flowers. The trees give fruit. Each woman is carrying a child. Cupid shoots his arrows every which way. The time of year may have been suggested by another passage in Lucretius. "Spring comes," wrote he in his 5th Book, "and Venus. . . ."

As to the Flora at the right, strewing flowers, she also appeared in the *De Rerum Natura,* but the lascivious puffing Zephyr seemes to have been taken from a passage in the work of Poliziano, a contemporary Florentine poet. We may also set down that Horace spoke of spring as the time when Venus led forth her band, and of the naked Graces dancing with measured tread before Mercury, who would presumably be the young man at the left.

For reasons made obvious by the paragraphs just above, strictures have often been leveled at Botticelli for being the originator (as he very nearly was) of the fanciful picture derived from literature. The practice, it is contended, tends to put the art of the painter in a secondary position. At best, or so we are told, the picture becomes a mere extension of the book; and at worst, a slavish illustration thereof. In either case, the painting would necessarily derive whatever merit it might possess, not from itself, but from the authority of the literary source.

There is much weight in the argument, and it can be applied with damning effect at various points in the history of art. It cannot, however, be used successfully against Botticelli. Living in an atmosphere of enthusiastic classicism, he took his inspiration where he found it. The crucial point is that the inspiration was genuine, by which we mean to say that the literary sources (none of which he followed closely, much less mechanically) merely set in motion feelings that were the painter's own. His affinities with the poets were real and deep, and he shared rather than borrowed their imagery.

Nothing we have yet said even begins to account for the sadness which fills the soft air of the picture. That nostalgic overtone, which lingers more in the memory than any other quality of the work, probably derived from contemporary persons and events, of which the reader will now require a recitation.

In 1469, Marco Vespucci had brought his bride home to Florence. She was Simonetta Cattaneo, a Genoese, sixteen years old; and so sweet and charming, said a contemporary, that all men praised her and no woman blamed her. In no time at all, the girl became the acknowledged belle of Florence. Giuliano Medici, the younger brother of the Magnificent Lorenzo, was specially her friend. It is a waste of time to speculate whether she was also his mistress; it can make no difference now, one way or the other. The important fact was that she was affectionately included within the intimate life of the Medici circle. In 1475, she was Queen of Beauty in a great tournament held in Giuliano's honor. That publicly established her, in a ceremonial sense at any rate, as the lady to whom Giuliano pledged his knightly devotion.

In 1476, Simonetta died after a short illness. Lorenzo the Magnificent, then absent at Pisa, kept his personal physicians in charge. He insisted upon daily bulletins. On the evening of her death, he went walking with a friend. Pointing up to a star of special beauty, he suggested that it might be a new star and "the soul of that most gentle lady."

Simonetta died in April. She went to her tomb with face uncovered in the sunlight. There was much remark, it is said, about the flowers that covered the earth like a blanket; always lovely in the Italian spring, they must have been specially so that year. The death of one so young amid so much beauty made dignified citizens cry in the streets of Florence. Everyone was reminded that spring cannot last.

In 1478, the Pazzi conspirators murdered Giuliano Medici. By coincidence, the date was April 26, the second anniversary of Simonetta's passing.

Those events, so brief in the statement, cast a pall over the intellectual life of Florence. Contrary to what we hear of domestic relations in some other families, the Medici brothers had been unselfishly devoted. Lorenzo was the older and more respected, Giuliano the more handsome and charming. The affection between Giuliano and Simonetta appears to have been a living symbol of the love and beauty which, for older and more serious persons, necessarily remained an intellectual ideal. It has long been a tradition that the *Primavera* was intended as a memorial for the two. With respect to Simonetta, that is probably true. Part of the tradition has it that the six female figures, all alike enough to be sisters, are each and all portraits of her. The Mercury at the far left is similarly suggested as a portrait of Giuliano; but if a memory of him was also involved, the timing was very close indeed.

Unhappily, the facts cannot be determined. Several portraits of the right kind and period have been labeled with Simonetta's name, but they depict several different women. None of them corresponds satisfactorily to the women of the picture, or with the Venus in the *Birth of Venus,* who is even more likely to be Simonetta. This evidence, however, is scarcely enough to contradict the tradition that she was Botticelli's model. Indeed, there is much in the nature of Florentine Neoplatonism, and its close involvement with the Medici family, to make it seem probable that her face and figure were at least the starting point for Botticelli's sublimations.

Her reputation gives us a woman of fragile beauty, strangely powerful in physical allure. Her temperament must have been, if we read the signs correctly, an appealing mixture of the mind and the intuition. Such women do not attract the common man, but their singular wisdom keeps the wiser male in constant wonderment. Simonetta alive had been the darling of her

Figs. 13.35-36 Botticelli. *Birth of Venus.* About 1485. Tempera on canvas 8 feet, 11 inches by 5 feet, 3¼ inches. Florence, Uffizi. (opposite) Detail: "Head of Venus." (Alinari; Anderson)

recondite friends, a walking example of femininity raised to a higher order. Simonetta dead easily became, it would seem, almost the definition of pure beauty. Happily, the supernal image was not nameless, but warm and personal. What better instance could there have been of the ideal within the thing? Of earthly loveliness as an emanation from heaven? Of the way in which the beauty of women might, upon occasion, turn the soul toward God?

The *Birth of Venus* (Figs. 13.35–36) was ostensibly a direct attempt at classical revival, a veritable school figure for the literal definition of the Renaissance. The imagery derived originally from Homer, who described the new-born goddess as being blown ashore from the Aegean Sea by the soft breath of the Zephyrs, while the Hours waited to spread a star-strewn robe over her white body, and countless flowers sprang from the grass her feet would tread.

The very same imagery had been used for one of the most famous paintings of the ancient world, as Botticelli well knew. That was the *Aphrodite Rising from the Sea* by Apelles, the most famous painter of the Greek Fourth Century B.C. and a figure closely associated with the court of Alexander. Apelles did his famous *Aphrodite* for the temple of Asklepios on the island of Kos. Augustus brought the picture to Rome and put it on exhibition in the temple of the Divine Julius in the Forum. The beauty of the nude figure,

especially the flesh tones in contrast with the cooler hues of the water, was the subject of much admiring remark. The supreme skill of Apelles was negatively made plain during a later reign when the painting was damaged in its lower parts, and no Roman artist could perform a restoration.

Statues more or less closely reproducing the appearance of Apelles' Aphrodite were popular in late antiquity; and the 15th-century Florentines thought they had recognized the type in several Roman copies, of which the best is the so-called *Medici Venus*.* Botticelli used the same pose, but not the same form for his Venus.

So much for the sources from which Botticelli worked. It would be hard to imagine a more pedestrian narrative; but fortunately, we have only reached the point where Botticelli came in.

Rather than confuse the right-hand side of the composition, he used only one personified Hour where the poets had mentioned three. In the matter of color, however, he was wisely governed by the reputation of his model; he tried to emulate what he knew of Apelles. The cool hues of the water modulate through the pearly tints of the shell, and transpose into the pink flesh tones. The sequence from cool toward warm culminates in the hair, which is a field of golden bronze. The highlights are brought out in pure gold, a circumstance that lends the event a supernatural aura and, incidentally, makes the painting unsuitable for hanging in a direct light.

It is doubtful whether Apelles, or anyone else, ever handled colors with greater delicacy. Surely no Greek ever used line better than Botticelli. Always sensitive to the movement of light and delicate things, his line here became a celebration, as it were, of the soft breeze over the ocean. With a sure cool strength, it lifts the draperies and moves the goddess' hair, and it blows her floating figure gently toward the land.

According to the ancient sources, Apelles's *Aphrodite* derived her loveliness from a living model. Two ladies, Phryne and Pankaspe, survive in name because one or both posed for the great Greek painter. It is difficult to know whether Botticelli may have been cognizant of the story or not; if so, he had classical authority for deriving an ideal figure from a mortal woman.

We have a special reason for making a shrewd guess that Simonetta was the model. She had been born at Porto Venere, the little harbor at the very tip of the peninsula closing the Gulf of Spezia on the west. The place gets its name from the Roman tradition that Venus stepped ashore there—and not on the island of Cythera, as the Greek myth tells it. There was material for a pretty compliment in the circumstance, and it is inconceivable that the gentlemen of Florence would have missed so obvious an opportunity to combine the chivalric tradition with classical lore.

The Birth of Venus could not have been started until several years after Simonetta had died. In order to understand the Venus for which she served as an inspiration, we must interpret the incident of her passing as an illustration of more general principles. The beauty of her body had proven transitory. Even the love directed toward her complete personality, body and soul together, was now denied an immediate object; such is the inevitable fate of all love that is personal. Forgetting Simonetta as a woman and realizing

* Discovered at Tivoli in 1680; brought to Florence in 1717. Botticelli must have seen one of the others.

that she merely furnished the starting point for an ideal and symbolic figure, we may think of Venus as Lucretius did.

The love Venus brought to the earth was the gift of life, but life is difficult indeed to explain. As a generative force, it carries forward into eternity. Inexorably, the race survives and increases, but individual men and women suffer loss, heartbreak, and death. For them, there is no permanence and no deliverance on earth. Any death, including Simonetta's death, evokes such thoughts; and they suggest why Botticelli gave Venus no joy in her birth, and why he filled her face with compassion.

Late in his career, Botticelli undertook to do one hundred drawings to illustrate a copy of Dante projected by one of the Medici. Of these, eighty-five are preserved in Berlin, and another eleven at the Vatican. All but a few are totally innocent of both hue and shading. Everything is rendered by unaided line (Fig. 13.37). Considered merely as technical demonstrations in the field of representation, the Dante drawings are a great monument. Botticelli had a linear device for every situation; the most esoteric necessities scarcely delayed his pen. Textures (fire, water, wood, flesh, masonry) were specified precisely. No sculptor could give a better indication of shape and weight. Within the represented space, the placement of things forward, right, back, and left was stated as unmistakably as any painter might indicate it with the full descriptive resources of hue, value, and intensity.

Such are great virtues, but not all. Insofar as words can describe an artistic experience, we may say that as the eye follows the movement of the artist's hand, the line itself comes alive. It swings, sparkles, and dashes. It sleeps and wakens. It becomes sad, or lifts like a song. Every smallest mark is an angle or curve of absolute beauty.

The most complete exposure of Botticelli's introspective sensitivity was furnished by his connection with the Savonarola episode. That affair had its start in a variety of matters; but in a broad way, we may interpret it as the violent reaction of the popular mind to the neopaganism of the Medici era.

When the great Lorenzo died in 1492, he left sons who lacked his ability. Their incapacity soon ended in disgrace, the occasion thereof being the investiture of Florence by the French in the course of their expedition of 1494. All Italy was humiliated, and the Florentines were ready to mend their ways.

Girolamo Savonarola was prior at San Marco. He was a man of extraordinary force and dignity, and of completely independent mind. He preached against the new worldliness; and in 1494, he pointed to the excesses of the Medici as the direct cause of his country's mortification at the hands of Charles the 8th of France. He presently assumed dictatorial power at Florence. His enemies, not the least of whom was the notorious Borgia Pope Alexander

Fig. 13.37 Botticelli. Illustration for Dante's *Inferno*, Canto 9. Rome, Vatican Library. Pen and ink on parchment. "Where in a moment saw I swift uprisen the three infernal Furies stained with blood, who had the limbs of women and their mien, and with the greenest hydras were begirt; small serpents and cerastes were their tresses, wherewith their horrid temples were entwined." (Anderson)

the 6th, at once began to intrigue against him. At length he was brought to trial, repeatedly tortured, and finally condemned. Sentence was carried out by hanging and burning in front of the Palazzo Vecchio on May 28, 1498.

There is a strong tradition that Botticelli came under the influence of the great Dominican preacher. He is said to have abandoned his Renaissance ways in a passion of guilt and remorse. He is further said to have assisted Savonarola's agents in collecting his own classical nudes for the Burning of the Vanities, a perverted ceremony of religious carnival staged in 1497 and again in 1498.

Some critics, probably with more caution than judgment, claim that the evidence sustains no such positive assertions. It is surely true, however, that a marked alteration in both the subject matter and spirit of Botticelli's painting coincides with the period of Savonarola, and it is perfectly plain from his latest work that his nervous stability had suffered a traumatic strain. Among the works that reflect the tumultuous state of his being, we may cite first the *Mystical Nativity* (1500) in the National Gallery of London, which has a Greek inscription referring to the Apocalypse and to the troubles in Italy.

An even more desperate expression is the violent *Crucifixion* now in the Fogg Museum. A Magdalen fiercely embraces the foot of the cross. An avenging angel holds by its left hind leg the heraldic lion of Florence, and whips it with a rod. Smoke and flame fill the right background, while to the left we see Florence lying under a sinister light. Admittedly obscure and possibly without specific denotation, the picture has with some justice been interpreted as predicting the doom of the city in punishment for Savonarola's death.

Botticelli was the last artist who belonged to the Early Renaissance, and the extreme conservatism of his style may be assessed if we make a comparison of dates. Botticelli was actually forty years younger than Leon Battista Alberti (1404–1472), whose career marked a new phase in the history of European culture. In fact, it was Alberti whose thought laid the foundation not only for the art, but for the entire outlook of the 16th century. With the introduction of his name, we appropriately pass on to the next chapter.

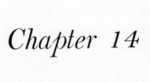

Chapter 14

LEON BATTISTA ALBERTI

L EON BATTISTA ALBERTI, the founder of the High Renaissance, was born as early as 1404. By the time of his death in 1472, the new movement was under way; and by about 1500, both its style and its philosophy were generally accepted.

Alberti was born at Genoa, the illegitimate son of a notable Florentine family banished to the north after losing a political fight at home. The Alberti were rich, and their ample funds made natural and easy the best education available, an opportunity which the young man followed up with incredible brilliance and acumen. His Latin was good enough to enable him, during student days, to write a comedy that was mistaken for the work of Terence. He was an accomplished musician. After graduating in canon law at Bologna, he later spent two years in the same place learning all there then was to know about natural science.

His name was enough to make him welcome anywhere; and that circumstance, in combination with personal charm and extraordinary ability, opened up splendid opportunities when funds failed at the death of his father. In 1428, he went to France and Germany as secretary to Cardinal Albergati (of whom there is a picture by Jan van Eyck). In 1431 he was invited to Rome as Cardinal Moulin's secretary. From there he went to a position on the learned staff of the Vatican. His routine duties left him plenty of time to acquire an expert knowledge of the antiquities, and for creative work. On several occasions, he accompanied the reigning pontiff on diplomatic journeys. He was with Eugene the 4th at Florence, in 1434, and with Pius the 2nd at Mantua in 1459. The first trip brought him into contact with Brunelleschi, Donatello, and other great Florentines, and the second resulted in his

546

THE HIGH
RENAISSANCE

drawing plans for Sant'Andrea at Mantua (Figs. 14.3–5), an extraordinarily important church.

Alberti's presence on the papal staff made the papal visits themselves memorable. The high regard in which he was held at Rome was excelled only by the impression he made everywhere else. His physical attributes did much to make him conspicuous, and thus enhanced the brilliance of his mind. Unbelievable tales are told of his feats of strength and skill. Without repeating them, we can say that much is indicated by this: in an age entirely dependent upon the horse, he was a world-famous horseman. His advice about training and breeding, moreover, was sought far and wide. All in all, he seems to have been the complete embodiment of the Renaissance ideal: the perfect body, the mind of universal genius.

♦ *Alberti's Writings* Although usually mentioned as an architect, Alberti often spoke of himself as a painter and sculptor. He surely had a right to, if we may judge from the incisive self-portrait (which exists in three slightly variant versions) done in low relief on a medal (Fig. 14.1). Unfortunately, it is the only thing of the kind from his hand. The buildings he designed all date from his middle age or later, and they number but a handful. It is evident that his original works of art were simply too few to account for the respect the man commanded during one of the most brilliant periods of Western civilization.

The fact of the matter is that Alberti spent most of his time writing. He wrote poems and plays. He wrote essays on ethics and sociology. But the great work of his life was a monumental exposition of artistic theory. It con-

547

sists of three parts: *Della Pittura (On Painting)* of 1435–36, with a dedication to Brunelleschi; *De Statua (On Sculpture)*, which dates from 1464; and *De Re Aedificatoria (On the Matter of Architecture)*, which appears to have been in hand from 1450 to 1472 and was posthumously printed in 1485.

As compared with the works of others who have from time to time written on the subject of art, Alberti's three books were uniquely successful. They are unique in being the words of a man who was himself a great artist—of a man, moreover, who lived in one of the great productive periods, and who knew numerous other artists of world reputation, what they did, how they did it, and what they thought. The value of practical experience has sometimes been overstated, but all highly trained technicians recognize by a kind of instinct the voice of a man who knows what he is talking about. Few of the greater philosophers have had the slightest influence upon the history of art, but Alberti stands as the paramount influence for the entire period between the middle 15th century and 1900.

Insofar as the artists of the Renaissance were concerned, the most important thing of all was that he purported to furnish them with a philosophy. Artists had never been admitted to the upper orders during the Middle Ages (page 429); and with significant exceptions, they still deeply felt the need of a theory to which they might refer. Alberti seemed to explain what they wanted to have made clear; namely, that the manual work they did was directed, not by mere craft rules, but by principles comprehensible only through the intellect. In order to understand how they felt, the reader must try to imagine a society where conceptual thinking was given an altogether arbitrary, but very effective prestige. Respectability itself hinged upon the difference betwen the liberal and the adulterine—on whether, that is, a man's activities were honorable or menial.

We cannot follow Alberti's thought in detail within the space of the present volume; let the student read over for himself the material so well selected and so well translated in Elizabeth Gilmore Holt's convenient publication.* Those who do may be disconcerted, for Alberti's theoretical writings are by no means so lucid as they ought to be. In perusing any book of an earlier day, one expects to be delayed from time to time by terms which now have a different usage or even a different meaning; but with Alberti, the reader will find himself puzzled by more than vocabulary. As a literary man, he lacked the compositional power he displayed as an architect. As a philosopher, he often did not perceive the inevitable implications of his own ideas. The meat of his thought comes in small pieces, surrounded by a dressing of manners and replete with allusions to matters that are no longer interesting. Nevertheless, anyone who wants to understand the Renaissance will find il-

---

* Elizabeth Gilmore Holt, *Literary Sources of Art History,* Princeton University Press, Princeton, N. J., 1947.

Fig. 14.1 Alberti. Self-portrait. Bronze. 7 29/32 inches high by 5 11/32 inches wide. Washington, National Gallery. (Previously in the Dreyfus and the Kress Collections.)

lumination on every page. Many of the ideas illustrate verbatim borrowing from the classical. Others attack problems that have been in the air since Alberti's time, and still are. Sooner or later, there is an explicit statement of almost every belief, hope, and desire which made the Renaissance operate.

Perhaps the most important idea put forward by Alberti was the notion that beauty was a philosophical reality beyond the reach of taste and fancy. The thought was not far out of line with the Neoplatonism presently to become popular at Florence (pages 529–534), a fact which gave it an extra chance for survival. Carried to its logical conclusion, such a concept might well have led Alberti in the end to a philosophy not unlike that of modern cubism. As it was, his favorite art was architecture, the nearest thing to complete abstraction socially acceptable in a world committed to representation.

It was imperative, of course, for him to reconcile his abstracted theories of beauty with the practical problems of art as he found it. It would have been useless to urge artists to abandon the representative convention (page 439), and ridiculous to suggest that a humanistic society find expression by way of some artistic vehicle other than the human figure. We do not say that Alberti ever wanted to bring about either; we merely say that the logic of his own philosophy would have forced him in such a direction had he followed it out.

As a matter of fact, his personal taste was altogether in keeping with that of his contemporaries, and not with his theories. Nature was his goddess.

He loved her, and could blame her for nothing. He broke into tears at the sight of a noble tree or pleasant field; and once when sick, he cured himself by looking at a beautiful landscape. We cannot doubt the intensity or the sincerity of his feelings. They were an expression of the most profound faith imaginable, but they surely imposed upon him the necessity of resolving a conflict between his heart and his head.

The task was to find a way to make abstract beauty seem a natural thing. In doing it, he was helped by the recently recovered text of Vitruvius (page 97). It was Alberti who put on the first full-powered effort to arrive once again at the lost canon of proportions of the Greek sculptor Polyclitus. "We have taken the trouble," he said, "to set down the principal measurements of a man. We did not, however, choose this or that single body; but as far as possible, we tried to note and set down in writing the highest beauty scattered, as if in calculated portions, among many bodies. . . . We have chosen a number of bodies considered by the skillful to be the most beautiful, and we have taken the dimensions of each of these. These we compared together, and leaving aside the extreme measurments which were below or above certain limits, we chose out those which the agreement of many cases showed to be the average."

In the end, Alberti compiled a table of dimensions, but the passage just quoted is indeed a tricky one. Every idea in it is slippery. Obviously it says that the *type* is more important than the single manifestation, but what reason was there (except for an apparent classical precedent) to imagine that the arithmetical average would be identical to pure beauty? Such worries did not delay the research, however. Alberti simply declared that his system enabled us to discover nature's intention. He did not raise the question as to whether nature was, or was not, attempting to produce ideal beauty; he simply assumed that such must be the case. Apparently, it did not bother him, either, that calling in "the skillful" betrayed a disloyal bit of doubt on his own part with respect to the infallibility of nature's judgment. But what did not embarrass Alberti disturbed no one else. One by one, Italian painters and sculptors went down the line, and the result was to give High Renaissance art an idealized figure style in considerable contrast with the realism which had remained standard almost until the end of the 15th century.

Alberti's interest in ideal anatomy was a manifestation of his general belief in the perfectibility of mankind, a subject upon which his personal endowments foreordained an exceedingly optimistic view. Nowhere can we read more eloquent and emphatic statements as to what might be accomplished. It was axiomatic in his thinking that man must be impelled upward by the power of his own humanity. With the will for a driving force, he urged men to work upon the raw material of themselves. Because natural gifts are unevenly distributed, he told every man to assess his own, to perfect the good qualities, and restrain the others. Having done that, he told men to live. And what would be the end of such a life? As much, said he, as a man might want to achieve.

Those ideas, if we apply them to the history of the past five centuries, have an endlessly ramified significance. No social force has been more powerful than the belief (essentially an artistic one) that mankind can be improved. Temporary, and perhaps peculiar to the era of the Renaissance and to Italy, was the further belief that important results might be expected within the span of a lifetime. Boundless enthusiasm for boundless achievement was the engine that made Alberti go; and he, more than any other figure of the time, personified the impulse for the innumerable beautified bodies destined to appear in Italian art. He also gave voice to the motive behind countless ensembles of architecture the world over, their cost incalculable, and their purpose to provide a setting for man.

It was the last-mentioned topic—the alteration of the environment for the better—that furnished the pretext for Alberti's book on architecture, which was intended as the crowning achievement of his career. It circulated widely in manuscript before being printed in 1485, about twenty years after the very first press had been set up in Italy. In its pages we may read one statement after another having to do with the general theme of the dignity of man.

With an unusual insight into what makes people want to live, Alberti, in the 2nd chapter of Book VI, set forth certain ideas about beauty which deserve wider credence. Beauty, he said, is a great power in society. Not a luxury, not merely worth its cost, but an essential food for the good life. Alberti praised the Greeks and Romans for insisting upon beauty in their laws, their ceremonies, and even their military affairs. He fastened on architecture as the most conspicuous of the arts, indeed the only art whose imagery we cannot escape, and he correctly pointed out that beauty was not an adornment of a building, but a necessity. Without beauty, he declared, the deepest resentments are fomented, and all classes of men get stirred up. There was an irony in his entertaining such a view at such a time, for in spite of the fact that beautiful buildings were continuously going up all over Italy, Italian society could hardly have been more continuously excited to acts of private and public cruelty and violence. We must remember, however, that Alberti was thinking of the ultimate effect upon mankind of an environment completely made over by the creative achievements of art. His ideas have a curiously familiar ring, because we so often hear exactly the same kind of thing today whenever housing, city planning, or any other aspect of human welfare may be mentioned.

Alberti's architectural imagination followed out his train of thought into conceptions of epic grandeur. He never forgot the importance of refinement in matters of detail, but his greater vision embraced whole cities. He visualized a metropolis composed according to artistic principles, with each handsome structure a harmonious element in the general design. The government, he thought, should have buildings of the most imposing kind (a conception that looked forward to Versailles and every modern capital). He counseled the leading citizens to maintain establishments proper for their station, warning them at the same time to avoid overt display.

Though his background and personality were aristocratic and though he plainly thought society depended upon a creative minority, he had the kindness and consistency to realize that the less gifted majority must also participate in the dignity of man. He carried that idea to its logical conclusion. Hospitals should be provided, he said, to keep cripples and beggars off the street. The relief of suffering, it would seem, was but a secondary motive; the central purpose was to save such persons from a degradation of their human dignity, and to prevent the sight of them from offending others. Going still further, he spoke strongly against contemporary prisons. Conceding that society must confine criminals, he declared that the vicious were entitled to decent jails.

Sociological preoccupations of the kind just described inevitably suggest that buildings ought to be useful, a point to which Alberti closed the eyes and ears of many readers by his strong emphasis on the value of beauty. It cannot be said, however, that he was guilty of anything worse than faulty weighting of the subject matter. In a number of places, and in different ways, he made it plain that he had no patience with an inconvenient building, or with one that cost more than it ought. His error was to think that practical requirements were easily fulfilled. "The having satisfied necessity," he says in Book VI, Chapter 2, "is a very small matter. . . ." Elsewhere, he urges the architect always to focus his attention on beauty, merely keeping function somewhere in the back of his mind. That thousands have followed this advice is all too evident; but as we have seen, the difference between Alberti's theories and those of the 20th century is far less than one might suppose.

One of the features which made Alberti's writings acceptable to artists was the fact that he never failed to point out how esthetic theory might be applied to practical problems. With respect to the creation of an architecture suitable to the dignity of the race, he thought he had an infallible formula. He depended upon Vitruvius. The inelegance of the Vitruvian Latin was doubtless a matter for regret to a man who was himself a stylist in that language, but every word nevertheless seemed golden. Where other classical authors made allusions to art, Vitruvius told how he personally had gone about putting up Roman temples, and gave directions for doing the same. If we consider the temper of the times, it is no wonder Alberti thought he was reading the word of God. At any rate, it would seem that he never discerned a significant difference between the architecture Vitruvius described and the perfect beauty for which his heart yearned.

In addition to what he could glean from Vitruvius, Alberti had expended an immense amount of his own time studying the classical monuments. His observations must not be confused with the mere contemplation of scenery which happened to be enhanced by Roman ruins; it amounted to a thorough course of self-discipline. He examined classical architecture by measuring it, and the data he took home would have enabled a good workman to build the like anywhere. With utter confidence, therefore, he furnished his readers with precise specifications for the classical orders.

When he published his tables for the classical orders, Alberti threw the door open to a more literal interpretation of classicism, to the implications of which we must now turn our attention. The reader will keep in mind, of course, that a classical revival of any kind is never a simple matter of cause and effect. Because classical Antiquity was no single thing, it is always necessary to know what department of ancient art was, in any particular instance, operating as a guide for the modern artists. We also need to know how thoroughly they understood it, and how strictly they were attempting to copy.

In the case of Alberti, it was the orders as used by the Romans for which he furnished dimensions. He knew nothing of Greek architecture. Neither did anyone else. The entire Renaissance went its way and ran its course, in fact, largely upon inspiration from Rome.

Neither were Alberti's findings final. His book proved to be merely the first in a very long series of similar publications. With respect to the orders, it was actually superseded rather soon by an even more minute analysis published in 1563 by Giacomo Vignola, who also worked for the popes at Rome. Nor was Vignola alone. In 1573, Andrea Palladio (page 642), whose country houses in northern Italy set the model for similar houses in England and America, published his *Four Books on Architecture*. These books and others like them set an Italian and Renaissance precedent for similar publication elsewhere. Figure 15.96, page 817, is a plate from a typical English volume of the early 18th century. The names cited are merely suggestive of many others, and the important thing to understand is that each and every one of the architects involved purported to furnish new and better information about classical architecture, plus the very latest ideas about how it might be adapted to the necessities of modern building. Penrose's work at Athens (page 93) merely capped the climax of the custom initiated by Alberti. The origin of the custom, it ought to be added, was Alberti's belief that the good architect must also be a scholar. The extraordinary number of publications resulting is but another index to the fact that his ideas prevailed and endured.

But the full meaning of Alberti's classical research has not even yet been made plain. His classicism, like every other brand of classicism, depended upon the belief that the ancient world, and the men in it, were better than the modern world may reasonably expect to become within the measurable future. It is to that faith we always refer when we speak of classical "authority," and it was Alberti who made classical authority all too accessible. His tables made it easy to copy the Roman orders. In itself, doing so might have been an innocent activity had not the very same tables tacitly labeled as ridiculous any further experiment with the orders. It would hardly be too much to say that he laid the dead hand of the past on architecture itself, and thus begot the dullest five centuries in the history of the art.

♦ *Alberti's Buildings* Alberti's travels on Vatican business took him now and again into northern Italy, and it was there that he received the commissions for his most important architecture. His relation to the buildings was new and different from what had been customary before. In part, the matter may have been decided by his responsibilities at Rome and by the impossibility of his remaining away for indefinite periods; but his procedure nevertheless reflected a modified conception of the function of the architect. Alberti merely drew the plans. He had a good knowledge of practical construction; but having furnished the design, he left the work to be carried out by others. His custom in that respect has remained the standard usage in Europe and America; and as a philosophical proposition, it will be noted that the net effect was to minimize the adulterine element in building and to maximize architecture's role as a liberal art.

At Rimini, Alberti worked for Sigismondo Malatesta. It appears not to have concerned him that the man was the quintessence of Renaissance paganism, or that the commission was to remodel a church originally dedicated to Saint Francis but now intended as a kind of shrine in honor of Sigismondo's mistress Isotta. The fabric of the building was Gothic. Alberti merely undertook to conceal it with an overlay of Renaissance forms. The plans were carried out only in part; and the renovation remains incomplete today. In its day, it was—with reference to the future progress of style—well ahead of its time.

Across the façade, Alberti put a Roman Arch Order (page 195), the first of its kind in modern architecture. Instead of pilasters, he used columns, and he rendered the entablature in ressault. The heavier proportions and

Fig. 14.2 Rimini. San Francesco. South side, as remodeled 1446–1455 according to plans by Alberti. (Alinari)

greater relief of the members constituted an important indication of the way Renaissance art was to develop. The remark applies not only to architecture, but to sculpture and painting as well; for where the 15th-century artists tended to deal in line and surface, those of the High Renaissance worked with mass.

Down the sides of the building (Fig. 14.2), Alberti designed a powerful arcade running the length of the nave. The arches are round. The soffits are very deep. Each arch might be described as a short bay of tunnel vaulting. The supporting verticals are substantial piers of masonry, with rectangular cross-section. The design appears to be derivative from the fabric of the Colosseum at Rome, but the proportions were more carefully studied, and the detail more elegant.

Under each arch, Alberti placed a sarcophagus. Sigismondo and Isotta were to have been similarly entombed on the façade, and these lateral arrangements were meant to accommodate illustrious members of their spectacular court. The custom of putting a sarcophagus under an arch in the thickness of a wall was a very old one, but Alberti's design opened up new vistas in

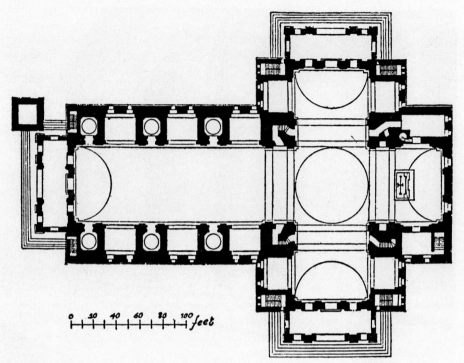

Fig. 14.3 Mantua. Sant'Andrea. Plan. (From Nikolaus Pevsner, *European Architecture*, Scribner, 1948.)

mortuary architecture. His means for expression were completely abstract: mass, line, proportion, light, shadow. Yet he was able to convey an impression as definitely as it might have been done in words, or by representative art. One can not think of these sarcophagi as coffins where lie the worn-out bodies of more or less forgotten men. It is obvious the place was built for heroes.

Sant'Andrea at Mantua (Figs. 14.3–5) was Alberti's most characteristic and influential design. He drew the plans for Ludovico Gonzaga, then head of Mantua's greatest family, and he left the construction to be carried out by the court architect. Most of the work was done after Alberti's death in 1472. The surface decoration of the interior (painted, not relief) was not designed by him. Typical North Italian work of the time and neither good nor bad in itself, it is out of scale with the proportions of the church. The arrangement of windows in the drum of the dome was likewise no plan of Alberti's. Otherwise, the church is much as he intended it to be.

The plan (Fig. 14.3) had been predicted by Brunelleschi's Santo Spirito at Florence (Fig. 13.23, page 516), and also by the arrangement of several North Italian churches. Sant'Andrea is nevertheless the key monument. It

Figs. 14.4–5 Mantua. Sant'Andrea. Built from plans drawn by Alberti. Started 1472. (below) Interior of the nave. (Anderson; Alinari)

conforms only in a general way to the basilican scheme. It is actually a new type, the first really successful modification of the traditional Christian church.

Alberti's manifest purpose was to give full expression to the plastic impulse already strong in his earlier work. He wanted a more emphatic modeling for the masonry, and a greater gravity of effect. He also wanted a more definite, more simple, and more lucid molding of the spatial volume enclosed. For such results, the traditional division of nave and aisles was unsuitable. He therefore canceled out the aisles. He eliminated the familiar nave arcade. He specified instead some immense and closely spaced verticals of masonry, so large that only three were required to run the length of the nave; the fourth belongs to the crossing. So ample were those uprights that it was practical to make them hollow; a small chapel is contained within each of them. Between each pair, there was room for a chapel of slightly larger area.

It would be difficult to name another interior so complicated as that of Sant'Andrea which has anything like an equal lucidity of arrangement. Alberti used large members in order to use very few members. When one enters the western doors, the furthest piers stand out almost as clearly as the nearest. The plastic shape of the enclosed space is completely free from impediment, encumbrance, or obstacle; and the same may be said of the tunnel vault above, the first of its kind during the Renaissance. Such features bespeak the inner spirit of classicism, so perfectly a part of the architect's nature as to be the material of his intuitions. The argument from classical authority (furnished by Alberti to lesser men, and for them poison) seems for himself to have been an esthetic food. It would be incorrect to say that Sant'Andrea marked the recapture of Roman architecture. It followed Roman principles, to be sure, but there were never any architects in ancient Rome good enough to design it.

The façade of Sant'Andrea (Fig. 14.4) was hardly less important than the interior. Much criticized because its height does not correspond with the height of the church behind, it is in reality a porch. As such, its function may be understood as simply to dignify the entranceway, and its artistic business is with the man outdoors, not with the nave behind. Within the limitations of such a scheme, Alberti's design may be considered a notable contribution in the vexed matter of adapting the classical orders to modern buildings (page 111). Originally worked out for temples of one story only, the orders fit nothing else perfectly. Modern architecture, however, almost invariably demands several floors.

Alberti's purpose seems to have been to give the world an academic demonstration to show how those disparate elements might be combined. Somewhat gratuitously (for there is no such division within), he gave himself three stories, and marked them with the aisle doors, and with windows at two levels above. Each window, it will be noted, rises from a horizontal of slight projection. The central entrance is a tunnel vault. Its height is the same as the higher windows to either side, and its shape is marked on the front by a pair of pilasters and a classical molding around the arch.

Above, around, and through the items of the ensemble, he ran the members of a complete temple front, also rendered in low relief. A pediment and entablature frame in the top of the façade. Beneath are four great Corinthian pilasters running unbroken to the ground. Those latter are of the proper classical proportion for their height. They are thus large in relation to every detail to which they are juxtaposed. Nothing is big enough to compete in any serious way with their vertical strength. They pass upward regardless of the delicate horizontals, and they pull everything together and tie the composition into one.

Any order that runs through several stories is technically described as a *colossal order*. The term has no reference to absolute size, and would be used for the colonnettes of a fireplace if they fulfilled the condition of running through two or more horizontal divisions. By giving the weight of his authority to the colossal order, Alberti unquestionably furnished Renaissance architecture with a useful compositional resource. Almost any collection of sculpture, openings, and what not can be brought into unity if a colossal order of sufficient strength is merely superimposed. But like everything else that is easy, the device has too often been relied upon to correct mistakes which never should have been made in the first place.

Sant'Andrea was too radical a building to become immediately popular, but in the long run, it exerted a great influence upon Renaissance architecture. Alberti was connected with the Vatican when Nicholas the 5th (regnal dates 1447–1455) decided not to repair the ailing Early Christian church of St. Peter, but to tear it down and build anew. We may fairly infer that Alberti had much to do with swinging the decision against sentiment for the past, and forward toward a grander modern Rome. When, at length, Bramante's first plans for the new building were approved by Julius the 2nd (1503), they were plans calling for a church more than a little like Sant'Andrea. Bramante died in 1514, leaving the work only begun. After various false starts with other architects, Michelangelo was finally put in charge in the year 1546. He revised Bramante's plans to make the immense structure even more like Sant'Andrea (page 614). The example set at St. Peter's laid down the style for almost all of the smaller churches built in Rome from that date forward. The Church of the Gesù, designed by Vignola and begun in 1568, is a typical example (page 689). The churches of Rome in turn set the type for baroque and rococo churches everywhere else. It may fairly be said, in fact, that Alberti's elimination of the nave arcade, with evident improvement in the floor space, very substantially modified the basilican tradition to which Europe had so long been unswervingly loyal.

♦ *Alberti, Bramante, and the Central Church*   Alberti also drew plans for another and less celebrated church at Mantua, and the type he chose for that second building has a special significance. We refer to San Sebastiano, probably designed in 1460. Because Brunelleschi's Santa Maria degli Angeli had never been finished (page 515), San Sebastiano was the first good-sized modern church to be completed on the central plan. Experimentation with the central plan might seem to indicate nothing more than one more revival in an age given to revivals; but knowing what happened afterward, we can see that a considerable movement was under way, with Alberti among the leaders. The difficulty of adapting the central form to the ritual was no less than it ever had been (page 249). What, then, was the appeal?

The answer seems to be twofold. In the first place, as Nikolaus Pevsner has so well put it in his brief but profound history of architecture, the central building seemed to be the perfect architectural expression of Renaissance individualism. By standing precisely at the floor's middle point, a man identifies his body with the axis of the design. He and he alone—for only one man can be there at a time—becomes for the moment the creature to whom the governing symmetry refers, the central integer that brings it significance. No other kind or type of artistic composition puts the single personality in a similar position. If the church has nobility of design, the sensation is glorious. If the church is enormous as well, the personality seems to gain scale in proportion with the architecture. The basilican interior invited no such feelings.

The second reason for the rather sudden popularity of central churches during the Renaissance had to do with a recrudescence of age-old ideas about the symbolic meaning of the domical shape. As made plain by evidence recently brought together and made accessible in E. Baldwin Smith's monograph on the dome, such notions may be traced back almost as far as the race. The precise symbolism has changed from time to time, but no race has ever become quite so controlled by its head as to disassociate itself completely from the impression that domes, as such, are animate with holy power. As soon as Florentine Neoplatonism started to do its work in Italy, the dome began to be specifically identified with the heaven from which mankind had been banished, and toward which it aspired to climb back. Neoplatonism also contributed the concept that beauty, especially the beauty of the primeval state of grace and glory, was an abstract and inaccessible ideal.

At any other time in the history of art, such difficult ideas might have

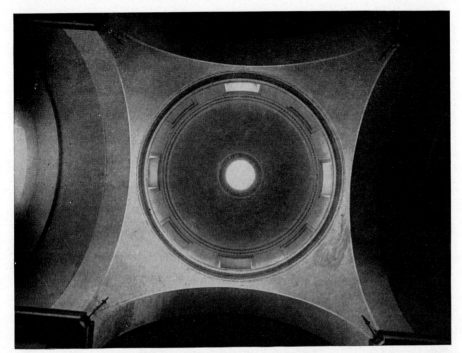

Fig. 14.6 Rome. Sant'Eligio degli Orifici. Interior. Looking up into the dome. 1509. Designed by Raphael. (Gab. Fot. Naz.)

received indifferent treatment in the visual arts, but Renaissance Italy was literally full of artists who wanted more than anything else to find means for expressing sublime concepts. A number of domes were designed with the deliberate intention of making the appearance, as seen from the interior, suggest heaven in all its transcendent, ineffable, and utter beauty. As a class, the domes of the period are distinguished by a deliberate separation of the dome from the drum (by one method or another) and of the drum from the pendentives beneath—in obvious parallelism with the Platonic scheme of an existence arranged in graded categories, each higher and better than the one beneath. Without doubt, the most perfect realization of such notions was the dome of Sant'Eligio degli Orifici (Fig. 14.6), which has the same ineluctable fascination as a crystal ball. It was designed by Raphael.

Alberti's endorsement of the central type set in motion a whole series of designs. Among the designers involved in the tendency, Bramante was the most important man; and among the centralizing churches he designed, we may mention the so-called "Tempietto" at San Pietro in Montorio, Rome, and Santa Maria della Consolazione at Todi (Fig. 14.7). When Bramante took charge of the works at St. Peter's, he firmly intended to make the great new building a central church on the Greek cross scheme. When Michelangelo succeeded Bramante, he had his own ideas about details, but he had no inten-

Fig. 14.7 Todi. Santa Maria della Consolazione. Church, 1508–1524; dome, 1606. Height: about 165 feet. Width: about 145 feet. (Alinari)

tion of changing the fundamental arrangement of the composition. He died, in fact, without ever imagining that St. Peter's would not be a central church.

While all that was going on at the capital, sizable central churches were going up in the provinces, of which we may mention San Biagio at Montepulciano, designed by the elder San Gallo and dating from 1518–1537. It looked, indeed, as though the basilica had been superseded and as though the central type would be remembered as the chief contribution of High Renaissance architecture.

The popularity of the scheme might, indeed, have endured a very long time had it not been for the Protestant Reformation. That movement, seemingly nonarchitectural in its implications, raised the question as to whether the ideals of the Renaissance had not been responsible, in part at least, for the Protestant defection. The general tenor of opinion at the Council of Trent, which sat from 1545 to 1563 and which was called to start the Counter-Reformation, held that the Church should turn its eyes and methods back to the usage of earlier generations. Among those usages was the traditional basilican plan for churches, the appeal of which was strong enough to dictate a fundamental alteration in St. Peter's itself. Carlo Maderna was therefore employed to ruin Michelangelo's composition by adding the present extended nave (Fig. 15.1). The work dates from 1606–1626; and with it, the central type crossed the great divide.

THE ARRIVAL OF THE HIGH RENAISSANCE

While it is hardly possible to exaggerate Alberti's part in starting the High Renaissance, there was a substantial interval between the time his ideas were made public and the time they took effect. We may think of him as a prime mover calling the new era into being, but the fact is that he was dead before we can note any considerable frequency in the phenomena which marked the arrival of another cultural climate. The actual transition from the Early Renaissance to the High took place during the last quarter of the 15th century, and we may pause here to note a few of the events and tendencies which made themselves felt, attracted approval, and finally changed the entire scheme of things.

For the art historian, the most conspicuous fact of all was the shift of the cultural capital of Italy from Florence to Rome. That had doubtless been inevitable from the moment when Nicholas the 5th decided to build a gigantic new St. Peter's, but various other happenings predicted the turn of the tide.

Among them was the construction of a new chapel at the Vatican, known as the Sistine Chapel. Esthetically undistinguished, the room was nevertheless notable for being bigger than almost any other private or semiprivate chamber designed up to that time. It is a tunnel-vaulted oblong measuring 133 feet long, 43 feet wide, and 85 feet high. It was designed with high windows and large areas of wall, doubtless with the idea of providing space for mural painting. The chapel was ready in 1481; and there being no competent painters at Rome, the Pope summoned prominent masters from Umbria and Florence. They painted the pictures which are still there on the side walls, but not one of them had the breadth of style requisite for the task. Botticelli, for example, did three frescoes which are curiously busy with delicate passages, and utterly empty of the monumentality that was needed. Perugino's *Christ Presenting the Keys to Saint Peter* came closest to success; but it, too, merely reached toward the "Grand Style." Obviously, the habits of visualization peculiar to the Early Renaissance were out of keeping with the taste of the incoming era. A new and larger imagery was requisite to fit the scale of the big pictures which alone were appropriate in a more pretentious setting. The men who had grown up in the tradition of 15th-century realism were unable to make

the change; but by a kind of instinct, the members of the next artistic generation knew just what to do.

The reign of Julius the 2nd (1505–1513) coincides with the actual achievement of artistic primacy at Rome. That energetic pontiff pushed forward the
procrastinated project for the new St. Peter's. It was he who appointed
Bramante architect, with the result that construction commenced in 1506.
He was the man who summoned Michelangelo to Rome to design and build
for him a tomb which, had it been completed, would have outdone the
Mausoleum at Halicarnassus. It was he, also, who commissioned the frescoes
of the Sistine Chapel ceiling. While Michelangelo was working on that stupendous task, Julius kept Raphael simultaneously at work on the frescoes of
the Vatican Stanze, the paintings which forever guarantee their author's place
in history. These are merely the most famous of the many enterprises in
progress, and the activity described is to be contrasted with the very few
commissions which had emanated from the Vatican during the previous two
generations.

The centralization of the Renaissance at Rome was concomitant with
the spread of the Renaissance to the rest of Europe—for it was during the
early 16th century that Italy began to furnish the modern world with a cultural leadership similar and comparable to that exerted by Athens during
later antiquity. As indicated by Ficino's immense correspondence (page 530),
there already existed a considerable tendency for northern intellectuals to
turn their faces toward Italy; but, as compared with the 15th century, the era
of the High Renaissance is chiefly different for the appearance all over
Europe of men who not only equaled the learning and genius of the Italians,
but thought in just the same way and belonged to the same culture. The
Dutchman Erasmus (1466?–1536), who published the first modern edition of
Aristotle and worked on more accurate translations of the scriptures, has been
remembered ever since as epitomizing in his person everything that was good
in the humanism of the period. Copernicus (1473–1543), a Pole who knew
Rome well but spent most of his life in East Prussia, may be cited as the
author of the most influential publication of the entire era. His *De revolu-
tionibus orbium coelestium* (1543) settled once and for all the perennially
disputed question of whether the sun was or was not the center of the universe. Contemporary with such men and upon terms of personal friendship
with them were men of similar caliber and similar interests in other lands—
Thomas More and John Colet, for example, merely to mention two names
which will be familiar to the English-speaking student. By pursuing the subject further, we would rapidly find ourselves building up a picture of a
Europe which more and more subscribed to a common philosophy of life
with its creative center in Italy. For the matter of our present interest, it is
necessary to add that Italian standards in art followed Italian standards of

every other kind: the 16th century was the period when almost all of the European world consciously cast off the Late Gothic and adopted the style of the Renaissance.

The first half of the 16th century is the only time when Germany produced artists of world importance. The best of them retained a certain measure of northern taste, but all were strongly conscious of the Renaissance. As compared with the great Italians, Albrecht Dürer (pages 652–658) and Pieter Brueghel (pages 658–665) stand out in history as men of similar mind and equal caliber.

France deliberately imported the Italian style as a result of the military expeditions into Italy, beginning with the invasion of 1494 (page 544). The wing added to the château of Blois in 1503 by Louis the 12th is generally mentioned as the first French monument in the new manner; but actually, it amounts merely to a sobering of the later Gothic. The same can be said with similar force for the more elaborate additions put up by Francis the 1st between 1505 and 1519, and it was that very same Francis who invited Leonardo to France. The great man died there in 1519 without having accomplished much, but his coming was reflective of a conscious policy. Francis imported other Italians, mostly second-string men, and some of them stayed. From that beginning sprang the exotic School of Fontainebleau, a deliberate negation of the native and northern tradition.

Spain, like the rest of continental Europe, embraced the Renaissance during the first generation of the 16th century. Her painters had hitherto been stylistically dependent upon Flanders (page 486). They now cultivated generalized forms and triangular compositions like those of Raphael (Fig. 14.16), and retained that habit until the coming of the Baroque. Even the exuberant Plateresque architecture, one of the great achievements of the Late Gothic, modulated its details toward the classical, and sobered down.

Only in England did the tide of the Renaissance fail to sweep all before it. Henry the 8th (regnal dates 1509–1547) is frequently nominated as the first Renaissance king of England, but that is more nearly correct with respect to his orientation and outlook than it is of English art. Hampton Court (1515–1540) and other buildings often catalogued as "English Renaissance" fit the characterization in date rather than style.

Thus in England—and especially in England because of the greater vitality with which native taste survived—we may note a major oddity of modern culture: the coexistence in the same society of a native and vulgar tradition beside an elegant and imported one. In Italy, the contrast is unknown, and its tensions never felt. Peasant and scholar alike inherit direct from Latinity. But in all northern countries, we are constantly confronted by a double standard—Chaucer on the one hand, and Milton on the other.

Or Hogarth's truculent assertion of a British art resistant to continental standards as exemplified by Sir Anthony Van Dyck and his followers.

The impression made upon Alberti by his long residence at Rome was symptomatic of the impression Rome now made on everybody. Florence had begun its artistic tradition with Giotto, and Florentine artists had continued in the progressive spirit, with an eye always on the future and a reputation yet to make. The shift to Rome was a shift to another world. Rome was and is overwhelmingly a city of the past. Ancient ruins of immense size loom up in every vista. To this day, no one can point to their equal; and the world hardly offers a similarly wholesale demonstration of scale combined with permanence. It was inevitable that artists would be affected by the spectacle. In subtle ways, their motivation changed from originality to emulation. A number of single incidents, none crucial or definitive in itself, contributed each in its own way to the state of mind described.

In 1506, the celebrated *Laocoön* group (Fig. 6.21, page 176) was dug up. Michelangelo himself examined it with minute care. His admiration was boundless. The experience doubtless turned his attention to the Pergamene division of ancient art from which he drew the inspiration for his later figure style. The *Belvedere Torso* (Figs. 6.22–23, page 177), a less conspicuous example of the same kind, had been in the possession of the Colonna family as early as the 1430's, but first came to public attention when Clement the 7th (regnal dates 1523–1534) brought it to the Vatican. To those monuments, it is perhaps worthwhile to add the name of the *Farnese Hercules,* which came to light in 1540.

Archeological activity is always interesting; but in the flamboyant musculature of those particular antiquities, Italian artists sensed something lacking in their own art. Apparently they felt that the statues revealed man's most complete and perfect physical development. All artists with a taste for force and power were impelled toward experiments along the same line. Even those, like Leonardo and Raphael, who had no special liking for power as such, became profoundly interested in the elaborate twisting of the body, the contrapposto, which has become almost a synonym for the figure style of the High Renaissance—as, indeed, it had been a synonym for the particular class of ancient statue then brought so much to the fore.

If, in our imagination, we add the news of lesser finds to such famous bits of excavation, it is easy to see that the recovery of antiquity was a lively topic at Rome, and kept on as a lively topic for a long while. Other things that were going on also contributed to the same effect, and gave men added reason to be conscious of Roman greatness.

When, for instance, it was desired to move the Vatican Obelisk from the Circus of Nero, where it stood, to its present position in the middle of the

Piazza San Pietro, no one knew how to do it. A conference of experts was summoned from all over Italy. They talked for weeks. Finally, the scheme presented by Domenico Fontana was adopted. After impressively elaborate preparations, he brought the job off in 1586. An immense amount of public interest came to a focus as the work went on. Everyone who watched was doubtless impressed by the fact that the Roman engineers, acting under orders from Caligula, had in A.D. 41 brought the very same obelisk all the way from Heliopolis on the Nile delta, across the sea, up the Tiber, and into its place about 250 yards from the spot to which Fontana had now moved it.

The events mentioned are but incidents in history. They will nevertheless suggest why so many artists of the highest personal accomplishment were willing to accept classical art as a guide. Some were even willing to accept it as a book of wise and just rules which, if faithfully followed, might be counted upon to yield success. Alberti had suggested such a course when he published his tables for the ancient orders, and the general nature of architecture made it easy for builders to follow his advice—especially those who wished to play safe. Painters and sculptors inevitably had problems which precluded so direct and precise a following of ancient rules, but they too became as classical as it was practical for them to be. In fact, one of the great over-all differences which signalized the advent of the High Renaissance was a turning away from nature, and a yearning for an idealized art comparable to that of antiquity.

The increased classicism of the High Renaissance, cogent though it was, did not exist in its own right, but as an expression of certain spiritual needs whch had become better understood and more openly asserted. The whole era had its genesis in a severe and more profound belief in the dignity of man. For that, the thought and writing of Alberti had prepared the way, but society had started early to move in the direction he seemed to indicate.

In spite of Alberti's generous concern for the masses of the population, one can scarcely find a page in his work which does not in some way or other suggest aristocracy. For leadership, safety, and progress, it seems implicit in what he said that mankind must rely not upon all the people, but upon certain selected persons of superior powers.

During the second half of the 15th century, Italian society had in fact tended to become more and more a court society—royal, noble, or ecclesiastical as the local conditions might require. In general, what was true in Italy was true everywhere; the famous Italian families merely furnished a pattern of life that was copied in other lands. The net result was to concentrate significance within the upper social orders, and the tendency to do so invited the expenditure of a prodigious amount of thought upon the general subject of superiority. What qualities gave a man a right to membership in the privileged circle? What behavior was appropriate for the members thereof between themselves, and in their contacts with the world outside?

Machiavelli's *The Prince* (1514) was an attempt to set forth a political method. Baldassare Castiglione's *The Courtier* (1527) was the most notable among a great many books which attempted to explore the question of how responsible persons ought to act in social situations. Alberti himself, it will be remembered, had raised the question of propriety with respect to architecture and other physical surroundings. Palladio's writings and his architectural practice were an even more thoroughgoing application of the same ideas. In every instance, it was not the generality to whom the discussion was directed, but the better man, supposedly in a position to make far-reaching choices.

The aristocratic mode of life in Italy became identical with the ideal of dignity and produced the standards of decorum which have been stereotyped in Western Europe and all its cultural derivatives. Solemnity was the emotion essential to the new era; people began to take themselves and the progress of their lives with high seriousness. Movement of the body was thought best and wisest when it partook of the cadence of a slow dance. The vocabulary, it came to be thought, ought to be carefully chosen, and the voice used like a musical instrument.

Above all, the new manners called for an impregnable adequacy on the part and in the person of the lady and gentleman. Grace of voice and of posture should, it was thought, be achieved without apparent effort. Ideally, such attributes existed within the character, were unconsciously possessed and employed, might even be instinctive. Overt elegance, either in dress, in bearing, or in one's belongings, logically became an offense; but the worst offense of all would be to prove inadequate to a situation, to be compelled to scramble for control of self and environment and thus to transgress the rhythm and tempo of the gracious life.

The Neoplatonic elements in the new concept of the dignity of man will be evident without specific citation; the ideal man of the High Renaissance would be the man who had completed the course of self-improvement recommended by Alberti and Ficino. A few persons, in the opinion of their contemporaries, actually exemplified the ideal in their own persons. Alberti was such a man, Leonardo and Raphael were others; but the person most often mentioned as the quintessential gentleman of the era was Frederick of Montefeltro, Duke of Urbino, of whom there is a fine portrait by Piero della Francesca. It is notable, however, that the praise directed toward Frederick makes an identity between the excellence of the man and the consistency with which his actions might be explained by reference to a code of behavior. It would be unintelligible, of course, to suggest a code of behavior unless it be assumed that the innumerable situations arising in life are known, can be classified according to type, and the best action prescribed for each. Once that truth is comprehended, the causal connection between Neoplatonism and the High Renaissance becomes obvious.

Unquestionably the people of the High Renaissance had good reason for self-respect. Equally without cavil, we must concede that they had a philosophy which moved the population of Europe far on the road toward achievement of humanity, and added much to Western civilization. But as reflected in the history of art, the increasingly elevated concepts entertained by the controlling members of society resulted in the elimination of certain points of view hitherto notable as fonts of creation. Direct delight in nature, the chief inspiration of 15th-century art, tended to pass out of the emotional pattern. The visual facts of the world no longer evoked the same response, and shortly ceased to furnish an adequate reason for painting and sculpture. At first thought, Leonardo's notebooks (page 572) might seem to contradict the statement just made; but in fact they sustain it: they were and remained entirely private; the work that made his reputation was typical of the new era.

Subject matter took on an imposing depth of significance as the High Renaissance developed and came into its own. Any theme that might be used for a picture, it presently appeared, had to be a theme of cosmic importance. An excellent example was Raphael's *Disputa* (Fig. 14.17), where the painter undertook no less than a visual demonstration of the truth of Transubstantiation, opened heaven before our eyes, and made Christ above the pictorial counterpart of the host on the altar below. It was a remarkable thing that such paintings were even attempted. Even more amazing is the fact that conceptions of similar magnitude were repeatedly and successfully brought off during the Italian 16th century. Most incredible of all was the magnificent clarity, both visual and intellectual, with which stupendous themes were presented. In the case of the Raphael just mentioned, it takes no wit to draw the inference that the wafer of bread is indeed Christ's body, and that the miracle of the Incarnation is repeated every time we perform the sacrament.

The grandeur of view which permeated contemporary society challenged and extended the artistic genius with which Italy was so generously endowed at the time. In the character of the 16th-century Italian artist, nicety of distinction may be said to have supplied something like the motivation furnished by realism a century before. Having once chosen a theme with judicious consideration of its suitability and import, artists and patrons alike put forth a terrific effort toward the analysis and understanding of every detail. Within the drama and meaning of the subject, they sought to recognize the significant facts and actions. To the limit of practical possibility, artistic emphasis was reserved for such; and by the same logic, everything extraneous to the grand purport of the matter in hand was sternly suppressed, even eliminated entirely, regardless of its truth in fact. The end product of the process was an iconography more complicated and elaborate than ever before. Easel pictures containing two or three figures are often inexplicable unless one has at his fingertips a great fund of erudite lore. As for the large wall paintings of the High Renaissance, it usually takes half a day merely to identify the characters depicted and relate each in the briefest way to the central theme (Figs. 14.19–20).

The tendency just described lent a lofty abstraction even to the smallest works of High Renaissance art (Fig. 14.22). The large ones often reached the level of the cosmic and sublime. The very same tendency was intimately operative in changing the figure style, a topic we shall presently consider in detail, but certain general aspects of which are apposite for mention here.

With respect to the human figure, Italian art, as of 1475 and after, found itself in much the same postion as the art of Greece during the generation when the Transitional period became the Great Age. Realistic studies were, of course, no longer an end in themselves. Personality was less interesting than certain more universal qualities of which the figure might be made expressive. Both realism and personality were therefore eliminated even in portraiture. Instead, the figure was refined, idealized, and generalized into a superior type. Nor was the idealization concerned with the body alone; almost every human being who appears in 16th-century Italian art seems to be thinking an important thought, or to be under the spell of profound insight. For the expression of such content (and in keeping with the contemporary taste for codifying everything under the sun) an entire system of pose and gesture was built up for the use of painters and sculptors, and presently became very nearly standardized. As was bound to happen, a writer ultimately appeared to set the matter forth in print. In 1593, a man named Cesare Ripa published a book called *Iconologia*—in effect, a quasi-official catalogue purporting to furnish artists with the right imagery for a great variety of situations and subjects. The headings were arranged alphabetically; and if the reader cares to spend an hour paging through, he will find brief articles, each illustrated by a clumsy woodcut showing an appropriate personification for *Ambition, Benignity, Confidence, Fecundity, Infelicity, Penitence, Tragedy,* and several hundred other rather abstruse conceptions. It seems odd that such a volume, to our notions both dull and presumptuous, could have enjoyed any currency among creative artists of the first rank; but it appears to have proved useful. Otherwise, why were there a number of editions, published in several different places?

The increased formality in behavior and the more analytical study of classical art also and inevitably evoked extreme formalism in the arrangement of works of art. Except for instances here and there and noted from time to time in the chapters above, composition as such had received very little systematic study at any period prior to the later 15th century. It then became a matter of general interest. By 1550 or thereabouts, the subject was as well understood as it ever has been, and nobody has added much to what was then a matter of general knowledge in Italy.

In keeping with their classical heritage, the 16th-century artists relied upon geometry as the governing principle of design. Buildings were almost always given a symmetrical plan on the Roman model (page 197). Pictures and groups of sculpture were universally composed according to the organic system of the Greeks (pages 66–67). As in Greek design, the geometry was (so long as the High Renaissance lasted) kept simple and lucid. Small paintings were generally arranged with reference to the vertical plane of the canvas only. Most of them compose on a triangular pattern (Figs. 14.13, 16). The circle and half circle came next in popularity (Fig. 14.22), followed in statistical frequency by arrangements of an elliptical nature. The immense wall paintings which were popular during the 16th century often included a very large number of figures. Space had to be represented in order to accommodate them, and the problem of arrangement was complicated thereby. The typical solution is once again illustrated by Raphael's *Disputa* (Fig. 14.17). It was geometrical and organic; but the governing geometrical figures—in that instance, half circles—lie in the horizontal plane rather than the vertical, and refer more to the space of the picture than to its surface.

LEONARDO DA VINCI

Leonardo da Vinci (1452–1519) was the man who created the style of the High Renaissance as applied to painting and sculpture. His relation to the new period was analogous to the service performed by Donatello for the artists of the 15th century; but in spite of his great influence upon European art, it is a mistake to think of him as an artist. He spent only a small part of his time painting, and the catalogue of his surviving pictures, according to Bernhard Berenson's latest list, numbers only nineteen examples, some of which are challenged by other critics and several of which are not entirely by Leonardo's hand. A more accurate and fairer view of this great man's career would make it necessary for us to describe him as a scientist and engineer. Inasmuch as our business is with his art, we cannot explore his other achievements in detail. The reader will find them well described in Parsons' book (page 509), the only one so far published by an author competent to follow Leonardo's scientific thought. A summary is appropriate here, however; indeed, without it, we could have no notion of the tremendous mentality behind the pictures.

In all its endless ramifications, Leonardo's genius seems to have derived from a single magnificent act of the imagination: he adopted, if indeed he did not invent, the experimental point of view. "If we doubt the certainty of everything that comes to us through the senses," we find him saying in his notes, "how much more should we doubt those things that cannot be tested by the senses. . . ." That position was probably unique at the time. It was not generally understood in a society devoted to the authority of the classics, a fact which made some of the humanists consider Leonardo ill-educated, giving rise to a rather resentful note which says, "Although I may not, like them, be able to quote other authors, I rely on that which is much greater and more worthy: on experience, the mistress of their masters." Leonardo, that is to say, would accept nothing as fact until proved right by rigid experiment or sustained observation of a more general sort. In all his writings, the underlying thought was the existence of fixed and demonstrable law which, if known, would permit man to conduct his affairs according to sure rules.

Proceeding on such assumptions, he spent his life accumulating evidence. His powers of observation were perhaps the greatest ever vested in a human being, and his acumen was unbelievable. It was his habit to note things down, with or without illustrative drawings, and we have inherited a substantial part of his records in the form of the so-called *Notebooks*. They amount to about 5,300 pages, and more may well turn up when, if ever, the libraries and archives of Europe are adequately catalogued.

Considerable mystery of an artificial kind surrounds his methods for recording what he observed. Being more or less ambidextrous like any good painter, and naturally left-handed, he preferred to write backwards. The cipher can be resolved merely by reversing the text in the mirror, and by understanding the abbreviations systematically used. Some of the latter, it must be conceded, still defy the student, and many passages remain unintelligible. With the help of the drawings, however, we can be sure of enough to establish him as a man about two centuries ahead of his time.

In the field of physics, he understood the pull toward the earth's center which Newton later reduced to a formula and introduced as the law of gravity. He investigated the acceleration of falling bodies, the trajectory of projectiles, and centrifugal force. He was familiar with the theory of the conservation of energy, and he put down what we know as the formula for work. His thoughts embraced molecular attraction and the idea of the vacuum, and looked forward to the atom and the electron.

As a painter, Leonardo naturally took a special interest in optics. Discarding the fantastic theory of sight entertained from the remote time of Pythagoras, he correctly reasoned that vision amounted to a triple play between the eye, the object under view, and the light source. He established the law that the angle of incidence of a light ray is equal to the angle of reflection, understood stereoscopic vision and the other geometric aspects of seeing, and was close to the theory of wave-motion by which today we explain both light and sound.

His investigations of color, undertaken along with linear perspective as a basis for a projected *Treatise on Painting,* led him into direct spectral investigation. He made himself a spectroscope, and hoped to develop from his findings something like a scientific basis for the art of representation. He got far enough with the project to note down some minute directions for the control of graded shadows in painting. In connection with his anatomical investigations (he dissected the human eye, and recognized the function of its parts), he discovered the so-called negative afterimage, now believed to be a photochemical reaction of the eye, and the phenomenon used as the starting point for all color theories deriving from the idea of complementaries.

As a geologist, Leonardo understood the difference between the earth's geographical center and its center of gravity. He recognized the stratification of the surface, the existence of fossils, and the general alteration of topography by erosion and deposit. From this, he was able to correct the contemporary notion that the world was about 5,000 years old.

As to whether he came into personal contact with Copernicus during the latter's sojourn at Rome and in North Italy, we cannot say, but the notes make it plain he understood and accepted the Copernican theory of a heliocentric universe. He knew, moreover, that the earth's orbit was an ellipse and that its axis was inclined to the plane of its revolution. Although the telescope is commonly believed a Dutch invention of about 1608, we find in Leonardo's notes a singular and unexplained reference to making "glasses to see the Moon magnified."

His botany was, if anything, more remarkable still. He discovered the relation between tree-rings and the passage of the years, and noted their variation in response to annual tricks and changes in the weather. He also observed and explained the phenomenon known as phylotaxis, that spiraling of branches and leaves which so simply and marvelously arranges for the sunning and ventilation of each leaf, and the systematic delivery of rain drops from leaf to leaf all the way down.

Most of the findings so far mentioned have now been more adequately explored or left behind; but the same statement cannot be made with regard to Leonardo's anatomical drawings. They date a full generation earlier than the eminent anatomist Vesalius, and are the first accurate and competent illustrations of their kind. As the only ones ever made in quantity by an artist who ranks with the great, they are still among the best. It is a matter of record that Leonardo frequented the hospitals and performed autopsies. In the course of such work, he recognized hardening of the arteries and was very close to Harvey's ultimate explanation of the circulatory system. His greatest anatomical researches, however, would appear to be those of a mechanical nature: he was the first to explore and explain the true location of various bones and muscles, and the tensions and leverages of movement.

In these modern days, the impracticality of the pure scientist often furnishes the theme for humorous anecdote; few such men have the least idea how to make their findings of any use at all. By exception to what seems a rule of the game, Leonardo was both pure scientist and engineer.

He instinctively recognized the vital importance of bulk transport, thus anticipating the ideas of Admiral Mahan and Sir Halford Macknider. Much of his active life, therefore, was devoted to the development of canals—until the railroad the one and only economical way to move freight across country. While working for the Sforzas he made a study of the hydraulic problems of the Lombard plain. He later did hydraulic engineering in the Arno valley, and one strong reason for his being called to France in 1516 was the hope that he might construct a canal to connect Tours, Amboise, and Lyon. He did not invent (as has been claimed) the lock gate, but he did improve it. Many locks in daily use today are mechanically inferior to those we see in his drawings.

As a mechanical engineer, Leonardo designed a great many machines. Most of them are the same in principle as modern machines, and many are better than anything put into service at any date previous to the later 19th century. It must be understood that many of them were built and operated, although most seem never to have got beyond the paper plans. A particularly interesting series are the rolling-mills. Leonardo appears to have designed them to roll out long iron bars which he then welded together to make barrels for cannon, a process necessary because of the unreliability of large castings. We have drawings for one of them. It was driven by a horizontal water turbine through worm reduction gears, one of two stages and one of three, thus giving a differential motion to rolls and bar. The notes say that this particular machine is his twenty-second of the same kind, and give formulas for determining the power required—the latter, he says, having been worked out after thirteen machines had been tried.

Smaller guns he was accustomed to cast, and developed new ways for keeping the bore central with the circumference of the barrel. His designs for firearms include multibarrelled weapons (Fig. 14.8), elevation screws, field pieces on wheels, and breechloaders. Mechanically, most of them are superior to everything in general use up to the time of the American Civil War, and better than most in use then. A mere machinist never made a good piece, and those accustomed to weapons will recognize in Leonardo's work the touch of the master.

The drawings show that he was not only interested in the guns themselves, but in the long-term implications of gunpowder. The multibarrelled field pieces indicate a grasp of the principle of fire-power. There are drawings

Fig. 14.8 Leonardo da Vinci. Fieldpiece with 36 barrels. Collection of the International Business Machines Corporation.

illustrating barrage fire, and plans for forts which include cushioning material for the walls—a principle used by Japanese engineers in World War II, and one that proved vexing for the American artillery.

Most famous of all are Leonardo's plans for an airplane. There can be no doubt that he would have been the first man to fly if, like the Wright brothers, he had possessed the gasoline engine. Less well known but equally ingenious are the drawings for a helicopter (Fig. 14.9) and several essays in the field of naval architecture. One of the latter is specially brilliant: a streamlined boat, shaped very nearly in accordance with William Froude's 19th-century findings which established the principle that each following square foot of wetted surface causes less resistance than the one immediately ahead of it—hence the exaggerated length of our modern liners.

In attempting to comprehend the meaning of all this research, probably the greatest total of original work ever accomplished by one man, it is important to appreciate that Leonardo's methods were instinctive, direct, and by rule of thumb. He tried many times to settle upon formulas covering such matters as the strength of beams, the capacity of columns, the breaking strength of wire and rope, and the pressure of water upon the surface of a lock gate. But in all such determination he was foreclosed from success by primitive mathematics. He could not figure out such comparatively simple variations, for instance, as those which come in terms of the square and the cube. That, perhaps, is one of the reasons why his immense and brilliant labors proved almost totally unproductive.

It is obvious that he contemplated a certain number of publications. For the *Treatise on Painting*, we have some parts that look like fair copy, but

Fig. 14.9 Leonardo da Vinci. Helicopter. Collection of the International Business Machines Corporation.

an incredible disorder is the only arrangement discernible in most of the material. The painful conclusion is forced upon us that Leonardo either lacked the inclination or the capacity to bring his work into a state of synthesis. He kept the notebooks with him as long as he lived. No one knows how many there may have been originally; a man who called on him at Amboise in 1517 describes them as "an endless number of volumes." When Leonardo died in 1519, his will directed that all his papers go to Francesco Melzi, a friend and associate. Melzi took them to Milan, and cherished them until he himself died in 1570. Melzi's heirs had no notion of their value. After making one or two ineffectual attempts to realize small sums for them, the later Melzi consigned the collection to the attic, and gave individual volumes away to friends and acquaintances who happened to be interested. Thus the great collection of papers became divided. Many must have been lost. Those that remain are scattered among the various museums and libraries of the world, some private and some public.

Had Leonardo's findings become even moderately well known in the early 16th century, world history would differ from the story we know. Among other things, it seems almost impossible that the Industrial Revolution would have delayed its arrival until the 19th century. But although the value of the papers became recognized early enough for Napoleon to order some of them transferred from the Ambrosiana at Milan to the Bibliothèque Nationale, and for the Italians to demand them back in 1815, almost everybody who saw the material looked upon it as a curiosity—hardly art and hardly science. The stupendous nature of the research has been generally understood only very recently; and, tragically enough, only after the bulk of it had been repeated by successful but more plodding men.

♦ *Andrea Verrocchio* With respect to his artistic education, Leonardo could scarcely have been more fortunate. He was apprenticed to Andrea Verrocchio (1435–1488). Although enrolled in the painters' guild under his own name in 1472, Leonardo appears to have remained as a member of Verrocchio's establishment until at least as late as 1477.

Verrocchio's personality is known to us mostly by inference, but the inferences are unusually strong and clear. Only a few works can with certainty be attached to his name, but those few are among the best that ever came out of Italy. Most famous, of course, is the bronze equestrian statue of Bartolommeo Colleoni at Venice, on which the master was at work from about 1481 until his death. It is surely one of the two best equestrian monuments in the history of art, excelling the *Gattamelata* in force, dash, and drama while remaining inferior to it in connotations and overtones. The bronze *David* (1476) in the Bargello is another important example. Where can one go to find a better treatment of youth in all its unformed beauty, its lithe grace, and its gawky strength-wasting movements?

From the standpoint of stylistic evolution, an even more important and revealing work is the *Boy with a Dolphin* (Figs. 14.10–12), the diminutive fountain figure which for a very long time has impressed its gaiety upon the ponderous architecture of the courtyard of the Palazzo Vecchio. The little statue might be said to put its small foot squarely on the divide between the 15th century and the High Renaissance. Nothing could be more definitively typical of the earlier period than so realistic an appreciation of the infant and his direct methods for enjoying life. At the same time, both the design and the technique exhibit a self-conscious, calculating esthetics rare at the date of the statue, but altogether typical of the 16th century.

The nature of the medium had evidently been much explored; the pe-

culiar virtues of bronze have, in fact, been exploited with the utmost sagacity. The capacity of the material to render textures was worked to the limit. Its tensile strength permitted the artist to poise the tiny figure upon a single delicate support, and invited him to indulge in a tour de force of projections which, in a more brittle material, would have been folly.

More remarkable still is the composition. The pose, seemingly so innocent and spontaneous, is in fact a contrapposto no less studied and elaborate than that of the *Nike of Samothrace* (Fig. 6.17, page 171) and quite worthy of Michelangelo. More interesting still is the fact that the figure, unlike the great majority of statues both ancient and modern, was designed not to be viewed from one angle only, but omnifacially. As our three views indicate, one may walk round and round it without finding a single station from which it does not compose with a subtle rhythm of statics and dynamics.

The entire performance explains why Verrocchio was at once the most admired and best loved master at Florence, and why his home was like a club for the leading artists and thinkers of the city. With respect to our present business of historical transition, the central point to be grasped is the academic nature of his outlook. To the direct and natural enjoyment of content and expression, he added a new interest: the esthetics of method. In addition to all its other virtues, his *Boy with a Dolphin* is a learned experiment, an attempt to explore still further the possibilities of what can and

Figs. 14.10–12 (opposite and right) Verrocchio. *Boy with a Dolphin*. 1465. Bronze. Florence, Palazzo Vecchio. (Brogi)

what may not be done with sculpture, and to demonstrate whatever findings the artist was able to make.

♦ *Leonardo's Easel Pictures and Mural Paintings*   Leonardo's debt to his eminent master was immense. It was nevertheless reserved for the pupil to realize and declare, as it were, the style of the High Renaissance. For convenience of explanation, we may discuss his contribution under two headings, taking easel pictures as one department of activity and mural painting as another.

Among the easel pictures, the first that belongs unequivocally to the High Renaissance is the *Madonna of the Rocks* (Fig. 14.13). The painting exists in two versions. The one in Paris probably belonged to Francis the 1st, and is listed in an early catalogue of the pictures at Fontainebleau. The one in London came to England in 1796 as the property of Gavin Hamilton. Superficially in better condition and more attractive, the latter is considerably less refined in the matter of drawing. The supposition is that the London picture was executed by members of Leonardo's staff, probably to replace the one now in the Louvre, which the master seems to have taken with him to France in 1516.

The classical precedent used by Leonardo and other High Renaissance painters has too rarely been pointed out. It was the so-called Alexandrian

formula (pages 161–163), one of the three recognizable divisions of Hellenistic pictorial art. The distinguishing feature was to bring the human figures forward on the stage, putting them in front of the landscape background, as it were, rather than within it.

Among the extant examples of classical painting, not one shows anything like the command over composition demonstrated by Leonardo. As seen on the surface of the panel, the figure group falls within a triangular outline. If we become conscious of the represented space, we begin to feel the design as pyramidal. In either instance, the principle of order is geometrical, and the form chosen simple, lucid, symmetrical, and stable.

The lucidity of the arrangement is perhaps better than that achieved by any other method of design, but it comes at a price. The four figures shown form a compact, self-contained, organic group; attention is so thoroughly con-

Fig. 14.13 (opposite and above) Leonardo da Vinci. *Madonna of the Rocks* and detail. About 1482. Oil on wood, transferred to canvas. 6 feet, 6½ inches high. Paris, Louvre. (Giraudon; detail, Alinari)

centrated within its area that the setting seldom receives its fair share of inspection. But the setting is important. We may not dismiss it as a mere memory of some young mother resting out the heat of the day in a cool spot. As usual with High Renaissance art, everything seen in the picture has a meaning.

In the opinion of Edgar Wind, the gloomy rocks, suggestive as they are of caves and dark chambers, stand for the rock of the Holy Sepulcher, and thus for the sacrifice of Christ. If that is so, we can make something of the gestures. The infant John can be thought of as symbolizing the human race for whom Christ gave his life. The Virgin's caressing him with her right hand endorses the sacrifice; her left hand, held like a halo over the baby Jesus, blesses him. The pointing finger of the angel to the right drives home the lesson.

The adult figures in the *Madonna of the Rocks* realize the standards of the High Renaissance less perfectly than some Leonardo painted later, but a comparison of the babies with those of Donatello (Fig. 13.11, page 493), or with Verrocchio's fountain figure (Figs. 14.10–12) will prove in itself a complete survey of the difference between the two periods. Both of Leonardo's children take poses indicative of mature religious feeling. John kneels in transfigured adoration. The little Christ is as full of authority as he is soft and young (Fig. 14.13). He raises his right hand in a gesture of blessing of which the Pope himself might be proud. The motions represented are, in fact, utterly unlike the impulsive actions normal among children. So are the poses. The Savior, for instance, rests on his left hand, turns at the waist, and raises the right with an utter completeness of nervous and physical adequacy. On earth, we witness such things only when some great athlete has taken holy orders and risen to high office in the hierarchy. The ceremonial nature of High Renaissance art could hardly be exemplified better.

The *Madonna of the Rocks,* like the *Mona Lisa,* is overlaid with dirt and varnish. Hence, we experience a submarine effect where more brilliant luminosity once reigned. For that reason, any remarks about Leonardo's employment of light and shadow must be made and accepted with caution. His *chiaroscuro* was, however, new, and destined to influence other artists.

Considered merely as a representational technique, his modeling served primarily to define contours, and only incidentally did it deal with the action of light from any definite source. In other words, Leonardo sought expression by way of mass and form, which is equivalent to saying that he continued the Italian custom of painting in the mode of relief. But the word *relief* is hardly expressive when applied to his work, and may even be misleading. The analogies are not with sculpture in relief, but with statues in the round.

By stipulating that his figures existed free-standing in space, Leonardo took the departure which, more than any other single thing, makes the difference between the style of the 15th century and the style of the High Renaissance. Not only did other painters follow his lead; sculptors began to produce statues rather than panels, and architects began to use columns instead of pilasters.

The above, factual though it is, may puzzle the reader. Knowing Leonardo for one of the most accurate observers of natural fact who ever lived, one might assume that he would have been interested in the mode of the total visual effect (page 481) but he was not, even though he was among the very first to shift over to the new oil vehicle recently made known from Flanders. The reason, it would appear, was that his interest in light and shadow was not representational, but emotional. He perceived that shadowy areas were in themselves mysterious, and illuminated areas revealing. In addition, he doubtless felt inclined toward the broader rhythms which could be developed with stronger contrasts. His method made each individual field of light (or dark) larger in relation to the total area of the picture. Thus, as convexities took the light and hollows fell into shadow (accent or node as the case might be) the alternation gained a scale and authority rarely encountered before. The eye was delayed longer by each successive obscurity and each illumination, and the tempo of the rhythm was slowed down. In contrast with the dancing lights and darks common in 15th-century painting, the impression given was of something more splendid, more solemn, and more imposing.

All of the elements just cited came into synthesis in Leonardo's *Madonna and Child with Saint Anne* (Fig. 14.14). Not a finished painting, but a *cartoon* (a monochrome drawing prepared as a rehearsal for a painting), the work might at first seem unsuitable as a basis for generalization; but on second thought, the reader will see that nothing could be more useful for our purpose. The drawing doubtless put forward whatever the artist himself considered essential; and when he made it, he gave himself no chance to become distracted by secondary thoughts and accessory notions.

The cartoon is extraordinarily useful as a demonstration of the figure style which was to become generally typical of the age. The two adult women are shown in the fullness of maturity. One would put Mary's age at 35 or older, and her weight at 140 pounds. A substantial layer of soft flesh underlies the delicate complexion; beneath its ample contours, the angularity of the skeleton is lost. The shoulders are large, and the bust deep.

Neither youthful nor active, such a woman would be incapable of sustained physical exertion, and yet her body is vividly alive. With the studied ease of a dancer, she twists at the waist, slightly lifts the left knee, and bends the torso gently forward. If not full of action, the pose is certainly full of grace. We may rightly infer that the picture presents the Madonna as a lady of standing. Her life, unless appearances deceive, would be a judiciously tasteful routine, and a certain cadence and repose would mark every procedure in which she might engage.

To render the clothing of such a figure with the curious particularity of a century earlier would have been impertinent. The artist's intention in that matter is made more baldly plain in the drawing than it might be in a completed painting, and the trend of the style is obvious. Details are completely lost in the darks; and by contrast to the busy little folds so usual in Early Renaissance art, we are given nothing but the grander undulations of the drapery. As to the nature of the costume, one can say only that it must have been made of heavy material. The cloth responds to the movement of the limbs, but remains static until the wearer alters position again. There is no

Fig. 14.14 Leonardo da Vinci. Cartoon for a painting of the *Madonna and Child with Saint Anne*. London, Burlington House, Museum of the Royal Academy.

indication as to the construction of the garments, or how they were buttoned, tied, or otherwise held in place. As compared to earlier work, the difference is once again as between specificity and generalization.

Let us now turn to consideration of Leonardo's mural painting. The much celebrated *Last Supper* in the refectory of Santa Maria delle Grazie at Milan was unquestionably Leonardo's greatest achievement in the field of art, and the earliest complete and perfect realization of High Renaissance painting. Such pictures reflect better than anything else the ideals of the period. They were grand in size, grand in style, and grand in conception. The work started, so far as we can tell, in 1495. Luca Pacioli, in a publication dating from February, 1498, spoke of it as though it were complete. From that date onward, its history is sad in the telling. Because he was philosophically unable to accept the bold finality of fresco painting, Leonardo wanted a medium that might be worked and reworked. Most unwisely, he attempted to employ an experimental technique for this important commission. He tried to waterproof the wall behind the painting, and he then proceeded to work with some combination of tempera, oil, and varnish. The experiment proved a disastrous failure. As early as 1517, the picture was in a ruinous condition. Vasari saw it in 1566, by which time it was a muddle of blotches. Some eighty years later, a visitor noted that one could not even make out the subject. Numerous restorations have taken place; there were at least four during the 18th century alone. A cleaning of 1908 helped somewhat; but during World War II, the roof suffered bomb damage, and the picture was exposed to the elements. The harm then done can scarcely be a matter for mourning because every speck of paint in view was of the 18th century at the earliest.

In spite of all such misfortunes and mischances, the great picture continues to haunt the Western imagination. By reference to drawings by Leonardo and his staff, Edgar Wind and others have been able to visualize the original to some extent. We may not retrace their studies here; suffice it to say that the over-all effect of their findings has been to refine the drawing and to correct the facial expression of individual heads—both items being intolerably bad in all extant reproductions after "the original." It is really better to refer to an engraving like the one shown in Figure 14.15. Objectionably sentimentalized though it may be, the engraving at least preserves Leonardo's compositional arrangements, and thus illustrates the theory which governed the great wall paintings of the period.

The setting was indoors, with the table of the Last Supper parallel to the picture plane. Christ sat in the center, with the Apostles on either hand. Emphasis upon the central figure was insured in two ways. First, the head of the Savior was put in silhouette against an open doorway at the far end of the chamber. Secondly, his head was placed at the vanishing point, and the location of the vanishing point was emphatically pointed out by an extra measure of beams in the ceiling, and other architectural lines. The scheme of the composition, it will be seen, had more to do with the arrangement of things on the horizontal plane of the stage plan than with the vertical surface of the painting—a condition that was destined to become typical of every large picture.

As usual in High Renaissance art, Leonardo made a masterly choice of the point of time. He chose the instant when Christ said, "Verily, verily, I say unto you that one of you shall betray me!" At that moment, shock was made to run outward from the center of the table, being felt less and less violently

Fig. 14.15   Engraving by Raphael Morghern (1753-1833) after Leonardo's *Last Supper*. Cambridge, Massachusetts, Fogg Art Museum.

by the disciples further away until the farthest of them needed to gesture back inward toward the center as though to make certain of what they thought they had heard. Judas alone did not gesticulate. Not isolated on the opposite side of the table as had been usual in earlier versions of the subject (Fig. 13.16, page 501), he was isolated by his guilty knowledge. Leonardo showed him as sitting in studied calm, almost with unconcern, dissimulating by a simple refusal to become excited.

The method of the composition also became strictly usual during the High Renaissance. It was the Greek organic method (page 66); but no other demonstration thereof, either ancient or modern, more perfectly realized all the possibilities of that excellent system. The diversity was great, and the unity intense. The physical arrangement was complete in itself and inseparable from the drama by reference to which it had cause and effect.

RAPHAEL

The brilliance of Raphael's career is manifest from its brevity. He was born at Urbino in 1483, worked at Perugia from 1500 to 1504, at Florence from 1504 to 1508, and at Rome from 1508 until his death in 1520.

When he left Urbino, he was a boyishly charming provincial painter. The *Dream of a Knight,* now in the National Gallery in London, comes from that time. At Perugia, he worked on the staff of Perugino, a master the world had already passed by. It was nevertheless no small achievement for the youth-ful Raphael to gain, almost at once and almost without effort, a complete command over Perugino's methods for representing deep vistas of space, and Perugino's quiet excellence in the figure style of the 15th century. From that second period of Raphael's career come the *Marriage of the Virgin* in the Brera Gallery at Milan and the *Colonna Altarpiece* in New York.

Realizing that Perugia was a small town, Raphael went to Florence at the age of twenty-one. He arrived just at the moment when Leonardo and Michelangelo simultaneously put on public exhibition the full-scale cartoons that were intended to eventuate in some great frescoes for the council cham-ber of the Palazzo Vecchio. Lost, and known to us only by indirect evidence, each was to commemorate a battle in which Florentine arms had gained memorable distinction. All indications characterize the two battle pieces, singly and together, as a veritable apotheosis of what the High Renaissance had to offer: dazzling technique, epic subject matter, force and power com-municated with dramatic clarity hitherto unheard of.

Raphael's natural gifts were lyric. Grandeur had to date been foreign to his art; but once again, he performed a spectacular act of assimilation. He set out to master the "Grand Style." By doing so, he illustrated both his genius and such weakness as can be urged against him. The willingness to make the change indicated a certain flexibility of temperament common among popular artists, and alien to the character of figures like Giotto, Donatello, and Michelangelo. Raphael's error can best be illustrated by such pictures as the *Entombment* of the Borghese collection at Rome. He labored infinitely, it is said, over the composition, the gesticulation, and the muscula-ture of the figures; but in the end, he produced a dud.

While admittedly requisite for certain themes, violence of action and feeling did not suit his temperament. Distinguished in his private life for lovableness and gentle manners, he was at his best when painting in a softer vein. It was fortunate, therefore, that he made easel pictures of the Madonna a specialty while at Florence. His work immediately became popular, and he had a great number of orders. As a result, he produced a whole class of paintings which are known collectively as the *Florentine Madonnas;* one of them appears in Figure 14.16. A description of one fits them all, though no two are alike. In fact, no other painter has ever maintained better standards of freshness and variety while continuing to manipulate a set formula.

The setting is usually out of doors. Neither cold nor heat obtrude them-selves upon our attention. The air is still and salubrious. Nature, as Raphael presented her, was a tranquil, compassionate power offering much to love and nothing to fear. Landscapes of the same kind had been Perugino's special stock in trade, but the figure style and the pyramidal composition came from

Fig. 14.16 Raphael. *Madonna of the Goldfinch.* 1507. Florence, Uffizi. (Alinari)

Leonardo. Raphael made both his own; they became so thoroughly his own, in fact, that he rather than Leonardo is usually cited as the definitive painter of the period.

The *Florentine Madonnas* were the best-liked paintings of their generation, and they remain the best-known and most popular Madonnas in existence. It is not too much to say that most of the European family gets its visual image of the Madonna from those pictures. It is nevertheless common to hear serious and responsible critics attack the reputation of the whole class, and of Raphael. Objection cannot be maintained if it takes off from a technical platform, or from considerations of abstract design: Raphael was superb in both departments. There is legitimate complaint, however, about the way he manipulated the theme. He made a questionable appeal when he decided to surmount an opulent Leonardesque anatomy with the face of a simple, childish girl. While it is to be supposed that the Madonna was young, healthy, gentle, modest, and that her maternal passion expressed itself in a decorous way, paintings which celebrate those qualities alone neglect history and close out innumerable connotations. The character of Mary is hardly a fit subject for light and sentimental treatment. Her career was tragic and supreme. To make it anything else is to deprive her of meaning. One suspects Raphael, in fact, of a studied policy calculated never to displease.

When Julius the 2nd called Raphael to Rome in 1508, the great Vatican program of artistic investment was already well under way. Michelangelo was at work on the frescoes of the Sistine Chapel ceiling, and Bramante had made significant progress on the new St. Peter's. Raphael, at that point, was merely a successful young artist who had yet to be awarded a single major commission. Bramante, it is believed, recommended him to the Pope; no matter what predictions he made when doing so, they fell far short of the truth the immediate future was to open up.

There is no parallel for Raphael's success at Rome. The Pope already had numerous artists on the ground. Most of them were men of standing. Some were men of fame. Within an unbelievably short time, almost all were summarily dismissed or made subordinate to Raphael. Much of their completed work was ripped from the walls, and instructions were issued Raphael to fill the spaces with work of his own. Bramante and Michelangelo were the only important men to survive the purge. The latter was perennially suspicious and hostile, but there is almost nothing to suggest that Raphael had conducted a malicious campaign for preferment. The amazing thing is the cordial regard which surrounded his name. His superior abilities seem simply to have been conceded by men who might have been his enemies, and his genius in human relations made it possible for him to organize and direct the work of a great corps of mature artists who normally would have been competitors. Such developments seem specially remarkable in view of Raphael's appearance. His face, even during his thirties, remained adolescent and unformed. He had the uncertain stance of a delicate boy. He nevertheless seems to have made upon everyone who knew or saw him an impression of prodigious ability. There was no limit to his resources of energy, patience, and creation. Everything he touched went fast and wonderfully well, and he did it all with such ease that there seemed to be no end to what he could undertake.

Raphael's fame soon spread far beyond Rome; indeed, it spread far beyond Italy. The reason? Raphael was the first great artist to appreciate the implications of the printing press. In 1510, there appeared at Rome an engraver named Marcantonio Raimondi (about 1480–1534), a man who had previously worked at Bologna and Venice, where he had scored a somewhat dishonorable success by counterfeiting plates by Dürer. In some way, Marcantonio attached himself to Raphael's circle. Presently, he formed some kind of partnership with Raphael's color grinder, Baviera, and the two (apparently with Raphael's aid and approval) opened a printing shop devoted almost exclusively to the manufacture and sale of engravings after paintings and sketches by Raphael himself and by his pupils. They did a big business all over Europe. In this way, hundreds of people who did not and could not know the other great artists of the Italian Renaissance were made familiar with Raphael's name and style. The novelty of the arrangement, it must be pointed out, was not merely the sale of prints—for Mantegna, Dürer, and others had sold prints. The innovation was to make engraving a secondary art devoted to the reproduction, and we might almost say the advertisement, of paintings.

Raphael's most important commission and greatest success at Rome began when the Pope assigned him the task of decorating the so-called "Vatican Stanze," a series of connecting rooms on an upper floor of one wing in the Vatican complex. The plan was to maintain a certain degree of system in the choice of subject matter. In general, the theme was High Renaissance Christianity as made manifest by significant instances in the ancient and modern history of the Roman Church and by the flowering of humanistic culture.

Raphael's first-hand contribution was largely limited to the *Stanza della Segnatura,* so called because the room was often used for the ceremonial signing of documents and for meetings of the *Segnatura di Grazia,* a papal court of justice. The chamber is architecturally undistinguished. It has a vaulted ceiling and measures about 30 by 35 feet on the floor. On the ceiling, Raphael put four round medallions containing personifications of Theology, Poetry, Philosophy, and Jurisprudence. Corresponding to them on the four walls below are the *Disputa* (Fig. 14.17), beneath *Theology, The School of Athens* (Fig. 14.19) beneath *Philosophy,* the *Parnassus* under *Poetry,* and under *Jurisprudence,* the personified virtues associated with the operation of justice: *Force, Prudence,* and *Moderation.*

Labored in the telling, ponderous and perhaps even tedious in fact, the iconography just summarized becomes a clear statement if we reflect upon it. Necessarily expressed in broadest generalization, does it not come close to being a succinct declaration of the conceptions which have controlled European culture since the Renaissance? A notable point in the ensemble is the even treatment, pictorially and otherwise, given to each subject. The others are in no manner subordinated to *Theology,* and we may conclude that the papal court of the moment felt that the world had arrived on a new plateau. Traditional religion, it would appear, was expected to remain as a great and essential part of the modern orientation; but the resources of secular philosophy and the richness of classical learning were also thought essential. Obvious necessity demanded the addition of a decent measure of social regularity as summed up in the institution of the law.

By general consent, the *Disputa* and the *School of Athens* stand out not only as Raphael's greatest pictures, but as the most felicitous expression ever attained in the style of the High Renaissance. The *Disputa* was the earlier of the two. The name is a mistake. It seems to have come into colloquial use rather early because certain gestures are similar to those used in debate, but as indicated by our earlier citation of the picture (page 569) there is no debate at all. In fact, the very notion of debate is opposite to the whole affair, the intention of which was to make people see the truth of the dogma of transubstantiation.

There can be no doubt that each of the many figures was intended to represent a particular personage, but accurate records do not exist to certify every identity beyond a reasonable doubt. Our diagram (Fig. 14.18) gives the probable identities, some of which are suggested by familiar physical types standard for certain characters and others by attributes like David's harp and Jerome's lion. It will be understood that variant readings exist, but they all indicate that the persons seen in heaven with Christ come from Biblical history, while those on earth around the altar come from the annals of the medieval church.

Although painting on a flat field in a square room, Raphael chose to make the picture simulate the semidome of an Early Christian apse. It will be noted furthermore that the resemblance does not stop with the familiar appearance; the theme involves a glimpse into heaven and thus repeats the supernatural setting standard in those earliest days of the faith.

While we can have no doubt that Raphael had it in mind to emulate the solemn dignity of such apses as that of Santa Pudenziana (Fig. 8.28, page 243), he had learned his lesson well from Leonardo, and he had at his disposal an art of composition unknown during the Middle Ages. As seen in black and white, the three horizontal registers appear more separate than they are in fact; the apparent fault is corrected in the original by color harmonies. By the date of this painting, Leonardo's resort to the vanishing point was the common property of all artists; everybody was using it as he had done to focus attention where desired. No one ever applied the principle more boldly, however, than Raphael did when working out this particular composition. By putting the wafer in its monstrance precisely at the spot of convergence, he succeeded in centralizing the entire ensemble around an exceedingly small spot on the surface of the picture. The history of painting contains no parallel for the performance, but there was a good reason for resorting to extreme measures. The bits of bread consumed in the ceremony of the Eucharist are small and ordinary and do not, as a matter of fact, change in texture or taste in the course of the service. The only thing that makes them important is the miracle which is believed to occur: the attributes of the wafer remain constant, but its substance has become divine. It takes great faith to comprehend what has happened, and it took great art for Raphael to present a visual demonstration of so beautiful and so intangible a reality.

Fig.14.17 Raphael. *Disputa*. Rome, Vatican. (Anderson)

Fig. 14.18 (opposite page) Diagram to indicate the identity of the various persons shown in the *Disputa*.

The composition is arranged in three registers. At the top, we see God the Father (27) raising his hand in benediction and holding the globe. To either side of him (23–26), 4–6) are angels and cherubim. In the middle register are Christ and Mary and John the Baptist (1–3) silhouetted against a glory; Christ raises his hands to show the stigmata, which are symbols of redemption. Immediately below (13–16) are four small angels, each with a Gospel Book, and the Holy Spirit descending in the form of a dove. The twelve figures to the right and left are prophets, apostles, and confessors; note that representatives of the old dispensation alternate with representatives of the new.

John the Evangelist writing the *Revelation* (20), David playing the harp (19), Stephen or perhaps Laurence (18), Jeremiah or perhaps Martin of Tours (17). Reading from the right: Paul (7), Abraham (8), Moses with the Tablets (9), James the Greater (11), George or perhaps Judas Maccabeus (12). The bottom register has an altar in the center, with the Host exhibited in a monstrance. The persons round about cannot all be identified; predominantly, they appear to be Christian writers who presumably find a common ground in faith. To the left of the altar is Gregory the Great (47) holding his treatise on Job and looking heavenward. Next to him is Jerome (48) meditating on the Scriptures. To the right are Ambrose (53), Augustine dictating *The City of God* (54), Thomas Aquinas (55), Innocent the 3rd (56), Bonaventura (58); Sixtus the 4th (60); Dante (62), and Savonarola (63). At the extreme left are portraits of Fra Angelico (30) and of Bramante (31).

In the *School of Athens* (Fig. 14.19) Raphael painted the picture which is probably the greatest produced during the Renaissance. The quality of greatness derives from a combination of things. The pictorial mechanics are superb. The iconography is of an intellectual profundity that can be appreciated only by the serious student, and only then after study. The physical relationship of the figures to each other, and of all the figures to the setting, conforms in miraculous fashion with the correspondence or contrast in the concepts and systems for which they, as persons, stand. Emotionally the content is mature and elevated beyond almost all else in the history of Western painting; if it is possible to comprehend philosophy through the feelings, one can do it by a study of the *School of Athens*.

So complicated a work of art demands a small explanatory volume of its own. As with the *Disputa,* much depends upon the identity of this figure and that, and there are many questions outstanding. The best brief essay available will be found in Baedeker's *Handbook for Rome.* A longer and better treatment was included by Eugène Müntz in his great work on the Renaissance, now all too seldom remembered. As this is written, Edgar Wind has in preparation a monograph which will summarize all the important suggestions in something like final form. Referring the reader to our own diagram (Fig. 14.20) for details, we shall confine ourselves below to such generalization as seems reliable and just.

Philosophy is the subject of the picture; but the word meant more in 1509 than it does now. It included everything taught in the universities, and it also included every science, every art, and every other activity that brought the rational faculty into operation. The subject matter is correctly understood, therefore, as a celebration of the earthly accomplishments of man: his physical productions and his perfection of himself.

Lucretius had spoken of "the temples raised by philosophy," an idea which doubtless suggested to Raphael the use of architecture for a setting. In primitive times, building had been the art of shelter; but in periods of high civilization, architecture meant what Alberti had so grandly imagined that it might and ought to be: it was the better environment for a race that knew dignity, the majestic symbol of man's reasoned control over the hostile forces of nature.

Because of Raphael's friendship with Bramante, it has often been suggested that the building we see here is Saint Peter's as Bramante would have built it. That is probable; but it is equally probable that Bramante got his ideas from Raphael. Why else would the latter have been appointed as superintendent of the works after Bramante died in 1514? All such matters are speculative, and however we fancy to work them out, the church in Raphael's painting is a better church than the overbearing one actually built by Michelangelo. Scale, in Raphael's design, was rendered easy by grace, and the oppressive weight of the vaulting was lightened by glimpses into the sky. The magnificent space of the nave was made more inspiring by the openings out into the air; the interior atmosphere thus gained the light, life, and movement of all outdoors.

It is hardly possible to say too much or to think too much about the setting as Raphael designed it, for the setting carries more meaning than the figures. No one can hesitate in ascribing pre-eminence to the two who stand at the vanishing point, centered on the stage in such a place. The elderly Plato is one (the face is perhaps an idealized portrait of Leonardo); he carries a copy of the *Timaeus,* and he points upward to indicate the locus and source of wisdom. Aristotle is the other man. He is appropriately represented in vigorous middle age; he carries a copy of his *Ethics,* and gestures in dignified remonstrance toward the world of men where all the daily choices must be made and the practical decisions taken.

Representatives of the abstract and practical sciences fall into an easy elliptical arrangement outward and downward on either hand. Except for a few contemporary portraits, every character is classical. There also seems to have been a governing sense of history in the arrangement. Pythagoras (6th century B.C.) is at the lower left, and Archimedes (died 212 B.C.) at the lower right; apparently those two were thought of as the beginning and the end of the Greek school.

It will also be noted from the diagram that the men famous for practical achievements are in general placed on the lower levels, and that we tend to climb upward before reaching the men who symbolize pure reason. But there are subtle distinctions over and above that obvious one. Old Socrates, it will be seen, still feels he must argue his point, while Plato's gesture is above and beyond contention: having produced the most perfect synthesis yet achieved by the human intellect, he merely expounds his doctrine.

Certain recent critics have refused to believe that Raphael was personally responsible for the philosophical erudition demonstrated in the *School of Athens.* The notion is even current that good artists, taking them as a class, never have been, and never ought to be interested in such matters. Such a view is mistaken, and derives from several sources, all rather recent.

The 19th-century movement known as Romanticism (pages 838–851) was in part an attempt to discredit the rational faculty altogether. Those who are under its spell find it peculiarly distasteful to have art connected in any way with learning. They reassure themselves by pointing to the occasional instances when worthwhile work has in fact been produced by men of little education, but they go too far when they suggest that knowledge is like poison to the creative imagination. As applied to Raphael, such thoughts are without contemporary documentation; indeed every bit of 16th-century evidence tends flatly to contradict the whole idea.

Fig. 14.19 Raphael. *The School of Athens.* Rome, Vatican. (Anderson)

Fig. 14.20 (opposite page) Diagram to indicate the identity of the persons who appear in the *School of Athens.* On the platform, in the middle, stand Plato (1) and Aristotle (2). To the left of them we see Socrates (49) and some of his famous pupils. Xenophon (48) leans against the pilaster. Alcibiades (45) is the young man in armor. The old man (46) listening so intently is probably one of the artisans with whom Socrates loved to talk because their minds were not cluttered with false ideas. From the far left, a young man (42) comes running in, eager to join the discussion. He is delayed by a Sophist (43), while Aeschines (44), the sausage seller who later became a famous orator, raises his arm in protest. The figures to the immediate right of Plato and Aristotle are difficult to identify. Further on, there are some Eclectic philosophers. One of them (13) is busy taking notes while a

Anaxagoras or Xenocrates. The old man writing (33) is Pythagoras. A pupil kneels beside him with the harmonic tables. The man crowded in behind Pythagoras (34) may be Terpander, who had also investigated musical scales. The Arab (35) is probably Averrhoës, who wrote a famous commentary on Aristotle. The jovial man with a wreath around his head (37) is probably Plotinus, to whom an old man (40) brings a pupil (39). At the lower right, we see Bramante (23) playing the part of Archimedes. Ptolemy (21) and Zoroaster (22) stand holding globes. The two young men at the extreme right are Raphael himself (19) and his colleague Sodoma (20). The statues in niches to the upper right and left (not shown in diagram) are Athena and Apollo.

The boy behind Plotinus (36) has been identified as Frederick of Mantua, who was brought up at the court of Julius the 2nd. The handsome young man (31) is said to be Francesco Maria della Rovere, Duke of Urbino.

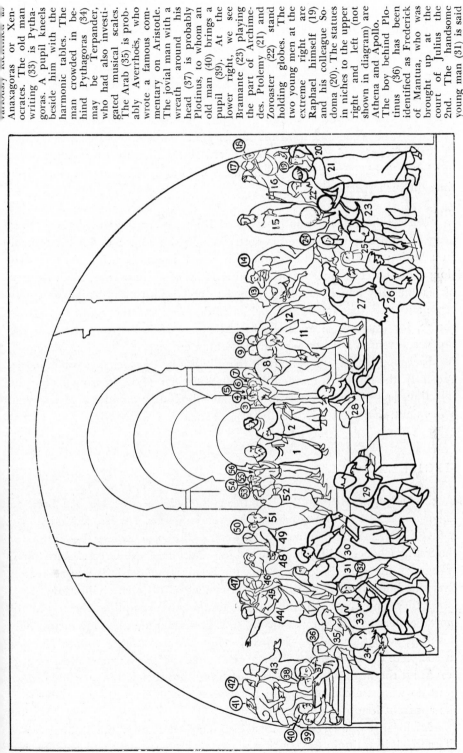

During the early years of the 20th century, furthermore, the British art critic Roger Fry promulgated the esthetic doctrine that subject matter of any kind had no legitimate place in the artistic transaction. If applied to the *School of Athens,* Fry's doctrine would tell the student to neglect the iconography entirely. It would even warn him to resist any impulse to become interested in the content of the painting—on pain of permitting "literary values" to intervene and spoil his capacity for "esthetic" experience. Because Fry's theories offered a sanction for modern abstraction, they have been popular; but it is obvious that Raphael, like Giotto and Michelangelo, wasted no time on such speculations.

During the twelve years he spent at Rome, every imaginable honor was heaped upon Raphael and every sort of enterprise placed under his control. In addition to the artistic and architectural responsibilities already mentioned, there were numerous other commissions of an important kind. Because of his affability and because he seemed to accomplish every assignment with grace and ease, the Vatican asked him to do more and more. He was put in charge, for instance, of an archeological survey of Rome, out of which was supposed eventually to emerge an elaborate new map of the area. Obviously, Raphael soon ceased to be an artist; like Phidias he became a statesman of art. Presently, the limit was reached. In 1520, at the age of 37, he caught an acute infection, lacked the strength to rally, and died after an illness of less than a fortnight. He was buried in the Pantheon.

MICHELANGELO

Michelangelo died in 1564 at the age of eighty-nine. He had been an important master before reaching his twentieth year. He left behind him a series of stupendous monuments: St. Peter's church at Rome, the frescoes of the Sistine Chapel ceiling, and the noblest sculpture since Greece. Recognized as one of the world's leading citizens, he was mourned like an emperor. Everyone knew that he had been an ornament of Western civilization.

And yet no other human being so thoroughly exemplifies the tragedy of mortal endeavor. Unhappy as a child, this very great man became increasingly downcast as mature insight clarified for him the meaning of things. He died in complete discouragement after a career marked by the most dazzling success in all the history of art. Before attempting to review his productions, we must do what we can to explain a temperament so far out of keeping with the apparent lesson of the facts.

Michelangelo was born into a distinguished family, the Buonarroti of Florence. His aptitude for sculpture asserted itself strongly and at once, but brought down upon him the wrath of his relatives: the medieval prejudice against manual labor was still strong enough to have effect.

Physically, Michelangelo was small and unbeautiful, a circumstance that contributed to morbid reaction in a personality endowed with a supreme passion for beauty and strength. As a youth, he received a severe beating in a fist fight and carried the mark of it the rest of his life in a badly smashed nose. As an adult, he several times yielded to cowardice when threatened by physical danger, a form of behavior in mortifying contrast to his heroic ideals.

Raphael's gift in human relations found its opposite in Michelangelo. He disliked and distrusted everybody. He could not get a block of marble out of the quarry without quarreling with the workmen, and he never found more than a handful of assistants whose presence in the shop he could abide. For his incapacity as an executive, he compensated by a prodigious expenditure of energy and by a rapidity of execution that passes belief even in the face of the incontrovertible facts.

Having few normal friendships and small outlet for the affections, he found it all the harder that bad luck frustrated every project he undertook. He was compelled to leave every one of them a mere fragment and suggestion of the nobler conception with which he had commenced. In all fairness, it must be stated that his imagination knew no limits. He lacked the most elementary grasp of costs, labor, and materials. He was obtuse in his judgment of those who employed him, and seems to have expected, as though by right, patronage with patience and single-mindedness never found anywhere in this world.

Powerful men were ready, it is true, to invest vast sums in art. Individual genius was never more highly respected. Personal capacity was never less restrained by the social order. Most educated persons, moreover, shared a common culture. The Italian 16th century was nevertheless the very worst period and the very worst place into which Michelangelo could have been born.

Modern nationalism was the chief product of the 16th century. England, France, and Spain each had a dynasty, and the Spanish Hapsburgs maintained a personal union with the German imperium. Each one of those nations was openly embarked upon a program of imperial aggrandizement. In such company, the Italian people were hopelessly outclassed. From the start of the Middle Age the peninsula had been the home of small city-states, intense local loyalties, implacable feuds and hatreds. Most Italians of Michelangelo's generation were quite incapable of comprehending even the notion of national interest, and the Italian despots literally invited (as Ludovico Sforza invited Charles the 8th in 1494) the great powers to invade Italy to interfere in Italian affairs. From that period onward, Italy was a battleground where foreign rivalries were fought out, only to flame up again from new sources and in new combinations. Mercenary armies marched wherever they wanted to go, and often did as they pleased. The crowning infamy occurred on May 6, 1527, when the Spanish and German troops of Charles the 5th sacked Rome. The details of the outrage are too revolting to repeat; in the roster of Christian disgrace, the event is second only to the Fourth Crusade. Thus during Michelangelo's adult life and by one of the great paradoxes, Italy was being degraded at the very moment when Italian culture was teaching the rest of the world how to live. It is impossible to exaggerate the degree to which political humiliation depressed the Italian spirit. The nation remained supine until the time of Garibaldi.

But even the political situation can hardly have borne down upon Michelangelo so heavily as the religious events simultaneously in progress. The first generation of the 16th century marks the nadir of Roman Catholicism. For some time the Chair of St. Peter had been occupied by popes occasionally marked by energy, often by intellectual distinction, always by culture, but never by religious pre-eminence. The evil side of Roman living became an international scandal in the behavior of some of these men. The details are scarcely fit for print, but may be read by the student in a number of places. All of the popes mentioned operated the Church as though it were merely another state in the general competition between governments. On the whole, the Papacy was competent and alert with respect to its temporal advantage, but none of the popes of the period fulfilled the obligation of spiritual leadership. Feeling began to run high in many places. Resentment became more bitter and more open; but with an incredible conceit, a whole series of pontiffs neglected the matter. They did not even try to find ways to correct the situation. The great and final break came with Luther's Reformation of 1517, followed by the Act of Supremacy (1534) which separated the English church from Rome.

Confronted at last with overt action of unmistakable cogency, the Papacy took measures of its own. The Society of Jesus was founded in 1540. The Universal Inquisition was established in 1542. With the avowed hope of finding a generally acceptable mode for reorganizing the Catholic polity, the Council of Trent held its first assembly in 1545, and met off and on until 1564. Among the dignitaries who attended the council, there was real difference of opinion with respect to the methods that might be used to heal the Reformation. In the end, the Church emerged with a program more intransigeant and authoritarian than ever before. However helpful in guaranteeing discipline within the Catholic organization itself, the so-called Counter-Reformation then undertaken proved a ghastly failure.

The Inquisition left a heritage of implacable hatred wherever it attempted to operate. In Germany and the Low Countries, the Hapsburgs identified their own political aims with the interests of Catholicism; although they staged a reign of terror more dreadful than anything known until the infamies of Hitler, they merely succeeded in making the population hate both the church and themselves. The same Hapsburgs sent the Spanish Armada against England in 1588, with much the same purpose; and again, they succeeded only in making patriotism synonymous with freedom from Rome.

Michelangelo's state of mind during those times can be imagined only if we fully appreciate that his Christianity was appropriate for a saint. The 13th century might have been more congenial for him than the 16th. His writings are replete with spiritual reflections, usually expressed in a tone of despair. His ultimate discouragement was the worse, moreover, because he was one of those who advocated a more moderate method for dealing with the Protestants.

Michelangelo's artistic education need not delay us long, but contains certain points of interest. In 1489, he entered the atelier of Domenico Ghirlandaio (1449–1494), a painter notable for philosophical insignificance. The man nevertheless had technical methods greater artists would have been wise to copy. The work went through his shop fast. It came out with scarcely a blemish. It has endured in splendid condition. No school could have been better for a youthful genius than one which taught him decision, dispatch, and the virtue of bringing work to a conclusion—it is on those very points that Leonardo was weak, and Michelangelo strong.

After a short time, Michelangelo moved on to become the pupil of the elderly sculptor Bertoldo, a man who had actually worked with Donatello and who conducted a kind of museum in the Medici gardens. The relationship brought the young man into contact with the classical style, and the immediate result was his rather youthful but powerful relief, now in the Casa Buonarroti, *Battle of the Centaurs.*

An even more significant incident was a sojourn of several months in Bologna. Having fled Florence in terror during a political crisis in 1494, Michelangelo stopped in just the place where he might be affected by the work of Jacopo della Quercia (Fig. 13.30, page 528). He remained long enough to carve two small marble saints and an angel to fill vacant stations on the elaborate *Shrine of Saint Domenic.* Vigorously personal like all his work, these statues still bear an obvious resemblance to one of the figures Quercia placed in the lunette over the doorway at San Petronio. From that point on, the force of Quercia's style became part of Michelangelo's own and remained with him the rest of his life.

The first work of permanent significance is the *Pietà* now placed in one of the side chapels at St. Peter's (Fig. 14.21). Generally given the date 1498–

Fig. 14.21 Michelangelo. *Pietà*. Detail. Before 1500. Rome, St. Peter's. (Alinari)

1500, it may be earlier. The style is an interesting combination of elements from the Early Renaissance, the 16th century, and the personal proclivities of the artist.

The composition is a Leonardesque pyramid, and one of the very first instances where that figure had been used in sculpture. We have already commented upon the capacity of the triangle to concentrate interest within itself (page 580), for which reason the form is perhaps more appropriate for sculpture than for painting. By making the work of art emphatically complete as a visual unit, there is no necessity for association with a niche or any other kind of architectural background.

Some authors have attempted to see a topical reference in the content. Does it refer to Savonarola's martyrdom? Or to the new crucifixion of Christ in the form of the infamous Borgia pope, Alexander the 6th, who was then in office? Without suggesting that such things failed to affect the spirit of the sculptor, a more general interpretation is in order. It is first of all evident that Michelangelo made the Madonna draw into herself, bearing her sorrow much as he had been compelled, by the contemporary world, to shut his personality away. Only the gesture of her left hand seems in any way to be addressed outward. That much is obvious. Less easy to account for is the distortion in which he freely indulged.

The distortion is of several kinds. In the first place, the Madonna is on a larger scale than the Christ; such a woman would be nine feet high if she stood up. Secondly, her dress contains a preposterous amount of cloth. These physical improbabilities and impossibilities are even less radical than a distortion of historical and biological fact. It is possible for a girl of eighteen to be a mother, but it is not possible for her to have a child thirty years old, as Christ was when he died.

Michelangelo himself explained the last point: a woman of perfect purity, he said, would keep her youth forever. As to the others, we are left to work out our own reasons. By exaggerating the Madonna's size, it was possible to make her handle an adult Christ as easily as a normal mother handles a baby; the entire group thus was made plausible. The extra bulk of drapery contributed to a broad, stable base for the statue, a less exalted purpose but an artistically important one. But we have not yet got to the bottom of the matter.

In the first place, no one can deny that the distortions, both physical and historical, constitute instances of emotional truth, but are quite untrue as facts. Seen in historical perspective, the resort to such methods signifies a potent attack by Michelangelo, even at the beginning of his career, against the whole philosophy of the representative convention. It took nearly four centuries for his point of view to gain a controlling position; but as this is written, there is little demur from the proposition that representative accuracy is actually unimportant by comparison with the efficiency of art as an expressive vehicle.

It is obvious that Michelangelo's methods partook of the nature of expressionism, but his particular application of that theory included a special element: Renaissance individualism in its most extreme form. He was perhaps the first artist to take the view that his art was his own. Raphael's *School of Athens*, to cite a recent comparison, was less Raphael's picture than a celebration of the culture of the age. In everything Michelangelo touched, the balance was adjusted in the opposite direction. He was often under pressure from his patrons, who tried to push him one way or another; but regardless of who paid the bill or what he wanted, the emerging work of art belonged to the artist. As to how that was possible, it is not enough to cite the privilege generally accorded genius during the Renaissance. It is necessary to appreciate that Michelangelo's personality was unique even in that great era. The most powerful men of the age felt actual fear when in his presence, and were glad enough to leave him alone.

The extent to which Michelangelo went in the matter of expressing his

Fig. 14.22 Michelangelo. *Holy Family*. About 1505. Florence, Uffizi. (Anderson)

personal opinions is well illustrated by the marble *David,* commissioned in 1501. Because David was a slayer of tyrants, the subject was a tactless choice for a civic monument at a moment in Florentine history when the question of tyranny was likely to stir up action as well as feeling. The net result, however, was to establish the young sculptor as one of the world's most admired artists. A trivial circumstance has lent the *David* an adventitious fame. Michelangelo carved it free-hand from a block of marble which had been badly mauled by a sculptor named Baccellino about thirty-five years earlier. Traces of Baccellino's chisel may still be seen on the back and on the top of the head. The incident is of course merely an illustration of the superior power of visualization common among professional artists. Set up in 1504, the *David* was taken to the Academy in 1873, to protect it from further weathering. Well displayed there, its gigantic size (height 18 feet) nevertheless renders the best possible indoor setting inadequate.

In 1505, Michelangelo received from Agnolo Doni (who had his portrait done by Raphael that same year) what is believed to be his first commission as a painter: the circular *Holy Family* (Fig. 14.22) now in the Uffizi. The work introduces us to a new class of Renaissance art, although it was hardly the first of its kind. We refer to the so-called "devotional picture," which derived from Neoplatonic concepts and requires, if it is to be understood, a frame of reference separate from that which applies to narrative painting.

The devotional picture has no story to tell. The artist may pose the figures as he wants; he is not governed by the necessity of making them do some particular thing. There is no point of time to bring up memories of the past, or to suggest future expectations. No local facts dictate the setting. All the factors which ordinarily control the imagination are removed; but by the same token, the artist is deprived of all those which ordinarily help him in the act of visualization. He is left free to perform the appalling task of presenting us with absolute beauty.

It was natural for any 16th-century master to assume that absolute beauty would find its best expression in the language of the human body, and specially natural for Michelangelo to find the body's greatest beauty in its shape and movement. Beyond that, the picture may be said to be abstract. The lighting has no parallel on earth. In a magnificent manipulation of the mode of relief, Michelangelo modeled the figures as no one else could possibly have done, and we see the Holy Family as though in a vision. "Had my soul not been created Godlike," wrote the artist himself in a passage which is surely apposite, "it would seek no more than outward beauty, the delight of the eyes. But since that fades so fast, my soul soars beyond, to the eternal form." The statement is enigmatic without such a picture to illustrate it, and needs in any case the supplement of another aphorism from the same source, namely, that "the heart is slow to love what the eye cannot see."

With such evidence in hand, we may justly infer that Michelangelo considered it his artistic destiny to find visual imagery adequate to suggest, and perhaps even to portray the most exalted concepts permitted to the human consciousness. The "eternal form" mentioned by him is probably to be understood in at least two ways: as a synonym for the glory of God from which humanity was banished at the time of creation (page 531); and as an artist's name for the divine quality felt whenever beauty is discerned in the shape of things on earth (page 532). "The wise," he said in still another statement, "believe all lovely things we see on earth approach more closely than anything else to that font from which we all derive."

In 1505, Michelangelo went back to Rome to discuss with Julius the 2d plans for a tomb suitable to the station, character, and taste of that most vigorous pontiff. The commission was in every way congenial, and the ideas of the Pope appear to have corresponded with those of the artist. Between the two, they projected the most remarkable tomb in the history of the world. It appears to have disturbed neither of them that their plans were fantastically impractical.

Fig. 14.23 The Tomb of Julius the 2nd as reconstructed by Erwin Panofsky: an attempt to visualize Michelangelo's original plan. (From Erwin Panofsky, *Iconology*, Oxford U. P., 1939.)

The original plan called for a small temple (Fig. 14.23) intended to stand inside the new St. Peter's. Julius had no intention of appearing in effigy as mortal, recumbent, and dead. Instead, we were to look up at his figure in the very act of entering heaven, into which place he intended to go seated bolt upright on his papal throne, riding on a catafalque carried by two angels, with his hand raised in the gesture of benediction and his eyes looking fearlessly forward into eternity.

No fewer than 47 full-scale marble statues were to be included in the composition, plus six panels of bronze relief. Except for the reliefs, which were to commemorate biographical episodes in the life of the Pope, the subject matter was to be a grandiose demonstration of the recondite iconography so satisfying to the taste of the period. Different scholars have developed different explanations, but we shall not be far wrong if we understand the tomb as an artistic parallel for Ficino's *Theologica Platonica*.

The elevation of the tomb was arranged in three levels. The purpose was to use the physically high and low to demonstrate the extremes of heaven and earth, and a stage of comparative grace between.

Around the exterior of the lowest story, there was to be a series of niches, with a *Victory* in each niche. On both sides of every *Victory*, nude and writhing *Captives* were to appear, each lashed to a slab (Fig. 14.25). Long recognized as reflecting to some extent the state of their author's own spirit, the *Captives* were intended (in the official iconography of the tomb) to typify the Neoplatonic concept of the immortal soul disgraced by imprisonment within the body, and struggling against the slavery of man's lower nature. In the

Figs. 14.24–25 Michelangelo. Figures intended for the Tomb of Julius the 2nd. (left) Florence, Academy. (right) Paris, Louvre. (Anderson; Clarence Kennedy)

same way, the *Victories* would also have an ethical meaning; they would stand for instances where reason had conquered the base emotions, giving man a taste of freedom and glory even here on earth.

On the second level, which corresponds to the top of the ground story, there were to be only four large statues, one at each corner. The characters to be depicted were Rachel and Leah, Moses and Paul. Moses and Paul had a special following at the time; they were often cited as men who had actually attained a synthesis of thought and action, thus enjoying spiritual grace during life. Leah and Rachel fell into a similar category. They symbolized the active and the contemplative life, both being considered necessary for the soul in its struggle back toward God.

As indicated above, the gates of heaven itself were to be the setting for the third and top level, occupied by the Pope and his angels. One of the latter, it is said, was to have a face full of rapture that so good a man should receive his reward. The other was to be in tears, because the world had lost him.

Very little work was actually completed in preparation for the tomb. Michelangelo spent an immense amount of time and disbursed tremendous sums accumulating a great stock of marble for the purpose, and the Pope himself lost interest as costs added up with little to show for it. In 1508, he diverted Michelangelo to painting the Sistine Chapel ceiling, originally intended as an interim project. In 1513, Julius died, and with him all hope of completing the plans.

After an enormous amount of delay and a tedious succession of revisions, the heirs, between 1542 and 1545, finally put together a simple wall tomb, using completed details intended for the full-scale project. The great Pope, as everybody knew, had intended to rest in his magnificent new St. Peter's; but by a maliciously ingenious reading of his will, the name San Pietro was construed in a generic way. The tomb of Julius was therefore placed within San Pietro in Vincoli, a small basilica which had been his titular church as the Cardinal Giuliano della Rovere.

The Moses, the only completed statue of the four projected for the second level of the tomb as planned, appears as the central figure in the arrangement at San Pietro in Vincoli. It is on the floor level, where it is probably even more awe-compelling than if placed as intended. To many, the force of the statue seems identified with rebuke, and the suggestion is made that Moses is shown as in Exodus 32:19. That is to say, we see him just as he is about to shatter the tablets of the law by casting them down in his wrath as he witnesses the celebration around the Golden Calf.

An eccentric detail tends to substantiate such an interpretation. Like Claus Sluter (Fig. 12.28, page 445), Michelangelo showed Moses with horns sprouting from his head. The error originated from a slip of the pen in Jerome's translation, which was then current. For a little further along in the narrative, Jerome misconstrued the verb qaran (to send out rays, to shine) of Exodus 34:35. He interpreted it as the noun qerem (horn). No one can blame him much because, in the Hebrew script, the two words differ only in their vowel markings, and are actually related to each other etymologically.

The moral dignity of the statue is inconsistent with Moses' somewhat childish behavior on the occasion mentioned; and on the whole, it seems likely that Michelangelo, as usual, intended to transcend historical narrative. If that be so, we may read the figure as a more general study of the Moses character, in which connection the last few verses of Exodus 34 seem apposite. They tell how Moses' face shone with light during and after his conversations with God. The Israelites were frightened thereby, and Moses had to put on a veil. It also seems likely that the statue was an attempt to depict the supernatural excitement known to all good students of Plato when, for an instant, the truth comes clear. In the words of Ficino, it "petrifies and almost kills the body while it enraptures the soul."

Among the other statues that were finished, or brought well along, are the *Victory* now in the Palazzo Vecchio, and some of the statues (Figs. 14.24–25) already cited as belonging to the lowest register of the arrangement as first planned. As a group, the *Captives* are colloquially known as "the Slaves." Two figures are in the Louvre, and four are in the Academy at Florence. The latter are believed to come from an abortive revision of 1532, which involved discarding all the work completed to date. They are larger than the statues in Paris, also more extreme. Their tortured bodies actually writhe back and forth in depth a greater distance than the total width across the shoulders.

Taking them as a set, the Slaves offer much provocation to anyone with a zeal for interpretation. Who can say what they mean? A number of suggestions have been put forward, all plausible. Perhaps they do not represent captives as previously stated, but the arts and sciences reduced to impotence by the death of so generous a patron. Another idea has it that they personify the political mortification of Italy, or even that they personify the foreign powers then reducing Italy, and show what Michelangelo wanted done with them. There can be no sure right or wrong in the matter. Neither do the various suggestions necessarily exclude one another; on the contrary, all may be true.

The truth is that except for the use of the human body in recognizable form, the Slaves are abstract. In that connection, it is of peculiar interest that several of the figures remain unfinished. Their condition can not easily be disposed of by reference to the sculptor's crowded schedule: Michelangelo's pre-eminence for speed in bringing work to a conclusion puts such a suggestion out of character. It therefore seems likely that he intended to leave things as we now see them.   .

What was the power that might be destroyed had he carried each statue further? The answer must in some way relate to the special strength of cogent but indefinite statement—a resource familiar in literature. Such statements set one off on his own. The artist names the train of thought, but does not map its course. So conceived, it seems that the unfinished marbles, which in physical fact are form emerging from matter, have something to do with humanity's struggle against the material incubus, and the beatitude vouchsafed when man realizes his humanity and later his salvation.

Michelangelo was at Florence when Julius sent for him to paint the ceiling of the Sistine Chapel. Having small taste for painting, and suspicious that Bramante and Raphael were at the bottom of the scheme (hoping to discredit him), he flatly refused to come back to Rome. After prolonged negotiations, Julius—a man not accustomed to negotiate with anybody—appealed to the government of Florence, asking that the artist be brought by force. "You have tried a bout with the Pope," said one of the Florentine officials, "on which the king of France would not have ventured. . . ." Nothing daunted, and realizing that Christendom would not be big enough to hold him, Michelangelo declared he would take refuge with the sultan of Turkey. Then presently he gave in.

At that time, the ceiling of the chapel was a mere field of decorator's work, blue and studded with stars. The Pope asked only that the twelve apostles be painted on the vault, but Michelangelo would have none of it. Disliking the task as he did, and with every reason to get it over with fast, he detested little plans even more. The scheme became increasingly big, and emerged as an attempt to provide an Old Testament foundation for the narrative frescoes painted on the walls of the chapel thirty years before (page 563). The main theme may be described as the Creation, God's subsequent wrath with mankind, and the survival of the human race by virtue of Noah's immunity. The narrative pictures are reinforced by seven Prophets and five sybils, thus recalling how one event foretold another, and putting classical mythology openly on a par with Christian history. In addition, there are innumerable subordinate figures of purely artistic utility; they are disposed for compositional purposes, to enframe units of narrative, or to lead the eye onward. The total area covered measures about 700 square yards.

Michelangelo is believed to have executed almost every inch of it personally, and his sustained expenditure of energy during the herculean performance is without a parallel in the history of art, or in any other history. He paused only when exhausted. In his creative fury, he neglected the simplest and most obvious routines of health and comfort. Forgetting to remove his shoes for a period of weeks, for instance, he pulled the skin off with them when finally persuaded to change his clothes. He worked almost entirely flat on his back; and as a result, he suffered serious ocular maladjustment for some time after completing the commission and resuming once again the normal posture.

Although individual pictures on the ceiling are among the greatest known on earth, the project as a whole could hardly have been more unwise. It being nearly impossible to bring the entire field into view at once, the surface had to be subdivided into panels, with scenes coming seriatim. The contour of the vault was no proper field for painting. It is often poorly lighted; and under the best of conditions, the height (about 85 feet) and the vertical angle of sight makes inspection of the paintings uncomfortable at all times, and often impossible. It is notable, in that connection, that few of them are genuine ceiling pictures in any case; most were designed as though to be viewed horizontally, like normal paintings.

After finishing the panels that told the story of Noah, Michelangelo apparently removed the scaffolding and studied the work from the floor. As a result, he very considerably simplified the compositions which dealt with the Creation, two of which we show in Figures 14.26–27. He reduced the setting to the lowest limit possible with any remaining correspondence to the narrative. The meaning is carried almost exclusively by the human figures. The latter were also reduced in number until there could be no fewer. Each was painted in the strongest possible application of the mode of relief; sometimes they make the impression of having been hewn from the block rather than painted.

The figure style shows the full effect upon Michelangelo of the Pergamene division of Hellenistic art with which he had recently become fascinated by way of the few decadent manifestations thereof visible at Rome. But his skill and judgment in posing the body showed incomparable improvement over either the *Laocoön* (Fig. 6.21, page 176) or the *Belvedere Torso* (Figs. 6.22–23, page 177). Starting with such flamboyant and empty sources, he arrived once again at standards of excellence comparable to those of the Greek Great Age.

His iconography was at once grand and pathetic, a truth best demonstrated by the *Creation of Adam* (Fig. 14.27). For a sincere Christian, the gift of life was no gift at all in Italy during the 16th century; and we therefore see Adam accepting it reluctantly, and God giving it, divine fire though it is, with sympathy and anxiety. It is also to be noted that Adam is placed on earth (from which he came) and near God (whose image he was to bear). The juxtaposition suggests a remark in Pico della Mirandola's *Oration on Human Dignity;* namely, that Adam had the right to choose: he might abase himself to the brutes, or become divine. The numerous figures enclosed within God's mantle amplify the meaning further. The lovely girl encircled by his arm must be Eve, whom God would presently give to Adam. It is significant that she is younger here than in the panel showing her own incarnation, and she looks out with fear and wonder upon the miracle of birth which she was destined so often to repeat upon the earth. The numerous babies suggest the descendants of Adam and Eve, but it will be observed that one of them is singled out from the rest. The fingers of the Almighty rest with painful weight on his shoulder, and the child feels the burden. He must be meant for the Christ child, and it would seem that the Almighty felt need of him at this significant moment.

The next important commission, and the first in Michelangelo's career to involve a substantial amount of architecture, was the new sacristy attached to San Lorenzo at Florence, often called the *Medici Chapel* because it was undertaken to provide a family mausoleum. Work began in 1521, and the project was abandoned unfinished in 1534.

Figs. 14.26–27 Michelangelo. Frescoes on the ceiling of the Sistine Chapel in the Vatican. 1508–1512. (top) *Creation of the Sun and Moon*. (bottom) *Creation of Adam*. (Anderson)

The architecture Michelangelo designed as a setting for the several tombs throws a new light on his personality. Uncompromisingly proud and completely aware of his own genius, it was his habit to respond to the opinions of others with intolerable arrogance. He was nevertheless capable of humility, and was occasionally more than gracious in his appreciation of other artists. Those he admired most seem to have been those opposite to himself: Gentile da Fabriano, for example, and Fra Angelico. On this occasion, he paid Brunelleschi the compliment of emulating his style. Michelangelo's handling of the decorative orders, and his employment of line and surface, echo the architecture of the modest and elegant nave just a few steps back through the entrance passageway. But at the same time, a master habituated to plastic expression and accustomed to make himself emphatic could not be Brunelleschi over again. Everywhere we look, therefore, we can feel the stronger relief and the greater weight of the High Renaissance.

Lorenzo the Magnificent and his murdered brother lie in a plain sarcophagus along the entrance wall; a more elaborate tomb for them was part of the original plan. The famous "Medici Tombs," one of which appears in Figure 14.28 (the other is almost the same in design), house two later and lesser Medici: Giuliano, Duke of Nemours, and Lorenzo, Duke of Urbino, who had died in 1516 and 1519 respectively. Into the iconography of those monuments we need not go in detail. Suffice it to say that it conformed to yet another scheme of Neoplatonic categories. Taken together, the two tombs were intended to set forth the dual concept of the active and the contemplative life, and into that theme was woven the notion of mortality and time, the latter being suggested by the recumbent statues of *Night, Day, Dawn,* and *Dusk* which lie so uncomfortably inclined upon the lids of the two sarcophagi. About the design, much is to be said.

Michelangelo was the founder of the Baroque (Chapter 15) in the same sense that Alberti founded the High Renaissance. As they stand, the two Medici tombs are incomplete. Both were to include a pair of river gods, probably reclining on the floor at angles opposite to the statues which now lie on the sarcophagi. The addition of those intended figures would tend to tighten the composition; but even as they stand, the tombs have an extraordinary finality of design. They are, in fact, the earliest demonstration of the principles by which baroque art was to be governed. As such, they belong to the next chapter rather than to this, and it is appropriate to defer discussion until that time (page 681). Equally a prediction of the Baroque was the immense *Last Judgment* on the eastern wall of the Sistine Chapel, upon which Michelangelo was at work from 1534 to 1541.

The *Last Judgment* proved to be his final important commission in either painting or sculpture. In 1535, Paul the 3rd asked him to become

Fig. 14.28 Michelangelo. Tomb of Guiliano de' Medici, Duke of Nemours. About 1523 to about 1533. Marble. Approximately 20 feet high. Florence, San Lorenzo, New Sacristy. (Anderson)

superintendent of the Vatican buildings, a position that did not mean much at the moment, but one which eventuated in his taking over the construction of St. Peter's (1546), the completion of the Farnese Palace, and the design of a piazza and a group of buildings around it for the Capitol Hill.

When Michelangelo took over St. Peter's, he found the fabric much as Bramante had left it in 1514 (page 596). The various interim architects had made a number of paper plans and a number of small wooden models, but they had accomplished little construction. It is difficult to say to what extent his decisions were dictated by circumstances over which he had no control. At any rate, he designed a central church around the existing piers at the crossing, with arms so short and a plan so compact that the body of the building would tell (much as it does today in the apse view) as a pedestal for the immense dome. The dome itself was a refinement of the one Brunelleschi had designed at Florence (page 509). There is no telling whether its present elliptical silhouette was designed by Michelangelo or by Della Porta, who took over after his death, at which time the work was complete to the top of the drum.

There can be no question that St. Peter's would be a better building had Michelangelo's central plan remained. The extended nave ruined the composition; any normal view including the present façade gives the church an unfortunately disjointed look. When all is said and done, the chief present interest of the design has to do with Michelangelo's manipulation of scale, a matter in which he made a significant historical contribution.

He took the fundamental shape of the nave from Alberti's Sant'Andrea at Mantua (Fig. 14.13, page 556), but he had a special problem because the building at Rome was intended to be immensely bigger. In making the adaptation, he proceeded in a bold new way. He discarded the idea of multiplying the conventional classical members. Instead, he merely gave the new church the usual number of parts but increased the size of each part in proportion with the gigantic scale of the whole.

Upon entering, one's sensibilities are affected in peculiar fashion. There is no chance to form a notion of size by the familiar method of counting parts, as we do at Hagia Sophia (Fig. 11.13, page 374) and at Amiens (Fig. 9.4, page 281). In fact, the exaggerated scale of familiar moldings and orders may at first pass unnoticed. Presently, however, the unusual surroundings begin to impart a feeling of their own size. The feet seem to wear seven-league boots, and every other capacity of the person becomes, for the present, enlarged in the imagination. Merely amusing at its inception, the sensation gradually becomes an idea seriously entertained. It is hardly too much to say that the end result is to impart a sense of personal grandeur to every man and woman within.

For the ensemble on the Capitol Hill (in Italian, Piazza del Campidoglio; colloquially, "the Campidoglio"), Michelangelo prepared a design that is surely one of the best in history (Fig. 14.29). A bronze equestrian statue of Marcus Aurelius, unique among classical antiquities, was chosen as the focus for the entire composition. Around it extends the pavement of the small piazza, bounded on three sides by palaces and opening on the fourth upon a tremendous stairway down the steep side of the hill. The Palace of the Senate closes the vista established by the axis of the stairs. It is a larger, slightly more ornate building than its flanking palaces. The latter are identical duplicates, and they lie at a moderate angle to each other.

Precedent for such an arrangement was not lacking; indeed, the inspiration may have come from a somewhat similar grouping at Pienza. But no earlier plan accomplished in the same measure an esthetic coherence between several buildings in a group. Michelangelo's success on this occasion inaugurated the modern tradition of working with units of architecture much as the painter manipulates single items within a composition. As compared with other essays along the same line, his design is perhaps still the very best.

Esthetic emphasis was produced by the size and central placement of the largest building, and yet the others have scale enough to stand in their own right, and not as mere outbuildings. Of particular interest is Michelangelo's care for the fall of the light. It was natural for him to approach architectural

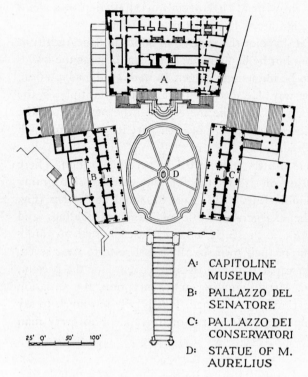

Fig. 14.29 (left) Rome. Plan of the group of palaces on the Capitol Hill. Designed by Michelangelo. Begun 1546. (opposite) Palace of the Senate. (Anderson)

A: CAPITOLINE MUSEUM

B: PALLAZZO DEL SENATORE

C: PALLAZZO DEI CONSERVATORI

D: STATUE OF M. AURELIUS

design from a sculptor's point of view, and it is said he would never permit construction until he had made and studied a model of the proposed building. In this instance, he demonstrated extraordinary judgment in the placement and projection of parts, with the result that cast shadows aid rather than harm the forms: the absence of parallelism in the plan guarantees that no two of the buildings will ever take the sun in the same way at the same time.

Considered separately, the Palace of the Senate can justly be hailed as the best, and probably the final solution of the Renaissance problem of combining the esthetic qualities of classical architecture with the demands of modern utilitarian buildings, most of which must have several stories. As such, it proved to be the model for so many derivative buildings in Europe, America, and elsewhere that it would be futile even to guess at the number; there are probably a thousand new ones under construction as this is written.

As a class, the Palace of the Senate and all derivatives take their original guidance from the Roman variation of the Greek temple (Fig. 7.7, page 190). Its three divisions (podium, order, entablature) are obvious on the façade, but Michelangelo's design called for a podium considerably higher and a colossal order much shorter than classical rules would suggest. In all such designs, it is essential to give the order (pilasters or columns as the case may be) sufficient vertical power to unify the elevation. It is correspondingly important to mini-

mize the horizontality of the several levels of floor, a result which was aided in this instance by a clever variation in the size and shape of the windows.

At the top of the building, Michelangelo found himself in the perennial trouble that besets every man who tries to adapt the classical orders to modern work. An entablature in proportion with the order would be too small to operate as a proper enframement for the whole building, while an entablature big enough to fit the height of the building would dwarf the order immediately beneath. Michelangelo's solution has been the standard one ever since: he added a decorative balustrade, by means of which he gained height without overbearing weight.

The great man was seventy-two years old when he redesigned St. Peter's, and the colossal spirit of that church remains as a testament to the regard in which he was held in Rome. His later years were more and more unhappy, however, and his isolation, seemingly grand, was in fact desperate. He could neither approve nor disapprove the policies of the Counter-Reformation, a fact which increased his personal turmoil. Certain minor aspects thereof even proved a direct embarrassment to him.

One of the matters to which the Catholic reformers turned their attention was the question of decorum. In view of the flamboyant sensuality marking

Fig. 14.30 Michelangelo. *Pietà Rondanini*. Milan, Castello Sforzesco.
(Anderson)

the immediate Italian past, their concern was appropriate, but it led them
into some artistically ridiculous notions. Nudity as such became suspect; and
Michelangelo himself, the most admired artist in the world, was accused of
impropriety because his *Last Judgment* contained many naked figures. Paul
the 4th actually had Daniele da Volterra (1555–1559) paint shorts on some of
the offending bodies. It was even suggested that the painting be removed
entirely.

Before Michelangelo was dead, both Catholics and Protestants were indulging in some of the worst cruelties known in the Western world. The excesses of the religious wars may be thought of as an outward and vulgar
counterpart of the spiritual stress within his own soul. His later writings
are replete with passages expressing a sense of utter futility. "Lord, what shall
I do unless thou visit me with thine ineffable grace?" he says in one place.

And again, "I have let the vanities of the world rob me of the time I had for the contemplation of God."

Among his later drawings many approach complete dematerialization, but perhaps the best and most intimate record from his old age is to be found in the medium he loved best. Only three sculptural groups survive from those years. All three deal with the entombment of Christ. All three utterly renounce the pagan ideals of beauty and strength with which he had amazed the world in earlier days, and still does. Figure 14.30 is the most pathetic of them all, but let the student also consult the grander group originally intended for his own tomb and now appropriately placed in the Cathedral at Florence. It stands all alone there, the last and by no means the least statement from the small, unhappy Florentine gentleman in whose person all the greatness of Italy was concentrated.

VENETIAN PAINTING DURING THE HIGH RENAISSANCE

The Renaissance came late at Venice, the reason being more or less evident in the character of the city. It is hardly accurate to think of Venice as Italian; in fact the place never has been so until rather recent times. From its foundation during the 6th century, the town was a maritime power and is still one of the busiest ports in Europe. The natural line of intercourse was with the Germanies by way of the Brenner Pass, and with the Levant by way of the Mediterranean. The important Venetian families had relatives resident at Constantinople, Saloniki, Tyre, Alexandria, and a host of other places. For the same reason of trade, colonies of Greeks, Arabs, Slavs, Syrians, Turks, and Germans lived at Venice to handle their end of the immense transshipment which flowed continuously through the city, leaving wealth in its train. It was natural enough that commercial considerations loomed much larger in the Venetian mind than philosophical or religious questions, and inevitable that materialism would assert itself strongly in the local culture. The cosmopolitan atmosphere of the place involved much more than mere trade, however. From the beginning of the 13th century onward, Venice held political and military control over many of the eastern islands, and over substantial portions of the mainland as far afield as the shores of the Black Sea. Except for a series of conflicts with Genoa, her only rival on the sea, Venice remained not so much aloof as unconcerned with Italian politics and Italian culture. Her interests lay over the horizon.

To identify one's self with Venice, moreover, was to call up visual imagery unique in all the earth. The reality of the place is like a dream. No other city was ever built on so irrational a site, with canals for thoroughfares and gondolas for transport. Venetian architecture is as fantastic as the idea of the town itself. Great palaces rise like lace out of the water, and all the ordinary customs seem replaced by farfetched romance. Nature has done her part to enhance the spectacle. The sea and clouds take on colors that are extravagant even for the Mediterranean. The very air often glows with golden light, bathing the colored marbles with bizarre opalescence.

It would be unreasonable to ask the inhabitants of such a place to spend their time wrestling with the severe abstractions of architecture, or to be content with the monotones of sculpture. Everywhere they looked, the view whipped them up to a lust for color. Their art may well have been delayed, in fact, by the lack of the right medium. Mosaic was too somber for the spirit of the times. Both tempera and fresco had proven fugitive in the damp atmosphere. The start of the school coincided, in fact, with a visit by Antonello da Messina who came there in 1475 to paint a large *Madonna Enthroned,* now broken up and preserved only in part. Antonello was one of the very few Italians who ever painted in the mode of the total visual effect, one of the earliest who habitually used oil, and one of the few men then alive who understood its properties.

The Venetians adopted oil instantly and made it their own. The best artists of the place have invariably been painters, and the historical contribution of the school depends upon their surpassing judgment in the development and perfection of methods for painting with oil. Most writers have erred by stating the matter too gingerly. They may perhaps be forgiven, because the truth of Venetian achievement and influence is so sweeping as to challenge the credulity of the reader.

As to the achievement of the Venetian masters, it may be said that their research was exhaustive and very nearly final. Except for the special and somewhat limited contribution made by the French Impressionists (pages 858–874), there has been nothing new in the way of technique since. It will be understood, of course, that the expression of mature men is ramified beyond description, and that when we state that such and such an artist painted by Venetian methods, we make no suggestion that his pictures look anything like Titian's or Tintoretto's. We merely mean that he accomplished his own purpose with the same tools and the same materials used in similar fashion. That being plain, we can make a very brief statement of the breadth of Venetian influence.

Through the agency of El Greco (about 1548–1614), who had learned his trade in Titian's shop before going to Toledo, the Venetian oil technique was transmitted to Spain. Every Iberian artist since might justly be called a Venetian derivative.

Through the agency of Rubens (1577–1640), who spent a full eight years in Italy and made many copies after Titian, the Venetian manner went to the entire north of Europe. Flemish, French, and much Dutch painting has ever since been Venetian in method. Rubens' distinguished pupil Van Dyck (1599–1641) took the same technique to England, and every British painter and all American painters have employed it since.

The influence so broadly described above has not yet lost momentum. As with most other instances of cultural invention and borrowing, the Venetian method was widely adopted because artists thought it better and more convenient; they instinctively recognized its theory as being fundamentally in keeping with the art of painting, and as opening up more complete possibilities of expression. Most of the technical stratagems in the work of Cézanne (pages 858–874)—all too often put forward as original inventions of his own—were matters of common knowledge at Venice during the 16th century, and he learned them from Venetian paintings he had studied in the museums. What was true of Cézanne is equally true of the followers of Cézanne. A retrospective exhibition of Matisse, held in New York in the autumn of 1951, showed that supposedly radical and modern master to be an immensely skillful painter indeed; but although the problems he had set himself were special and even new, his tactics in solving them were Venetian.

♦ *The Venetian Mode*   The Venetian mode, sometimes called the pictorial mode of the later Renaissance, was the fourth and last theory of painting to be promulgated successfully in the history of European art. It derived from the mode of the total visual effect (pages 481 ff.); in some respects, the two are often so nearly alike as to be difficult to distinguish. As the reader has doubtless inferred from what has gone before, the principal advantage of the Venetian mode over its predecessors was the fact that it offered greater flexibility to the art of painting. While producing pictures of acceptable verisimilitude, the new system set the painter free from the artistic lock-step which must be accepted as the inevitable consequence of maintaining a strict one-to-one relationship between the facts of the painting and the facts of nature.

It will be understood, of course, that the Venetian departure from nature was partial, and not complete. In Venetian pictures, the human anatomy is reasonably strict. Linear perspective is likewise correct. But in every department having to do with tonal relations, the Venetians did as they pleased, with only the slightest regard for the rules of light and color which Jan van Eyck had investigated so thoroughly and mastered so well.

Having cast aside natural fact as the law of art, they were able to make direct and arbitrary use of value, hue, and intensity in several ways from which painters had hitherto been foreclosed. Upon occasion, representation itself (especially the placement of objects forward and back within the represented space) was made easier by calculated contrasts between the tone of the near thing and the tone of the far thing. By an equally arbitrary manipulation

He took the fundamental shape of the nave from Alberti's Sant' Andrea at

Fig. 14.31   Tintoretto. *Presentation of the Virgin.* 1552–1556. Venice, Santa Maria dell'Orto. (Anderson)

of the tone, the Venetian painters threw the light, so to speak, upon a person in the act of doing something crucial in the drama of the picture. By a cognate use of shadow, they relegated other figures to subordinate status. Sometimes shadow has the opposite effect, and directs attention to a particular face by the simple power of our curiosity to explore the undefined.

An excellent instance of a comparatively simple picture in the Venetian mode is Tintoretto's *Presentation of the Virgin* (Fig. 14.31). One's attention is arrested at once by the flood of brilliance which carries up the stairs and stops at the small figure of the Virgin. Dramatically, what could be in more perfect order than the idea that a radiance as of divine grace followed her up the steps that day? And yet what could be more inconsistent with the logic of illumination as we observe it on earth? A single field here and there models, with reference to itself alone, in rational fashion; but the same cannot be said of the broader areas of light and shadow which form so essential a feature of the composition. Why does the light fall only where it does? How

Fig. 14.32 Tintoretto. *Miracle of Saint Mark*. Detail. 1548. Venice, Academy. (Anderson)

does it happen that the child herself merely leads the light up the stone stairs, and receives almost none of it? Why is there so exaggerated a contrast of value between the illuminated areas, which seem to get the full sun, and the shaded areas, which seem almost like nocturnes? What is there to say about the brightness of the amazed old man at the lower left? And what of the fact that the canvas divides into almost equal halves of light and dark along the diagonal?

So long as we insist upon finding a natural or mechanical cause for everything we see in the picture, it must remain an outlandish enigma. Immediately we accept the artistic propriety of using paint without reference to the facts of visual experience, the entire Venetian theory opens up. Because painting is in many respects more flexible than nature and much more under the control of the artist, it becomes feasible—once we accept as legitimate a substantial departure from the tone relations of nature—to create a pictorial world with effects of light and color which otherwise would remain quite out of the question. Out of the question, it is worth remarking, even in the modern theater with its battery of lights. The imagery of art, to put it briefly, can be different, more extended, and more responsive to the creative imagination than the imagery of sight.

In his well-known *Miracle of Saint Mark,* Tintoretto arbitrarily bathed some of the figures in light and some in shadow, and he thereby achieved emphasis and subordination as described above. Figure 14.32 reproduces a section from the upper right-hand corner of the composition; the purpose of the selection is to illustrate a modest instance of the Venetian habit of using contrasts of value, hue, intensity, or all three, as a method for making us read certain masses as being forward or back from certain others within the represented space of the painting.

The detail shows one figure entire, and part of another. The two lie approximately in the same vertical plane, and it was necessary for the painter to make both "come forward" from a background he wished to "place" about twenty yards away. Neither the drawing of the figures nor the drawing of the background would, in itself, furnish sufficient indication of the spatial relation he wanted us to comprehend. With respect to the two arms of the man at the lower left, he was aided in the representation by atmospheric perspective, and even more by the sharp contrast between the high value of the white gateway and the arms silhouetted against it. No such fortunate arrangement of contrasts existed to "place" the old gentleman at the upper right in the same manner, and he resorted to an arbitrary expedient.

Around the upper silhouette of the figure, he ran a ribbon of tint very near to white in value. Depending upon the variation in local contrast between the figure and its background, the whitish ribbon was made narrower or wider as circumstances required. The result, as seen either in the original or in a good photograph, was to make the figure "snap forward" into the desired position.

The convenience of these methods will be obvious. Most painters ever since have freely resorted to arbitrary modulations of tone, to calculated contrasts of local hue, and to any other manipulation of pigments whenever such would serve to supplement other indications of spatial displacement between objects seen in the picture. It was in this department of art that Cézanne, in particular, owed so much to the Venetians.

Although Venetian painting purported to be representative and was often stirringly dramatic, the going taste at Venice demanded, also, that paintings form an integral part of larger schemes of interior decoration. The picture, in short, was designed for the room in which it was to appear; and in that department, the Venetian artists preferred the principle of harmony to the principle of contrast. Thus, when composing a picture, they took care to keep the rhythm of lights and darks in appropriate relation to the architectural rhythm of the surroundings. Tintoretto's immense *Crucifixion* at San Rocco is a capital example, but it reproduces badly in black and white. Veronese's *Marriage at Cana* (Fig. 14.33) will illustrate the point as well as can be done with a book plate. If studied according to the theory of the total visual effect, its arrangement of values is irrational, but it is full of wisdom and merit if we understand that the painter intended to carry a decorative rhythm across a broad area. Lights succeed darks. Dark appears against light,

Fig. 14.33 Veronese. *Marriage at Cana*. 1563. Oil on canvas. 32 feet 5 inches wide by 21 feet 10 inches high. Paris, Louvre. (Giraudon)

and light against dark. The shadows are cast, or omitted, according to the rules of pattern and not according to the rules of natural illumination.

In similar fashion, the principle of harmony was applied to the color scheme of paintings. In theory, any hue whatever may be chosen to give a dominant tonality to a room; but 16th-century fashion at Venice called for paneling in rich brown woods (strictly, neutralized red-orange) with decorative accents brought out in gold.

While a quick look at a Venetian painting gives one the impression of experiencing all the hues in a more or less vivid state, a more systematic analysis (especially if it involves putting the Venetian picture in contrast with some other) corrects the original hasty reaction. If catalogued, diagrammatically or otherwise, all the hues in the Venetian painting will fall on the color circle in the general region of red-orange; and the picture, considered merely as a unit of area, will tell as a spot of that hue. Such a statement seemingly contradicts the evidence of the eyes; but the fields which tell as bright blue in Titian's *Europa* at Fenway Court, simply to name an example accessible to American readers, actually are very neutralized blue-grays. They tell as intense blues only because they are relatively cooler and more blue than the tones immediately adjacent to them. Because there is nothing to conflict in any serious fashion with the dominance of red-orange, the picture gleams with that tonality, and has the effect so often referred to as "the Venetian glow."

Able masters that they were, and preoccupied with decoration as they were, it was only natural that the Venetians produced pictures more gorgeous than any the world had seen before. At the same time, their strong interest in physical beauty tended rather often to result in beauty alone, and one looks in vain for the intellectual and spiritual qualities characteristic of all that art that stemmed from Florence.

By giving painters a sanction for modulations of color not to be justified by reference to nature, but acceptable by reference to their expressive power, the Venetian mode unquestionably opened up new doors. At the same time, it extended an invitation to bizarre effects. In his later years, Tintoretto in particular carried boldness to the point of violence, thus suggesting to the Venetian-trained El Greco the eerie wildness so appropriate to the perfervid Catholic art he produced after he took up residence at Toledo in Spain.

♦ *The Bellini* Jacopo Bellini (about 1400–1470) was the earliest important master native to Venice. Little of his painting survives, but his sketch books, now in the Louvre, show him as a member of the International style (pages 429–439). His immediate inspiration came from Gentile da Fabriano, and like Gentile (Figs. 12.20–21, page 438), he made a specialty of sweet Madonnas in half-length.

Jacopo had two sons, Gentile and Giovanni. Gentile Bellini (1429–1507) was an able but uninspired painter. He devoted his entire career to pictures of Venetian life and specialized in panoramic canvases recording the innumerable processions and ceremonies which seem to have been the chief joy of the official calendar in that picturesque city. Gentile may be said, in fact, to have established Venice as one of the perennial subjects of Western art. He was followed in that vein by Carpaccio (about 1455–1522) and by a long line of native painters culminating in Canaletto (1697–1768) and Guardi (1712–1793). Once started, the tradition of the Venetian view attracted painters from elsewhere. Claude Lorrain (1600–1682) did a number of harbor scenes suggested by the imagery of the canals. Turner (1775–1851) chose Venice for the setting of one impressionistic tour de force after another. The fantastic light and color of the place will probably never cease to excite the skilled technician, and for that reason some of the very best luminist experiments by both Manet and Monet are pictures of Venice.

♦ *Giovanni Bellini* Giovanni Bellini (1430–1516) was emotionally more profound than his brother or father and was much affected by his brother-in-law, Andrea Mantegna (1431–1506), the most powerful personality in

Fig. 14.34 Giovanni Bellini. *Madonna and Child*. Cambridge, Massachusetts, Fogg Art Museum.

Lombardy and Donatello's heir at Padua. Giovanni emerged in his own name about 1475, and from that date onward, paintings in large numbers came from his studio every year. Young painters were glad to work there—among them, Giorgione and Titian.

From the first, Giovanni's art was his own. A weaker man might have felt inclined to lean more heavily upon Mantegna, who was distinguished for his theoretical powers and marked in his work by a realism as passionate as the 15th century ever produced. Giovanni's gifts were gentler, however. His most characteristic painting might be described as visual poetry; it must be felt through the intuitions, or it will have no meaning at all.

As though by unanimous consent, Giovanni got the best commissions at Venice for thirty years and more. He did a number of large pictures. The *Frari Madonna* and the *Madonna Enthroned* of San Zaccharia, may stand as examples of his work in religious art; and we may refer to his *Feast of the Gods,* the subject of a monograph by Edgar Wind, to show his capacity in handling the classical themes.

Excellent though they are, ceremonial pictures in public places hardly spell Giovanni Bellini for those who care most about him. The pictures which reveal his nature best are the half-length Madonnas he turned out in large numbers. Figure 14.34 shows a typical example. All of them are arranged according to the same formula. The Madonna is seen behind a low wall, on which the child stands. A narrow screen is placed a couple of feet behind her. To either side, we get glimpses of the sky and sometimes of foliage. If the latter, the leafage is always of early summer, and the light and air are soft and still. The mood is as moderate and as unforgettable as that perfect time of year. Often the Madonna looks softly down. Sometimes her eyes open out toward us. In every instance, the expression is completely innocent of any effort to appeal or to impress. The affinity with Gentile da Fabriano is obvious at a glance; in fact, Giovanni's Madonnas might well be thought of as the International style brought up to date. His paintings remain unexcelled whenever and wherever a sentimental treatment of the Madonna subject might be appropriate. As compared with Raphael's Florentine Madonnas (Fig. 14.16, page 588), they maintain a level of dignity sadly lacking there. It is amazing that a single artist could so often repeat the same simple arrangement without precise duplication. It is even more remarkable that the content, which is delicate to the point of making each picture a serious esthetic risk, never once fails or cloys.

♦ *Giorgione* Giorgione of Castelfranco (about 1475–1510) was an even more lyrical painter than Giovanni Bellini, in whose shop he worked with Titian, his intimate friend. Unlike modern oil paintings, Venetian pictures were very slow in production; often a canvas would be turned to the wall after each stage of underpainting, and allowed to lie idle for months at a time, until the paint became utterly dry. It is not surprising, therefore, that a number of pictures were only half finished when Giorgione suddenly died in 1510. Titian took them over and finished them. An immense effort of connoisseurship has failed to separate the hands; and for the purist, there is a group of paintings known as "the Giorgione-Titians"—of which Figure 14.35 shows one.

The design is a demonstration of the manner in which the Venetian tonal rhythm, so obvious in larger pictures, can be applied to the composition of a small, portable painting. The meaning can be inferred from the faces of the three performers: the young and shallow singer to the left, the pedestrian countenance to the right, and the central figure who turns as though in appeal for some sign that the others share even a little of his learning and emotions.

Fig. 14.35 Giorgione. *The Concert.* About 1510. Oil on canvas. 3 feet 6½ inches high. Florence, Pitti Palace. (Anderson)

In the art of the modern world, it fell to Giorgione to perform the role of Praxiteles (page 136) and to establish the female nude as a subject in its own right, to be accepted as though out of obligation by Titian, Rubens, Rembrandt, Velasquez, Goya, Canova, Ingres, Bouguereau, Cabanel, and a host of others. The painting which set the tradition in motion was the well-known *Sleeping Venus* shown in Figure 14.36.

Any honest discussion of the picture involves the English-speaking critic in problems of the greatest social delicacy. The Victorian tradition is still strong enough to make some recent writers insist that sexual allure formed no part of Giorgione's expression. The same can hardly be said of the chaste Botticelli, who was steeped in a lofty Platonism. Much less can it be said of a painter who was popular at Venice during the 16th century, when that city included within its catalogue of luxuries a mature and refined taste for the sensual. It is irrational to suggest that Giorgione felt a distaste for matters which were the subject of direct and open interest among his friends and contemporaries, and it is fantastic to entertain the thought that the painting constitutes a kind of prophecy of the manners and customs of England and America during the 19th century.

The attempt to expurgate the picture is not only a failure; it is highly improper. It is far better to appreciate the painting for what it is, namely, a declaration of that physical attraction by which men are drawn to women and become devoted to them. The theme is presented tranquilly, without excitement. The fact of sleep, it will be noted, exerts a generalizing power over the warm appeal of the body. The essence of the matter, indeed, is a

Fig. 14.36 Giorgione. *The Sleeping Venus.* Oil on canvas. 5 feet 10 inches wide by 3 feet 7 inches high. Dresden, Gallery. (Alinari)

complete absence of narrative. Because no story is suggested, it is possible to contemplate the permanent reality of the universal desire to which all must respond in some measure. The subject of physical love thus attains the spiritual overtones without which desire itself remains incomplete, immature, and certainly no blessing.

♦ *Titian* Titian (1477–1576) enjoyed the longest career ever permitted a European artist. He was one of the world's best technicians before he finished his training under Giovanni Bellini; and when he died a few months before his hundredth birthday, he was not only still active, but capable of work that justifies the factual use of the adjective phenomenal. No other painter ever had the opportunity to acquire an equal measure of experience. No other was ever more fortunate—from the standpoint of technique—in the place he lived or the period he lived there, and certainly no other was better qualified by temperament and talent to advance in his chosen field. The reader will not be surprised, therefore, to be told that Titian had a broader influence upon subsequent painting than any other artist of the High Renaissance. His work, more than that of any other man, has set the standard and remained as the ideal and the norm for nearly 400 years.

In view of the length of his career, the development of Titian's style holds an unusual interest. An excellent example of his early manner is the *Sacred and Profane Love* (Fig. 14.37) in the Borghese Gallery at Rome. The odd name under which it has long been known is surely a mistake; but in spite of considerable effort scholars have not yet found an explanation that gives complete satisfaction. We can get some feeling for the content from the probability that the sarcophagus was intended for that of Adonis, whose

Fig. 14.37   Titian. *Sacred and Profane Love*. About 1514. Oil on canvas. 8 feet 7 inches wide by 3 feet 6 inches high. Rome, Borghese Gallery. (Anderson)

murder by the jealous Mars appears in relief on its face. If so, the nude woman is Venus, and the baby Cupid. A recent opinion would have us identify the clothed girl as Polia, a character who appeared in the *Hypnero-tomachia Poliphili*, a collection of allegorical and antiquarian love stories published at Venice in 1499. Polia was in the habit of frequenting a fountain which was kept filled with water from Adonis's stone coffin. If that is correct, Venus must be urging her to take a lover she has so far rejected.

As compared with the painter's later work, the modeling is strongly plastic, and the point of view not radically different from the mode of relief. The masses, both in foreground and distance, seem to assert their three-dimensionality by repelling the atmosphere around them. As time went on, Titian became less and less interested in sculpturesque definition, and more and more interested in the softening and blending of things much as they actually appear on the retina of the eye.

His output during middle life was immense. It included important commissions of every kind: religious, classical, portraits. Every writer has so many favorite paintings that he cannot choose one or two for discussion without doing violence to his own feelings, let alone the preferences of his colleagues. If, however, the citation of a "typical Titian" be required, there can certainly be no quarrel with the statement that it is the *Bacchus and Ariadne* of the National Gallery in London (Figs. 14.38–39).

The picture belongs to a famous chapter in High Renaissance taste. It was commissioned by Alfonso d'Este, Duke of Ferrara, who vied with his sister Isabella in the patronage of works of art intended to explore and make manifest the ramifications of the then-popular philosophy of love. Between them, the two scholarly aristocrats called into being a substantial corpus of refined erotica, most of it with classical subject matter. For the whole story,

Figs. 14.38–39 Titian. *Bacchus and Ariadne.* 1523. Oil on canvas. 5 feet, 9 inches high. London, National Gallery. (below) Detail.

we may refer the reader again to Edgar Wind's monograph, merely placing the Bacchus in the series by saying that it seems to deal with the frustrative aspect of the relations between male and female.

Wind pointed out that the imagery corresponds reasonably well with lines 505–508 in the *Fasti* III of Ovid, and he believes the scene is meant for the final encounter between the two lovers. Ariadne had long since been abandoned by the faithless god. But one day as she was walking on the beach bemoaning her condition and hoping for death, she suddenly found herself pursued by Bacchus. He was passing by in the course of his triumphant return from a trip to India. The presence of the Corona Borealis in the sky above Ariadne's head seems enough in itself to identify the moment, because the jewels of her crown became stars in heaven only as she died in Bacchus's arms on that occasion. Strangely enough, the literary source for the painting had, since the 17th century, been cited as a passage from Catullus (*Carmina* LXIV), which does not fit nearly so well in the matter of imagery, and tells, moreover, of the first and not the last meeting of the two.

Here, and elsewhere, it seems that Titian indulged his interest in visual esthetics even to the brink of contradicting what he purported to represent. The painting states that Bacchus has just jumped clean out of his chariot in a crazy dive toward Ariadne, but Bacchus is in fact a static figure. The same may be said of every other. The postures are those ordinarily assumed only under exertion; but there is no strain and nobody moves. We are reminded of the event Keats described on the Grecian urn: nothing is going to happen, and the future is the same as the present. The story was taken, that is to say, at a point when all its visual imagery fell into composition, and the artist's concern was less with the passion and tragedy of the narrative, and more with the inspired decorative surface Titian was better able to produce than any other man.

Accepting his scheme for what it appears to have been, no praise can be too high. The painting contains within it almost every expedient of design known to the art. No analysis in words can possibly do more than hint at the complexity and perfection of its organization.

The broader elements of the composition, for example, can scarcely be comprehended at all unless we analyze the arrangement in at least three different ways. As usual, the Venetian rhythm of value alternations carries the interest evenly over the entire surface in every direction. At the same time, a low triangular figure may be discerned, with Bacchus' head at the top; a moving Bacchus, it is worth remarking, would scarcely be appropriate at the apex of so inflexible a form. Either of the two systems mentioned (the rhythmic or the geometrical) would have been sufficent to give the painting order and intelligibility, but both coexist with a third scheme of composition which, because of its immense popularity since, requires special emphasis.

The system of arrangement is at least as old as the south front of the Erechtheum at Athens (page 110). The balance, that is to say, depends upon an asymmetrical arrangement of objects across the picture plane, and within the represented space. The principle involved is to work out a psychologically satisfactory equilibrium by producing an equation of subject matter. The method is in contrast with balance obtained through the stability of a geometric figure (Fig. 14.13, page 580), with balance established by an equilibrium of forces (Fig. 3.19, page 66), and with the familiar balance which depends upon the leverage of avoirdupois in symmetrical groups (Fig. 3.17, page 63).

Within the limits of the scheme, innumerable variations are possible, but the one Titian used here (which he appears to have perfected during his association with Giorgione, who had used it for his *Sleeping Venus*) occurs most often. It has been popular enough, in fact, to account for the composition of more than half the paintings since produced in Europe and America.

The eye, it will be noted, can reach out into the distance only at the upper left-hand corner of the picture. The opposite side is screened off from top to bottom by barriers which are very nearly impenetrable, and the foreground extends broad across the canvas from the bottom edge of the frame upward for about half its height.

The form depends for success upon our intense curiosity about what may be discovered in the far distance. We need not be conscious that such curiosity exists. Indeed, the appeal for attention operates effectively even though we may believe and declare that we look at nothing and care for nothing but the subject matter in the foreground.

In pulling an explanation out of the semiconsciousness as we do, we indulge in a method of argument admittedly susceptible of abuse. It may help, therefore, to point out that the pictorial function of a deep vista may escape the awareness of an observer for several reasons. The distance may seem, for example, to be neutral with respect to narrative, but inspection of a hundred paintings will show that the landscape chosen for each is ordinarily of a character likely to enhance the mood of the foreground content. Just as the sustaining instruments in the orchestra escape direct analysis, but are necessary, so the small areas of distance are not only vital to this particular form of pictorial composition, but powerful enough in their attraction to balance an immense weight of active subject matter on the opposite side of the painting.

In the instance under review, it will be observed that Titian took pains to make certain the vista he used would have ample power to attract attention. Bacchus and his companions enter from the upper right, and proceed over the ground in an arc that is roughly circular. The eye is led from right to left along one thing and another until Ariadne's right arm points directly out into the beyond; and the bluffs on the shore continue back and back in an un-broken curve.

Because the reader is destined to see similar compositions constantly as he studies the further history of painting, and because the scheme of arrangement analyzed here actually attained sufficient currency to make it a pictorial form comparable to one of the recognized musical or poetical forms, it will be useful to give it a name. We may refer to it as *the composition dependent upon a balance of mass against distance,* or more accurately as an arrangement of *mass against interest.* Although the small area of distance is usually at one upper corner or another, it obviously may be placed in the middle or anywhere else; the essential thing is to arrive at an equilibrium of appeal to the observer's attention. Distance, moreover, is merely the most usual subject matter employed for that purpose. Anything else which is comparatively small in scale but intense in the power to attract will do as well.

The intricate perfection of the composition of the *Bacchus and Ariadne* is matched by an equally accomplished handling of its most minute details. Throughout the painting, there runs a theme of harmony with respect to line and shape which is identical in physical fact with a great variety in the matter of hue and value.

The cloud above Ariadne, for example, has a silhouette that echoes her own, while the branch over Bacchus is an approximate repeat of his flying fold of drapery, but of opposite outline and in dark rather than light. The spaniel dog, on a smaller scale, has much the same outline as the leopard harnessed to the chariot; but once again, the value of its original is reversed. Repetitions of a V-shaped figure run all through the painting, sometimes flat on the plane of the picture, sometimes at an angle to it. The legs of the infant satyr may be said to announce the motive, which is symmetrically reflected by the front outline of the little dog and by the ears of the calf's head on the ground behind. Thence the V's go out to either side in the legs and arms of almost everybody else.

However honestly and thoroughly we make lists of such matters when we see them, the visual perfection of those interacting elements cannot be carried over into verbal description; it is merely hoped that the latter will aid the eye of the reader. Taking the history of painting as a whole, however, there are few who would quarrel with the assertion that Titian's mastery of the pictorial art was not only more facile and ramified than that of any earlier artist, but plainly more accomplished. To date, it must be added, no other painter has demonstrated a comparable fertility of imagination in those abstract inventions which he so easily incorporated into the design of some-thing that many persons have taken as no more than an unusually skillful performance in the field of representative painting.

Fig. 14.40 Titian. *Charles the 5th.* 1548. Oil on canvas. 10 feet 10¾ inches high. Madrid, Prado. (Anderson)

Portraits formed a minor but constant part of Titian's business. It may be questioned whether portraiture, as such, ever has or ever can open up vistas leading toward the full greatness of art; and were it not for Titian's paramount influence upon all future paintings of that class, we might skip the department altogether, except for the fact that Titian gave thought to the problems inherent in formal or ceremonial portraiture, solved them, and evolved what amounts to a standard recipe for all such art. The Spanish painters learned Titian's formula by looking at the Titians in the royal collection. Rubens took it up, and passed it on to the court painters in France, and to Van Dyck. Van Dyck's spectacular success in London established the same formula in England, and no other was used by Hogarth, Reynolds, Romney, Raeburn, or any of the other British portrait painters down through Sir Thomas Lawrence, who died in 1830. In details of style, portrait painting changed several times during the 19th century, but the original Titianesque formula is still often used for the arrangement. Wyndham Lewis used it once again, for example, when painting a portrait of Chancellor Capen (1937) for the University of Buffalo—a picture that is otherwise radically modern, being Byzantine in figure-style and cubistic in modeling.

Among the many available examples, none is better as a general demonstration than the *Charles the 5th* (Fig. 14.40). We may note in passing that the handling shows, by comparison to earlier work, considerably less plasticity and substantially more blending of the masses into the environment; but with respect to the formula now under review, the first point to be considered is the size of the canvas, which is grandiose for so simple a picture. Next, it should be observed that we find our line of sight directed upward toward the magnificently competent emperor, who wears his gorgeous armor as unconsciously as a peasant might wear a smock. The environment is appropriate to the majesty of the sitter: he rides not through wild country, but over the lawns of a great park. The occasion for the painting, moreover, was a significant moment in the history of the Hapsburgs and of Europe; Charles's army had just beaten the troops of the Elector of Saxony at Muhlberg, thus scoring heavily for the Catholic cause in the Counter-Reformation.

What went for the king, went also for the king's men, and official portraiture has ever since been much as Titian established it. The paintings, that is to say, have been in the Venetian mode. They have been made as large as possible, with the line of sight arranged to make it necessary to hang them abnormally high. Whatever the facts, the pictures have uniformly described the sitter as a person of superior physical, moral, and intellectual power, with the inevitable suggestion that he thought in large terms and was dependable in the world of great affairs. Aristocracy has been the true subject matter of all such portraiture, to which the average man must incline his eyes upward from a remove as though to admire his betters.

And yet it is always politic to remind the commons that however nobly the lords conform to the ideal of nobility, the lords are human and humane. It therefore became customary to include some object indicative of the sitter's private interests, or to show him doing something he liked to do. Scholars look up from a book. Scientists have an instrument in hand, or beside them. Sportsmen stand beside a fine horse. But best of all, from the standpoint of eliciting the ordinary man's sincere admiration, was an opportunity to show the sitter performing some everyday act in which he excelled. Titian set the fashion when he chose to put the emperor on a horse and make him hold a lance in his hand. Everyone who saw the painting was thereby reminded of a boastful complaint that had become a byword in Charles's armies, namely, that affairs of state had robbed them of the best cavalry commander in Europe—presumably to the disappointment of the monarch also.

In 1545, Titian went to Rome. He stayed there eight months. It is difficult to know the inward heart of such a man, or to tell how profoundly he was capable of being affected by an experience; but we may certainly note a change in his painting which seems to date from approximately that time.

The Rome Titian saw was Rome at the start of the Counter-Reformation, and the same Rome in which Michelangelo was spending the latter part of his career. It is evident from the later pictures that Titian felt some necessity for responding to what looked like a ground swell in European art and culture. Like Michelangelo, he moved in a direction that predicted the Baroque. Perhaps under the influence of the *Laocoön* and the other Hel-

Fig. 14.41 Titian. *Rape of Europa*. 1559. Boston, Isabella Stewart Gardner Museum.

lenistic pieces by which Michelangelo himself was being influenced, he made his later figure style more ponderous, and began to employ poses eloquent of muscular strain. We may note the same new stridency in both his religious and his mythological painting, and we may assume that he was attempting to supply the excitement which, foreign though it was to his temperament as we have known it to date, was to be of the essence in the art of the 17th century.

The *Rape of Europa* (1559; Fig. 14.41), one of the many classical subjects painted for Philip the 2d of Spain and now in Fenway Court in Boston, is typical of the later mythologies and unquestionably the best Titian in America. The experience of inspecting the picture is a strain on the sensibilities. To the right, the figure group performs a slashing diagonal across the vertical surface. The distance opens up on the left in no gentle fashion; the vista is a breakneck rush out into space. The color by no means diminishes the general commotion; it is bold in the foreground and alive with fire over the mountains. Tricks of perspective add a disquieting sense of the supernatural. We see Europa and the bull along the horizontal line of sight, but look down

Fig. 14.42   Titian. *Pietà*. 1573–1576. Venice, Academy. (Anderson)

from a great height into the landscape far behind and beyond them. Presumably we are up in the air with no platform to stand on, and looking two ways at once as we sometimes do in dreams.

Needless to say, the balance of such a composition is precarious, and the total effect of the painting strenuous rather than reposeful. The whole affair illustrates not only the trend of the times, but still further the odd relation between Titian and his subject matter. Why did he open up with such thunder about an abduction that amounts to a fairy tale?

Among the later religious paintings, we can do no better than study the last of them all, the *Pietà* (Fig. 14.42) Titian intended for his own tomb. The design dates from 1573, and the execution was not quite complete when the master died in 1576.

In the matter of style, the picture carries almost to a conclusion the predictions inherent in his later development. The technique bears no further relationship to the mode of relief, by which—whatever its merits—the art of painting had for so long taken its lessons from sculpture. The plastic reality of figures and objects was, in this last phase of his style, submerged in a vaporous harmony of atmosphere. Only by a conscious effort, in fact, can the eye separate out any particular shape for special inspection. Titian's control over tonal relations was more subtle and more profound than ever before. The tones themselves have the quiet of an elderly man. A soft golden light is reflected from the apse; it plays over the figures in this direction and that, bathing everything in gentle melancholy. The brushwork, which might be described as moderately impressionistic, is hardly that if the term connotes incomplete description; the technique is so magnificently competent that the slightest flick of the brush told its tale to the full. There is, as a matter of fact, almost no paint on the surface, and the grain of the canvas shows through.

The content, unfortunately, was slightly marred by the increasingly operatic taste of the later 16th century. What place has a pirouetting angel of the Cupid type in this quiet scene? Why is the Magdalen presented to us in a state of shock, yelling? Aside from those incongruous details, the scene is among the most dignified in the history of sepulchral art. Titian himself appears in the role of Saint Joseph of Arimathea. It is a notable characterization. The old gentleman kneels with courtly tenderness to assist the Madonna, accepting the inevitable tragedy as quietly as he accepted the certainty of his own early death.

♦ *Tintoretto* Jacopo Robusti (1518–1594), universally known as Tintoretto, was the last of the great figures in the Venetian School. He was apprenticed to Titian, but Titian disliked him and dismissed him from the shop before his time was up. An early account of the affair imputes jealousy as Titian's motive, which is incredible in view of the unchallengeable position he then occupied at Venice. The probable truth of the matter lies in their personal differences. Tintoretto's style derived from Titian's, but his taste and temperament were of a kind admirably calculated to offend the older master. Paradoxically enough, the offensive element was an early demonstration of the very qualities Titian himself tried to incorporate in his own later work. Tintoretto reacted, that is to say, vigorously and even flamboyantly to his subject matter. His most characteristic paintings are full of urgency and action. He seemed to consider it appropriate to whip up the observer's emotions by every device of technique and content. To study even his more moderate paintings is to be made conscious of a distinct heightening in the atmosphere.

The broader principles of his art have already been set forth in our general discussion of the Venetian mode. It now remains to summarize the innovations to which we have just referred.

No earlier painter employed directional forces with an equal prodigality.

Fig. 14.43 Tintoretto. *The Last Supper*. 1594. Venice, San Giorgio Maggiore. (Anderson)

His first consideration was to find an angle of sight so new, so odd, and so unfamiliar as to be startling in its own right. An upward angle of vision had been used before (Fig. 14.40), but hardly with the same temerity. It is one thing to ask the observer to raise his eyes, and another thing to put the central actors of the pictorial drama at the top of a near vertical incline going off diagonally from the surface of the picture (Figs. 14.31 and 43).

Having found an angle of vision sufficiently novel to meet his taste, Tintoretto would then figure out ways to enforce movement into the represented space. Every imaginable directional impulse was used in one picture or another: the gesture, the figure in motion, the glance of a startled eye, spectacular foreshortening, powerful perspectives of architecture—and the list has only begun. Because he almost invariably forced the movement inward, or somewhere near it, Tintoretto obtained a number of important and novel results. The space represented by the picture tends to impress the observer as a continuation of the volume within which he himself is standing at the moment, and the effect is to evoke a sense of personal involvement with the events already so strongly described. In extreme instances, Tintoretto may be said to blast his way into our sensibilities. However vivid, the experience is not without pain.

By historical chance, it was Tintoretto rather than any other man who first became synonymous in the European mind with everything suave, elegant, desirable, and Italian in the artistic manipulation of the human figure.

His women are unusually large, unusually soft of flesh, and unusually delicate in complexion. His men are fit mates for them. Both sexes were commonly made to sit or stand in exaggerated contrapposto; and in accordance with his habit, he usually presented both from some unusual angle of view. However insignificant for the narrative at hand, every figure was made to move like a dancer, and was made to seem in itself a thing of absolute beauty. These features became more or less standard in the figure style of innumerable painters and sculptors to follow.

In still another, and more philosophical way, Tintoretto's career was significant in the total history of art. He had a slogan lettered on his wall, to which he often called attention. It read: *The color of Titian and the drawing of Michelangelo.* Without impeaching the authenticity of his art, we must recognize that his deliberate combination of two recent styles bore a subtle but all-important contrast to the outlook entertained by Giotto, Van Eyck, Donatello, and the other men upon whom the history of art depends. Tintoretto's was a philosophy of derivation. In his case, the reader may well complain that we bear down too heavily upon a distinction which made small difference. In the world-view, however, the very existence of the distinction proved prophetic. The day Tintoretto put his slogan on the wall was the day Italian art crossed a great divide.

Tintoretto's career, especially his endorsement of amazement as a value in its own right, proved to be a signal that a new era in Renaissance culture was about to open up and swallow all within it. Not only does he mark the end of his era and the beginning of the Baroque; with him, the importance of the Venetian School ceased. Venice continued to have good painters right up to the Napoleonic era; but between Canaletto, Guardi, Tiepolo, and Longhi on the one hand, and Titian on the other, everyone must accept a difference in caliber. One cause seems to have been the loss by Venice of the special advantages which had formed the foundation of her materialistic philosophy. The discovery of the direct route to the Far East around the Cape of Good Hope (1498) opened that trade to shipping from northern Europe and gradually subtracted from the importance of the Mediterranean. The opening of the New World had a similar effect. To this day, the city maintains her local pride and a substantial prosperity; but her pre-eminence lies in the past.

PALLADIAN ARCHITECTURE

The north Italian architect Andrea Palladio (1518–1580) occupies a special place in history. In 1570, he published his *Four Books on Architecture,* a wonderfully practical work which came close to fulfilling, for future designers, the hopes originally fastened upon Vitruvius (page 552). It contained the first considerable body of measured drawings from ancient buildings, an excellent codification of the orders, and a number of drawings of buildings, and details of buildings, by Palladio himself. It would be difficult to estimate in any precise terms just how far and wide a circulation this book attained. Translated into various languages and reprinted a great many times, it went literally all over the Western world, and put into the hands of builders as far off as the American frontier precise directions for constructing moldings, columns, doorways, and porticoes quite as elegant as any to be seen in Europe.

It has long been customary to draw a contrast between Palladio and his older contemporary Michelangelo. Looking ahead to the art of the 17th century, we can discern two tendencies, usually called the "academic" and the "baroque." Palladio is said to be academic, Michelangelo baroque. The distinction is often a useful one, as we shall see (page 680), but the matter has usually been exaggerated.

The academics, we are told, were men of rules. They had derived their rules from successively closer and closer studies of Vitruvius, and had even founded (in 1542) a Vitruvian Academy at Rome. Michelangelo disapproved of rules, to which he referred as "toils and chains" imposed upon architecture. He declared he would be bound by none of them, ancient or modern. There was, of course, considerable bombast in what he said; and the academics, if we look at what they designed, were very much less hidebound than we might be led to suppose.

The differences, in short, sound larger than they were in fact. At any rate, any one who becomes acquainted with Palladio's architecture will be bound to say that the rules he followed (if rules they were) produced some of the finest buildings of the Renaissance.

He spent most of his life living and working at his native Vicenza, a small place about forty miles west of Venice. The little city is today virtually a Palladian museum. From the standpoint of scale, his greatest work there was the new exterior he designed for the immense covered market place of the town, a fabric known today as "The Basilica." This was a medieval building enclosing a central hall 173 feet long and 68 feet wide, with an interior height of about 80 feet. Palladio surrounded the great bulk with a Renaissance arcade in two stories, with nine arched openings on the long sides and five on the short. Except at the corners, he was bound by the intercolumniation of the original piers; but at the corners, he decreased the span of his arches in a manner that recalls the refinements of the Parthenon (page 100).

As a whole, the Basilica suffers somewhat from the handicaps imposed upon the architect, but in matters of detail, it is admirable, for it was here that Palladio gave full-scale multiple expression to the opening which has ever since borne his name. He did not use simple arches for his arcade;

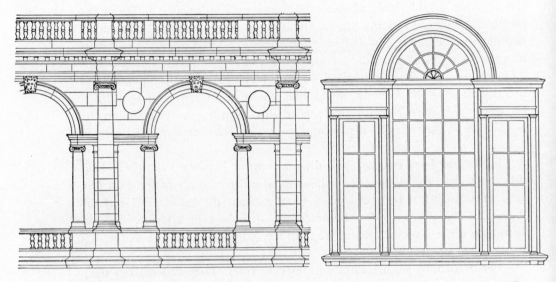

Fig. 14.44 The Palladian Motive. (left) Detail from the Basilica, Vicenza. (right) The Palladian Window.

rather, each one is an ingenious combination of a round-headed opening flanked by two that are lower and flat headed (Fig. 14.44). The motive is susceptible of innumerable variations and has been used literally thousands of times since, in both Europe and America, for doorways and windows, both small and large, high and low, singly and together, and in every color and material imaginable.

Palladio designed a number of city palaces at Vicenza: the Tiene and the Valmarana (1556), the Chiericati (1560), the Barbarano (1570), and the notable fragment of a larger project known as the "Casa del Diavolo" of 1571. He was twice called to Venice to design major churches: San Giorgio Maggiore of 1565 and Il Redentore of 1571. All of these demonstrate wonderfully tasteful adaptation of the orders to the necessities of modern architecture. No two of them are alike except that all of them are dignified and moderate—but an inspection of the details will correct the notion that the architect was "academic" in any restrictive sense of the word. Palladio was at his best, however, in the design of country houses, a fact which commended him to the taste of gentlemen in both England and America. He did several on the lower reaches of the Brenta, between Venice and Padua; and he left drawings for others which were never built. His most influential design proved to be the Villa Capra (better known as the "Villa Rotonda"), a short distance to the south and east of Vicenza itself (Fig. 14.45).

This remarkable building has a monumentality rarely found in domestic architecture. The theme was obviously suggested by the Pantheon at Rome

Fig. 14.45   Vicenza. Villa Rotonda. 1552. Designed by Palladio. (Alinari)

(Fig. I.17, page 950). The plan is symmetrical to the central vertical axis, with rectangular rooms grouped around a central domed chamber about forty feet in diameter. There is a Roman temple front (Fig. 7.7, page 190), complete with grand staircase, on each of the four faces. In elevation, the arrangement of stories follows the familiar sequence of podium, order, and attic originally invented for the Roman triumphal arch (Fig. 7.11, page 196).

Palladio's reputation as an academic probably derives in large measure from the fact that historical sources, like those just cited, are plain to be seen in almost every building he designed. It is less easy to explain the originality which enabled him to combine and blend these time-honored elements with a felicity never seen before, and never equaled by any of his innumerable imitators. What building ever took the light better than the Villa Rotonda? Where can we find the plastic better related to the open? In that latter connection, it will be noted that the corners of he central building block lack weightening, with the result that the eye moves easily on through the air to the space which interpenetrates the porches to right and left. This is the aspect of Palladian architecture which was destined to fascinate the painter Claude: the sense of life and movement in the sun-charged Italian atmosphere (page 784).

These delightful external effects, indeed the formal perfection of the building as a whole, were bought at considerable sacrifice of domestic efficiency. Even so, and quite without regard to the fact that the house was better adapted to Italy than the north, the Villa Rotonda provided a model that was irresistible to many an English and American architect. Unabashed imitations are a familiar part of our visual world. Adaptations are so numerous as to pass unnoticed.

Although handicapped by primitive mathematics (as all men of the 16th century were) Palladio had a considerable reputation as an engineer. He was a leader in the contemporary movement to improve and develop the truss, and he designed several extremely clever bridges. He thus became involved in a project which had been proposed, delayed, and brought up again at Venice for at least two generations; namely, to replace the old wooden Rialto bridge with an adequate, permanent, stone structure suitable to the dignity of the city. The idea had been proposed by Fra Giocondo as early as 1512. Designs, it is believed, had been submitted by Jacopo Sansovino, Michelangelo, and Vignola. Palladio's own plans are preserved, and they are considerably handsomer than the bridge actually started by Antonio da Ponte in 1587, the one that is still there. Had Palladio lived, the honor might very well have fallen to him, but he died at Venice in August 1580.

NORTHERN ARTISTS OF THE HIGH RENAISSANCE

As set forth in Chapters 12 and 13, the north of Europe had developed its realistic tradition direct from the Gothic; and whatever its content and however scientific its representational techniques, northern art remained Gothic in form throughout the 15th century. Only here and there do we find a detail or two to suggest direct influence either from Italy or the antique: for example, the architecture in the *Madonna with Chancellor Rolin* (Fig. 13.4, page 478) makes one wonder if the painter had been south of the Alps.

By about 1500, however, the situation was different. It was no longer possible for anybody to escape consciousness of an artistic garden, blooming with a new and gracious fragrance, stretching from the Piedmont to Naples, and full of beguiling southern flowers. As one might expect, a good many northern artists who otherwise might have continued in their own tradition made tours of Italy and tried as best they might to assimilate the lovely Italian style. Such men were most numerous in court circles or at metropolitan centers: at Fontainebleau, for example, and also at Antwerp, which by then had assumed its modern character of the greatest port in Europe, with an active trade leading to Italy and everywhere else.

As typical of the many Flemish artists who cultivated an Italian style, we may name Jan Gossaert, called Mabuse (1470–1541); Bernard van Orley (1493–1542); Jan Sanders, called Hemessen (1504–1563); and Frans Floris (1516–1570). Figure 14.46 may be taken as characteristic of their work.

Fig. 14.46 Jan Gossaert, called Mabuse. *Adam and Eve.* Berlin, Kaiser Friedrich Museum. (Stoedtner)

By the time such men felt its influence, the Italian Renaissance had passed into the grander and more idealized phase represented by the later work of Raphael and his contemporaries. Not one of the Flemings mentioned was strongly creative in his own right; it may be doubted whether any of them, if born in Italy, would have made a reputation there. All of them were too easily influenced and, worse than that, too quick to assume they understood the purpose and method of the great Italians.

It is difficult to explain the immense difference between authentic Italian art and the work of such Italianizing northerners, since the physical facts are so much the same. The complaint against the Flemings is not their inability to paint, for they painted well. It is the truth that the Grand Style, whenever the epic mind was lacking, has invariably proven the very worst art known to man. Unable to think or feel in heroic terms, the artists now under review considered their problem to be merely one of adaptation, not complete change. Instead of approaching the matter philosophically, they merely smoothed up the customary anatomy of 15th-century Flemish realism, and made it more ample and more sensual. The net result was a vulgar, uncomfortable, hybrid art with the faults of both its sources.

The painters just dealt with were popular. Without doubt they pictured

Figs. 14.47–48 Bosch. Details from *The Temptation of Saint Anthony*. Lisbon, National Fine Arts Museum. (left: Bulloz; below: Giraudon)

themselves as leaders if not creators of taste, in the act of opening new vistas for the northern imagination. But seen in historical perspective, they were faddish men who had nothing to do with the true worth of northern art during the High Renaissance. The latter depended upon the existence of several masters of grand scope and magnificent personality who, although very well informed about the Italian style, remained steadfastly Gothic in their idiom while demonstrating an imaginative drive and expressive power equal to the best of the Italians. We refer to Hieronymus Bosch, Albrecht Dürer, and Pieter Brueghel.

♦ *Hieronymus Bosch*   Hieronymus Bosch (about 1450–1516) was probably born at Aachen. He painted a good many pictures of the conventional Flemish kind, of which his *Adoration of the Magi,* a three-paneled folding altarpiece now in Madrid, may serve as an example. His special reputation depends, however, on works of quite another sort.

One of the most famous is a large triptych in the Museum of Fine Arts at Lisbon. The subject is a highly imaginative rendering of the temptations of Saint Anthony. The Anthony to whom we refer was the one born at Alexandria in the 4th century. He was a celebrated hermit. Even by the strenuous standards of that time and place, his asceticism attracted unusual interest and made him a special target for the schemes of the Devil. First, that Black Master undertook to torment the saint with all kinds of seductive thoughts calculated to drive him mad by filling his mind with images of the comforts and pleasures he might enjoy by a mere relaxation of the will. When that failed, the Devil resorted to physical methods. Delicious foods and drinks were set out to lure Anthony from his unimaginably austere diet. Lovely courtesans were sent to assail his chastity. When those measures also failed, the Devil lost his temper and sent demons and monsters to give the saint a brutal beating.

Bosch handled the subject with an intensity of detail typical of all northern art. Although the panels are large, items appear in such multiplicity as to render the whole painting unsuitable for reproduction on a small scale, and in Figures 14.47–48 we accordingly show two typical sections in close-up. Seen as a whole, the painting shows Anthony seated before a crucifix in a cell opening toward us in the middle of a castle ruin which fills the central part of the main panel; Bosch probably derived the idea from the tradition that Anthony lived in a cave. The courtesans disport themselves at table on a stone terrace outside. Around the ruin, there may be seen an unrivaled collection of real and imaginary monsters, all of the most sinister aspect. Every one of them seems himself to be tortured, morbid, or both, and every gesture is surcharged with ghastly menace.

The terrific scene is presented against a landscape which runs continuously through all three panels. The wings open up to a view of sea and harbor; doomed ships are there, either wrecked or sinking. A burning village appears in the background of the main panel, with a party of armed men traversing a bridge.

It goes without saying that Bosch worked in the region later to be entered by William Blake (1757–1827) and still later by Giorgio de Chirico, Salvador Dali, and the other surrealist painters of the present day. Surrealism abandons a setting in the world, and finds a locus elsewhere. Its method is always the same: to depict with devastating specificity the most radical concepts of the visual imagination. A generation ago, it was customary to explain Bosch's diabolism as an excursion of the fancy, usually intended to amuse. Whenever, in a particular instance, the appeal to humor failed to satisfy, the notion of satire came forward; and when that too seemed incongruous in the face of the painter's self-evident earnestness, one heard the phrase ". . . foolish superstition which the world has now outgrown." All such notions now seem like nonsense. Anticipating psychiatry by about 450 years, Bosch did his greatest work in the nether reaches of the mind, that realm more-real and yet not-real, before whose gateway all men pause in dread.

The subject matter with which Bosch dealt was different from any psychological malaise with which we are immediately familiar. He lived among a population largely illiterate, during an era when the Church was losing its power to soothe and reassure. Terrible imaginings came to the surface, more dreadful than any we moderns can comprehend because there was no way to explain them, and no hope of therapy.

Those who have traced northern art from its beginnings will of course recognize the pedigree of Bosch's grotesques; the genus is as old as the barbarian invasions of the ancient world. One effect of Christianity, however, had been to hold under control the violence of the northern temperament and, by the same token, its tendency to fantastic imagery. In general, that restraining influence was remarkably effective during the entire Middle Age, with the ever-existent turbulence of the barbarian taste breaking through only occasionally as in the Utrecht Psalter (Figs. 8.41–42, page 215) and the more extreme Romanesque tympana (Fig. 10.36, page 348). Bosch appeared just when the discipline of the Church was becoming less effective as a social reality. He was therefore free to roam where he pleased in an area hitherto quarantined. He appeared, also, at a time and place almost ideal for the purpose: in the Flemish region when it was impossible to be a painter at all without possessing an exhaustive knowledge of representative accuracy and the best techniques for achieving it. Without realism, surrealism is impossible; its power to convince depends upon its capacity to say that the outlandish is actual.

Fig. 14.49   Bosch. *Christ before Pilate*. Princeton, New Jersey, Princeton University Museum.

Again capitalizing upon the achievements of northern realism, Bosch may be said to have been the founder of the modern tradition of *vulgar genre*, an aspect of northern art destined to survive long after the patrician taste of the Renaissance had submerged every other remnant of Gothic feeling. The so-called *Prodigal Son*, formerly in the Figdor collection at Vienna, is perhaps the best-known painting of the class. As a general category, vulgar genre finds interest in the stable and the drunken party, and displays a liking for the company of farmhands, peddlers, tramps, whores, and bums. Bosch was simply the first of a notable line of northern artists, among whom we may name Adrian Brouwer (1605–1685), Adrian van Ostade (1610–1685), David Teniers the Younger (1610–1690), the 17th-century French painters called Le Nain, and the British Hogarth (1697–1764), who was the last of the great Gothic artists. To a man, such painters used all the skills of the Renaissance to assert the reality and validity of the unthinking majority who owned nothing, hoped for nothing, and worked with their hands. Their philosophy was opposite to the classical and Italian bent for selection by reference to some theory of beauty or edification. In the presence of their art, the heartbeat of Renaissance decorum inexorably slows and misses time. What are the deep racial instincts which pull us toward surroundings and behavior from which we are foreclosed by every tenet in the code of manners that all the world learned from Italy during the 16th century?

Bosch seems less to participate in his own vulgar genre than to tell its story with an overtone of heartbreak. Subtle and perhaps imperceptible in many paintings, his deep bitterness comes out plainly in *Christ before Pilate* (Fig. 14.49). The use of gross persons as actors in the sacred drama was in itself a shocking thing, but the device had to do with a judicious realism of thought as applied to Christianity. The meaning of the picture hinges upon the physical and even the mental contrast between Christ and the persons around him. In a world where shrewd officials train and control professionally brutal men to keep the mob in hand, is it intelligent to expect much from a little preacher who, as history tells us, got himself hopelessly caught? Although rarely stated so baldly then or now, there is much evidence, pictorial and otherwise, to indicate that more than one prominent person of the 16th century entertained the specific belief that Christianity had failed. Michelangelo certainly squared up to that possibility, even if he did not accept it. Pieter Brueghel, as we shall see, seems to have abandoned hope.

♦ *Albrecht Dürer* In the history of German culture, Albrecht Dürer (1471–1528) occupies a position comparable to the one held by Leonardo da Vinci in Italy. He had immense prestige among his contemporaries, prestige which rested only in part upon his accomplishments as an artist. He wrote a book on geometry with special reference to its application in art. Another book dealt with fortification, and still another with anatomy and the human proportions. He was an intelligent and profound scholar in almost every field of learning then available, a fact which greatly enhanced the contemporary authority of his art. He was, in addition, a friendly man.

Dürer has traditionally been introduced to students as a painter. His career in that medium may be evaluated by reference to the portrait of his father (1490), now in Florence, and to the three self-portraits—in the Louvre (1493), the Prado (1498), and the Alte Pinakothek at Munich (1500?). Supplementary reference should also be made to such religious paintings as the *Landauer Altarpiece,* an *Adoration of the Magi* (1511), now in Vienna, and the *Four Apostles* (1526) in the Alte Pinakothek. An honest estimate of such work is bound to suggest that we must hold Dürer's painting in less esteem than we hold the man. The technique was superb, but the style was an unsuccessful attempt to combine an exceptionally florid Late Gothic taste with the measured idealism of the Italian High Renaissance.

It is a mere affectation, however, to think of painting as a "major art" and print making as a "minor art"; the truth about Dürer is that he ought to be approached by way of his engraving, and judged by it. He had a personal taste for the medium, evidencing thereby the German genius for mechanics and for metal work in general. The unparalleled precision of the graver made a virtue, in fact, rather than a fault of the Gothic instinct for intensive detail. In Dürer's case, that was unusually fortunate and necessary, because he seems to have had an unlimited faith in the power of elaboration. As an architect, he would have been weak and tedious. As a painter, he was prolix. But with his own tools, he turned out a wealth of work which defies the faultfinder. Not only was he the greatest engraver who ever lived; engraving was par excellence the ideal medium for making the most of German taste at that period.

It is possible to have a personal fondness for almost every plate Dürer ever did. On the basis of technical perfection and on the basis also of spiritual profundity, three particular prints stand out from all the others. They are the *Knight, Death, and Devil* (1513) and the two plates from the next year, *Saint Jerome in His Study* and *Melancholia*. The three are about of the same size, and were evidently intended as a set. They were not meant to be shown as a single composition; the unity of the set depends, rather, upon an organic relation of the content. The *Knight* typifies the Christian faced with the problems of the daily world in which he must decide, act, and persevere. The *Saint Jerome* stands for the Christian scholar who secludes himself to make contemplation possible. The *Melancholia* refers to the creative faculty of mankind; it suggests that humanity is there closest to the divine, and yet sadly ineffective. The iconography of all three is complex; we can only suggest it here and refer the reader to the excellent account in Erwin Panofsky's *Dürer*.

It is probable that Dürer had been in northern Italy in 1494. He must inevitably have seen Donatello's *Gattamelata* at Padua (Figs. 13.13–14, page 494), and he must also have studied Verrocchio's *Colleoni* at Venice (page 577), which had been set up on its marble pedestal only a year or two before. In addition to those notable monuments, all the world knew that Leonardo was then at Milan, and had declared his intention of making himself the author of an even greater equestrian group. His notebooks contain many sketches which we now relate to the *Francesco Sforza* upon which the great Florentine did intermittent work from 1483 to 1493, in which latter year he was ready to put a full-size model on exhibition—presumably the same model that stood in the courtyard of the Castello when the French entered Milan in October 1494 (page 544) and put an end to the project by destroying both the model and the house of Sforza.

It seems inescapable that Dürer's interest in an equestrian composition

Fig. 14.50 Dürer. *Knight, Death, and the Devil.* 1513. Engraving.
9¾ by 7¼ inches. New York, Metropolitan Museum.

must have been stimulated if not suggested by his Italian tour, and scholars have amused themselves ever since by finding resemblances between the *Knight* (Fig. 14.50), the two completed statues in Italy, and the drawings of Leonardo, with which Dürer must in some way have become familiar. The rhythm of his engraved horse seems to be Donatello's, but the conformation of the animal and the armor of the rider are more like Verrocchio's. It is worth remarking as we pass that the triangular composition of the figure and its setting in a rocky pass are reminiscent of Giotto's *Flight into Egypt* (Fig. 12.40, page 463), a painting Dürer must have seen.

The content is both very ancient and very new. We see the knight riding across the picture, presumably making his way toward a beautiful city set high on a peak and appearing against the sky in the far distance. Death on a tired horse speaks to him and brandishes an hourglass. The Devil, half pig and half wolf, apparently also has tried to get a hearing, but the rider has already gone by. A big dog, something like our modern golden retriever, runs along intent on some errand outside the picture.

The image of the Christian as a warrior goes back to Saint Paul, whose epistles were often spiced with military vocabulary. Dürer also inherited the idea from the Crusades; and even more directly from Erasmus, who had used "Christian Soldier" in the title of one of his early essays.

For any well-informed German, the "breastplate of righteousness" was no mere figure of speech in 1513. The religious situation was volcanic. Violence was to be expected, and Erasmus tried to exert a moderating influence. In effect, it was his hope to bring about harmony by persuading both clergy and laity to embrace a better understanding of both Christianity and humanism. Sin, he contended, was not only prohibited by God, but beneath the dignity of man. If that much could be generally accepted, it followed that temptations would lose their power, and no one need fear them. Such, probably, was Dürer's reason for showing fiends as mere spooks. The Christian knight simply overlooks them, and the Christian dog doesn't even bother to sniff their scent.

The *Saint Jerome in His Study* (Fig. 14.51) can hardly be excelled as a celebration of the *vita contemplativa*. Although spatial realization had been a northern specialty for more than a hundred years, Dürer's elegant perspective—the work of an accomplished mathematician—opens up the room before us in extraordinary fashion. It is hard to believe we are inspecting a small picture; it seems much more as though we had actually looked in upon the fine old gentleman and saw him as friends might who had just come in the door. His lion looks sleepily up as Saint Bernard dogs do when familiars arrive; in a moment, the saint will finish his paragraph and look up also. In the meantime, we can envy the order and simple comfort possible only for bachelors: a few pieces of good furniture, and all one's gear ready at hand without any crowding. The windows face the south; and from the shadows, we may judge it is the middle of the morning on a fine day. No painter and no photographer could possibly rival the beauty of the light; not only does the engraver have sharper contrasts to work with, but also he can stipple and make the sun flicker with life in a manner from which even the French impressionists were foreclosed by the coarse tools they used.

From the *Saint Jerome*, in which the artist himself obviously took so much simple, genial pleasure, it is a disquieting experience to turn to the *Melancholia* (Fig. 14.52). If we may judge from the shadow cast by an hourglass hung on the wall above the head of the central figure, the setting is in

Fig. 14.51 Dürer. *Saint Jerome in His Study*. 1514. Engraving. New York, Metropolitan Museum.

moonlight. A comet blazes across the sky, and it is chilly enough to make the half-fed dog curl up. The personified Melancholy crowds herself heavily into the right foreground. Her face is sensitive, tired, and distraught. Her hair and her dress are in a mess. She has wings, but the idea of flight is ridiculous because they are too small for so gross a body. She sits in front of a partially finished building, with some fine tools in disorder around her. In her hand, she holds a beautiful pair of dividers, and there is a discarded book on her knee. A baby, perched uncomfortably on the rim of a grinding wheel, digs busily into a slate with an iron spike, doubtless making horrid squeaks as he does it.

The mood of the *Melancholia* is plain enough at a glance. Its more profound meaning involves an immensely complex excursion into medieval lore. The main features may, however, be explained without reference to details.

In its ultimate heritage, the theme goes back to the classical tradition which held that the nature of mankind might be explained by reference to four humors: the sanguine, the choleric, the phlegmatic, and the melancholic. Each humor responded to a physical cause in the form of a vital fluid sup-

Fig. 14.52 Dürer. *Melancholia I.* 1514. Engraving. New York, Metropolitan Museum.

posedly contained within the system. Ideally, all four fluids ought to be in what sounds like physical and chemical balance. Since they usually were not, individual men had to bear with a more or less warped temperament.

The four humors were also thought to have an astrological significance. The planet Saturn had come to be identified with the melancholic cast of mind; hence the adjective saturnine. Because Saturn was also an earth god who had much influence over agriculture, he was conceived as having a special and necessary interest in quantitative measure of all kinds. In particular, he was thought to hold jurisdiction over the survey of land. From that, it was no step at all to making Saturn god of geometry. The magic square on the wall at the upper right was, as a matter of fact, a talisman in sixteen compartments calculated to divert the gloomy influence of Saturn into constructive channels.

Among the 16th-century intellectuals, of whom Dürer was one, both melancholy and geometry had recently acquired new life and meaning. The entire representative convention (pages 439–441) owed much of its prestige to the sanction from geometry as reflected in the 15th-century research into the principles of linear perspective. As the Early Renaissance passed on into the High, a further attempt had been made to satisfy the esthetic sense by geometric compositions which, it had been hoped, would provide art with the finality and completeness of the antique.

Already connected with art through Saturn and geometry, the melancholic temperament had lately become identified with the creative imagination by another and yet stronger chain of reasoning. Marsilio Ficino had, among his other contributions, popularized a bit of Aristotle's mistaken but unbelievably accurate dogmatism.

Aristotle (384–322 B.C.) had noted that creative persons tend to be abstracted, that they exhaust themselves with effort, and that they often get downhearted. Neglecting the more exalted moments of the creative cycle, he flatly declared that every superior man is necessarily a melancholic. The discovery that Plato himself had been born under the sign of Saturn did nothing to diminish the popularity of that idea. To this day, intellectual snobs the world over cultivate melancholy, and creative persons often give the impression of it.

With such information to help us, Dürer's obscure plate may be understood. The little baby with his slate signifies the optimism of naïve and misdirected effort. The frustrated goddess symbolizes the incapacity of the mature mind to realize meaningful achievement. There is some reason to think that the geometrical apparatus, disposed in most ungeometrical arrangement, reflects Dürer's personal discouragement with geometry as such. The history of his critical writings indicates that he had first hoped to locate beauty by increasingly subtle geometric reasoning. After a great deal of work, he gave the idea up as impractical. In the absence of better mathematics, it would seem that he identified geometry with the rational faculty. The trouble with the rational faculty, as Dürer seems to have found out, is our inability to reason beyond what we can measure and count. In a word, every man must be enough of a mystic to know that the mind cannot keep pace with the imagination. It must be some such feeling that accounts for the inadequate wings Dürer gave his goddess and for her apparent realization that her keys would open nothing.

Inasmuch, also, as all three of the plates under review date from a time when religious issues were tense and grave, and when Dürer himself was in agony over which way to turn, it is possible to interpret the *Melancholia* as an expression of doubt with respect to the Renaissance itself. Humanism, particularly humanism as represented by such men as Alberti, inevitably involved some measure of departure from religion as the hope of grace, and an equivalent assumption by the self of the burden for achieving happiness on earth and ultimate salvation. The rational faculty was the principal tool to be employed in the process. Faith in the rational faculty was the essence of the new era; but Dürer, like Botticelli and Michelangelo, had evidently started to doubt.

♦ *Pieter Brueghel*   Pieter Brueghel the Elder (about 1528–1569) took his name from the place where he was born. Of the various villages of that name or something like it, the one near Bois-le-Duc seems most likely. Because Bosch came from the same locality, his powerful influence upon Brueghel is conveniently explained. The artist himself omitted the *h* upon occasion, making the name Bruegel; but for the spelling with the German diphthong *eu* there is no authority even though his descendants sometimes used it.

Because of his low taste, English-speaking critics have been slow to recognize Brueghel's greatness. The pictures so offensive to their delicacy are the numerous examples of vulgar genre, in which department of art he heartily outdid Bosch and everyone else who ever tried it. Examples are the *Peasant Dance,* the *Peasant Wedding,* and the *Parable of the Bird's Nest* in Vienna; also the *Wedding Dance* in Detroit, from which we show a detail (Fig. 14.53). In addition, there are numerous single figures depicting the same class of people. From the standpoint of the genteel, the enormity resides in the painter's apparent failure to feel distaste for such subject matter, and from the historical knowledge that he personally participated in similar revelries, did it habitually, and enjoyed it.

Some decorous critics, compelled nevertheless to admire, have tried to find a way out by interpreting Brueghel's vulgar paintings as pictorial tracts for our moral edification. In a few instances, like *The Blind Leading the Blind* (Fig. 14.54), there appears actually to have been a text (Matthew 15:14); but in other instances, if text there be, the sentiment expressed can hardly recommend the painter to the bourgeoisie. The parable of the bird's nest, for example, contains the disquieting conclusion that "He who knows where the nest is has the knowledge; he who steals it has the nest."

Without suggesting that Brueghel's wit is uniformly suitable for the drawing room, it must be conceded his offenses against daintiness are about the same as those of the poet Chaucer. In disposing of him as negligible because he was coarse, the Victorians overlooked some of the greatest painting ever done in Europe. It is now necessary to take another point of view.

In 1552–1553, Brueghel made a tour of Italy, apparently going as far south as Naples. He seems to have journeyed down by way of the Rhone Valley, and to have returned over the Brenner Pass. The things he saw furnished him with new and grander subject matter for his painting and had a

Fig. 14.53 Brueghel. *The Wedding Dance*. Detail. 1566. Detroit, Institute of Arts.

remarkable effect upon his artistic methods. In astonishing contrast with almost every other northerner who went to Italy, he remained completely his own man. Instead of being beguiled into imitation, he paid no attention to the superficial attractions of Italian art. At the same time, he was profoundly affected by its underlying fundamentals.

From Michelangelo, he learned how to pose a ponderous anatomy in complex and accomplished contrapposto; but he showed no interest in a classically idealized figure style. From Raphael and the Umbrians in general, he learned how to make space carry meaning. In fact, he seems at once to have understood the special power of Tintoretto's enforcement of movement into the represented space, and many of his landscape compositions are laid out on an inward diagonal. The most unusual circumstance of all, considering how much he gained from Italy, is the extreme rarity of instances where we can discern a one-to-one relationship with any specific Italian masterpiece. In fact, almost the only sure case of the sort is a drawing in Hamburg, in which the figure of a northern peasant is posed exactly like one of the incidental nudes on the ceiling of the Sistine Chapel.

Fig. 14.54 Brueghel. *The Blind Leading the Blind.* 1568. Naples, National Museum. (Anderson)

As a landscape painter, Brueghel has few equals and no superiors. Several of his best pictures record the winter scenery of the Low Countries; they are hardly to be surpassed for the excellence with which they communicate the damp, the cold, and the *gemütlichkeit* nowhere else to be found in the same combination at the same season of the year. The human figure, as rendered by him in such a setting, tends to take on the aspect of line and flat tone that forms actually take in nature when seen against ice and snow. By the outline alone, he was able to define mass and describe action. He demonstrated a genius for the silhouette, in fact, unknown elsewhere except in the Far East.

His true greatness had its genesis, however, in the Italian journey which brought him into contact with mountain scenery of a grandeur unknown in the Netherlands and which he employed in a series of magnificent paintings. The most famous are five which date from the two years 1565–1566. They are *The Hunters in the Snow, The Dark Day,* and *The Return of the Herd,* all in Vienna; *The Hay Harvest,* formerly in the collection of Count Lobkowitz at Raudnitz; and *The Corn Harvest,* now in the Metropolitan Museum. As distinguished from most other landscape paintings, either earlier or later, the pictures mentioned are important for the successful use of vast distances: not vistas of a mile or two, that is, but stupendous extensions of space as seen from an elevated station high in the hills, and imparting much the same sense of exaltation.

Had he lived in a happy world, Brueghel perhaps could have spent his life composing landscapes that were serene, noble, poetical, or intimate as inspiration might from time to time suggest. His career had its setting, however, amid horrors which until the time of Hitler were generally considered the worst ever perpetrated by an educated and Christian population. The Protestant Reformation had started in 1517. Because it was popular in the Netherlands, and because the Netherlands were also important for their wealth, the Catholic emperors Charles the 5th (Fig. 14.40, page 636) and his son Philip the 2nd made Brueghel's homeland the special object of their most resolute policy. Bosch had lived through some of their activity. Brueghel's maturity coincided with repressive measures of the utmost inhumanity. For the narrative at length, the reader should turn to J. L. Motley's *Rise of the Dutch Republic.* It is important to recall here that the 16th century was the period when the Spanish Empire was attempting to solidify its power not only in the New World but in England and on the continent. Events in Flanders and Holland, where most of the important churchmen, governors, and soldiers were Spaniards, formed merely part of the larger picture.

Protestant defection in the Low Countries had brought the Inquisition into vigorous activity. The infamous memory in which it is held springs from two sources. Its methods were diametrically opposed to everything summed up in the common law of England and America, or any other law possessed of a just procedure. Its sentences, moreover, were considered barbarous even during the 16th century. For so slight an offense as the oral discussion of theological matters, the average man was almost certain to suffer death if accused. His only hope was to establish repentance, in which case he would be hanged rather than burned.

In 1567, lesser measures having failed, Philip the 2nd sent the Duke of Alba into the Netherlands with the double purpose of suppressing heresy and crushing the liberty of the towns. Alba was one of the most competent Spaniards of the century. He came with a well-disciplined army. His sincerity cannot be questioned. His methods, however, remain a byword for ferocity and in the end failed to accomplish the calculated result. In the course of his administration, Alba brought about the torture, maiming, hanging, burying alive, and burning of innumerable individuals. He himself estimated one batch of executions at 18,000—a figure which must be interpreted in relation to the then population. He also mercilessly exacted ruinous taxation, and he missed no opportunity to subject both cities and citizens alike to calculated humiliation. He remained in the north six years, and returned in honor to Spain, where he died in 1583.

Brueghel's most definite description of the Spanish outrages is a drawing in the Royal Library at Brussels. It was used as copy for an engraving known as the *Justicia,* in which the details are reversed mirror-wise and seem strangely less immediate than in the original. In the middle, the Blind Goddess stands on a slab labeled with her name. A trial is being held over at the left. The space at the lower right is taken up by the figure of a man stretched on the rack. Simultaneously he is also receiving the water cure; his abdomen is already horribly distended, and men are pouring another jar full into his mouth through a funnel. The middle ground and distance give us a catalogue of punishments which were favorite at the time: a beheading, the crushing of a right hand, a flogging, a man suspended head and heels by a rope, tall poles surmounted by cart wheels to which men are trussed, half a dozen hangings, and a burning at the stake.

Among the major paintings which deal with the same sort of thing, two stand out from all the others: *The Massacre of the Innocents* and *The Way to Golgotha*. The former is conceived as an event in a Flemish village. The savagery and pathos of the action are brought into contrast with the magnificent discipline of the Spanish cavalry; a whole company of them remain in formation while the nasty work goes on.

As a picture, *The Way to Golgotha* (Fig. 14.55) is more complicated. Its implications are likewise more sweeping. It is set in barren ground. In some particulars, the spot may recall a site near one of the Lowland cities, but a pinnacle rock like those around Le Puy suggests a memory of the painter's route to Italy. The crucifixion will take place at the upper right-hand corner, where a great circle of spectators has already formed, in the manner of the time, around the two crosses already set up. A hole in the ground awaits the shaft of the third.

Christ may be found near the center of the middle ground. The point of time is the moment when he has collapsed under the weight of the cross. A bit to the left, a press gang has taken Simon of Cyrene, to make him help with the work. Simon's desperate wife protests, and a soldier callously repels her with a spear. The other peasants run away.

The Holy Mourners occupy the lower right-hand corner of the composition; they look like a group of Rogier van der Weyden (page 485). The rest of the picture is filled with Spaniards on their fine horses, yokels on their way to the show, and the detritus of yesterday's executions. The two thieves may be picked out as the men tied up and riding in a cart.

To understand the picture, it is first of all necessary to appreciate that Brueghel's dramatic method was fundamentally different from that of the Italian Grand Style. An Italian artist, in handling the same subject, would have approached his problem very much as a Greek might have done. To him, the human figure would have seemed the artistic vehicle par excellence. The unity of time would have been his primary artistic obligation. His procedure would have been to simplify the drama as much as possible by selecting the principal actors and eliminating the others, and then to pose the essential figures in such a way that the full meaning of their action would come into the field of attention instantly.

Fig. 14.55 Brueghel. *The Way to Golgotha*. 1564. Oil on panel. 66¾ inches wide by 48¾ inches high. Vienna, Kunsthistorisches Museum. (Braun)

Brueghel, however, was a northern artist, and one of the very few who ever attempted to use the northern and cumulative method of presenting subject matter (page 256) in an epic painting. He had no awe for the human figure, and he did not accept the classical theory of selection, elimination, and simplification. Indeed, we cannot find Christ himself without hunting for him; he is an obscure person in a crowd which itself is a mere part of the setting. Many things are going on at once. The eye must resolve them one by one, turning to the next thing in due time. Memory plays a part in the process. Comprehension is gradual, and the effect is built up piece by piece and item by item until we finally possess ourselves of the picture, total and complete.

Realizing that we cannot come into visual possession of the picture by a single act of inspection, and understanding also that its meaning is compound rather than simple, we can see that there is significance even in the bare mechanics of the method. Brueghel made the world a vast universe of space, the human population a detail, and the single person insignificant. Jesus is by no means obvious in such a place; and even when he has been found, it is patent that he influences the behavior of almost nobody. Some such intention must also have suggested rendering the Holy Mourners in a style then a hundred years out of date; the implication seems to be that conventional expressions of Christian regret do not moderate the march of contemporary events.

The analogy between the crucifixion of Christ and the 16th-century crucifixion of Flanders is obvious. Every historian has wondered how Brueghel managed to get away with it. None of the simple explanations fit the case. He was well known. His pictures did not remain hidden. No powerful patron protected him. The religious titles would not in themselves have fooled anybody. The Spaniards were the opposite of tolerant and liberal, and none of them admired good art enough to excuse the unflattering part the painter made them play on his stage. There can be no chance of our mistaking the intent, for we have Brueghel's own word for it. As he lay dying, he ordered his young wife to destroy a great many of the paintings then in stock for fear they would get her into trouble with the authorities. In view of what we still possess, it is appalling to imagine the content of those Martha Brueghel burned up.

16TH-CENTURY MANNERISM

It has long been customary to say that Michelangelo, Titian, and Tintoretto belonged to the High Renaissance, and they have been so presented in this chapter. The reader will recall, however, that we were more than once

at pains to suggest that those artists did not remain single-minded and assured. Especially as their activity drew toward a close, all three lost, now and
again, the decorum of their era. More and more frequently, they broke over
into expression marked by an absence of emotional control.

We used to say that whenever they did so, they predicted the Baroque,
but an increasing number of critics have begun to make the claim that the
matter cannot be covered by so simple a statement. More was involved, they
say, than the transition between two major styles. They contend that we
must recognize an interim period between the High Renaissance and the
Baroque—another epoch which would itself be a natural unit of art history—
to which, wisely or unwisely, they give the name *Mannerism*. The effect of
their thinking would be to readjust the familiar schedule as follows.

The High Renaissance, they suggest, must now be regarded as an extremely brief period starting shortly before 1500 and scarcely extending beyond
the death of Raphael in 1520. The epoch of Mannerism would then be made
to occupy the rest of the century; and the Baroque, according to the same
outline, would begin somewhere around 1590.

For reasons that will become apparent, the author of the present volume
rejects this rearrangement of the calendar. It is nevertheless important to tell
the reader what may be involved.

We rarely heard the word Mannerism until about thirty years ago. Today,
it is conspicuously present in almost every recent treatment of the Renaissance. Usually, the context suggests that both the author and the reader
know precisely what is being referred to. Unfortunately, that is almost never
the case. No two writers seem to use Mannerism in the same sense. Statements
which might give the term a clear denotation have been uniformly slippery
rather than definite. The situation, which sometimes impresses one as almost
ridiculously confused, is perhaps a normal reflection of the complexities of
16th-century culture and of our own uncertainty about the period. Pending
the publication of further research, the following may shed some light on a
vexed situation.

The High Renaissance, says the inadequate literature of Mannerism, was
an expression of confidence. It was typified by the great frescoes of Raphael;
and its philosophical foundation was belief in both the classical values and
the Christian values which Raphael so successfully seemed to combine.

Mannerism was the art of men who had lost confidence. The corruption
of the Catholic hierarchy brought about Luther's Reformation of 1517, with
an effect that worked two ways. On the one hand, men were made suspicious
of the church and, in extreme cases, suspicious of religion itself. On the other,
they no longer believed in the Renaissance with which the church had, of
late, been rather closely associated. In as much as the church was Roman and

Italian, it was the Italian artists who were most keenly confused. Their bafflement was further compounded by the political degradation of Italy, already cited in another connection (page 599).

But in their capacity as artists, all artists of the 16th century (and Italian artists more than any others) had professional reasons for concern. The stupendous achievements of Leonardo, Michelangelo, and Raphael were a matter of common knowledge. The very greatness of those great men laid an incubus upon younger artists and upon contemporaries with a reputation yet to be made. In view of what had already been accomplished, what further contribution could be made? In view of what was already known, what was there to learn?

To many, there seemed nothing else to do except study the figure style and composition of the great masters and to use the same formulas over again as opportunity presented itself. Vasari (1550) advised young artists to study nature and the old masters with care. After they had digested the accepted idiom, he suggested that they might develop their own *belle manière*. Vasari was merely expounding a policy which had been widely accepted for about a generation past. His choice of words probably accounts for the very general association of Mannerism with the eclectic theory. It also suggests the single element which is apparently common to all notions of Mannerism: a self-conscious striving by each individual artist for minor novelties which might attract attention.

It is evident that Mannerism has often been cited as a state of mind rather than a certain kind of art. For that reason, it is difficult to comprehend the frequent suggestion that Mannerism was a style. One reason for the difficulty is the simple fact that no one has given us an authentic list of the artists who were Mannerists. Some authors see Mannerism lurking behind every tree. The suggestion has been made that the venerable Leonardo was inclined that way, and that Pieter Brueghel was a typical member of the movement. Casting out such aberrations, we can at least deal with the work of various artists who have been consistently mentioned in every discussion.

As a descriptive term, Mannerism is natural (and easy to understand) if restricted to the work of certain artists who turned their backs upon content, either classical or religious, and conducted what amounted to a search for pure beauty. The sculptor Benvenuto Cellini (Fig. 14.56) was such a man, and so was Primaticcio (1504–1570), the chief founder of the exotic School of Fontainebleau.

These artists were Mannerists in the sense that they cultivated self-conscious, affected grace much as the Late Gothic Mannerists (page 414) had done, but they had a more sophisticated sanction for doing it. Disregarding nature, the classical, and the decorous idealism of Leonardo and Raphael, they attempted to generate pictures and statuary from an inner esthetic vision

Fig. 14.56 Benvenuto Cellini (1500-1571). Gold salt cellar for Francis I. Vienna, Kunsthistoriches Museum.

sometimes called the *disegno interno*. The notion was Neoplatonic, and depended upon the memory of divine beauty supposedly retained by sensitive men from that primordial period when humanity was at one with the deity (page 531).

Mannerism of this kind is best explained, perhaps, by reference to the work of its extreme exemplar, the painter Parmigianino (1503–1540). His *Madonna del Collo Longo* (Fig. 14.57) is a prime illustration. The nickname (literally, "Madonna of the long neck") is suggestive. The torso of the figure has a plausible proportion, but nothing else does. The thighs are extraordinarily long and heavy. Neck and head seem to combine the human with the swanlike. The pose is mellifluously serpentine; in order to produce it, the painter had to permit himself some remarkably loose linkage between the separate parts of the body. The operation of gravity, moreover, is vague indeed. If one gives thought to the position of the child, he is in peril of falling, but the sense that he might do so is strangely absent. As one critic has put it, the figures have volume but no "ponderation."

Obviously, Parmigianino's concept of the human figure was virtually abstract. He manipulated it in the spirit of pure calligraphy. And at the same time—with characteristically Mannerist paradox—he rendered the textures of flesh, hair, and cloth so vividly that his people are plausible. More than plausible, indeed, for the draperies which half hide, half reveal, are unmistakably erotic and even prurient.

The hypersensitivity of the demonstration is heightened by the strange world in which the Madonna is made to have her being. The space to the

Figs. 14.57–58 (left) Parmigianino. *Madonna del Collo Longo*. About 1535. About 84 inches high by 52 inches wide. Florence, Pitti Palace. (right) Pontormo. *Deposition*. 1525/26–1528. Florence, Santa Felicità. (both photos: Alinari)

left is stiflingly full of people who do not crowd each other as reason says they must. On the right, the setting takes a precarious drop, and we see a vista of columns ranging off toward an unhappy sky. In front of them, a "prophet" gestures as though in distress. The details of his costume are wonderfully clear and precise. In other words, the atmospheric perspective contradicts the linear, for the drawing tells us that the man must be further away than he seems to be.

The Florentine painter Jacopo Carucci (1494–1557), usually called Pontormo, has been included in every list of the Mannerists. His *Deposition* (Fig. 14.58) has sometimes been cited as "the paradigm of the style"—a description which is baffling in view of the obvious differences between Pontormo and the group of artists just discussed.

There are some eleven figures in the picture, and at first glance, they seem to be crowded into a conventionally triangular composition. Inspected with greater particularity, however, the arrangement takes on the aspect of a spiral movement swinging downward from the top around a curiously empty

Fig. 14.59 Pontormo. *Joseph in Egypt*. 1518–1519. 38 inches high by 43⅛ inches wide. London, National Gallery.

vortex. At the same time, some force from behind seems determined to compress everything forward and thus emphasize the flatness and verticality of the picture plane.

Taken individually, each figure looks like an example of the standard High Renaissance type so often seen in Italian art, but the draperies lack the Italian rhythm and seem somewhat Germanic. If one considers the anatomy in any detail, he becomes aware not only of considerable distortion but of various outright ambiguities, if not impossibilities. The gestures, moreover, belie their apparent extravagance because they are in fact stereotyped. The young man at the very bottom (the one who takes the weight of the body on his shoulders) glances out of the picture as though startled by some noise—which might very well have been made by our own footsteps as we approach the painting.

It is difficult and perhaps futile to attempt an interpretation. Is this Mannerism in the sense of seeking for a novel and startling effect? Is it an

Figs. 14.60–61 (left) Il Rosso Fiorentino. *Moses Defending the Daughters of Jethro.* 1523. Florence, Uffizi. (right) Bronzino. *Venus, Folly, Cupid, and Time.* 57½ inches high by 45¾ inches wide. London, National Gallery. (left: Alinari)

instance of groping toward a new style at a date when the nature of the Baroque had not yet become plain? Is it perhaps a veiled satire directed at conventional religion? If any or all of these things, is it not also the work of an artist who would have been a disturbed personality in any generation?

The febrile quality of Pontormo's art is made even more plain by the painting shown in Figure 14.59. The statue seen against the sky in the middle distance is Michelangelo's *Bacchus.* Most of the people who appear in the picture seem Italian, but the building which closes the vista is distinctly Flemish or German, and the whole composition vaguely reminiscent of Bosch.

The spatial relationships within the picture were deliberately confused by the artist himself. The figures seen at the lower left are monumental and rather near. Steps of no great length connect them with the crowd in the middle and bottom, but the members of the crowd (and there are more of them than the available room makes plausible) are diminished in scale and must be, by the logic of perspective, further away than the steps say they are. The placement of the statues is similarly ambiguous, and the people on the balcony at the upper right "come forward" in a manner the architecture contradicts. The effect of all these things is anything but comfortable, and it

Fig. 14.62 Bronzino. *Portrait of a Young Man.* Oil on wood. 37⅝ inches high by 29½ inches wide. Courtesy of the Metropolitan Museum of Art, Bequest of Mrs. H. O. Havemeyer, 1929. The H. O. Havemeyer Collection.

is no wonder that the artist, in his own day, was called "the unquiet Pontormo."

The reader may well beg to know whether Mannerism-as-of-Pontormo is the same thing as Mannerism-as-of-Parmigianino; and we obviously have still another kind of Mannerism in the painting reproduced by Figure 14.60, the work of Il Rosso Fiorentino (1494–1540). Its figure style is obviously derivative from Michelangelo, and the violence of its content is hard to reconcile with the sublimated refinement of the *Madonna del Collo Longo.*

Pontormo's pupil Bronzino (1503–1572) is usually, but not always, classified as a Mannerist. In some of his mythological pictures (Fig. 14.61) he did indeed go a little way down Parmigianino's road, but his portraits (the pictures for which he is remembered) were very different from anything yet cited as Mannerism. Yet we are told they belong in that category because the sitter in Figure 14.62 was obviously a self-conscious, introspective young man, because he dressed in the then prevailing and somber Spanish fashion, because the masks on chair and table were symbols of uncertainty, and because the surface of the painting is so smooth that it seems actually overfinished.

Giovanni da Bologna's *Mercury* (Fig. 14.63) has also been called the work of a Mannerist, but the classification seems to be one of mere convenience. Because of its grace and innocuous content, the statue was immensely popular

Fig. 14.63 Giovanni da Bologna (1524–1608). *Mercury*. About 1572. Florence, Bargello. (Alinari) .

a generation ago. It is true that the composition is clever, but Italian sculptors had been doing the same for over a hundred years (Fig. 14.12, page 579). There is nothing novel or remarkable to be noted; in fact, the piece is a perfectly normal example of High Renaissance work by a minor master.

Whatever affected painting and sculpture was bound to affect architecture also. If, therefore, Mannerism is a valid category, there must have been an architecture of Mannerism. The literature on this subject is, however, extremely slight, and the best of it is to be found in some of the writings of Nikolaus Pevsner.

In Michelangelo's Vestibule of the Laurentian Library (Fig. 14.64) Pevsner claims to discern the operation of Mannerism. The proportions of this anteroom are in themselves depressing. The floor plan is curtailed and the ceiling very high, giving one the impression of being at the bottom of a well. The colors are austere. The familiar classical members are almost malevolently arranged in situations which contradict their historical function. For example, instead of carrying an entablature, the paired columns are crammed into slots where they bear no weight. The staircase has an effect which has

Fig. 14.64 Florence. Vestibule of the Laurentian Library, with a view into the library itself. Designed by Michelangelo. The library and vestibule were designed in 1524 and 1526, respectively; the staircase in 1557. (Alinari)

aptly been compared to a dead flow of lava. And opening from this place is the vista of the library, which seems not so much to beckon as to suck us inward with the force of an unwelcome current.

The sensation has been described as "forced movement into space"— another element which, from time to time, has been put forward as a criterion for recognizing the existence of Mannerism. If so, Tintoretto was a Mannerist when he indulged in it (Figs. 14.31), and Vasari was another when he designed the familiar court of the Uffizi (Fig. 14.65).

With respect to tricks and novelties, however, the architect who best fulfilled the Mannerist recipe was Giulio Romano (1499–1546). After working under Raphael at the Vatican, he became artist-in-chief to the Duke of Mantua, for whom he designed and decorated an extensive new residence known as the Palazzo del Tè. The interior is replete with great frescoes, eclectic in style, but of a content always amusing and occasionally ribald. Giulio used a Doric order to decorate the walls of the courtyard of this palace; and, quite gratuitously, he had every third triglyph carved on the face of a keystone and

Fig. 14.65   Florence. Court of the Uffizi. 1560–1580. Designed by Vasari. (Alinari)

made arrangements to drop it several inches below the rest. The effect is more preposterous than successful.

He was more moderate when he built his own residence at Mantua (Fig. 14.66), but the design is full of newly conceived eccentricities. As in the case of Pontormo's painting (Fig. 14.59) a force from behind seems to flatten the façade as a whole. There is a notable variety of surface treatment which appears intended to give the masonry a texture like that of coarsely woven wool. Most conspicuous, and not entirely acceptable, are the ill-proportioned examples of the familiar temple front which appear in the windows—each one tucked under an arch and given a surface reminiscent of carved leather.

It is obvious that Vasari was prophetic when he put *belle manière* in the plural. Mannerism has been made to include so many different things that the term, at this date, is nearly meaningless. It looks as though a definition would be a long time in coming. Until we have it, there are serious objections to revising the outline of art history as some writers seemed determined to do.

Not the least of these objections is the word Mannerism itself. Its denotation and connotations have long been a familiar part of the language. At

Fig. 14.66 Mantua. Palace of Giulio Romano. About 1544. Designed by the owner. (Alinari)

times, it means *in the manner of,* to signify eclectic borrowing. More often, it means *mannered,* as we have used it in Chapter 12. In this second sense, it suggests excess and singularity, and is removed by a hairline from affectation. Both meanings have applied here and there in the present section, but neither can be extended to cover all of the ideas expressed, or all of the questions raised.

It is convenient, upon occasion, to stretch the scope of a familiar term, but never when the new sense must necessarily destroy accepted usage. This consideration has not bothered those who have written about Mannerism. Doubtless their intentions have been excellent; but it is always a mistake to cast semantics to the wind. The result has been that their words are often misunderstood, and Mannerism, instead of explaining anything, has served to make art history more obscure than before.

Readers with a feeling for dates must have been struck, as this section began, with the very narrow definition given to the High Renaissance by those who favor the Mannerist hypothesis. Exactly why is this curtailment desirable? If there are any facts which make it necessary, it ought to be possible to marshal them and make the matter clear. So far, that has not been done.

The reader must also have reflected, in the course of the discussion, that the period under review coincided with the maturity of Michelangelo, Titian, and Tintoretto, and with the early career of El Greco (page 722). Anything that governed art from 1520 to 1590 must, of necessity, have governed those great artists along with all the others. It is a curious fact, however, that the giants of the 16th century have rarely been mentioned in connection with Mannerism, and then diffidently. The question suggests itself: was Mannerism (assuming we can ultimately agree what it was) important enough to give its name to the whole era? The author thinks not. One reason is that all the Mannerist artists, so-called, played on the second team.

A final difficulty, if not a further objection, is the question of how Mannerism related to the Baroque. Here again, the literature is not explicit and seems vaguely self-contradictory. The Baroque, we are told, was a reaction to Mannerism just as Mannerism had been a reaction to the High Renaissance. Mannerism is said to have expressed uncertainty and frustration. The Baroque was an art of confidence and fulfillment. The notion is attractive, but the transition from Mannerism to Baroque requires more clarification than has yet appeared.

In other places, it seems to be hinted that Mannerism was a style transitional between the High Renaissance and the Baroque in the sense of being proto-Baroque. Again, the connection is not made clear. With regard to style, the author maintains that matters proceeded as described in the first part of the next chapter. Mannerism seems to have been a blind alley.

Chapter 15

HISTORY WILL probably show that the Renaissance ended in 1914, for until that fateful year, nothing happened to bring about a cultural change comparable to the difference between the Gothic and the Renaissance. The fundamental concepts which were first asserted at Florence shortly after 1400, and which were modified and developed a century later to make the philosophy of the High Renaissance, governed. In fact, the ideas which then went out from Italy to the rest of Europe still furnish most of the world with its values, its customs, and its ways of life.

It is true that great events have changed the outlook. Nationalism, which had never been an essential factor in European life at any time prior to the High Renaissance, emerged during the 17th century as the only political fact worth talking about. The national monarchies were in due course superseded by the national democracies, and democracy—a theory which at first seemed absurd—today is so firmly established as to be endorsed even in places where it does not exist in practice. Centralized government, coincident in date with nationalism and doubtless created by it, produced excellent conditions of public order, and made modern country life and modern city life possible. Science came into its own; and for the first time in history, the economy became geared not to agriculture, but to industry. The Americas were settled and civilized. Western ideas extended themselves to the Orient, with results which can not be foretold. The church ceased to exist as the primary patron of cultural enterprises, to be succeeded by the government, the wealthy person, and even the public at large. But not one of the things mentioned has been big enough to change the foundation of western civilization.

BAROQUE AND ROCOCO

Art history bears out that truth perhaps better than any other record of the era. The period since 1600 has been immensely productive. The 17th century alone witnessed the first important school of artists in Spain, the only Dutch art of any historical significance, the start of British painting, and the assumption by France of the artistic leadership of the world. But with respect to European art, all the crucial decisions (like all other cultural decisions) were, in point of fact, taken before Michelangelo died. All the definitive influences were at work. Every artist since then has been, in sober fact, a Renaissance artist. There have been numerous departures from the style of the High Renaissance, to be sure; but every one of them can be explained, and without much difficulty, as an extension of the Renaissance expression.

Even so, most of the buildings now in sight date from the past 350 years. The same is true of the innumerable pictures and statues on view in our museums. These circumstances pose an insoluble problem for the author of an introductory volume. If he conceives it his duty to mention every artist whose name may be known to the reader, the text will be reduced to a mere catalogue at best, and perhaps to a bare list of names. If on the other hand, an author declines to be lured into detailed treatment of matters that loom large only because luck has put them in our historical foreground, he can not avoid doing violence to some sentiment, some interest, some favorite material of the reader's—and indeed, of his own.

Limitations of space make it necessary that we restrict ourselves to principles, and avoid details. We must summarize in a paragraph questions which, in volumes of more intensive and more limited scope, appropriately are dealt with *in extenso*. At all times, we must keep in mind that the world has just passed through a dozen generations bearing to Italy much the same relation that the Hellenistic period bore to Athens, and we must remember that an understanding of the Renaissance is the key to comprehension of everything that has happened since.

The art of the 17th and 18th centuries forms a unit of style, with a recognizable difference which is reflected in the custom of referring to the 17th century as *The Baroque* and to the 18th as *The Rococo*. *Baroque* may come from the Portuguese *barroco*, an irregular pearl. *Rococo* may be a construction on the stem *roc*. The etymology of neither word is known, both are probably fanciful in origin, and take their present meaning from usage.

Our own usage makes them into chronological terms, but both are still occasionally used to designate distinctions of artistic style. Energetic and curvilinear monuments (Rubens, Bernini, Borromini) are some times said to partake of "the baroque tendency." At any given moment within the two centuries covered by this chapter, there were also artists of a more sober, more strictly classical kind (Poussin, Perrault, Inigo Jones) who are said to be of an "academic" trend. These distinctions are often useful, but must be accepted as distinctions rather than differences.

Similarly, *Rococo* has often been reserved for the more frivolous demonstrations of 18th century taste. Such usage appears to be nearly out of date, however. In any event, when the context makes either *baroque* or *rococo* appear to be a disparaging adjective, the implication is a mistaken one.

THE ORIGINS OF BAROQUE ART

Rome was the fountainhead of the Baroque, and the style is perhaps best approached in association with the Counter-Reformation.

That movement had painful beginnings and took a long time to get under way. The Society of Jesus was founded in 1534 and approved by Paul III in 1540. The same pope established the Universal Inquisition, in 1542, and called the Council of Trent, which met intermittently from 1545 to 1564. Guided largely by Jesuits, the Council arrived at findings which bear close analogies to the military theory of command and obedience—Saint Ignatius, it will be recalled, had been a soldier. The decisions of the Council were embodied in a series of pronouncements issued by Pius V between 1566 and 1570. These remain, with minor additions and revisions, the dogma of the Church.

The period described was anything but a happy one at Rome. It coincided with Michelangelo's most distressful years (page 617), and with the so-called era of Mannerism (page 665) in art. The difficulties of the papacy were not spiritual alone; every pope in a long list of popes found himself compelled to ride one swell or another in the endless maelstrom of French, Spanish, and German power politics, and usually Rome gained nothing. Austerity replaced buoyancy. Paul V is said to have eaten meat only twice weekly, and it was a matter for remark that even the cardinals were thin and dour.

It is history that the Counter-Reformation failed in its most important objectives. It gradually became plain that the Church could hope for no more than the preservation of Catholicism where it still remained. On the other hand, the Protestants turned out to be less vindictive than had at first seemed probable. It is true that Catholic residents in Protestant lands were often treated severely, but Protestantism as such made no world-wide move to destroy the entire Church of Rome. Thus, the militant phase of the Counter-Reformation was relaxed, and the modern religious situation started to establish itself. If the Church could not lure or force the Protestants back under its control, the Church could at least celebrate the glories of Catholicism wherever Catholicism was steadfast and strong. Sixtus V (regnal dates 1584–1590) was the first pontiff to undertake that policy.

He was one of the really great popes. He reorganized the government of the Papal States. He brought the local nobility under control. He enforced public order in the city, and he exterminated the bandits in the country roundabout. He put his own financial affairs in order, and he stimulated secular prosperity. He issued a new edition of the Vulgate, and he turned his attention to the beautification of Rome. He was the man who brought the dome of St. Peter's to completion, added to the Vatican Palace, and built the Vatican Library. He thus set the precedent for enthusiastic patronage of the arts by numerous popes and cardinals to follow, and by doing so, he became the man who gave modern Rome its baroque appearance and atmosphere.

Michelangelo founded the Baroque, although he was not of it. A prediction of almost everything typical of the era can be found somewhere in his work, or somewhere in his attitudes.

His most obvious legacy was the habit of thinking in terms of stupendous projects. During every previous epoch, works of art were undertaken one at a time, without any great regard for the relationship between them. During the 17th and 18th centuries, the absolute scale of artistic enterprises became bigger than anything ever dreamed of before, and it became standard practice to apply artistic principles to the arrangement of vast areas. St. Peter's and its magnificent piazza (Fig. 15.1) form a tightly organized composition. Versailles and its gardens (Fig. 15.2) form another. And these are merely single instances; the list could be almost indefinitely expanded. Wren's plan for a complete rearrangement of London (1666), a noble project even though it

Fig. 15.1 Rome. St. Peter's. St. Peter's was originally designed as a central church by Bramante and begun in 1506. After work had dragged on under a series of architects, Michelangelo took charge in 1547; by the time of his death in 1564, the drum under the dome was complete as redesigned by him. Giacomo della Porta built the dome (1588–1592), using a steeper pitch than Michelangelo had intended. Carlo Maderna was employed (1606–1625) to extend the nave and to build the façade. The great colonnades are the work of Bernini and date from 1656-1663. (Alinari)

never came to pass, is intimately illustrative of the mental climate of the time. The river front of Paris, from the Arc de Triomphe to the Louvre, was the work of many men and several generations, but virtually a single design. L'Enfant's plan for Washington (1791) was another example as well as many smaller enterprises which still deserve to be called noble: the new quarter at Nancy (1753), the Royal Crescent at Bath (1767), and Jefferson's design for the University of Virginia (1817), which perhaps falls outside the scope of this chapter but illustrates the principle perfectly.

By conceiving and carrying out projects like these, baroque artists actually changed the appearance of Europe for the better, and they contributed to our culture one of its most fortunate conventions. Whenever new buildings, streets, bridges, and parks are proposed, it is today taken for granted that artistic sanctions will be applied. Every school and college, indeed every institution of any kind, points to a "master plan"—which is to say an artistic composition by which all future construction will be brought into harmony and coherence.

The philosophy behind these great achievements had been implicit in Alberti's thinking (page 551). It remained for Michelangelo to demonstrate how the work could be done. His design for the Campidoglio (page 616) seems small in scale by comparison with those just cited, but it served as the prototype for them all. It also introduces us to the inner tensions present in all baroque art, and to the conflict and paradox from which the 17th century was never free.

The composition of the Campidoglio can be described as an intensification of the Greek organic type (page 66). Geometry furnished the order. Symmetry furnished the system. But the parts so arranged were different from those of every earlier style. A single Greek column can stand alone; it is a complete composition. But it became a cardinal principle of baroque design to make certain that no single part, taken by itself, would compose. Reference to the larger whole thus became necessary before the part made sense. Either one of the subordinate palaces on the Campidoglio would be curiously incomplete if removed to another site and viewed singly. The point at issue can be explained even better by asking the reader to imagine his sensations if, by chance, the *Night, Day, Dawn, or Dusk* were removed from the Medici tombs (Fig. 14.28, page 614) and set up alone in some museum. The piece would be unmistakably a fragment. Is it possible to imagine anything more homeless, more distressingly in need of the surroundings for which it was designed? Our sensibilities would grope for an esthetic answer much as they grope for the completion of an unresolved chord.

In order to maintain coherence between parts of this kind, it was necessary to make the geometrical relationships more pronounced. The two subordinate palaces of the Campidoglio have an angular reference to each other which was radical at that date. The same may be said of the pronounced pitch Michelangelo gave to the figures on the Medici tombs. The effect was to impose discipline and control upon material which otherwise might be confusing, and to force us to take account of the relationship between part and whole.

The situation just described was the greatest of many paradoxes within the Baroque, some times a blessing and some times a curse. When tumultous subject matter was relentlessly put into a state of order, a sense of regimentation, of confinement was certain to result. Many a baroque work of art gives the impression that the content has been imprisoned within the form; one thinks again of Michelangelo and of John Donne's poetry.

Michelangelo himself often strained his forms to the limit, and sometimes

Fig. 15.2 Versailles. (Courtesy of the French Government Tourist Office, New York)

seems deliberately to have offered suggestions that his well-ordered compositions might, at any moment, fall to pieces or even explode. Precarious equilibrium was one of his favorite devices. When called upon to design a new
pedestal for the *Marcus Aurelius,* used as the pivotal element in his composition on top of the Capitoline Hill, he chose to put the ponderous statue
on top of an unusually delicate support. Similarly, when designing the Medici
tombs, he put the heavy sarcophagi on trestles which do not look adequate,
and probably would prove inadequate if subjected to any unusual shock or
strain. The balance of the Medici tombs, moreover, is by no means at peace
with itself. The figure on the right is equal and opposite to its converse on the
left, but something more than simple equivalence is involved. The recumbent
Night, Day, Dawn, and *Dusk* writhe with an inner and spiritual compulsion.
Locomotion is denied them, but they struggle to have it. Should their energy
break loose, they would heave up and destroy the composition.

The balance, to put it in other words, is an opposition between forces
that strain away from each other, between emphatic opposites mutually frus-
tratory and bent on canceling each other out. The over-all impression is that
of great power governed by rigorous system. The method was always the
same: turbulent expression compressed into conventional order.

Fortunately or unfortunately, baroque art needed this discipline. With
the entire Renaissance behind them, artists of the 17th century were in possession of more skill than any others who can be named as a class or group.
Tours de force of technique were the order of the day, and matters often
got out of hand. The ideal baroque building was not only big, but confronted
the observer with a dazzling array of shapes, lines, and colors (Fig. 15.10).
The ideal baroque picture was an immense assembly of persons governed by
the terms of some extended allegory (Fig. 15.20). The most involved works of
the High Renaissance (page 592), it will be remembered, had been distinguished by a general lucidity no matter how many details they contained.
The baroque masters often left lucidity behind, but their most extravagant
productions were governed by ice-cold logic. Their iconography, however
recondite, was systematic. Their compositions will always yield to study.
Many of them were so minutely calculated, indeed, as to have earned the
sobriquet "machines."

If stupendous plans were out of place for reasons of cost, need, or otherwise, the baroque artists still attempted to amaze. By one method or another,
they undertook to move the observer to the depths, and to move him fast.
They aimed directly at his emotional vitals. The successful work of art was
the one that provided an almost painful heightening of the sensibilities and
the most vivid awareness of the experience of the moment. There are so
many ways to startle and dazzle that we need suggest only a few for the purpose of introduction, and leave the reader braced for the rest.

We ordinarily think of still life as being dramatically noncommittal, but in the hands of baroque painters, it attained a hyper-realism that takes the breath away (Fig. 15.45). The gentle subject matter of Vermeer has made him one of the best loved painters, but his handling of light and air literally strikes one—it is more vital than the light and air of actuality (Fig. 15.63).

Not content with actuality, it was standard practice among baroque artists to use their skill to create illusions. Opera and the theater were under intensive development during the 17th century, and the borderline between monumental art and stage scenery was often nonexistent. The greatest artists of the period did not hesitate to present misleading data to the eye. There was no conspiracy to deceive. The public was artistically sophisticated and could be counted upon to enjoy the demonstration.

Of the various devices that fall under the heading of tricks, none was more amusing than the constructed perspective. Theater sets (most of them permanent rather than movable) were usually built that way, and the same thing often added a fillip to otherwise formal architecture. Figure 15.3 shows a capital example. Ostensibly, we look down a long gallery at a life-size statue about a hundred feet away. The actual distance is less than twenty feet, and the illusion is so perfect that one might pass by without realizing the truth unless warned. And modest, minor illusions of this kind were as nothing by comparison with the stupendous ceiling paintings of the period (Fig. 15.20) which opened up an entirely new concept of architectural design.

Over and above such theories of design—in which they were intensely interested—the artists of Italy and other Catholic lands had a sober reason for making the optical illusion a standard resource of their trade. It was crucial to the Counter-Reformation to convince the public that transcendental things were real. Artists had the skill to call another world into being. They could literally show people what the church wanted them to believe.

The legitimacy of using art for such a purpose can not, as a theory, be attacked, but the advent of such ideas resulted in a corpus of religious art which requires explanation if not apology. The Counter-Reformation was a program directed at the mass of the population. The narrative subject matter for religious art was chosen accordingly. It almost always appealed to the sentiments, the emotions, the senses, and the credulity of people who could be swayed by the bizarre. It follows that cultivated persons, and above all intellectually inclined persons, sometimes find Catholic baroque art uncongenial and even offensive. To such, the Church has always been inclined to say: Beware of pride.

It is futile, perhaps, to speculate about what might have been, but it is strange indeed, and possibly was unfortunate, that the baroque era came hard after the High Renaissance, and was, in a larger sense, part of the

Fig. 15.3 Rome. Perspective Gallery in the Palazzo Spada. Designed by Borromini. (Alinari)

Renaissance. What would baroque buildings have been like had 17th-century architects been set free? As it was, convention demanded that every part of every building be recognizably classical in source, however freely manipulated. Was the figure style of the 16th century—a modernized version of the Greek and Roman—appropriate for the concepts entertained by baroque painters and sculptors? Surely this was the greatest paradox of them all: that the Baroque was produced by a society still firmly in the grip of classical taste.

17TH-CENTURY ART IN ITALY

♦ *The Church of the Gesù* Because of its style and its associations, and in spite of its comparatively early date, most people think of the Church of the Gesù at Rome (Fig. 15.4) as the first monument which is distinctly not of the High Renaissance, and belongs without question to the Baroque. It is the home church of the Society of Jesus.

Giacomo Vignola (1507–1573) is usually named as the architect because he was in charge when construction began four years after Michelangelo's death. Giacomo della Porta (1541–1604) added the façade after Vignola in turn had died. Michelangelo is known, however, to have offered to design the church, and recent opinion leans to the view that both Vignola and della Porta were very much directed, if not governed, by his advice, and possibly by drawings which he left behind.

The Gesù has been a tremendously influential building. It was the proto-

Fig. 15.4   Rome. Church of the Gesù. Façade. About 1573. Designed by Giacomo della Porta. (Alinari)

type for innumerable baroque and rococo churches in Italy, Spain, Germany, England, and America, and is thus, artistically speaking, one of the most important churches of all time.

The plan shows a tunnel-vaulted nave, a dome over the crossing, and a series of chapels where the aisles would ordinarily be (Fig. 15.5). This plan is the same type that Alberti had used almost exactly one hundred years before when he furnished drawings for Sant'Andrea at Mantua (Figs. 14.3–5, pages 556–557), but the interior of the Gesù shows some important changes in the relative size of the different divisions. These alter the emphasis without changing the form.

The nave is much wider, and the chapels smaller. Because the nave is wider, the dome is bigger, giving us a more ample view of the crossing. More important than that, the larger drum invited the use of big windows, and the light streaming in thus became a major factor in the composition. On bright days, it seems like a blazing fulfillment for the axial power of the nave.

The dramatic use of light is one of the most important features of baroque art; for the next two hundred years, painters and sculptors as well as architects outdid themselves in its manipulation. Recent findings suggest that the Jesuits were responsible, and that they got the idea from Spain where

Fig. 15.5 Rome. Church of the Gesù. Nave. 1568–1584. Designed by Giacomo Vignola. (Anderson)

their order originated. The matter is by no means definite, but some of the Late Gothic cathedrals of Spain (Gerona, for example; nave begun 1417) have a ground plan not unlike that of the Gesù and differ from it in elevation only as the Gothic differs from the Baroque. The suggestion is certainly consistent with the general political and cultural dominance of Spain in Catholic lands. And it throws light on the psychology of the Counter-Reformation. In no small measure, it was an attempt to turn the hands of the clock backward and recall men to the religion of medieval times.

The Gesù's façade proved quite as influential as the body of the church. With variations in detail, its essential form has been repeated and reiterated all over Christendom. The distinctive feature of the type was a reversion to the cross-section of the Early Christian basilica. The familiar clearstory rises in traditional fashion above a wider section.

Della Porta had discarded the notion of a unified temple front. His arrangement is best understood as piling a little temple on top of a bigger one: each story runs through the familiar Roman sequence of podium, order, and entablature.

The immense scrolls which provide a linear transition between the ground floor and clearstory were derivative from Alberti, who had used the same device for the present façade of Santa Maria Novella at Florence. Such scrolls are the modillions (page 190) of the Roman Corinthian cornice, immensely exaggerated in size and put to a use never dreamed of by the Romans. It is to be noted, further, that the columns and pilasters are in pairs, that the central entrance gets emphasis by the greater relief of its engaged columns, and that the pediment over the main door is doubled up, a segmental one enclosing a triangular.

The artistic merit of every expedient listed is self-evident. To our eyes, there is nothing sensational about the façade of the Gesù. To appreciate how advanced it actually was, we must remind ourselves that 1570 was the same year that Palladio (page 643) published his *Four Books on Architecture,* and that from the point of view of Palladio and other sincere academics, della Porta's new ideas were worse than liberties—they were virtually sins against the sanctity of classical rules.

♦ *Carracci and Caravaggio* Annibale Carracci (1560–1609) and Michelangelo da Caravaggio (1573–1610) were the first baroque painters. Both came to Rome from the north of Italy. Their personal relations seem to have been cordial, and they seem, also, to have agreed that strong measures were necessary in order to rescue Italian art from the confusion of Mannerism (page 665). Otherwise, they had nothing in common; in fact their methods were opposite, and their art was so different as to make it hard to believe they were contemporaries working in the same city.

Carracci came to Rome in 1595 from Bologna, where, ten years before and in association with two of his cousins, he had organized an academy which offered what amounted to a formal curriculum in the theory and practice of art. The approach was the eclectic one (page 667), and the Carracci have ever since been damned both for that and for the very notion that art might be taught in a systematic way. Their program was, in fact, very intelligent. No system of education, it must be pointed out, can teach greatness. The fair test of education is whether it equips men to make something of themselves, and it must be conceded that the pupils of the Carracci were excellent technicians.

The *Virgin Mourning over Christ* (Fig. 15.6) shows us Annibale at his best. He had profited by early acquaintance with the work of Correggio and the Venetians. At Rome, he had learned from Raphael. The composition has stability and repose. The space is easy and comfortable. The individual figures are much idealized, but remain warm and human. The clinical facts of death are softened by the elegance of the contours, and the gentle but brilliant light which plays over the form of the Savior. If not a great picture, it is undeniably an appealing one.

It is unfortunate, perhaps, for Annibale's reputation that he did not

Fig. 15.6 Annibale Caracci. *Virgin Mourning over the Dead Christ.* Rome, Doria Gallery. (Alinari)

restrict himself to easel pictures; but it was only natural that he would accept the bigger and more lucrative commissions then available at Rome. Indeed, there is reason to believe that he went to Rome in the first place at the invitation of Cardinal Odoardo Farnese, to decorate the grand salon of the family palace, then recently completed. The room was a vaulted one, about 20 feet wide and 65 feet long, and the Cardinal wanted the end walls and the ceiling covered with frescoes devoted to the theme "The Power of Love in Antiquity."

The commission, by its very nature, was an open challenge to equal or surpass both Raphael and Michelangelo. A glance at the result (Fig. 15.7) is enough to demonstrate that Annibale was not up to it. The scale of the operation made it necessary to call in assistants, but on the whole, the technical standards remained high. Annibale was capable of tenderness, as we have seen, but he lacked whatever qualities it might take to make the Grand Style grand. In the whole history of Italian art, there are no pictures more vacuous than these. They are also excellent illustrations of the eclectic theory at its worst—the reader can amuse himself by noting reminiscences of items seen here and there in the work of Michelangelo, Raphael, Titian, Veronese, and Correggio, but it is a question whether there is any profit in it.

Caravaggio took his name from the small town south of Bergamo where he was born. He learned his trade at Milan, and arrived in Rome not earlier

Fig. 15.7 Annibale Caracci. Ceiling of the Gallery of the Farnese Palace. 1597–1604. Rome, Farnese Palace. (opposite) Detail: *Triumph of Bacchus*. (above: Gab. Fot. Naz.; opposite: Anderson)

than 1590 and not later than 1592. He probably came there because the administration of Julius the 5th had made Rome a cosmopolitan center where painting was in demand and where wealthy patrons were ready to respond to talent. The Cardinal del Monte gave him quarters in his palace and protected him during his residence in the city. The painter's character and personality made protection requisite. Caravaggio was the archetype of the artist in rebellion, and still remains as an extreme instance of the artist as a self-conscious, thoroughgoing bohemian. He was in permanent revolt against authority of all kinds, artistic authority or civil authority as the case might be. Constantly in trouble with the police, he had to flee Rome in 1606 to escape a charge of manslaughter (the documents leave scarcely a doubt that he was guilty) and spent the next four years in Naples, Malta, and Sicily. He died of malaria on his way back to Rome in 1610.

The *Bacchus* (Fig. 15.8) is a good example of his earlier style. It is an insolent picture. In it, we see Caravaggio himself half-naked but, for the sake of symbolism, draped in a toga. His headdress is deliberately preposterous, but a remarkable demonstration of still-life painting nevertheless. The same may be said of the fruit, the wine, the cloth, and the flesh; indeed, the whole picture literally exudes a heightened sense of reality in the presence of which many persons feel discomfort and even distaste. Paradoxically, the control of the light is curiously unreal; the technique might be described as the mode of relief intensified by a rendering of textures more vivid than anything earlier. The picture, in sum, is a performance—a performance of skill, and a satirical

Fig. 15.8 Caravaggio. *Bacchus*. About 1595. 38½ by 33½ inches. Florence, Uffizi.

stunt intended to discredit the quasi-classicism of such portraits as Bronzino's *Andrea Doria as Neptune*.

Caravaggio's earlier pictures contain little suggestion of the profundity and scale of his greater works. Within a year or two of the *Bacchus*, he was producing some of the greatest religious painting of all time. *The Calling of Saint Matthew* (Fig. 15.9), one of a series in San Luigi dei Francesi, and *The Death of the Virgin* (Fig. 15.10) are but two of many of his pictures that are among the most moving in the history of art. It is obvious that the painter had brought all his force to bear: his skill, his brutality, and his tenderness. He had become a man with a mission. His purpose was to convince people that the holy stories had actually happened. His method was to tell the truth.

The reception of these great paintings furnishes us with an interesting sidelight on contemporary taste, and indeed on taste in general. Caravaggio got his commissions because members of the Roman aristocracy believed in his art, but the art itself was heartily disliked by the lower clergy and the people in general. Sacred history was certainly on the painter's side. Christ had described himself as having much to do with publicans and sinners, but the ordinary man was antagonistic to imagery which made those words visible. He still insisted that theological propriety involved the stately decorum of the High Renaissance. *The Death of the Virgin* was only one of many pictures which were actually rejected upon completion; but Rubens, who then happened to be in Rome, enthusiastically recommended its purchase by his patron, the Duke of Mantua, and with other artists, arranged for a public exhibition of the picture before it left the city. Great crowds, it is said, came to see it, apparently without making it popular. In a word, an art which said that religion was of the people and for the people proved disgusting to the people, but was understood by the learned, the wealthy, and the privileged. The phenomenon was all the more curious because the trend of counter-reformation religion was moving in a popular direction at the same time, as exemplified by the activity of Saint Charles Borromeo, Saint Philip Neri, and the *Spiritual Exercises* of Saint Ignatius.

The shock of Caravaggio's subject matter might have been tolerated, perhaps, had his methods been less aggressive. The most striking feature of his developed style was the evocation of sensation by violent contrasts of light and dark. The idea doubtless came originally from Venetian painting, but his scheme was more systematic and his purpose philosophical rather than decorative.

The end in view was to focus attention more vividly than ever before upon the dramatically operative areas of the canvas by bringing them strongly up into the light. Other areas were deprived of their power to attract attention by putting them into the dark. Caravaggio's scheme was new because he confined the light to a very small section of the picture surface. The important figure, or even the important part of the figure, was thereby given a stridency sufficient to stun the sensibilities.

His procedure was successful because it corresponded more closely than one might suppose with the actualities of sight. When viewing any scene whatever, the eye adjusts itself for the brightest light. Conscious readjustment is necessary to inspect material contained within the darks. Our visual world, therefore, is more like Carvaggio's painting than our habits of thought permit us to realize.

His methods were not capricious. He arrived at his effects by a systematic procedure often called "crowding the darks," an expression which describes the technique very well. Everything on the posed model or within the scene was crowded down into the lower range of the value scale if, in fact, its local tone was fairly dark. The upper half of the value scale, or more than that, was thus reserved for modeling the face, the hands, and other areas of lighter tone. Because strong contrasts of value are seen within, and only within, these lighter areas, mass and shape come out vividly there, producing a redoubled emphasis. The special merit of the system becomes plain when we reflect that the most expressive parts of the body are the areas which fall above the middle value.

Because of his personality and tastes, to say nothing of his way of life, Caravaggio no more founded a school than he belonged to one, but it is fair

Fig. 15.9 Caravaggio. *The Calling of Saint Matthew.* 1597–1598. 133 by 137 inches. **Rome,** San Luigi dei Francesi. (Anderson)

to say no artist ever had a wider influence. In Italy, the impact of his work produced a number of Caravaggisti, few of whom ever had personal contact with the master, and many of whom painted pictures which are some times mistaken for his own. In France, the work of Georges de la Tour and of the brothers Le Nain (page 696) was derivative from Caravaggio. Much the same can be said of the works of the Spaniard Ribera (1588–1656), and of the early period in the career of his great compatriot Velasquez (page 733). Rembrandt (page 746), the greatest of the Dutch masters, is hardly conceivable without Caravaggio as a spiritual forebear. It is notable, too, that baroque architects and baroque sculptors soon began to cultivate stratagems calculated to produce effects of light and dark that can only be described as Caravaggesque.

♦ *Bernini* Architect, sculptor, and painter, Gianlorenzo Bernini (1598–1680) was long the most prominent artist in all Europe. Most of his work is

Fig. 15.10 Caravaggio. *The Death of the Virgin*. Paris, Louvre. (Giraudon)

at Rome, but he was called to France in 1665, and was once commissioned to do a portrait of King Charles 1st of England.

It was an essential part of the Counter-Reformation to establish a literal belief in miracles. Because the continued and present reality of divine intervention was a burning issue, recent miracles were of more interest than miracles of greater import but more distant date. The new realism of Caravaggio might have lent itself to this program, but its value as propaganda was compromised by its unpopularity. There was a demand for an art that would accomplish the same result without offending notions of artistic and religious propriety—something, that is, which would combine Caravaggio's force with the elegance and decorum of the High Renaissance. It was Bernini who embraced this project with enthusiasm and success.

In the whole history of art, there is no experience at all equivalent to one's first view of Bernini's *Ecstasy of Santa Teresa* (Fig. 15.11). Attention is pulled toward the main subject by a magnificent architectural enframement rendered by dark marbles in combination with surfaces of gold, amber, and

Fig. 15.11   Bernini. *Ecstasy of Santa Teresa* (above) and (below) members of the Cornaro family. 1646. Rome, Santa Maria della Vittoria. (Anderson)

pinker tones. The broken pediment above swells out toward us, and then recedes as though in homage to the niche it encloses. Within the niche, we see the saint accompanied by an angel. The marble figures are carved with a relentless realism, but with a skill so exquisite as to defy belief. The scene is bathed in golden light, which comes through a yellow pane of glass concealed above, and its power to convince is by no means diminished by a set of gilt rods arranged radially behind, to simulate heavenly rays.

The saint is represented as a young and comely woman. She falls back and yet rises in voluptuous transport, swooning and losing consciousness of the earth, her body undulating with effort, pain, and delight. Above stands the angel. In compassion and understanding, he is about to thrust through her heart the dart of heavenly love which, by Teresa's own testimony, tore her breast when she had union with the divine.

So intense is the experience of viewing the central group that it is only afterward one becomes conscious of the bystanders; but they are present. On the walls to right and left, there are other niches unmistakably like boxes at the opera. In them sit the donors—in poses too casual by half—watching the show.

Such performances raise serious questions with respect to the propriety of much 17th-century religious art. Above all, we may challenge the use made of the subject matter. Santa Teresa (1515–1582) was a nobly born woman of Castile. She became a Carmelite nun in 1535, and she distinguished herself both as a mystic and as an executive of capacity and foresight. Her writings are excellent examples of the literary craft. In easy, elegant Spanish she set forth the difficult philosophy of direct religious experience, and her various publications proved among the most effective available for the Counter-Reformation. She brought about a revision of the Carmelite rule and founded a dozen new convents. Every memorial speaks of her common sense and good humor. Bernini's figure bears small resemblance to the chubby and somewhat jolly person of the saint herself, and the most ardent religionist should be given pause by the particular imagery he chose to evoke in his attempt to convince the public of her union with God.

Although his name is a synonym for all that was extravagant and bombastic in the Baroque, the very same Bernini could be thoroughly delightful when he turned his hand to less pompous material. His numerous fountains remain among the best on earth; they are deservedly the best loved landmarks in Rome (Fig. 15.12). In an occasional minor work, moreover, Bernini focused every resource of his formidable technique on fanciful themes. For an instance, let the reader turn to the *Elephant and Obelisk* (Fig. 15.13). The little obelisk is an ancient one, dug up in 1665. The official iconography of the statue is abstruse to a degree. Briefly: because it pointed upward and because the Egyptians had associated such monuments with the sun, 17th-century iconolo-

Fig. 15.12 Bernini. Triton Fountain. About 1637. Rome, Piazza Barberini. (Alinari)

gists construed the Egyptian understanding as prefigurement of Christianity, and made the obelisk into a symbol for Divine Wisdom. The elephant was chosen as a caryatid for a variety of reasons. Historically, elephants had often been used as emblems of strength and fortitude. Their well-known intelligence had served, moreover, to build up a veritable cult of admiration. People even believed them to be capable of such concepts as charity and credited them with a capacity for the religious impulse. Because Pliny had said that elephants courteously piloted lost wanderers out of the desert, the elephant was occasionally associated with the Savior himself.

Unquestionably, Bernini was familiar with all this ancient lore, but he must have known, also, about some live elephants recently imported into Europe, to the delight of young and old. There was much gossip about the tricks they could learn. One elephant, who had taken up his residence in

Fig. 15.13 Bernini. *Elephant and Obelisk*. 1667. Rome, Piazza della Minerva. (Alinari)

Holland, enjoyed his pipe of tobacco daily. So for all its ostensibly serious and ceremonial character, it is evident that Bernini took the same direct and delighted pleasure in the subject as a child. Only the hard of heart can think of a word to say against it.

Bernini was famous as a sculptor of portrait busts, and there are none better in the whole history of art. All but one or two of them were commissioned as ceremonial portraits; as such, they are admirable. But even while they flatter, they subject the sitter to an analysis of character both searching and unmistakable.

Bernini's painting is one of the mysteries not yet solved by historians of art. Reliable documents say that he did at least two hundred pictures. Only ten or a dozen can be located today, and not all connoisseurs agree about the authenticity of those. It is most unlikely that all the rest have perished.

Doubtless they exist, many of them unrecognized and many hung under other names. The weight of the evidence indicates that Bernini did not accept commissions for paintings, but painted for his own pleasure—a circumstance that makes the situation all the more fascinating and all the more maddening.

♦ *Bernini, Borromini, and High Baroque Architecture*   Previous to the 17th century, all architectural thinking had been curtailed by certain habits of thought.

When stones were taken from the quarry, they were squared. The builder relied upon the plumb and level when he assembled such material. Rectangularity was the result. Walls were vertical plane surfaces. Ground plans were defined by straight lines and right angles.

The reader will appreciate that we are indulging in over-simplification for the sake of illustration, and in exaggeration for the sake of emphasis. Innumerable exceptions will occur to him; for example, the absidioles of the Romanesque (page 335); the chevet of the Gothic (page 373). But were not all of these inventions, and any number of others, mere variations intended to beguile us from the domination of parallelograms? Is it not true that all sculptural embellishment, from the Greek to the Gothic and beyond, was conceived as something attached to a wall, placed in front of a wall, or incorporated into the thickness of a wall?

And taking an even broader view, is it not a fact that the Parthenon was notable because its refinements (page 93) did not conform to the usage of workaday building? Is it not also a fact that the curves of Hagia Sophia (page 278) were not usual even in Byzantine architecture? In other words, departure from the limitations cited had been not only exceptional, but very exceptional indeed.

It was Michelangelo who broke through these age-old conventions, opened the eyes of the world to an entirely new architecture, and thus paved the way for the Baroque.

By instinct and by training, he was a sculptor. The limitations of plane and solid geometry were intolerable to him. His original ideas came in terms of mass and the curvature of contours—which is to say, with an intense feeling for the third dimension. When he painted, he painted as though describing statues. When compelled to use the column, the pilaster, and the entablature (Fig. 14.28, page 614) he seems almost to have resented their angularity, he combined them with curves when he could, and he invariably attempted, by various devices which suggested movement in and out, to eliminate our thought of the wall as a plane surface. In the one project where practical and economic considerations did not impede his imagination, the tomb of Julius the 2nd (Fig. 14.23, page 606), he went even further. Taken as a whole, the tomb was neither architecture nor sculpture. Neither can it be adequately described as a combination of architecture and sculpture. It was, rather, a fusion of virtues, a new synthesis of the two arts. Nothing quite like it had even been seen before.

It is a tribute to the genius of Bernini to say that he understood Michelangelo's architecture, and brought about the results which were implicit, but only predicted, in the designs of that great man.

Bernini's first major commission, undertaken at the age of twenty-six, was for the baldacchino of St. Peter's (Fig. 15.14). No photograph can give any notion of the scale; the reader must ponder as best he can the dimensions given in the caption, and correlate these as well as possible with the size of the dome above (internal measurements: 137 feet, 6 inches diameter; 335 feet high). It is obvious that a tremendous baldacchino was essential in such a place, and yet Bernini kept it small enough to tell as an embellishment to the nave rather than as a counter-attraction.

The form he used helped in that effect, and was in itself an innovation. Traditionally, baldacchini had been little houses or temples, some times actually roofed over. Bernini made his in the manner of an open arbor and added realistic floral ornament to reinforce the suggestion. The gigantic corkscrew columns send the eye upward in an ascending spiral; it seems only natural that each should have an active angel for a finial, and still more so that volutes should swing still further upward and inward to make a base for the orb and the cross at the top of the entire composition.

No one can look at the baldacchino without knowing that contemporary Catholicism enjoyed a sense of triumph, and it is amusing to reflect that this monument has often been cited (especially its columns) as an instance of the tendency of the period to indulge in excessive display. The great columns were, in fact, nothing of the kind. They were a gracious tribute to tradition. On the right-hand side of Figure 15.14, just above the middle, there appear some smaller marble columns of much the same corkscrew kind. These had formed part of the fabric of Old St. Peter's, and were used again to emphasize the continuity of the Church.

When he designed the Shrine for the Chair of Saint Peter (Fig. 15.15; right of Fig. 15.14), Bernini outdid himself in the matter of display, but, as always, maintained strict logic with respect to iconography. Ostensibly, the cathedra floats on the clouds, with some aid from the four male figures stationed at its four legs. They represent Latin and Greek fathers who had in their day supported Rome's claim to central authority. The great throne encloses a wooden stool that once belonged to Saint Peter himself. On the chair back, we see a relief showing the Presentation of the Keys to Peter. Above, putti carry the papal tiara and key, and still further above, there is a transparency of the Holy Dove. The ensemble is thus a visual sequence of the

Figs. 15.14–15 Bernini. (left) Baldacchino. 1624–1633. 95 feet high. Rome. St. Peter's. (right) Cathedra of St. Peter. Rome, St. Peter's. (left: Anderson; right: Alinari)

reasons for obedience to the Pope: a reference to historical debates successfully completed, the delegation of office by Christ, the symbols of the pontiff's primacy in the Church on earth, and a reminder that he is at once and ever the special object of Divine Grace.

Considered stylistically, the monument is literally a thesis explaining everything we mean by the word *Baroque*. The theme is operatic, even melodramatic. The luxury of colors, textures, and myriad parts goes further than to defy description; it comes close to defying inspection. The sweep of the gestures, the draperies, and even the mechanical parts of the cathedra suggests the snap of a painter's brush, and we are reminded that Bernini once boasted that he had united the resources of painting and sculpture. And yet all this teeming vitality fits into an extremely strict composition—so strict, indeed, that one feels a certain lack of life in what purports to be vital activity.

The colonnaded piazza of St. Peter's (Fig. 15.1) was not only Bernini's greatest work, but perhaps the greatest monument in all baroque art. Its esthetic purpose is obvious, and its utilitarian excellence is familiar to every visitor. There was also a sincere religious reason for building it. The square in front of St. Peter's is a meeting place for great congregations and the traditional site for certain important ceremonies, especially the Pope's annual Easter greeting when he stands on a balcony above the doors and extends his blessing *urbi et orbi*—"to the city and to the world." It was that particular ritual which suggested the form Bernini gave his colonnades. They tell people

Fig. 15.16 Sant'Andrea al Quirinale. Rome. Designed by Bernini. (Anderson)

in vast numbers where to stand and where to look in order to have the Pope in view, and they surround the crowd in a manner to be described as all-embracing, thus providing an architectural symbol for the character of the Church itself.

Bernini once said that in his hands marble became as supple as wax. The remark is often quoted with reference to his sculpture, but it suggests also the essential nature of his architecture. One feels that he bent or molded rather than built those great curves. The sensation they evoke is strongly plastic. There is no better proof of the contention that Bernini made architecture an art of contours rather than an art of cubes.

St. Peter's is perhaps not the place for art that is gay and volatile; it must nevertheless be admitted by Bernini's admirers that his work there was imbued with an excess of gravity and earnestness, and seems at times to be overbearing. That impression is altogether corrected when we look at some of his smaller churches, of which Figure 15.16 is a good example.

The church has an elliptical plan, with the long axis in the transverse direction. Characteristics of the site suggested that shape, but Bernini was more than ready for the suggestion. Like other baroque architects of the time, he entertained himself by experiments; indeed, the bond of unity be-

Figs. 15.17–18 Rome. San Carlino alle Quattro Fontane. Designed by Borromini. (left) Façade. 1667. (right) Nave. 1633. (both photos: Alinari)

tween all small baroque churches was the certainty that each one would have a new and different ground outline. Seen in three dimensions, Sant'Andrea is a study in curvature, a remarkable piece of abstract sculpture that seems almost alive. It would be difficult to name another building that so nicely combines grace with austerity.

Francesco Borromini (1599–1667) was even more daring and ingenious than Bernini. His design for San Carlino alle Quattro Fontane (Figs. 15.17–18) was one of the most original of the Baroque or any other period; the tiny building relates to its era much as the Pazzi Chapel related to the Renaissance. The body of the church dates from 1633. The façade was Borromini's last design; it was added the year of his death.

For the plan of the nave, he took the shape of a cartouche in delicate, extended quatrefoil. The ground outline comprises curves both concave and convex, flowing into each other with slight breaks and joinings which seem so natural as to be foreordained. When projected upward as wall surfaces, the curves of the plan present the eye with rhythmic undulations hitherto unapproached in subtlety, and with modulations of light and shadow more delicate and various than any yet seen.

Fig. 15.19 Rome. Sant'Agnese in Piazza Navona. 1652. Designed by Borromini. (Alinari)

It is a pity that the little nave, in many ways the most exquisite designed during the 17th century, should have been marred by maladjustments. The curvature of the inner walls is somewhat obscured by the weight of a peristyle of Corinthian columns which, although engaged, project a full three-quarters of their diameter.

San Carlino is unfortunately situated; it is difficult to see its façade (Fig. 15.17) in comfort, or to photograph it properly; but no other design so perfectly fulfills the baroque ideal of a fusion between architecture and sculpture. The very walls seem to move, and the details have the nicest possible relationship to the whole. Often cited as the most extreme example of baroque architecture, it is, by exception, one of the few that seems to be at peace with itself.

Sant'Agnese in Piazza Navona (Fig. 15.19) is illustrative of Borromini's practice in buildings of greater size, and may be taken as typical of baroque ecclesiastical architecture in general. There is no other work of art which so thoroughly sets the critic against himself. Taken as a whole, the form is admirable, but an inspection of the details delights the eye with a succession of elegant motives then completely new, and familiar today because so many of them have been copied since. It is probable, for example, that no other building exhibits a like variety of door and window openings, all excellent. Novelty succeeds novelty at a rapid pace; we can scarcely see anything because something else is forever already in the corner of the eye. On this one façade, Borromini expended enough inspiration to have served for a dozen churches. In his case, content struggled within form in the sense that ideas came faster than they could be put to work.

◆ *Ceiling Painting* The Baroque taste for the spectacular brought ceiling painting into its own. Mantegna had done a proper ceiling painting at Mantua as early as 1474, and Correggio's *Assumption of the Virgin* (1524), painted on the underside of the dome of the Cathedral at Parma, remains an unsurpassed miracle of technique. But such things, when done at all, had been a special effort. During the Italian 17th century, they became almost a routine performance.

Among the notable examples, we may mention Guercino's *Aurora* in the Villa Ludovisi (1621–1623), Pietro da Cortona's *Triumph of Divine Providence* in the Barberini Palace (1633–1639), and Andrea Pozzo's *Glorification of the Company of Jesus* (Fig. 15.20), where, for the sake of legible illustration, we see only the central portion of the composition. Around the area covered by our book plate, there is a full story of baroque architecture, painted in bold foreshortening and conveying the illusion that the actual walls of the building rise continuously upward to their ultimate opening into the sky.

There could not possibly be a better illustration of the complex and subtle iconography of Catholic baroque art. At the vanishing point, where all lines of the architectural perspective converge, we find the Holy Trinity in the form of God the Father, Christ with his cross, and a Dove. Saint Ignatius is seen in ecstasy immediately below, rising heavenward on a cloud. Rays of light proceed from the Savior to the Saint. From the saint, the same rays run outward in four directions, ultimately coming to rest upon four figures (not seen in the book plate) who personify the four parts of the world: Europe, Asia, Africa, and America. As with all similar compositions, there is but one station on the floor from which an observer can look up and see all parts of the perspective in perfect order. The spot is indicated by a small circle of marble.

The more obvious meaning of the picture is indicated in a letter from the painter to Prince Lichtenstein. It has to do with the missionary enterprise of the Jesuit Order, to which Pozzo himself belonged. The imagery was suggested by Luke 12:49: "I am come to send fire on the earth. . . ." The fire referred to meant (to the painter) the fire of faith; and along with his personifications of the four continents, he included portraits of missionary saints who had distinguished themselves in each region.

A deeper and more subtle symbolism lay beneath the surface of the icon-

Fig. 15.20 Rome. Sant'Ignazio. Central portion of the ceiling painted by Andrea Pozzo, 1691–1694. *Saint Ignatius in Heaven,* sometimes called *The Glorification of the Company of Jesus.* The complete picture includes a full story of architecture beneath what we see here. The personifications of "The Four Parts of the World" appear below the portion shown. (Anderson)

ography. Pozzo was the author of a definitive work on perspective, which first appeared in 1693. It contains 100 magnificent plates, including several which illustrate his system for laying out the perspective grid on this particular ceiling. The author's foreword is addressed "To the Lovers of Perspective" and concludes with the admonition, "Therefore, Reader, my advice is that you cheerfully begin your work with a resolution to draw all the points thereof to that true point, the Glory of God; and I dare predict and promise you good success in so honorable an undertaking." The art of perspective, as conceived by Pozzo, was the artistic vehicle whereby one might make people see the direct and systematic connection betwen the Deity in heaven and each single and separate human being on earth. With that in mind, it is permissible to read a specifically Jesuit symbolism into the mark on the floor which tells one where to stand—an innovation of Pozzo's, lacking in similar and earlier situations where it would have been just as useful. The mark may be construed as a command, and the man who obeys may be thought of as submitting himself to the discipline of the perspective much as the artist had accepted the rule of the Society of Jesus. The inference is obvious that only those who so submit can hope to comprehend the divine scheme with clarity and truth; all others must accept a distorted view. The device itself (namely, the central placement of an observer) had been used during the High Renaissance (page 560), but with an almost opposite meaning.

The paragraphs above certify that Pozzo was a man of high intellectual power, with a profound grasp of theology and a formidable imagination. They also illustrate the farsighted wisdom behind the terrific emotional drive of baroque art. Pozzo's picture is exciting to a degree, but he knew that excitement doesn't last, and he produced a work which, when studied exhaustively, offers extended and continuous satisfaction for the mind. Certain reservations nevertheless remain.

No one expects to arrive at a mature understanding of any important matter, including a work of art, without knowledge and study, but only to a certain extent do we read paintings as we read literature. It is appropriate to ask that the eye be made keen by education, but another thing to substitute erudition for visual perception. It is generally thought the business of painters to find forms and figures which communicate the meaning, or most of it, to any man who is willing to use his eyes. It is a question whether pictures like this are even intelligible without a guide book and a schematic diagram.

Baroque ceiling painting opens up still another interesting question. In effect, such pictures were conceived as an indefinite upward extension of the volume enclosed by the walls. To the purist, such an illusion is hateful. "The picture blows the roof off!" he will declare. But are beams and masonry in fact sacred? How can we praise an architect for manipulating enclosed space in clever fashion, and then deny him the use of space that happens to be represented rather than actual?

BAROQUE PAINTING IN FLANDERS: RUBENS

Naturally and inevitably, our survey of the Baroque in Italy has involved us in continuous preoccupation with the Counter-Reformation, possibly to the exclusion of a proper concern for other matters. On the broader stage of Europe as a whole, other great forces were in motion, and the artist most concerned with them was Peter Paul Rubens (1577–1640), a Fleming by birth and, in the literal sense of the words, a man of the world.

His parents were of the minor gentry, and as a boy, he served for a time as a page in the household of Princess Margaret of Ligne. He was educated in the classics and soundly trained as a painter. In 1600, he went to Italy in the service of Vincenzo Gonzaga, Duke of Mantua, one of the greatest collectors of the period. Gonzaga's gallery contained some of the finest Titians, Correggios, Tintorettos, Carraccis, and Caravaggios.

Such pictures offered Rubens the best imaginable schooling in Italian are, and he made excellent use of it. As early as 1603, however, his talents as a courtier caused the Duke to divert him from painting into diplomacy, and Rubens was sent off to Spain, the first of several trips there, with a gift of horses and pictures for Philip the 3rd and a delicate mission to accomplish. Other missions for the Gonzaga took him at times to Genoa, to Venice, and to Rome. In each place, he did some painting and was most cordially entertained.

The death of his mother called him back to Antwerp in 1608. Flanders, it will be recalled, had remained Catholic, and was governed from Spain by the Regents Albrecht and Isabella. Relations with Protestant Holland were comparatively peaceful, and the region was becoming prosperous again. Almost as soon as he arrived, Rubens was made court painter to the regents, and immediately found himself besieged with more commissions than he could possibly handle personally.

The situation did not phase or delay him. He promptly organized a corps of assistants and set them to work in an establishment that has correctly been called a factory. It speaks well for both his ability and his character that he had no trouble hiring artists to do his work; in 1611, he said he had been forced to turn down a hundred applicants—a number which may be more indicative than precise.

He worked out an excellent technical procedure for the production of paintings. He himself made brief sketches to indicate the composition and the broader arrangement of colors. Assistants enlarged these, prepared the canvas, and laid on the essential undercoating, using transparent pigments. When these were partly dry, the master usually stepped in to add, with his own hand, the final touches (usually in opaque colors) which brought the picture to life.

Whenever events proceeded as described, the finished painting was very nearly as fine as though Rubens had done all of it himself. Rubens, however, was an exceedingly busy man. Some times he did much, and some times he did little. For that reason, many pictures that bear his name are curiously uneven and all too evidently the work of several hands. No deception was involved; in fact there is reason to believe his financial methods were scrupulously honest: patrons paid for what they got and knew what they had bought.

After the death of her husband (1621), the Regent Isabella turned much to Rubens as a counselor upon whom she could rely, and from that time until her death in 1633, he was almost continuously engaged in missions of one kind or another. He was in Paris off and on from 1622 to 1625, superintending the painting of twenty-one great pictures in the then new Luxembourg. Commissioned by Queen Marie de Médicis, they tell the history of her life, and have ever since been the paradigm for all art devoted to political propaganda. In 1625, the Duke of Buckingham persuaded Rubens to go to Spain as special envoy for England in the hope of negotiating a final peace between the two powers. He was there for nine months and was back again in 1628, only to be sent to England by the Spanish to do the same thing. After seven months at the court of Charles 1st, where he was cordially received, but less than successful in diplomacy, he returned to Flanders in 1629. In London, he had been commissioned to decorate the ceiling of the Banqueting Hall of the great new palace of Whitehall (page 818), and left sketches from which the work was done by assistants. It is worth noting, also, that he was knighted in both Spain and England.

Rubens seems to have derived his figure style from Michelangelo and his mode of painting from Titian. It took him some time to develop what we think of as his mature and characteristic manner. The familiar self-portrait (in Munich) with his first wife Isabella, probably painted shortly after their marriage in 1609, scarcely seems to predict the drama and exuberance which make his name literally a synonym for the Baroque. The picture has great sentimental interest, but considered critically, it must be described as an unusually competent attempt to do the Grand Style in northern terms. The detail is prolix, even tedious. The modeling is labored, and the figures and draperies are unpleasantly wiry. The conclusion suggests itself that when he found himself forced into mass production, Rubens was also forced to realize his own personality.

Fig. 15.21 Rubens. *Crucifixion*. 1620. Antwerp, Museum. (Stoedtner)

The *Crucifixion* (Fig. 15.21), more properly the *Crucifragium*, shows the painter in maturity and may be taken as typical of his religious work. Because sentence had been carried out on the day before the Sabbath of Passover week, the Jews were apparently able to persuade the Roman governor to respect the law stated in Deuteronomy 21:22–23 which held that a crucified man must be taken down and buried before night. The governor therefore sent soldiers to dispatch Christ and the two thieves, but the Savior was already dead when they arrived. Either in sheer brutality, or in order to make certain of death, one of them thrust a lance into his side. Blood and water gushed out, a circumstance which later gave rise to an assertion that Jesus died of a broken heart. Still another legend has it that the soldier who delivered the *coup de lance* was the same soldier who exclaimed, "Truly this man was the Son of God!" The Gospels are far from definite on the point, and the church has never endorsed the story, but rightly or wrongly this Roman soldier became known as Saint Longinus. In that character, and dressed in military costume, he occupies a conspicuous position in numerous paintings of the Crucifixion.

Fig. 15.22 Rubens. *Rape of the Daughters of Leucippus*. About 1619. Munich, Alte Pinakothek.

The diagonal perspective, reminiscent of Tintoretto, enabled Rubens to render musculature from a variety of angles. The writhing of the two thieves makes not only a physical but a spiritual contrast with the dignity of Christ, who seems resigned and accepting, even in death. The fine horses, the gleaming armor and the professional cruelty of the soldiers are fit symbols for the power of the Roman government, which seems strangely nonessential by comparison with the still, white figure on the cross.

If Rubens had any serious fault, it was the fault of his northern heritage which impelled him, to the very end of his career, toward myriad detail. The tendency was not diminished by the general trend of baroque art. For the purpose of understanding his style, a comparatively simple picture like the *Rape of the Daughters of Leucippus* (Fig. 15.22) is therefore more useful than some other compositions.

His debt to Michelangelo is obvious; indeed, he is the only artist who ever possessed sheer power in the same measure as Michelangelo. But there are important differences. Michelangelo remained a sculptor even when painting; his figures have a closer affinity to marble than to warm flesh. Rubens, even when defining contours, was more interested in texture and color than in shape. Taken as a whole, this picture has an excellent and complex rhythm of lights and darks, an accomplishment learned from the Venetians. Inspected for detail, the various textures are differentiated not only with formidable subtlety but with an enthusiasm that is absolutely carnal— an enthusiasm to which many persons refuse to respond, but one which was typical not only of the artist but of the era.

Michelangelo often presented us with ponderous figures struggling to move, but denied motion (page 685). Rubens unleased his people and let them go. Heavy masses in motion were not only a feature of his own art, but a feature of all baroque art; even in the abstract art of architecture, there is always the suggestion of activity. The movement might be fast, as it usually was in Rubens's own work, or it might be deliberate; but invariably, baroque movement was strong.

The dynamics of baroque subject matter posed difficult problems of composition. If allowed to run wild, such material could not be confined within the frame. Rubens's standard solution was to make the action proceed in a curvilinear manner, containing itself by the direction in which it goes. His geometry was admirably easy, but we seldom lose assurance that the moving figures mill about within the limits of a circular or elliptical figure. Some times the limiting outline falls flat on the picture plane. More often, it lies diagonally thereto, and frequently with a compound inclination as in Figure 15.23. In every instance, the principle is the same, and no different from that invoked by Little Black Sambo when he persuaded the tigers to chase each other around and around until they all turned to butter.

Rubens made something of a hobby, in fact, of hunting scenes like the one shown in Figure 15.23. In most of them, nude men and armed men are seen at intimate quarters with tigers, crocodiles, lions, hippopotami, and other beasts. Both sides are invariably raised to fury and fight with indescribable hate and desperation. The idea of using subjects of extreme violence may have occurred to Rubens when he saw and made a drawing after Leonardo's lost *Battle of Anghiari* (page 587). He had a classical source, as well, from what he must have heard about gladiatorial combats in the Colosseum; but it is doubtful whether the Roman mob was ever entertained by anything quite so impossibly sanguinary as the combats Rubens managed to conjure up. We may hazard a shrewd guess that such pictures were technical tours de force and that he was trying to see how much confusion he could depict and still make the scene compose.

Rubens's first wife, Isabella Brandt, died in 1626; and in 1630, at the age of fifty-two, Rubens married Hélène Fourment, then sixteen years old. The union was an extremely happy one. There are many portraits of Hélène; she appears nude in numerous classical pictures, and often as the Madonna. She had golden hair and an unusually opulent figure, conforming almost per-

Fig. 15.23 Rubens. *Lion Hunt*. About 1617. Munich, Alte Pinakothek.

fectly with the female canon so familiar in her husband's paintings. The
calendar makes it impossible, however, that she can have been the original
inspiration for the typical Rubens female.

His health impaired by incessant strain, Rubens retired in 1635 and took
up residence at Steen, his country house near Antwerp. Paintings from his
premature old age have a personal quality necessarily absent from his ceremonial art. Many, like the portrait of Hélène with her two children (Fig.
15.24) are moderately impressionistic, perhaps more oil sketches than finished
paintings. In Vienna, there is a half-length portrait of the painter himself,
done a year or two before his death, when he was still the perfect courtier,
but a weary man.

He was nevertheless able to make one more great contribution: he gave
the weight of his tremendous authority to landscape painting, a department
of art which had scarcely been in existence prior to the 17th century. Landscape settings had, of course, been familiar enough for more than two hundred years, but it is difficult to think of a landscape which was not secondary,
both in fact and in theory, to some classical or religious theme, or perhaps as
a mere contribution to the mood of a portrait.

Like other baroque artists, Rubens painted landscape for itself, without
a hint of apology. His *Landscape with the Chateau of Steen* (Fig. 15.25) has
always been a favorite. It is one of the happiest pictures he ever produced,

Fig. 15.24   Rubens. *Hélène Fourment and Her Two Children*. Paris, Louvre. (Giraudon)

more a celebration of country life in general than a portrait of a place. The eye looks out and down as though from an eminence. The space pulsates with light and air, and one feels the life of growing things. The picture is rich with incident, as though to demonstrate in a single view the great gentleman's pleasure in the life he led there. He died in 1640.

BAROQUE ART IN SPAIN

Spain was never a political unit until the marriage of Ferdinand and Isabella (1469), which united the ancient kingdoms of Leon, Castile, and Aragon. Those enlightened monarchs gave the peninsula a reasonably efficient central administration. Every one remembers their aid to Columbus, but contemporary opinion must have thought it even more important that 1492 marked the expulsion of the last of the Moors from Granada. That achievement was unique in history, for Spain, and Spain alone, has freed itself from the Arab Conquest which had started in the Near East a full seven centuries before (page 216).

Fig. 15.25 Rubens. *Landscape with the Château of Steen.* 54 by 92½ inches. London, National Gallery.

Juana, the daughter of Ferdinand and Isabella, had married Philip, Archduke of Austria, who died in 1506. Juana lived forty-nine years thereafter, but she was hopelessly insane. Her father therefore assumed the regency for her son Charles (born 1500) and held it until his own death in 1516.

Charles was a Hapsburg, educated in Flanders. He assumed the Spanish throne at once, and was elected Holy Roman Emperor as Charles 5th in 1520. Spain was thus only one of his territories. His nominal holdings included part of France, the Low Countries, most of what we now call Germany and Austria, plus Sicily and South Italy. During the 16th century, nominal holdings remained nominal unless a ruler asserted himself. Charles's ramified interests thus involved Spain in almost continuous warfare as the Emperor sought, without anything like real success, to assert and maintain what he claimed as his own. Titian's portrait (Figure 14.40, page 636) commemorates one of his many victories.

Charles's operations cost an appalling amount in both blood and money, and would have been impossible except for the success Spain enjoyed in the New World. He sent Cortes to Mexico (1519–1521) and he sent Pizarro to Peru (1531–1535). Those expeditions form a tragic chapter in American history, but the economic effect in Europe was pronounced. It was a regular occurrence for ships to arrive at Seville literally ballasted with gold. But gold was only one kind of wealth that was flowing into Europe. Vessels came and went to and from the Americas and the Far East, fetching into all the ports commodities of a variety and quantity never before imagined. If we wonder why the Baroque was inclined to be exuberant, let us remember this: the 17th century was the period when the resources of the entire globe were rapidly being made available to the inhabitants of western Europe.

Charles started to hand over authority to his son Philip the 2nd as early as 1554. The complicated procedure was complete by 1558. Charles formally abdicated and retired to a monastery. His act of renunciation had a profound effect upon the psychology of all Catholic lands, and the memory of it did much to govern Philip's policies.

Philip was a man of the very greatest ability. He never made a decision until after an exhaustive study of the facts, and only then with the utmost care about its results. His most important determination (doubtless discussed with his father) was to make himself known primarily as the King of Spain, and to make the Spanish dynasty the most powerful force in the entire world. It is beyond our subject to follow his political and military operations in all their fascinating detail, but the history of art does much to explain the character and purpose of the man.

Having decided to live in Spain, Philip chose Madrid for his capital. Not every one has been happy about the decision, but he had his reasons for it. The place was unimportant, badly situated, with a climate that has become notorious. The King did little to improve the small city, and it is a fact that well into the 18th century Madrid remained a shabby place with a shifting and unstable population. From the monarch's standpoint, however, Madrid had advantages. Because it had no historical tradition behind it, the crown remained impartial with respect to the claims of rival places, and even neutralized such rivalries. Because Madrid was an unattractive place to live, no one would willingly live there unless the King needed him. In part, this was no more than a reflection of the monarch's personal taste for solitude. In part, it was a shrewd measure calculated to reduce the horde of sycophants among whom most powerful men were compelled to live.

The new capital demanded a new royal palace, but Philip did not build it in Madrid. After searching some time for a site, he chose the village of Escorial, a full thirty miles to the north and west on the slope of the Sierra de Guadarrama. The immense fabric he erected there is officially named Real Monasterio de San Lorenzo del Escorial, and in English has always been known simply as "the Escorial." Preliminary work started promptly in 1559. It appears that the foundations were in place by 1563 when the original architect died and Juan de Herrera took over.

Fig. 15.26 The Escorial. 1563–1582. Designed by Juan Bautista de Toledo and Juan de Herrera. (Anderson)

As a work of art, the Escorial (Fig. 15.26) has never been popular with historians and critics. Indeed, as a work of art, it may even have been a failure, but no monument is more illustrative of its time and place. Philip had a variety of motives for building it, and it is remarkable how well he and his architect succeeded in combining and accommodating them.

The Escorial is more than a palace. It is a palace attached to a church and a monastery. The plan (675 feet by 530) is a square with a handlelike projection on one side. The resemblance to the gridiron on which Saint Laurence had suffered martyrdom has often been pointed out and was probably intentional. In one of his campaigns, Philip had been compelled to destroy a church of Saint Laurence with artillery fire, and the dedication was his penance.

In both plan and elevation, the most conspicuous feature is an immense church, approached through an atrium nearly two hundred feet long, with a dome over the crossing topped by a cross more than three hundred feet in the air. This church was intended to serve as the chapel for the convent, the buildings of which extend around it, and as a tomb for the dynasty.

Everything combined to make the Escorial one of the most austere piles in Europe. Outside and in, it was built from a local granite, yellowish gray in color. Both Philip and his architect had reacted strongly against the extravagance of Late Gothic architecture in Spain, and both were doubtless suspicious of the Italian Renaissance which had done so much to bring about the Reformation. They therefore chose to use their somber granite in the most academic manner conceivable. Baroque motives are unmistakable in the whole, but the details make Palladio's classicism seem almost frivolous. The capitals and pilasters are Doric. The statues are so few that they seem lonely. All the moldings are so chaste as to be negative.

As an expression of taste, the Escorial comports perfectly with the Spanish notions of propriety, dress, and manners which were then affecting Italy and the rest of the Catholic world. But the Escorial is much more than a reflection of what was fashionable for a period; it is a peculiarly consistent monument to the Spanish concept of religion and government.

Catholicism was the ruling factor in Spanish life. The long struggle against the Moors had made the people regard themselves as the chosen defenders of the faith. The ultimate victory over the infidel intensified this feeling. A fervid religiosity developed and took on a peculiarly ecstatic slant, which presently developed into self-conscious mysticism—sometimes exalted and sometimes merely sentimental.

The force of circumstances had, however, made the Spaniard a practical man of action. The Reformation, coming so soon after the capture of Granada, confronted him with the necessity for another crusade against heretics of an even more dangerous kind; and thus it was that the cause of the Spanish dynasty became identical with the cause of the Counter-Reformation. In the political sphere, Philip considered himself the special instrument of God, and his entire policy hinged around his determination to stamp out Protestantism.

There was an open analogy between the Vatican and the Escorial. Each was a palace attached to a church, and if St. Peter's was the larger church, the chapel of the Escorial was large enough and its dome looked very much like the one at Rome, a resemblance which was immediately noticed. But where St. Peter's extended welcome and offered a certain measure of joy, the Escorial did the opposite. Its grim walls forbade access, psychologically speaking, to any one who had the hardihood to make the journey to so remote a place. Within the vast complex, and in a set of rooms designed for privacy and even secrecy, the King conducted the government. Couriers came and went constantly, fetching and carrying an unbelievable number of papers, most of which Philip read himself, and in the margins of which his intelligent comments may be seen today. It was there that he received in March, 1587, the dispatch that told him of Mary Stuart's execution five weeks before—the event which swung the balance of his judgment in favor of an invasion of England, with results we all know.

It is scarcely too much to say that the monument which records this man, this philosophy, and this situation is also the prime monument of the entire Counter-Reformation.

♦ *Spanish Baroque Painting* The kings of Spain were great collectors, but Spain itself produced no great painters until the latter part of the 16th century. Until that time, the general run of native painting had been derivative from Flanders, with inevitable but usually temporary intrusions of influence from Italy (page 486).

Oddly enough, the first great Spanish painter, and the most Spanish of them all, was Domenikos Theotokopoulos (1541–1614) now universally called *El Greco,* who emigrated to Spain and arrived at Toledo about 1575, doubtless in the hope of participating in the decoration of the Escorial.

There has been a great deal of unnecessary speculation about the sources of El Greco's extreme style. His biography, which is now known with reasonable certainty, explains it easily enough.

The man was born at Candia, in Crete, at a time when Candia was a Venetian possession, but artistically still a Byzantine outpost. His earliest artistic experience, therefore, was with later Byzantine art of a rather extreme kind. If we knew more about Byzantine art, we could be more definite about the pictures El Greco recalled from his boyhood, but the Madonna in the apse at Torcello (Fig. 9.18, page 301) will serve to suggest what we mean.

In the natural course of events, El Greco made his way to Venice. A letter is preserved from 1570, when he went to Rome, introducing him to the Cardinal Farnese as a young and able "disciple" of Titian. While not conclusive, the evidence certainly suggests that he had worked in Titian's shop. If so, it was at the period when Titian himself was affected by the Counter-Reformation (page 637). Stylistically, however, El Greco seems to have learned more from Tintoretto. He doubtless learned much from any number of other Italian artists: the Bassani, for example, and Parmigianino. Although not often mentioned, the emotional influence of Michelangelo was profound even if stylistic analogies are far from close.

In attempting to know El Greco one must, in fact, always give unusual weight to emotional factors. His mature and characteristic art did not emerge until he had gone to Spain and lived there for some time. Undoubtedly he did much painting before he left Italy. Rather little of it has come down to us, and one can not help wondering whether some pictures are not labeled with other names. There is a half-length portrait of a Venetian gentleman in Copenhagen, for example, which long passed for a Tintoretto; and without the signature, the Naples portrait of Giulio Clovio might be mistaken for the work of Francesco Bassano. The portrait of Vincenzo Anastagi in the Frick collection is more than a little like Veronese. These are all excellent pictures

Fig. 15.27 El Greco. *The Assumption of the Virgin.* 1577. 158 by 90 inches. Courtesy of the Art Institute of Chicago, Gift of Nancy Atwood Sprague in memory of Albert Arnold Sprague.

in the sense of conforming to the best standards of Italian technique. They show nothing of the painter's Byzantine heritage, however, and if taken alone, they certainly would not suggest his Spanish future.

Even after he arrived at Toledo, El Greco's emotional intensification did not come at once. The *Assumption of the Virgin* (Fig. 15.27) was one of his first important commissions there. It is an uncommonly splendid picture, but it is still a Venetian rather than a Spanish painting—a frank and obvious adaptation, in fact, of Titian's own *Assumption* (1518) in the Church of the Frari at Venice.

Without much doubt, King Philip's brief interest in the newcomer resulted from El Greco's ability to paint like Titian, from whose hand the monarch had a number of canvases, some of them ordered directly from the master himself. In 1580, he summoned El Greco to the Escorial, and set him

Fig. 15.28 El Greco. *The Burial of the Count of Orgaz*. 1586. 192 by 142 inches. Toledo, Santo Tome. (Anderson)

to work on a *Martyrdom of Saint Maurice* (it is still there) intended for one of the altars. The picture is not like Titian. It is, indeed, one of the earliest paintings in El Greco's peculiarly personal manner. The King didn't like it, and commissioned no others.

The new manner which offended the King had the opposite effect among the citizens of Toledo, to which place the artist then returned, and where he enjoyed substantial prosperity. The picture which established his reputation was *The Burial of the Count of Orgaz* (Fig. 15.28), commissioned for the church of St. Thomas in 1586.

According to the legend, the good count had been a generous benefactor of that church. Some time after his death in 1323, and in accordance with his wishes, the body was moved for permanent interment within the building. Just as the priests were about to translate the body, Saint Stephen and Saint Augustine appeared from heaven and lowered it into the tomb with their own hands. No one seems aware of the miracle except the little boy on the left who looks out and calls our attention to it, and the priest on the right who alone is permitted a vision of the upper register where we see the count received in heaven by Christ and the Virgin.

This is a strange picture. It requires a readjustment of Renaissance standards of taste and vision, but, historically speaking, it is not a difficult picture to understand.

The faces are Iberian types, only slightly exaggerated for purposes of emphasis. Considered as portraits, they are incisive, very nearly realistic.

The canon of proportions is Byzantine, and as such, by no means extreme (page 226).

The poses come directly from Tintoretto (page 642), and the rendering of textures, both of flesh and of stuffs, is typically Venetian. It is only the Byzantine distortion of the vertical dimension which makes these people seem abnormal.

The lighting follows no logic; it is the lighting of the Venetian mode (page 621). Following in the footsteps of Tintoretto in this respect, El Greco manipulated the light calligraphically. It will be noted that the lighted areas are strips that bend and turn and often have a flamelike outline.

The setting is less easy to describe and to comprehend. The somber color scheme and the torches tell us that the time is night, and the ceremony is one normally carried on within a church—of which building, however, not a detail is in view. In this painting (but not in some others) El Greco maintained a distinction between earth and heaven, a boundary line which is obvious if not actual.

But are we to understand that this was a real church, the very one that still stands in Toledo? The manipulation of space makes an answer impossible; doubtless the painter intended the ambiguity. The foreshortening of the figures demands that we grant the existence of depth in some slight measure, and yet the whole picture has a curiously two-dimensional atmosphere. It would seem that the artist was yearning after the mystical and impenetrable background familiar in Byzantine art, at the same time using Renaissance techniques of representation. Thus we experience a sense of real people in an environment that is not so much abstract as super-sensory.

We do not know El Greco's biography in detail, but we know enough to say that no man could have been better suited by temperament to paint the perfervidly Catholic pictures that were so much in demand in Spain during the Counter-Reformation. He was a man who sat in darkened rooms on sunny days and talked of an inner light. He was a man who visited the insane and tried to see in their faces an insight denied to ordinary persons. He was a reader; among his books were the writings of famous mystics, with whose words he was familiar. He was a man, moreover, driven by inward passion, possibly a man who felt himself chosen to perform a particular mission on earth. Not everybody liked his pictures, and there were those who protested against them. Toward all such, he behaved with an arrogance that bespeaks more than mere confidence in his art.

Many contend that the *Burial* is El Greco's greatest picture. Certainly it

Fig. 15.29 El Greco. *The Vision of St. John the Divine,* sometimes called *The Breaking of the Fifth Seal.* 1608–1614. 88½ by 78¾ inches. New York, courtesy of The Metropolitan Museum of Art. Rogers Fund, 1956.

was a work in which moderation still tempered his tendency toward extravagant expressionism (page 496). Having discovered that his more extreme manner pleased not only himself but his patrons, it was only natural that his later painting would move in that direction. A comparison between the early *Assumption* (Fig. 15.27) and the very late *Breaking of the Fifth Seal* (Fig. 15.29) will tell the story better than a thousand words. The imagery of the latter is as visionary as the Apocalypse itself. The setting is strenuously ethereal, and the actors have become ectoplasmic.

Even to some of his Spanish contemporaries, El Greco's later religious painting seemed so vehement as to be unwise, but his portraits remained uniformly rational. The Metropolitan Museum has the most famous of them all, the *Don Fernando Nino de Guevara,* the Grand Inquisitor of Spain. It is a superbly decorative picture and a striking study of character, but there are those who prefer the *Fray Hortensio,* seen in Figure 15.30. The Dominican habit in somber black and white are perhaps even more impressive than the Inquisitor's red vestments, and it is hard to forget either the brilliantly intelligent face or the sense of animal power in the body. It is interesting that the date is 1609, the very time when the painter was accused of having cast discretion to the winds.

Any critical estimate of El Greco must take account of recent history. The fame he enjoyed at Toledo did not last long even there, and he literally dropped out of sight except for an occasional notice in the diary of some traveler who happened to pass by. The late Professor Mather recorded that in 1904, when he first visited Toledo, he actually did not know that the *Burial* existed, was taken by surprise when he entered the church and saw it, and was by no means prepared to understand it. As late as 1920, Max Dvorak gave a public lecture in Vienna * in which he undertook not only to explain El Greco to his audience, but to introduce them to his name.

During the last forty years, El Greco's reputation has increased not only greatly, but inordinately. Modern artists have praised him because he gave them a sanction for expressionism, surrealism, and a negation of the representative convention in general. Museums and private collectors have competed with each other for his canvases; today, even the most minor work commands a fabulous price. Historians and critics, often the very men who have been solemn and judicial when writing about other artists, have published page after page of enthusiastic comment, much of which reads like advertising. Members of the public, perhaps because dissatisfied with our secular and scientific environment, have found in El Greco an expression of spiritual values all too rarely thought of in this generation.

No painter could have achieved such prominence without a measure of greatness, but it is time we recognized El Greco for what he actually was and is.

It is significant that he made a habit of repeating the same composition again and again, making only minor changes which were not always refinements. It is thus obvious that his technical procedure was less passionate than the emotions he calculated to arouse. There is little doubt that his motives were mercenary, but that is perhaps beside the point. The important consideration is this: an artist of greater creative power would have had no need to repeat himself, and one must concede that the content of El Greco's art, while intense, is always very much the same. His positive virtues have been set forth above. They were considerable. They justify enthusiasm. It is nevertheless true that El Greco was a rather narrow artist, with nothing like the range of Giotto, Donatello, and many others.

None of these reservations militate against the truth that El Greco was brilliantly successful in giving an almost tangible reality to the ecstatic visions of Spanish Catholicism. His younger contemporary *Jusepe Ribera* (about 1591–1652) is to be remembered as an exponent of quite a different aspect of the same movement.

Probably because his father held a post in the Spanish government at

* English translation by John Coolidge in *The Magazine of Art* for January, 1953.

Fig. 15.30 El Greco. *Portrait of Fray Hortensio Pallavicino.* 1609. 44½ by 33¾ inches. Boston, Museum of Fine Arts.

Naples, Ribera left for Italy after early artistic training in Spain. He sojourned for some time in Parma, then in Rome, and arrived at Naples in 1616, where he soon married and where he spent the rest of his life. Tradition says that he was a notorious ruffian and the leader of a gang of ruffians. Doubtless the tradition reflects some measure of anti-Spanish sentiment on the part of the Neapolitans, but it is remarkably consistent with the pictures he painted.

In a general way, Ribera developed his manner of painting from Caravaggio. He chose his models from humble, even vulgar folk, and was especially fascinated by old men with dry skin and corrugated faces. Like Caravaggio, he crowded the darks, but his surfaces are very different. Caravaggio usually ended up with an almost mirrorlike finish. Ribera loaded the canvas with paint and streaked it into a state of coruscation. The method rendered the texture of elderly skin in a fashion almost painfully vivid and produced an uncomfortable sensation of much light and no air.

His studies of old men were easily adaptable to "character pictures" of various kinds, and he used them as apostles, saints (Fig. 15.31), and philosophers—demonstrating, in the last category, a preference for the vagrant

Fig. 15.31 Ribera. *St. Jerome.* Cambridge, Massachusetts, Fogg Art Museum.

thinkers (Diogenes, for example) who might appropriately be presented in terms of vulgar genre.

In more complicated religious paintings, Ribera made a specialty of martyrdoms, that of Saint Bartholomew (Fig. 15.32) being merely the most famous among many. In these pictures, he made it his duty to describe the event with a physical accuracy nothing short of brutal.

Regardless of their utility as Catholic propaganda, Ribera's martyrdoms are revolting to the modern observer, who must make a considerable effort to appreciate that the 17th century was a time when large crowds assembled to see hangings and burnings, in which they took an intense interest even when they sympathized with the victim. Even so, Ribera was a morbid personality. He sought out strange and unhealthy subject matter: deformed children, women who grew beards, and so on. It is significant that his most important classical pictures were a series of famous punishments, among which is a *Prometheus* that is shocking indeed.

At the time of which we write, the church employed, in one capacity or another, about one third of the Spanish population, and there were approxi-

Fig. 15.32   Ribera. *Martyrdom of Saint Bartholomew*. Madrid, Prado, (Anderson)

mately nine thousand monasteries on the peninsula. It will be recalled that
Santa Teresa had been active in reorganizing the Carmelite Order, and
what was true of the Carmelites was true of all the others: the period of the
Counter-Reformation produced improved administration, more rigorous discipline, and a general return to more austere standards of spiritual exercise.

Francisco de Zurbarán (1598–1644) was the great painter of Spanish
monasticism. It is true that he ultimately came to the attention of the court,
received an appointment there, and moved to Madrid in 1650; but he had
been born in a provincial place in Estremadura and retained throughout his
career a certain provincial calmness and solidity. His most famous painting is
the *Saint Bonaventure on His Bier* in the Louvre (1629), but it is scarcely more
impressive than some others. Simple piety is a trite phrase, but a refreshingly
descriptive one, especially when we compare Zurbarán with either El Greco or
Ribera. There is something sober and dignified even in his most emotional
work (Fig. 15.33). His art is a record of the sound and unspectacular faith
that still keeps Spain the most sincerely Catholic land in Europe.

Fig. 15.33 Zurbarán. *Saint Serapion*. 1628. Hartford, Wadsworth Atheneum.

Philip the 3rd (regnal dates 1598–1621) lacked both his father's ability and his taste for government. He limited his personal attention to the interests of the church, and left secular affairs to his *privado*, the Duke of Lerma, with unfortunate results. The administration became the subject of court intrigue, often of corruption. The noble families were able to assemble vast estates, which they, in turn, did not manage wisely. Many areas became depopulated from the loss of manpower in the wars. Emigration to the colonies contributed still further to the unfortunate situation. Agriculture declined, and so did the industry and trade which had flourished during the 16th century. Spain became simply a wool-raising country, and it is from this reign that we date the decadence and lethargy which was to characterize Spanish culture for the next three hundred years.

Philip the 4th, who reigned from 1621 to 1665, was an amiable prince, but he did not care to exert himself politically or economically. He was wise enough to put matters in the hands of the vigorous Count of Olivares, but the situation had already gone too far.

It was to this court that there came in 1623, through Olivares' good offices, the painter *Diego Velázquez* (1599–1661).* He had been summoned to try his hand at painting a portrait of the king. This proved so very satis-

* As with *Don Quixote*, the pronunciation has long been completely Anglicized.

factory that Philip at once made him court painter and declared that he would sit for no one else. The two men seem to have been remarkably congenial, and it was not very long before Velázquez found himself with other duties than painting. In the end, he became the chamberlain responsible for all public ceremonials, of which there were many, and for the operation of the domestic establishment of the royal family. On the face of it, it seems a pity that so able an artist should have been diverted into work of another kind, but the obvious is not always true. Velázquez was guaranteed an excellent living in circumstances that were entirely congenial to him; and far from interfering with his art, the King appears to have given him an unusually free hand to paint as he pleased.

We have all the essential details about Velázquez' biography before he arrived at Madrid. At the age of twelve, he had been apprenticed to the painter Francisco Herrera the Elder, a man of notoriously bad temper. Arrangements were made for a shift to the shop of Francisco Pacheco, whose daughter Velázquez married in 1618. Herrera was an aggressively realistic artist with a taste that seems curiously lacking in refinement. Pacheco might be described as an academic, but at least he was a cultured man, the center of a group of humanists and the author of a treatise on painting. Neither man, nor the two together, offer an adequate explanation for the early style of Velázquez, and it is worth remarking, also, that direct contact with the work of Caravaggio or Ribera, while conceivable, has not been proven.

But in some way or other, and while still a boy, Velázquez must have become familiar with the work of both those masters, and he soon made himself a specialist in painting genre pictures of the type known in Spain as *bodegon* (Fig. 15.34). Born with the best hands any painter ever had, he could, at the age of fourteen or fifteen, manipulate the pigments as skillfully as any one who ever lived. He seems, also, to have been born with the keenest imaginable sense for subtle optical phenomena; thus even these ostensibly derivative paintings contain passages at that date highly original and still startling. Except for his sympathy for the dignity, even the aristocracy, of the humbler folk of Spain, we might dismiss the *Mary and Martha* as a little domestic scene containing some uncommonly good still life. The main subject, however, is not what one might think. It is contained in the mirror at the upper right, where we see Christ with the two ladies before him. There was complaint then, and there still is, that a solemn religious story is a proper subject for neither genre nor a parade of technical virtuosity. Be that as it may, the composition is a picture within a picture, an achievement for which no praise can be too high. No amount of borrowing from older painters can possibly explain it. It is obvious that Velázquez himself had made an extensive and intensive research into natural phenomena.

When he came to Madrid, he was called upon to turn out paintings of

Fig. 15.34 Velázquez. *Christ at the House of Mary and Martha.* London, National Gallery.

a more formal and ceremonial kind. His royal portraits were so numerous that today lesser but still superb examples are rather widely distributed in the museums. It was fortunate for the royal family that he was there to paint them because it is difficult to imagine any subject matter less inspiring. As human animals, the members of the dynasty were not the best examples. They were accustomed to dressing themselves in costumes which would be flambuoyant were they not so hideous—one thinks of the Infanta Margarita, for instance, in a skirt wider than the total height of the wearer. There were no traits of character to ameliorate these unhappy physical facts. The then royalty was incompetent, degenerate, and dull.

The unhealthy situation apparently impressed Velázquez as a technical problem. The royal collections gave him access to any number of the best Italian paintings; and he gradually abandoned the thick impasto of his early *bodegones,* and developed a thin, semi-impressionistic technique something like that of the later Titians. He had a marvelous taste for the harmony of colors and the interplay of warm and cool tones. He was clever with the arrangement of things and posed his sitters in surroundings of furniture and hangings calculated to make the figure an organic part of an excellent composition. The resulting portraits remain among the most gorgeous of all time. The preposterous costumes became beautiful areas because of the way he used them. The vacuous faces seem almost benign amid the sheen of hair, the glimmer of satin, and the glitter of jewels.

His very success in this department of art illustrates, however, the limitations of the man. It is a tenuous rationalization to suggest that he felt an esoteric beauty in the delinquency of the aristocratic. The contention that he painted the principle of royalty, as contrasted with the person, is equally thin. There is really nothing to suggest that he was disturbed by sociological considerations, and much that points to the conclusion that he was merely devoting his great talents to the task assigned him by a master who paid him well.

Rubens was in Spain for a long visit during the year 1628. He and Velázquez were friendly, and it is generally assumed that Rubens advised a trip to Italy. An opportunity to go there in distinguished company was promptly at hand: the King was sending one of his ablest generals to represent the Spanish interest in some negotiations at Mantua. This man was Ambrogio di Spinola, by birth Genoese and member of a famous family. The painter attached himself to Spinola's train and set out from Barcelona in 1629, not returning until 1631.

While in Italy, Velázquez spent most of his time at Venice, and visited Rome. The association with Spinola was what made the journey important, however, because it resulted in *The Surrender of Breda* (Fig. 15.35), commemorating Spinola's greatest victory. The painting was finished in 1635, five years after Spinola's death and ten years after the event depicted. The dates are interesting. Spinola himself had experienced military reverses between 1625 and 1630, and worse than that, Olivares was his enemy and his machinations were successful. It must, therefore, have taken considerable force of conviction to gain royal consent for making Spinola the hero of a major canvas.

Magnanimity is the real subject of the painting. From the left, we see Justin of Nassau walking forward with the keys to the city, at which Spinola does not even glance. He is concerned, instead, with a gracious gesture of admiration and kindness, calculated to allay in some measure the heartbreak of defeat. The vast space of the background (much more effective in color) operates to lend an epic tone to the situation. The lances against the sky suggest the immediate presence of a great army and contrast with the uncertainly held pikes of the exhausted Dutchmen.

Velázquez' second Italian journey commenced in January, 1649, and was ostensibly undertaken to buy still more Italian art for the royal collections. One wonders whether Velázquez was not rather glad to get away. At any rate, he stayed away for what seems a very long time, and returned in June 1651 only after receiving repeated injunctions from the King to come home.

Fig. 15.35 Velázquez. *The Surrender of Breda.* 1635. 121 by 144 inches. Madrid, Prado. (Anderson)

While at Rome, the Spanish master was cordially received by Bernini, Poussin, and other artists; and Pope Innocent the 10th commanded a portrait (Fig. 15.36). The commission was only natural, perhaps, in view of the fact that Innocent had reversed the policy of his predecessor, and was favoring the Hapsburg interests rather than the French, but it is more than evident that the painter's duty to flatter the Hapsburgs did not extend to their allies.

The portrait is, in fact, nothing short of astounding. The colors are brilliant, but harsh and strident. Instead of the usual urbane repose, the composition is made uneasy by directional forces that pull the eye uncomfortably this way and that. It is significant that this gross male was notoriously under the thumb of a rapacious sister-in-law. Velázquez obviously recognized that his apparent force was choler and trickery, and that his sensuality lacked warmth. He felt, also, the enormity of having such a man in the Chair of Saint Peter.

The two paintings just discussed are, from the standpoint of content, the greatest Velázquez ever did; but, from the standpoint of technique, both were

Fig. 15.36 Velázquez. *Pope Innocent X.* 1650. Rome, Doria Gallery. (Anderson)

excelled by *Las Meninas* of 1656 and *Las Hilanderas* of 1657. The former appears in Figure 15.37.

Both pictures are interiors, and both might be described as majestic genre. *Las Meninas* gives us a view into a room where Velázquez, seen to the left, is painting a portrait of the little Infanta. Apparently, the child has been less than cooperative in posing, and her youthful ladies-in-waiting have been reasoning with her, only to be interrupted by the appearance of the King and Queen, whose images appear in a mirror on the rear wall. In the right foreground, we see a magnificent dog, a little boy, and one of the pathetic dwarfs maintained at the palace for the morbid amusement of the court.

The painting is a superbly complicated essay in the mode of the total visual effect, but its special character is best brought out by direct comparison with Vermeer, which we postpone to page 765. For the moment, it is enough to say that Velázquez, who had by this date been a great technician for more than forty years, outdid himself once again in rendering light and tonal relations.

In June 1660, the Infanta Maria Teresa was married to King Louis 14th of France. There was a stupendous ceremony, which took place on the Isle of Pheasants in the river dividing the two countries. The arrangements over-

Fig. 15.37 Velázquez, *Las Meninas*. 1656. 125 by 108 inches. Madrid, Prado. (Anderson)

taxed the physical strength of the chamberlain; he took a fever, and by mid-summer was dead. Rarely a philosopher and never a poet, he was perhaps not a great man, but he was indeed a great painter.

Because of his position at court, Velázquez could never be a popular painter. Indeed, it is doubtful whether any large number of citizens ever got a single look at most of his paintings. Zurbarán was likewise at a comparative remove from the public because he worked for the monastic orders and because his austere piety did not appeal to every one. At the very time those great men were going their great way, nine-tenths of the Spanish nation would have named as Spain's leading artist *Bartolomé Esteban Murillo* (1617–1682), some times called "the Raphael of Seville."

Engravings after Raphael's pictures were widely circulated (page 589), so there is no mystery about the stylistic resemblance between his work and Murillo's, and it is a fact that many a Murillo Madonna was literally an Iberian Raphael. There was considerable difference, however, in the caliber of the two men, and a different adjustment of the qualities they had in common. Raphael had been a great man occasionally guilty of relying too much on charm. Murillo was not a great man, but was gifted with an excess of charm. He studiously eschewed the vigorous and distressing parts of the Christian story, and in a corpus of about three hundred preserved works, less than a dozen deal with the Passion. He painted, rather, the subjects which made religion seem sweet and lovely. His sentiment may at times prove cloying, but the sternest critic can not deny that it was genuine.

Popular painters, like popular authors, have always cautiously avoided anything that might force the public to expand its emotional horizon, and it was Murillo's constant care to make his religious painting depend upon themes already accepted and loved. The little Saint Thomas of Villanueva (Fig. 15.38), seen giving away his clothes to beggar children, is an example in point, and but one of many canvases in which Murillo depicted famous instances where mere infants experienced precocious insight. In the nature of the case, many of these paintings are mawkish, but some show a delightful appreciation of the little boys of Mediterranean lands.

Like all other Catholic painters of the period, Murillo made it part of his business to depict miracles. He did a notable series about saints to whom the Virgin had appeared, and another about saints visited by the Christ child. The vision of Saint Anthony, done in nine or ten variant renderings, proved to be the most popular subject of all and is still popular. The Anthony referred to was Anthony of Padua, born in Portugal, who arrived, after a series of mischances, at Assisi. Unlike many of the earlier Franciscans, he was a learned man. Francis made him his coadjutor and bade him continue his studies. After a distinguished career of teaching at Bologna, Toulouse, and Paris, he came to the university at Padua, and was ultimately laid to rest there in the great church bearing his name.

His vision occurred while he was lecturing on the Incarnation. He looked up, it is said, to find the infant Jesus standing on the edge of his notebook, but Murillo varied the theme. In the large painting now in the Cathedral at Seville, he showed Anthony on his knees, welcoming the child as he descends in glory from above. Other versions are more intimate. The favorite one shows Anthony holding the baby in his arms.

Murillo's most famous paintings are those which deal with the Immaculate Conception, which was then a matter not only of interest but of dispute. All Catholics were bitter against the Protestants because the latter refused to believe in the traditional holiness of the saints, including Mary, but not every Catholic was willing to accept the doctrine of the Immaculate Conception. Feeling ran high; and in the end, the Church did its best to suppress discussion pending an official finding. The Spaniards were so vehement, however, that they could not be restrained. The peninsula became a veritable center of propaganda in favor of the doctrine. In 1617, when a Dominican preacher dared question it, he found himself expelled even though

Figs. 15.38–39 (left) Murillo. *St. Thomas of Villanueva.* About 1670. 86½ by 58½ inches. Cincinnati Art Museum, Mary M. Emery Collection. (right) Murillo (or a follower). *The Immaculate Conception.* London, National Gallery.

his query had behind it the authority of Saint Thomas himself. In 1644, an annual Feast of the Immaculate Conception was installed.

The citizens of Seville, where Murillo lived and worked, were the most ardent of all, and thus furnished him with his best theme for painting—the theme, in fact, that is almost synonymous with his name. He did at least fifteen pictures which are labeled as *The Immaculate Conception* (one appears in Figure 15.39) but which ought properly to be known as "Our Lady of the Immaculate Conception," because they do not depict the event (page 462) but show Mary in her aspect as the beneficiary of the event: conceived and born without original sin, by special grace free from sin during life, and eternally a virgin.

The imagery is from the first verse of Revelation 12: "And there appeared a great wonder in heaven, a woman clothed with the sun, and the moon under her feet, and upon her head a crown of twelve stars." As convenience suggested, Murillo omitted or included one or more of these attributes, and in all instances, he gave the miraculous subject disturbingly personal overtones. The true content of these paintings is the notion, almost universal in both Spain and Italy, that there exists an identity between spiritual purity and physical virginity on the part of the female—a notion that seems slightly incongruous when we consider the luscious femininity and warm actuality of the pretty Spanish girls who ride heavenward in the character of "la purissima."

Murillo's art was not addressed, however, to people accustomed to making fine distinctions between one emotion and another. No one bothered to cavil that a pretty girl was not necessarily a theological argument. The paintings were immensely popular. Furthermore, they were immensely successful. They were instrumental in keeping alive the Spanish interest in the mystery of the Immaculate Conception, and thus helped pave the way for its ultimate approval as a dogma, as announced in the bull of Pius IX, issued in 1854.

THE DUTCH SCHOOL OF THE 17TH CENTURY

The Dutch school was and remains a remarkable episode in the cultural history of Europe. It started at the end of the 16th century and lasted for a scant three generations. There had never been any important Dutch art before, and there has been very little since. But during the brief period referred to, artistic talent was virtually epidemic in Holland. Pictures were turned out at a rate that seems scarcely credible; so many exist that one wonders how the Dutch found time for anything else but painting—for, in addition to the professionals who earned their living from art, there were countless amateur painters known today only by a canvas or two. Even more remarkable than the corpus of material was the quality of workmanship. In the nature of the case, most Dutch painters could not be great men, but all of them seem to have known their business, with the result that one rarely sees a Dutch picture that has deteriorated to any serious degree. Most of them are as fresh and clear as they were three hundred years ago.

It is risky to dogmatize about the causes of this unique outburst of art, but it is fact that Dutch painting flourished during a period of political and economic buoyancy, and declined thereafter.

Holland became a Spanish province because Philip of Austria, father of the Emperor Charles the 5th (page 718), had owned it in his capacity as Duke of Burgundy. From Charles, it passed to Philip the 2nd of Spain. He installed his natural sister, Margaret of Parma, as regent.

The Dutch were Calvinists. The country thus became an object of Hapsburg vindictiveness. Margaret's repressive policy resulted in open revolt, which
broke out in 1568. With the earlier years of that struggle, we have already
been concerned (page 662).

After the Duke of Alba returned to Spain in 1573, Philip sent his half-
brother Don John of Austria, the celebrated victor of Lepanto; and when
John died in 1578, command was assumed by Alexander Farnese, Duke of
Parma, Margaret's son. These three men were among the ablest generals in
the history of Europe, and they commanded armies which were probably better
than anything since the Roman legions. They were not, however, able to
subdue the Dutch.

There was a truce of twelve years' duration, starting in 1609, after which
the Spanish resumed hostilities (Fig. 15.35). But by that time, Holland was
rich and powerful and able to hold its own. The Treaty of Westphalia (1648)
finally settled the matter of Dutch independence.

Philip had taken economic as well as military measures against the
Dutch. When he annexed Portugal (1580), he closed the port of Lisbon to
Dutch shipping. Instead of withering away for lack of Portuguese trade, the
Dutch sent their own vessels to the Far East. In a remarkably short time, they
drove the Portuguese out and established an empire of their own, admin-
istered by the Dutch East India Company (founded 1602). Similar operations
were successfully undertaken along the coasts of Africa, in Brazil, in the West
Indies, and in what is now New York State.

Amsterdam became the richest financial center in Europe, and it is interesting as a point of art history that its prosperity did not all come from over-
seas. This is the period when Holland established the flower industry which
still brings wealth into the land. An interest in color was so general that prize
bulbs were collector's items. Rich men bid against each other for them, and
their blooming provided Dutch society with a major topic of conversation.

The Dutch revolt was not an entirely propitious circumstance for the
development of Dutch art, and neither was Calvinism. For sixteen hundred
years, the Catholic church had been the direct patron or the indirect cause
of perhaps nine-tenths of Europe's art. Royalty and nobility accounted for the
rest of it. The 17th-century Dutchman wanted no part of either. From his
point of view, art had been one of the more reprehensible extravagances of
the Catholics; and in the course of the wars, he had perhaps engaged personally in destroying some of it. Art was also associated in his mind with the
incredibly elaborate pageants, so tedious to read about today, which were
staged whenever royalty appeared, and which are reflected in the imagery of
Rubens.

Having turned his back on the two causes that, historically, had resulted

Fig. 15.40 Pieter Saenre-dam (1597–1665). *Interior of St. Bavo, Haarlem.* 23-7/16 by 32½ inches. London, National Gallery.

Fig. 15.41 Simon Vlieger (1601–1653). *Vessels in a Breeze.* About 1640. 16¼ by 21-9/16 inches. London, National Gallery.

Fig. 15.42 Meindert Hob-bema (1638–1709). *The Avenue, Middelharnais.* 1689. 40¾ by 55½ inches. London, National Gallery.

g. 15.43 (above left) Avercamp (1585–
34). *Winter Scene*. 16 inches diameter. Lon-
on, National Gallery.

ig. 15.44 (above right) Gerard Dou (1613–
375). *Poulterer's Shop*. 22-13/16 by 88⅛
iches. London, National Gallery.

ig. 15.45 (right) Jan Davidsz de Heem
606–1683 or 1684). *Still Life*. 46¾ by 66¾
iches. London, Wallace Collection.

in the making of pictures, it would seem that the Hollander wanted no art
at all, but that was not so. He was an enthusiastic buyer of paintings that
depicted everything except religion and aristocracy, and he got them.

Patronage, in other words, came from individuals rather than institutions,
and from individuals with a bourgeois background and outlook. These domestic patrons were canny. They wanted to see what they were buying before
they paid for it. They shied away from the practice of commissioning an artist
to produce a work of art for delivery at some future date. They preferred to
let the painter take the risk of completing his picture in the hope of selling
it. Most Dutch paintings were marketed in that way.

Fig. 15.46 Frans Hals. *The Laughing Cavalier.* 1624. 33 by 26¼ inches. London, Wallace Collection.

The system had advantages and disadvantages. Because no patron dictated to him a list of demands and requirements, the artist was "free" in the sense that no one told him what to paint or how to paint it. On the other hand, he had nothing like the security his contemporary Velázquez was enjoying at the court of Spain. He was forced, in fact, to become a speculator in a very uncertain market; and he had to sell, in Holland, to a public which lacked the education in taste which comes, almost automatically, to members of aristocratic families.

Most Dutch painters met the situation by becoming specialists. Having found some theme that would sell, a man would stick to it rather than risk time and effort on experiments which might or might not pay off. Thus it was that some men painted nothing but still life. Others are remembered for nothing but country landscapes in the summer and autumn, skating scenes, church interiors, views of city streets and squares, nautical scenes, family parties, drunkards—and the list goes endlessly on (Figs. 15.40–45).

As a class, these paintings are the most cheerful in the history of art. To see them is sheer delight, but it is not for nothing that the painters have traditionally been called "the little masters." The phrase fits. The pictures were, in the first place, small in size, often tiny. The content, however refreshing, was similarly small, sometimes trivial. Religion evokes the sublime, aristocracy the heroic. The negation of both put Dutch art under serious handicaps.

♦ *Hals* But there were several Dutch artists to whom the term "little master" does not apply. The earliest of these was Frans Hals (before 1584–1666), author of the portrait traditionally but not accurately known as *The Laughing Cavalier* (Fig. 15.46). It is doubtful whether any other painting has been reproduced so often as this one. The picture is not profound in a philosophical sense, and yet it has never become trite. The arrogant pose, the swashbuckling costume, and the general air of confidence give us a record of the Dutch spirit at the time; and all those things are expressed with a technique as assured and dashing as the sitter himself. Holland had never before seen a painter of this caliber; neither had there ever been art so distinctively and characteristically Dutch.

The 17th-century Dutchman led a jolly life. He liked to get dressed up and go to meetings of every sort, and he made every sort of meeting an occasion for the consumption of food and drink on a scale that was always hearty and often excessive. His taste in that respect resulted in the painting of innumerable group portraits (the closest thing to official and ceremonial art ever produced in Holland) in which officers, boards of trustees, and others recorded both their association and their good times.

Hals had notable success with these pictures (Fig. 15.47). They presented some difficult problems. Ordinarily, every man in the picture paid his share of its cost; and while rank might offer the painter an acceptable excuse for putting one figure rather than another in the central position, no one was willing to pay good money unless his own portrait showed up clear and well. Ordinary standards of emphasis and subordination could not be maintained. Dutch taste demanded, furthermore, that every detail of costume and every piece of silver on the table be rendered with almost the same actuality as the faces. This latter requirement tended to force the painting into a minute realism entirely out of scale with the main theme of the picture, and likely to compete with it.

There is perhaps no way to comply with such stipulations and still produce a perfect composition. Counting upon it that observers would glance from head to head and thus establish a linear effect, Hals used to arrange the faces in such a way that they described a simple geometric figure, either on the picture plane or at an angle thereto. For the most part, however, he held his compositions together by a rhythmic alternation of light and dark which had the effect of spreading interest more or less evenly over every part of the canvas.

It is obvious from the zest of these pictures that Hals himself enjoyed attending just such parties. He also enjoyed parties of a somewhat less

Fig. 15.47 Frans Hals. *St. Adrian's Company*. 1623. Haarlem, Frans Hals Museum. (A. Dingjan)

decorous kind (Fig. 15.48) and thus became one of Holland's best painters of what we delicately describe as "gay life."

Hals himself painted the authentic if overt gaiety of the well-to-do, but not everybody in Holland was well-fed, well-clothed, well-housed, and cheerful. Hals had an assistant named Adriaen Brouwer who frequented the dives which catered to the poor, and was found dead in the street outside one of them in 1638, being at that time 33 years of age. The people in Brouwer's pictures (Fig. 15.49) are not the good peasant stock, but the foul, stunted, deplorable detritus of half a century of war. It is unkind to think of them as drunkards. Such men rarely have the money to get drunk. They came, rather, to smoke tobacco loaded with narcotic additives, and thus to gain a miserable surcease.

♦ *Rembrandt* Rembrandt, in the popular image, is a figure of pathos, but it is only fair to remember that he was almost forty years old before he experienced any real difficulty.

He was born at Leyden, the son of Herman van Rijn, a prosperous miller, who was determined that the boy should have every possible advantage. Originally destined for the law, Rembrandt was given the best formal education then available, but when it became clear that his bent was for painting, his parents interposed no obstacles. On the contrary, they made arrangements

ig. 15.48 Frans Hals. *The Merry Company.* 51¾ by 91¼ inches. New York, courtesy of The Metropolitan Museum of Art, Bequest of Benjamin Altman, 1913.

Fig. 15.49 Adriaen Brouwer (1606?–1638). *Boors Drinking.* 11½ by 8¾ inches. London, National Gallery.

for technical instruction: three years at Leyden with a certain Jacob van Swanenburch, and then a sojourn at Amsterdam to work with the more famous Pieter Lastman. Both those men were weak Italianates, and neither had the caliber to give Rembrandt direction. A painter named Gerard Honthorst was a more powerful force in the young man's development.

Honthorst (Fig. 15.50) was a native of Utrecht, to which city he had returned in 1622 after spending a dozen years or so in Rome. Unlike some northerners, he had been no mere hanger-on. He had, in fact, enjoyed important commissions from the Cardinal Scipione Borghese and others, and his small easel pictures were in demand everywhere. The Italians called him "Gherardo della Notte" (Gerard of the Night), a nickname by no means inappropriate. Honthorst was not a great master, but he was an authentic Caravaggian. His presence in Holland gave Rembrandt a direct line, as it were, to the great Italian who had died as recently as 1610. He at once adopted Caravaggio's "dark manner" and used it for the rest of his life.

Rembrandt became one of the greatest technicians in the history of art, but he was not precocious. He was apparently not satisfied with what his teachers had taught him, and he returned to Leyden in 1626 for a course of

Fig. 15.50 Gerard Honthorst (1570–1656). *Christ before the High Priest*. 106 by 72 inches. London, National Gallery.

self-education. Not needing to make a living, he spent his time experimenting. From the very first, he signed his pictures even though he had small reason to be proud of them. It was his habit to induce members of his family to pose for him, and he was usually able to persuade them to wear fantastic hats and exotic costumes—for he had already become a collector of odd and expensive bric-a-brac.

Some of these early paintings are so lacking in assurance that it is really hard to believe they are the work of a man destined to become a figure in world history. One thinks of the candle-lit portrait of his father as a money changer (1627) now in Berlin, of the several early self-portraits, and of the little picture in Boston showing the dogged young artist in his studio (Fig. 15.51).

It took four years of study to make Rembrandt satisfied with his own painting, but it is evident that he presently acquired more than a little confidence in himself. In 1631, he left Leyden for Amsterdam, where the opportunities were greater by far, and set himself up in business. His first important

Fig. 15.51 Rembrandt. *The Artist in His Studio*. Boston, Museum of Fine Arts.

picture was a great success. It was a group portrait showing Dr. Nicholaes Tulp lecturing on anatomy (Fig. 15.52).

It is a very uneven picture. Rembrandt crowded the darks, and used a spot-light effect to bring emphasis on the cadaver, but the cadaver itself looks strangely as though posed from a living model. The axis of the cadaver provides a moderate inward diagonal, and thus makes it reasonable to group the eight figures in an approximate semicircle. The composition is certainly no better than the best of Hals, but it was much better than the arrangement ordinarily given group portraits by the general run of competent Dutchmen.

It is disquieting to note that four of the seven listeners are not paying attention to Dr. Tulp's demonstration. Perhaps they were mature medical men who could follow without watching; indeed, that impression may have been intentional. At any rate, each of the eight heads demonstrates an insight of which no other living painter was capable. Even at this comparatively early date, Rembrandt knew that every mind and every spirit had a special and inward life which made each man an island.

It is questionable whether these subtleties were entirely plain to the average Dutch burgher, but successful men often have a kind of instinct for

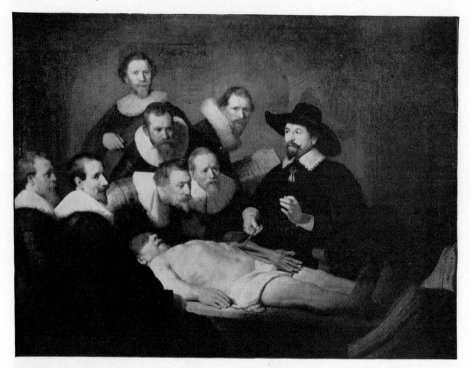

Fig. 15.52 Rembrandt. *The Anatomy Lesson of Dr. Nicholaes Tulp.* 1632. The Hague, Mauritshuis. (A. Dingjan)

quality even when they do not understand it. Almost at once, Rembrandt had more orders for portraits than he could possibly handle. Figure 15.53 shows a good example. The figures and objects are plastically defined, and the darker areas (in contrast to his use of the darks at a later period) function only in a pleasantly decorative way, to balance the lights.

Rembrandt's social career was as successful as his professional one. In 1634, he married Saskia van Uylenborch, an heiress who brought him a handsome dowry. They bought a fine house on the Bree street (now a museum). Rembrandt organized a corps of students and assistants, most of whom paid well for the privilege. His means now permitted him to purchase the most expensive pictures and objects, and he accumulated one of the finest collections north of the Alps. The familiar self-portrait in Dresden (1635) shows him at this time with Saskia on his knee, a sword at his belt, a plume in his hat, and a glass in his upraised hand. It is an emphatically carefree picture, if a vulgar one. Their way of life was high and wide, and became a subject for gossip. In 1638, Rembrandt and Saskia sued for libel two persons who had accused the young couple of wasting her rich inheritance on *prunken und prangen*. The suit was unsuccessful.

Fig. 15.53 Rembrandt. *A Lady and Gentleman in Black*. 1633. Boston, Isabella Stewart Gardner Museum.

The self-portrait of 1640 (Fig. 15.54) is perhaps an even better record of the painter's character during the years of his phenomenal prosperity. The picture merely confirms what we know from other sources. His gifts were evident and his accomplishments admired by all, but he was arrogant, avaricious, and perhaps none too scrupulous.

There are, for instance, about one thousand paintings which have, at one time or another, been attributed to Rembrandt. No one accepts more than about six hundred and fifty as genuine, and perhaps half of those are minor or even inferior works. It is obvious that Rembrandt's numerous pupils would imitate their master, and thus innocently contribute to the corpus of material. The conclusion is almost inevitable, however, that the master profited rather freely by selling work that was not his own. It is entirely possible he never once misrepresented the situation, but an extravagant man is likely to cut corners when money comes easily.

His material good fortune started to decline in the year 1642. It is possible to make a dramatic event out of what was doubtless a process; but Saskia died in June of that year, a few weeks after her husband had completed his

Fig. 15.54 Rembrandt. *Self-Portrait*. 1640. London, National Gallery.

most famous and most controversial picture, the group portrait popularly known as *The Night Watch* (Fig. 15.55).

The painting had been commissioned by one of the many militia or "shooting" companies of Amsterdam, some eighteen members of which had paid an average fee of one hundred guilders (some more, some less, according to their position in the picture). On delivery, the painting contained thirty-four figures and was not at all what the officers had expected. They made strenuous objections, some of which are understandable.

From their point of view, the picture was insulting. A company that prided itself on discipline was shown in most unmilitary confusion. The place, time, and purpose of the assembly were ambiguous. The pictorial emphasis seemed to fall on the adjutant (dressed in bright yellow) rather than upon the captain. Aside from those two figures, no one seemed to have any prominence at all, and the men complained that only four or five faces were actually recognizable. In the end, the disgruntled customers caused the addition of a plaque (seen at the top of the picture, slightly to the right) and had their names recorded on it.

The whole affair has been romanticized ad nauseam. Rembrandt has, in many minds, been made into a tragic hero and a sort of esthetic prophet

Fig. 15.55 Rembrandt. *The Shooting Company of Captain Frans Banning Cocq*, known as *The Night Watch*. 1642. 146 by 175 inches. Amsterdam, Rijksmuseum.

without honor among the coarse *bourgeoisie* of his own country. *The Night Watch* has been called "a thunderclap of genius," the equal of Michelangelo's ceiling, and the pictorial counterpart of Beethoven's "Eroica." The picture itself has become virtually the symbol (and to many, the proof) that artistic freedom must be absolute, and there has been precious little sympathy for the honest Dutchmen whose worst sin was merely to know what they wanted, and to ask that the painter cooperate.

It is obvious that communication was faulty between the painter and the patronage, but it was certainly no worse than it had been, at times, between Michelangelo and Julius the 2nd (page 609). At this date, there is no use in exploring further the ethics or legalities of the dispute; the question that concerns us today is whether, when he chose to do exactly as he pleased, Rembrandt performed as well as Michelangelo. On that point, critical opinion has been divided. Unfortunately, moreover, the condition of the picture handicaps analysis. It was cut down when moved in 1715; it darkened badly, and may or may not have been restored by cleaning in 1946–1947.

The painting is best understood as an attempt by Rembrandt to produce, in Dutch terms, a full-scale baroque composition: a pictorial spectacle vivid with glamour, a burst of movement dazzling in its complexity but governed by a strict system of coherence and unity.

For his point of time, he chose the moment before the company formed up. Supposedly, the men have just emerged from the archway dimly seen in the background. Captain Cocq has ordered the drummer to roll out the signal for falling into line, and is in the act of explaining a last detail to his adjutant. The picture is alive with the portent of great things, but the dramatic causation did not impress the contemporary Dutchmen and still escapes many a modern observer.

The National Gallery of London has Gerrit Lundens's copy of the picture which indicates that the composition was more spacious and comfortable before the original was cut down. A study of either the original or the copy will satisfy the reader that the directional impulses, which seem at first confusing, are in fact logical, and that the ground plan is similarly well organized. The dominating impression, however, is not one of arrangement in space, but a drama of light and dark that provides the strongest imaginable foil for the few areas of vivid color.

The real question, in short, is whether Rembrandt succeeded—or whether any one else could succeed—in organizing so large and complex a picture with primary reliance on contrasts of value. His personal attitude toward light and dark was involved. Caravaggio had been interested in the lights, but for Rembrandt, the operative areas of a canvas were often the luminous dark passages in which, miraculously, he almost always maintained the sense of hue. The darks, in other words, were the areas where secrets lay hidden, sometimes to be dimly revealed. Unless one searches there, his content is often missed entirely.

These considerations, which seem full of meaning today, failed to carry weight in Amsterdam, and the great painting was publicly condemned as a failure. It is doubtful whether that failure alone destroyed the artist's popularity and ruined his business. The affair was probably the simple climax of an accumulation of grievances, the inevitable result of his temperament and way of life. It is true, however, that he had fewer and fewer sitters for paid portraits, and earned increasingly less from other sources. Reduced in income, he spent capital in order to maintain his improvident habits; and like any number of other wealthy men, he sought to increase his fortune by speculation.

Saskia had left her money in trust for Rembrandt and their son Titus. As early as 1647, her relatives commenced official inquiries into the widower's administration of the estate. A general financial collapse hit Amsterdam in 1653, ruining many hitherto wealthy families. In one way or another, Rembrandt managed to hold out until 1656, when the family (in an attempt to salvage something for Titus) finally had him declared bankrupt. At a more fortunate moment, the sale of his splendid collection might have fetched a huge sum. As things were, it brought five thousand florins—in modern buying power, about a hundred and fifty thousand dollars. The fine house went, also; but even so, the painter was left with far too little to satisfy his creditors.

In the meantime, after having been sued for breach of promise by his housekeeper, Rembrandt had taken as mistress one Hendrickje Stoffels, a servant girl who had entered his house in 1649. The devotion of this woman, who asked little and gave everything, was undeviating until her death. Titus appears to have accepted her. In order to prevent creditors from seizing whatever his father might still be able to earn, he and Hendrickje had Rembrandt declared incompetent, and organized a small family corporation to handle the sale of prints and any paintings that might attract a buyer. Circumstances were worse than reduced; the family was sometimes in want.

Amsterdam was a commercial city where financial failure was identified with social and moral failure. Rembrandt lost not only his money, but his friends. His existence was that of a poor, unemployed man, prematurely beaten and old. Turned inward upon himself, he moved among the humbler members of the Jewish community. Any number of portraits, dark with mystery and yet phosphorescent with color, compassionately record the age-old wisdom of these folk who had been coming to Amsterdam for two centuries as refugees from Spain, Portugal, Germany, Poland, and Belgium. He wandered in the countryside, making the quick drawings which today are the admiration of the connoisseur and the despair of lesser artists. Occasionally, he painted some little, intimate event (Fig. 15.56) which still brought joy.

There is much to praise in Rembrandt's art at all periods, but the pictures which make us love him are those from the years after 1642. As his worries and adversities increased, he lost none of his intelligence, but he became gentler and less assertive. His spiritual qualities—sometimes obscured in the days of his vigor and enthusiasm—began to emerge. For their best expression, we must turn to biblical subject matter.

Calvin had denied the visual arts the right to serve religion. He asserted that any attempt to represent the holy personages tended to degrade them, and was an offense against the very notion of divinity. The severe simplicity of the Dutch churches—literally without decoration of any kind—reflects the thoroughness and rigidity with which these notions were enforced. The result, if we take Europe as a whole, was to eliminate religious art in every Protestant area.

Rembrandt was the great exception, and the only Protestant painter who has yet produced religious pictures which even compare with those that originated in Catholic countries. He turned out such work during his entire

Fig. 15.56 Rembrandt. *Hendrickje Bathing*. 1654. London, National Gallery.

career; in all, about 160 paintings, 80 etchings, and 600 drawings. The catalogue as a whole is evidence enough of his personal independence, but the immense corpus of drawings has a peculiar interest. Today, a drawing by Rembrandt is a collector's item of great price, but the drawings to which we refer were apparently never offered for sale. Rembrandt seems to have thought of them as notebook material of interest to himself alone. It seems obvious that he turned them out simply because religion was constantly on his mind.

The evolution of Rembrandt's religious art was what we might expect from his biography. *The Blinding of Samson* (Frankfort) and the *Sacrifice of Isaac* (Fig. 15.57) come from the years 1635–1636. The *Samson* is so overt as to make one wonder whether the painter was not attempting an ultra-baroque tour de force; it might actually be described as one of Rubens' hunting scenes with Dutch actors playing religious parts. The *Isaac* is only slightly less violent. With his massive left hand, Abraham has forced backward the face of his nude and helpless son, putting the vulnerable throat in position for the cut. At the last moment, the angel swoops in from the upper left to stay the father's right hand—from which the deadly knife falls, and apparently will land edge downward uncomfortably close to the bare thigh of Isaac.

If we are to understand the Bible as a narrative of physical events, we

Fig. 15.57 Rembrandt. (left) *Sacrifice of Isaac*. 1635. Leningrad, Hermitage. (right) *Sacrifice of Isaac*. 1655. Etching. New York, courtesy of The Metropolitan Museum of Art, Bequest of Ida Kammerer in memory of her husband, Frederic Kammerer, M.D., 1933.

can have nothing but praise for these two early paintings. They are superbly realistic, and all the more dashing because the drama of action is enhanced by a theatrical handling of light and dark. If, however, we think of the Bible as a source of wisdom, it becomes plain that Rembrandt's later work is incomparably more important.

In 1655, he did the sacrifice of Isaac again, this time as an etching (Fig. 15.57). It is a picture that moves much more slowly than the earlier version. That is appropriate because Abraham's trial was no sudden thing, but lasted a full three days. What can have been the thoughts of that aged parent as he journeyed with his son into the land of Moriah? The proposed sacrifice was not only contrary to his own instincts; it was, from the standpoint of social morality, considerably worse than murder. How could a man be sure that it was God himself who had directed that the deed be done? And it was a certainty that very few men on earth would accept, after the act, the explanation that Abraham had done what he did in response to a loftier ethic.

Genesis 22 does not state these considerations, but they are bound to occur to one who ponders the meaning of the story. The Abraham of the etching is a man who has wrestled with doubt, and who is not yet certain.

Fig. 15.58 Rembrandt. *The Three Crosses*. 1653. Etching. Third state. New York, courtesy of The Metropolitan Museum of Art, Gift of Felix M. Warburg and His Family, 1941.

The Isaac is not a youth who fears the pain of death, but a symbol of filial faith. The angel is not a divine thunderbolt but a gentle friend who calmly embraces the two, and compassionately makes clear the true will of God.

Rembrandt had been an etcher all his life. The excellence of his prints was attested by the existence of a loyal group of connoisseurs who promptly bought anything he might issue. Their judgment has been confirmed by time, and in the market. Shortly before 1650, he published a print which combined the imagery from various verses in Matthew 19, and showed *Christ Healing the Sick*. At some forgotten sale, probably later in the 17th century, a single impression fetched one hundred guilders—hence the nickname "The Hundred Guilder Print," which has stuck even though people were paying many times that amount not long after.

Price or no price, "The Hundred Guilder Print" was a notable work of religious art, but Rembrandt had still further to go, as we see in *The Three Crosses* of 1653 (Fig. 15.58). The imagery corresponds closely with the account given in Luke 23. The point of time is immediately after Jesus had died. In every ear, there still rings his cry of "Father, into thy hands I commend my spirit!" At almost the same instant, a centurion (seen at the foot of the cross) glorified God, and called out, "Certainly this was a righteous man!"

It will be recalled that there had been darkness over the earth for about three hours, and that just before Jesus died "the veil of the temple was rent in the midst." The veil referred to was the curtain which separated the holy place, into which all priests might enter, from the holy of holies, where only the high priest might go on the Day of Atonement. It seems doubtful that Saint Luke referred to the splitting of an actual and physical veil. He probably spoke figuratively, as Paul did in Hebrews 10:19–20, where he made the same veil a type for the body of Jesus, and suggested that its rending opened "a new and living way" for all believers into the very presence of God.

There can be no doubt that Rembrandt knew these cryptic passages and wondered what they meant. As a pictorial counterpart for the "rending of the veil" he rent the darkness with a blaze of light which seems indeed "a new and living way," a triumphant link between heaven and earth.

As with the work of Pieter Brueghel (page 663) it takes time to know the picture in all its wealth of detail: the rulers in the foreground who are departing after having derided Christ, the mounted soldiers near the cross to the left, and the Holy Women to the right, with Saint John standing in despair. Study is likewise requisite before one can appreciate the subtle and yet violent graduations of technique, from the rich modeling of the figures in the darker areas to the stark delineation of those in the full glare of celestial lighting. And yet, unlike the work of any other northern artist, this plate has an immediacy of impact which we associate with Italy and with the antique.

Nothing in all history could demonstrate better the folly of making conventional distinctions between the major and the minor arts. This etching is smaller than *The Night Watch,* but it has all the virtues of that great painting and none of its ambiguities. It is not only the greatest picture Rembrandt ever produced, but perhaps the most perfect realization of the baroque concept of religious art, and one of the two or three best Crucifixions of all time.

In a longer study, it would be possible to follow Rembrandt's life and art out to the end. The Frick Gallery has a fine self-portrait from 1656, the year of the bankruptcy, which shows the artist as still a great personage regardless of his troubles. From that point on, the self-portraits record the aging of his person and the reduction of his material circumstances, but it is heartening to note that one of the very latest shows him laughing. Hendrickje made a will in 1661 and died in 1663. Titus died in 1668. Rembrandt died

Fig. 15.59 Peter de Hooch. *Courtyard of a House in Delft.* 29 by 23⅝ inches. London, National Gallery.

the next year. He owned nothing except the clothes he wore and a kit of artists' tools and materials.

♦ *Cabinet Paintings* Of all the pictures that came out of Holland, none are greater favorites than the "cabinet paintings" or "conversation pieces," as they were called in England. A conversation piece is a domestic scene. The setting may be a parlor, a kitchen, a garden, or courtyard. There must be people in it, engaged in some unremarkable episode of daily life: taking a glass of wine, some one playing a musical instrument, or merely making a quiet visit. The painters particularly associated with this class of work were Gerard Terborch (1617–1681), Jan Steen (1625–1679), Gabriel Metsu (1629–1697), Peter de Hooch (1629–1684), and Johannes Vermeer (1632–1675).

These artists all had much in common and at first seem very much alike, but they were not. Steen was a gay fellow, more at home in tavern and kitchen than in the parlor. Terborch and Metsu did their painting upstairs. With honest but gentle realism, their pictures take us back into the 17th-century houses, so sumptuously furnished and so comfortably inhabited by

Fig. 15.60   Vermeer. *View of Delft*. About 1658. 38½ by 46¼ inches. The Hague. Mauritshuis. (A. Dingjan)

the well-to-do. With both these men, the setting seems to be there as a necessary but subordinate place for the people. With de Hooch, the situation was
reversed (Fig. 15.59). He was more interested in the setting than in the
people, and he outdid himself with architectural complexities, and light
coming from all sorts of angles.

A picture by any one of these men would be an ornament in any collection, but not one of them had anything like the stature of Vermeer.

Vermeer was born in 1632, at Delft. There is no evidence that he ever
made an extensive journey or that he ever lived or worked elsewhere. He
married in 1653, a girl who brought him some property. They had eight
children, and he died in 1675. Very little else is known about him.

There is reason to believe that he got high prices for his paintings, and
painted very few of them. That, perhaps, is why his name was virtually forgotten, and why dealers used to sell him as De Hooch or Terborch. He was
not recognized as a distinct personality until the middle of the 19th century

Fig. 15.61 Vermeer. *The Artist in His Studio.* About 1665–1670. 52 by 44 inches. Vienna, Kunsthistorisches Museum (Wolfrum)

when a few connoisseurs became interested in sorting his work out from the rest. The process is not yet complete. At present, various catalogues give him differing lists: some as few as thirty paintings, none more than forty-three.

Every list includes the wonderful *View of Delft* (Fig. 15.60) and the remarkable *Artist in His Studio* (Fig. 15.61), but most of the other pictures are small and much simpler in composition. Some are tiny portraits showing the head only (Fig. 15.62). Some include more than one figure. But the standard Vermeer is like Figure 15.63, an interior scene with the light coming from the left, showing a young woman engaged in some simple household task. It seems incongruous that these modest paintings which sold for eight or ten guineas about 1900 will today fetch fabulous sums, but for once, price is in harmony with artistic value.

There is no reason to doubt that Vermeer used his own house for a setting, and that his wife and daughters appear in most of the pictures. If so, the Vermeer family were fastidious in a sense that was not only uncommon, but —if we may judge by Dutch painting—virtually unknown in 17th-century Holland. The house was furnished with fine things, but there were not too many of them. As a result, Vermeer's pictures contain only such objects as

Fig. 15.62 Vermeer. *Young Girl with a Flute.* 7⅞ by 7 inches. Washington, D. C., National Gallery of Art, Widener Collection.

Fig. 15.63 Vermeer. *Young Lady at the Virginals.* London, National Gallery.

contribute to the pictorial design. The voids (areas of blank wall, for example) function in the composition, and we feel a sense of space and ease so often and so unhappily absent from the work of Terborch and Metsu.

The Vermeer ladies, moreover, dressed in the local fashion but with a taste that seems more French than Dutch. Their gowns and their hats were sometimes simple and sometimes obviously expensive, but they were always so nicely designed as to look quite as well today as they did three hundred years ago. It is difficult to think of any other women in Dutch art of whom the same can be said.

How did it happen that Vermeer had better taste than his contemporaries, and was, in fact, almost the only Dutch artist who never offended in that respect? If we knew more about his education and habits, we might be more definite; even so, a suggestion or two is possible.

As early as 1609, the Dutch had established a trading post at Hirado in western Japan, in competition with British, Spanish, and Portuguese interests. For some reason, the British found trade unprofitable, and they presently departed. The Spanish and the Portuguese had attempted to combine trade with a missionary effort. The latter stirred up suspicion and resentment in Japan. The Jesuits and Franciscans were killed. The Catholic traders were expelled. Japan, by 1641, had solidified the closed-door policy which lasted until Admiral Perry's expedition of 1853; but they made an exception of the Dutch, who were permitted to remain on an island in Nagasaki Harbor, and trade.

Oriental porcelains were imported in quantity by the Hollanders, and the celebrated potteries at Delft were set up in order to manufacture similar material at home. Vermeer, therefore, found himself an inhabitant of the very town where the subtleties of fine pottery were understood better than anywhere else except the Orient—which is to say, the town where the natural Dutch sense for color received its greatest refinement.

Vermeer's colors, particularly his yellows and blues, have an absolute beauty and a refined modulation very like the tones of china and porcelain. It is by no means far-fetched to suggest that he developed his palette by discussing tints and shades with his friends who ran the potteries. Porcelains, like enamels, often have extreme delicacy of coloration even when very dark in tone; and it is notable that Vermeer's painting was distinguished by a marvelous control in the darks.

Did he learn other things about art from Oriental sources? Did Japanese and Chinese pictures come to Holland in the ships that regularly plied to Nagasaki? Did Vermeer know them, and was it there that he learned to use a slightly elevated eye point? Did the Far East teach him the beauty of areas of line and flat tone? Was it there that he also acquired his special sense for the silhouette? All of this is possible, perhaps likely, but proof is lacking.

Such matters, while significant, are mere details by comparison to the "white magic" which makes Vermeer's technique one of the wonders of art history. The light in his pictures is more convincingly real than the light in any other paintings whatever. The sensation evoked is, in fact, notably more intense than the sensation of reality. Arthur Pope has aptly referred to it as "hyper-realism."

Vermeer achieved this effect because his paintings are, as yet, the most clear-cut, consistent, and perfect examples of the mode of the total visual effect (page 481). He was a man of taste, his sense for the harmony and contrast of lines and shapes was superb, and he was one of the best formal designers in the history of painting. But his chief passion, as a painter, was for the organization of tones, in which he found an abstract beauty quite separate from every other interest.

The Artist in His Studio (Figure 15.61) is much more complicated than most of his other pictures. Ostensibly, it shows Vermeer painting one of his daughters dressed up in some blue drapery, wearing a crazy floral crown, holding a book and a trumpet, and posing as a curiously demure personification of Fame. It is doubtful whether any one ever gave a thought to this "subject" without having it pointed out to him. The true content of the painting was

Vermeer's determination to render color relationships under conditions of light, both direct and reflected, which ran the full scale from sunlight into dark shadow.

No writer has yet found words adequate to express the general admiration for his achievement. A good black and white reproduction carries over fairly well the subtlety of the value relations throughout the painting, but the very best available colored reproductions can only suggest the precision with which Vermeer maintained the proportional contrasts between intensities and hues. Every painter knows that it is fairly easy to define tones in the plane of light, and very difficult to prevent the darker areas from becoming muddy. As but a suggestion of Vermeer's supreme ability, we may consider the contrast between the painter's jacket and his trousers. The jacket is a cool black, the trousers a warm black. Neither field receives the light direct from the window, and the contrast between the two fields is, at maximum, not a great one. The distinction between them is (in the original) perfectly obvious even in the extreme shadow where the actual contrast is almost nothing at all.

Vermeer's success depended, of course, upon an accurate compression of the natural value scale into the very limited range of values available in paint. A certain sacrifice was involved. It is obvious that a painting can not have every distinction of light and dark which is appreciable to the eye in the object the painting attempts to represent. Some of the distinctions which indicate form and texture in the object are thus, of necessity, lost, and were lost in all paintings by Vermeer—but that is what distinguishes him from his contemporaries.

Terborch, as a matter of habit, ran through the entire value scale when rendering any field he happened to be interested in. In his paintings, the shadows in an area of white satin are often as dark as any shadows elsewhere in the picture. His method enabled him to represent textures so vividly that he sometimes impresses one as over-insistent. Metsu did much the same thing, and both were popular painters; but when they extended the value range of individual fields beyond their proportional relationship to each other, they introduced an element of disorder which is keenly felt even when the reason for it is not understood. By limiting fields of yellow, of black, or of red, each to its fair proportion of the available values, Vermeer made his pictures lawful. His compositions impress us as absolutely right, even inevitable. Admittedly difficult to explain, the effect is so obvious that it is always mentioned.

The Artist in His Studio is much the same kind of picture as Velázquez's *Las Meninas* (Fig. 15.37), and the difference between them illustrates another quality which was unique with Vermeer.

The human eye, it will be recalled, is an instrument of narrow capacity.

If we adjust the eye for dimness, or moderate light, any area which receives intense illumination becomes nothing but a blank glare. If we adjust our sight for sunlight out of doors, we can perceive no details in the shadows. Conditions between those two extremes vary in proportional fashion. It is easy to deceive ourselves into believing that we have seen much that we merely infer, but the truth is that, at any given instant, our physical eye registers the facts only over a limited range of values, and we never perceive more than a small part of what is in view.

Many pictures by Rembrandt appear to assume that the eye is adjusted for very moderate light indeed, and any areas in strong illumination lack detail. In Velázquez' painting, it seems obvious that the artist accepted without question the conditions which he actually found in the rather badly proportioned room assigned to him as a studio. Details are indeterminate in the shaded areas much as they would be if we were there to look into the room. In the deeper darks, we see no details at all.

In sum, both Rembrandt and Velázquez (and most other painters) may be said to have taken account of the facts of physical vision. Vermeer did otherwise. He transcended them.

If the eye were adapted to viewing the tones in the brighter portions of the "Artist," it would require a special effort to make out distinctions of hue and intensity in the deeper darks. It is questionable, indeed, whether such an adjustment could in fact be made. In other words, Vermeer rendered subtle distinctions of tone which no human eye could comprehend simultaneously. This accounts for our heightened sense of light and space, and for the sense of exhilaration experienced when we look at his paintings. He painted not what we can see, but what our ideals tell us we might see.

During the second half of the 17th century, the Dutch were hard put to it to maintain their favored position in the world. Between 1652 and 1678, they fought two sea wars with England, had trouble with the Portuguese in Brazil, lost their foothold in New York, and experienced a land invasion by the French. These wars were costly in men and money, and ended with the commercial ascendancy of England over Holland. The Dutch, however, had experienced worse in the past, and were by no means impoverished. These troubles are always cited as coincident in date with the decline of Dutch painting, but the truth is that cause and effect is by no means obvious. The school stopped as mysteriously as it had begun.

BAROQUE ART IN FRANCE

From the standpoint of art history, the chief event of the 17th century was the shift of the artistic capital of the world from Rome to Paris, where it has remained ever since. We ordinarily say that the move coincided with the reign of Louis the 14th (1643–1715), and that Versailles (Fig. 15.2) was the monument which made all men recognize what had happened. The actual process started somewhat earlier.

During the entire 16th century, France had been almost continuously at war. The so-called Hapsburg-Valois Wars were scarcely over in 1559 when the Religious Wars (eight of them in all) commenced, and lasted until 1598.

No one can read the narrative of those three generations without being aghast at the destruction, suffering, and ruin which took place, but France has always had an incredible ability to rise again to prosperity and power. Henry the 4th (reigned 1598–1610) and his minister Sully inherited a bankrupt and lawless kingdom, but they were able to ride forward on the wave of French nationalism. They inaugurated the policy which, in the end, put all power in the hands of the central government, and made considerable progress in that direction.

The great Cardinal Richelieu (Fig. 15.65), who ran the government for Louis the 13th from 1624 to 1642, continued the process, and is generally remembered as the man who laid the foundation for the monarchy of Louis the 14th. Richelieu was succeeded by Mazarin, who negotiated the Peace of Westphalia in 1648, and the Treaty of the Pyrenees in 1659. By those treaties, he settled the perennial troubles between France and the empire and between France and Spain. The year 1660, it will be recalled, was the marriage date of the young French monarch and the Spanish Infanta. For the rest of his long incumbency, Louis the 14th was the most important human being in Europe.

The political history so briefly summarized is a narrative of constantly increasing centralization which, in the end, produced a monarchy as close to absolute as anything in history. The simple and brutal love of power was a motive in every step of the calculated procedure, but it would be unjust to suppose that no other motives were in operation. Any one who explores the matter in detail must be impressed with the broad and inclusive view of government entertained by the controlling members of French society.

They were concerned not only with military, fiscal, and judicial matters, but with French culture. In other lands, the artistic and intellectual life of the population has, with some exceptions, remained a private affair and no direct concern of the government. From the time of Richelieu, conditions have been different in France. It was he who first made Frenchmen conscious of their responsibility for the excellence of the language, the soundness of French science, the superiority of French craftsmanship, and the pre-eminence of French taste in costume, furniture, and the visual arts.

The great enterprise started with the founding of the Academy of Literature in 1635. The Academy of Painting and Sculpture was not established until 1648, but Richelieu without doubt visualized the grand design which was to be perfected during the reign of Louis the 14th (page 788). Once established, the academic principle survived, and still does. A detailed account of its development would not aid in our immediate purpose. We may therefore resort to popular parlance, and refer to the entire organization, in all its ramifications, as "the French Academy." Let the reader visualize it as a board of eminent gentlemen publicly declared to be the *grands seigneurs* of literature, art, and science, and empowered by the government to speak in the name of France.

Richelieu's establishment of the Academy merely formalized a cultural philosophy already accepted in France. The cornerstone of academic doctrine has always been the notion that the arts are primarily intellectual and therefore a fit subject for administrative control. The concept is also an aristocratic one: that the arts are the province of educated people, which is to say, people who have learned a considerable measure of restraint and are unlikely to respond to an appeal directed primarily to their emotions. The errors of this doctrine will appear in due course, but they were not apparent to Frenchmen during the 17th century. In any event, it is impossible to understand the history of French art unless we appreciate that the Academy was always there to protect its own and to undermine the prestige of outsiders. It has been like a rock, around which artistic currents swirl.

Preoccupied as he was by a thousand other matters, Henry the 4th nevertheless found time to inaugurate the policy which has made Paris the queen of all great cities. He thought in large terms, and the structures he put up are, as specimens of architecture, less interesting than his general ideas of city planning. It was he who conceived the splendid open squares surrounded by buildings of consistent design, the connecting avenues which sweep between them, and the grand big bridges across the Seine. In the space of about ten years, he completed the Pont Neuf, the Place des Vosges (formerly called Place Royale), and the Place Dauphine. He did not live to finish various other projects which he started; the important thing is that he left a legacy of common sense which has made Paris the most convenient metropolis in the world as well as the most spectacular.

Henry's improvements opened up whole new areas, and the great houses (called *hôtels*) began to go up there. Around his squares, it was his habit to invite private patronage by letting lots at a nominal rate on condition that a house be built according to his standard plan. The local effect of that enlightened policy is obvious to every tourist. Less obvious but more important is the fact that Henry made Paris the type and model for urban development in England, Holland, Germany, North America, and even in Italy itself.

Fig. 15.64 Blois. Château. Wing of Gaston d'Orleans. 1635–1640. (Copyright Country Life)

As Paris grew and spread and began to assume its modern appearance, every architect of reasonable ability had work to do, and most of them did it well. Their designs were controlled by theories of reason and order often referred to as "French classicism." In comparison to contemporary Italian work, their buildings seem elegant, but dry, sober, and severe. Figure 15.64 shows one of the best of them, and is generally typical of French work during the first half of the century. However lacking in warmth and spirit, this architecture was at least grandiose and impressive.

There was great demand for painting to decorate all the new buildings, and a great deal of painting was done. Most of the commissions were, however, schemes of interior decoration. Most of the artists involved were thought of, and thought of themselves, as decorators. The general level of quality is suggested by Marie de Médicis' decision to call in Rubens when, in 1625, she wanted a first-class master to work in her vast new palace of the Luxembourg.

It would be going too far to say that the modern art of interior decoration was invented at Paris during the first half of the 17th century. On the other hand, the notion of interior decoration as such certainly received more attention than ever before, appealed to more people, and has been part of our culture ever since. Even so, the French artists we now consider significant

Fig. 15.65 Philippe de Champaigne. *Cardinal Richelieu.* 1635–1640. 102½ by 70 inches. London, National Gallery.

had very little to do with decorative commissions, and the two greatest did not even live in France.

At Paris itself, the most important artist was *Philippe de Champaigne* (1602–1674). He was born at Brussels, but came to France at the age of 19, adapted himself completely to the contemporary French taste, became Richelieu's favorite portrait painter, and perhaps the greatest master of formal portraits in the whole history of French art.

His familiar portrait of Richelieu (Fig. 15.65) exists in four very similar versions.* The whole nature of French 17th-century culture is visualized in this single painting. Essentially, it is in the formula of Rubens, which Rubens had learned from the ceremonial portraits of Titian (page 636) and then passed on to others: the upward line of sight, the assertion of the sitter's aristocracy, the curtain, the architecture, and the suggestion of landscape. The different, and peculiarly French, qualities are these:

* The others are in the Louvre, at Buckingham Palace, and in the Chaix d'Est-Ange Collection.

There is a complete absence of the movement one always feels in Rubens, and indeed in most other baroque art. The figure is peculiarly erect and static. There is no real swing in the drapery, and the eye moves slowly among its curves and folds. The simple gesture serves merely to bring the left background into operation, and there we see some elegant but quiet architecture and some foliage through which no wind blows.

The absence of dynamics was, of course, deliberate. One feels the same quality in contemporary French architecture; and in both cases, the reason is that classical art had also been static. It is to be assumed that Champaigne had been studying ancient statuary and had noted its absence of movement (page 61), which he associated with dignity, nobility, and profundity of content. If so, the facial expression was in keeping with the character of his sitter, or at least with the public character he wished to assume. The Cardinal was fortunate in his painter; there is no face in the history of portraiture so perfectly definitive of logic and penetration. On the other hand, one wonders whether either Richelieu or the artist appreciated how accurately the picture recorded an absence of benignity and the difference between intelligence and wisdom.

While he will always be remembered for his official portraiture, Champaigne was an artist of considerable range. He did any number of more intimate portraits, usually in half length. He became interested in Jansenism, and produced some of the finest religious painting that was ever done in France. A notable example is the *Two Nuns of Port Royal,* now in the Louvre—one of them the painter's own daughter, who had been cured of paralysis by a miracle.

Recent criticism has focused a great deal of attention upon several French painters hitherto considered minor or provincial. Among these were the *Brothers Le Nain:* Antoine, Louis, and Mathieu, who were born in Lâon and were active in Paris from 1630 until the death of Antoine and Louis in 1648. About fifteen signed and dated pictures survive, all falling between 1641 and 1648, and none giving the Christian name of the painter. Modern connoisseurship tends toward the view that the brothers collaborated less than previously supposed, and that Louis was much the most significant artist of the three.

Louis Le Nain was remarkable in 17th-century France because of his subject matter. Instead of painting mythology and portraits of the great, he painted peasants (Fig. 15.66). It is all too seldom pointed out that his method of painting them was a perfect demonstration of French classicism; and in that connection, it is significant that all three brothers were ultimately elected to the Academy.

The sources of Louis' style are yet to be discovered. Obviously, he was

Fig. 15.66 Louis Le Nain (or possibly a follower). *Four Figures at a Table*. 18¼ by 21⅝ inches. London, National Gallery.

familiar with the vulgar genre of Holland. It is equally plain that he was a Caravaggian. There is some reason to believe he had sojourned in Rome, although the evidence is inconclusive.

His classicism was classicism of both form and content. He never satirized his sitters. He never patronized them by bringing out their eccentric or amusing qualities. Neither did he sentimentalize about them, as both Millet and Israels were to do during the 19th century. Le Nain simply painted peasants in a calm and sympathetic manner. One wonders whether he did not often reflect upon the durability of the peasant class: kings and armies and castles tend, at intervals, to get destroyed; no matter what happens, the humble agricultural folk endure. Whatever the painter's thoughts, it is a fact that his pictures evoke the sense of permanence. To see one of them is not unlike seeing the peristyle at Segesta, still there after twenty-five centuries of history.

Like Philippe de Champaigne and other contemporaries, Louis Le Nain gave his figures a classical immobility which, in his case, was spontaneous. Country people often seem very still and very silent when one looks at them. At first glance, the groupings appear easy and even haphazard, but any one

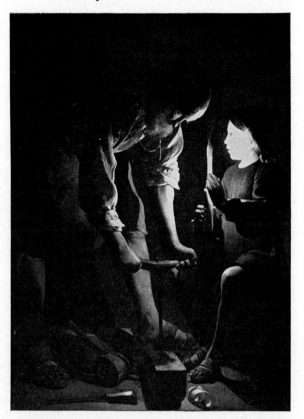

Fig. 15.67 Georges de la Tour. *Christ and Saint Joseph.* About 1645. 38½ by 25½ inches. Paris, Louvre. (Bulloz)

familiar with classical principles of composition (page 66) will appreciate at once that this artist was an accomplished formal designer. No one ever knew better how to play profile and frontal poses off against diagonal and foreshortened views of the figure, or how to close the composition in at both sides in the organic way.

Georges de la Tour (1593–1652) is another painter who has become a great favorite. He lived and worked at Luneville in Lorraine, about twenty miles east and a bit south of Nancy. His artistic education is still a matter of guesswork. It seems unlikely that he went to Italy or in any other way came into direct contact with the work of Caravaggio. Although it can not be proved, it seems probable that he had been to Utrecht and there picked up the manner of the local Caravaggians, of whom Honthorst was only one.

De la Tour was a gentle and elegant artist, by temperament almost exactly opposite to Caravaggio. His settings are always neat and clean even when they are humble, and the objects in them are few and well arranged (Fig. 15.67). He used the dark to eliminate sordid surface details; indeed, in his hands the dark became a force tending to simplify, generalize, and idealize the human figure. Some times he carried the process to the point of abstraction, and one is strangely reminded of the quattrocento sculptor Laurana and the modern painter Modigliani. His light, unlike Caravaggio's, comes from no external, horrific, and dramatic source; usually, it is the light of a candle seen in the picture itself, shedding a peculiar grace over the quiet people of the painting.

♦ *Nicolas Poussin and Claude Lorrain* Nicolas Poussin (1594?–1665) was the greatest French artist of the 17th century. He was revered as a world figure during his lifetime, and he is still remembered as the painter who most perfectly expressed the artistic ideals most respected in France. Strangely enough, he worked not at Paris (a place he detested) but at Rome.

He was born near Les Andelys in Normandy, the son of parents whom he later described as ignorant. Having picked up a certain amount of technical instruction in the provinces, he came to Paris in 1612, and seems to have supported himself by hack work. The single remarkable thing about his early life was his determination to go to Italy. He got as far as Florence in 1620, but came back to Paris where, in company with the young Philippe de Champaigne, he found employment in a minor capacity on the decoration of the Luxembourg. That episode is interesting because Rubens's florid masterpieces were being installed in the palace at the time, and Poussin seems to have paid no attention to them. Obviously, he already had a contrary artistic philosophy which involved study at Rome, where he finally arrived in 1624, and where he lived, with a single interruption, until his death.

In so far as we can discern it at this date, Poussin's fixed purpose was to discover and master the principles of classical art. We do not refer to the figure style of the ancients, which anybody could copy and many had copied. Neither do we mean the classical system of composition, which had been a matter of common knowledge from the time of Leonardo. Poussin was after the inner and spiritual meaning of antiquity. In the end, he came as close to making it his own as had Botticelli and Alberti, perhaps even closer. He was in no sense precocious, however, and he achieved his purpose only after some years of tenacious and intelligent study.

His earlier pictures were, as a matter of fact, singularly unlike those we most respect today, and his first important commission at Rome was considerably less than a success. In 1628, he was lucky enough to get an order from the Cardinal Francesco Barberini for a *Martyrdom of Saint Erasmus* (Fig. 15.68), originally intended for one of the subordinate altars in Saint Peter's. The opportunity was the kind of thing for which every coming painter longed; and it would seem that Poussin, not yet entirely sure of himself, tried to produce a painting which made a compromise between his own austere principles and the contemporary Roman fashion for baroque altarpieces.

Fig. 15.68 Poussin. *Martyrdom of Saint Erasmus.* 1628. Rome, Vatican. (Alinari)

The picture was an attempt to do the revolting work of Ribera in terms of French classicism. To see the original is to experience uncomfortably mixed emotions. Superficially, it is an elegant, even a beautiful painting until one appreciates, with some sense of shock, that the scene is disgusting. Contemporary sensibilities did not react to torture as we do, but the incongruity seems nevertheless to have been noted. People expressed their disappointment and disapproval, and Poussin never again attempted, at Rome, what is often referred to as "public painting."

He did, however, experiment further with scenes that involved typically baroque violence, and in the *Massacre of the Innocents,* now in the Musée Condé at Chantilly, he was more successful. The subject had been done any number of times before. In almost every instance, the harrowing essence of the scene had been deliberately mitigated by multiplying the number of actors on the stage, thus making it difficult to concentrate upon any single act of brutality or the personal anguish of any one mother.

Poussin's version shows us only three operative figures, who appear in the immediate foreground. A soldier has placed his foot on the neck of a fat infant, and is about to split the skull with his sword. With his left leg, he is blocking the interference of the kneeling mother, whom he also holds back by gripping her hair with the left hand. A few feet away in the right background, another mother, somewhat numbed by the awful reality, carries off her dead baby.

In the figure style, one can feel reminiscences of Venice and the influence of various baroque painters at Rome. It is obvious, however, that Poussin's study of ancient statuary had taken effect. Both heads and bodies are generalized, and every contour is simplified and smoothed out. The result is not entirely convincing; but the matter is unimportant in view of the masterly dramatic simplification of the composition as a whole.

Like Giotto, Poussin sternly eliminated every actor, accessory, and detail not absolutely essential to the significance of the narrative. His four figures are, as a medium of communication, more efficient than four hundred would have been. It is the most successful version of the subject on record, so harrowingly successful, in fact, that more than one onlooker has wished it never had been painted.

It speaks volumes for Poussin's courage and originality that he could move toward simplicity in a period committed to the opposite, but he was a thoughtful, introverted, analytical man who chose his own way. The relative failure of his *Saint Erasmus* coincided with a severe illness. Apparently, he had both reason for reflection and the enforced leisure to reflect. About 1630, he seems to have decided to change his course. He made no further attempt to compete for the big commissions in churches and palaces. He seems to have realized that his taste and talent was for easel paintings of modest size which might be conceived, developed, and completed in virtual privacy and in the absence of pressure from outside.

His determination has often been cited (and correctly) as an early instance of artistic independence, but no such policy ever succeeded by virtue of independence alone. Normans are traditionally prudent, and Poussin was one of them. His affairs were in good order. He had married Anna Maria Dughet, the young daughter of a French chef working for one of the noble families. With her dowry, he was able to buy a house on the Monte Pincio, where the two lived in quiet happiness for almost thirty-five years.*

Dowry or no dowry, an artist of modest means could not have turned his back on the patronage of the Church and the nobility without being sure of patronage from somewhere else. Of that Poussin was certain. He had made

---

* Gaspard Poussin, sometimes confused with Nicolas, was Anna Maria's brother. A very good landscape painter, he used the surname by virtue of adoption.

Fig. 15.69 Poussin. *Triumph of Flora*. Paris, Louvre. (Giraudon)

friends among the numerous scholars and antiquaries who shared his historical and archeological interests, and such men either were, or were acquainted with merchants, civil servants, lawyers, and bankers—persons capable of appreciating the painter's intellectual superiority and personal integrity. They did not, perhaps, command immense fortunes, but they had money, and they must have liked it that Poussin had established his own prices for his paintings, never raised them, and courteously returned the bonus sometimes sent by an admiring buyer.

One thing led to another; and in the course of time, Poussin became a kind of sage. He never pushed himself socially, it is said, but might be found strolling around of an evening, graciously ready to talk with anybody about any matter of serious interest. His reputation spread beyond Italy. Meeting him was one of the high points of a visit to Rome, and those who made his acquaintance corresponded with him after they returned home.

There is a tradition that Poussin's original desire to go to Rome had been inspired by seeing a collection of Marcantonio Raimondi's engravings after Raphael, shown to him by a friend in France. On the way to Rome, he sojourned at Venice, where he came to know and admire the work of Titian. He saw more Titians at Rome, notably three of the Este mythologies which left the Doria-Pamphili palace for Madrid as late as 1639. His earlier paintings were, as we have seen, too much affected by the overt action typical of contemporary Roman baroque art. In his new phase, he abandoned that and undertook a long series of so-called "bacchanals" that are distinctly Titianesque in both style and mood.

One of the most popular, in spite of damage from unwise cleaning, is the *Triumph of Flora* (Fig. 15.69). It is a lovely and lovable picture. The time seems to be early summer, when the light and air are gay and innocent, and the setting is nature in a friendly mood. It is a bit sober, perhaps, by comparison with Titian; but the individual figures are warm and alive even if they are a bit statuesque.

The bacchanals are but one illustration of Poussin's range; it is amazing that he could have shifted from the content of his *Massacre of the Innocents* into a lyric style. It is no wonder that he had many orders, several of them from Cardinal Richelieu. It is, indeed, but one more tribute to Richelieu's sagacity that he knew about Poussin and estimated his stature correctly. The association turned out, however, to be the most unfortunate thing that ever happened to the painter. About 1638, the King (doubtless at Richelieu's prompting) undertook to bring Poussin back to France. Attractive inducements failed to lure him from Rome, and presently inducement changed to pressure. In 1640, therefore, Poussin set out for the French capital.

He was cordially received there, provided with an excellent house and every other amenity. He was put in charge of decorating the Long Gallery of the Louvre and was asked to do several large altarpieces. The assignment was as much administrative as artistic: an operation of that scale, with pressure for completion, meant directing a corps of assistants, and it was very uncongenial to a man who liked to work in private on easel pictures. Poussin had to force himself as best he might, and the pictures which survive from that episode are concededly worked-up rather than inspired. We refer to a *Last Supper* and to the *Labors of Hercules,* all now in the Louvre.

It seems likely that Richelieu and the King had expected to put Poussin in charge of numerous royal enterprises, displacing incumbent French artists, some of whom were greater at the art of intrigue than at their stated profession. Sensing the danger, these men ganged up against the intruder and succeeded in putting him on the defensive. His schemes of decoration, they asserted, were so simple as to be ridiculously inadequate, and there were those who agreed with them. Poussin did not help matters by making contemptuous statements about his artistic rivals, and presently his situation became intolerable. "If I stay in this country," he wrote a friend in Italy, "I shall become a veritable swindler like the men here . . . he who is inclined to do well should keep away from this place." After eighteen months of it, he made an excuse to return to Rome, saying he had to fetch his wife. Obviously, he had no intention of returning, and he never did.

The Paris episode did him some good, however. He was able to renew

Fig. 15.70 Poussin. *Holy Family on the Steps*. 27 by 38½ inches. Washington, D. C., National Gallery of Art, Samuel H. Kress Collection.

old friendships, and make new ones. The fiasco at court made no difference to the intellectuals among whom he belonged, and with whom he was congenial. With people of that type, his reputation was greater than ever before. Once back in Rome, he found himself with an increased number of visitors and more correspondence to handle—also with a long list of loyal patrons who were glad to buy his paintings. In the ten years to follow, he produced the pictures which, then and now, stand as the best examples of French classicism.

In both form and content, his art took on a new solemnity. The religious pictures (Fig. 15.70) became more authentic than before; and in the classical field, the subject matter shifted from the pleasures of the gods to instances of Stoic philosophy: Coriolanus sacrificing himself for his country, Phocion suffering death with magnanimity, Diogenes casting material things aside. Concepts of the same sort occupied the attention of the contemporary tragedian Corneille; and it is important to remember that this was the generation which introduced into French art one of its ever-recurring themes, namely, the sacrifice of immediate and personal interests for the sake of an ideal, to serve honor, or for the social good.

The change in Poussin's art is best demonstrated by a comparison between his two versions of the *Arcadian Shepherds* (Figs. 15.71–72), one early

Figs. 15.71–72 Poussin. (left) *Arcadian Shepherds*. About 1630. 39¾ by 29½ inches. Chatsworth, Derbyshire, Collection of the Duke of Devonshire. Reproduced by permission of the Trustees of the Chatsworth Settlement. (opposite) *Arcadian Shepherds*. About 1650. 33½ by 47⅝ inches. Paris, Louvre. (Giraudon)

and one late. In both pictures, the setting and the incident are the same. The place is Arcadia, but we do not refer to the physical and geographical district of that name in the southern Peloponnesus—a rough and barren place. Arcady had been made into an ideal realm by Vergil and Horace. The peasants who lived there existed in bucolic joy, and they were in the habit (on a moment's notice, and quite without preparation) of breaking out into poetical expression of the highest quality. In both paintings, several of these peasants have come upon a tomb which bears the inscription "Et in Arcadia ego."

The expression did not come from classical literature, although it sounds as though it might. Apparently, it originated with some contemporary humanist. There is no way to be sure of the translation. If the initial *et* is conjunctive, the speaker is the deceased, and the words say, "And I, too, was in Arcadia." If the *et* is adverbial, it is Death who speaks, and says, "I, Death, am here, even in Arcadia." The alleged "rules" of Latin syntax (worked up by pedants to haze schoolboys) make the latter translation preferable, but there's small use splitting hairs about it. Either interpretation is good enough, and Poussin used them both.

The earlier painting is at first the more attractive of the two. A river-god lolls in the right foreground. A few feet beyond him, seen on the diagonal view, are two young men and a lovely girl, all lightly clad. In the course of their Arcadian wandering, they have come upon a tomb. Obviously, they

have been taken by surprise. The two men are engaged in deciphering the inscription, the force of which (in this instance) would seem to be admonitory. It is not the shepherds who are warned, so much as ourselves. "I, Death," we are advised, "hold sway even in Arcady."

The second version is less dramatic. Instead of the baroque diagonal, our line of sight is virtually frontal. The tomb and the figures are parallel to the picture plane. The composition is the simple geometric figure so often used by Raphael and Leonardo, and by most other Italian artists before Tintoretto started experimenting with new and startling vistas. The young men are relaxed and the girl so modestly draped as to eliminate the erotic overtones present in the earlier painting. There is no surprise; indeed, it is to be supposed that these folk know the tomb, and perhaps knew the deceased. They are thinking not of a fearful future, but of the past, which seems to have been beautiful. For them, the inscription is an elegy, and it means, "I, too, lived in Arcady."

There are numerous other instances where Poussin painted a certain subject, and then painted it again after protracted meditation, almost always with the result that the second picture is more mellow and mature than the first. In this case, even his first one showed reconsideration, for he got the idea from an *Arcadian Shepherds,* by Guercino, now in the Corsini Gallery at Rome.

The disciples of Roger Fry have often accused Poussin of depending upon "literary values" rather than "significant form"; but it is notable that *Et in Arcadia ego,* provocative statement that it is, does little more than embroider the meaning, so obvious and so subtly different, which we are compelled to infer from the pictorial facts of either version. The tomb (and every other tomb) does indeed evoke "associations" of a kind against which Fry warned us all, but Fry was blind and even rather stupid with respect to associations. The daily life of every human being is replete with them, and any picture that represents humanity is bound to fetch them up.

Some time in his middle forties, Poussin became interested in landscape painting. Unquestionably, he was affected by the success of his friend and neighbor Claude Lorrain (see below), and superficially, his landscapes are like Claude's. Both men, that is to say, produced easel paintings which give a broad vista out over an Italian landscape where trees and hills are punctuated here and there by the works of man: temples, forts, and bridges, some times in good repair, some times in chaste ruin. There is, however, a world of difference in the purpose to which each man put the landscape subject matter. Baldly stated it is this: Claude painted landscape for its own sake, and cared almost nothing for the narrative subject which he usually felt obliged to include as a conventional formality. Poussin's interest lay in the possibility of making landscape expound the deeper and inner meaning of some noble and solemn action.

It is very doubtful whether Poussin ever painted a portrait of any particular view. He usually placed the human actors in the near foreground, as in Figure 15.73, and he led the eye into the distance by a clearly indicated route, usually some kind of spiral which ends in the remote horizon. The light is always pure, cool, and equable, and he never took any interest in the vapors or shimmers inseparable from atmosphere in its natural state. Neither was he concerned with the aboriginal confusion in which inanimate nature actually exists.

Having decided on his purpose, Poussin constructed a landscape to fit. He did, for example, two paintings on the theme of the death of Phocion. The one in the Louvre shows two male figures carrying away the body which had been denied a decent funeral at Athens, and the one now at Knowsley, in the collection of the Earl of Derby, shows a lonely woman gathering up the hero's ashes. In both pictures, the landscape—somber, noble, and comprehended by the eye at a measured pace—carries the meaning. By contrast, the setting of the *Orpheus and Eurydice,* in New York, seems immanent with a sense of present emergency. Again, in Figure 15.73, there are flashes of revelation which provide a pictorial counterpart to the experiences of Saint John as he sat on his island writing the Apocalypse.

Because they were deliberately built and are as lucid as a mathematical

Fig. 15.73 Poussin. *Saint John on Patmos*. Between 1645 and 1650. 40 by 53½ inches. Courtesy of the Art Institute of Chicago, A. A. Munger Collection.

formula, some critics have called Poussin's landscapes "architectural," or "architectonic." Both words, while vaguely expressive of the facts, have confusing overtones and should be avoided. In any case, the important matter is not the logic of the construction, but the fact that Poussin, most of the time a figure painter, appreciated the small scale of humanity in relation to the environment, and the small significance of our greatest heroes in relation to history.

When Poussin died at the age of seventy-one, he was a man of great reputation, respected as much for his character and intellect as for his art. In our very short account of his long career, we have perforce concentrated upon his more successful paintings. A longer treatment would force us to deal with his failures, of which there were a good many. His severely rational methods foreclosed spontaneity and at times unquestionably inhibited his imagination, with the result that many canvases simply lack the spark of life and seem not solemn, but merely dead and heavy. At his best, however, he came very close to reincarnating the ideals of Fifth-century Athens.

The landscape painter Claude Gelée (1600–1682) has long been known in English-speaking lands as Claude Lorrain, and of late merely as Claude. He was born at Chamagne, near Nancy, orphaned early, and apprenticed to a baker. He must have learned his trade well because he secured employment as a pastry cook by the time he was about fourteen, and got a job in Rome. His employer was a minor painter named Tassi, and it would appear that the lad was soon working in the studio as well as the kitchen.

He was back in France from 1625 to 1627, when he returned permanently to Rome. On his journeys, he had passed through Venice, Marseilles, Genoa, Civitavecchia, and other ports; and about 1623, for some reason or other, he had been in Naples. To his inland eyes, the stately ships and the teeming life of the harbors were incredibly romantic, and the curve of the Bay of Naples, with Capri and Ischia in the distance, remained in memory for the rest of his life. He was equally fascinated by the Roman Campagna, and his favorite avocation was taking long walks, sometimes with Poussin as companion, sketch book in hand.

As we remarked above, Claude's classicism (if, indeed, it was classicism) differed from Poussin's. The man must have commenced his career as an illiterate, and he never became a scholar. Convention made it almost necessary that he attach religious or classical labels to his paintings, but when called upon to put an Apollo or Perseus into a landscape, he farmed the figure painting out to others, who were some times none too skillful. He must have picked up a good deal of information by talking with learned friends, and he must have reacted to the nostalgia every man feels when in Rome or near Rome; but it is probably an exaggeration to suggest that he attempted to reincarnate the life Vergil lived in his villa, or the Golden Age when Aeneas founded the Eternal City. It is notable, in that connection, that his famous series of "classical harbors" contain architecture from every period, including the Gothic, and ships of a type unknown before the 17th century (Fig. 15.74). They are harbors, to be sure, but more like Genoa or Venice than anything that existed in the ancient world.

The buildings that appear in Claude's pictures are questionably full of suggestion, but it is a mistake to single them out as the operative element in his art. He had inherited Palladio's peculiar feeling for the interplay between masonry and the air (page 645). The truth is that Claude was a painter of light and atmosphere, one of the first and still one of the greatest. If we may over-simplify for sake of emphasis: earlier painters had handled light as though it were an external phenomenon, shining into the picture in order to make objects visible. With Claude, light became the primary subject matter. His horizon lines are always shimmering. Masts and rigging become gossamers in the luminous mist. The architecture he painted lacks the solidity of Poussin's; it is replete with windows, porticoes, and arcades through which the luminous atmosphere can move and flow. He was perhaps the first artist who habitually undertook to make the light come out of the picture rather than into it; and, as in Figure 15.74, he dared to put the setting sun in the

Fig. 15.74 Claude (Lorrain). *Ulysses Returns Chryseis to Her Father*. Paris, Louvre. (Alinari)

central position. The rest of the painting is so full of fascinating detail as to be almost inexhaustible, and one will have difficulty in locating the maiden Chryseis, the titular heroine, who is about to embark. From the standpoint of design, all these things are subordinate; it is the source of light which governs.

Claude and Poussin, both separately and together, had an influence on European art and culture so far-reaching as to defy the art of declarative statement. Among French artists, Poussin was recognized as an ideal even before he was dead, and during the second half of the 17th century, the academicians (see below) accorded him virtually the same authority they gave the ancients. The early works of the 19th-century painter David (page 826) are more like Poussin's soberest paintings, and less like the antique than has commonly been supposed. Cézanne (page 879) publicly acknowledged Poussin as his inspiration, and without a knowledge of Poussin, no one can appreciate Cézanne.

The distinction between Claude and Poussin is plain enough to students of art, but they were often grouped together in the public mind. Of the two, Claude was the easier to understand because, instead of constructing land-scapes according to classical theories, he collected in his sketch books souvenirs of works of art by nature herself, with or without the embellishment of man-made architecture, and he then combined the samples into finished paintings —without, however, losing the mood of accident and spontaneity. The word "picturesque" was, in fact, invented during the 18th century to indicate views and vistas which looked like pictures by Claude. Where nature's success in composition had proven imperfect, it was possible for landscape architecture to intervene, and full many a park and garden (especially in England, where Claude was popular) is best understood as an attempt to reproduce the imagery he had introduced to our culture.

It would be impossible to draw up a list of every artist who, in one way or another, followed in the footsteps of Claude and Poussin and painted pictures containing architecture and land or seascape in some kind of combination. In Italy, the painter Pannini (1691–1765) made a career of painting the buildings of Rome, and the etcher Piranesi (1720–1778), a much better artist, circulated his prints all over the western world. Canaletto (1697–1768) and Guardi (1712–1793) painted the stones and the light of Venice respectively. The French artist Hubert Robert (1733–1808) ought to be cited for his paintings which were primarily architectural, and the Englishman Richard Wilson (1713–1782) for his, which were primarily landscapes. None of these men, delightful though they some times are, can be classed with Turner (1775–1851), one of the greatest technicians of all time, who took up the painting of light where Claude had left off, and never failed to express his reverence (page 852) for his predecessor.

♦ *The Era of Louis the 14th*   When Cardinal Mazarin died in March 1661, Louis the 14th at once announced that he would assume personal direction of the government, and thus commenced what was certainly the most spectacular, if not the greatest, era in French history. The internal administration prepared by Henry the 4th, Richelieu, and Mazarin was already so efficient that very little remained to be done in order to eliminate the last vestige of opposition to the central authority. Two decades of successful wars proved that France was more powerful than any other nation. Clever development of her economy supplied her with what, for some time, looked like inexhaustible wealth.

All of this was accomplished by a thoroughgoing application of the paternalistic and authoritarian principle. There can be no doubt that Louis entertained a high sense of his responsibility to France, but he either could not or would not consider any way of discharging his obligations except by the method of orders from above and compliance from below, with himself at the apex of the pyramid. He was interested in directing every detail of French life. He improved the roads, instituted improvements in agriculture, built up a merchant fleet, and replaced the authority of the old trade guilds with his own, imposing a new set of regulations in every instance. He did not limit his concern to material welfare, but took measures to direct the intellectual and religious life of the nation. He vigorously upheld the independence of the French church from the Pope, and at the same time stamped out any movements (Jansenism, for example) which might breed internal disunity. His famous aphorism, "L'etat c'est moi," was very close to the truth.

The royal program was not only successful, but (for a number of years) remarkably popular. All classes were ready to glorify the King, and the King was more than ready to glorify himself. There was genuine ability behind his conceit, and shrewd policy as well. He promulgated his public image as a modern Alexander, and as "Le Roi Soleil" (The Sun-King). There were plenty of people who maintained that modern kings were as great as any ancient kings, and that Louis was the best among them. And had he not, like another Apollo, made the sun to shine on France?

In Louis' scheme of universal direction, it was the business of the visual arts to magnify the personality of the monarch and provide a suitable setting for his person. In that enterprise, he was extraordinarly lucky in his lieutenants. From Mazarin, he had inherited an organizational genius named Jean-Baptiste Colbert who, until he died in 1683, might be described as the man who held the throttle (and very occasionally applied the brakes) of Louis' governmental engine. Colbert's responsibilities were multifarious, but he took a particular interest in art. "A king," he is quoted as saying, "is known by his monuments." He was therefore tireless in encouraging Louis in his natural taste for palaces, paintings, furniture, costume, and every imaginable kind of display. For such purposes, he systematically diverted a proportion of the national wealth which has yet to be justified by any economic theory, ancient or modern, but which was perhaps worthwhile for political prestige.

Colbert took care to keep the ultimate control of artistic investments in his own hands: he had himself made superintendent of buildings, and Protector of the Academy, and he was always comptroller of the public purse. In most practical matters, however, he delegated complete authority to the painter *Charles Le Brun* (1619–1690).

Le Brun had accompanied Poussin when the latter returned to Rome in 1642, and he stayed there about four years. From Poussin, he acquired the notion of a French classical style, and doubtless picked up, also, a number of ideas useful for survival in the competition and intrigue of the French court. Colbert and Le Brun were embarking upon a program of artistic investment which, for sheer scale and ramification, quite outdid anything since the collapse of the Roman Empire. They needed an army of artists and craftsmen who must be organized in accordance with the centralized theory of control, and most of whom were yet to be trained.

They made a distinction between artists and craftsmen, and with the latter, they were extremely successful. Le Brun took over the Gobelin tapestry establishment on the left bank, and converted it into a manufactury which could produce almost anything that might be made. Cabinetmakers, wood carvers, goldsmiths, founders, wheelwrights, and skilled workers of almost every other kind were recruited. At times, the working force approached three hundred men.

Le Brun was greatly concerned with the training of apprentices, and the system he established probably accounts for the extraordinary durability of the organization, which retained its identity through the Napoleonic era, and still exists in vestigial form. Le Brun himself was an ideal head of the organization. He could design almost anything, and design it well: a tapestry, a stage coach, a scheme of interior decoration, a piece of furniture or silver, the lock on a door. No praise can be too high for the standards of quality he established and maintained, and to him must go much of the credit for the association of France with articles of choice in every department of life.

The training of artists was a much more serious and difficult matter. The Academy furnished Colbert and Le Brun with a splendid piece of machinery for the purpose, and they turned their attention to strengthening it and making it efficient. Like everything else they did, their program was rational to a remarkable degree. If art were in fact an expression of pure reason, their system would doubtless have succeeded. Every one knows that, in a larger sense, it failed, but there was more good in it than some writers have been willing to admit.

It will be recalled that Richelieu had founded the Academy of Literature in 1635, and that the Academy of Painting dates from 1648. In fairly short order, other academies were established: the dance in 1661, science in 1666, music in 1669, and architecture in 1671. By a thorough tightening of the organization in 1663, Colbert and Le Brun had put all of these departments under a single authority. In 1666, furthermore, they had taken the important step of creating a French Academy at Rome.

Le Brun visualized a curriculum for teaching each one of the arts, and he undertook to develop it by a procedure which is not unknown in educational circles today. In spirit, each of the curricula was the same, and we may restrict our attention to that of painting.

Eminent painters, academicians and others, were asked to prepare lectures and treatises dealing with artistic theory in one aspect or another. Analysis and discussion were to follow; and it was assumed that, in the end, the principles of art would be defined. Knowing the principles, it would then be possible to lay down a set of rules to be followed in practice. A great many meetings were actually held, and numerous papers were written. Many of them are still available, and they are anything but light reading. In the end, a curriculum of sorts emerged.

An *École Académique* had been founded in 1648. It did not acquire its presently familiar name of *École des Beaux Arts* (colloquially "the Beaux Arts") until 1793. Now free to men and women between fifteen and thirty upon passing an entrance examination, the institution from its inception made available formal instruction under established masters. Attendance there has always been the easiest and most natural way for young artists to learn, and presently to put themselves (usually for a fee) under the personal tutelage of some leading figure of the day.

The formal curriculum involved both lectures and work in the studio— the lectures to inculcate the correct philosophy of art, and the studio to teach the right style. We need not dwell at length on the lectures because their purpose is already familiar to the reader. In brief, the students were urged to learn how to paint French pictures which would be very much like the great frescoes of the Italian Grand Style.

With respect to subject matter, the student was warned to avoid anything "low" and urged to seek only the "noble." By nobility, the academicians meant episodes from Greek and Roman history, from the Bible, or from some other tradition which had acquired an heroic aura.

It was conceded that painting must represent nature, but the artist's dealings with natural fact must, it was asserted, be governed by reason. Reason tells us that nature in the raw, while bountiful, is disorderly. The wise French artist, it was suggested, would discriminate, choosing only the most beautiful parts. He would then compose his picture with due regard for the unities of time, place, and action. The reader will recognize in this dogma merely a restatement of the idealism set forth by Alberti (page 550), but the 17th-century Frenchmen gave it some new twists which are interesting, and perhaps amusing.

It was stipulated that ancient art was very nearly perfect. It was conceded that Raphael had come close to reincarnating the ancient formulas, and Poussin always received reverent mention. By contrast, the Dutch and Flemish artists had painted with realism but no discrimination, and should be avoided. The great Venetians were to be studied with caution because they depended too much upon color (which was damned as transient, and appealing to the emotions) and too little upon drawing (which was the intellectual, and thus the respectable and reliable, element of art). As a practical proposition, it was pointed out that young artists, as individuals, could never hope to repeat the generations of research which formed the foundation for Raphael and the ancients, but they could save time by taking advantage of the findings of those great masters.

The studio program of the Academy was well calculated to implement these theories. Beginners were set to work making meticulous drawings in charcoal after ancient statues or casts therefrom. Because statues can not move and may be left in position with the same lighting for weeks and even months at a time, such instruction offered an opportunity for protracted refinement of the drawing. All the statuary used for the purpose was white (or some dusty variant). Shadows show up well on white, making it easy for the student to perfect himself in the modeling of contours. And all the while, because his subject matter was chastely monochromatic, the student was quarantined from the infection of color.

By drawing from the cast, the student made himself intimately familiar with the style of ancient sculpture; that was the first purpose and the first step in his training. Because the classical style, like any other style, is merely an habitual way of expressing oneself, those who learned from the casts formed habits considered eminently desirable. Consciously or unconsciously, they might be counted upon to put any figure in a classical pose and idealize its contours and texture. By that time, they were ready for the living model, and entered what has since been known as "life class" or merely as "life." The study of the model was an extension of the same pedagogy. The schools employed, when convenient, models who looked like classical statues. That wasn't always feasible; but every student who had learned his lesson knew exactly what to do. He corrected nature's oversight by abstracting the model's appearance in the general direction of classical idealism.

The academic curriculum was not only restrictive and authoritarian; it was tedious beyond description. Students of independent mind have been fighting it and cursing it for three hundred years. Nevertheless, there have always been plenty of students, and the reasons are easy to explain.

In the first place, to be a student at the Beaux Arts was to be recognized, socially, as a person engaged in an honorable enterprise. When the Academy of Painting was established in 1648, the French government (and probably with intention) put an end to the medieval worry as to whether the visual arts were liberal or adulterine, and nascent artists were henceforth assured of their own gentility.

Colbert and Le Brun, moreover, had been too shrewd to depend upon authority and honor alone; they offered inducements. Students who gained the approval of their masters were encouraged to take competitive examinations; the successful ones were sent off to the French Academy at Rome and generously maintained there for a period of five years. The prospect was enough to temper the thoughts of any young man, rambunctiously independent though he might wish to be. Who could not learn much at Rome? And 17th-century Rome, as we have seen, was not the museum of our own day, but a center of living art where one might see the grand baroque churches going up, the fountains being installed, and great frescoes being painted. And who could be so proud as to overlook the professional preferment beckoning in later years for those so privileged in youth? And who could be so reckless as to overlook the fact that significant commissions were likely to come from only one source, the crown? And who, finally, could be so impractical as not to reflect that the crown meant the Comptroller of France and his artistic administrators?

The failure of the academic enterprise was never fully demonstrated until the 19th century (pages 833 ff.). Its faults have been apparent, however, from the beginning and, in the nature of the case, have furnished material for many a polemic. Too seldom has it been pointed out that the instruction available at the Beaux Arts, whatever its errors and deficiencies, has always been the best that might be found in an imperfect world. That is why students from every country have come to Paris, and still do. Some of them have become remarkable painters, even great painters—usually, it is true, by breaking the rules they supposedly had learned. In any event, it is particularly unfair to blame the Academy because it did not immediately produce great artists in quantity. There is no evidence that the French population during the second half of the 17th century contained a single young man with the potential of a Bernini or a Rembrandt. All one can ask of any educational system is that its graduates reach a minimum level of competence, and Le Brun's students certainly became uniformly competent even though not one of them was inspired.

In view of the severity of Le Brun's theories, one might expect his painting to be chaste almost beyond belief. Pictures like Figure 15.75 therefore seem quite out of character; but, as Sir Anthony Blunt has put it, Le Brun found it much easier to be consistent in theory than in practice. His philosophy was neoclassical, but the arrival of an authentically neoclassical art was delayed until the 19th century (pages 825 ff.). In the meantime, Le Brun and his contemporaries conformed to the taste of their own time and place. Their art was baroque with some admixture of northern realism and totally without the passion which make the most extreme examples of Italian Baroque seem plausible and even acceptable. If we may steal another remark from Sir Anthony, Le Brun never painted a picture one feels inclined to dwell over. His real contributions were as an organizer and in the design of great schemes of interior decoration: at the Louvre, the Salon of Apollo, and at Versailles the Halls of Peace and War, and the Galerie des Glâces.

Le Brun's position as artistic dictator depended upon Colbert, who died in 1683. Colbert's successor Louvois favored Pierre Mignard (1610–1695), and Le Brun gracefully accepted the situation. He continued to receive occasional indications of royal regard, but the big commissions went elsewhere.

Fig. 15.75 Charles Le Brun. *Louis XIV Adoring the Risen Christ*. Lyon, Museum. (Camponogara)

Mignard was a professional rival, but his artistic principles scarcely differed from Le Brun's, and the same may be said of Hyacinthe Rigaud (1659–1745) and Nicolas Largillière (1656–1746), both of whom did a great many state portraits. The general state of French painting at the end of the 17th century may be inferred from Rigaud's familiar portrait of Louis the 14th at the age of 53 (Fig. 15.76).

This was perhaps the monarch's favorite representation of himself and has often been cited as the picture which shows him as he wished to be remembered. The colors are strong, but have a certain absence of appeal which might have pleased Le Brun. There is scarcely anything else about the painting which seems consistent with academic dogma. It is, in fact, a Frenchified version of the ceremonial portraits of Rubens and Van Dyck with the column, the familiar swirling curtain, the swaggering, twisted pose, the excessively elaborate costume, and the usual attributes—in this instance, objects from the treasury at St. Denis, including Charlemagne's sword. Opinions differ

Fig. 15.76 Rigaud. *Portrait of Louis XIV*. 1691. Paris, Louvre.

about this picture. Some critics find it the perfect expression of *la grandeur française*. Others say that there is no better demonstration of the conceit, bombast, and outright bad taste which existed at the court of Louis the 14th.

Colbert did his utmost to stave off the King's ultimate decision to move his residence and his government to Versailles. During the decade of the 1660's he therefore tried to keep Louis interested in Paris by proposing improvements and additions to the Louvre, which he hoped would remain the principal seat of the monarchy.

After fussing about with several French architects, some of whom he disliked and some of whom he appears to have bullied, Colbert decided to call in experts from Italy. After negotiating with several, he finally invited Bernini to come to Paris. Arriving in 1665, Bernini soon made himself unpopular. He insulted the local artists, who were not unnaturally against him in the first place. He annoyed the officials with whom he had to deal by

Fig. 15.77 Paris. Louvre. Eastern façade. About 1680. Designed by Claude Perrault, Charles Le Brun, and Louis Le Vau.

making comparisons between Paris and Rome which were distinctly unflattering to French traditions. But worse than that, he seemed unable to produce a set of plans which the King and Colbert could approve. His first project was so flamboyant and curvilinear that any one could have predicted it would not suit French taste. His later suggestions were impossibly expensive and lacked certain practical features Colbert demanded. In the spring of 1667, the King decided France had had enough of Bernini, and the famous Italian went home, having completed virtually nothing except the bust of Louis, now on view at Versailles.

The episode is worth remembering, not for itself, but because it stands as a historical landmark. It was the first plain signal that the artistic capital of the world was shifting from Rome to Paris, and it was to be followed by others. Italian authors began to publish books about art with dedications to the King of France or to Colbert. More significantly still, in the year 1675, Le Brun was elected President of the Academy of Saint Luke at Rome. It is true that Poussin had held the same post; but Poussin was an adopted Roman, and Le Brun a foreigner who had not been in Rome for nearly thirty years.

Having dismissed Bernini, the King called in Louis Le Vau, his first architect, Le Brun, and a man named Claude Perrault. Within three years, these men, acting in collaboration, designed and built the present eastern wing of the Louvre, with its justly celebrated colonnade (Fig. 15.77). There has been no end of debate as to the part played in the design by each of the three gentlemen, and the tendency has been to assign the most credit to Perrault, who was by profession a physician. He had, however, published an edition of Vitruvius and is known to have had some training as an engineer. In any event, the colonnade was not quite like anything ever designed before, was probably the best single work of architecture of the entire reign, and has been the model for countless public buildings since.

No building could possibly be a happier demonstration of French classicism in general or of the academic spirit in particular. With respect to the program of the academies, there could not be a better illustration of the truth that the neoclassical enterprise was much more practical in architecture than in painting. The painters had nothing to guide them but a fragmentary collection of inferior statuary, but the architects had a wealth of genuine Roman ruins; and occasionally, as in this instance, they were able to put up buildings which were classical in spirit as well as classical in detail.

In broad terms, the eastern front of the Louvre was a derivative from Michelangelo's Palace of the Senate on the Capitol Hill in Rome (Fig. 14.29, page 617). The flat skyline, familiar enough in Italy, was a novelty in northern Europe at this date, and it made possible the peculiarly successful emphasis on the central doorway by means of a slightly salient pavilion topped by a pediment which rises into the clear. The colonnade itself is much closer to the peristyle of a Roman temple than to anything in Renaissance Italy. It was a purely Parisian touch to put the columns in pairs, to bring them out from the wall behind, and to space them far apart—so far, in fact, as to render the span too wide for any lintel. Perrault designed some clever flat arches instead. No doubt the effect lightened the façade in a manner distinctly not classical, and distinctly better than most classical work. The large windows in the basement story operate, in similar fashion, to ameliorate the bulk and weight of the masonry, and the pilastered pavilions at either end define the limits of the composition definitely but not overbearingly.

Before the new wing of the Louvre was complete, Louis had made his decision to move to Versailles, and the colossal extravagance commenced and continued until the chapel there was dedicated, as late as 1710 (Fig. 15.22). A series of architects were employed to enlarge and remodel. Painters and sculptors worked on the decorations inside and out. One hundred sculptors, it is said, were employed in the gardens alone.

The word "palace" is scarcely adequate to describe Versailles. It is, rather, a small city laid out according to a complex but symmetrical plan; and in Louis' day, it housed not only the royal family and the numerous nobles who lived at court, but the bureaucracy of government as well. It was there that the King made his ceremonial appearances on state occasions. He received foreign ambassadors there. But above all, it was there that he entertained on a scale more elaborate than any Roman emperor. Operas and ballets, specially composed, were almost routine at Versailles, and great occasions called for out-of-door fêtes which lasted several days on end. Writers, actors, artists, decorators, costumers, and craftsmen almost without number were constantly at work putting on one display after another.

Versailles is the biggest palace on record and certainly the most expensive. Its formal gardens are the most extended the world has yet seen. Its interior décor is lavish, and was even more lavish when the original furniture (some of it silver) was in place. And yet Versailles is more a political and social monument than a work of art. It accomplished Louis' intended purpose of advertising the French monarchy, its success in that respect being attested by its great influence upon the design of other capitals, other gardens, and even country houses, all over Europe and in America. But not all French taste is good taste, and not all French art good art. The architecture of Versailles suffers from the very size of the buildings; it was of necessity mass-produced, and is more interminable than impressive. The interior decoration (mostly directed by Le Brun) is remarkably *sui generis,* but—if we are honest with ourselves—as objectionably ostentatious as the King himself.

THE ROCOCO

Although we Americans will always have a special place in our hearts for it, the 18th century was not a century of great art. It nevertheless put its mark on everything it touched, and its special contribution was to touch everything. Not a single artist of the period can be described as a world figure, but the absence of great men was compensated for by universal good taste which applied itself to the refinement and perfection of almost every man-made object. There is no ready explanation for the phenomenon, but it is a fact that gunsmiths in Pennsylvania demonstrated quite as nice an esthetic sense as painters in Paris, and worked in the same style.

The Rococo was, in fact, the last style to which all Western civilization subscribed. Most of the furniture, silverware, china, cloth, and wallpaper in use today follows 18th-century models so closely as to duplicate them. Most houses and public buildings still do the same, and variants are conspicuous when they happen. It has been truly said that the era embodied every advance made since the fall of Rome, including a great many more of the so-called mechanical conveniences than we might suppose.

The Rococo developed directly from the Baroque, and as a distinct variation thereof, it may be recognized in Paris during the last few years of the reign of Louis the 14th. Neither the King nor the court had anything to do with it. They remained resident at Versailles, where the daily routine of ceremonial living became ever more formal, pompous, and boring, until the more than timely demise of the monarch in 1715. In the meantime, the Rococo had been getting under way.

Fig. 15.78 Watteau. *Jupiter and Antiope*. Paris. Louvre. (Giraudon)

The artist who best illustrates every important feature of the style was *Antoine Watteau* (1684–1721), a painter of Flemish origin who arrived at Paris in 1715. He first supported himself by doing hack work. Presently he built up a patronage among the rich folk of the city. Many of them were newly rich; some had actually returned to Europe after making fortunes in the new world. All of them seem to have been specially endowed with the esthetic intelligence so common at the time, and instinctively, all seem to have appreciated that Watteau was the man who could make the Baroque over into a pleasanter, less bombastic idiom, suitable for the home as contrasted with the palace. In bringing about the required modification of the style, Watteau not only worked for and with the gentlemen who paid his bills, but with their wives as well. The emergence of the Rococo marks, in fact, the first important operation of feminine taste as a definitive factor in the history of art.

The difference between the Baroque and the Rococo is epitomized by the comparison between Figures 15.22 and 15.78, and the reader will find it helpful to supplement the latter by reference to Figures 15.79 and 15.80. Watteau's painting derived directly from Rubens. That fact comes out much more plainly in full color than in photographs, but the resemblance is clear enough in the latter nevertheless. Watteau had a daintier figure style than

Fig. 15.79 Watteau. *A Woman Seated*. Drawing. New York, Pierpont Morgan Library.

Rubens; it would be incorrect, however, to say that his canon was delicate. The poses he habitually used are much closer to Rubens than at first seems evident. As Rubens had done, Watteau conceived the anatomy to be an ensemble of several related masses. He almost always gave the figure a pronounced turn at the waist. He pitched the torso at an angle to the hips. He turned the head on the neck; and he lifted or depressed the chin. Such habits almost invariably made it necessary to present at least one part of the body in bold foreshortening, with consequent enhancement, on the part of the observer, of a sense of thrust in the shoulders, hips, bust, head, or elbows as the case might be. Watteau's dynamics, in short, were much the same as Rubens'; the important difference between the two artists had less to do with style than with content.

In sum, we may say that like the Baroque, the Rococo was an art of movement; but the movement was slower and gentler. The masses set in

Fig. 15.80 Watteau. *Two Studies of a Woman.* Drawing. London, British Museum.

motion, moreover, were lighter; the comparison between the two styles was the difference between power and grace. What applied to movement applied to everything else. The lighting was similar, but softer. The contours were convex, but less emphatically so. The textures were luxuriant, but more modest. And above all, the favorite subject matter, narrative or otherwise, was mild, charming, and for the most part inconsequential. Impact had been the most obvious effect of the Baroque upon the emotions; the Rococo merely sought to delight.

Watteau was, in fact, one of the very few authentically lyric painters in the whole history of art, and he made his reputation by painting a goodly number of pictures like Figure 15.81. As a class, they are known as *fêtes galantes;* the formula for one was the formula for all. The setting is always out of doors, usually in a baroque garden. The time of day is always dusk, or thereabouts. The time of year is always early summer, and the fresh foliage

Fig. 15.81 Wateau. *Les Champs Élysées*. Between 1717 and 1721. 16⅜ by 12½ inches. London, Wallace Collection.

is shown as growing half-wild, with consequent amelioration of the severity of such architecture and sculpture as may be in view. Ladies and gentlemen sit on the grass or stroll through the groves, making love to each other or simply enjoying that perfect time of day and year. There is no sense of hurry; but neither is there a hint of lassitude. The technique itself is peculiarly in keeping with such a mood; it is a moderate impressionism which describes everything adequately and pleasantly.

The remarkable thing was that Watteau could successfully multiply pictures of the same kind. He did not hesitate to use the same figure again and again in successive compositions; in fact, the same figure sometimes occurs more than once in the same composition. His methods of work were systematic and rational to a degree; and yet he never failed to evoke the elusive, indefinable, precious poetry which we think of as characteristic of Giovanni Bellini, Giorgione, and almost no one else.

As indicated above, the Rococo was an all-inclusive style. Paintings like those just reviewed were never intended to exist independently. All of the rococo artists were prepared to design entire schemes of interior decoration, and their pictures, however excellent in themselves, were meant to fit in. Watteau's position as prime mover in that new fashion has all too seldom been emphasized; Figure 15.82 shows one of his designs—the kind of drawing which might eventuate in a painting, an overmantel carved in wood, a panel of sculpture, or a tapestry back for a sofa.

Certain details of the style demand our attention because they are essential to an understanding of the Rococo as it expressed itself in architecture, furniture, silverware, and all the other arts which are relatively abstract and deal in solid materials. As in the Baroque, the individual forms were largely of classical derivation, and there is a similar sense of curvature and movement in and out. Every proportion was made radically lighter, however— lighter to such a degree, indeed, that the style remained only slightly plastic, and tended to become linear.

At whatever point the artist began to feel that he was expressing himself in line, certain new possibilities opened up before him. He made a study of curvature, with the result that the Rococo contains the greatest variety of graceful curves in the history of art, almost never simple circular arcs, and almost always with subtle variations in their curvature. In combining one curve with another, Watteau was meticulous to preserve the identity of both. His curves do not flow into one another, as in modern streamlining. Instead, he employed the principle of tangency. The drawing under review contains a great many examples, and the reader can find a great many more in the objects he sees around him at home: the handle of a tea pot, the leg of a

LES JARDINS DE BACHUS

Fig. 15.82 Engraving by Gabriel Huquier, after a drawing by Watteau. New York, Cooper Union.

chair, the trigger guard of a fine gun. In most instances, two curves of contrary direction are brought into contact, with the result that the motion of the eye is arrested and gently reversed.

The style Watteau had made popular was promptly taken up by the court and nobility as soon as Louis the 14th died. For that reason, we often hear the Rococo period referred to as "Louis Quinze." Because the existence of Versailles made further building superfluous (and also because the population felt strongly about the late king's depletion of the treasury for that purpose), there was almost no major construction in France for the rest of the century. A few sections of Versailles were subdivided, however, on a more intimate scale, and these were entirely redecorated and refurnished in the rococo manner. Figure 15.83 shows a characteristic example.

In Germany, however, the situation was reversed. The French language, French clothes, and French customs of every kind were immensely popular among the privileged classes there during the 18th century. As a result, the numerous noblemen who, as a loose federation, provided Germany with a collective government, each and all yearned to emulate Versailles on such scale as they could afford. Frederick the Great built a rococo palace at Potsdam and named it *Sanssouci*. As an instance of style, we shall be better

Fig. 15.83   Versailles. Apartment of Louis the 15th. (Archives Photographiques)

served, however, by Figure 15.84, which shows the Baroque just at the stage when it might first be called Rococo.

The ecclesiastical architecture of South Germany and Austria forms a special chapter in the history of the Baroque and Rococo. Building had come to a standstill during the Thirty Years' War. When that conflict finally came to an end in 1648, there was great need of new construction. In as much as both regions had remained Catholic, it was natural that they looked southward for inspiration. A number of Italian architects found a career north of the Alps, and German and Austrian builders made it a habit to sojourn at Rome. While there, they fastened on to the more extreme Baroque of Bernini and Boromini, made it their own, and returned home to execute statues and buildings considerably more extravagant than anything ever attempted in Italy.

As the 18th century did its work, German designers started going to Paris as well as Rome, with the result that the Italian Baroque merged with the French Rococo to produce some of the finest churches in all history. One of the best is the Vierzehnheiligen, seen in Figure 15.85. It is a pilgrimage church, standing alone in the country some dozen miles north of Bamberg. It is doubtful whether any other interior is quite so elaborately lovely. The eye is delighted by white and pink and gold, and by the surfaces which so subtly

Fig. 15.84 Dresden. The Zwinger Palace. Entrance of the northwest wing. 1711–1722. (Marburg)

define and yet open up fascinating effects of space. Let it be a lesson to us all that the somewhat Puritanical writings of Ruskin and Moore have persuaded English speaking students to overlook these wonderful churches for the past hundred years. We owe a debt to Professor Pevsner and Professor Faison for finally putting the matter right. As Pevsner correctly says, the best 18th-century German architecture is as good as the best German music of the same period.

In France, Watteau had two immediate followers, Lancret and Pater. Their principal function in history was to demonstrate the excellence of their

Fig. 15.85 Province of Franconia. Church of the Vierzehnheiligen. 1743–1772. Designed by Balthasar Neumann. (Hirmer Verlag)

master, for both failed every time as inevitably as Watteau succeeded. The reader may amuse himself at leisure by trying to ascertain why; the answer is by no means easy or certain—a painting by either man looks, in fact, enough like a painting by Watteau to be carelessly mistaken for one.

The Rococo continued to dominate French taste, and the taste of the world, until the Revolution of 1789. François Boucher (1703–1770) was its most prominent practitioner during his long career. As the favorite painter of Madame Pompadour, he made a business of erotica which, though superbly conceived and executed, were so cold as to remain innocuous (Fig. 15.86).

In due course, Fragonard (1732–1806) succeeded Boucher as the leading

Fig. 15.86 Boucher. *Cupid a Captive.*
1754. London, Wallace Collection.

artist of France. He made a tour of Italy, and to that experience we owe a
number of superb and sensitive landscape pictures, mostly of the baroque
gardens taken over by trees and shrubs which, by that time, were all of a
century old. His French patrons were interested in horticulture, however, only
insofar as it furnished a setting for human dalliance; and Fragonard delightedly supplied their demand. He became the prince among painters of
naughty gallantry (Fig. 15.87). It is doubtful, in fact, whether he ever painted
a single scene which represented love in its aspect as an honorable emotion.
The lovers who meet in his pictures seem always to be meeting clandestinely,
and he was unable even to permit a lady to receive a note without making
her look furtively up as though it contained a sentiment she had no right to
read.

Because both Boucher and Fragonard worked for the French aristocracy

Fig. 15.87 Fragonard. *The Swing*. Probably 1766. London, Wallace Collection.

and summed up in their painting all its elegance and irresponsibility, the end result of their art was to make the Rococo identical with everything the French Revolution was against. When at length the explosion took place, it was in the natural course of events for the new government to frown upon the Rococo as a style. Fragonard survived the Revolution. No one had anything against him personally; but during the later years of his life, he was

Fig. 15.88 Chardin. *House of Cards.* 23¾ by 28¼ inches. London, National Gallery.

unable to get work and existed in near poverty. The Rococo had in the meantime been replaced by Neoclassicism, to which we turn our attention in the next chapter.

Strangely enough, the man who now seems to have been the greatest French artist of the 18th century did not at all fit into the rococo scheme of things. He was Jean-Baptiste-Siméon Chardin (1699–1779), a painter of modest little pictures of still life and French domestic scenes (Fig. 15.88). The man was as unassertive as his art, and his biography is without a single notable incident. His father was a cabinetmaker who made a specialty of billiard tables, and when Chardin chose to become a painter, it is clear enough that he and his family thought of art as a trade. He gained some knowledge of Dutch painting because he happened to be a friend of the collector and portraitist Aved, of whom he did a picture now in the Louvre. He started exhibiting in the 1720's; there were always people who liked his paintings and were willing to buy them, but he never had a real vogue and never made much money.

Chardin's position among his contemporaries has been exaggerated by some writers, who not unnaturally want to put it into contrast with the oblivion he suffered during the 19th century. It is nevertheless true that he enjoyed considerable respect and appreciation almost in spite of himself, and the manner of its coming will suggest the right procedure for understanding the importance of his art. In 1728, he was exhibiting a few paintings in the Place Dauphine, hoping to sell some. Several members of the Academy happened to walk by. They admired the work, and suggested that the young painter apply for membership, something he himself would never have thought of doing. According to the records, Chardin was by no means confident of success, but did submit some pictures for the approval of the academicians. Largillière, the painter of royal portraits, instantly recognized their excellence. Chardin was elected with the somewhat condescending title *Peintre des fleurs, fruits, et sujets à caractères*. In later years (1752–1774) the Academy was good enough to let him act as treasurer, a tedious chore which carried a small stipend. He also served as *Tapissier* to the Louvre, which entailed the thankless duty of hanging pictures for the Salon. It is obvious that, in the eyes of those who considered themselves the leading artists of France, Chardin was a modest good fellow who deserved to be taken care of with jobs bigger men did not want. He was always generous and unassuming, but it might have been different had he claimed to be anything better than a painter of bourgeois subjects. It is comforting to know that his modest means were supplemented, eventually, by a royal pension and quarters in the Louvre.

Our historical perspective is indeed enhanced by the subject matter of Chardin's painting. It is refreshingly different from the art which records the life and pleasures of the great and the rich. Every housewife could see herself in it, her domestic routine, her furniture, her wardrobe, and the moods of her children. Every one likes Chardin's painting for those reasons alone, but it is not that which today makes the French rank with him Poussin.

He used ordinary indoor daylight, with an effect much less striking than Vermeer's, but with a control of the tones which often rivals the work of the great Hollander. He had an uncanny instinct for the balance between the human figure and the setting. His arrangements which look so casual at first glance become almost sublime on long acquaintance; there is nothing in view which does not contribute powerfully to the design. In his hands, a few humble objects attain the grandeur and monumentality ordinarily associated with primeval forces, great mountains, and space without limit (Fig. 15.89). It is not surprising that Chardin was in due time to offer inspiration to Cézanne.

ART IN ENGLAND, 1500-1800

England has always been conservative. Nowhere else has the line been so clearly drawn between the native and medieval culture and the imported tradition of the Renaissance.

We ordinarily say that the "English Renaissance" started with Henry the 8th (regnal dates 1509–1547). That is unquestionably true in many respects, but by no means does it indicate that the visual arts in England shifted over to the Italian style, which by that time had reached the stage of the High Renaissance. English architecture remained Gothic in form and spirit, with

Fig. 15.89 Chardin. *Tea Pot.* Boston, Museum of Fine Arts.

an occasional column or pediment rather timidly applied here or there. English painting and sculpture, instead of responding to Italian inspiration, were very nearly brought to a dead stop by Henry's conflict with the church. We need not repeat that entire narrative here; it is merely necessary to take note that, when the King suppressed the monasteries (1536–1539), he dealt a death blow to the patronage of the church. At the same time, the classical tradition in England was altogether too weak, or even nonexistent, to create any significant demand for the mythologies which had always been popular in Italy. The portrait remained as the only class of art in which British patrons were interested, and the English tradition in both painting and sculpture has ever since been overloaded in that direction.

Henry himself wanted portraits for the most practical of reasons, as we shall see; and it is probably just a bit of luck that he had available one of the keenest portrait painters in the history of art, *Hans Holbein the Younger* (1497–1543), a German, who had arrived in London in 1526, bearing a letter of introduction from Erasmus to Sir Thomas More. With brief visits to the continent, Holbein remained in London until he died in an outbreak of the plague in 1543.

From the time of Jan van Eyck onward, aristocrats did not temporize with portrait painters. They had no intention of enduring protracted and repeated sittings. They expected the painter to make a preliminary drawing and from the drawing to develop the finished picture in oils, often without bothering the sitter again. Such was the standard procedure, at which Holbein was preeminently competent. Hence the wonderful collection of drawings associated in the popular mind with his name, so sensitive, so wise, and so fresh as to make his sitters come alive. The drawings are so well liked, in fact, that today few people pay enough attention to the finished paintings, which if less immediately charming, are usually greater works of art.

Bluff King Hal had divorced Catherine of Aragon in 1533. In 1536, he brought about the execution of Anne Boleyn. Jane Seymour had died in October, 1537, leaving him a widower. He promptly started negotiations for a marriage with Christina, the younger daughter of the King and Queen of Denmark, and niece to the Emperor Charles the 5th. This girl had been married by proxy at the age of eleven and was still in mourning for her late husband, Francesco Sforza, Duke of Milan. Henry seems to have instructed the British ambassador at Brussels to send him a picture of the young lady, but apparently nothing really satisfactory was obtainable. At any rate, Holbein turned up on March 10, 1538, and on the 12th, was granted a sitting of three hours' duration. He was back in England a week later, presumably with his usual sketch in hand.

Nothing else is known about the purpose of the remarkable portrait reproduced in Figure 15.90, and very little of its history. The *cartellino* at the upper right is a later addition, and refers to Christina as Duchess of Lorraine—for either she, her family, or both turned Henry down, and she married the heir to that duchy in 1541. She was sixteen years old when Holbein saw her. The fact that he never saw her before and never saw her again, gives some indication of his astounding ability.

Even if these romantic details were not available (and they certainly add to our appreciation of the picture) there would still be plenty of well-informed critics willing to contend that no other portrait of a gentlewoman even compares with this. The rich, dark tones of the gown balance in remarkable fashion the white of the face and hands, and the lighter area of the floor. The panel has been cut down a little along both sides, and the composition was probably somewhat better than we now see it. The picture was always unusually tall and narrow, however, and the proportion itself is expressive of the patrician dignity of this princess, so childlike and yet already so experienced, and, at the time, perhaps about to be traded off to a husband thirty years her senior who, for all his brilliance, was a monster. It is no wonder that the beautiful hands, which are noted in various other records, betray somewhat less repose than the face.

♦ *The Van Dyck Tradition*   It is unfortunate that Holbein did not establish a tradition in England. He was followed by a succession of minor painters, some of them interesting to the antiquary but not to the general reader. The British portrait tradition really started in 1632, on the arrival in London of Anthony Van Dyck (1599–1641).

Van Dyck came there on the advice of Rubens who, on his visit in 1629,

Fig. 15.90 Holbein. *Christiana of Denmark, Duchess of Milan.* 1538. 70½ by 32½ inches. London, National Gallery.

had been immensely impressed both with the charm of the country and the free spending of its upper orders. Van Dyck had worked with Rubens, and had been to Italy. He was a talented man with the best training available, but there were many such in Europe, while in London there was no one with any real stature at all. Rubens had opened the door to cordial relations at court and with the nobility, and these Van Dyck exploited with considerable skill. He was soon running a large shop, and himself doing only the head and hands. He was knighted, lived sumptuously, entertained handsomely, and established the tradition that London's leading artists were important enough to associate on terms of equality with the great and the near great.

In England, the possession of a family portrait by Van Dyck has long been synonymous with aristocracy, with the natural result of exaggerating his place in the history of art. The best of his portraits (Fig. 15.91) are unquestionably fine pictures indeed; but there is almost nothing original about them.

Fig. 15.91 Van Dyck. *Portrait of Charles I, King of England.* 1635. 107 by 84 inches. Paris, Louvre. (Giraudon)

They are, in fact, routine if highly skillful exercises in the standard formula for state portraits originated in the first place by Titian and continued by Rubens. Van Dyck was perhaps more sensitive than Rubens. He was also a considerably weaker personality, and seems, at this remove, to have been a professional flatterer of uncommon skill.

The year Van Dyck died, Peter Lely (1618–1680) arrived to take his place. He was a competent man, with a style not unlike Van Dyck's. The same could not be said for Gottfried Kneller (1648–1723), a pretentious German who arrived in 1674, and established a portrait factory in London. It speaks volumes for the general level of British taste that Kneller did a good business, that people believed him when he boasted of studies at Rome and professional success at Venice, and that he was knighted. There was nothing about his painting to justify this success.

There was a feeling in England (as to some extent there still is) that the visual arts were properly the province of foreigners, especially foreigners of Latin extraction. Neither the court nor the nobility concerned itself with encouraging a native school, but there was obviously a market for art, and it was inevitable that local talent would eventually respond. William Hogarth (1697–1764) was the first English painter of consequence. He was followed

Fig. 15.92 Reynolds. *Lord Heathfield, Governor of Gibraltar.* 1787. 36 by 44¾ inches. London, National Gallery.

Fig. 15.93 Gainsborough. *Mrs. Siddons.* 1785. 49⅞ by 39¼ inches. London, National Gallery.

by Joshua Reynolds (1723–1792), Thomas Gainsborough (1727–1788), George Romney (1734–1802), Henry Raeburn (1756–1823), and Thomas Lawrence (1769–1830).

Although Gainsborough did landscapes (largely for his own satisfaction) all five of the last named earned their living, and a good one, by turning out innumerable portraits. It is to their credit that they were able to maintain a high level of charm and spontaneity when one picture after another conformed to the same set formula (Figs. 15.92–93). Reynolds' sitters had often figured in English history and literature; and the prestige of British painting has been immensely enhanced because he had social gifts even greater than his artistic abilities. He associated on terms of equality with royalty and with the circle around Dr. Johnson. His discourses before the Royal Academy (founded 1768) are fine pieces of prose and contain much artistic wisdom. But we must distinguish between our sentiments, and the real position of the British school in the history of art as a whole. The latter may correctly be inferred from the remark of the man who pointed to the painting reproduced in Figure 15.91, and declared, "My word, Sir, but that's the finest Gainsborough in existence!"

Fig. 15.94   Hogarth. *Captain Coram*. 1740. 94 by 50 inches. London, The Foundling Hospital. Courtesy of the Thomas Coram Foundation.

♦ *Hogarth*   Hogarth was the only one of the school of any significant stature or force. Incredible but true, every Englishman has always paid him the tribute of knowing him well without ever thinking of him as a great artist. The reason is not far to seek, but has rarely been stated. Reynolds and the others belonged to the imported tradition of the Renaissance. Hogarth, if properly understood, stemmed from the same northern and Gothic background as Pieter Brueghel.

The statement may at first seem paradoxical because he painted a great many portraits which conform to the Van Dyck recipe even if they are somewhat less consciously flattering than most. In fact, his *Captain Coram* (Fig. 15.94) might well be cited as the best of all British portraits. The important thing is that Hogarth was not content to limit himself to the portrait trade.

At Saint Bartholomew's Hospital, he did some large murals with religious subject matter. They were unsuccessful in the sense that he got no further commissions of the same sort, but there are worse pictures on view

Fig. 15.95 Hogarth. *A Midnight Modern Conversation.* 1733. Engraving.

in France and Italy. He tried narrative painting in his famous *Harlot's Progress,* and tried it again in *The Rake's Progress, Marriage à la Mode,* and *The Election.* Each of the four is a set of pictures, each individual canvas adding an episode to the story; and every one of the compositions is crowded with the intensively defined detail that had always been typical of northern art.

He had, however, learned much from the Renaissance, and his compositions are among the most tightly organized on record. It was his custom to hire hack artists to make engravings from his oils; as engravings, most of them are coarse indeed, but they sold well and brought in most of his income. Figure 15.95 shows a favorite example, and suggests the humorous and satirical temper of the man. A straight edge laid along any horizontal or vertical line will demonstrate that no one ever knew better how to use the vanishing point as a system for tying things together and leading the eye from one place to another.

In addition to being considerably more than a competent designer, Hogarth was a superb technician. Many of his papers have survived, but they contain no mention of the Dutchman or Fleming who probably taught him the simplest fundamentals of painting. It is a fact, however, that he used materials which were chemically superior to those of Reynolds and Gains-

Fig. 15.96 Hogarth. *The Shrimp Girl*. London, National Gallery.

borough, whose paintings are often badly cracked and some times colorless in the darks. Hogarth's gleam.

He enjoyed sketching in oil, and there have been few painters who used the brush with greater virtuosity. Among the numerous oil sketches which survive, the favorite is *The Shrimp Girl* (Fig. 15.96). There is a wonderful harmony between the slight and momentary subject and the thin, fast-handling with which it was rendered; and it is significant that he carried the matter no further. This little picture which has (with pardonable exaggeration) been called the finest bit of painting that ever came out of England, now belongs to the nation. Hogarth never attempted to sell it, and when his widow's effects were auctioned off after her death, it fetched six guineas.

♦ *Architecture* Inigo Jones (1573–1652) was the first British architect to reject the Gothic. He did it with a vengeance, and thus set the precedent for sporadic instances of extreme classicism in British building, which, when they occur, still seem curiously out of character. Jones had been to Italy. He made a special study of Palladio's buildings in and around Vicenza (page 643). He had visited Rome, and made friends with Maderna and other prominent architects there. When he returned to London, he was determined to introduce England to Italian architecture, and he had the ability to do it. Unfortunately, his greatest project never came off.

Fig. 15.97   London. Westminster. Whitehall. Banqueting House. (National Buildings Record)

He prepared plans for an immense palace at Whitehall, between the Thames and Saint James's Park. There were to be seven courtyards, the main one measuring 800 by 400 feet, or about twice the size of the court at the Louvre. Because of the troubles between Charles I and his Parliament, only a fragment of the grandiose fabric was ever completed, the Banqueting House (Fig. 15.97). The style is Palladian, and any architect in Italy would have been proud to call it his own work. It is anomalous that so advanced a building should have been built in a country that was resistant to the Renaissance, but the circumstances should not be exaggerated. Jones' architecture was court architecture, and its effect upon the population at large was slight.

In 1666, a disastrous fire swept what is now the eastern section (called "the City") of London. In keeping with the spirit of the times, it was decided that the rebuilding should proceed according to a master plan. Sir Christopher Wren (1632–1723) was selected to draw the plan, and to superintend the work, but local traditions and interests were too strong, so the scheme, excellent as it was, succeeded only in part. The notion of city planning did, however, receive more attention than ever. In both Europe and America Wren's frustration was remembered as a public misfortune, and people were more cooperative when the time came to design the Royal Crescent at Bath (1754ff),

Fig. 15.98 London. St. Martin's in the Fields. 1721. Designed by James Gibbs. (From James Gibbs, *Book of Architecture*, London, 1728.)

the New Quarter at Nancy (1753–1757), and the city of Washington (plan drawn 1791).

Our present interest is less concerned with Wren's plan as a whole than with the numerous parish churches he was called upon to design to replace those that had been lost. It was his first intention to give them the appearance of classical temples, but British churchgoers protested. One rector wrote Wren a sharp letter demanding a spire "pointing up to God." This put Wren in a quandary.

The spire, of course, was a northern, linear, and Gothic form, primarily vertical and of dissolving silhouette. Wren was committed to the Italian and classical style, which, in spite of all variations, clung to the spirit of the ancient temple—a building one story high, with an outline severely enclosed by cornices, and fundamentally plastic in character.

To pile one temple on top of another; to destroy the horizontal divisions intended by the Greeks to stop the eye; to lead us upward within a light, airy silhouette to a sharp point; and to do this with forms that are classical in appearance and plastic in nature—such were the preposterous elements of Wren's success. It is true that he had a few Italian precedents to help him, but none of them explains exactly how he accomplished the impossible so well.

Because most of the London parishes were poor, the little city churches Wren designed had to be inexpensive, and were distinguished only by the lovely spire each raised against the sky. For illustration, therefore, we reproduce a more elaborate building, St. Martin's in the Fields, then on the outskirts of town and now facing Trafalgar Square (Fig. 15.98). It is the work of James Gibbs, one of the ablest architects in the Wren tradition. It has a special importance because it represents a distinct type in ecclesiastical architecture: a church modeled as closely as possible upon the classical temple, with a temple front and a spire of the sort Wren had been the first to design. Our illustration comes from a book of plans, which will explain how easily the type was imported to America and thus became the standard model for all colonial churches.

Chapter 16

WE ARE STILL too close to the 19th century to see it in adequate perspec
tive. We all too often hear that the world experienced vast and significant changes during those hundred years—changes that were more radical
than at any other time, and faster moving. There is truth behind such assertions, but it is easy to exaggerate. No other period except the 20th century
puts an equal obligation upon the historian, art historian or any other kind,
to tread lightly. In the nature of the case, every judgment must be more than
usually subjective, and even though the principal phenomena of the period
are known, today's estimate of cause and effect may have to be revised to-
morrow.

So far as we can now tell from the indications of the history of art, the
19th century was the twilight of the Renaissance. The era started in normal
fashion, and for something more than its first generation, artistic tendencies
and developments are easily understandable by reference to points of view
established during the 16th century. We then begin to find ourselves confused by situations for which there had been no earlier parallel.

The great single fact of 19th-century art was the exclusive importance of
France, and within France the exclusive importance of painting. Nothing else
counted. Even men so great as Turner (page 852) were off the main track.
The Italian sculptor Canova (Fig. 16.1) might for a time have been considered the most prominent living artist, but the decisive history of the Neoclassical movement to which he belonged was written in France and conducted by painters. The French sculptor Rodin (1840–1917) likewise had a
great vogue in his day; but he was a follower of the painters rather than a
leader, and played no important part in bringing about the several major
shifts of style by which the century was marked.

822

THE 19th CENTURY

Within the history of French painting we may recognize three such shifts during the century, to each of which a section of the present chapter is devoted. The *neoclassical style* was well under under way during the 18th century. It became the official art of France during the Revolutionary era, and in the hands of the French Academy, it dominated both art and the education of artists until about 1850. It has not yet ceased to function, but as the central phenomenon of French art it was succeeded by the varigated work we may loosely classify under the name *Romanticism*. Romanticism also had its beginnings several generations earlier; as a distinct movement in France, it came to public attention about 1820, gained momentum during the next two decades, and finally attained general acceptance about the middle of the century. Romanticism was, indeed, the very last artistic philosophy ever to enlist the cordial sympathy of the public at large. To this day, most people still subscribe to that theory of art; thus the *French Impressionists,* who became identifiable as a school about 1870, had always to work against an onus of unpopularity. A more complete outline might list the so-called "Realism" of Courbet, which is better understood as an eccentric excursion within the romantic movement. The century ended, and modern art began, with Paul Cézanne (1838–1906), who started out as an Impressionist, turned his back on both the style and its theory, and promulgated the statements which gave a sanction for 20th-century abstract art.

There are various remarkable sidelights to the narrative just summarized so briefly. One of them is the apparent lack of connection between 19th-century art and the ostensible course of 19th-century life. One may study the political, social, military, and economic history of all nations during that era

Fig. 16.1 Antonio Canova (1757–1822). *Pauline Bonaparte as Venus*. Finished 1808. Marble. Life size. Rome, Borghese Gallery. (Anderson)

without gleaning much useful information about its art. Except for the French Revolution which, as stated, left an artistic record in the neoclassical style, the various wars, shifts of government, social advances, and even the Industrial Revolution itself seem to have arrived and passed on without doing more than to supply incidental subject matter for artists.

As the century proceeded, a significant change took place with respect to the position of artists in society. During every earlier period (pages 474–475), fame and fortune were the prompt reward of every successful artist. The 19th century also had its successful artists. Some of them received generous patronage and made huge sums of money. But very few of the men who enjoyed approbation a hundred years ago remain in honor today. Most of them have gained the contempt of every serious scholar. The great painters of the period (those whose pictures hang in the Louvre and the Luxembourg and in the major museums of England and America) had to wait a generation or more for the most rudimentary kind of fair treatment.

The phenomenon of the great artist unable to make a dignified living from his art will probably prove in the end to be more significant than any other event, and perhaps more significant than all other events of the 19th century. While the causes are still obscure, we can trace the gradual separation of the artist from other men. Merely troublesome at the beginning, the misunderstanding proved devastating in the end. A chasm opened up between the creative mind and society. By the time of the Impressionists, the barrier had become impassable. By then, the average solid citizen frankly disliked the creative art of his own day and was all too willing to express his antagonism. Instead of beckoning with opportunity, the career of the artist became synonymous with renunciation. By 1900, artists as a class had lost any rational and workable connection with the economic system. Most of them lived as they could, and those who elected to make peace with the going order were stigmatized as "commercial artists."

It is an unpleasant duty to contemplate a society which denied itself the fundamental outlet of expression by way of the visual arts; but it is true that the 19th century drove artists into a world of their own. That will be the chief lesson of the present chapter. As to the elusive cause, it is still up in the historical air. No one has come forward with a provable analysis of why things happened which we know did happen. The best we can do is to sketch the main outlines of the general picture as it affected art, suggesting reasons where we can.

THE FRENCH ACADEMY
AND THE NEOCLASSICAL STYLE

Destruction of the old regime was important to the purposes of the revolutionary government, and that intention accounts for the abrupt end of the Rococo, an art identified in the popular mind with royalty and aristocracy.

Far more important was the positive program of the new era. The political events of the late 18th century were epic events, and everybody knew it. The vision and wisdom of the men then in control can not be overstated. History contains no equivalent demonstration of the creative imagination exercised in the field of government. The French and American republics constitute the grandest expression of the Renaissance belief in the perfectibility of the race.

Looking forward to a new world order, Frenchmen of education and culture felt a manifest necessity for having a new art capable of commemorating the great things which had just happened, and the better life to come. Their point of view was, as a theory, identical with that of Colbert and Louis the 14th (page 788); in practice, they merely wished to use art to glorify a new and different France.

The Academy was ready-made for the purpose. It had immense prestige, and its prestige was fortunately identified with France rather than with the government which had just been overthrown. Its procedures and techniques might easily be turned in the new direction. An artistic executive of the highest skill—one who looked like a man of genius and destiny—was on the ground, moreover; and he had a plan which offered every political advantage, was congenial to both the learned and the ignorant, and, at the moment, looked so perfect it must have seemed God-given.

The man to whom we refer was *Jacques Louis David* (1748–1825), a painter. We may skip the details of the royal patronage he had received shortly before the Revolution, of his personal connection with the revolt, and of his brilliant and unscrupulous shifts of loyalty as one faction succeeded another in the years after 1789. Suffice it to say that no matter what he had done in the immediate past and no matter how black it looked, he was always able to turn it to his personal advantage whenever a change took place. History, it would seem, was rolling in his favor with loaded dice. His greatest single achievement was to convince himself and everybody else that the particular kind of art in which he happened to be interested was and always had been an ethical expression identical with the morals of the new order.

At the time of which we speak, David was a conspicuous exemplar of the stricter and narrower Neoclassicism to which we have alluded before (page 790). The movement had been gaining momentum for the past generation, and is best described as a literal application of the notions which had been entertained and stated in the days of Le Brun.

As a young painter, David had started in the rococo style. In 1776, he won the Prix de Rome, and after four years there had scored a great success at Paris with his *Date Obolum Belisario,* the painting which secured his election to the Academy. During the next seven years, he followed up his advantage with *The Oath of the Horatii, Andromache Mourning the Death of Hector, The Death of Socrates, The Lictors Bringing Back to Brutus the Bodies of His Sons* (Fig. 16.2), and *Paris and Helen.* Several of these pictures had been purchased by Louis the 16th. Not all of them were susceptible of an edifying political interpretation, but most of them were. As compared with the work of Fragonard or Boucher, the style was much simpler. The pictures bore, in fact, a marked resemblance to the more static works of Poussin, and the content had weight and solemnity.

At a time when resentment was mounting against the aristocrats and the court, it was easy to popularize any contrast with the Rococo. David's simplicity became "nobility" and his solemnity "greatness." Almost every government on record has represented itself as subscribing to both those abstractions, but there was a special reason of a more logical sort for drawing an identity between Neoclassicism and democracy.

While all students of government recognize important constitutional differences between the French and American democracies and the republics of the ancient world, the notion was nevertheless prevalent that the new system had been drawn up in sagacious disregard for about eighteen centuries of error. The citizens thought they had jumped back over all of that, and they believed that their new tradition invoked sound principles originally established and proven in the city republics of Greece and the awesome republic of Rome. It is a waste of time to analyze their error with respect to technicalities. The possibility of making a direct association between the new era and classical times was enough to swing the artistic decision.

One of the great original intentions of the Renaissance had, of course, been to recapture the civilization of antiquity. In the pages above, we have noted how data accumulated and how practicing artists felt increasingly obliged to provide themselves with a more and more precise acquaintance with the facts of classical art. From the middle of the 18th century onward, however, a series of events had served to redouble classical enthusiasm all over Europe and to make all previous archeology seem inadequate, erroneous, and out of date.

In 1757, the modern excavations had commenced at Pompeii and Herculaneum. Everybody who could read was delighted and fascinated by the news. An ancient city preserved in fairly good repair, even to the incinerated bodies of citizens, was a new kind of archeology, much more lively than the usual battered ruins.

In 1760, there appeared in London a book called *The Antiquities of Athens,* the work of two young Englishmen named Stuart and Revett. The volume contained some fine big plates showing the Parthenon and the other temples still encumbered with nondescript medieval buildings, but standing nobly forth nevertheless. Athens had been a very inaccessible place for a long time, and even the existence of such a treasure trove came as a surprise to most western Europeans. The book had a wide effect in a world which hitherto had possessed only the foggiest notion of Greece as something separate from Rome and perhaps finer, and its publication doubtless paved the way for Lord Elgin's machinations of 1801–1810, which resulted in the shipment to London of most of the remaining sculpture on the Parthenon, and its ultimate assignment to the British Museum.

But the event that really made the difference was the publication in 1764 of Winckelmann's *History of the Art of Ancient Times,* with which we have already had to deal in an earlier connection (page 9). Winckelmann's great success was due only in part to the fact that he addressed a public already well disposed. His intellect was of an order to command respect, and his language, in contrast with that of most other writers on similar subjects, was clear and carried conviction. His greatest single contribution was an exposition, which then had the force of a thrilling announcement, that classical art had two divisions—Greek and Roman—and that the Greek was better. "Causes

. . . of the superiority of Greek art beyond that of other nations" we may read in his very first chapter heading. The statement opened up an entirely new perspective.

His fundamental thesis was reinforced by corroborating analyses of a newly definite and newly rational kind. Let those who wish to understand David read some of the other chapter headings: *The essential point in art: the drawing of the nude figure based on beauty. Ideal beauty formed from beautiful parts of individuals. The conformation and beauty of the male deities and heroes. The conformation and beauty of the female deities and heroines. The expression of beauty in features and action. Beauty of the individual parts of the body.*

Such words sound trite because we have so often heard them paraphrased, and still do whenever artistic taste is discussed. It was Winckelmann, however, who first set down on paper the neoclassical theory which today survives in good measure. Contemporary esthetics is colored by it, and so are the press notices which celebrate the "conformation and beauty" of such female deities and heroines as we are permitted to view in the cinema. Mistaken though he may have been in matters of detail, the merit of Winckelmann was the merit of being right: he had a just estimate of the methods by which the Greek artists had arrived at their high idealism, and his recommendations were practical. How fortunate, from the standpoint of David and the Academy, to be able to claim such a man as their philosopher!

There is something very attractive about Neoclassicism as just described, and it is easy to see why the French public was genuinely enthusiastic. David was far too shrewd, however, to depend upon public support alone. He turned his remarkable political talents to perfecting the methods which made it possible for the Academy to control French art. Such jurisdiction was exercised in two ways, both legal: control of exhibition and control of education.

With respect to exhibition, it is important to appreciate that the showing of pictures had long been controlled by law. Members of the Academy could exhibit their work in public only at the official exhibitions sponsored by the Academy. Artists not associated with the Academy were forbidden to exhibit at all.

Shows of paintings had begun to assume great importance from the beginning of the 18th century onward. The "Salons," as they were called, were first held at Paris only every other year; but from 1737 onward, they had been annual. As time went on, more and more people came, and painting began to reflect the taste and needs of the middle class as well as the nobility. Finally the king himself, once the sole arbiter of taste, became merely the greatest among a large number of patrons.

The members of the Academy did not hesitate to exercise their control for their own benefit. An indicative statistic is the following: the Salon of 1789 was the last held under the monarchy; only 350 pictures were hung. The Revolution forced, for the time being, a more liberal policy. The degree of previous restrictions may be gauged from the fact that there were more than 800 paintings in the show of the next year, more than 1,000 in 1793 (the year of the Terror), and over 3,000 in 1795. The restrictive policy was not, however, brought to an end by the Revolution. Throughout the 19th century, the Academicians found ways to control the exhibitions; and at every opportunity and upon a variety of pretexts, they denied a showing to persons, styles, and subjects of which they disapproved. In 1863, for example, they excluded more than 4,000 pictures, causing a national scandal. Even then the fight was not over; however, we need not pursue the narrative further. Enough has been said to illustrate the nature of the operation.

David was equally astute in controlling the education of young artists. His methods have for so long been rejected that we must remind the reader that David, and any number of his contemporaries, sincerely looked forward to a great new democratic, and French, era in art. It may be doubted whether any enterprise in the history of culture was better planned or seemed more certain of magnificent success. The monumental subject matter was at hand. A style was ready which was not only popular, but combined present advantage with an aura of history. The need was there and was expressing itself as an insistent demand. And yet Neoclassicism, which started out with high hopes, was destined to end in tragic and even miserable failure. What was wrong?

A satisfactory answer to that question remains to be found, but certain facts are obvious. One such circumstance was the lack of good ancient art upon which to build a neoclassical style. Let the reader peruse again Chapters 3 and 5. He will be more than ever impressed with the newness of most of our data; it is not too much to say, in fact, that by Thanksgiving holiday, the average freshman knows more facts about classical art than either Winckelmann or David could possibly have known. The archeological knowledge available to them was not far better than the statement made long before by Alfonse du Fresnoy in his *De Arte Graphica* (1668), namely, that ancient art ". . . is that which has been made from the time of Alexander the Great to the time of Phocas." Obviously du Fresnoy didn't know what he was talking about, for Phocas was a Byzantine emperor of bad character who ruled at Constantinople between A.D. 602 and 610. Historical mistakes of that order can have an important practical effect. In the case of David, the result was to lead him into a gross error when he selected, from the classical monuments then available, the model for his own figure style.

The model he chose was the *Apollo Belvedere* (Figure 6.24, page 178), which he believed to be an example of the best Greek art—and which, in point of fact, comes as close as any other statue to fulfilling the specifications laid down by Winckelmann. It was a dangerous move in any case for a painter to adopt a statue for his model; but the choice was not made blindly. The cold and static nature of classical marbles appealed to David as desirable. The white monotone of the surface seemed to him expressive of purity. The absence of movement signified, by a similar train of thought, stability, permanence, strength, and inexorable dignity.

David personally mastered the style of the *Apollo Belvedere;* indeed, he improved upon it. He directed the Academic curriculum toward teaching that style, and he succeeded in doing so. Neoclassical painting has long ceased to be popular, and countless pictures have dropped out of sight. Any number of them were produced, however; and a general description of one would fit all the others. Like the major paintings of David himself, they show one or more figures similar to the *Apollo Belvedere,* composed in the organic manner.

With respect to the particular department of ancient art from which he elected to choose, nothing could have been more unfortunate. We no longer think highly of the *Apollo Belvedere,* but the statue—and all cognate pieces— must be conceded a certain elegance and grace. Neither elegance nor grace may be overlooked as artistic desiderata; but when those qualities are sought to the exclusion of others, art becomes a vehicle foreclosed from certain types of expression.

As pointed out in various other references (page 46), the nude figure is artistically useful only because the muscles can be manipulated to indicate innumerable states of emotion. Statues like the *Apollo Belvedere* are distinguished, however, by a refined absence of musculature and by a chaste refusal to display feeling. Neither element can have been overlooked by so intelligent a man as David; both must have been misinterpreted as expressing lofty detachment or some kindred content. But the fact remains that when the die had been cast, Neoclassicism found itself enslaved by the very kind of ancient model least capable of carrying epic subject matter, or any other meaning which might be strongly and deeply felt. Another choice, even from among the monuments then available for choice (and we still lack a sufficient number to make a neoclassical enterprise feasible) might have brought more fortunate results. As it was, neoclassical painting, which sprang from a bloody revolution, was condemned from the beginning to be a bloodless art.

The miscalculations which are now so easy to discern did not appear as such to David and his contemporaries. With a genuinely classical faith in the superior dignity of events from remote history (page 64), the doctrine was promulgated that Greek and Roman literature contained somewhere every subject worthy of serious artistic treatment. Such a notion—which had the

Fig. 16.2 David. *The Lictors Bring Back to Brutus the Bodies of His Sons.* 1789. 36 by 27½ inches. Hartford, Wadsworth Atheneum. (There is another, slightly larger, version in the Louvre.)

effect of supplying a substitute for the Bible—fell in with the anticlerical program of the Revolution. Almost any classical subject was virtually certified as acceptable, and David himself was not above painting a few that were distinctly racy. The kind of subject to be taken seriously, however, was epitomized in the *Brutus* (Fig. 16.2).

The Brutus of the picture was Lucius Junius Brutus, nephew to Tarquinius Superbus, the last king of Rome. In 510 B.C., the Tarquins were expelled and Rome became a republic, with Brutus as one of the first two consuls. His sons, however, became involved in a conspiracy to restore the dynasty, which would have meant the end of the new republic. Brutus ordered the execution of the young men as impartially as he might have directed that of any other young men; the painting shows him sitting shattered, broken-hearted, and alone, having lost not only his dead sons but also his living womenfolk, who shriek with horror as the bodies are brought home.

The date was 1789, and the moral of such a painting was too obvious to escape the dullest citizen. The incident depicted was an example of conflicting

Figs. 16.3–4. David. *The Sabine Women Stopping the War between the Romans and the Sabines*. 1799. Paris, Louvre. (Giraudon)

loyalties: private loyalty on the one hand, civic loyalty on the other. The strength of the picture derived from its honesty; the cost of putting state above self was made ghastly plain, while the intangible reward of heroism was left to the imagination.

David's developed style is better exemplified by the painting he himself is said to have considered his best, *The Sabine Women* (Figs. 16.3–4) of 1799. Not only was the picture concerned with the civic welfare; to a certain extent, it was even a civic project. David had announced that he intended to paint the subject, but indicated that he could hardly do it justice without the help of models of both beauty and character. His male friends were cooperative, of course, and we have an index to the high seriousness with which his art was regarded when we read that their wives and daughters were equally ready to pose. Ladies appeared in a concourse, it is said, to undrape their forms before him, and he was able to choose as he wished.

The unusual method for choosing models doubtless accounts in some measure for the disquieting element of personality in figures otherwise as smooth as marble. The news that such had been the procedure contributed, equally without doubt, to the popularity of the painting—which was unprecedented. David put it on view as a commercial exhibition. He promised his staff and pupils a dinner should the take exceed 24,000 francs; but even at the then substantial admission of 1 franc 80, three times that amount, and over, was realized. The delighted pupils demanded three dinners, for which the delighted master paid. With the balance he bought himself a country estate. Although well pleased with himself, he did not try the same trick again. The critics got after him, suggesting motives that were less lofty than the obvious lesson of the painting.

The latter, it is necessary to add, applied to the internecine strife within the government, which by that time had become the Directoire. The Rape of the Sabines, said the picture, gave just cause for grievance; but the Sabine women were right when, as shown, they came between their avenging kinsmen and the Romans, thus saving irreparable bloodshed.

Like many another revolutionary, David became an admirer of Napoleon. By still another act of the formidable rationalization at which he had so often proved expert, he converted to the glory of that despot the very art which he had first brought into being as a celebration of democracy and freedom. When the Bourbons returned in 1816, David was exiled because, as a member of the Convention, he had voted for the death of the king when that matter came up in January, 1793. He spent his last years in Brussels.

♦ *The Decadence of Academic Art*   Academic art was decadent even before the Neoclassical enterprise got well under way. Classical literature contains a number of episodes which, instructive though they may be, are unlikely to edify. David's early *Paris and Helen* had been one such example; his later *Cupid and Psyche* was an unmistakably salacious picture. The power of ancient authority is well illustrated by the fact that such a work, in every way antithetical to 19th-century mores, proved not scandalous, but acceptable.

David left Paris forever in 1816. His position as the semi-official dean of French art was presently assumed by his former pupil *Jean Auguste Dominique Ingres* (1780–1867), who had won the Prix de Rome in 1801, had been unable to depart for Italy until 1806 but had spent the next fourteen years at Rome, the following four at Florence, and had arrived back in Paris in 1824. The technique of Ingres sums up everything that was good in the Beaux Arts system. No one ever knew how to draw better. Of his painting, Delacroix wrote in 1855, "After examining the Homer picture [Fig. 16.6] I am bound to say I have never seen anything approaching the way it is executed. . . ." The skill to which we refer is best illustrated in a long series of pencil portraits like Figure 16.5, which Ingres used rapidly to run off during his stay in Italy.

Upon his return to France, he became almost ashamed of them, and refused to do more. Slamming the door in the face of a lady who inquired, "Is this the place where the gentleman lives who does little pencil portraits?" he declaimed, "No, Madam! This is the place where a history painter lives!"

As to his history painting, it is all summed up in his greatest single effort, the *Apotheosis of Homer* (Fig. 16.6), where we see Homer being crowned by Victory, with the personified Iliad and Odyssey at his feet, and in the presence of a carefully selected group of the world's great from ancient to modern times—Shakespeare and Goethe being excluded from the delegation as being insufficiently classical. It is doubtful whether an equal measure of intelligence and skill was ever expended on so complete an absurdity; in addition to its conceits of content, the painting was intended as a ceiling decoration for one of the galleries of the Louvre. It is now hung vertically.

Ingres had in mind to emulate and even to surpass Raphael's *School of Athens* (Fig. 14.19, page 594). The essential folly of the Academic theory is well demonstrated by his failure to evoke anything like the same sensations. The reason would appear to be his sole reliance upon the human figure as a vehicle of communication, and the absence of the space which Raphael had used so well.

It will be noted, also, that the theme was laboriously contrived, and was not, in strict truth, classical history. Obviously it was intended to elevate; but the conception lacked the epic proportions to which the painter pretended. The whole affair is illustrative of another serious error in the Academic dogma. The classical literatures simply failed to contain the inexhaustible supply of inspiring subjects which, as an article of faith, the neoclassicists had loudly claimed were there, ready and waiting.

Figs. 16.5–6 Ingres. (right) *The Stamaty Family*. 1808. Pencil drawing. Paris, Louvre. (below) *Apotheosis of Homer*, 1827. Paris, Louvre. (both photos: Giraudon)

Figs. 16.7–8 (left) Ingres. *La Source*. 1865.
5 feet 5 inches high. Paris, Louvre. (below)
Thomas Couture (1815–1879). *The Romans of
the Decadence*. 1847. 15 feet 3½ inches high.
(Giraudon; Alinari)

Other painters began to do what Ingres had done. They tried to make up, that is, stories and situations which were classical only in the sense of including classical characters, showing them in actions that were plausible. A prime example was Couture's *Romans of the Decadence* (Fig. 16.8). The picture was famous in its day and immensely popular, especially in New England, where it was understood as proof positive that wine and women would be fast poison for any civilization. No one stopped to calculate that those corrosive agents had taken all of 476 years to ruin Rome, but doubtless some characters were stiffened by a perusal of the original or one of the prints after it.

Large and complicated paintings continued to be the Academic stock in trade and to have the best hanging at the annual Salons. Because there was no private market for ceremonial art of that size and kind, many of them were bought by the nation and may be seen today in the provincial museums of France—where, presumably, they fit the taste of persons insufficiently knowledgable to appreciate the better pictures shown in Paris. But in order to appeal to the individual buyer, the Academic painters provided, almost from the first, a class of smaller and simpler pictures including only a couple of figures, or perhaps only one. Some such actually had classical subject matter: the *Oedipus and the Sphinx* (1808) of Ingres, for example. More often, however, the classicism was far-fetched, as illustrated also by Ingres in his *Bather* of the same year. The latter shows a single female nude, seen diagonally from behind, seated by the edge of a sunken bath. The allusion to Praxiteles (page 133) was obvious, but it is significant that no one ever refers to the painting as an Aphrodite. It is representative, rather, of a whole class of Academic nudes known as "studies"—demonstrations by mature masters, that is to say, of the single-figure pictures which formed an essential part of the neoclassical curriculum for students. Many such are extremely lovely; Ingres' *La Source* (Fig. 16.7) is perhaps the favorite work of the kind.

It is difficult to understand how it was possible for such paintings to maintain the approval of 19th-century society; but they did. As time went on, the display became more and more daring, as seen in Figures 16.9 and 10. Ultimately, even the custom of idealizing the model was forgotten in what amounted, as Mather once said, to a cult of the "heroic altogether," and the pictures became no more than pretty girls posed undressed on the model stand, with incidental landscape painted in later (Fig. 16.11). It is interesting that certain classes of patronage, innocent in all probability of neoclassical theory, understood perfectly what such pictures implied. Before the First World War, canvases of the sort referred to found an appropriate hanging behind the bottles and above the gleaming mirror of the "gentleman's bar" in many an old-time saloon.

Fig. 16.9   Adolphe Bouguereau (1825–1905). *Birth of Venus.* 1879. Paris, Luxembourg. (Archives Photographiques)

ROMANTICISM

It was inevitable that there would be a reaction to the activities of the Academy; and it came in the form of the so-called "Romantic Revolt," the start of which we may date from the Salon of 1819.

In that year, *Théodore Géricault* (1791–1824) exhibited *The Raft of the Medusa.* The painting would never have been hung except that, under a technicality in the rules, the artist had the right to bypass the jury—and did. It was exhibited as "A Nautical Scene"; but the equivocal title fooled nobody. All the world knew that a French naval vessel named *Medusa* had been sent to sea in questionable condition, had been badly navigated and run ashore on the sands off Cape Bon on the west coast of Africa, that the officers had not acted properly, that the surviving enlisted personnel had drifted in agony

Figs. 16.10–11 (top) Alexandre Cabanel (1823–1889). *Birth of Venus*. 1863. Paris, Louvre. (bottom) Raphael Collin (1850–1916). *Floreal*. 1886. Paris, Luxembourg. (Giraudon; Archives Photographiques)

on a raft until rescued by a British corvette, and that the Admiralty intended to cover up the whole affair. It was likewise a matter of common knowledge that Géricault had been incensed by the whole business, had dug out the truth, and had painted his picture on the basis of first-hand conferences with the men who still lived. In addition to all of that, it was an immense canvas which by virtue of size alone asserted the same demand for serious attention as any neoclassical history.

The modern reader will find it difficult to understand why the painting stirred up so violent a reaction in Paris, not only among artists, but from everybody else as well. It is necessary, once again, to emphasize the strength of faith behind the Academic program; that alone can explain why Géricault's art impressed so many persons as dangerous and hateful. The style, it is important to stipulate, was reasonably sculpturesque, and except for the use of darker and broader shadows could not in itself have been particularly offensive. It was the content that mattered. Instead of an incident dignified by history, it depicted an event still classified as topical. The question raised by the event, moreover, had not yet been settled; there was burning difference of opinion on the matter. In addition to that, the painter took sides, and the painting attacked the integrity of an armed service. It was impossible, under such circumstances, to maintain even for a moment the judicial type of contemplation which, according to the neoclassicists, was equivalent to artistic propriety. As though that were not enough, by representing human beings in helpless agony, the artist attacked all established conventions with respect to the dignity of man.

It has been truly said that the French Academy never slept peacefully again. Its entire program had been challenged, and with some success, by another program so thoroughly opposite that the two could not possibly live and let live. Géricault had in effect issued a manifesto which denied the right of the Academy to direct French art, and which, in the same breath, asserted the right of the artist to make art whatever he pleased. Géricault's position was peculiarly strong because it contained the magic word *freedom,* which was something the Academy dared not openly oppose. In understanding the situation, however, it is extremely important for the reader to recognize that historical chance was also playing its part at the moment.

There was no essential connection between the content Géricault chose to paint and the personal freedom of artists. He wished to be free to paint subject matter which he found greatly exciting as well as profoundly moving. The Academy was then insisting upon a calculated subject matter which appealed more to the mind than to the feelings. As of 1819, individual freedom was identified, that is to say, with the emotional values, and civic pressure was identified with the intellectual values. Today the tables are turned. Romanticism in due course undermined the Academy, and a habitually romantic public is today shocked by art that fails to enlist its feelings. Picasso, Braque, and others are demanding personal freedom as vehemently as ever Géricault did; but they want to exercise it for an art more highly rational, colder, and more elaborately calculated than anything the Academy ever advocated.

The epoch-making picture of 1819 was Géricault's greatest work, but it was a somber, ponderous composition and not at all a standard example of his expression. With an ingenuity that, to the Academy, must have seemed perverse, he collected material which, though morbidly interesting, was nevertheless bound to fascinate: the faces of madmen, the heads of dead men, stallions fighting. His interest in horses is suggested by the last item, and as one

Fig. 16.12 Constable. Detail from *The Hay Wain*. Shown in London 1821; in Paris 1824. London, National Gallery.

of the most competent painters thereof on record, he was once again sure to be successful in a world where every intelligent man had to be concerned with the subject. He was not interested in the horse as a philosophical expression, but in the horse as a means for action and speed. His best pictures defied the statics of Academic art by showing splendid animals and daring riders engaged in stirring feats which could not help but thrill anyone who had ever been in the saddle. He himself owned stallions and rode them with marvelous abandon, and his untimely death came as the result of complications following injuries received in a heavy fall.

When Géricault died, the leadership of the Romantic Revolt devolved upon his good friend *Eugène Delacroix* (1798–1863), an equally brilliant and much sounder character. From the standpoint of the Academy, it was unfortunate that Delacroix was born into a distinguished family. Throughout his life, he had powerful friends who were able to steer good commissions his way in spite of all contrary influence. From earliest childhood, his manner of life, like Géricault's, was the opposite of safe and sane. The affairs of his family were habitually conducted in an impulsive way, and his becoming a professional rather than an amateur artist was decided only in 1819, when he suddenly found himself without funds upon the demise of his mother. Reckless and careless at all times, he managed during a single year of his boyhood to get poisoned, to experience near-suffocation, to set fire to his bed and nearly burn alive, to hang himself—not in attempted suicide but while demonstrating the details of a case that had been in the news—and to be rescued at the last minute from drowning in the sea. It was no wonder that he grew up without awe for convention and without fear of anything or anybody.

His first important painting was the *Dante and Vergil in Hell,* shown in the Salon in 1822. The subject would not seem radical today, but the notion of finding merit in a 14th-century poet was equivalent, in the neoclassical mind, to absurdity; the picture was vilified as exaggerated and detestable. For the first adjective there was in fact some justification because the damned souls represented as swimming in the water of the River Styx were in fact adaptations from the figures Michelangelo had used on the Medici Tombs (Fig. 14.28, page 614).

Delacroix seems to have found his way to his developed style as the result of an incident of 1824; this constitutes one of the very rare occasions upon which the course of French art was affected in any profound fashion by outside influence during the entire 19th century. In that year the British painter John Constable (1776–1837) sent over to the Salon his *Hay Wain,* a detail of which appears in Figure 16.12. Constable's reputation derives from his unsurpassed interpretations of the English countryside. Most of his pictures are gentle and quiet, depicting some ordinary scene and humble activity; but he had developed a technique often not recognized as dazzling simply because of the peaceful themes to which he devoted it. Most of the elements of French Impressionism (pages 858–874) are there. Delacroix was not the only Frenchman to enthuse over the brilliant play of light and color Constable had found ways to make possible. It seemed warm, hearty, and welcome as a change from the cautious tinting the neoclassicists had been using in their attempt to combine the appeal of the living nude with the appearance of marble statuary. Delacroix therefore took himself off to England in 1825 and returned a moderate impressionist with an addiction to brighter colors.

The direct inspiration of Constable seems to have brought Delacroix's temperament into a state of synthesis. He had an early taste for Venetian painting and for Rubens, and for the rest of his life he seems to have been engaged in bringing Rubens back again by handling the paint in the manner originally suggested to him by Constable. His industry may be judged from the corpus of material that still survives: about 800 major paintings, about 1,000 small and minor ones, and some 6,000 drawings. The most notable feature of that immense catalogue is the catholicity of its subject coverage. Classical and religious paintings are there, also material from Dante, Shakespeare, from new and unproven authors like Byron and Scott, and from contemporary events like the Greek War of Independence and the Revolution of 1830.

A particular category of content stands out from all the rest as specially significant with relation to the developing philosophy of the romantic movement. We refer to Near Eastern subject matter. Various artists had been painting Turkish and North African scenes, and Delacroix had also tried his hand at it. In 1832, he made a trip to Africa as a member of a diplomatic mission. He never went again, but the experience cemented his taste for oriental material, and he kept on painting it the rest of his life (Fig. 16.13). More was involved than a tourist's memory of the sights he had seen. More was involved than the impulse which, three centuries before, had sent men exploring the New World. More, also, was involved than the peculiar satisfaction such material gave to Delacroix personally.

Whether he appreciated it or not, he had found expression for a great unsatisfied—and until that date undefined—yearning in the European heart. We refer to the desire for escape, which has ever since been of the essence in Romanticism, and which crops out in strange ways and in strange places. That such a desire should be most keenly felt by the creative minority within the population is an important and disturbing phenomenon. To say that the grass is greener in the next field is to say that the grass is not green enough where one is. One does not depart to improve his lot unless unhappy with

Fig. 16.13 Delacroix. *Lion Hunt*. 1861. Chicago, Art Institute.

the present situation. We must face up to the probability that Romanticism, insofar as it involved the idea of escape, amounted to nothing less than a philosophical negation of Western civilization which, in Delacroix's day, was already rapidly being transformed by the materialism resultant upon the Industrial Revolution.

As expressed in art, the desire for escape has so far found two avenues for making itself articulate. Both are represented in the work of Delacroix.

One may escape by going somewhere else, as he had done when he went to Africa. It is not easy to account for the satisfaction he took in the experience. For the Arabs and Moors who lived there, North Africa was a dull place; but for the highly educated Frenchman, it was full of fascination and worth not to be had at home. It becomes still harder to account for the impulse to go when we reflect that artists by the hundreds have annually come to France from other lands to find the inspiration Delacroix left France to get. When Gauguin abandoned France for Tahiti in 1891, he merely felt the same yearning and sought the same surcease.

Those who cannot escape in physical fact must escape into the realm of the imagination, which is feasible in art and literature simply by choosing a setting in some era different from one's own. Delacroix did that frequently. He did it when he painted two versions of the *Abduction of Rebecca*, both

Fig. 16.14 Delacroix. *The Death of Sardanapalus*. 1827. Paris, Louvre. (Giraudon)

with the Castle of Torquilstone burning in the background while the wicked Sir Brian de Bois-Guilbert swings the fainting maiden onto his war horse. He did it once again when he painted *The Crusaders Entering Constantinople in 1204* (page 296); and he outdid himself when he painted the *Death of Sardanapalus* (Fig. 16.14).

Delacroix was doubtless familiar with Byron's *Sardanapalus* (1821), but the imagery of the painting differs from that of the play. Both, however, derived from a rather free use of Assyrian history. The actual identity of Sardanapalus remains a mystery, but there is some correspondence with the character of Asurbanipal, who perished when the Babylonians destroyed Nineveh (page 23) in 612 B.C. Convinced that the city was doomed, the fierce king ordered all his dogs, horses, and women killed in his presence. He ordered the palace set on fire; the smoke may be seen already rolling in. Then he calmly slit the veins of his wrists.

The painting is illustrative not only of the romantic escape, but of certain other tendencies destined to become operative whenever and wherever the romantic impulse took effect. Delacroix's crusade, as we have seen, was for the value of emotion in art. Emotional satisfaction is surely a good thing in art and in life, and it had admittedly been absent from Academic art. No one needs to be told, however, that emotion is unreliable and at times unsafe. It sometimes directs the judgment properly and provides the fuel for good action, but it also tends to feed upon itself. Excellent though it was in its aspect as a necessary readjustment in French art at the time, Romanticism exemplified one of its chief faults in works of art like the *Sardanapalus*. By making excitement his measure of value, Delacroix—unwittingly, we may suppose—opened the door to the assumption that where some excitement was good, more would be better. The best picture, according to such reasoning, would be the picture which contained excitement in the greatest variety and in the highest degree.

The same train of thought inevitably was applied to the technical process by which pictures were painted. Exciting subject matter, that is to say, seemed to demand exciting technique; and exciting technique came to be identified in the public mind with visual evidence that the artist had been excited while he worked. The excitement of the artist as he worked came, by another step of the process, to be classified as a supernatural condition, often colloquially referred to as a "divine passion."

The notion was not invented during the 19th century; it had the specific sanction of the most honorable authority. In the *Phaedrus,* Plato had spoken of ". . . the madness of those who are possessed by the Muses," and likened the creative impulse to "inspiring frenzy." In the *Ion* he had elaborated more specifically upon the same theme. "For the poet," said he, "is a light and winged and holy thing; and there is no invention in him until he has been inspired and is out of his senses, and the mind is no longer in him. When he has not attained to that state, he is powerless, and is unable to utter his oracles." As for those who had "no touch of the Muses's madness," Plato by direction and indirection wrote them off as incapable of significant creation, no matter how hard they tried or how clever they might be. The same thing, we may infer from what he said, would apply to the potentially creative personality at all times except when possessed by the Muse.

Plato has always been in the European air; as George Santayana once remarked, a great many people are Platonists who don't in the least realize it. While it is still too early to speak dogmatically about the philosophical basis for the romantic movement, there is serious reason to believe that Plato's notion of the psychology of creation was supplemented in the mind of the 19th century by certain vulgarized excerpts from the ethical theory of Immanuel Kant (1724–1804) and borrowings from the social theory of Jean Jacques Rousseau (1712–1778).

According to Kant, for a perfectly rational being who was also completely informed, there was no choice except to do the right thing. Upon such a being, as it is usually explained, the ethical problem was no problem at all; the correct action was a *categorical imperative*. A moment's reflection will show that Kant's theory is scarcely susceptible of general application in day-to-day living, for who except the Deity can ever expect to be perfectly rational and completely informed? The 19th-century public was not delayed, however, by such refinements of thought. Ordinary men were sufficiently sure of themselves to resent any suggestion that they might be ignorant or unreasonable. Kant was generally understood to say that each man had within himself an infallible and automatic mechanism for deciding matters of right and wrong. By letting one's "conscience" be the guide, as it was colloquially put, a man could decide things for himself. Originally intended for application to moral questions, it was easy enough to apply the same technique of decision to artistic questions; and the artistic good or bad presently became, or so it was contended, not a matter for social judgment but a matter for personal judgment.

Rousseau had been the first philosopher to challenge in any fundamental fashion the essential righteousness of Western civilization. Although his vast influence is still underestimated, we may not take space to pursue his ideas in detail. The concept that interests us in connection with Romanticism was his assertion that people, if left in a state of innocence, would be good. Evil, he contended, was to be accounted for by the pressure of social institutions upon the individual. Here again, a simple transference to the problems of art gave Rousseau's dicta the force of saying that artists, if not put upon by others, would turn out good art.

By pondering the ideas just summarized, the reader can put himself in a postion to account for much that has occurred in the history of art since the start of the Romantic Revolt. By following Plato out to the end, works of art would inevitably be removed from the reach of the intellect. Such never actually came to be the case; but in the words of the late Irving Babbitt, Romanticism did in fact become a systematic conspiracy to discredit the rational faculty.

As part of the creed they were prepared to assert and defend, romantic artists began militantly to impeach all criticism. From Rousseau they had it that critics were the agents of society; because social pressure forced the individual toward evil, criticism was to be resisted and resented. From Plato, they had it that even the artist was foreclosed from a critical analysis of his own work. For how, when in the normal state of mind, could he deal with the products of divine madness?

These notions soon began to affect the technical process by which pictures were painted. In the art of Géricault and Delacroix, the change was for the better; as compared with the tightness of Academic technique, their brushwork was free, alive, and thrilling. But as the century wore on, the internal logic of Romanticism became more and more literally to be asserted and applied, with results Delacroix and Géricault could not have foreseen, and which neither would have approved. Taking a broad view of all painting from about 1850 onward, the result of the romantic doctrine has made itself conspicuous in at least three ways. It has dictated the medium used. It has changed the fashion with respect to pictorial composition, and it has made coarse impressionism the standard method for handling details.

As to the medium, protracted procedures similar to those used in Flanders (page 479) and at Venice (page 628) were inconsistent with the romantic concept of artistic creation. Fast work was essential. Otherwise, the Muses might loosen their grip on the painter, and go away before he could finish. For such work, the right kind of paint was the kind that gave the desired tones at once, covering with a single coat and permitting every field within a painting to be finished at a sitting. Complicated pictures have never been turned out so rapidly, but the impulse to do so was always present.

Because Romanticism made calculation suspect, the past three generations have witnessed a general decline of interest in the art of formal arrangement. Judging by their work and what we know of their methods, rather few artists of the later 19th century even attempted to visualize in minute detail the completed canvas before they began. Instead, they improvised as they went along. Thus, it has become increasingly rare to see a picture which gives the feeling that everything in it has an inevitable placement and a function necessary to the whole. All too often, compositional relationships seem haphazard and even sloppy.

The value sought, of course, was the value of spontaneity, but where does one draw the line between the spontaneous and the impulsive? "Sir, you do not paint," said Cézanne to Van Gogh, "you *attack the canvas!*" Bold work inevitably meant coarse work, and there is no denying that the fashion for it has made us the richer by some very lively painting—painting that makes the observer feel in empathetic fashion the actual sensations felt in the muscles of the painter as he manipulated the brush. Impetuous methods are unreliable, however.

It took about a generation for Romanticism to gain public support, and its ultimate victory over the Academy may perhaps be dated in round numbers from Delacroix's final election to that body in 1857. In attempting to understand why and how such a theory won the hearts of the population, we must first remember that while, at their inception, both the democratic revolution and the neoclassical style had started with high civic idealism, the Napoleonic Wars left Frenchmen disillusioned and ready for some philosophy which might give meaning to individual existence by reference to something warmer and more immediate than one's sense of membership in society.

The appeal of Romanticism is still further not to be understood without reference to the personalities of the artists and poets who were its leaders. To a man, they were as charming as they were dashing and brilliant, and very easy to love. Because they claimed to be abused, and because they were fighting a brave battle against odds, they became, as a class, the first artists in history who, in their professional capacity as painters and poets, were heroes.

Because the history of art inevitably tends to become a history of styles, it is specially important to emphasize that romantic art was never a style. Because of its individualistic platform, Romanticism could not, without self-contradiction, govern artists in the matter of style, and it was therefore impossible for the movement to bring about sufficient uniformity to make the word "style" intelligible in connection with it. The reverse, in fact, has been true. Romanticism brought about complete artistic freedom; and it was the latter, more than any other influence upon European life, which in turn brought about the clamoring chaos which has dominated Western taste for some time.

Even more important, and indeed the most far-reaching of all phenomena resultant upon the general acceptance of the Romantic doctrine, was a fundamental alteration of attitude with respect to the function of art in Western civilization. With the significant exceptions of Michelangelo and Rembrandt, it is fair to say that, before the outbreak of the Romantic Revolt, no artist had presumed to work for himself alone. For generations, in fact, it had been a point of honor among established masters to offer the patron, when the picture he had ordered was ready, an opportunity to refuse delivery, and to refuse payment as well, unless perfectly satisfied.

By virtue of its emphasis upon the self, Romanticism made art into self-expression. How very rare it is at this date to hear the worth of a picture estimated by reference to the satisfaction it gives the owner. How equally seldom do we hear any significant emphasis upon the picture in its capacity as a visual synthesis for some important truth or inspiring idea. And how commonly are we told, both directly and by implication, that the crucial question, from beginning to end, is whether the work of art gave satisfaction to its creator.

The general acceptance of Romanticism, it is necessary to add by way of a final word, must be understood by the reader in a broad rather than a literal way. The movement was not a movement within the world of art alone; it was a system of ideas which, if accepted, would in the end alter one's whole orientation to the world. As with most other philosophies, it has functioned as an influence and not as a set of rules. Its literal application has never been attempted except in extreme cases, but its influence goes on, and tends to account for much that is otherwise inexplicable in the motivation of western society.

♦ *Courbet's "Realism"* The capricious nature of 19th-century taste is well illustrated by the cycle which began to make itself apparent as soon as the romantic movement was well under way. Throughout the century, every new thing in art had its genesis not in and of itself, but as a resentful reaction to some established situation. As an illustration of what we mean, we cannot do better than to give the reader a brief account of the career of the painter Gustave Courbet (1819–1877), who had arrived in Paris as a youth of twenty. He came prominently into the public eye in connection with his rejection by the jury in his early years there, and the hanging of two paintings in the Salon of 1849.

Romanticism had not brought about the discontinuance of Academic art. Both had plenty of life and force in them. Courbet declared that the one was arrogantly abstract and the other exotic. He wanted no truck with either; and in the name of what he called "realism" he announced his intention of painting "things as they are." "Show me a goddess," he said, "and I will paint her."

Those who have read the earlier chapters of the present work will appreciate that he was announcing a policy which was physically impossible. It is not easy to say what a thing is. Complex questions, both philosophical and technical, confront every artist who attemps to paint visual truth. Realistic art is not a straightforward business, but a problem.

In a superficial way, however, Courbet did succeed in being photographic. Although his artistic instincts often betrayed him into excellent compositions, he cultivated chance arrangements, especially with regard to the broader areas of light and shadow. As shown in Figure 16.15, he accepted the accident of a cast shadow falling across the face of a nude model. As the same picture also demonstrates, he systematically refused to idealize the human figure in any way whatever.

His most famous painting, and the only one that even approaches greatness, was the *Funeral at Ornans,* which he was able to hang in the Salon of 1850 as a matter of right, by virtue of having won a prize the year before. The picture is grim, but straightforward. The setting is in the rural district of the Jura Mountains, from which the painter had come. There is an open grave, unrelieved by flowers. Around it stand the friends and family of the deceased; they are working people dressed in their miserable best. A priest, whose face is equally common and whose vestments seem shabbily elaborate, reads the service. A bird dog is among the mourners.

The painting did much to give the word "realism" its modern connotation of having to do only with the poorer and coarser classes within the community, with the overt description of brutal and depressing facts, and with the studied avoidance of gentle feeling, noble thoughts, and heroism. Because of such usage, we have been under the necessity in earlier chapters of quali-

Fig. 16.15 Courbet.
Sleeping Bather. 1845.
Detroit, Institute of Art.

fying the word and giving a special application to the phrase *objective realism*
page 19).

As a defiance of both the Academy and the romantics, Courbet's picture
had considerable success, and the success got him into serious trouble. No one
knows whether he had it in mind to stir up sympathy for the underprivileged
classes, but it was so assumed. His painting was hailed as the art of socialism.
More conceited than shrewd, he adopted that doctrine, parading his sincerity
and increasing his vogue by refusing the Legion of Honor when Napoleon
the 3rd offered it to him. In 1871 he took part in the Commune, was elected
to the Chamber of Deputies, and became President of the Commission on
Fine Arts. In that capacity he had something to do with the destruction of
the column in the Place Vendome, and after the suppression of the Commune, his enemies fastened the responsibility for that act upon him. He was
sent to jail for six months and ordered to restore the monument personally
at an impossible cost. He therefore fled the country, and died in Switzerland
a few years later.

Courbet's "realism" is less interesting for itself than as a ramification of the romantic impulse. Contrary to what he thought, his contentions did not militate against the fundamental tenets of the romantic faith; in fact, they had the opposite effect. He endorsed the validity of emotion with the same emphasis as Delacroix. He merely denied that such satisfaction must be sought in the strange and the remote. His real contribution, and it was a great one, was to assert the truth that stimuli for significant emotions lie all around us. The end result was to establish the dignity of humble things, and to set art free from the formal preoccupations of the High Renaissance.

♦ *Joseph Mallord William Turner* (1775–1851)   The British painter Turner was the great exception to the general rule that the history of French painting was equivalent to the history of art during the 19th century. Born in Maiden Lane, Covent Garden, he was the son of a barber. His formal education amounted to nothing. Throughout his long and successful career, he was disadvantaged by lack of learning and by a certain vulgarity of taste retained from his early background. A drawing is preserved which dates from his ninth year, and by the age of thirteen he was regularly employed doing wash drawings for architects and coloring for engravers. He also turned out little pictures of his own which he exhibited in his father's shop window and sold for a few shillings apiece.

As a youth, he formed a taste for landscape. There is reason to believe he had covered most of England on foot before he was twenty-one, omnivorously collecting scenery. Throughout his career, it was his habit to disappear for weeks at a time, usually on some prodigious walking trip, sleeping anywhere and eating whatever came to hand. Before he was through, he had covered Scotland, much of France, the Rhine Valley, Switzerland, and the Italian cities. It is impossible to say precisely where he went because he liked to travel under an assumed name. His exceedingly secretive nature has, in fact, closed the book on most of the details of his private life. It is thought he had an unhappy love affair, certain he never married, probable that he fathered several illegitimate children. He was elected a full member of the Royal Academy in 1802 and became one of its most honored professors. Throughout his maturity, he had close friends in the topmost circles of British society, but appears simultaneously to have maintained another way of life about which he did not talk. When he died in 1851, it was not at his official residence, but in a small house maintained for a mistress known to the neighbors as "Mrs. Booth." Turner himself was locally thought to be a retired naval man who had taken to drink.

Turner's output was terrific. The inventory of his estate included a corpus of 282 paintings and 19,000 drawings and water colors, for which material he had twice refused offers in the amount of 100,000 pounds sterling. In order to form a notion of the complete catalogue, we must add to these

Fig. 16.16 Turner. *Pont Aberglaslyn*. Cambridge, Mass., Fogg Art Museum.

the pictures, prints, and drawings which had enabled the man to accumulate other assets probated at 150,000 pounds. Obviously, Turner was a brilliant businessman, but his lack of schooling betrayed him at the end. His will, which he wrote himself, did not make his wishes definite. A great part of the estate was eaten up by litigation, but in 1856, his pictures were finally handed over to the nation, and are today conspicuous in the great museums of London.

Turner belonged to the romantic movement in the sense that all landscape tends to be romantic and involves the paradox that man can best fulfill himself in society by solitary communion with nature. Turner recorded such experience in innumerable drawings, one of which is reproduced in Figure 16.16.* The history of art contains nothing more sensitive, more powerful, or more lonely. Indeed, it is doubtful whether any landscape drawings, even those of Leonardo, Dürer, and Brueghel, are on a level with these. No other master so wisely eliminated extraneous subject matter to the benefit of the total effect. No one ever knew better how to summarize textures by abstract

---

* At irregular intervals between 1807 and 1819, he published a set of engraved plates, mostly after his drawings, known as the *Liber Studiorum*. Five plates were issued at a time. The original intention was to publish one hundred, but only seventy-one actually appeared. There was an obvious parallel to the *Liber Veritatis*, a similar publication by Claude.

twists of line, or how to indicate spatial displacement by all the devices of disconnection and the arbitrary selection and suppression of detail.

In his painting, Turner was romantic, but considerably more than that. He seems never to have lost consciousness of his humble beginnings. At the same time, he was fully aware of his own capacities; it is a simple statement of fact that, judged on a purely technical basis, he was the equal of Titian, Velázquez, and the incomparable Tiepolo. The situation engendered an unfortunate spirit of competition. On occasion, he painted pictures in the manner of Van Goyen, Rembrandt, Richard Wilson, Salvator Rosa, and others. These were not derivatives so much as demonstrations that he could "outpaint" masters of established reputation. His principal rival, and his greatest admiration, was Claude.

He took up the study of light and atmosphere where Claude had left off. Doubtless the climate of England, with its incessant smoke and mist, gave him an advantage Claude had not enjoyed. In any case, if he did not surpass Claude, he certainly carried the matter further. His *Dido Building Carthage* (1815) shows a fanciful harbor of exactly the kind Claude liked to paint, with the sun casting a streak of light down the middle. Superficially, the picture looks like a Claude, but Turner adjusted the balance between the atmosphere and the solids. The Palladian architecture counts for rather little; indeed, the marble buildings seem about to dissolve in the fiery light and the molten air. The painting was one of those willed to the nation; by the artist's wish, it hangs in the National Gallery adjacent to the Claudes.

Had Turner left us nothing but a series of technical achievements, we would think of him as a small man. He took a much more serious view of the function of an artist; and difficult as it may be to understand, he was more profound than any other artist of the 19th century.

It is significant that the *Dido Building Carthage* was followed, in 1817, by a *Decline of Carthage*. In the foreground of the latter, there are objects which remind us that luxury and self-indulgence brought about the surrender and destruction of the city; and lest the message escape us, the picture has two subtitles. One is an explanation in prose, and the other six lines of verse, perhaps a fragment from the *Fallacies of Hope,* an epic poem to which Turner often alluded as being in process, but of which no manuscript was found among his papers.

It is possible that the two pictures of Carthage were intended as an admonition to England at the moment when the Napoleonic menace had at last been conquered. If so, that topical reference was a mere subheading in Turner's general philosophy, to which we must not allow ourselves to be blind. But in order to appreciate it, let us admit that one must make an effort to overlook his childish use of words, and the tarnished melodrama which so often handicapped his painting.

Fig. 16.17 Turner. *The Fighting Téméraire*. 1838. 35¾ by 48 inches. London, National Gallery.

How often, in Turner's work, do we see the decayed castle next to the rustic bridge, and the indestructible peasants laboring for subsistence amid the ruins of a heroic past? Carthage and castles alike were, for Turner, not mere archeology, but symbols of the hope and ambition of mankind. As the late Chauncey Tinker once put it, Turner's pictures depict ". . . the insatiable pride which goads men to undertake tasks more and more stupendous until at length both they and he are plunged into a common ruin." It would be careless, however, to suggest that Turner was simply a painter of tragedy and disaster. More importantly, he was a painter of change, and the only painter who, in any fundamental fashion, dealt with the Industrial Revolution.

Figure 16.17 shows such a picture. The vessel under tow is the *Téméraire*, 98 guns. On October 21, 1805, she had held station on *Victory's* starboard quarter and was immediately behind Nelson when he broke the French line at Trafalgar. She was sold out of the service in 1838, and here we see her being taken from Sheerness to the ship breakers at Rotherhithe. The first three miles of the channel involves an easterly course to round the Nore. The glow which bathes the stately ship is the sunset of the age of sail. The primitive steam tug, then an innovation of less than twenty-five years' standing, belongs to the future, much of which was destined to be as efficient, as ugly, and as dirty as the little side-wheeler herself.

The 1840's were the heroic age of British railroading, some times referred to as the decade of the "railroad mania." In the hope of driving each other into bankruptcy, competing companies some times built parallel lines through the same territory, terminating at rival station hotels in the same town. In 1800, few people had even dreamed that it would ever be possible to make any extended journey on a schedule; by shortly after the middle of the century, England had almost all its present network of rails. Figure 16.18 shows an express train crossing a trestle at Maidenhead, bound away from London. The bridge itself was a daring and controversial piece of work designed by Isambard Kingdom Brunel, who was later to build the enormous iron steamship *Great Eastern*. Tennyson, after riding, it is said, on this very train, wrote the line, "Let the world spin forever down the ringing grooves of change!"

The extreme impressionism of the handling was characteristic of Turner's later style. A monochrome reproduction conveys some suggestion of the train's driving movement through the resistant rainy atmosphere, and perhaps a hint of the glow diffused through the mist. Color, however, does most of the work in the original, and the reader must imagine as best he may the reds and oranges savagely burning in the fire box, and the interplay between those hot tones against the blue of the locomotive and touches of cool in the sky.

It might seem that Turner, in *Rain, Steam, and Speed* (Fig. 16.18), had gone the limit in sacrificing plastic form to the enveloping atmosphere. Yet two years earlier, he had painted another picture, also in the National Gallery, to which he gave the lengthy but provocative title, *Snow Storm—Steamboat off a Harbor's Mouth Making Signals in Shallow Water and Going by the Lead* (Fig. 16.19). It is questionable whether reproductions in black and white are even intelligible. In the original, one can with an effort make out the mast of the vessel, but the borderline between the heaving water and the swirling sky is confused indeed. As a marine subject, it is a landlubber's picture; but as a work of art, it is an unexcelled expression of a passenger's reaction to a severe storm in the narrow waters of the Channel. More than an expression, it is indeed a capital instance of expressionism itself. Without the title, one might be confused as to what the picture represented. Even so, it is unlikely that any sensitive observer would go far wrong about the content. The colors are in themselves an emotional experience, and the sense of their manipulation by the muscles of the artist even more so. But as visitors to the Tate Gallery of London know very well, even this painting was moderate by comparison with some others—a number of them, to be sure, oil sketches probably never intended for sale.

Fig. 16.18 Turner. *Rain, Steam, and Speed: The Edinburgh Express Crossing a Bridge at Night.* 1844. 36 by 47 inches. London, National Gallery.

Because of his date, his impressionism, his interest in light, and the existence of easy travel between France and England, it would be natural to suppose that Turner's art was a major source of inspiration for the French Impressionists, even that French Impressionism derived from Turner. It is astounding to realize that the exact opposite was indeed true. It would have been impossible for any French painter not to have known Turner by name, in view of his reputation, but none of them made any real effort to become intimately acquainted with his work. Monet and Pissarro, who were in London during the winter of 1870–1871, found it convenient to study Turner; but from what little they said about it, it is obvious they had never done so before, and while interested, were by no means certain they had much to learn.

As we shall see in the next section, we can have no quarrel with them. Turner was concerned with the cosmic forces of fire and water and with the larger history of mankind in relation to the environment. Nothing could be more different from the doctrine of instantaneity (page 864) to which all the French Impressionists subscribed. In a word, Monet and Pissarro instinctively recognized that their philosophy was different.

Fig. 16.19 Turner. *Snow Storm—Steamboat off a Harbor's Mouth Making Signals in Shallow Water and Going by the Lead.* 1842. 35½ by 47½ inches. London, National Gallery.

FRENCH IMPRESSIONISM

The Impressionists became a force in French art about 1870, and the history of their doctrine followed the usual 19th-century cycle. Denounced as radical and dangerous in the beginning, the kind of painting they advocated gained grudging acceptance by about 1890 and is today the conservative way to paint.

The Impressionists remain the last artists who can by any legitimate reasoning be grouped together as a school. The name is a mistake, and it gained currency more by accident than design. In 1874, Manet and a group of artists who had come into association with him held an exhibition at Nadar's Gallery to show a number of their paintings, some of which had previously been turned down at the Salons for several years back. Manet's catalogue mentioned the possibility that the purpose of a picture might be to render "an impression." The word *impression* appeared in the titles given to several paintings: *An Impression: the Sun Rising, Impression of a Cat Going for a Walk, Impression of a Saucepan.* The critic Jules Claretie, when writing up the show, called it the "Salon des Impressionistes," and the name stuck.

Luminism would have been a more descriptive title. These Frenchmen were impressionists, to be sure, but their impressionism was merely a single tool toward the end they sought. Their common interest was in the action of light, and their central doctrine may be very briefly stated. Namely, that *the dullest object on earth becomes a thing of beauty when transfigured by the light*. The reader will recognize this as a special application of Courbet's "realism," and thus will appreciate that there was more connection between Impressionism and the romantic movement than has often been allowed.

The achievement of the French Impressionists resulted from the essential truth of their thesis; and in order to implement it, they developed a brilliant new variation of the Venetian mode (pages 621 ff.)—a technique for symbolizing in paint the life of the sun as experienced in nature. This technique has frequently been explained by reference to 19th-century science; but, in the opinion of the author, such a view has proven fallacious, although we shall deal with it in a paragraph below. A sounder and more practical analysis may be offered by reference to four essential factors: (1) new pigment materials; (2) the additive mixing of hues; (4) a special method for suggesting the flicker of light; (4) a system of modeling which compensated in large measure for the short value scale available in paint.

It is all too rarely that we reflect upon the debt of Impressionism to the chemical industry, but there is no question developments in that field furnished painters with some powerful pigments. The first chemical pigment is generally believed to have been Prussian blue, discovered by Dresbach in 1704; but that was a comparatively isolated incident. The real harvest of new pigments began to come in toward the end of the 18th century. Zinc white, chrome green, cobalt green, and cobalt blue all date from around 1800. In 1826 Guimet discovered how to make artificial ultramarine blue, thus replacing the genuine ultramarine which had to be made from powdered lapis lazuli brought all the way from the Far East. Cadmium yellow appeared in 1846. The years 1859–1861 produced mauve (the first coal-tar color), cobalt yellow, and magenta. Several new reds arrived during the late 1850's, and from then on there seems literally to have been a deluge of chemical pigments. Many of the new pigments proved fugitive and have since dropped out of the artist's palette; but many proved good and remain. It would be going rather far to say that the old organic and mineral colors dropped out of use, but let the reader judge the upshot for himself. When walking quickly in a museum from a room of earlier pictures into a room where the Impressionists are hung, one experiences a stimulating sense that the color has been heightened, not a little but a very great deal. The new and brighter paints were used, moreover, at highest possible intensity, by a method next to be described.

When we take some blue paint and stir it up in a pot with some yellow paint in the usual way, we indulge in *subtractive mixing.* Constable (page 843) was one of the earliest artists to attempt mixtures of any other kind, and his motive for experimenting was the fact that subtractive mixing is almost invariably a disappointment. Different pigments and different vehicles combine capriciously, and it is impossible to lay down a general rule about what to expect. The subtractive mixture, however, will usually be both darker and less intense than either of the colors which were combined to make it.

Additive mixing, in the literal meaning of the term, is possible only with the aid of equipment which enables us to blend two or more beams of colored light. Such mixing is a daily routine in the theater, but it is hardly available to those who must use paint. A near substitute for true additive mixing had been used in the textile industry for hundreds of years, however, and the French Impressionist painters took it over and made it their own.

Most gray tweed, for example, is woven not from thread of a uniform gray, but from whiter and blacker threads in a predetermined proportion. When one looks down at the sleeve of his jacket, the separate strands are in plain sight; but when one looks at the same jacket from twenty feet away, he can no longer resolve details so small. The dark tones tend to lower the value of the field. The lighter tones tend to raise it. When asked to name the local tone of the whole, the observer deals neither with the lighter or the darker threads, but with the tone produced by the blend of them as seen from his particular station. The principle involved can be applied to any other mixture of values or hues; essential phenomena are the juxtaposition of one color with another and the blurring of small spots as seen in the distant view.

It will be obvious from what we have said that the effect of green can be had by a judicious spotting of a surface with blue and yellow, or that a red can be made into an orange by arranging flecks of red and flecks of yellow in much the same way. The reader will find it amusing to prove it with his own paints. He will doubtless find it disciplinary as well, for it takes an immensely subtle judgment to produce a specific tone. Such experiments carried a bit further will also illustrate how a tint of any hue can be produced (and a very lively tint, too) by spotting in with pure white. As for the production of shades, the matter is not so simple, as we shall presently explain.

Various names have been given to the Impressionist technique which brought about the additive mixing of the hues. "Broken brush work" and "divisionism" are excessive. "Pointillism" (that is, *pointillisme,* but the word should be Anglicized) is the most common designation; strictly it applies to doctrinaire applications of the theory as seen in the work of Signac and Seurat (Fig. 17.2, page 879).

In the majority of instances, however, there was no standard or accepted size or shape for the single touch of the brush or palette knife. Neither did most of the painters attempt to maintain the same type of dab throughout an entire picture. Monet now and then approached the spirit of mosaic almost as closely as Seurat; but at other times, he simply cross-hatched or flecked with the several hues he wished to mix, without attempting to maintain uniformity in the size, shape, or direction of the stroke, and varying the pressure upon the brush as judgment indicated. Van Gogh often used serpentine strokes, leaving stripes of paint a quarter of an inch wide or more, and as long as he pleased. Renoir, in much of his work, was apparently averse to anything that might deny the liquidity of the vehicle; his colors, while broken, seem to flow against each other, and to be in hydraulic rather than mechanical juxtaposition.

Every author who has attempted to describe the broken-color technique has stressed too heavily the phenomenon of the blurring of the juxtaposed spots whenever Impressionist pictures are seen from a normal remove. Our own paragraphs on the subject are no exception; and we must now qualify what we have said. In every typical painting of the kind, the individual spots or flecks of color are significantly large. When seen from any distance short of a hundred feet or so (which surely is farther away than one would stand to look at a painting), they do not blend completely together. Each spot retains a certain measure of its own identity. Additive mixing takes place, to be sure; and one is conscious of the new tone thereby built up. The additive mixing, however, remains incomplete just the same, and one is almost equally sensitive to the several hues which go to make up the mix. The latter phenomenon is almost as important as the first.

Because it was part of the Impressionist system to use every pigment at highest possible intensity, the contrast between any two contiguous spots of paint was perforce (and intentionally) the maximum contrast possible between those two hues. The surface of an Impressionist painting might accurately be described as an infinite number of such contrasts, tiny in size but violent with respect to the clash of colors. The psychological effect upon the observer has often been described as "vibratory." Purists in the language may protest that no vibration exists, but thousands of persons have felt that sensation under the circumstances we mention.

This was, in fact, one of the most vital achievements of the Impressionist technique. The response of the optical system is not only similar, but may well be the same response that we experience whenever we see the leaves of a tree flicker as they move in the sunlight or whenever we see reflections on clear and rippling water. As a reinforcement to the other representative aspects of the painting, we instinctively read the vibratory effect as indicative not only of the living sunlight, but also of movement in the air.

As set forth in Appendix II, the principal handicap of all representative painting derives from the infinitely short contrast between black paint and white paint, as compared to the immense contrast in nature between the darkest shadows and the brightest high lights. It was the great merit of the Impressionists to develop and perfect the best artistic compromise yet known for dealing with that inexorable fact.

The most familiar and conspicuous consequence of their method was the bright purple which they painted into the darkest parts of their pictures. We often hear it said that they were "the first artists to realize that shadows are in fact purple," but nothing of the sort is true. Purple shadows are familiar in nature under certain conditions and unknown under other conditions. Shadows of every other hue occur as often as purple shadows. The use of purple by the Impressionists did not result from naturalistic motives, but from a well-calculated artistic scheme.

Their theory in that respect was extremely simple for so excellent a stratagem, and it may be stated briefly. Pissarro followed the formula more literally and consistently than most of the others, and the reader will find in his work a number of paintings which might be classified as laboratory demonstrations. The rest of the school conformed more to the spirit than to the letter of the rule; but if the principle is understood, the reader will be prepared for variations and approximations in practice.

The crux of the whole matter was to substitue violent contrasts of hue (which were available in paint) for the terrific value contrasts of nature (which could not be duplicated by paint).

Let us assume that a single field contains both the darkest shadows and the brightest highlights within the entire picture. In modeling such a field, the doctrinaire Impressionist would paint purple at highest possible intensity into the darkest areas. He would reserve his brightest yellow for the areas in full illumination, and white for the high lights. In grading from the dark up toward the light, the painter would then shift from hue to hue around either the warm side or the cold side of the color circle (page 973). And, in doing so, he would use every hue at highest possible intensity. A "warm" field" would thus go from absolute purple through red-violet and the reds, and thence into the oranges up to yellow. A "cold field" would follow a similar sequence of shifts by way of the blues and greens.

It will be understood, of course, that it is extremely unusual to be confronted with the necessity for modeling a single field which, within itself, contains both the brightest and the darkest areas of the picture. Yellow and purple, as noted in Appendix II, lie on the vertical axis of the color circle simply because they happen to be the two hues which, when at highest possible intensity, give the maximum contrast with respect to value. For any hue other than yellow, the maximum possible contrast is not obtained from purple, but by using the complementary. If he inspects Impressionist paintings with care, the reader will find numerous instances where that fact, also, was employed for modeling fields within which the full range of value was either inappropriate or not desired. The lighter complementary, that is to say, would go in the lights, and the darker complementary, whatever it happened to be, in the shadows. In similar fashion, spots of the complementary were often introduced by the pointilist method whenever it was desirable to "gray" a particular area.

The merit of the analysis just given is that it corresponds with the physical facts of Impressionist paintings, and offers a reasonable explanation for them. Many writers have stated it as truth, however, that the Impressionist technique was developed in direct response to recent scientific discoveries in the field of physics and optical psychology. The names of prominent scientists like Rood, Chevreul, and Helmholtz are sometimes appended to such statements, and we are told that this painter and that had the writings of such men in his library. As to the use the painters made of information gleaned therefrom, we are usually told something like this:

Since the spectral colors result from the disintegration of white light and may be reintegrated once again into white light, the painter can produce an illusion of white light if he lays on the canvas a full selection of spectral tones in a pure, unmixed state. When seen by the eye, it is asserted, such tones will be "mixed on the retina," with the desired result. To the points already listed, almost every writer who fancies this particular rationale for Impressionism has added a word or two about complementaries, with a hint here and a hint there that the complementary relationship between tones was of the greatest practical use. Still further, mention is usually made of recent psychological investigation, and we are reminded of the photochemical reactions of the eye (page 573), the familiar optical illusions, and the color top.

The reader may make what he can of the notions just summarized. He will certainly be able to assure himself that there was some interchange between artists and scientists. The artists bought scientific reports and read them. The scientists were interested in the possibility of making a contribution to art. Chevreul, who was a chemist, published in 1838 a paper on contrasting colors, for example; and while director of the Gobelin tapestry works, made some practical experiments.

Any one who pursues the matter very far, however, is bound to become impressed with the inadequacy and probable error of the view which wants to make Impressionism a department of physics. The allusions made to science and to psychology are provocative, to be sure, but they are not proof. Proof would require detailed analysis of particular paintings on the one hand, and precise demonstration that such were in correspondence with specific points established by science. Nothing of the sort is available; and the writer, years ago, arrived at the opinion that a one-to-one connection between optical physics and French Impressionism was a will-o'-the-wisp. The simpler, more workmanlike explanation previously stated seems, however, to fit the case.

The technical system just discussed—no matter what analysis we happen to prefer—was a major development in the history of art. It opened up for painting an entirely new jurisdiction. It made it possible for artists to offer visual experience of a new kind and for pictures to evoke emotional experiences hitherto unfamiliar, and unquestionably of value. What were the philosophical assumptions that called French Impressionism into being?

Like every other art, Impressionism derived from a series of assumptions about the reality of our visual world. The visual experience of the race is no single thing. Circumstances alter not only what we see, but what we are able to see, and we change our techniques to fit the occasion.

When, for instance, we study biology, we inspect the specimens continuously for a considerable period of time. Such vision is always under the constant direction of the mind. It is purposeful. It is, moreover, a process involving consecutive acts of sight. Let such work be compared to the vista which suddenly comes into view through the window of a moving train and as suddenly is taken away. Of the latter, one lacks a *knowledge,* but he may retain a most vivid *impression.* The suggestion of the moving train indicates that there was a time element in the imagery of the French Impressionists, aptly styled *the doctrine of instantaneity.*

The doctrine of instantaneity gets its strength from a statistical argument; namely, that controlled, systematic, and intellectually directed inspection of the world is rare, so rare, indeed, as not to be part of daily life at all. The momentary view, received as from the train window, sums up—or so they alleged—so great a part of our visual life that, for the practical purposes of art, it may be taken as the totality.

That much being accepted, it followed that the painter's problem was first of all to make certain of what went on in the mind and in the feelings during experiences of instantaneous, simultaneous, and summary vision. Various statements have been made which purport to be descriptive of our sensations at such times; all contain a measure of truth, and all are inaccurate in the sense of being incomplete and inconclusive. Every single suggestion, however, has this much in common with every other, namely, that we almost never see the view clearly. The mode of the total visual effect, that is to say, presents things as they might be seen by the perfect eye directed by the perfect mind, a situation not to be hoped for on earth. The mode of relief depends upon an assumption about the superior reality of mass; that assumption, according to the Impressionist doctrine, is an abstraction contrary to experience.

From such reasoning, it followed that the French Impressionists would, as a matter of principle, be impressionists indeed (page 164); they would perforce describe objects in the same fuzzy way that the eye receives them during moments of instantaneous vision.

Further analysis of momentary vision suggested that its most cogent effects depended upon the state of light at the instant when sight took place. We are all aware, of course, that every object and every area within the field of view has a local hue: red, green, yellow, violet, gray, or whatever. But these local hues, when observed from a distance, do not carry through to the eye unaltered. Local hues, on the contrary, are changed (some times radically) whenever, and as often as, the light changes. Not only is it close to the truth that "the eye sees nothing but color"—the colors seen by the eye are colors resulting from the action of light.

These painters became, upon occasion, almost morbidly self-conscious about the action of light. We learn in school that the sun traverses fifteen degrees of longitude every hour, which is to say one minute of arc every four seconds of time. Expressed in linear measure, the same data indicate that, in the latitude of New York, the sun passes over slightly more than two-tenths of a statute mile every single second, and a bit less than that in Paris or London.

The French Impressionists were not preoccupied with this arithmetic; but, when attempting to render what the physical eye actually sees, they were chained to the facts. They were luminists in the sense that they tried, as best they might, to paint imagery which was never the same for two moments on end because the source of light moved so very fast. They were impressionists in the sense that they sternly eliminated every detail which might (with the aid of memory, perhaps) be *inferred* from the visual data, but not registered upon the retina (Fig. 16.20).

There is no question that the Impressionists were correct when they insisted upon the validity of instantaneous vision. Such pictures deal with something that happens. The immediacy of our reaction is apology enough. At the same time, when they decided that the action of light must govern painting, they put themselves under a very unstable jurisdiction. Objects, dull and otherwise, get transfigured by the light at intervals which are most fleeting, putting the painter under an obligation to record an infinite number of transfigurations.

Fig. 16.20 Monet. *Houses of Parliament*. Washington, National Gallery, Chester Dale Collection. (Vizzavona)

Monet, in particular, faced up to the task with an industry as immense as the problem itself. It was his habit to paint a number of pictures of the same subject seen from the same station, shifting one canvas for another as soon as the light changed. His "series" of the façade of Rouen Cathedral (1892–1894) is perhaps the best known production of this sort, but it is only a single series among a series of series. He arranged for a room on the second floor of a shop opposite the cathedral, and set to work. Before he was through, he had painted at least thirty (some say forty) "cathedrals." Twenty of them were exhibited by Durand-Ruel in 1895, and a selected half dozen were in the great Monet show in New York in the spring of 1960. The principal difference between individual canvases is merely that the light had changed—not much, it must be understood, but enough to make a distinction for a connoisseur of light.

No one can deny that the Impressionist doctrine was interesting. Its premises were both valid and vital. Indeed, when recited one by one, they carry conviction in a remarkable manner. Why, then, was Impressionism unpopular? Why, when the leaders of the movement were demonstrably the ablest artists alive, were they denied the fame and fortune to which major artists had traditionally been entitled? The reasons are as yet far from plain, but some of them can be stated.

In the first place, we must remind ourselves that Impressionism was necessarily addressed to a public accustomed to art of a very different kind. The conservative citizen of 1870 still believed in neoclassicism, and still thought that Academic pictures were superior to all others. More liberal persons doubtless had assimilated the romantic values, but the apparent contrast between Impressionism and Romanticism was also very great. The Impressionists were, in effect, asking that contemporary habits of thought be cast aside and that taste be founded upon new and unfamiliar principles.

Any whole-hearted endorsement of Impressionism put people, for example, under the necessity of discarding all previous definitions of subject matter. With respect to any work of representative art, the *subject* had always been what was represented: a man, a woman, a building, a landscape. The things, that is, which the picture purported to *show,* the objects one could *see* in the picture. But that idea did not apply to Monet's "series" of Rouen Cathedral or similar productions. As representations of the cathedral itself, Monet's paintings left much to be desired. As studies, indeed as celebrations of the transitory light passing over the architecture, they were superb. In other words, the subject of the series was not the building, but the light.

There was plenty of merit in making light the subject matter for paintings, but the majority of viewers were unwilling to adjust their age-old habits of observation, interest, and appreciation—if, indeed, they understood the adjustment demanded. They might have done so gradually, however, had it not been for a certain inconsistency in the policy of the Impressionists themselves.

If light was to become subject matter, it made very little difference what objects the light played over, so long as the light effect itself was worthwhile. Ideally, it would seem that the best material for the purpose would be objects with neutral connotations. That situation is well illustrated by Monet's *Haystacks at Giverny* (mostly from 1891), a "series" showing the same two haystacks from the very same station, at different times of the year, and recording in admirable fashion the changes in the light. Unfortunately or not, and wisely or unwisely, the Impressionist painters did not, as a rule, choose "subjects" that were strictly neutral.

The entire movement had got off to a bad start, actually, when its elder statesman Edouard Manet (1832–1883) put on exhibition two paintings which proved extremely offensive, the *Olympia* (Fig. 16.21) and *The Picnic on the Grass* (Fig. 16.22). Although some critics have tried to, it is a waste of time to suggest that Manet was oblivious to the implications of the figures we see

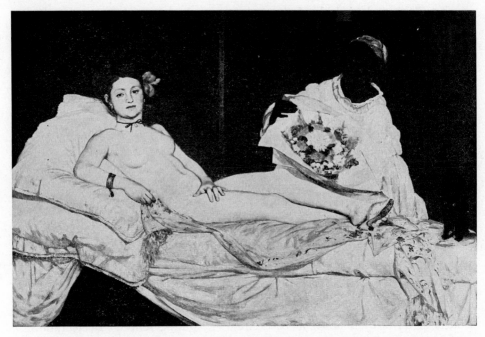

Fig. 16.21   Manet. *Olympia*. 1863. 51¼ by 74¾ inches. Paris, Louvre. (Giraudon)

in these pictures. Both seem perfectly understandable and decidedly healthy today when understood for what they were; namely, a proper dressing down for persons who misinterpreted as interest in art their taste for the girl shows provided by Bouguereau and Cabanel (Figs. 16.9–10). Olympia was a naked strumpet who looked out of the painting not with the sweet allure of Venus, but with an actuality bold as brass. The same might be said of the healthy young woman in the other picture. It was the latter, strangely enough, which aroused the stronger reaction. The close juxtaposition of clothed male and nude female figures was, people declared, an elaborately contrived insult to public morals. The suggestion was seriously advanced that the picture would undermine the French home. A similar grouping of male and female figures had long been on view at the Louvre without having had that result, but it was by Giorgione, who had been dead three hundred years and had lived in another country.

As long as the leading Impressionists lived, they continued to needle the accepted taste of their generation, but deliberately offensive pictures were occasional rather than common. More often, the paintings seemed to show material that struck the average viewer as egregiously ordinary (Figs. 16.23–24). Except for those erudite in the doctrine of luminism, any number of canvases seemed actually trivial (Fig. 16.25) and were in fact trivial if considered merely as representations.

Fig. 16.22   Manet. *Picnic on the Grass.* 1863. 84¼ by 106¼ inches. Paris, Louvre. (Giraudon)

It is not surprising that the public was baffled by Impressionist subject matter. Public misunderstanding of Impressionist technique was even greater.

The necessity for recording fleeting moments of visual experience had imposed upon these artists an intense pressure to work fast. Monet, on one occasion, allowed himself only seven minutes to paint a leaf, and while working on the *Haystacks,* the sun often drove him crazy by setting faster than he could keep up with it. No wonder his correspondence contains frequent expressions of frustration, even of despair—and that during periods when his technique was as thrilling as any in the history of art.

Speedy execution, even when performed by a great master, cuts both ways. Such methods can not produce paintings comparable in finish and refinement to those produced by equally good artists working more deliberately. By all previous standards, French Impressionism was remarkably bold, but boldness is not invariably an attractive quality. There were many people who disliked it for itself, and they accused the Impressionists of being sensational, and of trying to get away with hasty, sloppy, careless, and inferior workmanship.

Was there any merit in these strictures? It is all too easy to say that the accusations were made merely because Impressionism was new and unfamiliar, and that its brilliant pigments (juxtaposed for maximum possible contrast) demanded adjustment from eyes accustomed to the suave harmonies of Vene-

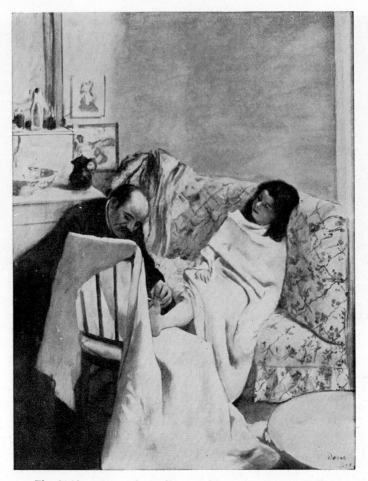

Fig. 16.23 Degas. *The Pedicure*. 1873. Paris, Louvre. (Bulloz)

tian painting and the chaste tints of Academic work—eyes perhaps not yet comfortable with the cautious use of broken color by Constable and Delacroix. But more than the normal cultural lag was involved. Impressionism had some serious limitations. More important than that, Impressionism now appears to have been a symptom of an uncomfortable cultural change.

The cult of the instantaneous had both virtues and faults. The worth of the momentary was the value of spontaneity, an inheritance from the romantic movement. Impressionist paintings often have a wonderful immediacy, but the immediate is only rarely the profound.

How great, moreover, can a painter become when he restricts himself not only to the instant, but to the visual? "Monet is nothing but an eye," said Cézanne, "but *what an eye!*" The remark does not settle the question, perhaps, but it suggests an answer.

Figs. 16.24–25 (top) Degas. *Cotton Exchange at New Orleans.* 1873. Pau, Museum. (bottom) Monet. *The Breakfast Table. Paris, Luxembourg.* (top: Bulloz; bottom: Vizzavona)

Figs. 16.26–27 (top) Monet. *Argenteuil-sur-Seine*. Chicago, Art Institute. (bottom) Manet. *The Folkstone Boat*. Philadelphia, collection of Mr. Carroll Tyson, Jr.

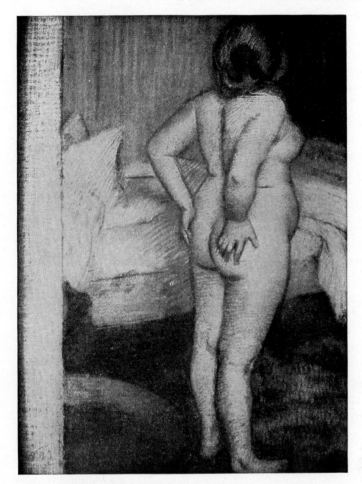

Fig. 16.28   Degas. *Woman Stretching Herself* (Bulloz)

Spontaneity itself, to carry the matter further, underwent a subtle change in the hands of the Impressionists. A curious by-product of Romanticism is the popular fallacy that an equation exists between the sincere and the spontaneous. Many an Impressionist canvas seems to suggest that its author took care to furnish evidence that he was innocent of contriving. The pictures seem all too often to depict natural accidents in all their original disorder. More than one critic has said that the Impressionists either composed badly or simply refused to compose.

All of these reservations stem from the fact that French Impressionism was, in an extreme sense of the phrase, a highly specialized art. At its best, it recorded vivid, perfect moments of intense vision, something that had never been done before with anything like the same success (Figs. 16.26–27). The very virtues of the school nevertheless leave a fundamental qustion still outstanding: Did the Impressionists create beauty, or did they merely recognize it?

None of these reasons, nor all of them together, quite account for the cultural discomfort evoked by Impressionism. A more fundamental point remains to be made.

Our emphasis, naturally enough, has so far been directed to the relation between the Impressionists and the contemporary public, and the relation between the movement and the art within its immediate past. It is now necessary to look down a broader perspective.

The matter with which we are to deal is best illustrated by reference to the work of Degas. It is scarcely unfair to say that he went out of his way to find subjects hitherto considered unsuitable for major painting. He produced, for example, any number of female nudes. One may search for a long time among them without seeing a single figure which could possibly be cited as that of a lovely woman. Rather often, moreover, he presented his nudes in surroundings and under circumstances that did not comport with bourgeois notions of social delicacy (Fig. 16.28).

It was difficult to accept such art as a demonstration of light's power to transfigure. It remains difficult. People felt that Degas was attacking the dignity of man, and they were not entirely mistaken. For we must face up to it: French Impressionism was the beginning of the end of the Renaissance, and the start of a new and confusing era in which we exist today, and which we do not yet understand.

Chapter 17*

PAINTING

A book's division into chapters gives us the idea that a sharp line can be drawn between one century and another, between one art development and another. But of course it can not be—not even in the case of the 20th century, when the revolutions that we call "modern art" seem to have developed so suddenly after the dividing line of 1900.

While the impressionists were still at work, and even while they were still fighting for recognition, the art of the 20th century was being born within the chronological limits of the 19th. The artists who set out in new directions at that time are grouped together as "postimpressionists," for want of a better term. No term has been invented that includes the variety of their styles, but *postimpressionism* at least indicates their common point of departure, which was a dissatisfaction with impressionism and an effort to go beyond its principles in order to find new ways of expression.

The impressionists themselves did not leave impressionist principles unquestioned. The freshness, vivacity, and sparkle of impressionism carried with it a sacrifice of certain other values. Its appealing spontaneity of effect was sometimes achieved at the expense of the formal definition, the order, and the calculation through which so many great works of art have translated the chaotic material of human experience into meaningful terms. And on the other hand, impressionism's preoccupation with the material of everyday life precluded exploration of the world of mystery and fantasy that has also been part of man's incessant curiosity about his place in the scheme of things.

As early as 1882, Renoir began to abandon the loose, semi-improvisational impressionist technique to retrain himself along the lines of the masters of

* Chapter 17 was written by John Canaday for this revised edition.

POSTIMPRESSIONISM
AND 20th-CENTURY ART

the Italian Renaissance, with their studied compositions and strong definition of form. His *Bathers* (Fig. 17.1), a large picture that occupied him between 1884 and 1887, served as a disciplinary test piece. Although the background echoes the shimmering vibrations of impressionism, the picture is a carefully studied one and the figures are as tightly executed as the most conventional academic ones against which the impressionists had revolted.*

Even more emphatically, the "neoimpressionists" examined the impressionist achievement and found it wanting. With George Seurat as its spokesman, neoimpressionism set out to retain the vibrant surface of impressionist painting while yet establishing a set of rules that would correct the improvisational nature of, for instance, a Monet canvas. Seurat's *Sunday Afternoon on the Island of the Grande Jatte* (Fig. 17.2) is the neoimpressionist masterpiece, a huge, almost painfully meticulous canvas covered by thousands upon thousands of tiny dots of color of uniform size, their combinations calculated by formulas as nearly scientific as any ever followed by an artist. Similarly, the composition is rigidly controlled on a semimathematical basis. Each figure and each landscape detail is reduced to simplified geometrical form in the neatly joined and fitted whole.

The *Grande Jatte* (which was begun the same year as Renoir's *Bathers* and completed a year sooner) is an impressive painting, but there is a real question as to whether its extreme discipline has not sacrificed the virtues of impressionism in the process of correcting its shortcomings. The brief life of neoimpressionism is explained by this question, and by the early death of

---

* After this period of self-imposed discipline, Renoir returned to a looser, freer style, seeking at the same time to retain some of the volume and solidity of traditional painting.

877

Fig. 17.1 Auguste Renoir (1841–1919). *Bathers.* 1884–1887. 45¼ by 67 inches. Chestnut Hill, Pa., Collection Mrs. Carroll S. Tyson.

Seurat. Other painters who had been converted to his theories soon abandoned it or, like Paul Signac, who inherited the leadership of the movement, relaxed the severity of its formulas.

But in the meanwhile, in seclusion near the city of Aix-en-Provence in southern France, an obscure painter named Paul Cézanne was reaching his own solution of the synthesis of impressionism with tradition—and in doing so was creating an art that made him the father of modern painting. His *View of Gardanne* (Fig. 17.3) was painted while Renoir was working on his *Bathers* and Seurat on his *Grande Jatte,* and in it are the seeds of the most revolutionary aspects of 20th-century theories.

We have become so familiar with these revolutions, especially the revolution of abstract art, that *View of Gardanne* seems mild enough in its departures from conventional ways of representing nature. But in the context of its time these departures are extreme, and of a nature entirely different from Renoir's or Seurat's.

The problem Cézanne set himself was in essence to correct the same impressionist shortcomings that had bothered Renoir and Seurat, but he went about solving it in a different way. Where Renoir hunted a correction by a return to the methods of the old masters and Seurat tried to crystallize impressionism through a semiscientific formula, Cézanne set out to go beyond

Fig. 17.2 Georges Seurat (1859–1891). *A Sunday Afternoon on the Island of the Grande Jatte.* Detail. 1884–1886. 81¼ by 54 inches; the entire painting is 120¼ inches long. Chicago, Art Institute, Helen Birch Bartlett Memorial.

either of these ideas. He wanted to discover a new way of painting rather than to harmonize impressionism with older ways, or to formalize it. He said that he wanted to "do Poussin over again after nature" and wanted to "make of impressionism something solid and durable like the art of the museums" (two ways, really, of saying the same thing), but he recognized that the classical, monumental art of the 17th-century master could not be merely hybridized with the mundane subject matter and the transient effects of impressionism—or rather, that such hybridization could not be achieved by the usual techniques without creating a monster. It would have been like trying to cross an oak tree with a wild rose.

In a lifetime of experiment, abandoning Paris and isolating himself in his native Provence, this moody, uncommunicative, even quarrelsome and difficult man created a body of work that has since been studied, dissected, analyzed, and reanalyzed by innumerable critics and painters, few of whom

Fig. 17.3 Cézanne (1839–1906). *View of Gardanne.* 1885–1886. 31 by 25½ inches. New York, Metropolitan Museum of Art, jointly owned with Dr. F. H. Hirschland, Harrison, N.Y.

would agree entirely with one another as to exactly what means Cézanne employed or exactly why he employed them. Yet all would agree that he created a new art.

By Cézanne's own statement, he failed of consummation. Yet his revolution was so great that it is often compared in importance to Giotto's, which seeded the Renaissance in the soil of the Middle Ages. Few historians or estheticians would deny that the revolutionary bedlam of 20th-century painting finds its genesis, more than in any other single source, in our effort to assimilate Cézanne's innovation. Basically, this innovation consisted of two parts: the concept that natural form serves the painter best not as something that should be imitated or idealized, but as something that may be warped, bent, flattened, distorted in any way the artist pleases for the purpose of creating a pictorial structure; and second, that color is not merely a decorative, descriptive, or expressive accessory to a form, but an integral part of it.

By the usual standards of accurate perspective or photographic reality, a Cézanne still life (Fig. 17.4) is absurd. Tables tilt, planes break and drop or rise, vases or similar objects stand askew and their two sides don't match. If we try to imagine how such a picture looked to people at the time it was painted, we can understand why Cézanne was considered either a madman or

Fig. 17.4 Cézanne. *Still-life with Commode.* About 1885. 25¾ by 31⅞ inches. Cambridge, Mass., Fogg Art Museum, Maurice Wertheim Collection.

a fantastically incompetent draftsman. Even impressionism was by comparison a kind of soft-focus photography.

The idea of deliberately drawing objects out of perspective and in conflicting perspectives, of flattening a round object by arbitrarily striking in a strong dark line along one side (a line which of course had no counterpart in nature), of drawing a straight line where the eye—or the camera—would see a curved one, or a slanting one where reality supplied a strictly vertical one, of changing the shapes and dimensions of objects at will—all this seemed absurd, not only pointless but self-defeating of the painter's imitative or idealizing function. Instead of imitating, Cézanne distorted. Instead of idealizing, he seemed even to uglify, to create awkwardness instead of endowing with grace. An extreme example is his *Great Bathers* (Fig. 17.5), where nude female figures are given forms that, as those of living women, would be grotesque, although as forms in an abstract composition they have an impressive architectural quality.

What, in truth, did Cézanne gain by such distortions? He gave his painting *as a painting* a kind of life, a kind of energy, independent of our associations with the painted objects. Individually the volumes and planes of his still lifes or landscapes or figure studies may be shifted, splayed, and broken in what seems an unreasonable way. But in combination they balance and counterbalance one another. These "tensions" may be compared to the ten-

Fig. 17.5 Cézanne. *The Great Bathers*. 1898–1905. 82 by 99 inches. Philadelphia Museum of Art, Wilstach Collection. (A. J. Wyatt)

sions, the thrusts and counterthrusts, of architecture. Like great architecture, a great Cézanne painting has an inner energy in spite of the fact that by literal definition it is static. Thus, without dissolving his objects in the flickering light of impressionism, Cézanne endowed them with the sense of life that, in impressionism, is inherent in the shimmering surface.

In developng his theories of color, Cézanne drew upon impressionism in a very direct way. Impressionism had divided color into the component parts of the spectrum and had applied the pure tints without blending them into one another. Cézanne kept the concept of unblended strokes of color, juxtaposed, but he added to it the idea that color, in addition to simulating light, could express form. Other artists, especially Delacroix, had had something of the same idea, but none had developed it to the point that fascinated Cézanne.

Expression of the distance or closeness of an object by relative color intensities based on observation of nature has been familiar in painting for centuries. Distant hills have been painted blue because they appear blue to the eye; colors in the immediate foreground have been painted in strong tints while those behind them have been painted in reduced tints, and so on. It is only a step from this principle to the question of whether the roundness of a single object might not be expressed by color as much as by light and shade.

Is this possible? Theoretically, yes, since certain colors tend to "recede," others to "come forward." A spot of yellow on blue paper, for instance, will appear to be in front of the blue. On the other hand, a spot of blue on yellow will look more as if it is behind the yellow and seen through a hole in the paper. In general, yellow, orange, and red tend to project; blue, green, and violet tend to recede.

But this generality is subject to a thousand variables, or ten thousand, and when a painter tries to apply the principle it is complicated by the fact that the objects he paints—red apples, green pears, yellow lemons, and so on —refuse to change their local colors for the convenience of a theory. Nevertheless, Cézanne believed that an object could be divided into a series of planes, that each plane could be made to recede or project by a slight color change. Thus a round apple painted by Cézanne may become a faceted object, each facet slightly changing color. Cézanne's version of "broken" color thus retained the brilliance of impressionist color, and at the same time served to keep his objects from dissolving in light, to solidify them, to make them "solid and durable like the art of the museums."

But any effort to analyze a single painting by Cézanne on these principles will be frustrating. These and his other stated principles seem to be violated from picture to picture, for—unlike Seurat—he did not begin with a set of rules to which he bound himself. Each canvas was an experiment.

Cézanne once said that all objects in nature could be reduced to the cube, the cylinder, and the sphere. This preoccupation with the simplest geometrical forms (which are associated in our minds with basic enduring values, with strength and mass) contributes greatly to the feeling of permanence that in a Cézanne coexists with the sense of vivid life and energy. And yet in his very late work, particularly in landscapes like *Mont Sainte-Victoire from Les Lauves* (Fig. 17.6), the geometry of individual objects is lost in an almost totally abstract surface. The central mass of the mountain is clear, but the houses, roads, foliage, fields and sky surrounding it all but disappear in a construction of planes that exists for its own sake rather than for description.

We must repeat our warning that a single canvas of Cézanne's may be conflictingly analyzed by a dozen critics. What Cézanne said and wrote about his theories is incomplete and contradictory. What we know of his ideas has come from reports of conversations with him, from an occasional letter. It is quite probable that many an element in a Cézanne painting that seems to us to be a brilliantly successful adjustment of form according to his theories as we have formulated them, was unsatisfactory to the artist himself. We must

Fig. 17.6 Cézanne. *Mont Sainte-Victoire from Les Lauves.* About 1904. 27⅞ by 36⅛ inches. Philadelphia Museum of Art, George W. Elkins Collection.

accept the possibility that some of our ideas about his painting might have surprised him.

Ultimately, however, these reservations are beside the point. We might ask likewise how many of our ideas about Giotto might have surprised the father of Western painting. What were Giotto's theories, in comparison with what we have discovered in his work? By the standards of the following century, Giotto's realism was technically inept, his figures malformed, and his perspective curious indeed. Nevertheless, his innovations were the foundation for later developments, and his expressive power is not reduced for us because he only partially achieved, technically, the realistic statement toward which he directed painting.

Cézanne's statement that he was "the primitive of the way I have discovered" indicates his own recognition of only partial achievement. Yet he remains the father of modern painting, and when the artist appears who is to Cézanne what Masaccio was to Giotto, Cézanne's art will remain as powerful and complete in itself as Giotto's has remained all these centuries.

It is a mistake also to think of Cézanne only in context with his innova-

Fig. 17.7 Cézanne. *The Card Players.* 1890–92. 25¾ by 32 inches. New York, Collection Stephen C. Clark.

tions, as if he were an artist interested only in a way of painting rather than one with a response to the world that he wanted to express in pictures. His insistence that a landscape be painted in the presence of nature is sufficient proof that whatever theories he held were developed not for themselves but in the service of expression.

The world Cézanne reveals is one that combines the vibrance of life that we sense in momentary aspects of things with the eternal imponderables that lie in deeper experience. Above all, Cézanne affirms the quality of enduring majesty in nature and the dignity of man. In *The Card Players* (Fig. 17.7) he selects a subject that could be—and frequently has been—one of only genre interest. In Cézanne's treatment we take no interest in the card game, nor are we supposed to do so. The players bent over the table have the solidity and the power of great natural forms or, a closer parallel, of architectural ones. Over the plane of the table they create a domelike volume, while the figure in the background has the strength of a great pillar. By such means, rather than by story-telling, Cézanne affirms the nobility of man in an essentially classical way as opposed to the romantic, emotionalized concepts that his century built upon the theories of Jean Jacques Rousseau.

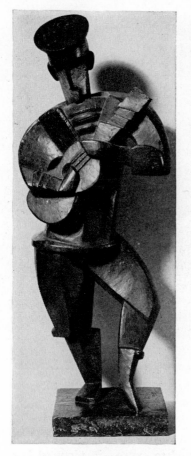

Figs. 17.8–9 (left) Lipchitz (1891–). *Sailor with Guitar.* 1914. Bronze. Philadelphia Museum of Art. (right) Duchamp (1887–). *Nude Descending a Staircase* (No. 2). 1912. 58 by 35 inches. Philadelphia Museum of Art, Arensberg Collection.

During Cézanne's lifetime, other artists, such as Vincent van Gogh and Paul Gauguin, were exploring in other directions. But we might follow first the geometrical-abstract movement that Cézanne set in motion. From the picture we have just seen, *Mont Sainte-Victoire from Les Lauves,* it is not very far to the 20th-century revolutionary experiment of cubism.

The most obvious principle involved in cubism is implied by its name— the reduction of all form to simple geometrical equivalents, whether cubes, pyramids, cylinders, spheres, or what-have-you. Jacques Lipchitz's cubist sculpture *Sailor* (Fig. 17.8) is evidence of one cubist work in which the principle dominates the composition. But cubism was more adaptable to painting, by reason of its second principle, that of "simultaneity."

The concept of simultaneity is based on the idea that the painter should not be limited to a single point of view in representing an object—a function

Fig. 17.10 Metzinger (1883–1956. *Tea Time*. 1911. Panel. 29¾ by 27⅜ inches. Philadelphia Museum of Art, Arensberg Collection.

that photography could perform mechanically—but should find a way to show the totality of an object all at once—front, back, sides, even cross-sections. In a very simple way Jean Metzinger does this by showing a tea-cup (Fig. 17.10) divided down the middle by a line that separates two points of view. On one side we see the cup straight-on, on the other, from slightly above. In a more complicated way, Marcel Duchamp's celebrated *Nude Descending a Staircase* (Fig. 17.9) shows us a single object in a multitude of positions. Planes grow transparent and overlap, fade and merge, yet in the right-hand side of the picture we can distinguish with some clarity a puppetlike figure with the head, bust, an arm, the torso, pelvis, and legs all reduced to simple geometrical approximates.

Nude Descending a Staircase was a curiously prophetic picture. It involved not only cubist theory, but had the element of impertinence (in its subject and title) and eeriness that were to combine, as we shall be seeing, in the art of surrealism. Also, the picture can be connected with the strong impulse felt by artists of its date to express the driving, frenetic nature of the 20th-century world. "Dynamism" was the favorite word of a group of Italian artists whose theories overlapped those of cubism—the Futurists. Russolo's *Dynamism of an Automobile* (Fig. 17.11), as an example, is an effort to express the forward lunge of the machine that is discernible beneath, or within, the abstract pattern that expresses its force and direction.

Eventually, cubism's effort to represent multiple aspects of an object may

Fig. 17.11 Luigi Russolo (1885–1941). *Dynamism of an Automobile*. 1913. 41½ by 55 inches. Paris, Musée National d'Art Moderne.

make the object completely unrecognizable, as in the case of Picasso's *Female Nude* (Fig. 17.12). Paradoxically, instead of representing a total image the artist ended by destroying that image. Pictures of this kind represent the end point of what is called the "analytical" phase of cubism. Even so, *Female Nude* can still be recognized as a close relative of the planes in Cézanne's *Mont Sainte-Victoire from Les Lauves*.

Having finally established the painter's right to reject completely the photographic image, the cubists abandoned the extreme abstractions of studies like *Female Nude* and evolved a second phase, sometimes called "decorative," but more properly "synthetic," cubism. In this phase the painter played freely with objects to derive from them whatever shapes (quite arbitrarily colored) seemed to him most ornamental or expressive. Juan Gris' *The Violin* (Fig. 17.13) plays freely with forms that remain recognizable in spite of his arbitrary dislocations. The color is a highly ornamental scheme of blacks, grays, white, and rosy tan, a combination that in its subtlety, quietness, and rightness can be called poetic.

Gris is often called the poet of cubism, but the appellation must not lead us to expect the kind of poetic sentiment that can be translated into literary terms. Only by forcing associations could we find "poetry" in the subject. But in color and arrangement the picture suggests a poetic mood

Figs. 17.12–13 (left) Pablo Picasso (1881–   ). *Female Nude.* 1910–1911. 38¾ by 30⅜ inches. Philadelphia Museum of Art. (right) Gris (1887–1927). *The Violin.* 1916. Panel. 45½ by 29 inches. Basel, Kunstmuseum.

almost in the way a Corot does—and Corot was indeed among the painters whose work Gris admired and studied.

Georges Braque's *Musical Forms* (Fig. 17.14) is a similarly harmonious combination of whites, blacks, soft blues, and tans, and also plays curved lines derived from the silhouette of a guitar against straight ones derived from a table top. The picture, if it can be called a picture rather than simply an ornamental composition, is a *collage,* made up largely of pieces of paper and cardboard.

Collage, which has developed in many directions in contemporary art, originated with the cubists and was an additional symptom of the artist's effort to free himself from the usual exhibitionism of dextrous brushwork. In using actual materials instead of paint to imitate other materials, collage substituted a kind of literal reality—the reality of actual materials and textures—for what used to be called "realism" when materials and textures were accurately imitated.

All of this begins to sound highly theoretical and indeed it is, of course. The layman has little interest in esthetic theories, and cubism marks the

Fig. 17.14 Braque (1882–   ). *Musical Forms.* 1918. Collage. 30⅜ by 37⅜ inches. Philadelphia Museum of Art, Arensberg Collection.

point of divorce between the general public and the contemporary artist that is so unhappily characteristic of our day. Although *Nude Descending a Staircase* was painted in 1912, it, like cubism in general, still has the capacity to irritate or enrage the public even though it seems old-fashioned to painters who have long ago discarded cubism for even more abstract forms of painting, which we will shortly mention.

The most important difference between the art of Cézanne and cubism, in spite of the great role the former played in the conception of the latter, is that Cézanne remained always an artist who was intent upon interpreting nature, while the cubists were most intent upon developing theories for their own sake. In other words, Cézanne's theories were necessary to what he wanted to say, while the cubists theories *were* what they wanted to say. To the lay observer, who is first interested in what a picture says rather than in how it is said, this makes a tremendous difference, and from this point of view Cézanne remains a 19th-century artist, closer to the Impressionists who relayed to the observer their response to nature than to the modern artist who, so to speak, expects the observer to come into the studio and listen obediently while the painter theorizes about art.

Fig. 17.15 Léger (1881–1955). *The City.* 1919. 91 by 116½ inches. Philadelphia Museum of Art, Gallatin Collection.

Cézanne was a painter who, like other 19th-century artists, regarded art as a form of communication. The cubists are among the painters who, typically in our century, regard art as something created for and understandable by only the initiates of a limited circle of intelligentsia. One critic has compared modern painting to the sport of fencing. Before the invention of firearms, he says, skill in swordsmanship was necessary to the defense of a man's life and honor. But fencing exists today only as a residual sport for those who are interested in doing it for its own sake or in watching it. Just so, painting used to be a part of life; today it is, or may be becoming, a residual art without vital connection with the life of our time. Although this comparison is extreme, it is supported again and again in 20th-century painting. And cubism, in the first years of the century, was and remains an art for "those interested in doing it for its own sake or in watching it."

Yet cubism proved to be a remarkably fertile source for variations ranging from forms of ornament enjoyed by the general public to new forms of expression for painters. Its frequent suggestions of mechanism—its angularity and precision—contributed to the typical style of Fernand Léger, who after

Fig. 17.16 Picasso. *The Old Guitarist*. 1903. 37⅜ by 28 inches. Art Institute of Chicago, Helen Birch Bartlett Memorial Collection.

some early cubist experiments decided that a painting in the 20th century should have the smoothness and uncompromising definition of a machine part. He once stated that his daily contact with machines during World War I might account for his interest in a mechanistic art, and he also said that "contact with violent and crude reality" at that time completed his divorce from the hyper-refinements of analytical cubism. He set about to express the clangorous excitement of contemporary urban, hence mechanized, life. The sharp, purely colored forms of *The City* (Fig. 17.15) are a visible credo. But although *The City* is a rejection of cubist theorizing, it draws eventually upon cubism for its manner, and could not have been painted if Léger had not passed through the cubist experience.

Picasso, one of cubism's inventors, continued to employ its principles in modified ways as he passed through a multitudinous sequence of styles. He even adapted cubism to passionate social statement, to which it would seem utterly unsuited.

In his earliest work Picasso had been concerned with pathos—for instance, in his precubist *The Old Guitarist* (Fig. 17.16). When this fantastically inven-

Fig. 17.17 Picasso. *Guernica*. 1937. 138 by 308 inches. New York, Museum of Modern Art, on loan from the artist.

tive artist emerged from pure cubism, he returned to emotionalized statement. There is a good chance that his *Guernica* (Fig. 17.17) may one day be considered his masterpiece. Certainly it is as highly charged dramatically as any of his works. It involves cubist-derived forms, but far from being an intellectual exercise, *Guernica* is one of the most fervent statements of the first half of the 20th century, as a personal protest and as a social one.

More than 25 feet long, *Guernica* suffers badly in reproduction on the page of a book. It is a condemnation of the action by which Guernica, an ancient and holy city of Spain, was attacked by German bombers in the service of General Franco in the Spanish civil war. This was in 1937, and the destruction of the city was a test run, the first practical application of the military theory of saturation bombing. Much of Guernica and many of its innocent inhabitants were destroyed.

Picasso's version of this crime and tragedy shows a farmyard or courtyard in which human beings and animals shriek and die hideously. Purposely grotesque, brutal and violent, *Guernica* draws equally upon the structural principles of cubism—not in themselves expressive—and the emotionalism of expressionist distortions.

Expressionism was a logical continuation of the romantic movement. It developed concurrently with cubism, and we must now drop back to the end of the 19th century to follow its course up to *Guernica*.

The four major names among the postimpressionists are Seurat, Cézanne, van Gogh, and Gauguin. The latter two led lives so conspicuously bizarre

Fig. 17.18 Paul Gauguin (1848–1903). *The Moon and the Earth*. 1893. 45 by 21½ inches. New York, Museum of Modern Art, Lillie P. Bliss Collection.

that almost anyone with the slightest acquaintance with art is familiar with their tragic or pathetic adventures, which have been the subject of numerous biographies, pseudo-biographies, and motion pictures—to such an extent that their painting is seen, to an exaggerated degree, purely as an illustrative corollary to their lives.

Gauguin was a successful businessman and a collector with a fondness for the impressionists. At first he painted as an avocation, but he ended by sacrificing his business, his family, and eventually his life to a passion for art that was deeply romantic. Romanticism as a way of life had created the image of the artist as a free soul associated with exoticism. This concept led Gauguin to the South Seas, where he expected to find the perfect life in an exotic natural setting surrounded by simple people of unsurpassed physical beauty and natural nobility of spirit. Added to this, his interest in the dark world of superstition as manifested in the lives of simple people made of the islands a never-never land of deep mystery as well as surface beauty.

The reality was less enchanting than the preconception. But in spite of the afflictions of poverty and disease, Gauguin became an islander, returning

Fig. 17.19   Van Gogh (1853–1890). *The Starry Night.* 1889. 29 by 36½ inches. New York, Museum of Modern Art, Lillie P. Bliss Bequest.

only briefly to Paris to exhibit his work. And if his life in the islands was not quite idyllic, and if the European bureaucrats and missionaries had introduced serious adulterations of the noble primitive spirit, Gauguin nevertheless fulfilled his dream by painting what he had expected to find. From corrupted reality he synthesized pictures like *The Moon and the Earth* (Fig. 17.18).

The 19th-century romantic idea of art as an adjunct to personality most strongly colors our response to the painting of Vincent van Gogh. We are a bit overfamiliar with the picture of an ugly and intense man frustrated in sexual love, in his yearning for human affection, and in an early career as an evangelist, and subject to periods of irrationality that finally led him to suicide. Although he sold only one picture in his lifetime, he was sustained by his conviction, richly justified as it turns out, that the future would know and recognize him through pictures that he was forced to paint largely for himself.

Fictionalized biographies have presented van Gogh as the archetype of the mad genius and his art is almost always called "tragic" because his life was pathetic. Actually, even his most intense pictures are not tragic. In *The Starry Night* (Fig. 17.19), a fervent and mystical joy in nature, which van

Gogh saw as an expression of cosmic energy, approaches religious ecstasy. This ecstasy is so intense that it is all but agonizing, but it is a kind of fulfillment rather than a tragic expression.

It is important to remember about van Gogh, also, that while his technique is often so violent and so slashing that we can imagine his pictures pouring forth in unthinking and inspired frenzy, he was a thoughtful and even analytical painter. His romantic turbulence may be emotionally inspired, but it is controlled, not spontaneous. His voluminous letters tell us that he pondered, theorized, and made careful preparatory studies even for pictures which, in their final versions, might be painted with great rapidity.

By definition, expressionism is a form of art in which the freest distortions of natural appearances are invented as means for the intensification of emotional response. Among the old masters, El Greco is the most obvious expressionist, and indeed he may be called one of the great ones of all time or even the greatest one. But as a term limited to modern art, expressionism is more concerned with intimate, directly personal expression. We might say that in *The Starry Night,* a canvas on which writhing pattern and vivid color are used almost as symbols of an emotional state, there is not much that was not anticipated by El Greco. The difference is that El Greco, in his religious subjects at least, translated into pictorial images a basic mystical concept. The passionate intensity with which his paintings are charged is not his personal, individual response to the Christian mysteries, but his generalization for all of humanity that holds to them. *The Starry Night,* on the other hand, is one man's vision of nature, an ardently personal release of feeling which we are free to share. It is certainly not a generalized concept of a starry night, which most people would associate with quiet, peace, and deep skies, rather than with an explosive universe.

We feel extraordinarily close to the artist when we stand in front of *The Starry Night,* and part of this immediacy comes from the artist's manner of applying the paint. Its very texture reflects his emotional impetuosity; we are closer to him because the canvas still bears so vividly the impress of his brush. Here, too, we may relate van Gogh to the past, but this time within his own century and to an artist whose work we know he studied— Delacroix. The great romantic was one of van Gogh's models, and in breaking away from the smooth, precise surface of neoclassical painting he began, or revived, a tradition of free painting that continued through the Impressionists, was developed in van Gogh, and has found its temporary end result in those contemporary painters who actually fling, drip, and dribble their paint onto their canvases.

Delacroix, who was essentially an intellectual painter, spoke often of the absolute necessity of creating an *effect* of spontaneity. His agitated pattern, rich paint surface, and intensified color were all calculated to produce an

Figs. 17.20–21 (left) Heckel (1883–   ). *Portrait of a Man.* 1919(?). Color woodcut. 18¼ by 12¼ inches. Washington, D.C., National Gallery of Art, Rosenwald Collection. (right) Munch (1863–1944). *Anxiety.* 1896. Color lithograph. 16¼ by 15¼ inches. New York, Museum of Modern Art.

emotional effect although if the effect were to be complete the calculation needed to be hidden. In van Gogh the calculation is even less apparent (although we know he made many preliminary studies for *The Starry Night),* the agitation of pattern more extreme, the paint surface even more active, and the colors much brighter—thanks in part to the more intense pigments developed in the latter part of the century. On all these scores, van Gogh is a primary source of inspiration for the early 20th-century painters for whose work the term "expressionism" was coined.

Expressionism was an international tendency, but the disturbed social climate of Germany preceding and following the First World War was most sympathetic to its spirit, which is generally one of tragedy and pathos, of violence and moody introspection. Erich Heckel's *Portrait of a Man* (Fig. 17.20), with its air of neurotic apprehension, is a summary of the psychological atmosphere at the core of German expressionism, but the movement as a whole covered a wide range of emphatically personal styles.

The first of several organizations of German expressionist painters was *Die Brücke,* meaning The Bridge, founded in 1905 by young painters strongly influenced by van Gogh and by two other Northern artists, the Norwegian Edvard Munch (Fig. 17.22) and the Belgian James Ensor (Fig. 17.21), both

Figs. 17.22–23 (left) Ensor (1860–1949). *Self-portrait with Masks.* 1889. 47½ by 31½ inches. Antwerp, Collection Cleomire Jussiant. (right) Kirchner (1880–1938). *The Street.* 1913. 47½ by 35⅞ inches. New York, Museum of Modern Art. (left: Museum of Modern Art, New York)

of whom were eccentric personalities who created worlds of fantasy in which human suffering and vulnerability to evil were dominant themes. Ernst Ludwig Kirchner is usually thought of as the most typical painter of The Bridge, and his *The Street* (Fig. 17.23), painted in 1913 just before World War I, reflects a frenetic and sinister social atmosphere as perceived emotionally by an introspective onlooker.

The second expressionist group called itself *Der Blaue Reiter* (The Blue Rider). Formed in 1911, it eventually absorbed The Bridge, and was international in character rather than specifically German although it had its center in Munich. Munich was then a stronghold of conservative painting, and in revolting against traditional standards The Blue Rider had tremendous historical importance. Its influence was felt most emphatically through the Russian Wassily Kandinsky, one of its organizing members, who is given credit for producing the first completely abstract painting in 1910 and whose treatise *Concerning the Spiritual in Art* has been a handbook on abstract painting since its appearance in 1912. Cubism, burgeoning in Paris at this time, also influenced The Blue Rider, which combined the emotionalism of The

Fig. 17.24 Grosz (1893–1959)
Street Scene. Date unknown.
Lithograph. 10½ by 8½ inches.
Philadelphia Museum of Art,
Harrison Fund.

Bridge with the intellectualizing that was beginning to dominate European painting. By this time 20th-century art had, in fact, entered into that period of concurrent and often conflicting revolutions and experiments that have made it the fascinating welter of multiple directions and heated argument that it still is.

As a final confusion in German expressionism, a group of painters appeared at the end of World War I under the not altogether appropriate title of *Die Neue Sachlichkeit* (The New Objectivity). Hardly objective, they turned the first introspective and then intellectual character of expressionism to violent social criticism. Among them, George Grosz with his bitter satires and brutally drawn indictments of the times (he could also be an exquisitely delicate draftsman on appropriate occasions) left some of the most appalling records. His lithograph *Street Scene* (Fig. 17.24) shows a city inhabited by grotesque figures of poverty, stupidity, and corruption, while the three windows of a single house are vignettes of lust, murder, and suicide.

Morbidity and violence of the kind so frequent in German expressionism are foreign to the French spirit, and the nearest French cousin to German expressionism is a cousin at least once removed. Georges Rouault, after some early works strongly infused with the spirit of social protest, evolved a more generalized and meditative manner that he frequently applied to religious

Figs. 17.25–26 (left) Rouault (1871–1958). *Crucifixion*. 1918. 41 by 28¾ inches. Philadelphia, Collection Henry P. McIlhenny. (right) Belgian Congo. *Head*. Wood. 13¾ inches high. Philadelphia, University Museum.

subjects, making him one of the few modern painters who have made a religious statement except in terms borrowed from the Renaissance. In his *Crucifixion* (Fig. 17.25), the strong black lines common to much German expressionism are apparent, but they are even more closely related to the lead joints in medieval stained-glass windows. The areas they define are filled with color of similar nature.

The French expressionist art, however—with which Rouault had an early association—was *fauvism,* which might be partially defined as a contrastingly happy response to the stimulus in the air that was leading painters to investigate strong colors and abrupt forms as means of emotional expression. Very brief in its duration as anything like an organized movement, fauvism was an art of pure, bright color usually applied in flat areas, with Gauguin's pattern as one of its multitudinous sources. Among the other sources, African sculpture (Fig. 17.26) was potent. The bold, simple, and vigorous geometry of such primitive yet oddly sophisticated work had a great impact on European art at the beginning of the 20th century, having been a factor in cubism as well as in the concurrent development of fauvism.

Figs. 17.27–28 Henri Matisse (1869–1954). (left) *The Green Line*. 1905. 16 by 12¾ inches. Copenhagen, Statens Museum for Kunst, Rump Collection. (right) *Lady in Blue*. 1937. 36½ by 29 inches. Chestnut Hill, Pa., Collection Mrs. John Wintersteen.

Matisse, as the great name of fauvism, is often called the great colorist of his generation. Certainly he is one of the great ornamental painters of any time. His early fauve portrait of his wife (Fig. 17.27) is called *The Green Line* because an arbitrary band of bright green runs through the center of the face as one vivid element in a color scheme that exists for its own sake as much as for any other reason. The picture is two things at once: it is quite obviously a strongly defined representation of a woman's head and shoulders, but simultaneously it is a pattern or, to use a stronger word, a structure of pure color that has its being independently of the object represented.

But Matisse was not an artist who was ever ready to settle for any purely theoretical values in painting, and his color and structure became more and more the servants of an art so fresh and joyous that it can logically be included in the French tradition that includes the art of the 18th-century court and of Renoir. Matisse and Picasso are usually accepted as the dominant figures in the first half of 20th-century painting, but certainly they are at opposite poles expressively in spite of the fact that their innovations combined to shatter our concept of pictorial form. Where Picasso explores dark and violent areas of the spirit (along with other areas), Matisse is dedicated to the joy of life, its graces and pleasures. His *Lady in Blue* (Fig. 17.28), a late work, is equally with *The Green Line* a color structure, but its sinuosities of pattern and its general elegance of effect are more typical of the mass of his work than is the earlier picture.

But both pictures, with their emphasis on color as a structural element, are of the kind that has led other artists to ask an important question: If color can exist as structure to such an extent that it becomes as important or even more important than the object represented, why not try eliminating the object altogether? Why not let color exist alone, without the confusion of association with a natural object? Likewise, expressionist paintings suggested the question: If the mood of a picture like *The Starry Night* is created largely by the colors used and the manner of their application, why bother about a subject? Why not use pure color and pure shape to create a mood, instead of confusing them with whatever mood a subject suggests?

It began to seem to many painters that ever since impressionism, art had been trying to free itself from the representation of the visible world. Cézanne had violently distorted nature for purposes of pictorial structure, van Gogh for purposes of intensification. Cubism had very nearly destroyed the object but then had backtracked and had more or less re-established the reference to nature. Why not go all the way, and free painting from its bondage to representation?

As said some paragraphs ago, Wassily Kandinsky is usually credited with the first completely abstract painting. In a series of compositions like *Improvisation* (Fig. 17.29) he used high color and agitated pattern not as overlays on a subject from nature and not in distortion of nature, but for themselves. The "meaning" or the "mood" of the painting is not defined for the observer, either by objects represented or by any clue in the title. The painting simply exists, for whatever effect it may have on the observer who is willing to open himself to its impact. He may find in it emotional stimulations of one kind or another, or he may find in it only a variety of colored shapes that do or do not please him as something to look at. Or, of course, he may find in it nothing at all, depending on his willingness or his capacity to accept its premise and on the degree of his cultivated or innate esthetic responses.

We might define here the term *abstract* as well as can be done in relation to painting. By philosophical definition, "abstract" means "separated from closely associated ideas or perceptions." Thus an abstract painting is one that is not closely associated with the idea of a tree, a head, a vase, a flower, or any other objects. There are all degrees of abstraction. Picasso's *Seated Nude Woman* is almost, but not quite, completely abstract. Its title helps us to associate it with the idea and perception of a natural object. But Kandinsky's *Improvisation* is completely abstract in that no natural objects are recognizable in it or hinted at in the title. To distinguish such paintings from ones that are partially abstract like *Seated Nude Woman* or the even

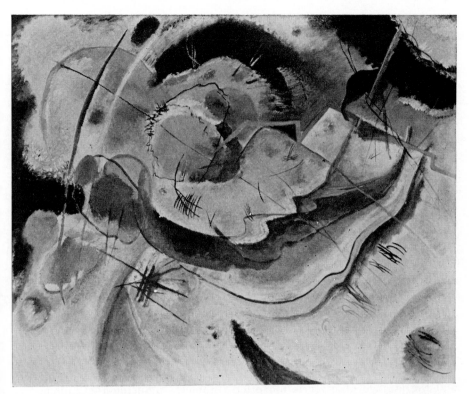

Fig. 17.29 Kandinsky (1866–1944). *Improvisation*. 1914. 30¾ by 39⅜ inches. Philadelphia Museum of Art, Arensberg Collection.

less abstract *Musical Forms,* efforts have been made to establish the terms "nonfigurative" or "nonobjective." But the word "abstract" persists in general use.

During the decade 1950 to 1960, abstract painting came completely into its own in the salesrooms, with most critics, and with many collectors. For the first time, America rather than France took the lead in avant-garde movements with *abstract expressionism,* a further development along the lines of Kandinsky's *Improvisation.* The most spectacular subdivision of contemporary abstract expressionism is "action painting," a term yet to be unequivocally defined but indicating a vigorous application of paint in free and at least partially improvised patterns. The American Jackson Pollock originated a technique of dripping, flinging, and spattering paint from above onto a canvas laid flat on the floor (Fig. 17.30). This and derived or similar techniques (such as spreading the paint with a wide board or other implements) should, theoretically, bring us as immediately as possible into the presence of the artist. Any freely painted picture—like a van Gogh—evokes the presence of the artist at work in a way that a very smoothly painted one does

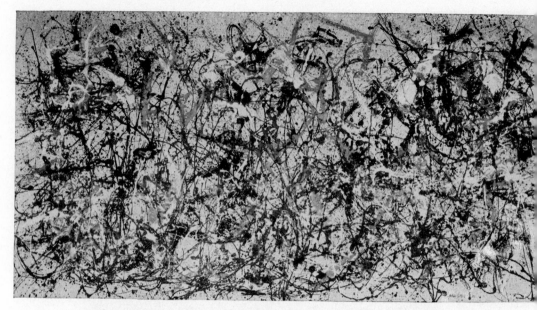

Fig. 17.30 Pollock (1912–1956). *Autumn Rhythm*. 1950. 105 by 207 inches. New York. Metropolitan Museum of Art, Hearn Fund.

not. But the theory does not always work; the divorce between the painter and the average observer is too often complete—reducing the audience for painting to narrow limits.

Opposed to the extremely personal, emotive style of abstract expressionism is the school of geometrical abstraction in which Piet Mondrian occupies the position of fountainhead. Mondrian's meticulously impersonal rectangles are an extreme application of the idea that the greater the disciplined economy of means, the purer the art. Mondrian—once a conventionally realistic artist— arrived at his style by limiting himself not only to straight lines, but to horizontal and vertical ones, and thus to the rectangle, the simplest of geometrical forms. He also limited himself to the primary colors—pure red, pure yellow, and pure blue—plus black and white. For the sympathetic esthetician, Mondrian consummates the classical ideal of purity, order, and intellectual control, while abstract expressionism summarizes the opposite romantic ideal of personal emotional release at any cost. Both schools of abstract painting, with infinite gradations and variations in between, have hundreds of practitioners.

The development of 20th-century painting as outlined here has, then, been progressively toward abstraction of one kind or another. But figurative painting has, concurrently, continued in conventional forms and has spurted in a few specialized ones, ranging from social propaganda to fantasy.

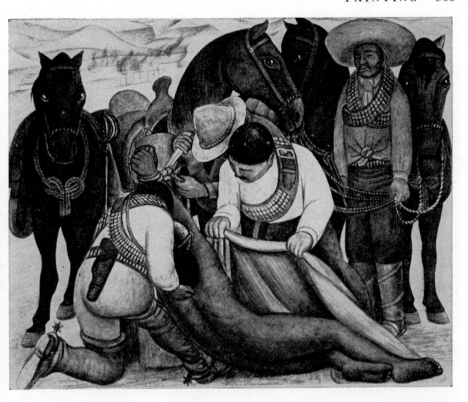

Fig. 17.31 Rivera (1886–1957). *The Liberation of the Peon*. 1931. Fresco. Variation of fresco in Ministry of Education, 1923–1927, Mexico City. 74 by 95 inches. Philadelphia Museum of Art, Gift of Mr. and Mrs. Herbert C. Morris.

In the 1920's, a group of Mexican muralists headed by Diego Rivera (a former cubist) revitalized the art of fresco and also painted the first government-sponsored art with a social purpose since the Renaissance. For a people just emerging from oppression and illiteracy as a result of the Mexican agrarian revolution, these painters decorated public buildings with scenes from Mexican history and with strong, obvious allegories of the new political ideals. Rivera's *Liberation of the Peon* (Fig. 17.31) shows a naked peasant, his body scarred by the lash, receiving the minstrations of revolutionary soldiers while a hacienda, symbol of the landowner's oppression, burns in the background. The "Mexican Renaissance" lost impetus after a few years, but it produced a great expressionist, José Clemente Orozco, who combined his social message with more general statements of human dignity under oppression.

In the United States, a much milder but somewhat similar movement flared up in *regionalism*. A group of middle-western painters who rejected Europeanisms, especially such esoteric ones as cubism, began to sing the

Figs. 17.32–33 (above) Burchfield (1893–   ). *Back-yards in Spring*. 1946. 33 by 44 inches. Philadelphia Museum of Art, Gift of Mrs. Herbert C. Morris. (left) Wood (1892–1942). *American Gothic*. 1930. 29⅞ by 24⅞ inches. Art Institute of Chicago.

Fig. 17.34 Sloan (1871–1951). *Greenwich Village Backyards.* 1914. 26 by 34 inches. New York, Whitney Museum of American Art.

folksy glories of rural America, and occasionally to satirize our limitations. Grant Wood's *American Gothic* (Fig. 17.33), which is in part satirical and in part a bow to homespun virtues, has become the standard example of the slightly too self-conscious Americanism of the school.

But where regionalism failed, the American scene supplied material to many artists who were interested in exploring it without propagandizing special virtues or criticizing shortcomings. Among these, Charles Burchfield (Fig. 17.32) found in shabby small towns, in backyards, along railroad tracks and in similarly unpoetic places a kind of poetry in which the growth of trees, the lights in windows, the weathering of unpainted wood, and the familiar sky are components of the eternal poetry that springs through the overlay of commonplaceness and shoddiness that men impose upon the world.

The American city, too, was discovered. Early in the century it had been seen impressionistically by the painters of the Ash Can school—painters like John Sloan (Fig. 17.34) who abandoned conventional prettiness to record the streets and hall bedrooms of New York and Philadelphia with a brash, vigorous interest in the everyday that was a counterpart to the French impressionists'

Fig. 17.35 Hopper (1882–   ). *Early Sunday Morning*. 1930. 30 by 40 inches. New York, Whitney Museum of American Art.

interest in the life of the boulevards. Today the Ash Can painters seem to fall somewhere between the regions of fine painting and skillful illustration, an unhappy position. They roamed the city with a lively eye for a new kind of picturesqueness—the clerks, the stenographers, the vagrants, the shoppers, and their background of the trafficky street, the architectural hodgepodge, and the tenement.

But the Ash Can painters offered little comment except on the surface appearances of the city and its mores. It remained for Edward Hopper to explore the American city as something more than a haphazard spectacle.

As a poetic painter, Hopper chose the dingiest aspects of the urban world to show that light is unconquerable even when it must play upon sooty bricks, fireplugs, and dreary rows of windows (Fig. 17.35). He commented, at the same time, on the nature of urban life, revealing the loneliness that can exist even in places where men must shoulder one another in going about their ordinary business. He also painted the cottages and lighthouses of the New England coast, disposing a few simple elements—a rise of ground, a building, a cloud—with such assurance and dignity of pattern that he brought to realistic painting the quality of abstract art without the dehumanization that abstraction so frequently entails.

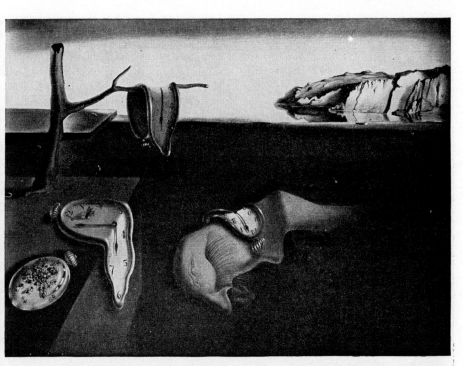

Fig. 17.36 Dali (1904–   ). *The Persistence of Memory.* 1931. 9½ by 13 inches. New York Museum of Modern Art.

The United States also produced painters who commented as directly as the Mexicans on politics, oppression, and the kind of mind that creates or tolerates social evils. The dean of the group was Ben Shahn, who had the first, the imperative, qualification that distinguishes the socially conscious artist from the mere propagandist: his paintings were at once scathing indictments by a man who held strong and usually nonconformist political and social convictions, and esthetically pleasing works by an artist with full command of his technical resources. He also, especially in his later work, painted allegories of the contemporary world. *Epoch,* painted in 1950, shows two figures riding wobbly bicycles, one of whom carries a placard saying "Yes," the other, "No," while between them a little figure balances precariously in a handstand, a hand on each head. The background suggests a carnival— the false, giddy brilliance of our hazardous times.

Social comment as a reaction against abstraction—or as indifference to it —was limited largely to the North American continent. In Europe the reaction took an entirely different form although this form was acutely representational—not realism, but sur (or super) realism. The surrealist recipe is simple: precise realistic definition of every detail of a picture, but the combination of these details in startling and irrational ways. The resultant dream-

scapes were, more often than not, morbid or perverse and drew heavily on Freudian symbolism. At its best, surrealist art created a dream world of disturbing concreteness, as in Salvador Dali's *The Persistence of Memory* (Fig. 17.36). Surrealism's weakness was that when imagination failed, shocking perversities were substituted for poetic images. Never content to be less than startling, surrealism as an organized movement proved before long that nothing is more tiresome than repetitions of the bizarre. Nevertheless it has remained a persistent force in the work of individual painters and has even infiltrated realistic painting by increasing an awareness of the extent to which the most commonplace subjects may take on mysterious suggestions when thrown slightly out of kilter with their surroundings.

Surrealism also has its abstract form. The Spaniard Joan Miró is sometimes listed with Matisse and Picasso as the third most widely influential painter of the first half of the century. Developing through a semicubist period and then through surrealist fantasy of a figurative kind, he finally developed a style in which curious abstract forms sometimes suggestive of amoebae, sometimes of bones, sometimes of sea or land creatures, yet never quite representing anything, engage in encounters half-humorous and half-sinister (Fig. 17.37). Somewhere between Miró's flat, highly ornamental ab-

Fig. 17.37 (opposite) Miró (1893–). *Painting.* 1933. 51 by 64 inches. Philadelphia Museum of Art, Gallatin Collection.

Fig. 17.38 Tanguy (1900–1955). *Shadow Country.* 1927. 39 x 31⅝ inches. Birmingham, Mich., Collection Mr. and Mrs. Harry Lewis Winston.

stract surrealism and the precisely defined images and landscape in such surrealist pictures as Dali's *Persistence of Memory* are the dreamscapes or nightmarescapes of Yves Tanguy (Fig. 17.38). Here the forms continue to be precisely defined, as concise and nearly as tangible as sculpture, yet they are forms that never existed on earth although we can imagine their existence on the lunar plains or at the bottom of the drained sea suggested by the topography of Tanguy's invention.

The world of enchantment and dream that surrealism was to explore against a background of abnormal psychology in the 20th century was entered unaware by the extraordinary painter Henri Rousseau in the 19th. His birth and death dates (1844–1910) nearly coincide with Cézanne's, and he occupies in the realm of 20th-century fantastic art a position comparable, on a smaller scale, to Cézanne's as a precursor. Usually nicknamed "Douanier" because he was a toll-collector, Rousseau was a simple man and an untutored artist who differed importantly from the hundreds or thousands or tens of thousands of other people who paint, without instruction, as a hobby: He had a natural talent for decorative pattern, he cultivated it assiduously over many years, and he possessed a combination of naïve faith and fantastic imagination that found expression in his obsessive dedication to painting.

Figs. 17.39–40 (above) Rousseau. *The Sleeping Gypsy.* 1897. 51 by 79 inches. New York, Museum of Modern Art, Gift of Mrs. Simon Guggenheim. (left) Rousseau (1844–1910). *Village Street Scene,* 1909. 16¼ by 13 inches. Philadelphia Museum of Art, Arensberg Collection.

Even Rousseau's earliest known paintings (Fig. 17.40), while marked by the curious perspective, the persnickety detail and the odd stiffness typical of other "modern primitive" painting, have the additional quality of enchantment, a translation of the facts of this world into a realm where every detail is realistic yet the sum of details is unreal. As he progressed, Rousseau recognized this quality in his art (or it was recognized for him) and he cultivated it.

Fig. 17.41 Chirico (1888–). *Melancholy and Mystery of a Street.* 1914. 34⅜ by 28¼ inches. New Canaan, Conn., Collection of Mr. and Mrs. Stanley Resor.

His jungle pictures are his most famous because they are his most decorative, but his masterpiece may be *The Sleeping Gypsy* (Fig. 17.39), in which, totally inexplicably, a figure in a striped robe sleeps in a desert while a lion watches nearby, beneath a sky in which a few stars shine. The magical effect is produced by the combination of absolute definition, which insists upon the reality of the subject, with the impossibility of the subject's existence in this world. This is the basic recipe of surrealism, but the picture is without the efforted and programmatic quality that makes much surrealism suspect.

Surrealism's other immediate precursor was Giorgio de Chirico, a painter who was never officially connected with the movement. His most typical painting is an eerie cityscape in deep perspective (Fig. 17.41) illuminated by unnatural lights and peopled sparsely by statues and by equally immobile personages, in which time is suspended in a never-never land at once utterly convincing and utterly fantastic.

Surrealism developed most directly, however, from a movement known as *Dada,* which, like surrealism itself, was as much a literary as a painterly revolution on small scale. Dada was the paradox of an anti-art art. Developing like the German New Objectivity out of World War I, and in fact overlap-

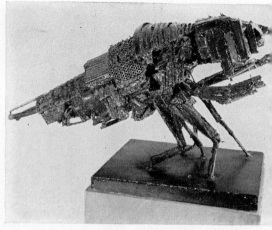

Figs. 17.42–43   (left) Schwitters (1887–1948). *Merz K*
struktion. 1921. Painted wood, wire, and paper. 14½
8½ inches. Philadelphia Museum of Art, Gallatin Coll
tion. (above) César (1921–   ). *Galactic Insect.* 1953–1⁹
Welded iron. 19⅜ inches high, 36½ inches long, 1
inches wide. New York, Museum of Modern Art, Gift
G. David Thompson.

ping the German school, Dada was a protest (in, unfortunately, negative
terms) against a society that for centuries had tried to regulate itself on reasonable principles but had come to the unreasonable end of self-destruction in
war. Hence Dada rejected art as the expression of man's supposedly rational
efforts. In view of the defeat of the rational, Dada "literature" was written by
pulling words out of hats and Dada "paintings" were created by such illogical
processes as tearing pieces of paper into bits and pasting them onto another
piece of paper in the positions in which they fell when dropped onto it.
The absurd, the impertinent, the mocking, were Dada's stock in trade. But
Dada frequently produced works of disturbing psychopathological associations,
and from them surrealism, in great part, developed.

But Dada experiments were often rational in spite of themselves, or because maintenance of irrationality for a period of time is difficult for a rational
person. Kurt Schwitters' *Merz Konstruktion* (Fig. 17.42) is a case in point.
Schwitters was disinherited by his dadaist colleagues because into such as-
semblages of trash, the three-dimensional equivalent of collage, he introduced
a sense of design, a combination of colors, textures, and in this case shallow
volumes, that transformed the "found" objects into a cohesive abstract pattern. Currently, the found object is an important element in the conception

Fig. 17.44 Klee (1879–1940). *Jörg*. 1924. Watercolor. 9¼ by 11¼ inches. Philadelphia Museum of Art, Arensberg Collection.

of sculpture like César's *Galactic Insect* (Fig. 17.43), in which bits of metal from the junk heap have been assembled into an image of disturbing half-reality, as if natural forms had suffered dreadful mutations.

In surveying a period of art some arbitrary use of categories is necessary for any kind of clarity. When we are speaking of our own century, of a time so close at hand and so unusually complicated, this categorizing may be misleading. The movements and "isms" that we have outlined here are not so neatly bounded as this summary has, of necessity, made them appear. Matisse, the fauvist, has been influenced at times by cubism, and Picasso, a parent of cubism, has learned from his rival, Matisse. German expressionism included variations of analytical cubism. And there are painters whose work is unclassifiable and all the more impressive for being so.

An example is Paul Klee, an artist who would be some critics' selection for the most representative painter of the first half of the 20th century although his pictures may seem to the uninitiated to be only entertaining whimsies. A single example, *Jörg* (Fig. 17.44), may carry hints or echoes of cubism, of the art of children and savages, and of expressionism. Klee deals at different times or simultaneously in terms of irony, wit, formal philosophy, and an investigation of abnormal states of mind. Beginning as a representational draftsman, he was in turn influenced by Cézanne, van Gogh, and others before joining an early expressionist group. There was not a subsequent movement in European art that he did not study or that did not affect him.

This sounds, on the face of it, as if Klee could be only an eclectic artist, creating a pastiche of bits of this and bits of that. Actually he is as individual an artist as his time produced. His tremendous importance lies in his philosophy as an artist and the successful expression of that philosophy in his art.

At the heart of Klee's belief was the conviction that no amount of intellectualizing can explain the ultimate mystery of existence. He was, hence, a mystic first and a theorist second, an intellectual who, when all was said and done, admitted that the irrational was a more powerful force than the rational. When his art is puzzling to laymen, or seems inconsequential, it is because we associate mystical expression in art with vague or solemn figures rather than the witty ones invented by Klee. But these apparently thin and weightless images take on more importance when we understand that Klee often regarded them as being close to magical devices.

The earliest art we know, that of the caves, was magical in intention. The representation of the animals upon whom man's life depended gave man a power over them and also insured their fertility. And the idea of art as necromancy was never far beneath the surface even in later ages. The materialization of men's gods in stone or in paint, and men's reverence for these images as a medium of communication with his gods, is based on magic, an idea that affects most religious art whether it is Egyptian, Greek, medieval, or even, in some cases, later. We could even argue that until the invention of the camera there was a kind of magic in man's ability to create by his own hands images of his world, to reduce a vast landscape, for instance, to a few square feet of canvas, and to open that flat canvas into the landscape's vast depth.

The quality of magic was lost in 20th-century intellectual theorizing. Even surrealism's exploration of a nether world was only speciously magical since it depended so largely on the intellectual formulas of Freud. Everything about surrealism can be explained; in fact, it can be regarded as an illustrative explanation of theories that are frequently too pat.

But Klee believed that true art is inexplicable. All our explanations have as their purpose a clearing of the way toward the inner mystery of existence— but in the end this mystery must be sensed, not known. The contradiction in Klee's art is its combination of intellectualism and apparent innocence. It frequently resembles the art of children and savages because in these forms of expression Klee felt as direct a communion with magic through images as an uninnocent man can feel.

Fig. 17.45 Klee. *Diana.* 1931. Panel. 37½ by 23⅜ inches. St. Louis, Collection Mr. and Mrs. William Bernoudy.

In the light of these ideas, a painting like Klee's *Diana* (Fig. 17.45) becomes extraordinarily complicated. It is connected with Greek legend by its title; with primitive magical-symbolical art by the goddess' arrow (which has its own eye to direct it), resembling signs scratched or painted on cave walls or in aboriginal decorations; with Seurat's pointilism in the manner of execution; with medieval art perhaps in the wheellike device under the goddess' foot, which occurs in medieval sculpture as a means of indicating miraculous transportation. But finally Klee's design is inexplicable. It exists for itself, enriched but not explained by these associations. Klee's dilemma, and the dilemma of the observer of his pictures, is that the sophistication required to understand him and the innocence required for belief in magic are incompatible. But among contemporary painters, Klee comes closest to giving us a door into an all-but-lost world to which the artist has always been our guide.

SCULPTURE

Sculpture found no Cézanne in the 19th century, but 20th-century sculptors, like the century's painters, have worked in new ways that reject realism

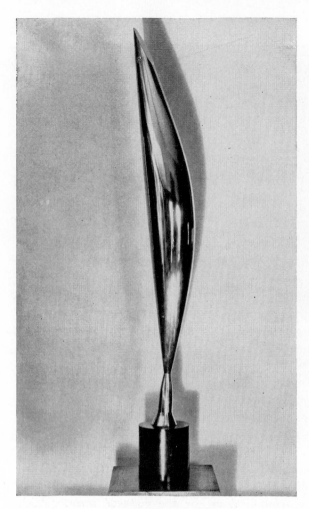

Fig. 17.46 Constantin Brancusi (1876–1957). *Bird in Space.*
1925. Polished bronze. 49¾
inches high. Philadelphia Museum of Art, Arensberg Collection.

Fig. 17.47 (opposite) Moore
(1898–   ). *Reclining Figure.*
1935. Elm wood. 19 inches
high. Buffalo, Albright Art
Gallery, Contemporary Art
Collection.

for one degree or another of abstraction. Yet, a work of sculpture depends
upon one emphatically and unchangeably nonabstract factor: to exist at all,
it must exist as a tangible and concrete physical object in wood, stone, metal,
or whatever material. The tangibility of painting is of a less emphatic order
and may be involved with illusion. But the concreteness of the materials of
sculpture has been a stabilizing force in modern experiments without being an
inhibiting one.

Also, modern sculptors have developed a new respect for their material.
Metal, stone, or wood are only the mediums through which the realistic sculptor presents a reproduction or idealization of a natural object, and although
the beauty of the material is part of the quality of any great statue, it is asked
to sacrifice some of its own quality to the creation of an illusion of another
material—flesh, foliage, hair, feathers, drapery, and even such unstony, un-
metallic, and unwooden things as water, clouds, and rays of light. If Bernini's

Ecstasy of Santa Teresa (Fig. 15.11. page 698) is compared with Brancusi's *Bird in Space* (Fig. 17.46), we have a vivid contrast between traditional and contemporary attitudes toward materials, forms, and expression.

Bernini's material—in this case, marble—is asked to simulate a dozen others of antithetical texture and solidity. His technical brilliance is gauged by the degree of his success in changing marble to something as different as possible from stone. But the modern sculptor Brancusi's technical brilliance, less obvious although he is working in extremely difficult material, is gauged by the precision with which he tools and polishes a piece of brass so that its innate beauty as brass is fully revealed. Expressively, *Bird in Space* does not tell us a story, as Bernini's work does, but abstracts an idea. The long, clean, gleaming form represents neither a bird's body nor the trajectory of a flight in space, but gives physical being to a concept to which the sculptor's title gives us a clue.

This clue is, actually, the weak point of the work. Ultimately the association with "bird" and "flight" is much less important than the abstract beauty of the form itself. This is the argument for totally abstract sculpture. Without a title, *Bird in Space* might be even more enjoyable, and our enjoyment might be more pure.

Henry Moore's *Reclining Figure* (Fig. 17.47), carved from an enormous piece of elm wood, might at first glance seem to have been conceived along the same principles as *Bird in Space*. Certainly the respect for material has had much to do with the conception of the forms. The wood's grain, and wood's adaptability to forms at once bulky and sinuous, has been a determining factor in the design. But the design is remarkable for the emphasis it gives to hollowed-out spaces, and here we have an example of the "negative volumes" with which much contemporary sculpture is concerned. According to this idea, a void is not a mere shapeless nothing, but a shape in itself, defined by surrounding solids. Thus regarded, *Reclining Figure* is an interlocking of solids and voids. The tunnelings through the wood can be compared to forms eroded by air or water in nature, even, specifically, to the hollows in trees. Thus Moore's sculpture has a strong relationship to natural forms—especially since he likes to emphasize the natural quality of his materials—although it is far from imitative of natural objects.

The concept of the shaped void, or negative volume, is not unique to modern sculpture. The extreme undercuttings in *Ecstasy of Santa Teresa,* the tunnelings between figures or up into the separations of folds of drapery, similarly create a union between the solids of the sculpture and the space that surrounds and penetrates it, but the sculpture's illusionistic character is so dominant that this factor in its design is generally lost sight of. In contemporary sculpture, as in contemporary abstract painting, the quality of illusionism is often rejected to call attention to space and volume as sculptural components of primary rather than secondary importance.

An extreme example of the contemporary sculptor's investigation of abstract space is Naum Gabo's *Linear Construction* (Fig. 17.48), if this can be called sculpture rather than a kind of three-dimensional linear drawing. The object is an exquisitely precise threading of nylon string on supports of transparent plastic. Since all the materials are transparent, the object comes as close as any tangible one can to defining space without recourse to solid boundaries. The precisely calculated pattern of strings creates subtly warped planes, and one sees front, back, and sides simultaneously. Here, in its own way, a three-dimensional object that can be called sculpture overlaps the cubist principle of simultaneity—the revelation of the "total object" without the necessity of examination from a variety of different points of view. But the object is not one of nature—not Picasso's *Seated Nude Woman,* for instance. There is no object, but rather only shaped space—although the object created to shape this space happens to have considerable decorative beauty of its own.

Contemporary sculptors have also explored the world of fantasy that surrealist painters staked out as their own, although the sculptors have seldom called themselves surrealists. In that connection, we have already seen César's *Galactic Insect* (Fig. 17.43) in which bits of junk that we would ordinarily connect with neither art nor fantasy serve as the raw material for fantastic art.

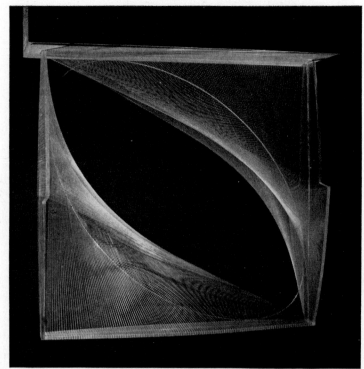

Fig. 17.48 Gabo (1890–   ).
Linear Construction. 1942–1943.
Plastic with nylon string. 24¼
inches high. Washington, D.C.,
Phillips Collection.

ARCHITECTURE

In spite of the excitements they offer, contemporary painting and to a large extent contemporary sculpture impress many thoughtful people as vestigial arts. Painting and sculpture used to be part of the fabric of society, demanded by the church for the decoration of temples and cathedrals, by the state for its celebration, by the individual either for the decoration of his habitation or the perpetuation of his memory. Today painting and sculpture have almost entirely lost these functions, which have been replaced by the idea of art for art's sake, just, as we have noted, as fencing exists for fencing's sake.

But no one could say the same of architecture. It is the one art that our time has not only demanded and demanded imperiously, but of which it has demanded new and revolutionary forms to satisfy the conditions of a changed society.

The most spectacular development and the one that may stand as the symbol of our age with all its aspiration, its technical inventiveness, and its emphasis on practical values is the skyscraper. Our modern cities, with millions of people crowded into small areas, had to grow upward instead of outward. The condition has existed in no other society. And in no other society did the technical means of solving such a problem exist. Without the modern materials of steel and concrete and without the engineering principles invented to capitalize upon their structural potentials, the contemporary world as we know it could not have come into being.

In the matter of design, skyscrapers virtually imposed an esthetic upon the architect. The earliest multistoried structures were efforts to pile one temple or other outmoded architectural form on top of another. The architect soon learned that he could not simply multiply old forms, but had to invent new ones dictated by his material and by the uses of his building. Thus developed the idea of *functionalism*—that "form follows function." In the case of the skyscraper, this was first recognized in Chicago, where architects like William LeBaron Jenney and Louis Sullivan, who invented the phrase, established the idea of the skyscraper as a vertically rising skeleton in which walls were only skins, not supports. When large portions of the skins were made of glass, the problem of light in city buildings was solved and the "Chicago window," precursor of the total skin of glass that was to appear later, was born.

Yet the conventions of architectural design were so ingrained, especially in the consciousness of the public which commissioned and used the buildings, that suggestions of columns, cornices, window frames, and all the other architectural elements that were no longer inherent in structure continued to be applied, even if in a vestigial way, to the outsides of buildings. Residences continued to be designed in imitations of old styles. But eventually, with the popularization of the functionalist theory of esthetics, commercial buildings took on the clean, spare lines and surfaces that we think of as "modern," and residences also began to be conceived in untraditional patterns.

Not the most recent, but still many people's candidate for the title of the most beautiful skyscraper, is Lever House (Fig. 17.49), built in 1952. Devoid of ornament, it is extraordinarily handsome because its materials are used with elegance in a design as carefully proportioned as any piece of abstract sculpture. We must emphasize that in proportioning the building harmoniously the architects did *not* observe the idea that esthetic effectiveness would automatically follow the practical disposition of interior space by the purest functional standard. Not only are the masses of the building carefully adjusted to one another, but such details as the sizes of glass panes, the width and degree of relief in their joining elements, and other purely structural details were designed with as much eye to inherent beauty as to efficient functioning. In other words, the architects remained designers as well as engineers. And the enlightened client, in spite of the fact that Lever House is a commercial building, sacrificed some practical values to esthetic ones. To achieve its beauty of proportions and to set the building in adequate space—free space being the most expensive luxury of all in a city like New York—

Fig. 17.49 New York. Lever
House. 1952. Skidmore, Ow-
ings & Merrill.

the architects were allowed to sacrifice a good percentage of the office space
that would have been possible under New York's zoning laws.

Although force of circumstance produced the skyscraper, the functional
ideal was clarified and formulated by theorist-builders. Lever House is a
skyscraper development that finds its ancestry equally in the early Chicago
skyscrapers and in the "international style," largely a European crystallization
of the esthetic inherent in functionalism. One of the leaders in this crystallization was the Frenchman Le Corbusier, whose Stein House of 1927 (Fig.
17.50) is typical in its concept of architectural design as spare, pure, and elegant geometry. Although the structure does not look sensationally original
today, the fact that it does not is a tribute to the combination of intellectualism and imagination that produced forms that seemed outrageous to
most people in a day when the pseudo-buttress, pseudo-arch, and pseudo-wall
were still the stock in trade of the average architect. Le Corbusier was also
an early theorist of modern city planning, which he regarded as a mammoth
architectural problem. His ideal terms have affected the work of men who have

Fig. 17.50 Stein House. 1927. Le Corbusier (1887–   ).

to deal with the problem more practically. Le Corbusier conceived of the city as a single piece of design in which buildings, streets, bridges, everything, were parts of a predetermined organic whole.

The practical dissemination of the functional-international style in circles wider than those reached by Le Corbusier began in Germany with the Bauhaus, a school of the arts centering around architecture, under Walter Gropius. Gropius' design for the school's workshop wing (Fig. 17.51) soon became the best known advertisement for the new architecture. Actually, "international style" is a somewhat misleading term. For although both Gropius and Le Corbusier were practitioners of the "style," and although their work bears the common hallmark of clean geometrical form with strong emphasis upon glass, steel, and concrete as the revealed components of structure, the two men exemplify the contrasts that existed within the general concept.

Le Corbusier was essentially an imaginative theorist, an explorer of architectural form who was as much affected by love of pure abstract geometrical composition as by practical considerations. It is significant that as a painter (Fig. 17.53) he designed forms that reappeared in his three-dimensional structures.

Gropius, on the other hand, was a stricter functionalist, and it is natural that his most successful designs were for institutional buildings, in which the functional premise is most legitimate as the dominating one of a scheme. Le Corbusier's own apartment in Paris (Fig. 17.52) is less a "machine for living"

Fig. 17.51   Dessau, Germany. The Bauhaus Workshop Wing. 1925–1929. Gropius (1883–   ).

—a definition of a house coined by Le Corbusier—than a piece of abstract sculpture which a human being may inhabit. The Bauhaus workshop wing by comparison is engineering made palatable by successful, but still secondary, recognition of detail and proportion as adjuncts of good building design.

The culmination of the functional idea combined with worship of pure proportion may be seen in the work of Miës van der Rohe, an architect and designer who has been active in the development of contemporary architecture since the early days, when "contemporary" meant revolutionary, to the present, when the stylistic triumph is complete. Miës' designs, whether of architecture or furniture (in which field he has also had tremendous influence) have been marked from the beginning by understatement. All dramatic flourishes are eliminated to reveal an austere and elegant drama of beautiful materials in carefully studied patterns from which the last suggestion of ornamental complication has been pared. His Seagram Building in New York City (Fig. 17.54) is a bronze and glass shaft with every dimension, from total height to smallest bevel, determined by an arbitrary modular system.

Miës is always referred to as the classicist of contemporary architecture. His use of the module, his extreme formal purity, the beauty of materials, do relate him to the classical standards of ancient Greece, although it would be difficult to find a single architectural form in which a direct stylistic resemblance could be found. We should add that this idea of "classical" takes no recognition of a major aspect of Greek architecture—its vivacity, its color, and

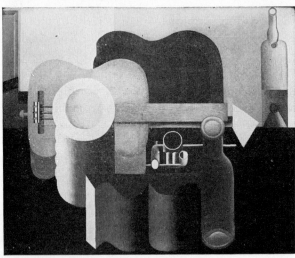

Figs. 17.52–53 (above) Le Corbusier. Paris. The architect's apartment. 1933. (left) *Still-life*. 1920. 31⅞ by 39¼ inches. New York, Museum of Modern Art.

the elaborate sculptured and painted ornament that was originally part of buildings that we now see unnaturally bare.

The functional premise, the international style, and their variations are easily abused, and evidence in dozens of mediocre buildings surrounds superior buildings like the ones we have been discussing. Any person with sufficient knowledge of construction can seize upon the same structural elements and produce a building that has all the component parts of a contemporary archi-

Fig. 17.54 New York. Seagram Building. 1957. Miës van der Rohe (1886–   ). (© Ezra Stoller)

tectural masterpiece except the one thing that makes it a masterpiece—the adjustment of its parts into a harmonious whole. Abused or misunderstood, the functional styles have been used as excuses to line the streets of our cities with ungainly, impersonal, and monotonous buildings of a style best called "contractor's modern."

But even at its best, architecture of the Le Corbusier-Gropius-Miës kind impresses many people as chilly, skeletal, and forbidding. In opposition, another school of architects has insisted upon more romantic designs, even though they also take advantage of contemporary building techniques and materials. The leader of these was Frank Lloyd Wright, who, although a pioneer in the theories from which functionalism developed, always insisted that architecture was an art that dealt with the most personal, the most intimate spiritual needs of mankind.

Fig. 17.55 Green Spring, Wisconsin. Taliesin. 1925. Frank Lloyd Wright (1869–1959).

Although Wright's structures include hotels, factories, office buildings, laboratories, stores, and a museum, into all of which he introduced a degree of fantasy, his enduring contribution may finally be considered his concept of domestic architecture. He loathed the "box with holes punched in it" of the traditional residence, yet he equally loathed the "machine for living" concept of the purely functional habitation. In Wright's thinking, architectural theory and poetic philosophy were inextricably mingled, with the result that when his designs failed they failed badly. But when they succeeded, his new forms not only served their purposes better than the ones he discarded, but also served the spiritual need that was the determining factor in his theorizing.

Taliesin, the residence Wright designed for himself at Spring Green, Wisconsin, best exemplifies several of his basic ideas. He believed that a structure, especially a residence, should seem to grow naturally from its setting. The long horizontals of Taliesen echo and merge with the long gentle horizontals of the countryside around it (Fig. 17.55). The materials—warmly textured wood and stone from the area—continue to suggest their origin in the natural world while they serve as parts of a man-made structure. Exterior garden areas are treated as integral parts of the floor plan of the house, which becomes at once an expression of man's union with the natural world, and his refuge. This idea has infiltrated contemporary residential design, especially in the United States, to such a degree that Miës' doctrine of "less is more," Gropius' idea that a building is simply an anonymous container for life, and Le Corbusier's concept of the architect as a painter-sculptor-builder, have been warmed and humanized in designs at whose heart is Wright's romantic feeling for the life of man in the world.

Wright's early writing on architecture was prophetic of the developments that eventually produced the International style, and were in fact an immediate source of the theories of the architects of the generation that included Gropius and Le Corbusier. It was the essentially humanistic Wrightian ideal that they missed, and this lack which led to Wright's rejection of, so to speak, his own grandchild. Even when Wright designed commercial or industrial structures he held to the idea that architecture could not be produced by any hard-headed or hyperesthetic standards.

His buildings for the Johnson Wax Company in Racine, Wisconsin (Fig. 17.56), are his most famous and probably his most successful designs outside residential ones. The interior of the administration building (Fig. 17.57) combines an unusual engineering form (the downward tapering columns with flaring caps) and a most emphatic element of fantasy. The columns are designed to support tremendous weight, but are used in a portion of the area for their purely decorative effect, supporting, as the illustration shows, nothing but the air above them. Only an artist with Wright's extraordinary combination of ingenuity as an engineer (the columns were his invention and had to pass qualifying tests imposed by building laws before they could be used) and almost mystical imagination could have created so exceptional a structure, combining expressions of modern administrative efficiency with a statement of the imponderables that nourish mankind spiritually.

The third quarter of the 20th century has opened as the most prolific period of building in history, following the destruction of cities in World War II and the population explosion that demands more and more houses and buildings of every kind. Much of the building is of course wretched; our acres of unimaginatively conceived and jerry-built opportunist housing developments are usually deplorable, esthetically and socially. But we are probably justified in saying, even from such close range, that we have entered a great period in architecture. A new generation of architects has absorbed the good from the functionalist principle and has also been strongly affected by the romanticism of Wright. Current solutions of architectural problems change almost from day to day with the expansion of materials and building methods that continue to pour forth through modern technology.

At the same time, the most thoughtful young architects have re-examined

Fig. 17.56 Racine, Wisconsin. Johnson Wax Company. 1949. Wright. (Photo courtesy S. C. Johnson and Son, Inc.)

Fig. 17.57 Interior of Administration Building. Johnson Wax Company. Wright. (Photo courtesy S. C. Johnson and Son, Inc.)

the past to discover what it can teach them. They are no longer interested in borrowing its columns, its capitals, its flying buttresses, or any other forms for use at second hand. But they have discovered that while modern man has special needs that demand special solutions in architecture, man in general is not a contemporary phenomenon. The architecture that served him in the past is studied for its connection with the life of man that is continuous over the centuries. The most encouraging facts about the arts in the second half of the 20th century is that architecture, which is traditionally their mother, is in vigorous health.

Appendix I

The primary purpose of architecture is to enclose useful space, thus permitting human beings to keep themselves warm, dry, and nourished. Without buildings of some kind, life could not be maintained on this planet except in the favored climates. In most places where people live, rather elaborate and expensive buildings are necessary because of the severity of the weather. If daily life is to be conducted with comfort and dignity, buildings must be considerably more complicated and much more expensive than mere subsistence demands.

The architect is obviously an important public servant, but he is by no means so free as the painter and poet. His responsibility to the economic system is great: buildings cost so much that no building is a good building if it costs more than it ought—and in estimating the value received, all sorts of factors must be considered in addition to the mere necessity of the moment. Appearance, durability, economic efficiency, and practical convenience are among them. In other words, the function of a building is no simple thing; it involves emotional as well as mechanical elements.

The responsibility of the architect for the physical safety of the population is a matter we may not take for granted. The smallest building demands that he take care of ponderous weights and dangerous forces. A large fabric puts in his hands the safety of hundreds, even thousands of people. Contrary to popular opinion, not every structure is safe.

The history of architecture is punctuated, in fact, with hideous accidents. One recalls that the dome of Hagia Sophia fell in more than once (page 280), that the original vaults at Beauvais collapsed, and that the 500-foot tower of the same cathedral tipped over (page 378). And lest the reader suppose that

932

STRUCTURAL
PRINCIPLES

modern science has rendered similar disasters impossible, let him reflect that the bridge over the Firth of Tay blew over on a December night in 1879, and that the train from St. Andrews for Dundee simply ran off the end and plunged into the water.

It is thus obvious that no man can make a rational estimate of any building unless he is familiar with the forces at work and understands the members designed to withstand and sustain them. It may not be so obvious, but it is more than true, that knowledge and appreciation of structure form part of the esthetic transaction. The physical principles involved have an order and a beauty of their own. It is history that those principles have often pointed the way to a theory of design, most notably in the Gothic era and during our own generation. In a word, there never was a good architect who was not also a good engineer.

The unchanging force of gravitation makes the problems of construction constant, the same for every century and every style. It is convenient to summarize these problems in this Appendix, for general application throughout the text.

For the sake of completeness, we must mention that all building begins with the foundation. Because the foundations are out of sight below the ground, we may omit detailed consideration here; it is one of the rare instances where engineering may legitimately be separated from art and relegated to another department of study. Even so, it is worth remarking that very few of the world's great buildings stand on firm rock. The ledge comes close to the surface at Athens, providing an ideal substructure for the Parthenon,

933

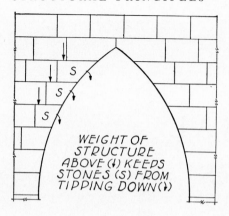

WEIGHT OF STRUCTURE ABOVE (↓) KEEPS STONES (S) FROM TIPPING DOWN (↓)

Fig. I.1   The corbeled arch.

but the entire metropolis of London, probably the most densely populated area in the world, rests on wet mud. It is a considerable problem to build any large building there. Skyscrapers are nonexistent in spite of the high land values in the City and elsewhere. It is probable that the foundations of some of the great buildings in the British capital actually represent more intelligence and judgment than the superstructure which interests the art critic. Recording that truth, let us pass on.

Foundations having been provided and vertical supports having been set up in the form of columns, piers, or parallel walls, the problem of enclosing space resolves itself into spanning the opening between supports. The methods for doing so are few and involve physical principles of an elementary kind; it is their application which is tricky, expensive, and dangerous. In application, moreover, the several methods for spanning a gap are severely limited by the materials available.

Until structural steel and glass became available in large sizes and at low cost, construction was limited to wood and masonry. Metal and glass were known, of course, but came only in little pieces—enough for a window or a hinge. The architect had to think of them as accessory rather than fundamental. Limited to wood and stone, he could span an opening *(a)* by using a *beam* or *truss,* both of which fall under the generic term of *lintel;* or *(b)* by using the *true arch.* A third method, the *corbeled arch* (Fig. I.1), might be listed for the sake of completeness; it has seldom been used except in Mycenaean Greece and for some of the buildings put up in Central and South America before the arrival of the Europeans.

One often hears the word *arch* applied to any opening that happens to be curved at the top, but such usage is loose and misleading. The term has no essential reference to appearance and is best reserved for spans which in fact conform to the principle of the *true arch,* to be explained below. When the theory of the true arch is extended to the construction of an entire roof of masonry, we speak of a *vault.* Vaulting was the only fireproof roofing available until very recent times. There are several kinds, none perfect. We shall describe presently the three types of vault which gained an important place in architectural history, either because they were mechanically convenient or especially good-looking.

The advent of cheap steel opened up two further principles for the architect: *cantilever* and *suspension.* Both had been known since time immemorial, but primitive materials precluded the use of either one in major construction. As yet, neither cantilevers nor suspension are sufficiently seasoned to have had much effect on design, but it is a safe prediction that both will operate to make our future buildings very different from anything we are now used to.

THE POST-AND-LINTEL SYSTEM

The post-and-lintel system of construction has already been covered at some length in the chapter about Greek architecture. Every child has invented it once again for himself. He sets two of his blocks endwise on the floor and lays a third across them to span the gap. The vertical blocks are *posts,* and the horizontal block is the *lintel.* However simple in theory and elegant in application, the post-and-lintel method presents some serious practical difficulties (or did until steel became available) whenever applied to a building any larger than a shed.

Because stone is brittle, lintels of that material will crack of their own weight unless the span between posts is kept very narrow (page 80); and even then, no stone lintel may safely be loaded with any great amount of weight—as, for example, the upper stories of a high building. Large blocks of stone present serious problems, moreover, in the matter of procurement. Few quarries furnish sound material in big sizes, and even where available, great lintels of stone demand either an excellent system of roads, conveniently located rivers and harbors, or a system of canals—before the railroad, they could not otherwise be transported from the quarry to the site of the building. It is only in Roman times and our own that the necessary transport has been feasible; in other periods, some other method had to be used if big buildings were to be constructed at all.

Whenever columns or piers are placed close together, the floor space must be inconveniently curtailed and the vista of the interior crowded. For that reason alone, the Romans had a strong motive for developing the vaulted roof. But at any time and in any place where the principle of the arch was not understood, or where its application was out of the question for whatever reason, the wooden lintel was the only member that would serve to span any substantial gap.

Simple wooden lintels of large size demand primeval forests, such as have been unknown in most of Europe since ancient times. That being so, the only available expedient was to bridge a wide span by some sort of *truss*. We may define the truss as an open-work lintel made from a number of short pieces bolted together, the object being to arrange the pieces so that they cooperate in stiffening the member as a whole. The roof of the church shown in Figure 8.25, page 238, is supported by a wooden truss of familiar pattern.

The truss has been developed in a variety of forms. All look complicated, but the system behind every arrangement can always be resolved by reference to the triangle—a figure which can not be made to change its shape unless one or more of its legs be broken. The most intricate truss, therefore, amounts to no more than a collection of small triangles, each defying distortion.

Because it can be made from comparatively small pieces, the truss involves no serious problem of transport. It is also an exceedingly efficient device mechanically, but very rarely is it good-looking. In first-class buildings, therefore, the trusses of the roof are usually concealed by a ceiling, a custom to which the only notable exception is the English *hammer-beam* truss of the late medieval period (Fig. 11.32, page 400).

Like every other wooden member, the wooden truss is subject to rot, fire, and destruction by insects. One might jump to the plausible notion that all those faults were corrected when steel trusses became available, but unhappily such is only half the truth. Steel is fireproof only in the sense that it will not feed the flames. The material loses strength rapidly at elevated temperatures, and buildings framed with steel do not enjoy a high rating with the underwriters. Most steels so far put to use are, moreover, subject to rust. They are subject, also, to the phenomenon known as the fatigue of metals, a gradual and unpredictable loss of strength culminating in sudden failure.

For all of that, steel offered a degree of tensile strength immensely greater than any other building material hitherto known to man. Tensile strength made it possible to bolt members together more solidly and more reliably than ever before. Many a structural problem hitherto vexing or impossible of solution rather suddenly became easy. Hence the almost infinite variety of steel trusses in plain sight today, supporting immense roofs and forming mighty bridges. Some of the more familiar forms are shown in Figure I.2.

PRINCIPLES OF THE ARCH

The practical application of the arch principle is of great antiquity, but to this day no reliable formulae exist for predicting within close limits the

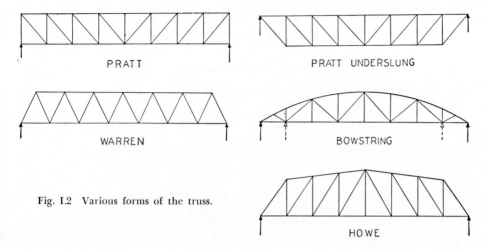

PRATT

PRATT UNDERSLUNG

WARREN

BOWSTRING

Fig. I.2   Various forms of the truss.

HOWE

carrying capacity of a particular arch or the various forces it will generate. The statements made below must therefore be general where the reader might often hope for something definite, but they may be taken as a fair summary of the time-honored assumptions to which engineers refer when they design arches and vaults.

The principles of the *true arch* can best be explained by reference to Figure I.3, which shows, in several views, a semicircular arch built of cut stone. Arches of any other shape may be constructed at the option of the builder without any change in the fundamental procedure, and with little more difficulty than it takes to produce this simple shape. Figure I.4 shows some of the shapes that have gained currency at one time or another.

A great many arches are not built of cut stone. Concrete, either pure or reinforced, has often been used, in which case the arch becomes virtually monolithic as soon as the cement has set. One often hears it suggested that a monolithic arch is stiff enough to exert no thrust (see below), but such is not the case. For no matter how we build it, any arch consists of two separated legs supporting weight in the middle, and so long as gravity is with us, the weight must perforce attempt to shove the two legs further apart. Therefore, regardless of how we put our arches together, we must make much the same provision for the safety of the structure; and for purposes of understanding, the reader may assume that what goes for the arch in Figure I.3 also goes for all other arches of any sort whatever.

In our discussion, we will proceed as one might in looking over an arch already completed, and not in the sequence followed by the builder in putting up a new arch. To the latter concern, we shall return later.

The upper drawing of Figure I.3 shows that the silhouette of the arch is defined by two concentric arcs struck in from the center marked with the

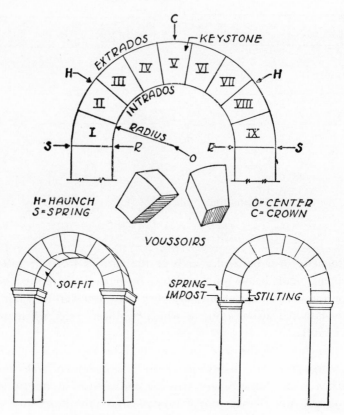

Fig. I.3 Elements of the true arch.

letter *O*. It is frequently necessary to refer to the inner curve and the outer curve separately. The inner curve is called the *intrados,* and the outer the *extrados.*

The point where the arch begins to curve upward and inward (marked with the letter S) is called the *spring*. The spring may or may not be the same as the *impost*. The drawing in the lower left-hand corner shows an arch which springs directly from the upper surface of the capital of its pier; in such an instance, spring and impost are synonymous. Arches are rarely built in that manner, however. The drawing to the lower right illustrates the normal design. The masonry of the arch, it will be noted, rises vertically for a slight distance above the capital before actual curvature commences. The amount of the vertical rise is the *stilting* of the arch, and where stilting exists, we refer to the capital beneath as the impost, reserving the word *spring* for the start of curvature. Stilting is used in the great majority of cases simply because it enhances the appearance of the arch in relation to the piers beneath it. During the Gothic period, stilting was used in order to get certain structural advantages (see page 381).

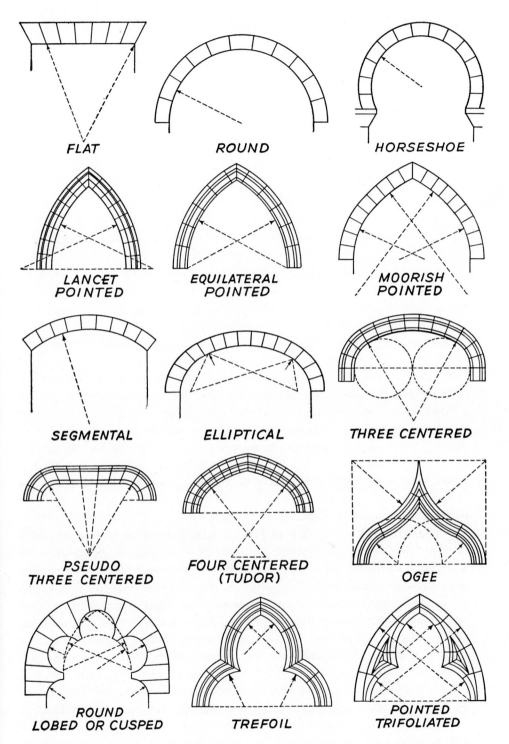

FLAT ROUND HORSESHOE

LANCET POINTED EQUILATERAL POINTED MOORISH POINTED

SEGMENTAL ELLIPTICAL THREE CENTERED

PSEUDO THREE CENTERED FOUR CENTERED (TUDOR) OGEE

ROUND LOBED OR CUSPED TREFOIL POINTED TRIFOLIATED

Fig. I.4 Drawing to illustrate the great variety to which the principle of the true arch lends itself.

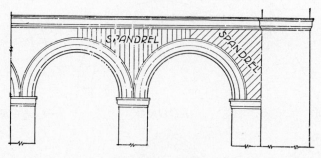

Fig. I.5   An arcade.

Certain further terms are essential. The *crown* of the arch (marked with the letter *C*) is the topmost point reached by the extrados. The general region about halfway between spring and crown is known as the *haunch* (marked with the letter *H*). The under surface of the arch into which we look from below is referred to as the *soffit* (see lower left-hand drawing). The same word is used for the under surface of any vault.

Arches very rarely stand alone. Almost every vault rests on a framework of arches, as we shall see presently. The simplest use of arches in combination, and the most frequent, is the *arcade* (Fig. I.5). In an arcade, similar arches are built one after another in a row. Almost every arcade has a cornice, a molding, or some other horizontal immediately over it, clearing the crowns by a short distance, a juxtaposition that gives a certain visual significance to the small area of wall space where adjacent arches melt together. As labeled in Figure I.5, such wall space is called the *spandrel;* and the same word is used for any wall surface that may be thought of as being in the esthetic vicinity of an arch. Obviously the spandrels offer an ideal field for a bit of decorative sculpture, and are often so used.

The arch drawn at the top of Fig. I.3 is made up of nine separate pieces of stone, each labeled with a Roman numeral. Each piece is in the shape of a wedge, and the technical term for any one of these wedges is a *voussoir*. Two voussoirs are drawn in perspective at the middle of Figure I.3. There is of course nothing sacred about the number nine. Most arches actually have more than nine voussoirs, but there is no use in complicating our drawing and making it hard to read. Whatever the number chosen, it is usual to make it an odd number, for reasons that will appear in a moment. As drawn, each of the nine voussoirs subtends an angle of 20 degrees measured at the center of the arch. The central and highest voussoir is known as the *keystone* (No. V on our drawing), a distinction that has a certain practical reason behind it.

Consideration of the data so far presented will show why the arch is usually preferable to the post-and-lintel system. A very large arch can be built from small stones; indeed the greatest medieval cathedrals contain hardly a

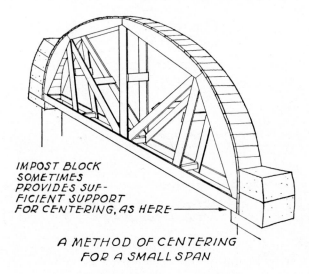

IMPOST BLOCK
SOMETIMES
PROVIDES SUF-
FICIENT SUPPORT
FOR CENTERING, AS HERE ⟶

A METHOD OF CENTERING
FOR A SMALL SPAN

Fig. I.6   An arch under construction, illustrating the use
of wooden centering.

stone that could not be lifted into place by a gang of twenty or thirty men
aided by the block and tackle, the inclined plane, and other simple devices.
In Roman work, spans of forty or fifty feet pass unnoticed, and the dome of
the Pantheon (in effect an arch; see Fig. 7.5, page 186) swings no less than 142
feet between supports. Such heroic dimensions are impossible in masonry by
any other known method of building. It is worth noting in this connection
that a wooden truss can be built with a wide span. The hammer-beam roof of
Westminster Hall in London (about 92 feet between walls) long had the
reputation of being the greatest span ever achieved in wood; but during
World War II, improved methods of fastening timbers together were developed in response to the shortage of steel—resulting in some tremendous trusses
bridging even wider gaps.

A well-constructed arch can be loaded with an almost unbelievable
amount of weight, which is a vital consideration in a large building or a high
building, where several thousand tons of masonry may have to be carried by
a spanning member. Inspection of Figure I.3 will show, however, that any
increase of weight above the crown will result in squeezing the voussoirs more
and more tightly together. No matter how intense, the strain on each voussoir
is compression, a force that good stone is well able to endure. Twisting and
bending strains, which stone cannot sustain, are altogether avoided.

We must now turn our attention to the faults of the arch, which are two
in number and both serious. For assembly, every arch requires *centering;* and
when built, every arch requires *abutment* or it is unsafe.

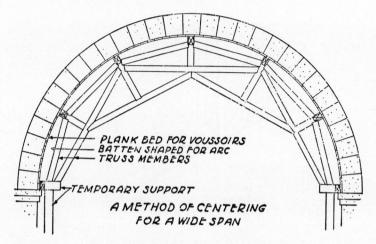

PLANK BED FOR VOUSSOIRS
BATTEN SHAPED FOR ARC
TRUSS MEMBERS

TEMPORARY SUPPORT

A METHOD OF CENTERING
FOR A WIDE SPAN

Fig. I.7 An arch completed, with centering yet to be removed, illustrating an economy of material as compared to Figure I.6.

Centering is the technical name for the wooden form over which the
arch must be constructed. As indicated by Figure I.6, the form must remain
in place until the keystone is dropped into position; otherwise there would
be nothing to prevent the voussoirs from falling to the ground. The essential
feature of any piece of centering is that its upper surface correspond precisely with the true shape of the soffit of the arch, and obviously it must be
strong enough to hold this shape without any distortion whatever against the
very considerable weight of all the voussoirs. It is no easy matter to build
such a form. Excellent design and much sound timber are requisite. Timber
being scarce and expensive, all sorts of stratagems have been employed from
time to time to reduce the cost of centering. Figure I.7 shows one method of
building the form with slightly less timber than Figure I.6 would require.

Abutment is made necessary by the *thrust* of the arch. Thrust results from
the fact that every voussoir is a wedge, and acts like any other wedge. For
purposes of understanding the principles involved, we may concentrate our
attention upon the keystone and postulate extreme conditions. Let us assume
that a giant with an immense hammer strikes a blow vertically downward,
hitting the keystone plumb in the middle. Figure I.8 is an attempt to visualize
what would happen if the keystone was driven downward, the other voussoirs
failing to slide over each other: the arch would expand beyond its original
boundaries which are represented by the dotted lines. The slow force of
weight tends constantly and inexorably to accomplish the same result as the
giant's hammer. Any arch bearing a considerable burden is forever trying to
bulge outward along the extrados. This is the force we call *thrust*. Figure I.8
was drawn merely to introduce the conception of thrust; it oversimplifies the

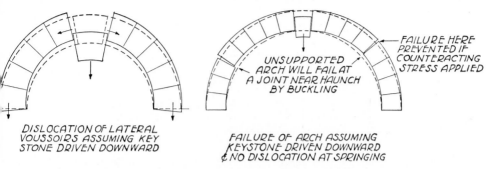

FAILURE HERE
PREVENTED IF
COUNTERACTING
STRESS APPLIED

UNSUPPORTED
ARCH WILL FAIL AT
A JOINT NEAR HAUNCH
BY BUCKLING

DISLOCATION OF LATERAL
VOUSSOIRS ASSUMING KEY
STONE DRIVEN DOWNWARD

FAILURE OF ARCH ASSUMING
KEYSTONE DRIVEN DOWNWARD
& NO DISLOCATION AT SPRINGING

Figs. I.8–9 (left) Schematic drawing to illustrate the phenomenon of thrust. (right) Diagram illustrating the points of first failure when an arch is overloaded.

action of that force in actual cases. Figure I.9 comes nearer to illustrating what happens when an arch fails. Assuming that the spring is held in place, the first breaks will occur in the region of the haunch. In practice, abutment of one kind or another is usually brought to bear against both spring and haunch, in which case the arch is assumed to be safe.

It will be noted that both Figures I.8 and I.9 make sense only if we assume that the voussoirs can slide over each other, and such has been the assumption upon which we have been proceeding in our present discussion of thrust. Everything that we have said would be literally true if, in the laboratory, we made some voussoirs of polished steel, oiled them, and put them together to form an arch. But no one builds that way—hence the existence of certain writings which challenge our conventional theory of thrust.

The writings referred to point out that stones under compression can scarcely be made to slide at all, that stones joined with mortar tend to stick together as though glued, and that concrete, once set, becomes virtually mono-lithic. They bring forward instances where keystones have been removed, leaving the two sides of an arch hanging in mid-air by virtue of the adhesive quality of the mortar. They also point to cases where the supporting piers have sunk, departed from the vertical, and have actually spread further apart at the top—thus stretching the span of an arch of vault. Instead of falling in, the much abused arch or vault merely shows cracks on the soffit.

As indicated earlier, none of these arguments has as yet impressed the engineer. All of them depend upon the assertion, direct or tacit, that masonry may safely be subjected to twisting and bending strains, any and all of which produce tension somewhere or other. Masonry will sometimes endure a moderate amount of tension for a very long time; there are instances where masonry has endured it for centuries. It is nevertheless a fundamental principle of structural design that no brittle material shall ever be deliberately subjected to tension. No one can tell when it may crack and collapse.

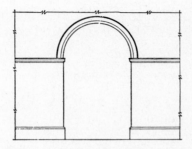

Fig. I.10 Arch opening through the thickness of a wall.

♦ *Methods of Abutment*　There is no way to keep an arch from changing shape and collapsing except to provide a compressive force opposite in direction to the thrust and equal to it. The act of doing this is denoted by the verb *to abut,* from which we derive the generic noun *abutment.* The noun *buttress* and the verb *to buttress* are near-synonyms. If there is any difference in meaning, usage seems to prefer *buttress* when we refer to a particular mass of masonry of specialized design, placed in position to perform the act of abutment for an individual arch.

The simplest form of abutment (simplest in theory, that is; often hardest to provide) is a mass of masonry to either side of the arch, a familiar instance being an arched doorway opening through a wall as in Figure I.10. In such a case, the thrust of the arch, even though very powerful, would almost certainly be insufficient to overcome the inertia of the masonry, and no movement can take place.

The arrangement shown in Figure I.10 is not very subtle. It demands only the vaguest knowledge of how thrust really acts. But quite apart from its rationale, abutment by a mass of masonry to the right and left of an arch, opposing the thrust by sheer weight, is altogether impractical if not downright impossible in the majority of buildings. If, for instance, an arch springs from a point a hundred feet above the ground (and that is not uncommon), an extravagantly ponderous substructure would be required to support the necessary material. The cost would be prohibitive, the cubic measure of masonry being a rough indication of expense. The appearance and utility of the lower parts of the building would be ruined.

In order to escape this necessity, architects have resorted to all sorts of arrangements, all intended to reduce the amount of buttressing. Individual applications vary in appearance, but the most important principles to be borne in mind are the following:

To reduce the thrust of the arch: This can be accomplished in two different ways: *(a)* by reducing the weight of all parts of the building, thus reducing the pressure upon the arch and hence its capacity to generate thrust; *(b)* by changing the shape of the arch until a form is found that thrusts less for a

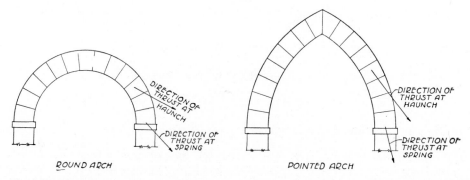

Fig. I.11 Direction of thrust at spring and haunch as predicted for a round arch (left) and a pointed arch (right).

given load over a given span. In general, the flatter the arch the more it thrusts. Steeply pointed arches thrust least of all. To understand the last statement, refer to Figure I.11, which shows the familiar semicircular or "round" arch in contrast to a pointed arch approximately like those used in the French Gothic cathedrals. In each case, arrows indicate the predicted direction of the thrust at spring and haunch; and in both instances, the direction is along a downward diagonal. There is probably small difference in the poundage of the thrust exerted by either arch, but that of the pointed arch is substantially closer to the vertical—or as the physicist would put it, its horizontal component is less. Less masonry is therefore demanded to prevent it from spreading sidewise.

To introduce a tension member in the fabric of the arch: The so-called "tie rods" familiar in Italian work of the Gothic and Renaissance periods illustrate this method (Fig. I.12). The tie rod binds the arch together across the spring, thrust to the right pulling against thrust to the left with equlibrium resulting. Made of wood or iron, the tie rods are quite able to sustain the tension; and mechanically, the expedient is excellent. Tie rods are also the cheapest form of abutment, but everybody agrees they are hideous. They introduce an extraneous line into the composition of the arch but were nevertheless so common in Italy that painters often included them when making pictures of arches (Fig. 13.29, page 525).

To arrange an opposition of equal thrusts: This method is illustrated in its simplest form by the normal arcade, as seen in Figure I.5. Used by all designers from the Romans onward, the arrangement results in an equilibrium of compressive forces, each arch pushing against its neighbor and canceling out its thrust. Buttressing is not needed except at the extreme ends of the line, where only enough is required to stabilize the last arch in the row. Precisely the same principle, but in more complex application, was employed to contain the thrust of the largest Roman and medieval vaults.

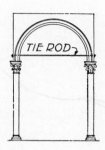

Fig. I.12 Arch buttressed by a tie rod.

To group arches of comparable size together in such a way that thrusts are concentrated at a few predetermined points: Similar in principle to the method just cited, this technique is primarily a solution to the problems of vaulting where many arches may be thrusting in several directions. We shall postpone further explanation until we discuss the cross vault.

To refine the shape and placement of the buttress, thus making it possible to reduce its size: The flying buttresses of the French Gothic are the best example. See Figures 11.20, page 383, and 11.23, page 385. These delicate members contain the thrust of some very large vaults. Nothing of the sort could have been possible without the supreme knowledge of thrust—its amount and its direction—possessed by the master builder during the 13th century. No other abutment has been equally daring. It is important to emphasize that the knowledge to which we just referred was not arrived at by mathematical calculation; in fact, mathematical analysis of the arch remained completely impossible until the development of the calculus during the 17th century. Practical builders learned by trial and failure, and passed their knowledge on to favorite apprentices by word of mouth. Often they were very close-mouthed indeed; hence the frequency with which the "mysteries" of one craft or another are mentioned. In the absence of anything resembling our modern formulas and building codes, accidents were common.

PRINCIPLES OF THE VAULT

♦ *The Motive for Vaulting* The construction of any sizeable vault is obviously an expensive, laborious, and dangerous operation, but there is still no better way to enclose a reasonable volume of space beneath a fireproof roof.

The modern reader can not possibly feel the fear of fire as the ancient and medieval builders felt it. Fire protection is now so efficient that every insurance company, as a matter of conservative financial practice, assumes risks many times its total assets. Indeed, almost the only serious conflagrations within recent memory are those which resulted from bombing during World War II.

A few examples will perhaps suffice to show how bad conditions were in other generations and will demonstrate that the risk of fire is enough to account for the tremendous energies expended in the development of vaulting. We need seek no other motivation.

In 1120, an inflammable church at Vézelay, the predecessor of the present Madeleine, burned with a loss of 1,127 lives. In 1134, the basilican cathedral at Chartres was totally destroyed, an event that accounts for the start of the present church on the same site. During the single year 1188, the cities of Rouen, Troyes, Beauvais, Provins, and Moissac were all laid waste by fire. In 1194, a second blaze swept the cathedral at Chartres; the loss of life is not accurately known, but all records say it was terrific. During the first 25 years of the 13th century, Rouen burned six times.

All of these fires are believed to have been accidental. To see the risk as the medieval builders saw it, we must add to this partial citation from the awful total all of the burning deliberately set during wars, disorders, and punitive measures. An inspection of the pictures by Hieronymus Bosch and Pieter Brueghel will furnish visual evidence enough; the backgrounds contain many a burning farm and village.

Those who have read descriptions of the great fire of London in 1666 can form for themselves an impression of the fire risk in a medieval city. What could be done when inflammable buildings were conglomerated along miles of narrow, crooked alleyways? In the complete absence of adequate organization and equipment, such a place, once well alight, would burn until there was no more fuel for the flames.

The designer of a building was thus compelled, at any period prior to our own, to assume that the town around his church, cathedral, or temple would be entirely consumed by fire not once or twice during the life of his edifice, but many times.

By use of the vault, however, it was possible to make almost certain that the major buildings would endure. They are in plain sight to this day all over Europe. The grand old Pantheon at Rome has lasted for more than eighteen centuries without significant repair. Churches more than 500 years old are in daily use in almost every city. Indeed we may say that well-designed vaulted buildings will, with any reasonable care, resist the attrition of nature indefinitely. Their chief enemy is man—either the peasants coming to purloin ready-cut building stone, or the government deliberately removing a monument as the French did with the old abbey at Cluny toward the end of the 18th century.

It is necessary, of course, to surmount almost every vault with a peaked roof of wood, the function of which is merely to protect the masonry from rain and snow (Fig. I.13). These wooden rain-sheds are inflammable, but they

Fig. I.13 A view underneath the wooden roof super-imposed to keep the weather from the tunnel vaulting of a French church of the Romanesque period. (Archives Photographiques)

Fig. I.14 The cross vaults of the Cathedral at Chartres as they appeared after the burning of the wooden roof in 1836. (Archives Photographiques)

can burn with surprisingly little effect upon the masonry below. The wooden roof over the vaults of Chartres burned in 1836. A drawing made after clearing the debris shows the fabric of the church almost undamaged (Fig. I.14). In 1914, the cathedral at Reims was subjected to shelling, and its wooden superstructure burned with the same comparatively innocuous result—the damage done to the church at that time was almost entirely the work of explosion, not fire.

♦ *The Dome* The dome can best be described as a vault whose shape is generated by rotating a simple arch around its central vertical axis, much as we generate an ellipsoid by rotating an ellipse around its long axis.

Figure I.15 shows a dome built from cut stone, and Figure I.16 illustrates what a similar dome would look like when about half finished. From the

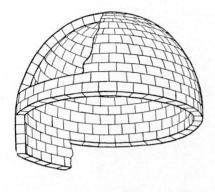

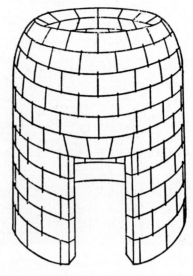

Figs. I.15–16 (above) Cut-away diagram showing a dome made from cut stone. (right) A domed structure with a large open oculus.

latter, it will be noted that each voussoir has a compound bevel; it is cut on a slant, that is to say, in both the vertical and the horizontal plane. As a result, the dome consists of a series of rings, or *courses,* of masonry. Each course is self-sustaining as soon as the last voussoir is dropped in place. There is no necessity for a keystone at the top; and more than half the time, this space is left open to help solve the difficult problem of lighting the interior. In other words, a dome can have a hole where the crown ought to be. If left completely open, as it was and is at the Pantheon (Fig. I.17, and Fig. 7.5, page 186), we call the hole an *oculus.* If covered with an openwork tower, as in most Renaissance and baroque examples (Fig. 15.19, page 707), the word *lantern* is used—for the opening, for the tower, or for both together if convenient.

Few domes of great size have been built of beveled voussoirs as shown in Figure I.15. All the famous big ones depend, in fact, upon some sort of framework, sometimes imbedded in concrete and sometimes not. No variation in construction will change the fundamental action of any dome, however; and for purposes of understanding, the reader may assume that any dome will behave very much like the one seen in Figure I.15. In other words, thrust results from the *shape* of the dome regardless of how it may be assembled; and in practice, one must provide abutment for a continuous pressure of thrust all around the circle, extending upward as high as the haunch.

The thrust of a dome puts the architect upon the horns of a dilemma. If adequately buttressed by inert masonry as in Figure I.17, the exterior silhouette is almost entirely concealed. If lifted into the air where its majestic form

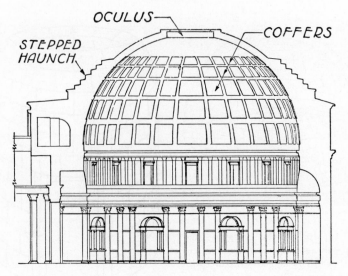

Fig. I.17   Rome. Pantheon. Cross section. The rotunda is 142 feet in diameter and 142 feet high. Note that an abutment of inert masonry (about 20 feet thick at the widest part) is carried as high as the haunch.

can show up, chances must be taken with the abutment—a hazard attested by more than one disastrous collapse.

Accepting the risk, the designers of the largest domes built during the past 500 years have deliberately raised their domes high in the air, setting them up on a circular ring of masonry technically known as a *drum* (Fig. I.19; see also Fig. 15.1, page 682). In such a situation, abutment must be provided by tension. Several great wooden rings, or *chains,* hold in these domes as a belt holds in the belly. Thus the handsome appearance of the exterior is bought at a steep price: when they fail, tension members fail suddenly, and there is no way to ascertain their future endurance within reasonable limits. Because no one can give utter assurance that such a dome may not one day fall down, the use of tension for abutment has never gained absolute approval. It is possible that wire rope woven from some superior and noncorrosive material may one day nullify these reservations.

♦ *The Dome over a Rectangular Ground Plan: Squinches and Pendentives* Another consideration militating against the frequent use of the dome is the fact that its shape does not make an easy fit with any ground plan convenient for ordinary use. The Pantheon has a circular plan. Its substructure may properly be described as an immense drum, artistically harmonious with the dome above. But a circular room, even a big one, lends itself only to a few purposes; for most functions, a worse shape can not be found.

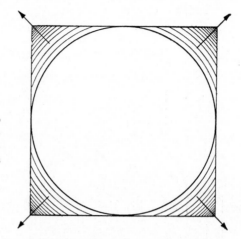

Fig. I.18 Schematic drawing in plan view to illustrate the necessity for transitional members whenever a dome is placed over a rectangular ground plan. The shaded portions represent pendentives.

Furniture fits better into a rectangular room, and the same is true of almost all work and all play.

It is also necessary to point out that almost every service and ceremony entails a focus of attention by an audience or congregation, which is the same thing as saying that many eyes should be directed along a horizontal line of sight toward a speaker, an altar, or whatever. But the dome, by its very shape, insists that we give attention to the vertical axis around which it is generated, the effect being to emphasize a spot on the floor. Excellent for tombs, baptisteries, and other small and specialized buildings, the centralizing effect is often undesirable, as any picture taken inside St. Peter's or St. Paul's will show. The drum of the dome opens up a hole in the ceiling; one wonders what in the world can be up there—an innocent revery in itself, but not identical to attention upon the altar. In spite of all this, the exterior beauty of the dome has dictated its choice in many instances. In almost every case, the dome has been raised over a rectangular room for the reasons stated; and in almost all cases, also, the dome is supported by four piers describing the corners of a square.

Figures I.18 and I.19 are intended as an aid in visualizing the situation. A dome raised over a square ground plan may have a diameter shorter than the length of one side of the square. Many domes do. But, plainly, no dome may have a diameter longer than the length of a single side of the square, and geometry tells us that the diagonal of any square must be longer than one of its sides. A square amounts to two right triangles, each being subject to the law that the square on the hypotenuse is equal to the sum of the squares on the other two sides—hence if the square shown in our figures is 50 feet on a side, its diagonals must measure 70.71 feet. No matter how we try to get out of it, the circular dome above will not cover all the floor space described by the square beneath. We are left with four vacant spaces at the corners as

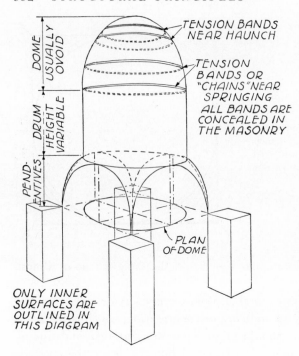

TENSION BANDS
NEAR HAUNCH

TENSION
BANDS OR
"CHAINS" NEAR
SPRINGING
ALL BANDS ARE
CONCEALED IN
THE MASONRY

DOME
USUALLY
OVOID

DRUM
HEIGHT
VARIABLE

PEND-
ENTIVES

PLAN
OF DOME

ONLY INNER
SURFACES ARE
OUTLINED IN
THIS DIAGRAM

Fig. I.19 Schematic drawing illustrating the component parts of an architectural fabric involving a dome raised on a drum above pendentives.

shown in Figure I.18; and we must fill them up with transitional members as shown in Figure I.19. The problem, of course, is to design a transitional member which will modulate the shape of the square into the circular shape from which the dome can spring, and which will be, at the same time, both structurally sound and esthetically acceptable. Various devices have been tried; two, the *pendentive* and the *squinch,* have excelled all others in popularity.

Generally considered the more elegant of the two popular solutions to the problem just outlined, the pendentive was selected to support the dome at Hagia Sophia in Constantinople (Fig. 9.4, page 281), for St. Peter's at Rome, and for St. Paul's in London—to say nothing of almost every other domed building where prestige was a special desideratum.

A *pendentive* (Fig. I.20) is a spherical triangle. Four are needed. One must spring from each pier, spreading upward and inward to meet the others. A circular base is thus provided from which the dome can spring. In most cases, the radius used for each pendentive is approximately equal to one-half the length of the diagonal of the square below. But this is by no means necessary. By using a longer radius, the pendentives can be made to sweep further inward over the floor, meeting in a smaller circle and providing a base for a smaller dome.

The shape of a pendentive is handsome. By using it in connection with

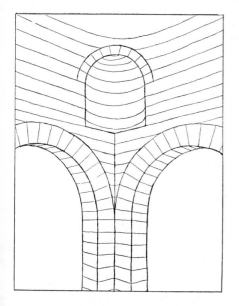

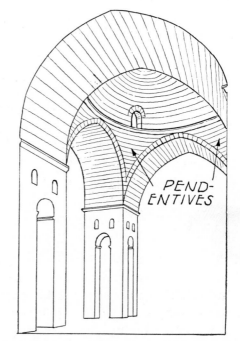

PEND-
ENTIVES

Figs. I.20–21 (above) An arch squinch.
(right) Pendentives as seen from below.

the dome, the architect opens up for himself the whole realm of curvature, an area scarcely entered as yet except for the brief period of the Byzantine 6th century. Because our modern ferroconcrete lends itself to curves more conveniently than does any earlier building material, we may perhaps look forward, when modernism becomes mature, to seeing parabolic and hyperbolic contours where we now see angles and unrelieved straight lines.

But like everything else, the pendentive is not without its drawbacks. Because it partakes of the nature of an arch, a pendentive exerts thrust, and the pressure of the thrust will be distributed, more or less, over its entire outer surface. The direction of the thrust will, moreover, be along the diagonals of the square beneath the dome. Logical abutment can be provided by a substantial mass of masonry with its own axis along the same diagonal; or, on the principle of vector diagrams, the diagonal force may be subdivided into its components and buttresses built to suit. A neat and perfect solution to this special problem of abutment has not to date appeared in the history of architecture; even Hagia Sophia, the queen of domed buildings, leaves much to be desired in this respect.

Used mostly for the smaller and less famous monuments of Byzantine and other medieval architecture, the squinch has more to recommend it than one might at first suppose. Various shapes have been used. In principle, they all boil down to the typical form shown in Figure I.20. Arches are

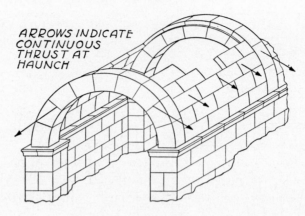

ARROWS INDICATE
CONTINUOUS
THRUST AT
HAUNCH

Fig. I.22 A ribbed tunnel vault.

thrown across the gap between the four piers as before, giving support to a square wall surface. Across each corner of the square thus established, smaller arches are thrown, converting the square into an octagon. Because the octagon approaches the shape of a circle, the dome may be allowed to spring from it if care is taken to adjust each course of masonry in or out a bit as the case may be. The fit is not perfect, but it is good enough.

Most writers seem to suggest that the squinch is something to be pitied— a makeshift to be tolerated when the pendentive cannot be had. They base their feeling upon the obvious disharmony of shape between the curved contour of the dome and the rather abrupt transition of the squinch. The squinch does give a bump to the eye: the act of seeing it is not a smooth, flowing motion as it is with the pendentive, but a series of starts and stops. There is more to design than harmony, however. Contrast is just as useful: for example, the juxtaposition of dissimilar shapes which squinches provide. While pendentives are admittedly more suave, squinches are rugged and direct. Incontestably, one can take solid satisfaction in the looks of them.

♦ *The Tunnel Vault* Considerably more adaptable to general utility, the *tunnel vault* (often called the *barrel vault*) has a shape as simple and lucid as the dome. The shape can be described as that of a simple arch indefinitely extended in the horizontal direction (Fig. I.22). The tunnel vault has the very great advantage of making a natural fit with a rectangular ground plan. Its shape also tends to produce a strong emphasis on the long horizontal axis of an interior, an emphasis corresponding with the ceremonial requirements of churches, law courts, and other public buildings.

But in spite of its pleasant form, the tunnel vault shares certain faults with the dome. Abutment is required along every foot of its length. Such abutment is automatically supplied in the New York subway system, but is difficult and expensive to provide whenever a tunnel vault is raised high in the air. Unless lighted by electricity, the tunnel vault is also almost certain to be gloomy because it is unwise to place windows higher than the spring. Windows often appear there, but it is impossible to guarantee the stability of any vault pierced above the spring.

Like the dome, many tunnel vaults are finished smooth or have the soffit decorated with some surface pattern. In a number of excellent examples, however, the problem of continuous thrust was ameliorated by the use of ribs. The Romans did this when vaulting the so-called Baths of Diana at Nîmes, and the ribbed system was popular in the Romanesque architecture of the 12th century (Fig. 10.11, page 324). A series of duplicate arches were first swung transversely across the rectangular chamber below. A single piece of centering doubtless sufficed for all, being moved on to the next station as each arch was completed. The vault was then in frame, and the primary ribs divided the whole into compartments, or cells. Each cell was then filled in with much lighter masonry as suggested in Figure I.22. Every cell of masonry between a pair of rib-arches became, in effect, a short section of tunnel vaulting, but because of its light weight, logic could be cast aside and its thrust neglected. For all practical purposes, the stability of a ribbed tunnel vault can be insured by placing buttresses against each of the main ribs. In effect, a division of the total thrust had been brought about, with pressures localized at a series of points along the sides of the building. Usually such buttresses take the form of salient piers standing against the outside walls, as seen in Figure 10.14, page 325.

Esthetically, the ribbed tunnel vault is extraordinarily satisfactory. By repetition, the curves of the primary arches emphasize the character of the shape. Line is combined with mass simply and lucidly. The shadows cast by the ribs change with the light. There is also a sense of rhythmic progression established by the view of one rib after another, off to the far end of the building.

♦ *The Cross Vault* The *cross vault,* also called the *groin vault,* has a shape too complex for convenient verbal description, although it may be worth repeating the loose statement that the form would result if two tunnel vaults were built intersecting each other at right angles. Such vaults may be constructed from beveled voussoirs, but most of those in existence depend upon a framework of six arches with the cells between closed in by light material. Figure I.23 shows the framework of a single ensemble, or *bay,* of cross vaulting, and Figure 11.18, page 382, gives a good idea of the appearance of a number of bays joined together to cover the oblong nave of a great church. In medieval vaulting, the ribs of the frame were almost invariably left in plain sight. Roman and Renaissance architects almost always

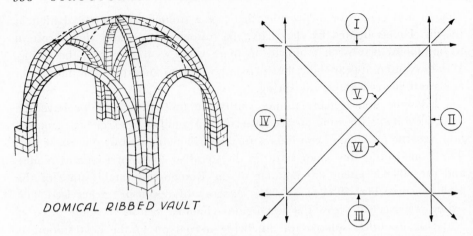

DOMICAL RIBBED VAULT

Figs. I.23–24 (left) Framework of a single bay of ribbed cross vaulting. The dotted lines suggest the contour of the lightweight masonry which will later be constructed to close the interstices between the ribs. (right) Thrust pattern of a single bay of cross vaulting as seen in the plan view.

used a frame similar to that shown, but concealed it in some way or other in order to produce a smooth soffit.

The two special advantages of the cross vault are these: For covering a long, narrow interior like the nave of a church, no other vault can be buttressed so easily or so cheaply; and the shape of the vault automatically provides spaces for large windows at a very high level. It is natural that such considerations would appeal to the engineer. We have, however, been subjected to a plethora of quasiesthetic praise based on the untenable notion that anything that is efficient must also be lovely. The truth of it is that unless very well-designed indeed, the cross vault produces a chaos of line and contour. On purely formal grounds, the best of them are none too good.

Figure I.24 shows Figure I.23 in plan view, the six arches of the frame being symbolized by straight lines on the paper. Each of the six arches will be exerting thrust both ways in the normal manner, as indicated by the three arrows drawn at each corner. Obviously, the thrust pattern is so complex that it would be a great nuisance to provide abutment for a single bay of cross vaulting. A single bay, in fact, is no good at all, and is never used. The real merit of the system begins to appear only when several bays of such vaulting are grouped together in sequence as in Figure 11.18, page 382 and as indicated in the schematic plan presented in Figure I.25.

Rather complicated at first glance, Figure I.25 will make sense as we proceed. Overlooking its details for the moment, let us give the separate ribs the names they ordinarily bear in such an ensemble. The arches which lie in the same plane as the walls of the building are called the *wall ribs*. The arches that swing directly across the interior at right angles to the long axis of

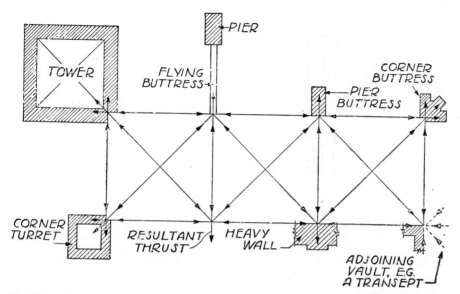

Fig. I.25 Schematic drawing of several bays of cross vaulting arranged as they would be to cover the nave of a church, with indications of various methods for abutment.

the building are called the *transverse arches*. Those that go diagonally from corner to corner, intersecting at the crown of each bay, are called the *diagonal ribs,* or simply the *diagonals.*

The notable properties of the cross vault become manifest when we consider what happens to the thrust pattern every time a pair of contiguous bays come together at a common corner. Figure I.26 is an attempt to illustrate the situation; its intelligibility depends upon the reader's capacity to visualize several arches rising up toward him, each being indicated here only by lines on the flat surface of the paper. The two wall ribs act like any duplicate arches in an ordinary arcade; their thrust being equal and opposite, they merely cancel each other out. The transverse ribs necessarily press outward at right angles to the building. There is nothing in the frame itself to hold them in, and buttresses must be placed to contain them. The two diagonals press against each other, and combine to produce a resultant thrust also at right angles to the wall of the building. We might prove this by vector diagrams, but the principle will be plain if the reader will merely put his palms together with the forearms diagonally behind them. By exerting an equal pressure on each palm, he will force his hands directly forward in the manner of the diagonal ribs of the vault. It follows that the thrust of the diagonals simply has the effect of increasing the thrust already exerted by the transverse ribs. Both may be stabilized by the same buttress made a little heavier.

Various shapes and kinds of buttresses have been used from time to time to provide abutment for cross vaulting. Figure I.27 shows a reconstruction of

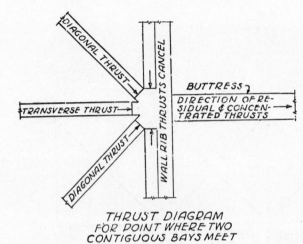

Fig. 1.26 Diagram to illustrate the interaction of thrusts where two contiguous bays of cross vaulting come together at a common corner.

a great Roman building with cross vaults. The immense windows and small buttresses are impressive testimony to the efficiency of the mechanics of the cross vault. The dainty flying buttresses of the French Gothic cathedrals (Fig. 11.14, page 379) stand as the ultimate refinement in the art and science of abutment.

Another detail needs to be mentioned for the sake of completeness. In Figure I.25 we see that a mixed-up pattern of residual thrusts is left outstanding at each extreme corner of the building. This is inevitable in the nature of the form, but the fault has done more good than harm in the history of architecture. The twin western towers that originally appeared in the Romanesque of Normandy and went on into the Gothic of the Ile de France, in appearance superb (Figs. 10.31, page 340, and 11.7, page 365), perform the simple function of weighting down the corners. The same thing may be said of the transepts and apse of many a church. The drawing also attempts to suggest various types of buttresses placed at other points.

By way of a final word, it is necessary to stipulate that our discussion of cross vaulting has, in this Appendix, been limited almost entirely to matters that might be illustrated or inferred by reference to the plan view alone. The interaction of the arches as seen in elevation is also important, but it has never been a vital feature in any architecture except the Gothic. For a discussion, see pages 381–384.

STRUCTURAL STEEL AND GLASS

The Industrial Revolution provided architecture with two new media: steel and glass. At any date prior to the 19th century, metal of every kind had been a luxury item necessarily reserved for small parts: nails, screws, hinges, locks, and the like. Iron was cheap as early as 1840; and during the latter half

Fig. I.27 Rome. Basilica of Constantine. Reconstruction. (From J. Durm, *Die Baukunstder Römer*, Stuttgart, Kröner, 1905.)

of the century, structural steel became available in large pieces at low cost. For architectural purposes, the principal use of the material has, to date, been in one of three forms: wire rope, reinforcement for concrete, and beams.

Glass in significantly extensive plates had been literally unknown. Big windows, when made at all, were necessarily assembled from many small panes. Larger panels appeared long before 1900, but the very large ones which are commonplace today were a special item before World War I. At this writing, glass is actually a raw material for building.

In the whole history of all the arts, there had never been a comparable situation. Even the arrival of the oil vehicle (page 479) did not change the conditions of painting to the extent that steel and glass altered the architectural outlook. Any estimate of recent architecture must therefore take into account the necessity for experiments on the lowest level of primitive groping —the kind of trial and error which results from blank ignorance and which, for every other known architectural material, took place so long ago as to be forgotten. We have no right to be surprised, therefore, if some experiments have turned out very badly indeed. An immense number of failures must be accepted as the cost of ultimate success; and it is still too early to say what the ultimate effect will be.

To whatever extent the modern style in architecture has arrived, the novel appearance of the latest buildings seems to key in with a more and more complete understanding of the internal logic of steel and glass. Until World War II, steel was the dominant medium. Recently, we have seen a shift of emphasis toward glass; and we even hear complaints that some architects have used too much of it. The most important monuments of modern architecture have so far been called into being by commerce (office buildings) or by the transportation system (bridges), and the chief effect to be noted is a vast increase in scale. Single buildings of immense volume and dizzy height, notable in any earlier era for their size alone, are today a routine performance all over the Western world.

The mechanical principles of steel construction are not new. Some of the most spectacular modern forms are, as forms, of primeval antiquity. The important advances made during the past century were easy enough to figure out in the imagination, but hitherto were forbidden in practice by lack of the right material. From the standpoint of its absolute capacity to carry out any plan an architect can visualize, the special qualities of steel have opened up a new world and have made architecture more nearly a liberal art than ever before.

These words of praise must be tempered with admonition. Steel used as reinforcement for concrete is subject to corrosion and has an uncertain life. During the author's childhood, it was bruited about that ferroconcrete buildings probably would not remain structurally safe for more than fifty years. That estimate proved overly pessimistic because many such buildings are today much older than that. Nevertheless, the reservation still holds.

The production of reliable steel beams entails the existence of manufacturing plants where the control of quality is superb. This was vividly demonstrated on the night when the train fell into the Firth of Tay with the loss of everyone on board. The great bridge had collapsed. The reasons were never completely determined, but it seems probable that while the design of the structure was adequate, the individual parts were defective. And even today, the best metals remain subject to the insidious phenomenon of fatigue (page 936).

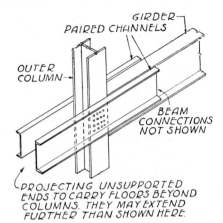

Fig. I.28 A method of using steel beams as cantilevers.

The fire-resistant properties of steel are exaggerated in the public mind. The material rapidly loses strength at elevated temperatures. In the great Chicago fire of 1871, the damage to steel-frame buildings was worse than that to structures of traditional material.

In spite of these faults, steel offers advantages that have made it our standard medium for every large fabric. Its principal difference from stone is that steel may be put under tension. A host of compact and efficient assemblies are therefore practical which were completely out of the question so long as architecture remained an art of wood and masonry. The assembly shown in Figure I.28, for example, would be impractical in wood. The ends of the beams would split open. Triangular bracing would be required to secure the joint against any stress which might give either member a tendency to turn over the other with the joint as a center. The point is well illustrated by what usually happens whenever an abandoned barn finally collapses. The beams and the uprights rotate at the joints, and the building subsides one way or the other.

The modern bridge has assumed four different forms, ilustrated by Figures I.29–32. The choice has depended upon the footing available and the special purpose of a particular bridge.

The so-called "arches" shown in Figures I.29–30 are not in fact arches but trusses hogged up in the middle to resemble the profile of the true arch. If loaded heavily enough, either would exert thrust, as would any other member of similar shape. Both have internal triangular bracing, however—seen in Figure I.29 and concealed by the cement in Figure I.30. Any force which tends to distort the shape of the truss will put the triangular bracing under tension, making both forms very stiff indeed.

The cantilever bridge is merely a pair of big steel brackets which stick

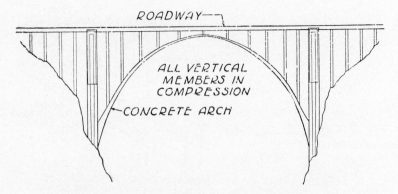

Fig. I.29 Bridge supported by a modern arch of ferroconcrete.

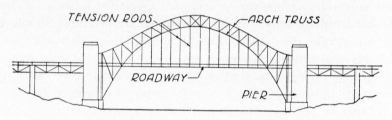

Fig. I.30 Bridge carried by a steel truss in the form of an arch.

out over the space to be spanned, and meet in the middle. (See Figs. I.35–36 for illustration of the cantilever principle.) As drawn in Figure I.31, the bridge might be called a balanced cantilever, because each extension has its equal and opposite to the other side of the fulcrum.

Steel arches and steel cantilevers tell as linear outlines seen against the sky, elaborated by internal tracery. Some are ugly because their designers thought of themselves as engineers only, and were indifferent to linear grace and to the action of light and dark. Others are superb.

The suspension bridge (Fig. I.32) has a power over the imagination not even suggested by the others. The principle has been known as long as men have known anything, and there is a primordial satisfaction in our final achievement of the capacity to build the form as it ought to be built. By comparison, all other methods of bridge building seem wasteful of material and clumsy in appearance. Because the supporting cables inevitably fall in a catenary, it is impossible for the most maliciously anti-esthetic engineer to design a suspension bridge that lacks grace. By the same token, the type offers the sensitive artist an unparalleled opportunity to integrate form and function. The great British engineer Sir Marc Brunel designed some beautiful suspension bridges as early as 1830. Some of the smaller ones executed by

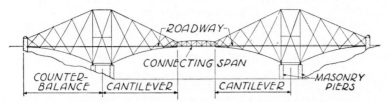

Fig. I.31   The principle of the cantilever bridge.

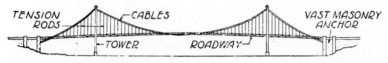

Fig. I.32   The principle of the suspension bridge.

W. A. Roebling around the turn of the present century are the quintessence of both art and engineering.

The suspension bridge has one fault, however, and it is a bad one. Like its primitive prototype made of grass rope in the jungle, the great modern bridge can swing and sway. In a few instances (apparently when the wind has set up a vibration in key with the period of the wires) dangerous conditions have resulted, and traffic has had to be prohibited.

The construction of steel-frame buildings seems prosaic by comparison with the drama inherent in a bridge, but there can be no question of its utilitarian virtues. The availability of large steel beams made feasible the now familiar "bird cage" system of framing, illustrated by Figure I.33. The method is simply a special application of the post-and-lintel system, longer spans being permitted because of steel's tensile strength and because we can give the material a cross section that makes for stiffness. It is important to note, however, that the whole pattern of the fabric has been immensely simplified by the compact joining of members, as illustrated by Figure 1. The beams cross the uprights at a ninety-degree angle. Triangular bracing is conspicuous by its absence.

Such a fabric forms a structural integer. It may be bolted down to bed rock or its base may be sunk in a socket like a flag pole. Both expedients have been tried innumerable times in the case of water towers, windmills, and other comparatively small structures; larger buildings depend for stability on their shape and weight. But all steel-frame buildings are measurably flexible and bend a little as the wind hits them.

As noted in Chapter 17, there was much confusion of mind before it was possible to develop an architectural esthetic based upon the realities of steel-

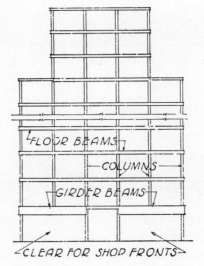

Fig. I.33   Modern steel construction.

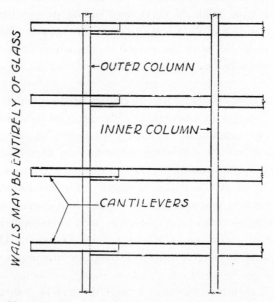

Fig. I.34   Use of internal columns and extending cantilevers in modern steel construction.

frame construction. Jenney and Sullivan (who worked in the Middle West during the 1880's and 1890's) promulgated the first acceptable philosophy of the matter. Their theory dealt with the exterior appearance of buildings and suggested that the verticality of skyscrapers ought to be emphasized by repeating the vertical lines established by the uprights of the steel frame.

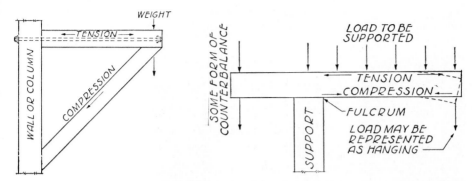

Figs. I.35–36   (left) The principle of the cantilever. (right) Forces upon a steel beam used as a cantilever.

This point of view is still popular, but a certain reaction set in; and the notion has become current that buildings should be designed "not from the outside in" but "from the inside out." The accommodations provided indoors, says this new theory, are paramount; and if good accommodations demand compromise with respect to exterior design, the sacrifice ought to be made.

The most obvious result of such thinking has been to make glass the primary medium and to make steel the servant of glass. This is possible because steel-frame construction enables one to locate the vertical supports of a building in a number of different ways. In Figure I.34, we see the columns placed well in from the outer surface. The floors are then extended out for a considerable distance beyond the columns. The latter do not cast shadows across the windows as they must when used, as Sullivan used them, to make vertical lines on the exterior.

Such an arrangement is feasible because steel beams may be cantilevered outward for a reasonable distance, as shown. Figures I.35–36 illustrate the principle of the cantilever. A cantilever is a bracket. A bracket is a cantilever. The mechanics are the same whether we use wood or metal, and whether the cantilever holds up a kitchen shelf or a directors' meeting. As applied to the floors of a building, where the loading is very light in proportion to stiffness, steel cantilevers have the merit of being extremely compact. They take up scarcely any useful room. The model shown in Figure I.37 was intended to emphasize what might be done. The McGraw-Hill Building in New York was one of the first to make frank use of the cantilever method, and Lever House (Fig. 17.49, page 923) was similarly designed.

Lever House is also believed to be the first major fabric to take advantage of still another possibility inherent in steel-frame construction. The idea had been put forward in a number of drawings and in several houses actually built to the plans of the French architect Le Corbusier: the bulk of the build-

Fig. 1.37 Miës van der Rohe. Model for sky-scraper with walls of glass. (Stoedtner)

ing was set up on stilts. The ground story, that is to say, was eliminated. The number of vertical supports was reduced to a minimum, and the intercolum niation appropriately increased. One may walk at will underneath. A general adoption of such a scheme may in time prove to be the cure for the infamous congestion of our growing cities.

Appendix II

THE DESIRABILITY of a systematic way for discussing color is suggested by the annual crop of tricky names invented for the dress trade, by interior decorators, and for the colors of motor cars: Sahara Yellow, Rose Beige, Glengarry Green, Endeavor Blue, Safari Brown, Faded Denim, Aqua, Mocha —and the list goes endlessly on. Admittedly, some of the names are attractive and a few may even be poetical, but it is obvious that efficient communication demands something more reliable.

Various authors have published books which purport to analyze the phenomena of light and color. The system summarized here is the one developed by the late Denman W. Ross and by Arthur Pope.* As compared with other theories, the system of Ross and Pope is lacking in certain refinements which may occasionally interest the scientist; but for our purposes, it has the incomparable advantage of furnishing a vocabulary which is simple, accurate within practical limits, and entirely adequate for the discussion of painting.

The word *color,* although all of us continue to employ it conversationally in a more particular sense, had best be understood generically. It is the name for the study which embodies and contains all the phenomena mentioned herewith. The word *tone* is often convenient as a near-synonym.

The different "colors" like red, blue, green, yellow, and violet are best referred to as *hues.* The difference between red and blue, for example, is a contrast of hue; and the similarity between blue-violet and red-violet is a harmony of hue.

---

* The latest and most complete exposition will be found in Pope's *The Language of Drawing and Painting,* Harvard University Press, Cambridge, Mass., 1949.

968

COLOR THEORY

Grays are tones which we recognize as being more or less light or dark, but which lack any recognizable hue. For that reason, grays are usually referred to as *neutrals*. The darkest neutral is named *black,* and the lightest neutral, *white.*

The difference between black and white is referred to as a contrast of *value*. Because *value* is current in other meanings, its choice in this denotation was unfortunate, but it is too late to attempt a correction. The reader will simply have to make a special effort to construe the term in its technical sense; and we shall presently find it useful to construct a *value scale* in even steps between black and white, thus making it possible to name particular *value levels* with the expectation of being understood.

In addition to possessing hue, any tone that gives us the sensation of red, green, orange, and so on, obviously possesses the quality of value also. If we wish to name a particular tone approximately, we simply call it a "dark red" or a "light green," as the case may be. If we want to name it exactly, we must name the precise hue, the precise value level, and the degree to which the hue is in contrast with the neutral gray at the same level of value. The latter quality—the amount of contrast with the neutral of equivalent value—is referred to as the *intensity* of the hue.

To recapitulate: *We may name any tone by naming its hue, its value, and the degree of its intensity.*

It is obvious that intensity varies in much the same manner as value. It is possible to imagine that every conceivable hue might be produced at every conceivable level of value, and in all degrees of intensity at each level.

969

Possibly painters may find that true in heaven. On earth, they have to accommodate themselves to the action of pigment materials. One of the most important limitations thereof is the tendency of any paint to lose its hue (that is, to neutralize) the minute one attempts to darken it or make it lighter. To put it another way, for every recognizable hue, there is but one value level where we may have that particular hue at its maximum intensity, usually referred to as the *highest possible* intensity. Yellow, for example, can be had at highest possible intensity only when the tone is very close to the value level of white. Absolute violet, neither reddish or bluish, is most intense only when nearly as dark as black. Red-orange comes to highest possible intensity at about the middle value, and the other hues behave as indicated diagrammatically by Figure II.3.

Hues at their highest possible intensity were, as a matter of historical fact, very rarely used in painting at any date earlier than about 1870, when the French Impressionists assumed the identity of a school and style (page 858). It therefore becomes a matter of interest to have an expression which indicates the degree of intensity of any hue at whatever value level we care to name. If we want to use red-orange (which comes to highest possible intensity at about the middle value) at a value level halfway between middle and black, the strongest intensity *available at that particular value* is best called *full intensity;* but the term *full intensity* is meaningless unless we simultaneously name the value level to which we refer. At any given level of value, a tone may of course be used, and often is, at considerably less than full intensity. As convenience indicates, we then refer to it as "half-neutralized" or "at half-intensity"—or any other degree of intensity or neutralization—as the facts demand.

◆ *Naming the Values* We can save much laborious explanation if we establish a system for naming a reasonable number of values between black and white. Figure II.1 indicates in abstract fashion how such a scale may be constructed. The reader may rightly wonder why the diagram does not appear in successive stages of gray, but it is still unfortunately true that the most painstaking work of the best printers can accomplish nothing better than approximate reproduction of the tones as they might appear in a carefully executed water color or oil. Let the reader, therefore, take his own box of paints, and proceed as directed below. If he has an instructor to help him, so much the better; and if not, he is bound to learn much if he is willing to be severe with himself and use his eyes.

Nine levels of value will prove sufficient for all practical requirements. If using water color, one begins by laying successive coats of charcoal black over the lowest circle in the diagram until it becomes as dark as the pigments in use permit. The top circle may be left without paint, the white of the paper standing for white.

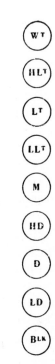

Fig. II.1   The value scale.

The next thing to do is to establish the middle value. Upon the manner of doing it, one's entire understanding of color depends, and the next few sentences have a special importance.

The middle value is defined as the value which contrasts equally with both white and black. We must find a gray, that is, which compares to black precisely as it compares with white. The judgment must be made with the eye. It is a subjective judgment, but experienced observers working with the same pigment materials tend to arrive at identical results. In any case, we must remember that paintings are never sent to the physics laboratory for analysis. They are hung on the wall for people to look at.

Once the middle value has been satisfactorily arrived at, the rest of the scale may be constructed by following the same method. *Dark* is defined as the value which compares to middle precisely as it compares with black. *Light* has a similar station between middle and white. *High light, low light, high dark,* and *low dark* must likewise contrast equally with the grays immediately above and below them. In theory, an infinite number of steps might be worked out; but, as stated, nine are sufficient.

The reader doubtless has already been bothered by the thought that a value scale executed in water color, as suggested, would not and could not demonstrate the full range of values available in all the pigment materials on earth. Black enamel, for example, is much darker than any black we can produce with water color, but the circumstance is of no artistic importance. One does not shift from water color to enamel in the course of painting a single picture. For the artist, the important thing is to know the range that is possible within the limits of his chosen medium. Thus, the useful chart is the chart that is consistent with itself and that demonstrates what can be done with the materials in hand.

The value scale, while laborious to construct and tedious to read about, is vitally important because it demonstrates in conclusive and unmistakable fashion the chief reason why the painter cannot possibly copy what he sees. As it appears on these pages, the diagram measures about three inches from black to white. Were we to symbolize the value relationships of nature in the same way, using vertical length to indicate the difference between black and white, we would require a scale as high as a house. The blackest darks of a sunlit scene, that is to say, contrast with the brightest lights so violently that the difference between white paint and black paint is insignificant by comparison. If the painter is to describe such a scene at all, he obviously must have a well-conceived system for making the feeble medium of paint suggest, symbolize, hint at, or otherwise recall to the observer the imagery of the natural world.

♦ *Naming the Hues* The hues are best named by laying them out on a circular diagram, as in Figure II.2, usually called the *color circle,* or *color wheel.* Similar diagrams have often been published without much explanation, and perhaps with small understanding of the method of construction or the significance of the result. The principles involved are the same as those used for the construction of the value scale; namely, the governing conception is to maintain an equal contrast between each hue and the two on either side of it.

The circular diagram permits us to range the so-called "warm colors" on one side and the "cool colors" on the other. In order to maintain mutual consistency between our diagrams, it is worthwhile to keep the graduations of the color circle in step with the value scale, an operation demanding slight departures here and there from theoretical accuracy, but one that involves no practical inconvenience. All hues are produced at the highest possible intensity. Yellow and violet fall on the central vertical axis because yellow comes to full intensity at high light, and violet at low dark. The contrast between them is not only a contrast of hue, but the strongest value contrast available between any two hues. In order to define yellow and violet, we resort to the familiar notion of the warm and cool colors. Absolute yellow must not contain a hint of orange or a hint of green. Absolute violet is the hue that tends neither toward blue nor toward red.

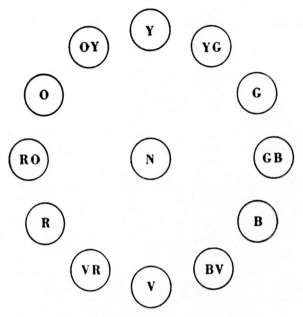

Fig. II.2 The scale of hues.

When actually constructing the twelve-hue color circle indicated in Figure II.2, one does not establish yellow and violet first. In order to avail ourselves of the principle of equal contrasts, and at the same time to produce a color circle that corresponds with the value scale, we start out by laying in yellow, red, and blue—which fall at equal angular intervals around the circumference and are defined as having equal contrasts, each with the other two. Violet, orange, and green then fall in place, each being defined as the hue in equal contrast to the two on either side of it. Orange-yellow, yellow-green, green-blue, blue-violet, red-violet, and red-orange may then be put in as intermediaries betwen the hues already located.

It takes skill to construct a reasonably accurate, self-consistent color circle. The beginner will be continually vexed by mistakes and adjustments; but if he perseveres, he will be in a position to make on his own authority some very cogent observations about the operation of colors. Perhaps the most important of these is the interaction of value and hue, as set forth above and as indicated by Figure II.3. It will also be found that the color circle has a beneficial and sharpening effect upon one's colloquial vocabulary. Almost every "red" in common use is in fact a red-orange. Practically all the "browns" are neutralized oranges. Most of the "pinks" are tints of red-violet.

It will still further be noted that every hue, as laid out on the color circle, falls on the same diameter as its *complementary,* which we define as the color that gives the maximum possible contrast with respect to hue. From physics

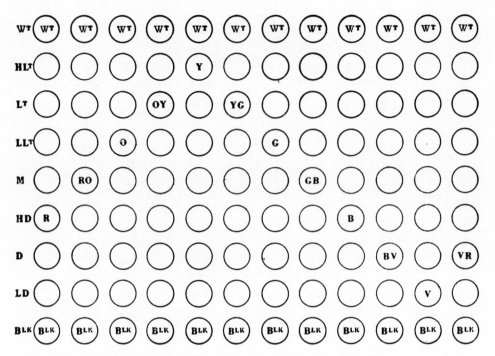

Fig. II.3 Abstract diagram to indicate the construction of a chart demonstrating the particular level of value at which each hue comes to its highest possible intensity. (The three figures in this appendix are from Arthur Pope, *The Language of Drawing and Painting*, Cambridge, Mass., Harvard University Press, 1949, pp. 7, 8, 14.)

we know that pigment materials obtain their capacity to exert the force of hue because they act like filters when light falls upon them. A blue pigment, for example, absorbs every part of white light except for the blue rays, and an orange pigment reflects only the orange rays. Theoretically, blue and orange (or any other two complementaries) ought to cancel each other out if mixed, producing a neutral as indicated by the small circle labeled *N* in the middle of the color wheel. That matter requires considerable explanation, however, because mixtures of paint do not produce the same results as mixtures of colored light (page 860). It will suffice here to point out that the hues at opposite ends of each diameter in the color circle may be thought of as approximate *pigment complementaries*. When mixed, any two give a gray. The diagram seems also to suggest that every neutral formed by the mixture of any two complementaries will also be a neutral at the middle value. Such, however, is hardly the truth. Paints are capricious more often than not. No one can predict within narrow limits what any two pigments will do when mixed. Trial and error is the only way to learn.

Another defect of the color circle also requires mention. By direction and definition, each hue on the circumference is at its highest possible intensity; but as laid out on the diagram, each hue is also equidistant from the center, which is to say from neutral. The inference would seem to be that every hue makes an equal contrast with its neutral gray of equivalent value. The notion is contrary to fact. In general, all the warm tones seem to differ from neutral more than the cool tones; and every hue in the lighter ranges strikes the eye as being less gray than any of the darker colors.

Once in command of the principles outlined above, it is possible to describe a tone with considerable assurance and precision. A few other terms occasionally are useful.

For all hues above the middle value, *tint* is an expressive designation. Everything darker than that is a *shade* of orange, violet, blue, or green, or whatever else the hue may happen to be.

A *field* is any area within a painting which constitutes a natural unit of a single hue. A grass plot, for example, would form a field of yellow-green. A red dress would be a field of red; and a sapphire set in a ring would be a tiny field of blue. In each instance, the yellow-green, the red, or the blue, would be called the *local tone* of its field.

INDEX

Index

NOTE ON THE USE OF THE INDEX

The Index and the Table of Contents must be used together. Refer to the latter for the major styles, periods, and topics covered by the text.

Because technical terms are defined and discussed at some length in the body of the text, the Index undertakes to perform the function of a glossary. Page references to definitions and definitive passages are printed in **bold face**.

References to buildings and museums are indexed according to city, then alphabetically by name. Unless otherwise indicated, the reader may assume that the principal museum of the place is indicated.

Whenever custom has made a prefix part of a proper name (*de, della, la, le, van, von*), the name is indexed according to the initial letter of the prefix.

Surnames became universal only a couple of centuries ago, and any number of artists are ordinarily known by their Christian name, or even by nicknames. In such cases, the name is indexed according to the initial letter of the noun that has become standard.

When saints are referred to in their capacity as individuals, they are indexed under their Christian names, with the title following. When the word "saint" forms part of the accepted title of a work of art, look for an entry under the letter "S."

There is no usage which might offer guidance for the indexing of the numerous esthetic, critical, and philosophical topics to which the text from time to time refers. These have been indexed, therefore, in accordance with the author's best guess as to what might be in the mind of a reader searching for information, seeking to refresh the memory, or on the prowl for argument. If all such readers will be kind enough to run the eye down the columns, perhaps they may find what they want.